Rock and Roll

an introduction

Michael Campbell

James Brody

SCHIRMER BOOKS
New York

A Marie Joséphine, "my cherie amour":
tu es le soleil de ma vie.

For Jane (Stones Rule!) Brody, whose courage
and conviction have been an inspiration.

Copyright © 1999 by Michael Campbell and James Brody

Schirmer Books
An imprint of Macmillan Library Reference USA
1633 Broadway
New York, NY 10019

Library of Congress Catalog Card Number
99-10095

Printed in the United States of America

Printing Number
1 2 3 4 5 6 7 8 9 10

Library of Congress Cataloging-in-Publication Data

Campbell, Michael, 1945–
    Rock and roll : an introduction / Mike Campbell, James Brody.
        p.   cm.
    Includes bibliographical references (p.403) and index.
    ISBN 0-02-864727-0
    1. Rock music—History and criticism.   I. Brody, James.   II. Title
    ML3534.C26   1999
    781.66—dc21   99-10095
                                                                             CIP

This paper meets the requirements of ANSI/NISO Z.39.48-1992
(Permanence of Paper).

contents

preface

Rock as Music

Rock is many things to many people and probably something different for each of us. It can be an escape to good times, a window to the soul, a vehicle for rage or frustration, ecstasy or empathy, an instrument of empowerment, and much more. It can tell us about ourselves and our culture, and about other cultures and subcultures. For most of us—or at least most of us reading this book—rock is a big part of our lives. For some, even, "rock is a way of life," as Geoffrey Stokes once wrote.

Most fundamentally, however, rock is music. Accordingly, the main focus of this book is on rock as music.

Active Listening

We hope that as readers listen to the music discussed in this book and read the commentary, they will further develop what might be called "active listening" skills. That is, they will become more aware of all that's going on in a performance. To some extent, this will involve becoming more attentive to such features as the bass line and the changing harmonies it often implies, or subtle rhythms from extra percussion instruments. But it will also involve simply becoming aware of what we already hear. Most of us have had the experience of being able to identify the style of a song without having heard it before. One of the goals of this book is to help you discover *why* you are able to do this.

Active listening is not the same as recreational listening: it requires attention and detachment, as well as involvement. It is a skill that can be cultivated, like learning to shoot a jump shot. It can be developed by listening *for* specific details, repeating as necessary until they can be easily identified, then listening again to hear how all the features work together to create the performance.

Active listening offers a particular kind of pleasure—the pleasure of discovery. We feel very strongly that when the discoveries have been made, and when the skills needed to make them have been acquired, then *all* listening will be enhanced, because you will hear more. You needn't listen actively all the time, any more than you would think about squaring your shoulders while taking a jump shot in a game. If you've practiced well, it will simply happen automatically. The benefit should be substantial: To hear more is like going from eight crayons to 24—or 64. The development of that skill is one purpose of the first chapter.

Listening Goals

As we develop our active listening skills, how do we put them to use? There are three ways we will ask you to apply them in this book:

1. Relating music to other music
2. Relating music to words
3. Relating music to cultural context

RELATING MUSIC TO MUSIC One of the main objectives of this book is to provide a historical framework for *all* the rock-era music that you listen to, not just the music discussed in this book. Here's a case in point: Before class begins, Mike plays music that students bring in. Toward the end of the semester, one student brought in Beck's *Mellow Gold* and recommended the song "The Loser." As they listened to it a second time, Mike asked the students when was the first time they'd heard particular features of the song. They traced the form back to the 1840s (the minstrel show song), the talking verse and sung chorus back to the 1930s (Willie McTell's talking blues), the use of a repeated electric guitar riff back to the late 1940s (John Lee Hooker), his talking/singing style back to the mid-1960s (Bob Dylan), and the beat back to the late 1960s. And we noted that the main melodic idea bore an uncanny resemblance to the signature riff of the Beatles' "Hey Jude." All of the song's salient features had been part of the popular music for at least 25 years!

The point was not to denigrate Beck. Just the opposite: originality in popular music is often a product of innovative recombination of well-known musical elements, instead of making something entirely new, as we'll discover again and again. By focusing on each feature and relating it to music that they had studied, students were able to put the song in historical perspective. When they were done, they had a sharper sense of what aspects of the song built on the past, and what features were original.

RELATING MUSIC TO WORDS Another useful application of active listening is connecting the musical setting of a song to the words, to hear if the music amplifies—or at least comments on—the meaning of the lyric and, if so, how it does so. This, too, is a recurrent theme in our discussions. To cite one example among many: we will suggest that it was *necessary* for Dylan to "go electric," because of the changes in the lyrics to his songs.

RELATING MUSIC TO ITS CULTURAL CONTEXT Many students suffer from the "ten-second problem": they decide within a few seconds whether they like a particular song. If they hear intense distortion and have already decided that they don't like heavy metal, then they immediately stop listening.

To address this problem, we have tried to relate songs and the styles they represent to the environment in which they developed. Our intent is to encourage readers to listen to *all* the music presented in this book on its own terms, rather than from a single fixed point of view. When we listen to punk or rap or Motown or alternative or Southern rock, we can try to connect the music to its time, place, and audience by considering the messages that musical choices send. Again, an example: We will suggest that the combination of simple finger snaps with sophisticated symphonic-sounding strings helped Motown stake out a position in the pop middle ground.

By doing this, we shift the emphasis from "Do I like it or not?" to the more objective "What signal does a musical choice (e.g., a heavily distorted power chord) send to its audience?" By putting ourselves in that audience, by shifting our frame of reference from style to style, we almost surely will broaden our understanding of not only the music, but also the cultures from which it emerged.

Presenting Rock as Music

The approach and the design of this book emerged from the interplay of two considerations, our focus on music and the awareness that this book is an *introduction* to the music of the rock era, not a history. The opening chapters introduce the idea of musical style and trace the evolutionary paths that led to rock. The remainder of the book is divided into three time periods: 1945–1964; 1964–1974; and 1974–1989. Individual chapters within each time span explore particular themes. For example, Chapter 9 explores several rock substyles with artistic aspirations: progressive rock, rock opera, glam rock, and so on.

Preceding the first chapter in each time span is an overview of important social trends and developments in music business and technology. The overviews provide context and chronology for the discussions within each chapter.

Where Are My Favorite Bands? My Favorite Songs?

As you look over the playlists, you may ask "How could you leave off Blue Cheer, or the Jefferson Airplane, or Kiss, or Mötley Crue?" Or you may think, "Well, you've got Van Halen, but why did you pick *that* song?" Or you may say to yourself, "You've got this African song on the CD set, but no Black Sabbath. Why?" Here's why.

There were three factors that dictated the choice of songs: our preferences, cost of the CDs, and our ability to license recordings for the CD package. In selecting the songs for discussion, we wanted to introduce rock-era music in depth (to study in some detail the achievements of rock's most important acts) and breadth (to show the extent of rock's impact). For instance, we discuss 11 songs by the Beatles and music that is well outside the rock middle ground: e.g., the gospel music of Andraé Crouch and the zouksoukous of the Guadaloupe band Kassav'.

Within these general parameters, our decisions were driven mainly by cost. We have discussed over 300 songs in the book. If we could license all of the songs, we would have about a 15–16 CD set, which would be far too expensive for most student budgets. (Still, there'd be a lot of great songs.) But it's a moot point, because it's impossible to license almost all white rock after 1960, and many important black acts, as well. That means no Beatles, no Stones, no Who, no Springsteen, no U2, no Paul Simon, no Michael Jackson . . . it's a long list.

So we have licensed much of what we can—keep in mind that this is the first rock text to have a CD set—and tried to find the most cost-effective way of obtaining the rest.

Recordings cited in the book come almost exclusively from five sources:

1. The CD set that accompanies the book
2. Three Time/Life anthologies
3. Greatest hits collections
4. Important albums by individual artists or groups
5. The CD set that accompanies Michael Campbell's textbook on American popular music, *And the Beat Goes On*

We chose the Time/Life sets because:

a. they contain a lot of great songs;

b. they are likely to stay in print;

c. they provided the least expensive way to cover a lot of rock music of the seventies and eighties.

Their song choices for particular artists may not agree with yours—or ours: In our discussion of Peter Gabriel, we mentioned "Sledgehammer" because it is on a Time/Life set, but focused on "In Your Eyes," which we felt was more representative of his work.

For unlicensable songs not on the Time/Life sets, we opted next for "greatest hits" packages. We typically chose them over single albums for much the same reason: more songs for the buck. When we had to choose a single album, we normally opted for a critically acclaimed album released at a crucial point early in a group or artist's career: Joni Mitchell's *Blue*, David Bowie's *Ziggy Stardust*, and Deep Purple's *Machine Head* are good examples.

We understand that you may not agree with all of our choices, but we hope that you will appreciate the difficulties we faced and our desire to keep the cost as low as possible.

Acknowledgments

Jim's acknowledgments: I wish to acknowledge the following individuals for their contributions and support in the creation of this book: Bill Kearns (who convinced me, almost against my will, to teach a class in this topic far before it was fashionable to do so); Bill Maakestad (who provided me with a music appreciation course I'll never forget); Peter Muste (who has been there from the beginning); Andy Schneidkraut (who has contributed his encyclopedic knowledge); my students and teaching assistants (especially John Gray and Christa Garvey) for enlivening the process; and my family for their unwavering support in whatever I've attempted to accomplish.

Mike's acknowledgments: I wish to thank all the people who have helped me, directly and indirectly, in my work on this project. Jan LaRue and Allen Forte have inspired me through their example and their support. I have used LaRue's comprehensive framework for style analysis in virtually all of my professional work for over twenty years. Those familiar with LaRue's ideas will see his influence on every aspect of the book: approach, design, and musical discussions. I had long admired the clarity and compelling logic of Allen Forte's thinking. In 1995, I had the privilege of experiencing it firsthand. To the extent that my part of the writing is lucid and logically developed, it betrays Forte's influence.

Two other scholars have, by example, shaped my work. Peter Brown has taught me that it is possible to know virtually everything about something. Through her writings and presentations, Susan McClary has taught me the crucial importance of situating music in its cultural context. Their examples have been inspiring and instructive.

John Covach graciously provided a prepublication copy of his book, *The Analysis of Popular Music*, and has taught me more than he knows in our toofew conversations. We are also grateful for his contribution to the aural glossary.

Guthrie Ramsey generously agreed to read and comment on sections of the manuscript.

I am indebted to several of my colleagues at Western Illinois University: Paul Paccione, who read several chapters of the manuscript and offered helpful suggestions; John Murphy, who has patiently listened and responded to my ideas in progress; and Jim Caldwell, who has given his technical assistance and interest.

To my family, I owe a long-term debt for their constant support. Thank you.

Both of us would like to thank Jim's sister Jill for her interest in the project and her helpful comments on part of the manuscript. We wish to thank Mike's agent Donald Cutler for his work on our behalf and for his prudent advice. We are indebted to the staff at Schirmer books. Special thanks to senior editor Richard Carlin, for his support, advice, and skillful editing of the manuscript: more scalpel and less cleaver this time around.

Finally, we both agree that this book, whatever its shortcomings, is far better than it would have been if we hadn't worked together on it.

Michael Campbell
James Brody

Introduction: Blues Basics

Rock began with the blues, and so will we. To understand rock and rhythm and blues, we must be thoroughly familiar with the basics of blues form. The best way to learn blues form is by creating and performing our own blues. Here's how:

The Three "Rs" of Writing a Blues Lyric

Begin by writing a sentence about something that's on your mind. Here's an example.

> *I'm gonna sit right here and write a blues today.*

Now, write virtually the same line again.

> *Yeah, I'm gonna sit right here and write a blues today.*

Think of a word that rhymes with "today." Then make up a line that ends with the rhyming word.

> *If I can rhyme "today," my blues will be okay.*

If you've done this, you've written one *chorus* of a standard blues. That's all there is to it. To review: the three "Rs" of writing a blues lyric are:

WRITE

REPEAT

RHYME

To perform the lyric, simply change "write" to "read." So, the pattern becomes:

READ

REPEAT

RHYME

To test your new skill, think of an incident or feeling that's on your mind: what you did last night, how you're getting along with your "significant other," something you heard on the news. Then relate the incident or feeling by writing three choruses of a blues lyric. Use everyday speech. Blues lyrics typically tell their story in plain language, and the story usually involves an immediate experience: the cliché opening for a blues is "I woke up this morning . . . ."

Musical Elements of the Blues

You've written the lyric. Now, how do you sing it—or say it—with the band? Before we take that step, we need to learn, and experience, some basic elements of the blues—and of a lot of other music.

BEAT One meaning of "beat" is a foot-tapping regular rhythm. A regular rhythm divides time into equal segments. Regular rhythms can occur at many speeds, from very fast to very slow. We usually locate the beat somewhere in the middle, at a speed to which we can respond easily and comfortably. So, to get a beat going, simply tap your foot at a medium speed, or *tempo*. (Tempo refers to the speed of the beat.)

BAR Beats typically group by twos, threes, or fours. These groups of beats are called measures, or *bars*. The blues form that we've learned has twelve measures per chorus, so it's often referred to as a twelve-bar blues. Each bar in our blues will contain four beats. So as you tap your foot, say "1-2-3-4," over and over.

BACKBEAT A backbeat is a percussive accent on the second of a pair of beats. An *accent* is a sound that stands out in some respect—because it's louder, longer, higher, etc. A percussive sound begins with a sharp attack and dies away quickly. Snap your fingers—that's a percussive sound.

To coordinate the backbeat with the beat, we can do this: start tapping your foot, count "1-2-3-4," then snap your fingers, or clap your hands, on "2" and "4."

Say	1	2	3	4
Snap/Clap		X		X

Practice this until it's so easy that you can count in your head and talk to your neighbor without skipping a beat.

BLUES HARMONY Our next task is to learn the standard bass line to a twelve-bar blues. In the blues, and most other popular music, the bass line supports the chords that make up the harmony. If you know—and can sing—the bass line, the rest of the harmony follows.

Let's begin by singing up and down the first five notes of a scale, using numbers for each note: "1-2-3-4-5-4-3-2-1." When that's easy, then sing just the first, fourth, and fifth notes: 1-4-5. When *that's* easy, sing the pattern shown below.

First four bars:

I-2-3-4//I-2-3-4//I-2-3-4//I-2-3-4//

Second four bars:

IV-2-3-4//IV-2-3-4//I-2-3-4//I-2-3-4//

Third four bars:

V-2-3-4//IV-2-3-4//I-2-3-4//I-2-3-4//

In music, numbers are used to count beats, to identify notes of a scale, and to identify chords built on the notes of the scale. To reduce confusion, Arabic numerals are used to count beats and identify notes of the scale, while Roman numerals are typically used to identify chords. In the previous pattern we used Roman numerals to identify the chord used at the beginning of each measure and the Arabic numbers to count the remaining beats in the measure. You'll sing the bass note of the chord identified at the beginning of the measure on every beat of the measure.

Notice that you'll sing the bass note of the I chord for four bars, shift up to the bass note of the IV chord for two bars, then back to the I chord for two more bars, shift again, up to V for a bar, then IV for another bar, and then back to I for the final two bars.

Then find a partner—or, better, a group of four or five people—and sing the blues bass line together while tapping your feet and snapping or clapping on the backbeat. When you're all comfortable with doing all three things, take turns reading and/or singing your blues lyric. Use the change in harmony to tell you when to say each line:

Read at the beginning of each chorus.

Repeat a little bit after your partners change to the IV chord; try to finish around the time the bass line returns to I.

Rhyme just after your partners change to the V chord.

Let's review what we've learned to this point. We can:

1. Write a standard blues lyric.
2. Mark the beat with our feet and the backbeat with our hands.
3. Sing the bass line to a twelve-bar blues.
4. With the help of a partner, sing or say your lyric so that it lines up with the harmony.

So far, we have four layers of activity: the lyric, the foot-tapping, the backbeat, and the bass line. To make our blues a little more interesting, we're going to add another layer. It will introduce two musical features common to a lot of blues: riffs and syncopation.

RIFFS AND SYNCOPATION   A *riff* is a short melodic idea, usually with some rhythmic interest. Riffs are usually short, consisting of two to eight notes; ours will have two: "Oh, yeah!" We'll sing the first syllable on the second beat of every measure and the second syllable some time before the third beat. We want to stress "yeah!" We'll use a higher version of the bass note for "oh" and let our voice drop a little for "yeah!"

Beat	1	2	3	4
Riff		Oh,	*yeah*!	

When you sing it this way, the riff ends with a *syncopation*. A syncopation is an accent that conflicts with the beat (or other regular rhythm—the backbeat is the most basic syncopation in popular music), rather than lining up with it. If we stress "yeah!," we place an accent between the second and third beats, rather than on either beat.

To practice coordinating the riff with the lyric, beat, backbeat, and bass line, get back together with your practice group. Everybody keeps time. Men sing the bass line, women sing the riff, and the designated lyricist reads his or her lyric. Then, so everybody gets practice, exchange roles: men on the riff, women on the bass line, other lyricists/lead readers.

If we want the complete package, we need a band. It's too much to conjure up a live band, but we have a nice karaoke-like alternative: Booker T. and the M.G.s' recording of "Green Onions."

The recording begins with a four-bar introduction. In these four bars, we can find the beat, which is marked by the organ; the backbeat, marked on the

> The neighboring higher (or lower) version of any note is called an *octave*. Octaves are considered a different version of the same note, rather than a different note, because they vibrate in the simplest possible ratio, 2:1. The top and bottom strings of a conventionally tuned guitar are two octaves apart. The bottom string vibrates at 82.5 cycles per second (cps), the top string at 330 cps, creating a 4:1 ratio. The octave in between vibrates at 165 cps, twice as fast as the bottom string and twice as slow as the top string.

sock cymbal; and the starting notes for the bass line and riff. Those who are singing the bass line will hear the right bass note at the beginning of each bar. Those singing the riff can get their bearings from the organ riff. The first two notes of the organ riff are identical to our sung riff, but the second note comes more quickly in ours. By the end of the fourth bar of the intro, you should be in the groove.

A sharp guitar chord signals the beginning of the first chorus; that's your cue to enter. If you're singing the riff, remember that the starting note for our riff moves up and down with the bass line. If you're reading your blues lyric, use the bass line to time your entrance.

If you practice performing the bass line by yourself, with your classmates, and with "Green Onions," until it's easy, then practice singing or talking over the recording until that's easy. You should be able to write a blues song, then walk into a blues club and sing it with a band.

Elements of Music

The ability to write a blues lyric, sing or say it with a band, keep our harmonic bearings through a blues chorus, and do all of this while marking the beat and backbeat: all are valuable skills. However, there is another useful dimension to this exercise. Working through these steps, we have introduced important elements of almost any performance—its beat, melody, harmony, instrumentation, form, etc.—and have specific examples of each feature. Here's a list that shows all of the elements and how they work when we sing or say our blues over "Green Onions."

RHYTHM   We've already learned beat, measure or bar, backbeat, and syncopation. And we can also notice that *rhythm* is not just the beat, but the interaction of the beat with the backbeat, riffs, the pattern of harmony change, and even the delivery of our lyric.

MELODY   If you're singing your lyric, then that's the melody of your blues. However, there are other melodic ideas present, especially if you sing along with "Green Onions": in the first part of the song, there are also instrumental riffs.

HARMONY   We know the three basic chords of the blues—I, IV, and V—and the pattern of change in a typical blues song.

INSTRUMENTATION   You supply lead "vocal," backup singers, and a fingersnap or clap on the backbeat. Booker T. and the M.G.s provide a complete rhythm section. A complete *rhythm section* contains at least one chord instrument, one bass instrument, and one percussion instrument. The M.G.s have that and more.

TEXTURE Texture is a new concept here. It simply refers to how the various parts of a performance—vocals and instruments—weave together. Here, the parts, including yours, are layered on, until there's a lot going on. In the first chorus, the texture includes the bass riff (and your bass line), organ riff, drums (both backbeat and cymbal pattern), guitar, vocal riff, fingersnap, and the blues lyric.

FORM You have learned the basics of blues form: lyric form, phrase structure (three four-bar phrases, twelve bars in all), and chord pattern.

This survey of the elements—rhythm, melody, harmony, instrumentation, texture, and form—gives us a framework for constructing our own blues performance. It also builds a framework for listening actively to performances—recorded and live—by others. The things we did ourselves—keeping the beat and backbeat, and singing riffs and the bass line—give us features to listen for in other performances.

c h a p t e r   1

The Motown Sound

It is impossible to talk about rock without using labels. In fact, "rock" itself is a label. When we use rock as a noun or adjective to describe music, we imply a certain sound, or range of sounds. It is not classical, or folk, or pop, or jazz, or country. It is rock—we expect loud guitars, dense, up-front rhythms, hooks, rough-edged vocals, etc. Without question, a lot of rock music has none of these qualities. Still, when we go to a rock concert, we don't expect to see and hear a symphony orchestra or a Frank Sinatra-type pop singer. But what does "rock" mean? Or, for that matter, heavy metal, punk, new wave, industrial, rap, soul, or funk?

Labels such as these are a shorthand for style. They enable us to communicate in a word or two key information about the sound of a particular performance or group of performances—even the music of an era. Mention "heavy metal" and a distorted guitar sound should come to mind (as well as "love it" or "hate it" associations). But why do labels work? How do they condense countless performances into a word or two?

When musicians create a song, they make choices: what instruments to use, how to play them, the basic beat and tempo, how the beat is realized, and so on. When the same—or at least similar—choices recur from song to song, they produce style.

Style is comprehensive: it is the sum of shared features. Some features may be immediately apparent—the distortion of a guitar, the rasp of a lead singer or the rap of a rapper, the slapping of an electric bass. Others, such as form, may take a while to unfold. And still others, such as the faint strum of a rhythm guitar, may require careful listening to detect. But all are part of style.

Style also occurs on different levels (see Figure 1.1). We can talk about the style of a song ("My Girl"), the style of an act (the Temptations), the style of several acts with a similar sound (the Motown sound), a larger group of acts with some shared choices (sixties rhythm and blues), the sound of a generation (rock in the sixties), the sound of an era (the rock era).

FIGURE 1.1
Style pyramid

"My Girl"
Temptations
Motown Sound
Sixties R&B
Sixties Rock
Rock Era Music

At each level of a style pyramid, the shared choices define the style, while some of the differences identify subgroups within the style. For example, we could confidently assert that all of you who followed the three "Rs" of blues songwriting wrote a blues song. While each song was unique, they were all blues, because they shared the same harmony and form with each other and countless other blues songs.

Style and Musical Relationships

To describe style, we need a comprehensive framework—a checklist of choices—so that we can observe and evaluate all the elements that shape a performance. Fortunately, we already have one well underway, as a result of our experience writing and singing the blues. Recall that we learned about:

1. rhythm (beat, measure, tempo)
2. rhythmic conflict (backbeat, syncopation)
3. instrumentation (rhythm section plus vocals)
4. melody (riffs)
5. harmony (I, IV, and V)
6. texture (layered textures)
7. form (blues form)

In this chapter, we'll add to this list as we work through a case study in style description: a profile of the Motown sound.

The Sound of Young America

Berry Gordy, the founder of Motown Records, billed the music coming from his Motown studio as "the sound of young America." He was right. During the mid-sixties, the Motown sound spoke to young Americans of all races and backgrounds. Thirty years later, many of the songs are classics, known not only to those who grew up with them, but also to their children and grandchildren.

Our goal here is to analyze the Motown sound. We want to identify its distinctive features. We also want to discover how much of its distinctiveness was due to the groups in the spotlight and how much was the result of the songs and their settings. To this end, we will focus on three songs. All date from 1964, the year the Motown sound became a truly international phenomenon—the Temptations' "The Way You Do the Things You Do" and "My Girl," and the Supremes' "Come See About Me." We'll start by expanding our understanding of rhythm.

Rhythm

Let's begin with "beat." When you counted the blues bass line, you experienced the most fundamental meaning of "beat": marking off time. The counting pattern produced two regular rhythms, the beat (i.e., a regular rhythm at foot-tapping speed) and the measure (in our case, a group of four beats). Here, we'll introduce another rhythmic level and two more connotations of "beat."

BEAT DIVISION In addition to the beat and the measure, there are usually other regular rhythms in rock era songs. Some move faster than the beat. The

The Temptations, c. 1966. PHOTO COURTESY CORBIS/BETTMANN.

first question we ask about these faster-than-beat-speed rhythms is "do they divide the beat evenly or unevenly?" The title phrases from two songs will show us both possibilities. In "The Way You Do the Things You Do," the beat divides unevenly, into a long/short pattern. In "Ain't Nothin' Like the Real Thing" (another Motown song that we're "borrowing" from Chapter 6) the beat divides evenly, into two shorter segments. Figure 1.2 shows this.

FIGURE 1.2A
Even beat division

Beat	1		2		3		4		1
Division									
Lyric			ain't	no-	thing	like	the	real

FIGURE 1.2B
Uneven beat division

Beat	1		2		3		4		1
Division									
Lyric		the	way	you	do	the	things	you	do

The beat division in the other two songs—"My Girl" and "Come See About Me"—is not apparent in the title phrase, but it is heard in the drum part, especially in "Come See About Me." Both songs have even beat division. The "foot-tapping" beat and the backbeat are our points of entry into the rhythm of the songs. Beat division is our point of entry into a second meaning of beat: the rhythmic foundation of a song or style.

"STYLE" BEATS   Most rock songs from the sixties have a "rock beat." In this context, "beat" is verbal shorthand for a set of expectations regarding rhythmic organization, not the foot-tapping regular rhythm. In the case of a rock beat, we expect a backbeat, and a regular rhythm that moves twice as fast as the beat (i.e., even division of the beat). Figure 1.3 diagrams a measure of rock rhythm.

FIGURE 1.3
Diagram of a rock beat

Rock beat layer									
	rock	and	roll	and	rock	and	roll	and	rock
Beat	1		2		3		4		1
Backbeat			X				X		

> Here's a good way to practice this rhythm. Tap the beat with your foot, clap your hands or snap your fingers on the backbeat, and say the words: "Rock and roll and" over and over. The words mark the rock beat layer. Make sure the backbeat comes with the word "roll."

Figure 1.3 shows three rhythmic layers. Note that the layer that defines "rock beat" is the fastest one, the rhythmic layer that divides the beat into two equal parts. From this, we understand that "Come See about Me" and "My Girl" have a rock beat. By contrast, "The Way You Do the Things You Do" does not have a rock beat (even though it's also from 1964), because the beat is divided unevenly, not evenly.

You can test this for yourself by tapping a rock rhythm (the fastest layer) and saying the title phrase of each song. In "My Girl" and "Come See About Me," every syllable will come on a tap. You can't do that with "The Way You Do the Things You Do."

The rock beat layer doesn't even have to be explicit for us to feel a rock beat rhythm. Consider the beginning of "My Girl." The rhythm accumulates, layer by layer—first bass, then guitar and finger snap, followed by drums and lead vocal. We hear the rock rhythm marked only when the drummer enters; he plays it on a closed hi-hat. But we feel the rock rhythm from the start, because both the bass line and—later—the guitar part line up with the rock beat (see Figure 1.4).

FIGURE 1.4

The opening of "My Girl"

Beat	‖1		‖2		‖3		‖4		‖1
Rock beat layer	|	|	|	|	|	|	|	|	|
Finger snap			X				X		
Bass	x	x		x	x	x		x	
Guitar	—			x	x	x	x	x	

In its most general sense, a rock beat is the expectation of rhythms that move twice as fast as the beat, or that line up with that faster moving layer. The marking of this layer can be strong and explicit, as in the beginning of "Come See About Me," or more delicate, as occurs later in the song. Or it can simply be implied by less regular rhythms and their interaction, as in the opening to "My Girl." Still, the expectation is there, regardless of how it's realized. That's what produces a rock beat.

BEAT NUMBER AND STYLE BEATS A rock beat is also known as an "eight-beat" rhythm. The eight refers to the fastest equally emphasized regular rhythm. In an eight-beat rhythm, the fastest regular rhythm (i.e., a rhythm that divides time into equal segments) moves twice as fast as the beat, or eight attacks (or "beats") per measure. The opening of "Come See About Me" lays this rhythm out as plainly as possible.

To this point, we have identified two meanings of beat: "foot-tapping" beat, and "style" beat. Both are quite specific in their meaning. A third meaning of "beat" is more subjective, as we will see in the following section.

By contrast, the blues that we created in the previous chapter uses a four-beat rhythm, which you counted when you sang the bass line. In our blues, and in "Green Onions" and "The Way You Do the Things You Do," the fastest regular rhythm moves at beat speed, or four attacks per measure. All the faster rhythms divide time unequally, into long/short patterns.

When the long/short pattern is strongly and consistently emphasized in the rhythm section, it becomes a shuffle rhythm, or simply a "shuffle." A shuffle is a stronger version of a four-beat rhythm, simply because the long/short pattern makes the four-beat rhythm more obvious.

There are two other "number" beats, a two-beat rhythm and a sixteen-beat rhythm. (Note that all four beats are powers of two.) A two-beat rhythm alternates bass notes (the fastest equally emphasized layer) with the backbeat. If we use the backbeat as a reference—it sounds on two and four—there are four beats per measure, as before, but the bass only sounds on one and three. That's the fastest regular rhythm. We hear a clear two-beat feel in Chuck Berry's "Maybellene," a rock and roll classic.

THE BEAT OF THE MOTOWN SOUND We also commonly use "beat" in a third way, to describe the overall rhythmic feel of a song. This usage is more subjective than the other meanings of "beat." One person might think that the Sex Pistols' "God Save the Queen" has a great beat, while another might be repulsed by its obviousness. (By contrast, we have a very specific expectation for a rock or eight-beat rhythm, which we noted earlier.)

Most people agree that Motown songs have a "good" beat, one that makes people want to snap their fingers, tap their feet, and maybe move their body to the beat. By listening carefully to the three songs discussed in this chapter, we notice that they approach rhythm in much the same way. The Motown approach has six main features, all of which are largely independent of the "style" beat used. They are:

1. a medium groove tempo, between 100 and 120 beats per minute;

2. a strong backbeat, especially when compared to the other rhythmic layers;

3. light timekeeping at faster-than-beat speeds, usually on percussion instruments;

4. only moderate syncopation, both in the vocal line and in other parts, such as bass and guitar;

5. a bass line that is often in free rhythm, and often moving at beat speed or slower;

6. a dense, multi-layered, heterogeneous texture.

This approach makes rhythm accessible and infectious, but not overpowering. It's accessible because the strong backbeat provides an easy point of entry, and the rhythms of the vocal line usually confirm the beat. It's infectious because of the carefully orchestrated balance between beatkeeping and rhythmic play. It's not overpowering because the faster rhythms are usually in the background.

The Motown rhythmic approach allows for considerable variety, because the most prominent rhythmic layers—the main melody, other riffs and melodic lines, and the bass line—are specific to each song and seldom regular. Still, there is a consistent rhythmic feel in these Motown songs, even when they use different "style" beats, because the six features identified above recur from song to song. This rhythmic strategy, which is at the same time both simple and sophisticated, is a crucial component of the Motown sound, as we shall see.

Melody

A melody is a series of pitches or notes. When a group of pitches come in a series, especially one we can sing, it often produces a melody.

However, the vocal line is not the only melodic collection of pitches. What—other than the fact that it's sung—makes it catch our ear? Typically, it is some combination of melodic and rhythmic interest. Melodic interest grows out of variation in melodic contour, the pattern of rise and fall in the melody. Similarly, rhythmic interest is the result of variation in the duration of the pitches or other kinds of rhythm. When a series of pitches has some combination of these qualities, it can grow into a melody—or at least a melody-like idea. So, although the vocal line is the most prominent melodic idea, there can be—and usually are—other melodic strands in a song.

"My Girl" is a good case in point. The opening bass riff (recall that a riff is a short, rhythmically interesting melodic idea) has a distinctive contour and rhythm, and the guitar riff is memorable enough to identify the song before we hear the first sung note. As the song progresses, we hear trumpet flourishes and active violin lines in addition to the guitar riff and the vocal lines. There is melody-like material everywhere: not only the vocal lines but so many of the instrumental parts have melodic interest.

Indeed, many of the memorable melodic ideas in this and other Motown songs are riffs. The most notable are their signature phrases. The shortest is "My Girl." It finishes a longer phrase, but is clearly distinct from the first part, because of both words and music. Notice that it has a sharply defined rhythm and melodic contour, so that it stands apart from the music around it. The other extreme is the eight-syllable "The Way You Do the Things You Do." This riff, with a nice peak on the first "do," also has a distinctive profile. The same strategy also applies to instrumental riffs, as we heard in "My Girl."

Riffs tend to be rather short and isolated—or at least showcased—so that they are easily remembered. They are also frequently repeated throughout the course of a song, for the same reason: so they stick in our memory. Vocal riffs, simply because they are attached to words, can afford to be on the long side. Instrumental riffs, which must operate without the benefit of words, tend to be shorter and more clearly defined. That is the case throughout "My Girl": not only in the bass and guitar riffs, but also in the trumpet flourishes that appear later in the song.

MELODY AND THE MOTOWN SOUND There is a Motown approach to melody. As with rhythm, the approach is flexible enough to accommodate considerable difference from song to song, yet consistent from song to song. This consistency helps define the Motown sound. Its key element is saturation: Motown songs are saturated with melody; melodic writing permeates the entire texture. Almost any instrument that can play melodically does so, even accompanying instruments. For instance, the guitar riff in "My Girl" outlines the chord melodically instead of simply chunking out the harmony.

All the songs contain a lot of melodic activity. Some of its elements, especially the vocal and instrumental hooks, are very much in the foreground. Other strands are less apparent, but enrich the overall sound. As with rhythm, there are obvious points of entry to draw you in, and there is enough going on to keep your ear busy once you are there.

Harmony

Our experience with the blues taught us three useful things about harmony:

- We hear harmonies from the bass up.
- I, IV, and V are the three basic chords of the blues—and of early rock.
- The change from one chord to the next creates a rhythm.

We can use this information to make a couple of observations about harmony and the Motown sound.

HARMONY AND THE MOTOWN SOUND We have already noted one characteristic of the Motown approach to harmony, that chords are often presented melodically. Another more subtle feature is the harmonic ebb and flow. All of the songs start with simple harmonies. As they build toward the end of a section, the chord rhythm quickens and new harmonies are added. For example,

"My Girl" starts with a simple alternation between I and IV. During the approach to the hook ("I guess you'd say"), however, the chord rhythm gets faster, and two new chords appear. When the section reaches the climax, usually the title phrase, the harmony becomes simpler again and the chord rhythm slows. The harmonic ebb and flow—faster/slower chord rhythm, more/fewer chords—help outline the form of the song, as we'll see below.

Instrumentation

We describe the instrumentation of a performance by listing the voices and instruments we hear and discovering how they contribute to the performance. Some may stand out, others may remain in the background. Some may play throughout, others may drop in for a few seconds, then disappear. All add to the overall sound.

From our blues experience, we already have a nucleus in place: lead vocal, backup vocals, a hand clap or finger snap on the backbeat, and (thanks to Booker T. and the M.G.s) a four-instrument rhythm section. As we listen to "My Girl," we hear other instruments added to this nucleus and observe how they interrelate.

INSTRUMENTS AND THE MOTOWN SOUND "My Girl" uses a lot of musicians: lead vocalist, backup vocalists, violins, trumpets, guitars, bass, drums, fingersnapper. That in itself tells us a good deal about the song. We can sense a "melting pot" approach to music making: the sophistication of symphonic strings (the violinists on this recording were moonlighting from the Detroit Symphony) mixed with something as everyday as a finger snap.

The sequence in which they enter tells us even more. We hear bass, guitar and finger snap, drums, lead vocal, and backup vocals. Only later do the brass and strings join in. The sequence tells us which instruments are essential and which are optional.

The introductions to all three songs showcase the rhythm section. A rhythm section contains three types of instruments:

- bass instrument (stand-up or electric bass)
- chord instrument (guitar or piano)
- percussion instrument (drum kit or individual drums [tambourine, etc.])

Within this general framework, there is considerable latitude. There can be more than one kind of instrument type: on "My Girl" we hear drums and finger snap. And no specific instrument is required within each instrument type: on "My Girl" the main chord instrument is guitar; on much of "The Way You Do the Things You Do," the primary chord instrument is piano; and on "Come See About Me," it is, rather unusually, a vibraphone. What's more important is that all three roles are filled.

In "My Girl," the rhythm section stays pretty much in the background, except for the introduction and its reprise about halfway through. Most of the time, the spotlight falls on the vocalists. Behind them, the brass instruments add sustained chords and little flourishes. The strings are even busier, with active melody-like lines, as well as more sustained background figures.

The choice of instruments and their roles suggests Motown's priorities. Voices and rhythm section are essential to provide the melody, its harmonic support, and the beat. The use of additional instruments not only enriches the sound but positions the music squarely in the mainstream: the extra percussion sounds have strong black roots, while the strings have a classical, or at least classic pop, connection. There are familiar sounds for almost everyone.

Performing Style

By surveying instrumentation, we learn what voices and instruments we hear. Performing style tells us how they are played. Both describe sound, but observations about performing style offer a more detailed and individualized portrait.

PERFORMING STYLE AND THE MOTOWN SOUND   The clearest evidence of a distinctive performing style is an individual sound. In Motown's case, this takes place on two levels. Most of the Motown singers share a basic sound concept: a blend of gospel and pop, with perhaps a touch of blues. The singing of the Temptations and the Supremes exemplifies this. Although each artist or group has its own sound, their singing represents gradations within the Motown style.

The Motown vocal sound represented a stylistic midpoint in the popular music of the sixties: unquestionably black, but a black pop sound, not the gritty singing of soul singers such as James Brown and Aretha Franklin. It helped position Motown music in the center of pop. The vocal style also represented a midpoint in the overall Motown approach to instrumentation and performing style. It sits comfortably in the middle, between the extremes of street-derived finger snaps and symphonic strings.

Dynamics and Inflection

Dynamics refers to loudness and softness. It is perhaps the most obvious of all musical elements: Deep Purple and Black Sabbath are loud—ear-damaging loud; new age pianist George Winston is soft. Yet dynamics can be presented with considerable subtlety, as we will discover.

Inflection is dynamic variation on a small scale, a stress of one note over another. In rock-era singing, inflection is often used to intensify the normal accentuation of a song lyric. This can produce a kind of heightened speech, a way of conveying a degree of emotion that exceeds what is possible with speech alone. For a clear example, listen to the Temptations sing the title phrase "My Girl" over and over. Inflection is also an expressive device in instrumental performance. Used in this way, it often mimics vocal inflection—or at least uses it as a point of departure.

DYNAMICS, INFLECTION, AND THE MOTOWN SOUND   In our three Motown songs, there is a clear hierarchy in dynamics. The vocal lines are the most prominent. The bass line, melodically presented harmony, and the backbeat are typically the next loudest. That gives us the nucleus of the sound: the most important line and its primary rhythmic and harmonic support. Other melodic lines, e.g., string parts, come next; other percussion instruments are more in the background.

Moreover, the recording does not encourage excessively loud or soft playback. Like other elements, dynamics finds the middle path between extremes. So does inflection: the singers' delivery is more inflected than a fifties pop singer, e.g., Perry Como, but less than a blues- or gospel-influenced singer, such as Ray Charles.

Texture

In the preceding discussion, we have identified several layers of musical activity. Recall that in "My Girl," we heard them enter one or two at a time. Some of the layers, like the lead vocal line and the guitar riffs, stand out. Others, like the bass line, backbeat, or vocal harmonies, are easily identifiable if we simply turn our attention to them. Still others may be very much in the background. Like the hum of an air conditioner or fluorescent light, we are most aware of them when they are not on.

We use the term "texture" to describe the relationship of these layers. To get a feel for texture, try the following. Pick any of the three songs, play the recording, snap your fingers on the backbeat, and sing along with the lead vocalist. Do this over and over until you know the song pretty well. Then try snapping your fingers and singing the lead vocal line without the recording. You'll notice that there's a lot missing. Texture is not only the parts you've been performing, but everything else as well: in Paul Harvey's memorable words, it's "the rest of the story."

THE TEXTURE OF THE MOTOWN SOUND The texture of the Motown sound is remarkable in rock-era music both for what is there and what isn't there. What we hear is a rich musical fabric, woven together from strands of melody (or at least melody-like lines) a strong backbeat, and light percussion. What we don't hear is heavy reinforcement of the faster-than-beat rhythms: either the rock rhythm of "My Girl" and "Come See About Me," or the shuffle rhythm of "The Way You Do the Things You Do." There's no guitarist pumping out a rock rhythm a la Chuck Berry, and the rock rhythm pounded out on the drums at the beginning of "Come See About Me" is definitely the exception.

The result is an open-sounding texture: heavy on voice, bass, and backbeat, but pretty light everywhere else. When the texture becomes thicker, it's usually through the addition of vocal harmonies, sustained string or wind chords, or additional melodic layers. Strong, steady reinforcement of the prevailing rhythm and harmony is rare.

Even more than other elements, texture in these Motown songs consists more of a set of preferences than a set of prescriptions. These preferences begin with easy rhythmic and melodic points of entry: a strong backbeat and catchy hooks. They are surrounded with other active rhythms and multiple melodic strands, even from rhythm instruments, as we have already noticed. The details differ from song to song, but the basic strategy remains consistent: voices, backbeat, and bass prominent, other melodic lines swirling around, and light beat-keeping in the rhythm section.

A final note on texture: a persistent feature in Motown recordings is call and response, rapid exchanges between two different sonorities. The most obvious call and response exchanges occur between lead and backup vocalists: in the verse of "Come See About Me," the "response" figures by the Supremes complete Diana Ross's statement. Call and response exchanges come out of the black church. It was absorbed into almost every black style—e.g., blues, jazz, rhythm and blues, doo-wop—as we'll discover in the next several chapters.

Form

Form is the organization of music in time. We cannot apprehend the form of a song all at once, as we can with much visual art. As we listen, however, we hear memorable musical events—riffs, rhythms, refrains. When they repeat or return, they give shape to the performance, marking off temporal boundaries and outlining the overall pattern.

Changes in other elements also help bring the form of a song into focus: louder or softer dynamics, addition or subtraction of instruments or voices, thickening or thinning of the texture, and the like. A tour through "My Girl" shows how both memorable events and coordinated change in several elements shape the song in time.

The sequence of events coalesces into an introduction, two statements of a melody, an instrumental interlude, a third statement of the melody, and a fadeout ending. Table 1.1 outlines the form.

Each statement of the melody contains four distinct sections. The first two are a phrase and its repetition, which we've called a and a'. (A phrase is a musical idea that's more than a riff but less than a complete thought. Think of it this way: A phrase says enough to deserve a comma, but it is not long enough to require a period.) The third section presents a new, shorter melodic idea and its more active repetition (together they make b). The fourth section consists mainly of several repetitions of the title phrase (c).

The melody remains more or less the same from statement to statement, although the third statement is in a higher key. The lyric follows a different plan: it changes from statement to statement in the a and a' sections, and remains the same in b and c. The part of the melody where the lyrics change is often called a *verse*. The part that remains the same in both words and music is called the *refrain* or *chorus*.

The memorable events in "My Girl," and especially the periodic return of the refrain, help us find our way through the song. They are the aural equivalent of the dots in a dot-to-dot puzzle: as we connect each dot in time, the formal outline comes into focus. However, form is not only outline, but shape—the ebb and flow of the music in time. (Again, when we finish the dot-to-dot puzzle, we know what the object is, but we also recognize that it is far from an accurate rendering of the object.) "My Girl" is an "end-weighted" verse/refrain form. That is, the refrain is not only a milestone but a point of arrival. Throughout the verse, the music gradually builds up, peaking on the many restatements of "my girl." We feel the music gain momentum as voices and instruments gradually enter and both the chord and phrase rhythms quicken. The energy from the buildup spills over into the "my girls," but other elements relax: for example, we settle on the I chord for eight beats, after moving through four chords at two beats per chord. This sudden stability signals that we've arrived at an important formal destination.

This sense of building toward a goal is also evident over larger time spans. We sense the two statements of the melody as one larger unit because the strings and brass, which weren't even playing at the beginning of the first verse, become more active during the second verse; and because of the sudden dropoff—just bass and wordless vocal continue—after the second refrain. And we sense that the final destination of the song is the very end because the third statement of the melody is in a higher key, the strings are even busier, and the final refrain is extended by mixing in the verse.

TABLE 1.1
The Form of "My Girl"

Introduction.

0'00"	Bass riff begins song.
0'05"	Signature guitar riff layers in.

First Statement of the Melody.

0'10"	a	Verse	Lead singer enters, singing first phrase of the melody.
0'19"	a'	Verse cont.	Backup singers join in with sustained harmony as lead singer repeats the first phrase with different words.
0'28"	b	Refrain (bridge)	New, shorter melodic idea (with longer notes) and its repetition; brass double vocal harmony.
0'37"	c	Refrain (hook)	Title phrase tossed around among voices; strings take over sustained harmony.

Second Statement of the Melody.

0'46"	a	Verse	New words sung to a varied version of first phrase of the melody, this time with sustained string accompaniment and brass flourishes.
0'55"	a'	Verse, cont.	New words sung to the repetition of the first phrase. As before, backup vocals support lead singer on the restatement.
1'04"	b	Refrain (bridge)	Like [0'28"] in both words and music, plus a string countermelody.
1'13"	c	Refrain (hook)	Like [0'37"] in both words and music, plus a string countermelody.

Interlude.

1'22"	Like [0'00"], plus wordless vocal line.
1'27"	Like [0'05"], plus sustained notes from strings.
1'31"	New string melody based on harmony of [0'10"].
1'41"	Beginning of a move to a new key.

Third Statement of the Melody.

1'50"	a	Verse	Third statement of the first phrase of the melody, with brass flourishes and string countermelody. More new words.
1'59"	a'	Verse cont.	Third statement of the first phrase repetition, with same accompaniment. More new words.
2'08"	b	Refrain (bridge)	Third statement of second phrase, almost identical to [1'04"], except that the string part is more active.
2'17"	c	Refrain (hook)	Third statement of title phrase, almost identical to [1'13"], except that the string part is more active.

Tag and "Outro."

2'26"	Several repetitions of chords and instrumental texture of [2'17"]. Vocal lines combine the first phrase text [0'10"] sung by the lead singer with the title phrase sung by the backup singers.
2'46"	Fadeout over final line of text ("talkin' 'bout my girl"), sung over and over.

In describing the form of "My Girl," we began by outlining the form as a series of aabc verse/refrain statements, framed by an introduction, interlude, and "outro." This first step helps us "auralize" several minutes of music as an easily perceived pattern. However, by fleshing out the outline with a description of the activity within each section, we were able to hear how the song is end-weighted over increasingly larger time spans. Each return of "My Girl" is set to a more powerful climax. As this example shows, form is more than a mold into which songwriters dump melodies. It is the product of the interaction of every element: not only melody, but also harmony, rhythm, texture, instrumentation, etc.

Form and the Motown Sound

Smokey Robinson, who wrote "My Girl," recalls that Berry Gordy told him very early in their association that a song must tell a story. Motown songs do that—or at least paint pictures. For example, the lyric of "My Girl" offers a succession of images that give us a character portrait of "my girl."

The form of the song amplifies and reinforces the verbal message through a well-coordinated set of strategies. Most obvious is the alternation of verse and refrain: the repetition of the refrain keeps our focus on the central message of the song—"my girl"—while the verse fleshes out her portrait. More subtle, and ultimately more telling, is the musical highlighting of the refrain: it appears as the climax of each section, prepared by a transition from the verse that increases the tension.

This basic plan is also used in "The Way You Do the Things You Do" and "Come See About Me," with some difference in detail. Although the details of form may differ, the underlying strategy remains consistent: putting the spotlight on the refrain, and repeating it again and again.

Summary of the Motown Sound

Table 1.2 outlines the framework that we've developed and reviews terms that we introduced and how they are realized in "My Girl."

In the process of constructing the framework, we've also created a profile of the Motown sound. We learned that songs could differ in obvious details— the featured singers, the beat or instruments used—yet maintain a consistent sound. The Motown sound included specific features, e.g., a strong backbeat. But most of its identifiable features were principles and approaches that could be realized in many different ways. These included:

1. light timekeeping, by both percussion and chord instruments;
2. melodic saturation, including melodic presentation of harmony;
3. moderate syncopation, especially in accompanying riffs;
4. rich instrumentation, with only bass, drums, and voice as constants;
5. hierarchical dynamics, with bass, backbeat, and melodically presented chords second in importance to the voice;
6. the Motown singing style;
7. dense, multilayered textures; and
8. verse/refrain forms that reached a climax at the title phrase.

TABLE 1.2
Review of Terms with Examples from "My Girl"

Rhythm: Beat and tempo	"My Girl" = about 100 beats a minute
Rhythm: meter	four beats a measure; beat divided evenly
Rhythm: backbeat	finger snap
Rhythm: "style" beat	rock beat/eight-beat rhythm
Rhythm: rhythmic conflict	syncopation mainly in bass part and lead vocal
Rhythm: rhythmic texture	dense, multi-layered
Melody	riff figures in vocal lines, bass line, guitar line, brass figures, and strings
Harmony	song built mainly on I, IV, and V
Instrumentation	lead vocal and nuclear rhythm section plus backup vocals, brass, strings, extra percussion (finger snap)
Performing style	two level sound concept: Motown sound (gospel/pop/blues blend), then Temptations' sound
Dynamics	recording suggests mid-level volume
Inflection	"My Girl" and other phrases, especially during the ending
Texture	lead vocal line is the main focus, but texture is dense and layered
Form	"end-weighted" form

Similarly, the appeal of Motown recordings was the product of several factors. Among the most significant were:

1. *An exquisite balance between melody and rhythm.* The best Motown songs had great, but not overpowering, beats and catchy melodies. No one did it better.

2. *Multiple points of entry.* The backbeat was always there to lock in the rhythm, and most songs had not only a memorable vocal hook but an instrumental one as well.

3. *A fresh new vocal sound close to mainstream taste.* The gospel-inflected yet pop-oriented singing style of the Motown acts was a new black pop sound, one that struck a balance between novelty and familiarity.

4. *Something-for-everyone instrumentation.* Motown recordings typically fleshed out the nuclear voice and rhythm instrumentation with the strings and horns associated with pop and jazz and the extra percussion associated with R&B. A wide spectrum of listeners would find familiar sounds in Motown recordings.

5. *Easy-to-follow forms.*

Motown's success was no accident. Rather, it was the result of Berry Gordy's carefully calculated strategy: he created a style positioned to appeal to as broad an audience as possible. He was lucky to be in the right place at the right time. But in his case, luck was largely the by-product of design. The Motown sound, Gordy's "sound of young America," lived at the top of the charts during the mid-sixties. The best songs live on as classics. They bring back floods of memories to the young Americans of the sixties and are almost as familiar to their children.

If we read his autobiography, we know what Gordy wanted to achieve. If we look at the charts from the mid-sixties, we know that Gordy reached his goal. By profiling these three 1964 hits, we have learned how Gordy achieved his goal, because we have identified the musical components of the Motown sound and how they work with the lyrics of the songs.

So we have answered two questions. The first, more specific one is, "What is the Motown sound?" The second is, "By what method can we identify its elements?" In the process of describing the Motown sound, we have also created a framework for observing and evaluating musical events that we can use to discuss all the music of the rock era—and some that comes before.

We have also generated a number of other questions: What did Gordy and his Motown stable take from the past? What was truly innovative? How did Motown relate to other rock and R&B styles in the sixties—Stax soul, the Rolling Stones, the Beatles? We will address these and other questions through the course of the book, using our style checklist to generate musical insights. We begin with a tour through rock's roots.

K E Y   T E R M S

Style	**Syncopation**	**Performing Style**
Beat	**Rhythmic conflict**	**Dynamics**
Measure	**Riff**	**Inflection**
Rhythmic layers	**Harmony**	**Texture**
Rock/Eight-beat rhythm	**Instrumentation**	**End-weighted form**

C H A P T E R   Q U E S T I O N S

1. Review the three distinct meanings of beat discussed in this chapter: beat 1 (timekeeping at a comfortable speed); beat 2 (rhythmic foundation of a style); and beat 3 (overall rhythmic feel). Then practice shifting between a rock beat and a shuffle beat.

2. Explore the idea of melodic saturation in "My Girl" by finding at least one melodic fragment from each of the following: lead vocalist (easy), backup vocalists, bass, guitar, trumpets, strings. Then sing or hum along with the melodic fragments.

3. Review the "Motown sound" profile in Table 1.2. Then listen to a Motown hit not included in Chapter 1 or Chapter 6 and describe each element as it's heard in that song.

4. Using the same Motown hit, outline the form. Is it an "end-weighted" form, or something different?

5. In the discussion of instrumentation, we suggested that the use of strings and finger snaps helped broaden the appeal of Motown because it linked the style with both classical music and rhythm and blues. Do you agree with our suggestion? If yes, can you find other aspects of the music that imply this symphonic/street-corner mix? If not, can you offer an alternative explanation?

c h a p t e r   2

The Roots of Rock

Rock fomented a revolution, but it was also the product of a long evolution. It grew out of musical traditions that go back centuries, and popular music styles that were over a century old by the time Elvis Presley's "Heartbreak Hotel" hit the airwaves. What follows is a whistle-stop tour through more than a century of music, from the 1830s to the 1950s.

Early Sources of Rock Style

Rock is an integrated music. It has roots in European and African culture. From the British Isles came music of both "high" culture (or "classical") and "low" culture (usually labeled "folk"). The slave trade brought people from all over west Africa, with little regard for family or tribal bonds. However, the musical values of west Africans survived in the New World, although they took on markedly different forms in the United States, Cuba, and Brazil.

The African Influence

We don't know much about the music of the slaves in the early nineteenth century. We have some anecdotal evidence, mostly written by white observers who found their music baffling. But we do know that drums were largely out-lawed on the Southern plantations, because slave owners feared that blacks were using them as a means of communication. As a result, heavy use of per-cussive instruments, perhaps the most crucial element of African music mak-ing, was all but eliminated. In Cuba, Brazil, and elsewhere in Latin America, African retentions were stronger, because slaves were allowed to re-create their drums, rattles, and other instruments.

Perhaps the most interesting aspect of the evolution of popular music is the gradual, but relentless, infiltration of African musical values into main-stream pop. That this has occurred, despite suppression of African rhythms and instruments during slavery and then strong resistance from the cultural-ly dominant white majority, is remarkable.

From African music, rock inherited, above all, key features of its rhythm. It also inherited other elements:

- percussion instruments and percussive playing techniques
- riff-like melodic ideas

- layered textures
- open forms

A field recording of Yoruba tribesmen from Africa shows the unmistakable affinity between African folk music and rock-era popular music. It's evident in the rhythms, riffs, and sounds. Some of the correspondences between it and a contemporary example, Kool and the Gang's "Ladies Night," are uncanny in their similarity:

- a dense, syncopated rhythmic texture built around "eight-beat" time-keeping
- melismatic vocal lines (a *melisma* is several notes sung to a single syllable)
- a layered texture made up of voices, percussion, and pitched instruments

The Classical Influence

In the early nineteenth century, the upper and middle classes in Europe and America shared a common musical language. We know its most sophisticated statements as classical music: the music of Beethoven, Schubert, et al. However, there was also a vast body of "popular" song and music for social dancing that used a simpler form of the same musical language. Unlike today, there was a smooth continuum between classical music and popular song, as we can hear in Henry Russell's "Woodman, Spare That Tree."

> Classical music, from which Russell borrowed so freely, also embodied cultural prestige. Throughout the twentieth century, new popular styles assumed classical trappings to "legitimize" themselves. A few examples: Joplin's ragtime opera, *Treemonisha*; Paul Whiteman's "symphonic jazz," which was responsible for George Gershwin's *Rhapsody in Blue*; the Beatles' concept albums, art rock, the Who's *Tommy*.

Henry Russell was an Englishman who studied composition with the Italian opera composers Rossini and Bellini before he emigrated briefly to the United States. During his heyday in the 1830s and 1840s, he was the most popular and influential songwriter in America. In "Woodman, Spare That Tree," he used a simpler version of the Italian operatic style of the period.

"Woodman, Spare That Tree" may seem miles away from rock, and it is. Nevertheless, its "popular" classical style contributed three important musical ingredients to rock:

- the use of harmony to support a melody (rock uses chords, and it got them from "classical" music; neither African- nor Anglo-American folk music use harmony);
- a clear rhythmic hierarchy—beat division, beat, measure, and two or four measure phrase;
- clearly outlined form.

All three elements would be integrated into rock and rhythm and blues.

The Folk Influence

The people who emigrated from the British Isles to North America brought their music with them: ballads and dance music that date back centuries. Ballads were unaccompanied storytelling songs. The most popular dances were uptempo jigs and reels, played by a fiddler. We have no way of knowing exactly how this music sounded in the early nineteenth century, but we can infer some of the key features of the style from the earliest country recordings and contemporary accounts.

Like classical music, Anglo-American folk music is also far removed from rock. Nevertheless, we can find antecedents of rock style in several of its features. Among them are:

- a story told in plain everyday language;
- sung with a rough, untrained voice;
- heterophony (i.e., multiple versions of the melody, played simultaneously);
- a form that alternates scene-painting verses with a recurrent refrain; and
- an uptempo dance rhythm.

We can hear all of these qualities in Ben Jarrell's 1927 recording of the popular folk song, "Old Joe Clark." One of the first country music recordings, it is an example of "old time music." Because its performers are from the rural South, the style probably dates back to the nineteenth century.

The First Synthesis

If American popular music has a birthday, it could easily be March 7, 1843. On that evening, the Virginia Minstrels, a four-man troupe of experienced blackface performers, presented the first complete minstrel show at the Masonic Temple in Boston. Gilbert Chase described the Virginia Minstrels' show as a freewheeling affair, "a combination of singing, dancing, and instrumental music . . . interspersed with jokes, anecdotes, and repartee in pseudo-Negro dialect."

The music of the minstrel show was the first American popular music. There had been music that was "popular" in the commercial sense. Russell's songs, for example, were widely known, and they sold well. But the minstrel show brought qualities into popular music that stamped it as distinctively American. Two stand out: an irreverent attitude that had little tolerance for the airs of genteel society; and a vibrant new sound synthesized from African music and both European traditions.

Anglo-American folk music was the catalyst for the creation of a vernacular popular style. It infused popular song with the energy and high spirits of its jigs and reels. Songs such as "Boatmen's Dance" became vibrant alternatives to the slow and sentimental songs of Russell, et al.

African Americans provided minstrelsy with images and instruments. White and, after the Civil War, black entertainers used to perform in "blackface." They applied burnt cork to their faces to simulate the appearance of African Americans, or at least an African-American stereotype. Their depiction of black speech and movement was likewise stereotyped. Three of the core instruments of the minstrel show gave the music an African tinge. The banjo is, by most accounts, an instrument of African origin; bones and tambourine add percussion to the texture. Only the fiddle comes from white folk music.

There is a painful irony that the first popular music recognized as American—in both the United States and Europe—was a grotesque parody of a largely enslaved minority. To add insult to injury, it was white performers who portrayed blacks to white audiences until after the Civil War. And even after the Civil War, when black minstrels began to take the stage, they had to put burnt cork on their faces so that they looked like whites felt they should, not like themselves. These vicious stereotypes persisted, on posters, sheet music covers, and elsewhere, until well into the twentieth century. Al Jolson "blacked up" in the twenties, and Eddie Cantor and others performed in blackface in several Busby Berkeley movie musicals from the thirties.

Dan Emmett's "Boatmen's Dance," re-created here in Robert Winans's conscientious 1985 recording, was one of the first minstrel songs. It is a synthesis on two levels. First, it mixes folk song and folk dance: we hear the fiddle playing a reel-like tune while the singer(s) tell a story. Second, it blends in elements of European classical and African-American music. It took harmony and regular form from classical music, and, as we have noted, most of its instruments come from African-American culture.

However, the folk influence is dominant. The song is written in the verse-chorus form that was popular among folk musicians, with a loose set of verses leading up to a singable, and easy-to-remember, refrain. The melody is based on a pentatonic (five-note) scale, commonly heard in Anglo-American folksongs. The tempo is upbeat and lively, the subject matter drawn from a common American experience.

Post-Civil War popular song shows the influence of minstrelsy in two innovations: the use of dance rhythms and forms that alternate storytelling sections with a recurrent refrain. Popular songs prior to 1840 seldom had either, while the majority of the songs written between the Civil War and the 1910s had both. In other respects, however, popular song retreated from the freshness and vitality of the early minstrel songs. Around 1900, the most popular songs of the time were waltz songs, such as "Take Me Out to the Ball Game," a big hit in 1908. To be sure, these songs used verse/refrain form and were set to a dance beat, but there was little else in the style that we associate with the minstrel show, or rock. Popular music was still miles away from rock and roll.

Table 2.1 shows the three main sources of rock style and their interaction in the first vernacular style to become a commercially popular music.

One need look no further that the logo of the Rolling Stones to discover how the irreverence that began with the minstrel show has carried into the rock era. Indeed, some writers have accused Mick Jagger of being a minstrel-without-portfolio—or at least burnt cork—because they consider his performing style to be a grotesque parody of black blues singing. (Not our opinion, we should add.)

TABLE 2.1
Sources of Rock Style and the First Synthesis

African: "Yoruba Chorus"	dense, complex rhythmic texture with lots of syncopation
	percussion instruments
	riffs
	raw vocal sound
Classical: "Woodman, Spare That Tree" (1837)	harmony
	clear forms
	melody plus accompaniment texture
	social prestige
	idea of art music
Anglo-American Folk: "Old Joe Clark" (1927)	storytelling songs (ballads)
	fast dance rhythms (jigs, reels)
	nasal vocal sound
	lack of pretense
	verse/refrain form
	heterophonic texture
	down-home lyrics
First synthesis: "Boatmen's Dance" (1843)	introduced idea of vernacular popular music
	first important synthesis of classical music, Anglo-American folk music, and African-American musical traditions
	down-to-earth lyrics
	dance rhythms
	I-IV-V harmonies in folk-inspired popular song
	percussion instruments
	heterophonic texture
	verse/refrain form

"Boatmen's Dance" also exemplifies the most fundamental creative process in popular music: forging new styles by blending together musical elements that are seemingly incompatible, both musically and socially. This synthetic process is also part of the minstrel show's legacy to rock. As we learned in the previous chapter (think finger snaps and symphonic strings), it was certainly alive and well in the 1960s.

A New Century—and a New Sound

A revolutionary change in popular music began just after the turn of the century with a healthy infusion of black music—ragtime, blues, and jazz—into the prevailing popular styles. By 1930, when the revolution would be complete, popular music would have changed more substantially than at any time before or since.

This transformation of popular music began in the 1890s, when the cakewalk (a social dance fad borrowed from the minstrel show) and the "coon song" (also borrowed from the minstrel show) introduced syncopation into popular song and dance.

> The 1890s was not a politically correct decade. Indeed, it was probably the low point in post-Civil War race relations. Few whites seemed bothered by racial slurs such as "coon," and the Supreme Court passed the "separate but equal" ruling in 1896.

Ragtime and Its Impact

Ragtime, a more syncopated style, caught on around 1900, soon after the publication of Scott Joplin's "Maple Leaf Rag" (1899). Although printed by the obscure St. Louis publisher John Stark, it was an overnight sensation. Both whites and blacks bought the sheet music to play in their homes. Soon, ragtime was in the air: not only piano rags, but also ragtime songs and dances. Any music with a hint of syncopation, or even with a bouncy beat but no syncopation at all, was considered ragtime. (Irving Berlin's 1911 hit, "Alexander's Ragtime Band," is a good example of a "ragtime" song without a shred of syncopation.)

Scott Joplin, c. 1915.
PHOTO COURTESY FRANK
DRIGGS COLLECTION.

The piano rags of Joplin and others were, in essence, African-American interpretations of the European march, performed on the piano. They retained the form, beat, and harmony of the march, but "ragged" (i.e. syncopated) the melody.

Ragtime also provided music for the notorious animal dances of the 1900s and 1910s: among them the turkey trot, chicken scratch, monkey glide, and bunny hug. These watered-down versions of African-American social dances became popular with many white youths during the first years of the century. As such, they were the forerunners of the social dances popularized on Dick Clark's American Bandstand.

Ragtime was a crucial step on the road to rock. It introduced authentic African-American rhythm into popular music, a rhythm that would eventually evolve into rock. Moreover, it gave black music a commercial presence. Even at the peak of its popularity, ragtime remained a minority music, commercially as well as racially. But it was a start. And, like rhythm and blues in the forties, it was the first harbinger of another major revolution in popular music.

Early Blues Styles

Blues began to infiltrate popular music in the teens and early twenties. It came in three waves. The first blues appeared as popular songs and dance music. They introduced some blues basics: its melodic and harmonic form, and a little of its feeling. Jazz bands followed with their own instrumental blues. Finally, in the early twenties, record companies began to record black performers, including commercial blues singers like Bessie Smith.

BLUES AS POPULAR SONG AND DANCE MUSIC The first "popular" blues came in vocal and instrumental versions. W.C. Handy's best known blues song was a vocal: "St. Louis Blues" (1914). It was the most frequently recorded popular song before rock. Handy's "Memphis Blues" (1912) was the first published blues; it was also the first fox-trot. Irene and Vernon Castle, accompanied by black society bandleader James Reese Europe, created the dance after hearing Europe improvise on Handy's composition.

The fox-trot quickly caught on: it was the first big dance fad of the twentieth century. By the early twenties, syncopated dance orchestras, both black and white, had sprung up everywhere. Fletcher Henderson, an African-American pianist and arranger, led one of the most important of these orchestras. His 1924 recording, "Copenhagen," is a "hot" blues dance number. Although not particularly "bluesy" by rock-era standards, "Copenhagen" offers a clear example of the fox-trot beat, clearly marked by a rhythm section. The most prominent rhythm instruments in this recording are the tuba and banjo: they alternate between bass note and crisply played chord (the backbeat) in a *two-beat rhythm*.

The syncopated dance music of Henderson and others presages rock in several ways. Most fundamentally, it paved the way for the widespread use of the fox-trot rhythm in popular music. Almost overnight, popular song was sung over a black beat, instead of the European rhythms of the waltz, march and polka. Dance orchestras (and jazz bands) fleshed out rhythm sections to mark the beat, as well as a heavy backbeat. Both the rhythm section and an African-American rhythmic conception (including a strong backbeat) are core elements of rock style. As we can hear, their roots go back to the twenties.

BLUES AND JAZZ   The second wave of blues sounds came in 1917, with the release of the Original Dixieland Jazz Band's recording of "Livery Stable Blues." For most early jazz bands, both black and white, blues songs comprised about half the songs in their repertoire. The classic blues performance in early jazz is "Dippermouth Blues," recorded in 1923 by King Oliver's Creole Jazz Band. In it we can hear the roots of jazz in the march and the blues.

Like the ragtime pianists, jazz musicians had transformed the march into an African-American music. Indeed, jazz kept more of the march sound, at least in its instrumentation. The early jazz band—cornet, clarinet, trombone, brass bass, drums, banjo, and piano—is nothing more than the nucleus of a marching band plus two chord instruments. It is also the predecessor of the soul bands of the sixties, and the funk bands of the seventies and beyond. Change clarinet to saxophone, brass bass to electric bass, and banjo to electric guitar, and you have the Blues Brothers' backup band.

At the same time, jazz brought more African-derived elements into popular music. These include denser, more syncopated rhythms; a thick, interdependent texture; the use of riffs; and blues-inspired inflection. The four-beat rhythm chunked out by the banjo moved popular music closer to rock's eight-beat rhythm, and there is more syncopation than in either "Maple Leaf Rag" or "Copenhagen." The interplay among the horns fore-shadows the interaction among voice and instruments so characteristic of much rock-era music.

> Beginning in the twenties, notes such as the first note of Oliver's solo were called "blue notes." We hear them clashing with the I and V chords in the blues progression. They clash because they are borrowed from the African pentatonic scale. They were called "blue notes" because they occurred even more frequently in classic blues songs.

"Dippermouth Blues" is a blues in both form and style, especially during Oliver's cornet solo. Right from the beginning, we hear key elements of blues style: a gravelly sound, clearly imitating blues vocal style; repeated riffs; beat-defying rhythmic freedom; moaning blue notes. All these elements were in the service of blues feeling: it's not difficult to imagine Bessie Smith (see directly below) singing the opening riff to the words "Ma man's gone." However, Oliver develops the riff in a purely instrumental way.

This excerpt shows how close blues and jazz could be, and how they remained different. It also marks the beginning of a tradition of blues-based improvisation. That line passes through the honking saxophones of forties and fifties rhythm and blues before arriving at the extended jams of Hendrix and Clapton.

CLASSIC BLUES   African Americans, especially women, had been singing the blues professionally since just after the turn of the century, and a few had made recordings. However, "classic" blues—vocal blues songs that had blues form, style, and feeling—didn't appear on record until the twenties. In 1920, Mamie Smith recorded "Crazy Blues." Like many so-called blues songs of the era, it was not really a blues, but a vaudeville-type song sung in a bluesy style.

*Bessie Smith, wearing
one of her many fancy
stage hats, c. 1925.*
Photo courtesy Frank
Driggs Collection.

However, its success made record companies aware that there was a substantial market for black performers, among them Bessie Smith.

These recordings were called "race records," recordings by black performers intended primarily for the black community. That designation remained more or less in place until 1949, when—at Jerry Wexler's suggestion—it was replaced by "rhythm and blues."

Bessie Smith, nicknamed the "empress" of the blues, was the most popular and artistically successful of the women blues singers. Her audience included both blacks and whites. Her recordings, of which "Back Water Blues" (1927) is a good example, put real blues feeling and style on record. In the song, we hear all the elements we associate with blues singing:

- a gritty vocal quality
- conversational phrasing
- inflection that heightens the normal accentuation of speech
- blue notes
- phrases that start high and finish low
- a narrow melodic range

These qualities invest the somber lyric with the emotion of deep blues. Both style and feeling would trickle slowly into the mainstream, moving one branch of popular singing closer to rock and rhythm and blues.

From our perspective, the blues recordings included here seem tame in comparison with the "deep blues" of Robert Johnson or Muddy Waters. Only Smith's singing has the emotional commitment we expect from the blues, and James P. Johnson's piano accompaniment undermines its potency. However, from the perspective of a white American, ca. 1925, it was pretty heady stuff. A generation that has grown up on rap may find it difficult to understand that the infusion of black musical values into music that was lily white in 1900 was a long, gradual, and often reluctant process.

A New Kind of Popular Song and Dance

In the twenties, America got a new kind of popular song: the fox-trot song. It had conversational lyrics set to syncopated, riff-based melodies, which were played by dance orchestras and jazz bands, who laid down a black beat with a backbeat. All of these features surfaced in popular music as the innovations of ragtime, jazz, syncopated dance music, and blues filtered into popular song and its performance. As they appeared in popular song, these innovations were considerably toned down from their original black forms. Still, they completely transformed the sound of popular music in less than a generation. Sentimental ballads were out; syncopated, danceable popular song was in.

Both the songs and the performances of them were more upbeat than they were around the turn of the century. Danceable recordings of the songs of the twenties and thirties began to emphasize the chorus; the verse was either sandwiched between two statements of the chorus or simply discarded. The chorus unfolded quickly, typically in four eight-measure phrases. By far the most common formal plan was AABA: an opening riff-based phrase (A); its restatement (A); a contrasting phrase, often called a bridge (B); and a final restatement of the opening melody. (This is the form used in "If I Had You.") At brisk fox-trot tempos, it was often possible to include three statements of the chorus on a 3-minute recording. We hear a nice example of up-to-date popular song in a 1930 recording of "If I Had You," by the Sam Lanin Orchestra, featuring a young Bing Crosby.

Black music also reshaped the *function* of popular song: by the twenties, it had to be danceable as well as singable. Before the teens, most popular songs, even those with an obvious dance beat, were strictly for singing. After 1920, however, almost all up-to-date popular songs were fox-trots.

Furthermore, social dancing to syncopated popular song had become socially acceptable. The hectic animal dances of the first decade of the twentieth century, which had provoked such moral outrage, had been transformed by a kind of musical alchemy into the elegant fox-trots of the thirties. Dancing "Cheek to Cheek" was about as classy and elegant as Americans could get, as Fred Astaire and Ginger Rogers showed us in a series of film musicals. Most people found the image quintessentially romantic; only the most hidebound traditionalists objected.

Electrical recording and amplification, both adapted from radio broadcasting, not only made for better-sounding performances, but also opened the door for new kinds of singers. Singers no longer had to belt out their songs. Instead, crooners such as Bing Crosby and jazz singers such as Louis Armstrong could sing in a more intimate, personal manner.

Blues and Jazz, 1926–1940

In the fifteen years between 1926 and 1940, blues diversified and jazz matured. Country blues began to appear on record, and new blues styles such as boogie woogie and urban blues took shape. By the thirties, jazz had begun to swing consistently. In its most dance-oriented form, it also became the basis for a new, more rhythmically vital dance music: big band swing.

By the mid-thirties, popular music had come to an evolutionary fork in the road. One path, blues and jazz, would eventually lead to rock. The other, the increasingly conservative pop of the same era, would lead to the music that rock would react against.

Blues, 1926–1940

Changing taste, continuing evolution, and the Depression completely transformed the sound of blues on record. The barely blue pop songs and the up-tempo blues of the syncopated dance orchestras went out of fashion. The Depression, which hit African Americans especially hard, eroded their support of Bessie Smith and the other classic blues singers. Their careers were effectively over by 1930.

In their place came a number of blues styles, some old, some new. Among the old—but new to records—was country blues. Paramount Records advertised the country blues of Blind Lemon Jefferson, the first major country blues singer to record, as "real old-fashioned blues by a real old-fashioned blues singer." Among the new styles were hokum and boogie woogie, both blues styles with a strong beat. At about the same time, Louis Armstrong showed both jazzmen and pop singers how to infuse their performance with the sound and feeling of the blues.

COUNTRY BLUES From 1926, the year of Jefferson's first recording, until about 1940, country blues was a small but viable niche in the record industry. The bluesmen who recorded in the twenties and thirties came from all over the South and Southwest. Blind Lemon Jefferson and Leadbelly came from Texas, Blind Willie McTell from Georgia. However, the spiritual center of the blues, then and now, was the Mississippi Delta region, just south of Memphis. It was home to a host of legendary bluesmen, including its two most influential: Robert Johnson and Muddy Waters. We discuss Johnson here, and Waters in the next chapter.

Johnson is the most compelling personality in the history of the blues. His is the kind of story that fans, musicians, historians, and just about anyone else interested in popular music find irresistible: unsurpassed musical genius coupled with a live-hard, die-young life about which we know very little.

If his life is a mystery, his music is not: no one has sung and played the blues better than Johnson. He excelled at each phase: writing, singing, playing. His music communicates on an elemental level. It speaks to us directly. Its power is present in both words and music, in both singing and playing.

His lyrics can speak about life issues in vivid, to-the-point language ("If she gets unruly and thinks she don't wan' do/ Take my 32-20, now, and cut her half in two" is about as direct as it gets) or powerful metaphors ("Blues coming down like hail . . . hellhound on my trail").

Johnson's performing style intensifies their already potent message. His lyrics may tell us what the message is, but his delivery helps us feel the emotions behind the words—or, at times, beyond the words. "Come On In My Kitchen" is an especially good example of his style. Most of the time he sings clearly and comprehensibly, so we can savor his words. However, he occasionally slurs words, drops spoken asides, or simply hums a line. His singing intensifies speech, like so much great blues singing. Similarly, his non-verbal sounds intensify the feelings we express without words—a sigh, a moan, a laugh.

Johnson modeled his melodic playing on his singing. In the opening of "Come On In My Kitchen," the guitar line not only matches the notes of the sung melody fairly closely (a good example of blues-style heterophony) but also parallels the inflection of his voice. Johnson's singing and playing are different forms of a more basic expressive conception.

Johnson's music is all of a piece. It is self-consistent in a way that very little music—of any kind—is. In every respect, it resonates with life experience of the most elemental kind and at the same time transcends it. Perhaps it is this elemental quality that has given his music such universality, and it may explain how music from one of the least known and appreciated American subcultures—African Americans in the Mississippi Delta—could reach across oceans and generations.

> Eric Clapton says of Johnson's singing, "His music remains the most powerful cry that I think you can find in the human voice . . . ." Keith Richards recalls hearing Johnson for the first time, wondering "who's the other guy playing with him?" and not realizing until much later that what sounded like two guitars was actually one person—Johnson—playing two parts, often simultaneously.

By the time Johnson made his last recordings in 1937, country blues had peaked as a commercial style, at least in the eyes of the record executives. It went into decline for about two decades, resurfacing as part of the folk revival around 1960. Johnson's recordings were among those reissued on LP about this time.

Country blues, and especially Johnson's music, hit British blues-based rock musicians like a heavyweight's right hand, partly because it leapfrogged a generation, and partly because it defined the essence of the blues. Its impact on rock was sudden and dramatic. Other blues styles would trace a more continuous path to rock. Among them were two upbeat sounds, hokum and boogie woogie.

HOKUM New, more urban blues styles also began to appear on record in the late twenties. They featured singers who sounded bluesier than pop or jazz singers but not as emotionally charged as Bessie Smith or as raw as the country bluesmen. The accompaniment, typically piano and guitar, gave the music a stronger, more consistent beat than country blues, but it was not as elaborate as the jazz accompaniments of the classic blues singers.

Among these new blues styles was *hokum*, a blues novelty style that was popular between the two world wars. Hokum songs showed an entirely different side of the blues: upbeat, salacious, good-humored, light-hearted. They were miles away from the elemental power of Johnson's blues.

Perhaps the most famous hokum blues is "It's Tight Like That," a 1928 recording featuring pianist Georgia Tom and guitarist Tampa Red, aka the Hokum Brothers. Its naughty good humor connects to much forties rhythm and blues, not to mention Little Richard's uncensored version of "Tutti Frutti." It is also an early example of a verse/refrain type blues form. Here, the first four bars of each chorus tell a story; the last eight repeat a refrain. Verse/refrain blues forms resurfaced in the jump band rhythm and blues of Louis Jordan, et al., and in many of Chuck Berry's breakthrough hits.

The song also had another strong—if less direct—link with the music of the rock era. Georgia Tom was Thomas A. Dorsey, who, shortly after making this recording, gave up performing on Saturday nights for preaching on Sunday mornings. We will discuss his seminal role in the development of black gospel music later in the chapter.

BOOGIE WOOGIE   Boogie woogie, an idiomatic blues piano style, emerged in the twenties, mainly in the cities north and south of the Delta: Chicago, St. Louis, Memphis, and New Orleans. It took root in nightclubs and bars, where a two-fisted piano style was needed to be heard over noisy crowds.

The recording that put boogie woogie on the popular music map was Pine Top Smith's "Pine Top's Boogie Woogie." Smith recorded the song in 1928, less than a year before his death at 24 from an accidental shooting. The song was an early crossover hit, and became an even bigger hit in 1938, when Tommy Dorsey recorded it as "Boogie Woogie."

"Pine Top's Boogie Woogie" is classic medium-tempo boogie woogie. The pianist's left hand plays a repetitous figure low on the keyboard that outlines basic blues harmony. Except for the occasional breaks, the left-hand figure maintains a shuffle rhythm throughout. Meanwhile, Smith's right hand plays riffs: usually one per chorus, or one for the first eight bars and another for the last four. The riff figures, typically featuring double notes or chords, are idiomatic to the piano, just as Robert Johnson's guitar lines are idiomatic to that instrument.

"Pine Top's Boogie Woogie" gave its listeners a preview into the future of popular music. The shuffle rhythm heard here and in so many of the blues recordings of the thirties is a stronger, more intense form of a four-beat rhythm. It became the standard beat of the rhythm and blues of the forties and fifties, and a common alternative to rock rhythm in the sixties: we heard a "lite" form of it in "The Way You Do the Things You Do."

Equally forward-looking was Smith's melodic approach: building a phrase by simply repeating a short riff. This approach, seldom used either in popular song or classic blues, became standard practice in the swing era. And like the beat, it would carry over into rhythm and blues—if anything, it became more common in that music.

What happens when you play boogie woogie at a fast tempo? The beat changes. At slow to medium tempos, the shuffle rhythm divides the beat in a 2:1 ratio. At faster tempos, a shuffle becomes uncomfortable—if not impossible—to play. So pianists edge closer to even division of the beat—in other words, the eight-beat feel that would define rock rhythm. There is a direct link between these kinds of left-hand patterns and Chuck Berry's breakthrough guitar accompaniments. The genesis of rock rhythm in boogie woogie is clear in Joe Turner and Pete Johnson's 1938 classic, "Roll 'em Pete." Moreover, the piano style would profoundly influence keyboard playing in the rock era.

The recordings of Robert Johnson, the Hokum Brothers, Pine Top Smith, and Joe Turner and Pete Johnson link directly to rock style. In their own time,

The idea of an "eight-beat" rhythm dates back to at least 1940: one of Glenn Miller's hits that year was a song called "Beat Me, Daddy, Eight to the Bar."

however, they were little known outside the black community. In fact, Johnson was hardly known outside of the Delta. Much more visible was the jazz singing of Louis Armstrong and the big band swing of Count Basie.

Jazz Singing and Swing

Through much of the twenties, jazz was strictly an instrumental music, played by small groups. Some of it was danceable, but it was not strictly a dance music, at least in the minds of its best musicians. In the thirties, jazz became a truly popular music for the first and only time in its history. It shaped a new kind of popular singing and gave birth to a new, vibrant dance music: swing, both of which are discussed in the following.

LOUIS ARMSTRONG Louis Armstrong, the dominant figure in jazz before World War II, was perhaps even more influential as a singer. His distinctive rough-voiced style brought blues feeling and the freedom of jazz rhythm and phrasing into popular singing.

We can hear this in his 1932 recording of "I Gotta Right to Sing the Blues." Despite the assertion of its title phrase, "I Gotta Right to Sing the Blues" is a popular song. It was written by Harold Arlen, a white songwriter with a real affinity for black music. Although the song is already "bluesy" by pop standards, Armstrong completely reworks the melody, flattening it out, floating over the beat, and varying the inflection, at times from syllable to syllable. All this makes his singing much more blues-like than almost all of the popular singers of the day. (A notable exception was Bessie Smith's versions of popular songs, such as "Alexander's Ragtime Band.")

Armstrong's singing is a milestone along the evolutionary road to rock. His blues- and jazz-inflected interpretations significantly broadened the expressive range of popular singing. They would not only influence the song interpreters of the next generation (Frank Sinatra, Nat Cole, Peggy Lee) but also indirectly touch much of the music of the early rock era, most notably the reworking of standards by Ray Charles and doo-wop groups. In this way, it primed the pump—helping to move popular music closer to rock values and pave the way for its acceptance.

SWING Big band swing broke out in 1935. It had bubbled under for the greater part of a decade, mainly in the music of urban black dance orchestras, most notably those of Duke Ellington and Fletcher Henderson, and midwest territory bands, like Bennie Moten's, which used Kansas City as their base. (Count Basie took over Moten's band after Moten's death.)

Benny Goodman was the first bandleader to find a big white audience. His rise to popularity come after a 1935 cross-country tour. Other white bands quickly followed his example: both Dorsey brothers, Glenn Miller, and Artie Shaw. Count Basie, Duke Ellington, and other black bandleaders found a wider audience, although it wasn't as big as that of the white bands. For the rest of the thirties and into the forties, a line was drawn. It was swing, the energetic new dance music, vs. sweet, the fox-trot song, now grown more melodious, less syncopated, and (usually) slower.

Swing moved popular music several steps closer to rock, as we can hear in an excerpt from Count Basie's 1938 recording of "Jumpin' at the Woodside." Among the swing-style elements that anticipate important features of rock style are:

- *Four-beat rhythm.* The four-beat based swing beat is the intermediate step between the two-beat rhythm of the fox-trot (the first African-American rhythm in mainstream popular music) and the eight-beat rhythm of rock.

- *A complex, syncopated rhythmic texture.* The performance, often featuring piles of riffs over a steady groove, anticipates the dense textures of the Rolling Stones, James Brown, and many other rock-era acts.

- *Call and response exchanges.* Here, they're between horn sections. In the Motown songs discussed in Chapter 1, they occur between lead and backup singers or melody instruments.

- *A melody built from a repeated riff.* Chuck Berry does much the same thing in "Rock and Roll Music."

- *Simpler harmony.* Like many James Brown songs, the harmony remains the same through entire sections.

Rock musicians have acknowledged Basie's legacy. Indeed, Rolling Stones drummer Charlie Watts has repeatedly expressed his admiration for the Basie rhythm section.

Country and Folk Music

The influence of Anglo-American folk music on rock dates back to the minstrel show, as we have noted. More recently, it shaped rock through two direct antecedents, country music and the music of the folk revival. Country music began in the early twenties, when white Southerners began to perform their traditional music on radio and records. This converted a true folk music into a commercial music, although it was certainly small-time at first. The impetus for the folk revival (usually called "folk music") came about a decade later, when John and Alan Lomax began recording white and black folk performers throughout the South.

The wellspring for both was, of course, the folk music of the British Isles. And both country and folk wrestled with the ever-present creative tension between tradition and innovation. In country music, this tension was mainly in the music; for folk music it was in the words. Innovation in country music meant absorption of outside musical influences: pop, jazz, blues, swing. Tradition meant holding onto country music's defining qualities. Innovation in folk music meant writing about what happened yesterday, while tradition was rediscovery and presentation of the past. As we will hear, country brought the music of the Anglo-American folk tradition into the twentieth century; folk music brought the words into contemporary society.

There was also an insider/outsider difference. Country music was created by Southerners. Those most responsible for the folk revival came from outside the South. Even Woody Guthrie came from the Southwest. Country moved away from its musical roots; the first folk revivalists tried to preserve them. By the beginning of the rock era, they had crossed paths: rockabilly vs. the folk revival.

Country Music

The conversion of Anglo-American folk music into country music began in Atlanta. A local radio station broadcast the first country music performance in 1922, and Ralph Peer recorded Fiddlin' John Carson there the following year.

The music that they played was not new. The songs and dance music of the first country musicians had been passed down through several generations. So had the singing and playing styles.

What was new was the idea that "old-time music" (as it was called) was commercially viable. Both the record companies and the newly established radio stations found an audience for this music. It was small by pop standards, but enthusiastic and supportive enough to justify opening up this new market.

The success of country music on records and radio had three far-reaching consequences. It created a nucleus of professional—or at least semi-professional—musicians. (Most didn't give up their day jobs, at least early on.) It improved country musicians' access to each other: a guitarist in Oklahoma could now learn Maybelle Carter's innovative guitar style from her recordings. It also enlarged country musicians' contact with other kinds of music. This outside contact gave country music its evolutionary momentum.

COUNTRY MUSIC'S FIRST STARS Jimmie Rodgers and the Carter family, the two biggest and most influential acts in early country music, began their recording career in the same place and on the same day: Bristol, Tennessee, on August 4, 1927. It was one of the most remarkable coincidences in the history of popular music. The Carter family and Jimmie Rodgers represented two enduring, and conflicting, trends in country music. The Carters preserved its heritage, in both repertoire and style. By contrast, Rodgers pointed the way to the future with his assimilation of blues, jazz, and pop influences.

Carter Family, c. 1930. L to r: A.P., Maybelle (with guitar), and Sara (with autoharp). PHOTO COURTESY FRANK DRIGGS COLLECTION.

The Carters' best-selling record was "Wildwood Flower." A popular song published in the northern United States in the 1860s, "Wildwood Flower" had been familiar in oral tradition throughout the South for several generations. Recorded in 1928, it sold extremely well, making it one of the most popular early country recordings.

Its three most traditional features are the song itself, Maybelle's singing, and the absence of contemporary influences. Maybelle's singing—nasal, unadorned, with no vibrato or other vocal devices, and straightforward in its presentation of the melody—is a sound that we associate exclusively with country music. Moreover, there are no drums, horns, riffs, or other evidence of pop or jazz influence.

However, there are departures from the style of "Old Joe Clark." Most noticeably, there is no fiddle or banjo. Instead, Maybelle accompanies herself using her trademark "thumb brush" style: she plays the melody on the lower strings and interpolates chords using the upper strings. This guitar style would be copied by dozens of other folk and country players.

By contrast, Rodgers embraced the musical world around him. "Waiting for a Train," the best-selling recording of his short career, shows an eclecticism unprecedented in country music. It mixes Rodgers's singing and Dean Bryan's guitar playing with the sounds of a steel guitar and a small jazz band: cornet, clarinet, and string bass. The performance blends country, blues, and New Orleans-style jazz into a unique mix.

Rodgers also recorded a series of "Blue Yodels." Like the "country blues" of black bluesmen, they are blues: in form, feeling, and style. They have a far greater affinity with Robert Johnson's blues recordings than they do with those of the Carter family and most other early country music recordings. Indeed, if Rodgers had been black, at least one of his blue yodels would almost certainly have found its way into a blues anthology. Rodgers's affinity with black blues style presages the white takes on black music at the beginning of the rock era, especially those of Elvis and Jerry Lee Lewis.

Jimmie Rodgers, holding his deluxe Weymann autograph guitar, c. 1931. PHOTO COURTESY FRANK DRIGGS COLLECTION.

WESTERN SWING Partly because of Rodgers's presence, the Southwest became the center of country's "avant-garde." No one typified Rodgers-like openness to non-country music more than Bob Wills, the man most responsible for western swing.

Western swing mixed old and new country sounds with jazz and pop styles. Wills's recording of "Steel Guitar Rag" features not only steel guitar (of course), played by Leon McAuliffe, but also a full rhythm section and horns. The sound is an expanded and updated version of the instrumentation heard in Rodgers's "Waiting for a Train."

HONKY-TONK A honky-tonk is a place where working class whites go to drink and dance. Following the repeal of prohibition in 1933, honky-tonks sprang up all over the South and Southwest and in Northern cities where southern whites had moved. Honky-tonks were usually rough places, with loud, often unruly crowds.

> Recall the scene in John Belushi and Dan Ackroyd's film *Blues Brothers* where the band is mistakenly booked into a honky-tonk: chicken wire around the bandstand, beer bottles flying, etc.

To be heard above the crowd, country musicians working in such places soon learned to fill out the sound of their band by adding drums and replacing acoustic guitars and dobros with electric guitars and pedal steel guitars.

They wrote songs that related to the lives of their audience. The most common were songs about woman/man troubles, told from varying points of view. Other popular themes included the trials of living in a new place (usually in or near a city) and homesickness, drinking, and traveling, especially trucking.

"Your Cheatin' Heart," a 1952 recording by Hank Williams, Sr., epitomizes honky-tonk style, as well as the best that country music has to offer. The words to "Your Cheatin' Heart" say what they have to say in plain, no-frills language. Williams's singing, which he called "moanin' the blues," invests the words with an intense emotion that brings them to life and makes them meaningful; the effect is almost cinematic.

The instrumental accompaniment features fiddle and steel guitar, country's old and new instrumental trademarks. Non-country elements include a full rhythm section (guitar, string bass, and drums) to give rhythmic and harmonic support. This particular blend of country and pop instruments helped define the sound of honky-tonk. So did the beat they marked: a fox-trot beat with a crisp, emphatic backbeat.

Honky-tonk and western swing brought country music to the verge of rock and roll. Bill Haley, Elvis, and the other rockabilly artists would take the next step. They would follow much the same strategy as their progressive country predecessors. Rockabilly would be, in Carl Perkins's words, "blues with a country beat."

While country evolved from "old-time music" to honky-tonk, the more conservative music of the Carter family and others retreated to a niche within the country music world. Their songs would resurface during the folk revival in cover versions by Joan Baez and others, as we'll hear subsequently.

Folk Music

The folk revival that got underway in the thirties had two main agendas. One was the preservation of Anglo-American folk music, both in print and on record. The other was the use of a simple folk style to talk about the life of everyday people, usually to further a politically progressive populism.

Five men gave the contemporary folk tradition its sound and its message: John and Alan Lomax, Leadbelly, Woody Guthrie, and Pete Seeger. Beginning in 1933, under the auspices of the Library of Congress, John Lomax and his son, Alan, recorded white folk musicians in the South (as well as many others, both white and black, throughout the United States). In addition, they transcribed many of the songs, which they published in a series of songbooks.

WOODY GUTHRIE Woody Guthrie brought folk music into the twentieth century. In the course of his career, he wrote or adapted over 1000 songs. Some were new songs; others simply fitted old songs with new lyrics, in true folk tradition. Nearly all were influenced by his travels, the people he met, the situations he encountered. There were storytelling ballads and incisive commentaries on hard times, political injustices, and social inequities. They covered a wide range of topics, from the hardships of the Great Depression (many of which romanticized the role of the labor union) to simple children's songs. Although Guthrie was constantly on the move, his branch of folk music found a home in New York's Greenwich Village and a following among the politically left.

"This Land Is Your Land," perhaps his best-known composition, *sounds* like a traditional folk song. It has a simple, memorable, singable tune, with a guitar accompaniment borrowed directly from Maybelle Carter. The images that it presents are evocative and pleasing—at least until the later verses. When Woody sang it, it had the natural, direct quality of traditional folk music. Still, it was *Guthrie's* song, his own commentary on contemporary life as he saw it.

Beginning in 1939, Pete Seeger worked closely with both the Lomaxes and Guthrie and provided the strongest link to the folk revivals after World War II. In 1948, he helped found the Weavers, a traditional-style folksinging group. They enjoyed tremendous commercial success as the fifties began, but their politics cut their career short. Senator Joseph McCarthy's House Un-American Activities Committee brought them in for questioning in 1955. Their subsequent blacklisting turned them into pariahs within the music industry, although Seeger would return as a major figure in the civil rights movement.

The use of music as a vehicle for social commentary and protest was the most important contribution this urban folk movement made to rock. Guthrie's music inspired Bob Dylan, who in turn raised rock's consciousness.

Black Gospel Music

Black gospel is an African-American religious music that blends white Protestant hymnody, the African-American spiritual, and more fervent religious music with a touch of the blues. It emerged as a new style around 1930 and flourished in the next two decades.

Gospel came by its blues tinge naturally. Thomas A. Dorsey, the father of gospel music, had begun his musical career as the blues pianist Georgia Tom, whom we met performing "It's Tight Like That." Dorsey didn't turn his back on the blues when he devoted himself to gospel music. The opposite is closer to the truth. Anthony Heilbut observed that:

> Dorsey says he didn't deliberately use blues melodies and rhythms but "You see, when a thing becomes a part of you, you don't know when it's gonna manifest itself. And it's not your business to know or my business to know."

The message of gospel was quite different, however. Blues comments on everyday life. Sometimes it is a lament; on other occasions, it talks about good times. Gospel, by contrast, is good news. Again in Dorsey's words:

> This music lifted people out of the muck and mire of poverty and loneliness, of being broke, and gave them some kind of hope anyway. Make it anything [other] than good news, it ceases to be gospel.

Dorsey gave the new music its name:

> In the early 1920s I coined the words "gospel songs" after listening to a group of five people one Sunday morning on the far south side of Chicago. This was the first I heard of a gospel choir. There were no gospel songs then, we called them evangelistic songs.

Although Dorsey considered C. A. Tindley the first gospel songwriter, he himself was the person most responsible for creating both the music and the environment in which it flourished. His first gospel hit, "If You See My Savior, Tell Him That You Saw Me," written in 1926, was a sensation at the 1930 Baptist Jubilee convention. After it caught on, Dorsey devoted himself full-time to gospel.

In its first two decades, gospel was a world unto itself. Performers traveled from stop to stop along the "Gospel Highway," churches and conventions where black believers congregated. The music remained virtually unknown outside the African-American community. Some white Southerners knew and liked Dorsey's songs, but the rest of the country knew little or nothing about this new music.

Gospel represented both a repertoire and a way of performing. Gospel songs included traditional hymns such as "Amazing Grace" and African-American religious songs such as "Golden Gate Gospel Train," and newer compositions by Tindley, Dorsey (e. g., "Precious Lord") and W. Herbert Brewster ("How I Got Over"). There were two distinct performing traditions in early gospel music: male quartets and female solo singers. Mixed gender groups were not unheard of, but they were the exception, even in the forties and fifties.

Male Quartets

Male quartets were not unique to black gospel music. The Dinwiddle Colored Quartet had recorded in 1902, and the Mills Brothers, a popular pre-rock black vocal group, began their career in the early thirties, about the time gospel was getting off the ground.

However, gospel quartets, who sang without instrumental accompaniment, developed their own sound. "Golden Gate Gospel Train," recorded by the Golden Gate Jubilee Quartet in 1937, is a spectacular example. While the lead vocalist sings the melody, the rest of the quartet imitates the sound of a locomotive—an early instance of using the voice as rhythm instrument.

"Jesus, I'll Never Forget," a 1954 recording by the Soul Stirrers, features a more contemporary version of this practice. As before, the rhythm is in the voices, first in their riff-like responses and later in the vocal bass line. As both recordings demonstrate, rhythmically oriented backup vocals were very much part of the male quartet singing tradition. They would carry over into up-tempo doo-wop.

The lead singer on this recording is Sam Cooke. His singing is notable not only for its beautiful sound, but also for its rhythmic freedom. Except for the ends of phrases, Cooke soars over the riff rhythms of the voice parts, secure enough in the beat that he can feel it or float over it as the spirit moves him. Cooke would leave the Soul Stirrers two years later to begin a short but spectacular career as a pop singer.

Female Soloists

Gospel performances that spotlighted female vocalists such as Mahalia Jackson and Clara Ward typically included other features that further distinguished gospel. Three stand out:

- *A blues-tinged vocal style.* Gospel solo singers during this era sang with rich, resonant voices. They occasionally colored their singing with blues-like inflection and, more distinctively, expressive melismas.

- *The use of two keyboards, the Hammond organ and piano.* The Hammond organ, invented in the 1930s, did not get a toehold in popular music until the late sixties, but it was widely used in gospel from the start.

- *Gospel harmony.* During the thirties and forties, gospel took its harmonic language from nineteenth-century European hymns and colored it with blues harmony. This produced a distinctive harmonic vocabulary: richer than blues, country, and rhythm and blues, but more African American than pop. All these are heard in the next recording.

Mahalia Jackson's 1947 recording of "Move on up a Little Higher" showcases her rich, yet blues-inflected voice. Dorsey may have brought the blues into gospel, but it was Mahalia Jackson who adapted the feeling and style of her idol, Bessie Smith, to gospel singing.

A Mixed Choir

Roberta Martin was an early associate of Dorsey and one of gospel's most beloved performers: her funeral in 1969 drew 50,000 mourners. Unlike most of the other groups on the gospel highway, her Roberta Martin Singers included both men and women. Their 1949 recording, "The Old Ship of Zion," a traditional song arranged by Dorsey, is unusual for the time in that it features a male lead singer, baritone Norsalus McKissick, backed by a mixed choir. In other respects, it is an exemplary gospel performance.

McKissick's sound and singing style are squarely in the gospel tradition. He has a rich voice, far warmer than a blues or country singer but far less sugary than a crooner. And, like other gospel singers, he uses melisma as an expressive device. Melismatic singing is part of most African-American vocal styles, including the blues, but it is used more frequently and with greater elaboration in gospel than any other mid-century African-American music. Melisma would become the most widely used—and abused—gospel-derived vocal technique of the rock era.

The rhythm and harmony of "The Old Ship of Zion" are also of particular interest. At slow tempos, the basic gospel beat is divided into three equal parts, and occasionally subdivided further. This is the processional rhythm, the rhythm the choir uses to get to the altar. As they walk, they step on the bass note, bring the other foot up on the chord, and use the momentum of the triplets and their divisions to swing to the next step. While a procession is not dancing, it is rhythmic movement, and the rhythm that supports it remains the most identifiably gospel rhythm, both in and out of church.

Afro-Cuban Music

Afro-Cuban music was the "silent partner" in the rock revolution. The two elements of Afro-Cuban music that most influenced rock and rhythm and blues were its instruments and its rhythms. We can hear both in a familiar example: the Rolling Stones' "Honky Tonk Women" begins with a *habanera* rhythm played on a cowbell. Its familiarity—and the country theme of the song—may cause us to overlook its obvious Afro-Cuban connection. Indeed, the example epitomizes Afro-Cuban influence on rock: often present but infrequently acknowledged.

Afro-Cuban groups typically include a battery of percussion instruments: conga drums, timbales, bongos, maracas, claves, and cowbell. Of these, the most widely used are the conga drums. They have been especially popular in African-American music: They were part of the Motown sound almost from the beginning. They were used to thicken the rhythmic texture or provide a gentler alternative to the drum set.

Other instruments appear less frequently. And when they do, they are often woven discreetly into the fabric of the song. Still, there are conspicuous examples on occasion: Bo Diddley's use of maracas is a noteworthy early example.

The Rumba

In 1930, Don Azpiazú, a white Cuban bandleader, had a surprise hit with a song entitled "El Manisero" (The Peanut Vendor). The song sparked a new dance craze, the rumba, and prompted many Tin Pan Alley songwriters to write Latin songs.

Azpiazú's song introduced two essential elements of Latin music into popular music, Afro-Cuban instruments and *clave*, its most distinctive and fundamental rhythmic feature. The clave pattern is best understood in relation to its rhythmic context, which is much more African than American popular rhythms.

Afro-Cuban rhythm de-emphasizes the beat in favor of other rhythms. It begins with the clave rhythm pattern, played on claves (two wooden cylinders that are struck together). Other rhythms that move twice as fast as the beat overlay the clave pattern. Figure 2.1 shows the relationship between the clave rhythm, the underlying rhythm, and the beat and measure.

Clave is to Afro-Cuban rhythm what the backbeat is to American dance rhythms: its most elemental feature and main point of reference. Playing "in clave" is to Afro-Cuban music what rocking is to rock or swinging is to swing. In stylistically authentic Cuban music, other rhythms conform to clave or react against it in a specific way.

We can hear the clave pattern and the Afro-Cuban instruments in an excerpt from "El Manisero." The sharp percussive sound of the claves clearly

Figure 2.1
Clave rhythm

Beat/measure	|	*	*	*	|	*	*	*	|
Overlay rhythm	x x x x x x x x x x x x x x x x x								
Clave rhythm	X	X	X		X	X			

articulates the clave rhythm, here played with the second measure first. The rest of the band is "in clave": the accents in the rhythms of the accompaniment and the vocal always map onto the clave pattern.

Mambo

The final pre-rock Afro-Cuban dance fad was the mambo. Unlike earlier Latin dance fads, it was homegrown, not imported. The mambo developed during the early forties in uptown New York. Latin musicians, some of whom had worked in the swing bands, crossbred big band swing with Latin rhythms and percussion instruments and came up with a hot new dance music. By the late forties, non-Latins were filling up ballrooms. The mambo craze peaked in the fifties. By the end of the decade, the much simpler cha-cha-chá had become the Latin dance of choice.

Like the authentic rumba, mambo uses Afro-Cuban rhythms. However, they are much denser than those of the rumba, as we can hear in an excerpt from Tito Puente's 1958 recording, "Complicación." (Puente is a percussionist, bandleader, and one of Latin music's most vibrant personalities.)

Americanized versions of Afro-Cuban rhythms often ignored the clave pattern but kept its "eight-beat" rhythm and something of its rhythmic density. Before rock, Latin rhythms were exotic. They were less so after 1955, because they mapped onto rock rhythm perfectly. By the late fifties, Latinish rhythms would be an occasional alternative to rock rhythm, as in the Champs' "Tequila" (1958) and Ray Charles's "What'd I Say" (1959).

Summary

Two hundred years ago, there was no popular music as we know it. Deep cultural, class, and racial boundaries divided rich from poor, rural from urban, white from black. The notion that a popular style could cut across these boundaries, as Motown did in the 1960s, was unimaginable.

One hundred and fifty years ago, minstrelsy had just exploded into American life. Its music injected energy and humor into popular song. Minstrel songs were the first American popular music, and their synthesis of classical, folk, and African-American elements established a precedent that other new styles would follow.

One hundred years ago, ragtime brought the syncopations of African-American music into popular music. Soon, Americans would be singing and dancing to syncopated songs.

Seventy five years ago, jazz bands brought rhythms, riffs, and rhythm sections into the popular music mainstream. Jazz, blues, and country music found their way onto recordings, while popular song filled the airwaves.

Fifty years ago, rock and roll was almost ready to roll. The music scene in the late forties included not only pop and jazz, but also a broad spectrum of rhythm and blues, Afro-Cuban mambos, and country music edging ever closer to rockabilly.

In this chapter, we have traced the roots of rock back to the pre-history of popular music. We have shown the gradual accretion of rock's style features. Some date back over a century; others emerged after World War II. Rock's diversity grows out of the diversity of its sources and influences. We have tried to account for the most important ones and show how they led to rock. In Chapters 3 and 4, we will see how they transformed into the new music of the fifties.

The table on the following pages shows the twentieth-century styles discussed above, their main contributions to the development of rock, and the styles of rock they influenced. They are arranged chronologically.

TABLE 2.2
Musical Styles of the Twentieth Century

Style and song	Main contributions	Influence
1890s		
Ragtime ("Maple Leaf Rag" [1899])	Syncopation	All of rock-era music
1920s		
Syncopated dance music ("Copenhagen" [1923])	Social dancing to syncopated music, rhythm section, two-beat rhythm, riffs, blues form	All of rock-era music
New Orleans jazz ("Dipper-mouth Blues" [1923])	Rhythm section, four-beat rhythm, blues-like inflection on an instrument, dense, multi-layered texture with several melodic parts, blues form, R&B band instrumentation	Big band swing; rhythm and blues; all rock-era music
Classic blues ("Back Water Blues" [1927])	Deep blues feeling into commercial music; standard blues lyric and musical form; blues/jazz synthesis; rough vocal style	All of rock-era music
Hokum blues ("It's Tight Like That" [1928])	Danceable good-time blues; repeated riffs; verse/refrain form within blues form; expansion of rhythm section in blues accompaniment; naughty lyrics	Forties rhythm and blues; fifties rhythm and blues; rock and roll; electric blues (expanded rhythm section)
Traditional country music ("Wildwood Flower" [1928])	Innovative guitar style; nasal singing style	Thirties folk revival; fifties folk revival; Dylan
Progressive country music ("Waiting For A Train" [1928])	Mixing country music with jazz	Western swing; honky-tonk; rockabilly
Boogie woogie ("Pine Top's Boogie Woogie" [1928])	Shuffle rhythm; melody constructed from repeated riffs; heavy bass sound	Big band swing; swing-based rhythm and blues; rock and roll

TABLE 2.2
(continued)

1930s

Fox trot song ("If I Had You" [1930])	Songs for singing and dancing; conversational lyrics and singing style; absorption of African-American influences: rhythm section, two-beat rhythm, jazz/blues inflected singing and playing	All of rock: moved popular music closer to rock; pop-oriented rock, e.g., the Beatles and Motown
Rumba ("El Manisero" [1930])	Clave rhythm, Latin percussion instruments; dense, percussion-enriched rhythmic texture	Rhythm and blues, especially New Orleans-style, Ray Charles, Motown
Jazz-influenced popular singing ("I Gotta Right to Sing the Blues" [1933])	Broadened range of pop singing styles—greater freedom in reshaping melody, jazz swing, blues feeling	Laid groundwork for acceptance of blues and jazz-based rhythm and blues singing
Western swing ("Steel Guitar Rag" [1936])	Drums and strong dance beat in country music	Honky-tonk; rockabilly
Delta blues ("Come on in My Kitchen" [1936])	Virtuoso guitar patterns, deep emotional commitment, profound lyrics, expressive model	Blues-based rock of sixties
Male quartet black gospel ("Golden Gate Gospel Train" [1937])	Black vocal group sound; call and response between lead and backup vocals	Fifties rhythm and blues, especially doo-wop and uptempo vocal groups
Big band swing ("Jumpin' at the Woodside" [1937])	Dense, layered, riff-based texture over driving four-beat rhythm, slow chord rhythm, simple riff-based melody, highly inflected horns	All of rock
Fast boogie woogie ("Roll 'Em, Pete" [1938])	Eight-beat rhythm, blues form, repeated riffs, heavy bass figures	Rock and roll
Early folk revival ("This Land Is Your Land" [1938])	Topical song, direct lyrics, plain singing, transfer of Carter-style guitar playing to folk revival	Folk revival; Dylan; folk rock; singer-songwriters

1940s

Solo female gospel ("Move on up a Little Higher" [1947])	Gospel vocal style; organ as chord instrument; good-feeling counterpart to blues; call and response; vocal melismas	Fifties rhythm and blues; sixties soul, most notably Aretha Franklin
Gospel choir ("The Old Ship of Zion" [1949])	Slow triplet feel; gospel vocal sound; intense feeling	Doo-wop; rock and roll ballad; slow soul

1950s

Honky-tonk ("Your Cheatin' Heart" [1952])	Deep emotion in country singing; plain-spoken lyrics that express feelings in direct language; country two-beat; blues-nuanced vocal sound	Rockabilly; rock and roll; country rock

TABLE 2.2
(continued)

| Male gospel group ("Jesus, I'll Never Forget" [1954]) | Rhythmic freedom in lead singing; model black vocal sound | Black pop |
| Mambo ("Complicación" [1958]) | Augmented percussion section; dense, complex rhythmic texture | Fifties rhythm and blues, sixties soul, fusion, Latin rock, funk |

KEY TERMS

Melisma	Hokum	Western swing
Layered texture	Boogie woogie	Folk music
Heterophony	Shuffle rhythm	Gospel music
Ragtime	Swing	Afro-Cuban music
Country blues	Four-beat rhythm	Rumba
Two-beat rhythm	Call-and-response	Clave rhythm
Fox-trot song	Country music	Mambo

CHAPTER QUESTIONS

1. Listen again to "Woodman, Spare That Tree" and "If I Had You." Then compare the two songs, element by element, using the left column of table 1.2 as a checklist. Summarize the differences, then write a paragraph or two outlining the influence of African-American music on popular song in the early twentieth century.

2. Review the blues basics presented in the introduction. Then listen to each of the blues songs presented in this chapter. Determine the extent to which each of the songs conforms to "standard" blues practice: in lyric form, phrase length, and harmony. Then, in a few words, try to describe the "mood" of each song and consider how elements of blues style help create that mood.

3. Listen to "Old Joe Clark" and "Your Cheatin' Heart." Using the two songs as references, describe the changes in country music between the early twenties and the early fifties. Note what features of country music were retained and what new elements were added.

4. Listen to "Waiting for a Train" with "This Land Is Your Land." Then compare the lyrics and the musical setting. What do they discuss, and what kind of mood do they create? What common ground do the two songs have? What are some of the key differences?

5. Listen to "The Peanut Vendor" and clap the clave rhythm along with the band. Then start clapping at eight-beat speed and accent the clave pattern, like this:

    X x x X x x X x x x X x X x x x

American Society and Popular Music

1945–1964

This overview spans the early years of rock, covering twenty years: from 1945, when postwar rhythm and blues began to find a white audience, to 1964, the beginning of the British invasion. It has two main purposes:

1. To place the rock-related music of these years in the cultural context in which they developed.

2. To connect it to the music business.

The discussions of social trends, the music business, and technology will provide a context for the musical discussions in the next three chapters.

Social Trends

World War II reverberated through American society long after the atomic bombs were dropped on Japan and the peace treaties were signed. It resonated through every aspect of American life: politics, the economy, demographics, race relations, technology, and social and cultural attitudes. All would touch popular music in some way.

The Postwar Boom

Through the 1930s, America suffered from one of the greatest economic downturns of its history. Known as the Great Depression, it put millions of people out of work and crippled the recording industry and other entertainment media. World War II put an end to the Depression, thanks to the mobilization of the armed forces and the investment in plants to make the armaments needed to win the war. After the war, the economy continued to boom. Economic growth meant more disposable income. Much of it was spent on entertainment. During the fifties, the television changed from luxury item to essential household furniture, and record sales grew at an annual 20–25 percent rate. Prosperity trickled down to a newly enfranchised segment of society, the teenager.

Fifties teenagers, no longer burdened by farm chores or the work-to-survive demands of the Depression, had far more leisure time than their predecessors. They were also better off: parents gave them allowances and many found after-school jobs. More time and more money inevitably led to the emergence of the new teen subculture.

Teens defined themselves socially ("generation gap" became part of everyday speech; so, unfortunately, did "juvenile delinquent"), economically (they put their money where *their* taste was), and musically (many had a taste for rock and roll). They rebelled by putting down high school, by idolizing Marlon Brando, James Dean, and other "rebels without causes," and by souping up cars (celebrated in the rock and roll of this era from Chuck Berry's "Maybellene" to the Beach Boys' "Little Deuce Coupe" and "409"); but the most obvious symbol of their revolt against the status quo was their music.

Rock and roll and rhythm and blues epitomized this new rebellious attitude. Although most of it seems tame to us now, the music was, by contemporary pop standards, crude and obviously black—or black inspired. Some songs reeked of sex: Jerry Lee Lewis's "Great Balls of Fire" was a prime offender. Elvis and his fellow rock and rollers talked differently, wore their hair differently, dressed differently, danced and walked differently. All of it—the music, the lyrics, the look—horrified the teens' prudish parents.

Little Richard's high-pitched hysteria in hits like "Long Tall Sally," Elvis's hip gyrations to "Heartbreak Hotel," and Chuck Berry's "duck-walkin'" antics may seem miles away from the misogyny of heavy metal and gangsta rap,

James Dean and Natalie Wood in a scene from Rebel Without a Cause. *PHOTO COURTESY CORBIS/BETTMANN.*

Madonna's overt sexuality, and the grotesqueness of Marilyn Manson. But fifties teens and the music they claimed as their own planted the seeds of a new morality. It was a turning point in American life. From it would come "Sex, Drugs, and Rock and Roll" in the 1960s and the "No Future" motto of the Punks in the 1970s.

As the sixties began and fifties teens matured, social activism replaced simple rebellion. The civil rights movement and the anti-Vietnam war protests shook the core of American society. The generation gap widened.

America on the Move

During World War II, most automobile production was stopped in order for car makers to focus on building airplanes and tanks. After the war, there was an enormous, pent-up demand for cars. With newfound wealth, families could afford to own two or even three cars; teenagers suddenly had the ability to get away—far away—from mom and dad. Teen hot spots—from the local car-hop to the drive-in—were by-products of the new "car culture." And every car was equipped with its own built-in entertainment system: the AM radio, home of the "top of the pops."

Cars also meant mobility. Congress passed the Interstate Highway Act in 1956 to make travel by car easier. It's fitting that the automobile symbolized the massive population shift that had begun in World War II.

The migrations of rural Americans, both white and black, accelerated during World War II. Many joined the armed forces and never returned home after the war. Others moved to cities to work in the defense industries. They came from the South and Midwest, and moved to the North and West. This trend continued after the war.

As laborers and their families filled the cities, many of the middle and upper class fled to the suburbs. Sleepy towns mushroomed overnight; families filled block after block of tract houses. The suburbs became self-contained worlds, with schools, services, shopping, and entertainment close at hand. Dad might commute to the office every day in his new car, but the rest of the family stayed home, except for special occasions.

Not surprisingly, city life declined as urban centers decayed. Deepening divisions by class, race, and geography joined the generation gap in fragmenting American society even as network television portrayed the country as one happy—and very conservative—family.

Race Relations

The early rock era witnessed the most concerted drive for racial equality since the Civil War. Black and white soldiers had fought for the United States during World War II, sometimes side by side, but more often in segregated units. The irony of blacks fighting to defend freedom in a country which did not treat them as free men was not lost on President Truman. In 1948, he signed an executive order demanding an end to discrimination in the armed services. This was one of numerous postwar developments that moved the United States—however painfully—closer to integration.

A major step in race relations was the Supreme Court's 1954 decision, *Brown v. Board of Education of Topeka*, which rescinded the "separate but equal" policy sanctioned by the Court's 1896 decision in *Plessy v. Ferguson*. In *Plessy*, the Court had held that blacks could be educated in separate (or segregated) schools as long as they were "equal" in quality to the schools whites attended. Now, the Court was saying that there could be no equality unless blacks and whites had *equal access to all schools.*

Following this decision, the civil rights movement gained momentum in the courts and on the streets. In 1955, Montgomery, Alabama native Rosa Parks refused to give up her bus seat to a white person. When she was arrested and sent to jail, blacks in Montgomery boycotted the municipal bus service for a year. Two years later, Dr. Martin Luther King, Jr. organized the Southern Christian Leadership Conference, which advocated non-violent protest modeled after that used by Mahatma Gandhi in India. As the sixties began, whites joined blacks in protesting racial inequality. Over 200,000 people marched on Washington in the summer of 1963. As part of the march, popular performers like Joan Baez; Peter, Paul, and Mary; and Bob Dylan performed. The enormous social pressure created by the civil rights movement—not to mention common decency—led to two legislative triumphs, the Civil Rights Act of 1964 and the Voting Rights Act of 1965.

Rock and roll was not directly involved with the civil rights movement. A few pop and R&B performers recorded songs that directly commented on the struggle for equal rights, such as Sam Cooke in his posthumous hit, "A Change Is Gonna Come." However, rock and roll and rhythm and blues were not without influence. White teenagers grew up listening to—and enjoying—black performers. This helped breed respect for blacks as individuals, and raised questions about why society was segregated, if music was not.

At the same time, rock and roll's detractors linked the music with race and moral degeneracy, and implied that the two went hand in hand. Those who wanted to preserve an America in which whites had the upper hand used the

Rosa Parks riding in the front seat of a bus, photographed right after the famous Montgomery, Alabama, bus boycott, December 21, 1956. PHOTO COURTESY *CORBIS/BETTMANN.*

music to show what would happen to the country if blacks were given equal rights. Pro and con, rock and roll and rhythm and blues were part of the struggle for racial equality—just because of what they were and what they represented.

Music Business and Technology

In the fifties, entertainment media went through their most dramatic and tumultuous period of change since the twenties. The rise of television, its impact on the film industry and radio, improvements in recording technology, and the development of new musical instruments all had an impact on rock-era music.

Television, Films, and Radio

Between 1949 and 1963, television went from novelty to fixture in the American home. In 1949, fewer than a million households owned a TV; four years later, over 20 million had a set. By 1963, it was almost as common in American homes as a refrigerator or stove.

Television quickly became the dominant mass entertainment. Variety shows, news programs, situation comedies, mysteries, westerns, children's shows, cartoons, soap operas, talk shows, sports, and more: all became part of television programming. Choice was limited. Throughout the fifties and early sixties, there were only three networks. Among them, they pretty well monopolized programming.

Because of its immense popularity and its penetration into almost every home, television quickly became the most influential advertising medium. For the advertisers, the bottom line was simply how many people watched a particular program. As a result, programming was conservative; it was designed to appeal to the widest possible audience. Although teenagers were part of that audience, there were only a few programs specifically designed for them. One of the most influential and important was *American Bandstand*, Dick Clark's Philadelphia-based dance show broadcast live after school. This was one of the few outlets for rock music on the air.

Prior to television, radio had been an all-purpose form of entertainment. However, with the ascendancy of television, many of the network series—soap operas, comedies, etc.—moved over to television. Almost all the radio series had gone off the air by the mid-fifties. Most of the new radio programming was music. The musical variety missing from television programming could be found on radio, with not only pop, but classical, rock, rhythm and blues, and country.

Radio was also more portable than television. Car radios, an extra in the thirties and forties, became all-but-standard equipment in cars from the fifties on. The invention of the battery-powered transistor radios, available from the late fifties on, enabled people to take radios anywhere: beach, mountains, or backyard. They could listen to their music almost anywhere they wanted.

The Format Battle

Through World War II, the only commercial recording format was the 78 rpm disc. Pop records came on 10-inch disks, with a playback time of about 3 minutes; classical and other more serious recordings usually came on 12-inch disks, which lasted a minute or so longer.

In 1948, Columbia Records began making commercial long playing (LP) records. These 12-inch disks, which revolved at 33 1/3 rpm, could contain over a half hour of music. One year later, RCA introduced the 7-inch 45 rpm disk. Forty-fives held the same amount of music as a 78, but they were less bulky, lighter, easier to make—a new technology that injected liquid into a mold resulted in faster production and much better quality control—and tougher to break.

By the mid-fifties, the 78 had become obsolete. Although 45-rpm singles were popular among teens, album sales generated most of record company revenue. (In 1960, for example, sales of singles accounted for only 20 percent of record companies' gross earnings.) Some albums were singles compilations, but most of the best-selling albums were Broadway and film musical sound tracks, or recordings by pop stars. Album sales were primarily to adults.

Counterrevolution by the Suits

Like other elements of American society in the fifties, the music business was conservative. Rock and roll music did not appeal to the major recording company executives, who tended to be middle-aged, male, and white. It is not surprising then that the first hits came from tiny, independent labels—like Sun Records (which first recorded Elvis) or Chess (which recorded Chuck Berry).

However, by the mid-fifties, the great success of rock and roll acts could not be ignored. The major labels reacted in several different ways to the rock phenomenon:

- They bought out the contracts of hot artists from the small labels. RCA purchased Elvis's contract and past recordings from Sun Records in 1956, establishing themselves as instant "leaders" in the rock field.

- They had more conservative (white) artists "cover" the hits of R&B stars. Pat Boone made his career out of covering the hits of Little Richard and others.

- They denigrated rock and roll as debased music suitable only for primitives.

- They issued songs that were "rock and roll" in name only, like Georgia Gibbs's "Rock Right." Gibbs was a pop performer who had no understanding of the new style, but was simply trying to climb on the bandwagon

- They recruited teen singers who more or less looked the part—Fabian is a good example—but sang in a pop style palatable to parents and teenagers without taste.

In the long run, none of these strategies would work; rock was too powerful to be repressed.

Payola

The biggest threat to rock's survival was not the music business's attempts to repress or shape it. It was a scandal that erupted over paying disc jockeys to play records on the air, or so-called "payola." Rewarding people for promoting songs was almost as old as the music business. In the fifties, disc jockeys were the people to bribe, because they controlled airplay. Representatives of the smaller, independent labels often resorted to bribes of one kind or another in order to

L to r: Conway Twitty, Chubby Checker, and Dick Clark Do the Twist,
September 7, 1960. PHOTO COURTESY CORBIS/BETTMANN.

get their records on the air. The established labels had clout with the stations
because of their large advertising budgets and presence in the industry; the
smaller ones had to resort to either paying for play or bribing disc jockeys by
offering them partial songwriting credit (and thus a piece of the royalties).

In 1958, Congress convened a special committee to study abuses within
the pop music industry, particularly among purveyors of rock and roll. It
didn't help that rock was identified with teen rebellion, and that many hoped
the music itself could be kept off the air. Alan Freed, the most popular deejay
of them all—and the one who presented the most racially diverse shows—was
a prime target of the hearings, and was subsequently discredited and lost his
job. On the other hand, another influential deejay, Dick Clark, who had his
hands in many aspects of the music business from record production to song
publishing, was able to use the hearings to burnish his own squeaky-clean
image. The fact that he promoted white acts only, and that his *American
Bandstand* show was aimed at a white audience, undoubtedly did a good deal
to help his cause.

While the payola scandals set back the rock industry, ultimately the music
survived.

A Revolution in Recording

The rock revolution also produced a revolution in sound recording. In its own
way, the recording revolution was just as radical as the musical revolution of
which it was such an integral part. The more revolutionary developments were
new sounds produced by innovative recording techniques and multitrack
recording. Together they expanded rock's sound world, helped establish the

recording as the document of a song, divorce the recording from live performance, and even transform the creative process.

The modern era in recording began at the end of World War II, when Allied soldiers confiscated a Magnetophon, an early version of the tape recorder developed by German scientists. Using it as a prototype, Ampex Corporation began selling tape recorders in 1948. Their products would remain the industry standard through the early rock era. The tape recorder was the crucial component in modern recording technology, because tape can be manipulated in many ways:

- It can be cut and spliced, so a single "performance" can be made out of many takes.

- Parts can be added or "overdubbed" so that a vocalist can sing harmony with himself, or one guitar player can record two complementary parts.

- Effects can be added to a recording, including echo and tape delay (one part sounding slightly after another).

- With the growth of "tracks" (or number of individual parts that could be recorded at the same time) from 2 to 4 to 8 and more, the engineer could have greater and greater control over the balance of a composition. Tapes could be "remixed" after a recording session was completed to create the optimal sound.

This growth in technology made the record's producer much more important in the entire process. In the past, company A&R (Artist and Repertoire) men were responsible for discovering talent and overseeing the recording process, to make sure a good performance was captured on record. Now, producers became increasingly important in crafting the performance itself. Producer Dave Bartholomew—the architect of the New Orleans sound and the genius behind Fats Domino's hit records—was one of the first. Not far behind were Jerry Leiber and Mike Stoller, who went from writing several of Elvis's early hits to producing the Coasters and the Drifters. In the early sixties, notorious producer Phil Spector used an interchangeable cast of singers and musicians to give his "groups" a unique sound. Spector was the ultimate example of the producer-as-artist; he only needed singers and musicians to carry out his ideas.

New Instrumental Sounds

New electric instruments went hand in hand with recording innovations. The two most important were the solid-body electric guitar and the electric bass, although electronic organs and pianos would also add color and variety to rock recordings.

THE SOLID-BODY ELECTRIC GUITAR From the time of its introduction in the mid-nineteenth century, the guitar was a popular instrument for an individual to play to accompany songs. However, it had a hard time being incorporated into a larger group, because it was easily drowned out. Guitar makers came up with some ideas on how to solve this problem, ranging from making very large-bodied guitars (the larger the body, the louder the instrument, the thinking went) to making all-steel bodied instruments with built-in resonators (the famous National Steel guitar). Naturally, when electrical amplification became available in the thirties, some instrument makers added a "pickup" (or small microphone) to their acoustic guitars in order to allow their sound to be amplified.

Early electric guitars suffered from several problems, however. They were large and heavy, which made carrying and holding them difficult. They tended to have poor sound quality, because the built-in microphones picked up much extraneous noise, including the echoing of the sound within the guitar's body itself. Many musicians and instrument makers thought there must be a better way.

One of the first to tackle this problem was guitarist and electronic hobbyist Les Paul. Paul figured that, because the guitar's sound would be amplified electrically, it was unnecessary to have any sound chamber at all. The guitar's "body" was necessary simply as a place to anchor the strings at the end of the neck. He also reasoned that the many vibrating surfaces of a guitar's body were interfering with producing a clean reproduction of the string's sound. The more solid the guitar's body, the less extraneous vibration would occur, and the better the sound. With this in mind, he experimented by attaching a guitar neck to a railroad tie, christening his new instrument "the log." Lo and behold: his solid-body instrument had excellent sound, notes would sound seemingly indefinitely, and there was none of the boom or echo heard on amplified acoustic guitars.

California-based instrument builder Leo Fender refined this notion in his electric guitar designs. He placed pickups directly under each string, so that the strings' vibration would be immediately turned into an electrical signal. The Fender Telecaster and Stratocaster guitars, with their fiberglass solid bodies, offered a variety of settings for these pickups, so that new sound possibilities were immediately opened up to the guitarist. They were light and easy to play, and could not be easily damaged. (Pete Townshend, famous for his guitar-smashing antics as lead guitarist for the Who, discovered that it was impossible to smash a Stratocaster; when he threw it down on the stage, it bounced rather than breaking in two!)

Amplification offered guitarists a wide palette of special effects that were previously unknown. Distortion was the first sonic experiment: electric blues guitarists like Guitar Slim and Buddy Guy discovered that they could get a dirty, overdriven sound from their guitar through distortion. That distortion gave their riffs an edge, a sound that complemented the rough vocal sound—either theirs, or the singers that they were backing. Although bluesman Willie Johnson had experimented with overamplified guitar sound in 1950, and Jackie Brenston's 1951 hit, "Rocket 88," had a distorted guitar sound (supposedly because the speaker cone tore when the amp fell off the top of the group's car on the way to the recording studio), Guitar Slim's 1953 recording, "The Things I Used to Do," was the first to purposely use distortion.

Another major innovation, the fuzz box, came a decade later. Like the pocket radios that went everywhere, the fuzz box was powered by transistors. As a result, they were small, light, and cheap. They enabled guitarists to get distortion under control, and they expanded the range of effects, from sustained tones to a heavily distorted sound. The wah-wah pedal, which gave the guitar a crying sound, was another early effect that was used by many rock players.

ELECTRIC BASS Leo Fender invented the electric bass in 1951 as the bass counterpart to his innovative solid body guitars. Despite its obvious appeal—it was not nearly so bulky as an acoustic bass and it could play more loudly—

it took a while for bass players to switch over. As amps got more powerful, the electric bass became a virtual necessity. As the sixties began, the acoustic bass was on its way out. By the middle of the decade, it was a rarity.

The electric bass required much less effort to play. This opened up the possibility for faster moving and more melodic bass lines. James Jamerson, the bassist on most of the early Motown recordings, led the way in exploring this new direction. His playing inspired Paul McCartney, who acknowledged Jamerson as his major influence. The liberation of the bass from its thankless job as rock's stodgy beatkeeper was a crucial element in rock and roll's maturation into rock. No instrument's role changed more.

ELECTRIC KEYBOARDS   Electric keyboards began to appear on rock recordings in the late fifties: The opening riff to Ray Charles's "What'd I Say," which he plays on the newly invented Wurlitzer electric piano, is a familiar example. However, the first efforts at portable electric keyboards were primitive at best. Better days were ahead.

c h a p t e r   3

Rhythm and Blues, 1945–1959

Rhythm and blues came of age after World War II. Between 1945 and 1959, the music got its name; broadened its audience, especially among white listeners; added new sounds; and gave birth to rock and roll.

During World War II, rhythm and blues was just an occasional blip on the radar screen of popular music. After the war ended, rhythm and blues took off—maybe not as fast as Jackie Brenston's "Rocket 88," but quickly enough to claim a significant market share within a decade and powerfully enough to transform popular music. It began to expand its niche in the pop marketplace, even as it carved out its distinctive sound identity. Within fifteen years, rhythm and blues had become an integral part of a new pop world. Crossovers were common: in 1959, the Platters and Lloyd Price shared top pop honors with Frankie Avalon and Bobby Darin—all four had No. 1 hits. Four years later, *Billboard* would suspend the R&B chart because there was so little difference between the R&B and pop charts. In less than a generation, rhythm and blues had grown from a commercial afterthought to a major player in pop music.

Crossover Appeal

The postwar success of rhythm and blues owed much to the emergence of new styles with clear crossover appeal. The most pervasively popular was doo-wop. Other rhythm and blues styles also charted: the gospel-tinged solo singing of Sam Cooke, Ray Charles, and others; the novelty songs of the Coasters; "big beat" songs by Louis Jordan, Wilbert Harrison, and others; and the smooth rhythm and blues of Fats Domino.

Crossing over typically meant mixing black style with mainstream popular music. The best case in point was doo-wop. Much doo-wop was neither rhythm nor blues, but a new kind of pop. Groups such as the Platters and the Flamingos transformed pop "standards" (popular songs that remained popular well past their original release) so radically that they created, in effect, a new style. Their transformations of popular songs was a much more extreme version of what Louis Armstrong, Billie Holiday, Nat Cole, and others had done. In effect, they did to popular song what black gospel had done to white hymns. Another good example is the music of Sam Cooke. Cooke and "Bumps" Blackwell, his first producer, sought to carve out a niche in the pop market by overlaying his unique gospel-derived singing style with a sumptuous pop accompaniment.

Other black music enjoyed a kind of trickle-down popularity. As the biggest stars—Fats Domino, Sam Cooke, the Platters, the Coasters—became regular visitors to the pop charts, other African-American acts also got a bigger slice of the commercial pie. Even black artists whose music made little effort to find a pop middle ground found a growing audience. The electric blues of Muddy Waters, Howlin' Wolf, B. B. King; the Latin-tinged R&B coming out of New Orleans via Professor Longhair; Ray Charles's early, gospel-tinged R&B—all enjoyed some commercial success.

The growing popularity of such acts during the fifties reflected the deepening interest of whites in all kinds of rhythm and blues. Indeed, the career of Fats Domino is a perfect example of how this change occurred. Before 1950, Domino was all but unknown outside New Orleans. Beginning with his 1950 hit, "The Fat Man," he began to develop a nationwide following, mainly among blacks. Still, between 1950 and 1955, only two of his string of R&B hits crossed over to the pop charts. After 1955, however, almost all of his R&B hits also charted on pop.

Domino's commercial success—he sold over 65 million records in his career and was the most popular black recording artist during the early years of rock and roll—is evidence of the changing taste of whites, or at least young whites. Domino's songs and style remained remarkably consistent throughout his career. He made little effort to modify any aspect of his music in order to attract a wider audience. Unlike many black performers of earlier generations, Domino let the white audience come to him, rather than catering to their taste.

Musical Trends in Postwar Rhythm and Blues

In the first fifteen years after World War II, the major musical trends within rhythm and blues were:

- an emphasis on stronger, more active rhythms
- the introduction of gospel vocal styles into pop song
- the emergence of a black pop sound
- the incorporation of Latin rhythms and instruments

These were not mutually exclusive developments, but simply sounds in the air. As such they could be combined and recombined in almost endless variety. Many of these combinations can be expressed as simple formulas:

- Strong, upbeat rhythms + hokum blues + small-band jazz instrumentation = jump bands (Louis Jordan)
- Heavy rhythms + country blues + electric guitar = electric blues (Muddy Waters, Howlin' Wolf)
- Gospel harmony + pop material = doo-wop
- Smooth but expressive gospel solo singing + lush strings + pop ballad material = Sam Cooke
- Intense vocal style + blues + jump band instrumentation + Latin, gospel, or shuffle rhythms = Ray Charles or James Brown

- Raw vocal style + jump band instrumentation + heavy triplets or Latinish rhythms = New Orleans sound

Overall, the R&B experience is a mixture of styles that are combined and recombined in fascinating ways. With that in mind, we will examine rhythmic rhythm and blues, doo-wop, gospel-influenced solo singing, and electric blues. We will consider each style more or less chronologically. Although we are studying each style individually, keep in mind that the Coasters, the Platters, Muddy Waters, Fats Domino, and Ray Charles were all busy around the same time—and, in many cases, listening to each other.

After World War II, these new styles found a biracial audience that grew steadily through the fifties. The combination of fresh new sounds and commercial success was the clearest signal that the musical times were changin'.

Rhythm in Rhythm and Blues

After World War II, black music got serious about rhythm. Rhythm had been a defining element of black commercial music since the ragtime era, and by World War II, African-American rhythms had evolved into the toe-tapping grooves of swing. After 1945, however, rhythm became even more prominent in several black styles. In some cases—most notably postwar jump bands, Fats Domino's rhythm and blues, and electric blues—the beat got stronger and more insistent. In Latin-influenced styles, first in New Orleans, then elsewhere, it became more complex and loose-jointed. In both cases, rhythm was front and center, in a way that it had not been before the war.

Jump Bands

Jump bands stripped down big-band swing and souped it up with boogie woogie and a bluesy vocal style. They retained the rhythm section of the big band but reduced the horn section from twelve or thirteen to two or three. They appropriated the shuffle rhythm of medium-tempo boogie woogie, and strengthed the backbeat and overlaid it with layers of riffs.

Along with the reduced instrumentation, jump band songs were distinguished from big-band swing by an even greater reliance on riffs. Saxophone players such as Illinois Jacquet, Earl Bostic, and especially Jay McNeeley could build mountainous solos out of nothing but riffs—or less. The saxophonist would often climax his solo by honking out a single note over and over while he twisted and turned, or writhed on the floor. His act was part showmanship, part orgasmic ecstasy, and maybe part possession by the spirit. Whatever its source, the honking saxophone was *the* instrumental sound of rhythm and blues in the late forties and fifties. By contrast, swing band solos typically featured a more continuous and flowing line.

The interaction of the shuffle rhythm, which intensifies the beat, with a stronger backbeat and syncopated riffs, produced unprecedented rhythmic energy. This was real foot-tapping music.

LOUIS JORDAN The man most responsible for putting the rhythm in rhythm and blues was Louis Jordan. People danced to Jordan, the most popular rhythm and blues artist of the era. There were other rhythm and blues artists during

Louis Jordan, c.1950.
PHOTO COURTESY
CORBIS/HULTON-DEUTSCH
COLLECTION.

the forties, but none had Jordan's sustained commercial impact. From 1943 to 1950, he had a string of hits, many of which crossed over to the pop charts: his 1944 hit "G. I. Jive" topped both pop and R&B charts.

In songs such as his 1946 hit, "Choo-Choo-Ch-Boogie," Jordan strengthened the basic four-beat swing rhythm by reinforcing it with a boogie-woogie bass line (clearly heard during the piano solo). Riffs now permeate the entire texture. All the melodic material—not just the tune and horn accompaniments, but the solos as well—grow out of simple riffs. The most simple and memorable is the refrain: "Choo-Choo-Ch-Boogie . . . ." Almost every other melodic idea is either a riff or a more extended but riff-based figure that is repeated with little or no variation. (The opening phrase of the verse is a good example of an extended phrase built on a repeated pattern.)

The form of "Choo-Choo-Ch-Boogie" expands the verse/refrain blues heard in "It's Tight Like That." Here, the storytelling verse sections are set over a 12-bar blues form. But the refrain does not use blues form: it is a simple eight-bar section. Songs such as "Choo-Choo-Ch-Boogie" (and there were many) link Georgia Tom's hokum blues to Chuck Berry's blues-based storytelling forms, which began to appear about a decade later.

Heavy Rhythms

In the fifties, the already strong shuffle rhythms of Jordan and others got even stronger. Three recordings, Jackie Brenston's "Rocket 88," Joe Turner's "Shake, Rattle, and Roll," and Fats Domino's "Ain't That a Shame," show us different ways in which the beat was made stronger—and a good deal more about rhythm and blues during the fifties.

Jackie Brenston's "Rocket 88" (1951) was a big rhythm and blues hit with a big beat. Although Brenston was the singer on this date, it was pianist Ike Turner's band that Brenston fronted. The most distinctive sound on this recording is guitarist's Willie Kizart's distorted guitar, not Brenston's singing. The story of how it found its way onto a record is the stuff of rock and roll legend.

According to most accounts of the making of this record, the band was driving from Mississippi to Memphis, with their instruments strapped on top of the car. At some point, the guitar amp fell off, or was dropped, and the speaker cone was torn. As a result, the guitar produced a heavily distorted sound, even after Kizart had stuffed it with paper. When recording engineer Sam Phillips heard it, he decided to make an asset out of a perceived liability, so he made the guitar line, which simply adapts a shuffle-style boogie-woogie left hand to the guitar, stand out.

Both the distortion and the relative prominence of the guitar were novel features of this recording. They are the elements that has earned "Rocket 88" so many nominations as "the first" rock and roll record. From our perspective, it wasn't, because the beat is a shuffle rhythm, not the distinctive eight-beat rhythm of Chuck Berry and Little Richard. Still, the distortion and the central place of the guitar in the overall sound certainly anticipate key features of rock style.

In other respects, the song is right in step with the up-tempo songs of postwar rhythm and blues. The lyric tells a story set against a blues form accompaniment—unlike "Choo-Choo-Ch-Boogie," there is no refrain. Its subject touches on a recurrent theme: cars. "Rocket 88" was inspired by Joe Liggins's 1947 recording, "Cadillac Boogie," and it is one link in a chain that passes through Chuck Berry's "Maybellene" to the Beach Boys' "Little Deuce Coupe." There is the obligatory honking sax solo—a good one—and a nice instrumental out-chorus (the final statement of the blues progression) that's straight out of the big-band era.

Joe Turner's 1954 hit, "Shake, Rattle, and Roll," stands out because of its heavy backbeat, which is much stronger than in any earlier recording we've studied. In this respect, it anticipates rock and roll. In every other way, the song continues the jump band style of the forties. The song is a "verse-chorus" blues, with both verse and chorus set over blues form. The lyric sandwiches some salacious metaphors into Turner's unflattering portrait of domestic life. The band behind him is typical uptempo R&B: horns playing riffs plus rhythm laying down a solid swing beat. The strength of the backbeat is the new element.

FATS DOMINO Fast triplets, an even more insistent rhythm, came into rhythm and blues mainly via New Orleans. They were not unknown in early rhythm and blues—Ike Turner plays them now and again in "Rocket 88." However, in the New Orleans style popularized by Fats Domino, they are present throughout. Domino introduced the sound indirectly in recordings such as Lloyd Price's "Lawdy Miss Clawdy," a big R&B hit in 1952, and more obviously in his own music.

We hear an early version of this sound in "Ain't That a Shame" (1955), Domino's first crossover hit. Domino cowrote "Ain't That a Shame" with producer Dave Bartholomew, as he did most of his hits. Here, his trademark heavy triplets are woven into a typically dense New Orleans rhythm and blues

Fats Domino, c. 1956.
PHOTO COURTESY
CORBIS/BETTMANN.

sound. It's thick in the middle: Domino's voice and piano triplets, sustained horns, and guitar riff all sit in the same basic register, and most are active parts. Even more than rhythm, this density, especially in middle and low middle register, identifies New Orleans music in the fifties. We'll encounter it again in Little Richard's "Lucille."

Domino's heavy triplets help link the shuffle rhythm of forties rhythm and blues and the new beat of rock and roll. On one hand, the triplets simply intensify the shuffle beat. In Domino's recordings and others like them, the triplets mesh perfectly with the long/short shuffle pattern: the first two parts of the triplet on the long note, the third part on the short note. This is shown in Figure 3.1.

On the other hand, the triplets add a regular rhythmic layer that moves faster than the beat, like a rock beat. However, the underlying rhythm is still the shuffle rhythm. One important consequence of this new rhythmic layer was the partial liberation of the bass line. In "Ain't That a Shame," the bass is freed from the strict timekeeping of the four-beat walking bass line. Instead, bass and saxophone play a riff. Both the faster-than-beat steady rhythm and the freed-up bass line would resurface in sixties rock.

Both the lyric and Domino's singing show his laid-back approach. The lyric is economical: most of it is repeated; there are only three different verses, all terse. The first verse describes the heartbreak of breaking up in nine words.

FIGURE 3.1
Shuffle rhythm and triplets

Shuffle	1		2		3		4		
Triplets									

The title phrase of the refrain that follows seems to shrug its shoulders: "Ain't That a Shame" (i.e. too bad, better luck next time). So does Domino's singing, which is pleasant and earthy, but not passionate.

The song, and Domino's performance of it, help explain his crossover popularity. Compared to a song like Jerry Lee Lewis's "Great Balls of Fire," this is "safe" rock and roll. For teens, it was the right sentiment without much emotional weight; for their parents, it was non-threatening music, even if it was by a black man.

Electric Blues

The electric guitar, already a staple in country music and jazz by the early forties, also began to find its way into the blues. Muddy Waters began playing electric guitar in 1944, so that he could be heard over the crowd noise in the bars where he performed; others followed suit. It came together over several years and would flourish only in the fifties. However, even early electric blues, such as John Lee Hooker's blues hit, "Boogie Chillen'," would prove very influential.

"Boogie Chillen'," which topped the rhythm and blues charts early in 1949, shows a transitional stage in the urbanization of the Delta blues. Its success was surprising because its sound was unprecedented: the sound of raw Delta blues, with amplified guitar accompaniment.

Hooker abandons conventional blues form. Instead, he tells a story over a repeated riff. The electric guitar amplifies its ominous quality, evoking images of the Delta in the dead of night.

The chord used by Hooker in the riff is what would become a power chord. Both the chord and the lack of harmonic change link this song to rock. However, it's safe to say that every element of Hooker's style would influence sixties rock, at least to some degree. He was one of the most popular bluesmen of that decade's blues revival.

Electric blues came of age in the fifties. It completed its transformation from a rural to an urban music and its migration from the plantations of Mississippi to the bars of Chicago's south side.

Blues kept its soul through the journey. Muddy Waters's singing and playing retained its earthiness and passion after he moved north; however, he added the power of amplification and a full rhythm section. Both voice and guitar gained a presence not possible with the "man and his guitar" setup of country blues.

As the fifties progressed, electric blues found its groove. By the end of the decade, it had evolved into the style which it has retained to this day. Its most consistent features include:

1. regular blues form, (or an easily recognized variant of it);
2. rough-edged vocals;
3. vocal-like responses and solos from the lead guitar or harmonica;
4. a dense texture, with several instruments playing melody-like lines behind the singer;
5. a rhythm section laying down a strong beat, usually some form of the shuffle rhythm popularized in forties rhythm and blues.

At the same time, its stars attracted a loyal following. Recordings by Muddy Waters, B. B. King, Howlin' Wolf, Lowell Fulson, Elmore James, and

Bobby Bland consistently found their way onto the R&B charts. They were not as well-known as the pop-oriented groups, but better known—within and outside the black community—than their country kin from previous generations.

"(I'm Your) Hoochie Coochie Man," the 1954 recording that was Muddy Waters's biggest hit, epitomizes the fully transformed electric blues style. It retains the essence of country blues in Waters's singing and playing. Blues singer Big Bill Broonzy described Waters's appeal in this way:

> It's real. Muddy's real. See the way he plays guitar? Mississippi style, not the city way. He don't play chords, he don't follow what's written down in the book. He plays notes, all blue notes. Making what he's thinking.

And certainly it is all of a piece: Waters's singing brings Willie Dixon's lyrics to life. It makes the references to love potions and voodoo charms, sexual prowess and special status seem believeable. It is easy to conjure up such a world, with him as the hoochie-coochie man. That much remained virtually unchanged from the rawest country blues of the twenties and thirties.

The great achievement of electric blues, however, is that everything else that goes on simply amplifies Waters's message. Instrumental support includes what amounted to Chess Records' house blues band—bassist (and blues songwriter) Willie Dixon, pianist Otis Spann, and drummer Fred Below—plus guitarist Jimmy Rogers and harmonica player Little Walter, Waters's musical alter ego. Together they weave a dense musical fabric out of riffs and repeated rhythms.

The song alternates between two textures: the stop time of the opening (an expansion of the first four bars of the standard twelve-bar blues form), where an instrumental riff periodically punctuates Waters's vocal line, and the free-for-all of the refrain-like finish of each chorus. The stop-time opening contains two competing riffs, one played by the harmonica, the other by the electric guitar. In the refrain, everybody plays. Harmonica trills; guitar riffs; piano chords, either lazy Fats Domino-style triplets or on speed; thumping bass; shuffle pattern on the drums: all are woven together with Muddy's singing.

All these different melodic and rhythmic strands are an important part of the mix, but none is capable of standing alone. This kind of dense texture, with independent but interdependent lines, was almost unprecedented in small-group music before rock. The closest parallel would be early New Orleans jazz band recordings, such as those by King Oliver. And it works. No one gets in anyone else's way. There is no stylistic inconsistency, as is so often the case when country blues singing is mixed with horns or strings.

The electric blues of the fifties also brought nastier guitar sounds into popular music. The distorted guitar in "Rocket 88" may have been an accident, but the overdriven guitar sounds that jumped off numerous blues records was intentional. Almost as soon as they went electric, blues guitarists began to experiment with distortion in order to get a guitar sound that paralleled the rawness of singers like Muddy Waters and Howlin' Wolf. Among the leaders in this direction were Buddy Guy and Elmore James, both based in Chicago through much of the fifties.

Elmore James's 1959 recording, "The Sky Is Cryin'," features James singing the blues and playing slide guitar. There is a bite to the sound of James's lines, particularly at the bottoms of phrases in the guitar intro.

Although his sound is a far cry from the distortion that Hendrix would use less than a decade later, it was certainly a new style in 1959.

ELECTRIC BLUES' CONTRIBUTION TO ROCK   The legacy of electric blues to rock came in two installments. The first arrived in the mid-fifties, when Chuck Berry adapted the basic blues band instrumentation—prominent lead guitar, second chord instrument, bass, and drums—to his rock and roll.

The second arrived a decade later, when rock musicians dipped so deeply into the blues. The Rolling Stones took their name from a 1950 Muddy Waters recording. Rockers adapted the blues attitude, as expressed in words and music. The Stones covered Muddy Waters's "I Can't Be Satisfied," then reworked it into "I Can't Get No Satisfaction" (even though the story behind the title came out differently). Bluesmen like Howlin' Wolf inspired the onstage persona and singing of Jagger and countless others.

Rock also took its dense texture most directly from electric blues and found inspiration in the overdriven sounds of blues guitarists. The sound of the Rolling Stones, the Who, Hendrix, Clapton, and other major sixties acts have deep blues roots.

Although it was innovative and influential in many other ways, electric blues was certainly in the R&B rhythmic mainstream. The tempos were slower, but the shuffle rhythm heard in so many jump-band recordings was also the mainstay of electric blues. More active rhythms that paralleled the rock beat came via Afro-Cuban music.

The Latin Tinge

The rhythmic evolution of rhythm and blues during the fifties began conservatively and ended innovatively. Even as rock and roll broadcast a new beat, most rhythm and blues held onto the shuffle beat of the forties. The rock-defining music of Chuck Berry and Little Richard—both African Americans, of course—immediately stands apart from the music of most other black artists of the mid-fifties because of its rhythm. By the end of the decade, however, Latin-inspired rhythms were used increasingly as an alternative to rock and shuffle rhythms in a wide range of R&B styles. These were generally richer and more complex than the straightforward timekeeping of rock and roll.

Afro-Cuban influenced rhythm and blues first surfaced in New Orleans. It blended Afro-Cuban rhythmic elements with the feel of rhythm and blues. Afro-Cuban rhythm and rock rhythm have this essential feature in common: a rhythmic layer that moves at twice beat speed. This even division of the beat immediately distinguishes both rhythms from the long/short shuffle rhythm. This "Latin tinge" had been part of the New Orleans rhythm and blues mix almost from the beginning. It is evident as early as 1949 in a series of recordings by Roy Byrd, better-known as Professor Longhair.

AFRO-CUBAN INFLUENCE IN NEW ORLEANS   Professor Longhair was arguably the most important musical influence in New Orleans rhythm and blues, although he was virtually unknown outside of the city. His only hit was the 1950 recording, "Bald Head," which briefly visited the R&B charts. In town, however, his influence was considerable. Many of the great New Orleans piano players—Huey Smith, Allen Toussaint, Mac Rebbenack (Dr. John)—acknowledge his impact on their playing. Professor Longhair, Byrd's professional name, confirms his stature: Among New Orleans musicians, a "professor" is a skilled pianist.

Longhair's influence on the rhythms of New Orleans music was even more far-reaching. In several of his early recordings, Professor Longhair blended Afro-Cuban rhythms with rhythm and blues. The most explicit is "Longhair's Blues-Rhumba," where he overlays a straightforward blues with a reverse clave rhythm (see Chapter 2), played on claves on this recording.

"Tipitina," a 1952 recording, shows a more subtle blend of blues and Latin rhythms. The recording features two key New Orleans studio musicians, tenor saxophonist Lee Allen and drummer Earl Palmer. Palmer's playing—most prominently the patterns played on drums with brushes, but also the off-beat snaps of the hi-hat cymbal—seems a blend of New Orleans street-drum style and the Afro-Cuban eight-beat rhythm played on the conga. Although he works within an eight-beat feel (which Longhair's piano riffs also reinforce), Palmer usually varies the pattern from beat to beat, often interpolating double-time bursts.

As a result, "Tipitina" not only forecasts rock rhythm—making it one of the very few early fifties rhythm and blues recordings to do so—but also anticipates the African-American response to rock rhythm: more complex and less-explicit variants.

BO DIDDLEY   The influence of Afro-Cuban music was not confined to New Orleans. Bo Diddley created the most unusual synthesis of the early rock era—the country cousin to the Latin-blues fusion of New Orleans. Like so many other blues artists, Bo Diddley, born Elias McDaniel, came to Chicago from Mississippi—as a young child in his case. And like other artists—Howlin' Wolf, for example—he assumed a stage persona: Bo Diddley comes from the "diddley bow," a homemade single-string instrument played by African Americans in Mississippi that is derived from an African one-string guitar.

In his breakthrough hit "Bo Diddley," which topped the R&B charts in 1955, Diddley drew on both the raw but electrified blues style of John Lee Hooker and early Muddy Waters and Afro-Cuban music to create what can best be described as a grown-up version of a children's song.

Two Latin elements stand out. One is Diddley's trademark "hambone" rhythm, a subtle variant of the Afro-Cuban clave pattern. The other is the use of maracas, a staple of Latin bands in American since Don Azpiazú's 1930 hit, "El Manisero" (see Chapter 2). These blend with Diddley's take on the one-chord Delta blues style heard in Hooker's "Boogie Chillen'." Rhythms and chords provide a continuing undercurrent to a repetitious, sing-song melody. The lyric is true stream-of-consciousness: diamond rings, private eyes, animals slaughtered for Sunday clothes, now-you-see-them-now-you-don't people. Even in an era of genuine novelty, Bo Diddley's music stands apart: it truly was one-of-a-kind.

MAMBOS AND R&B   Afro-Cuban influence on other fifties rhythm and blues artists was generally less direct. For many, it came by way of the mambo. With the mambo craze in full swing by the early fifties, most rhythm and blues bands included a few Latin numbers in their repertoire. Ruth Brown topped the R&B charts in 1954 with "Mambo Baby." She was not alone. Both of Ray Charles's two live sets recorded in the late 1950s, from the 1958 Newport Jazz

Festival and a 1959 concert in Atlanta, feature one Latin number among rhythm and blues and jazz songs.

THE IMPACT OF AFRO-CUBAN MUSIC ON SIXTIES BLACK MUSIC

Afro-Cuban and rock rhythm share an eight-beat rhythmic foundation, but the rhythmic foundation of Afro-Cuban rhythm is more complex than the rhythmic foundation of rock. Its basic texture is richer, yet more open, and the beat is less explicit than in rock and roll. When black music eventually assimilated rock rhythm in the early sixties, it gravitated to more Latinish rhythmic textures, instead of simply aping the prevailing rock style. Afro-Cuban influence is apparent in both the more "open" sound of the Motown songs (see Chapter 1) and the new rhythmic approach that James Brown announced in "Papa's Got a Brand New Bag" (1965). Indeed, both occasionally used the clave pattern (cf. The Miracles' "Mickey's Monkey" and Brown's "Get It Together"). The frequent use of Latin percussion instruments (conga, bongos, etc.), especially in Motown recordings, provides additional evidence of Afro-Cuban influence.

Through the first half of the twentieth century, black musicians had driven the rhythmic evolution of popular music. Ragtime brought in syncopation. Syncopation brought in the two-beat. Jazz introduced the four-beat rhythms of swing. During the latter half of the fifties, however, rock and roll was rhythmically more progressive than rhythm and blues, in the sense that the eight-beat rhythm of rock and roll would become the beat of sixties and seventies rock. Little Richard and Chuck Berry, both black men, laid rock and roll's rhythmic foundation, as we shall see. However, it was white musicians such as Jerry Lee Lewis, Buddy Holly, and Eddie Cochran who latched on to this new beat in the late fifties, while most rhythm and blues artists shuffled along to a four-beat rhythm.

However, by absorbing Afro-Cuban influence, rhythm and blues leapfrogged over rock in the early sixties. Its richer, more complex rhythms anticipated the rhythms of funk, disco, and a host of eighties styles. Once again, it was black music that forecast the new rhythmic directions of popular music. Afro-Cuban music was not the sole source of the new black rhythms of the sixties. Still, its influence was certainly significant, even though it is largely unacknowledged.

Gospel-Influenced Rhythm and Blues

The most pervasive and most recognized changes in rhythm and blues came from a large-scale infusion of gospel style. Gospel entered rhythm and blues via doo-wop, the new group singing that surfaced after World War II. In the late forties, doo-wop was only a small drop in the rhythm and blues bucket. After 1950, however, doo-wop groups began to frequent the R&B charts more regularly and began to cross over to the pop charts.

By mid-decade, gospel-influenced solo singers also began to make their mark. Ray Charles made the first big splash in 1955 with "I Got a Woman." Others, most notably Sam Cooke and James Brown, would follow soon after. By the end of the decade, almost all rhythm and blues would show some gospel influence.

Doo-Wop

The term "doo-wop" most often identifies the music created by vocal groups between the late forties and early sixties. Doo-wop embraces several different branches of black music during the fifties. The common thread seems to be the gospel influence—group singing by African-Americans, mostly male—and the names, which identify the groups as a unit: the Platters, the Penguins, the Cadillacs, the Drifters, and countless others.

DOO-WOP IN THE EARLY FIFTIES By the beginning of the fifties, there were two main doo-wop styles: fast (jump-style) and slow (pop ballads). Uptempo doo-wop typically adapted jump-band style to a singing group. The Dominos' "Have Mercy, Baby," which topped the R&B charts in 1952, shows how this was done. As in jump-band rhythm and blues, the group includes a lead singer (in this case, Clyde McPhatter) a saxophone soloist, and a driving rhythm section. The other vocalists in the group are the new element: they sing the riff responses that would have been played by a horn section.

In most other respects, "Have Mercy, Baby" is straightforward rhythm and blues. It uses blues form to tell a story—about the most common of blues subjects. It has a strong shuffle beat and a crisp backbeat, a honking saxophone solo, and melodic phrases and vocal responses built from riffs. It is the singing that distinguishes it from the big-beat rhythm and blues of Joe Turner. The most obvious difference is the presence of both lead and backup vocals. However, McPhatter's singing features the melismatic melodic embellishments so characteristic of gospel style.

Billy Ward's Dominos were one of the hottest doo-wop groups in the early fifties. They were also a springboard to success for their lead singers. Clyde McPhatter left the Dominos to form the Drifters. After military service, he went solo, becoming one of the better-known black pop stars of the late fifties and early sixties. Jackie Wilson, McPhatter's successor with the Dominos, also left the group for a successful solo career.

Although uptempo songs such as "Have Mercy, Baby" popped up consistently on the rhythm and blues charts, the sound most closely associated with doo-wop was the slow pop ballad. This branch of doo-wop offered gospel-inspired interpretations of mainstream pop. Its most direct antecedents were the vocal styles and close harmonies of the male gospel quartet and the pop songs and stylings of black vocal groups like the Mills Brothers and the Ink Spots, not rhythm or blues.

The Five Keys' "The Glory of Love" (a No. 1 R&B hit for them in 1951) shows how early doo-wop groups transformed popular song into a new style. The song is a Tin Pan Alley pop standard; it had been a No. 1 hit for Benny Goodman in 1936. Both the song and the unobtrusive rhythm section accompaniment are standard fare, ca. 1950. In a posh supper club, both song and accompaniment would blend smoothly into the background.

What takes it out of the restaurant and onto the street corner (where so many doo-wop groups got started) are three gospel-derived features:

- the singing style of the lead vocalist
- sustained harmonies that float softly behind him
- very slow tempo

The tempo of the song moves about half as fast as the original recording. This severe slowdown parallels the comparably severe drop in tempo that is customary in black gospel performances of white hymns like "Amazing Grace."

Another innovative rhythmic element is introduced by the backup vocalists: slow triplets. These would become much more prominent in doo-wop by mid-decade.

THE HEYDAY OF DOO-WOP   From the mid-fifties to the early sixties, doo-wop crossed over to the pop market more consistently and with greater success than any other rhythm and blues style. The Orioles' 1953 hit, "Crying in the Chapel," blazed the trail. Its history foreshadows the blurred genre boundaries in the early rock era: "Crying in the Chapel" was a country song that crossed over to the pop charts and was then covered by a R&B group whose version also made the pop charts!

The breakthrough hit, "Sh-Boom," came the following year. The original rhythm and blues version by the Chords hit both pop and rhythm and blues charts the same week: July 3, 1954. A cover version by the Crew Cuts, a white singing group, hit No. 1 a week later. The higher chart position of the Crew Cuts' cover has often been hauled out as Exhibit A in the case against white covers of early rock and roll hits. Certainly, the financial and racial implications of white covers give an unflattering picture of the practice.

However, details of the "Sh-Boom" story show that the business of covers was not as one-sided as it may seem. "Sh-Boom" was the "B" side of the Chords' single—almost an afterthought. The "A" side was their cover of Patti Page's hit from earlier that year, "Cross Over the Bridge." Page, like the Crew Cuts, recorded on Mercury. So, from the point of view of Mercury record executives, the Crew Cuts' cover simply returned the favor.

Many doo-wop songs were, in effect, cover versions—i.e., remakes of existing songs—before the idea of covers surfaced. Typically the songs reconceived by the early doo-wop groups were standards that had been around for a while. However, "Cross Over the Bridge," like "Crying in the Chapel," was a current hit. In doo-wop, at least, song covering was a two-way street. The repertoire that doo-wop groups recorded clearly suggests that they were trying to locate the pop middle ground.

The injustice of covers is not so much a musical issue. The blacks who sang doo-wop were borrowing liberally from white pop. The greatest musical injustice here is bad taste: the pop music establishment superimposing their conception of a sound with mass appeal, and enervating the music as a result. (RCA won the bad taste contest hands down, having sugarcoated both Elvis and Sam Cooke.) Instead, it's a financial and racial issue: that blacks did not have easy access to the pop market; that many were naive about the music business and never saw the money that their records made; that the labels that signed and recorded them could not compete with the majors.

In any event, the Chords' eye toward the pop charts is clearly evident in "Sh-Boom." "Sh-Boom" is an uptempo song, not a ballad, but it is in most other respects far removed from upbeat R&B songs such as "Have Mercy, Baby." The beat is discreet: a light shuffle rhythm, very much in the background. The harmony and form come straight from Tin Pan Alley standards such as "Heart and Soul" and "I Got Rhythm." The nonsense words of the title and group singing are a pleasant take on a popular R&B practice—undoubtedly borrowed from bebop jazz—that produced such hits as Lionel Hampton's "Hey! Ba-Ba-Re-Bop" and "Stick" McGhee's "Drinking Wine Spo-Dee-O-Dee."

Although the nonsense syllables didn't provide any verbal information, they did energize the song rhythmically. ("Doo-wop" got its name from one widely used pair. We hear it later in the Flamingos' "I Only Have Eyes for You," where the backup vocalists sing, "doo-wop-chi-bop.") In this respect, they are one expression of the African-American practice of "percussionizing" instruments, including the voice. We have already heard the walking bass and the "chunk" of the banjo and guitar. We will encounter other examples later: "slapped" bass, "choked" guitar. Rap would represent a more extreme version of using the voice as a percussion instrument: it would reinstate words, but eliminate pitch.

Other doo-wop hits soon crossed over. The first and most enduring was the Penguins' "Earth Angel." The song blended old (Tin Pan Alley-style melody, harmony, and form plus the swing rhythm in bass and drums) and new (triplet rhythm overlay, the refreshingly untutored singing of Cleveland Duncan and the rest of the Penguins). This distinctive mix transformed "Earth Angel" into one of the most recognizable sounds of the fifties.

Others mined the same lode countless times, from the Moonglows' "Sincerely," which followed on the heels of "Earth Angel," to the appropriately titled 1961 hit "Beat of My Heart," the first big hit for the Pips, and beyond.

For whites, doo-wop put a fresh coat of paint on familiar-sounding material. For the majority of white teens who had heard their parents' Tin Pan Alley pop growing up, the familiar elements must have made the music more accessible. They also made it easier for white singers to copy.

Doo-wop's old wine/new bottle relationship with mainstream pop undoubtedly contributed to its popularity. Other big hits by black singers that either reworked Tin Pan Alley standards (e.g., Ray Charles's version of Hoagy Carmichael's "Georgia on My Mind," his first No. 1 hit) or reworked Tin Pan Alley formulas (e.g., Sam Cooke's "You Send Me," a No. 1 hit in 1957) also suggest this strong connection between commercial success and doo-wop's mix of new sound and old style.

THE PLATTERS Early doo-wop hits such as "Sh-Boom" and "Earth Angel" were more commercially successful in their cover versions. When white listeners began to turn more to black singing groups, it was the Platters, the most popular of the doo-wop groups, who scored first, with two No. 1 hits in 1956, "The Great Pretender" and "My Prayer." They led the way into the sixties with a string of hits, including two more No. 1 records.

The Platters were not only the most successful of the doo-wop group, but also the slickest, most sophisticated, and most symphonic. Guided by their vocal coach Buck Ram, who wrote or adapted most of their material, they found commercial success with a real middle ground style.

What stands out in their early hits is the fullness of their sound. What's remarkable is that it's achieved with such limited resources: lead singer, vocal harmony, saxophone, and rhythm section. Lead singer Tony Williams has a warm tenor voice of extraordinary range. The sustained background harmonies give rich support. Modest, unobtrusive instrumental accompaniment underpins the voices: drums playing brushes, bass playing every other beat, piano triplet chords or arpeggios. It's clear that their "symphonic" sound comes from the voices, not the instruments—and with plenty of help from the recording engineer.

"My Prayer" adds another "symphonic" connection: classical music. The song was adapted from a violin piece by Georges Boulanger. Its classical roots are especially apparent at the beginning of the song, which sounds like a gypsy violin melody with words.

Although "My Prayer" is the only Platters record with such an overt connection with classical music, all of their songs betray a musical sophistication that sets them apart from most other doo-wop groups. At the same time, there is an immediacy to their vocal sound that beautifully counterbalances the sophistication. That combination was their "Magic Touch." It captured the ears of millions of listeners.

The Platters were extremely influential, especially on the music of the early sixties. One can hear reverberations of their sound in the music of Roy Orbison (another great tenor voice), Phil Spector, and early Motown.

VOCAL STORYTELLERS: THE COASTERS The Coasters—so named because they came from the West coast, unlike most of the other doo-wop groups—were really doo-wop in name only, because their music is so different from the Five Keys, the Penguins, the Orioles, the Platters, and almost all the other groups of the time. They had formed as the Four Bluebirds in 1947, and became the Robins in 1950, singing backup behind Little Esther. They reformed in late 1955, renaming themselves the Coasters.

The group's fortunes changed when they met Jerry Leiber and Mike Stoller in 1953. Leiber and Stoller were a white songwriting and (later) producing team, also from Los Angeles, who had grown up listening to rhythm and blues. Active from 1950, they had scored big in 1953 with "Hound Dog," sung by Big Mama Thornton, and had written several songs, including "Jailhouse Rock," for Elvis.

However, their most distinctive early songs were what Leiber called "playlets"—songs that provided slices of ghetto life. These were humorous stories, but with an edge. Through the mid-fifties, the Robins/Coasters were the vehicle for these songs. Their list of hits includes "Smokey Joe's Cafe," "Charlie Brown," "Yakety-Yak," and "Young Blood," which topped the R&B charts and reached the top ten in the pop charts in 1957.

The story told in "Young Blood" deals with youthful infatuation, but it is a far cry from the starry-eyed romance of "Earth Angel"—and with no happy ending. The musical setting, with its medium groove, heavy backbeat, loping bass riff, and biting sax breaks, is a long way from the soft cushion heard in so many doo-wop ballads. The Coasters' singing sounds slick, but not sweet. Frequent breaks showcase their trademark: a humorous aside that drops down the vocal ladder, with bass singer Bobby Nunn getting in the last word(s). As "Young Blood" shows, the Coasters' songs were the opposite of most doo-wop: steely-eyed, not sentimental, and darkly humorous.

LATE DOO-WOP BALLAD STYLE Even as the Coasters' popularity peaked, the romantic doo-wop ballad continued to evolve—and continued to sell. Musical evolution continued along the path marked off earlier in the decade: slower tempos and interpretations that depart even more dramatically from earlier pop styles. A comparison of the Flamingos' 1959 hit, "I Only Have Eyes for You," with the "The Glory of Love," recorded eight years previously, shows how far along the path doo-wop groups had gone.

Like "The Glory of Love," "I Only Have Eyes for You" dates from the thirties: it was a hit in 1934 and became a favorite of Frank Sinatra and many other singers over the years. The Flamingos' recording is consistent with earlier doo-wop in several respects: use of a pre-rock pop song, slow tempo, insistent triplets, rich vocal sound. What distinguishes it from the earlier recordings are its harmony and riff-laden texture.

The opening of the song is drastically reharmonized from the original version. Here, static harmony supported by a low riff replaces more conventional chords. This is clearly by choice, as most of the song retains the lush harmonies of the original—beautifully sung. The other notable feature is the "doo-wop-chi-bop" riff that stands in counterpoint to the lead vocal and low riff during the opening. By adding this "signature" riff and changing the harmony so drastically, the Flamingos are not merely reworking a standard, but virtually creating a new song.

The presence of a "signature" riff here shows a crucial stage in the evolution of doo-wop into black pop. Memorable riffs outside of the main melody were common in much fifties rhythm and blues, including uptempo doo-wop (cf. "Have Mercy, Baby" and "Sh-Boom"), but not earlier doo-wop ballads. The "doo-wop-chi-bop" riff of this song finally puts rhythm in this, the most melodic rhythm and blues style of the era. And it anticipates the diffusion of melodic interest that characterized Motown and so much other sixties black pop.

Although it died out in the early sixties, doo-wop was the main source of the new black pop style of the sixties. It would inspire both the girl groups so popular in the early sixties and Motown, which was just getting started as doo-wop was dying out.

Gospel-Influenced Solo Singing

Gospel's influence on rhythm and blues went far beyond doo-wop's gospel/pop blends. The full range of its influence becomes apparent only in the work of gospel-influenced solo singers. Three performers whose careers took off in the mid-fifties marked off innovative paths. Each blended gospel with another style.

- Gospel-Pop: Sam Cooke blended smooth-voiced gospel singing with pop, defining a new black pop solo singing style in the process.
- Gospel-Rock and Roll: Little Richard combined gospel's ecstatic side with the old/new beat of boogie woogie/rock and roll.
- Gospel-Blues: Ray Charles secularized the uninhibited passion of the sanctified church and mixed it with the deep feeling of the blues.

Sam Cooke and Ray Charles are discussed below; the profile of Little Richard more properly belongs in the discussion of rock and roll (see Chapter 4).

The careers of Cooke and Charles run parallel in several important respects, and opposite in others. Both were commercially successful, especially within the black audience. They were also the best at what they did. In the late fifties, their music epitomized the possibilities within black pop solo singing and the blues/gospel merger that would soon become soul.

However, the paths of their careers ran in opposite directions. Cooke started on the outside (i.e., with gospel, a non-commercial style) and came "inside" in search of pop success. Charles, on the other hand, started out on the inside, emulating the popular style of Nat Cole, then made his mark by creating a new "outside" style.

They also differed in the amount of adversity they had overcome. Cooke, whose looks matched his talent, seemed to be sailing through life, as much as any black man could sail through life in the fifties and sixties—signing with a major label, headlining at the Copacabana—until his sudden, shocking death. By contrast, Charles had to battle through numerous problems—most obviously his blindness, but also a well-publicized drug problem. He has overcome both to become one of the icons of the rock era.

SAM COOKE Cooke, the lead singer for the gospel group the Soul Stirrers through 1954, was the golden voice of black pop between 1957, when he scored with "You Send Me," and 1964, when he was shot and killed at a motel in circumstances which are still a mystery.

"You Send Me," his first and biggest hit, remains the classic example of his pop singing. Record producer Jerry Wexler commented:

> Sam was the best singer who ever lived, no contest. . . . he had control, he could play with his voice like an instrument, his melisma, which was his personal brand—I mean, nobody else could do it—everything about him was perfection.

In "You Send Me," there is little change in Cooke's singing from his gospel recordings. First and foremost, there is his beautiful, effortless sound, a rock era analogue to Nat Cole. Then there are the elements he brought from gospel, most notably the melisma that Wexler found so distinctive and the rhythmic freedom that allows him to soar over the beat. Aside from Cooke's singing, however, "You Send Me" is pop. Both the song and the setting—discreet backup, white chorus—are closer to Patti Page or Perry Como material than rhythm and blues.

Cooke's career continued to follow a mainstream, pop path. During the course of his tragically short career, the disparity between the expressiveness of his singing and the treacly pop settings widens. Cooke's voice, which was completely in harmony with The Soul Stirrers, never finds a perfectly complementary acccompaniment on his commercial pop recordings. For most of this material there is only one reason to listen: Cooke's singing. For every "Bring It on Home to Me," there seem to be ten trite songs, like "Sad Mood" and "Ain't That Good News."

Wexler was right about Cooke's singing. Still, for many, his gospel recordings showcase it better than any of his pop material. It is the stylistic inconsistency between his singing—a beautiful and genuinely new sound—and the conventionality of its accompaniment that flaws his legacy.

RAY CHARLES The music of Ray Charles presents a puzzle of a different kind: Why did a musician who had created such an important new direction suddenly turn his back on it? Unlike Cooke, who simply brought his voice, Charles brought the whole gospel package to rhythm and blues: the songs, his uninhibited singing, the open-ended "getting happy" exchanges, the beat, the feel of the music.

"I Got a Woman," the 1955 recording that integrated this full gospel sound into rhythm and blues, marked an abrupt change from his earlier recordings. For him, and for the world of popular music, it was a brand new sound, as new in its own way as rock and roll. It brought him a measure of success, especially within the black community—much more than he had enjoyed previously. For about five years, he refined and expanded this new concept, producing some of the most distinctive music of the decade.

Then, just as abruptly, he switched gears again—not once, but three times—with excursions into pop (1960), jazz (1961), and country music (1962). These excursions brought him unprecedented success: while his gospel/blues fusions made him a top artist among blacks, his gospel/blues/jazz/pop/country fusions made him one of the most successful and influential artists in all of popular music during the early sixties.

By his own account, Charles listened to, and absorbed, all kinds of music when he was growing up, and it has all come out in his music over the course of his career. He has brought to popular music one of the most unusual dualities in its history: one of the most personal, immediately identifiable voices in all of popular music, paired with an eclecticism that embraces almost every popular style of his generation.

Charles's two live recordings, from performances at the 1958 Newport Jazz Festival and in Atlanta a year later, show how he filtered a broad array of music through his gospel experience—and vice versa—to come up with a range of new sounds. They include blues, rhythm and blues, Latin dance music, jazz, secularized gospel, and even minstrel songs (Stephen Foster's "Old Folks At Home" becomes "Swanee River Rock").

They also document the two most remarkable features of his blues/gospel synthesis: its range and its power. In effect, he infuses all the blues strains in rhythm and blues with a gospel tinge and updates their sound. It is not that Charles's blues become more powerful than Bessie Smith's or Robert Johnson's, but that they are powerful in a different way. The sad blues find a new way to communicate their melancholy, while the happy blues convey a heaven-on-earth ecstasy that could only arrive by way of gospel.

This ecstasy comes through loud and clear in "The Right Time." Charles's (and Margie Hendrix's) gritty vocals and the persistent "night and day" vocal responses of the Raelets (Charles's female backup singers) are gospel-influenced, but a long way from church.

So is the beat: Charles's approach to the Fats Domino-style triplet rhythm synthesizes electric blues and New Orleans-style versions. He slows the beat way down and underpins it with a hard shuffle rhythm, not only in the bass but also the baritone saxophone (the strongest New Orleans connection). The throbbing beat that grows out of this marriage is more emphatic than it would be in a blues band, and nastier than it would in a Fats Domino recording. Both the beat and the vocal styles give the song a down-and-dirty quality very much in keeping with its subject.

"What'd I Say" adds another dimension to Charles's blues/gospel synthesis. Like "The Right Time," it is a good-time blues that celebrates earthly pleasure. However, it is not one song, but three: an instrumental, a solo vocal, and a rapid-fire call and response dialogue between Charles and the Raelettes.

The instrumental section features Charles's take on Latin rhythm. The opening piano line sounds like an American cousin of the piano *montunos* (i.e., a vamp in a mambo or salsa song) of Afro-Cuban music, and the drum part is much closer to Americanized Latin drumming than standard rock drumming, circa 1959. In most other respects, the song is straight rhythm and blues.

The solo vocal section alternates between stop time and the instrumental riffs, which are now part of the background. Although the solo vocal section uses the by-now venerable verse/chorus blues form, it does not tell a story. Instead, it offers a series of images, mostly of dancing women. The sequence of the images in the live recording differs from the studio version, further suggesting that the real message is in the feeling behind the words, not the words themselves. The final section, which often transcends verbal communication in its moans of pleasure, confirms this impression.

"What'd I Say" defined a crucial juncture in the relationship between gospel and blues. The song revisits a blues tradition—in subject matter (the pleasures of sex), narrative style (pictures, not a story), upbeat mood, and form (verse/chorus blues)—that began with songs like Thomas A. Dorsey's "Tight Like That" (see Chapter 2). Soon after Dorsey recorded "Tight Like That," he brought the blues into African-American sacred music. Charles closes that particular circle by bringing gospel music into a "Tight Like That"-type blues song.

The up-tempo songs were Charles's biggest hits from this period. However, his most emotionally charged music comes out at a slow tempo. Perhaps the best example is "A Fool for You." In this song, he sings with the deep feeling of the blues, enriched with the most expressive devices of gospel singing—the melismas, the soaring phrases, the high-pitched wails—all set to the stately swing of slow gospel.

Charles's fusion of blues feeling with gospel style was a unique synthesis and an expressive milestone in the history of popular music. Few popular performers have communicated with such emotional intensity, and only Aretha Franklin followed in Charles's footsteps with comparable artistic success.

His influence has come in two installments. The first grew out of his work in the late fifties, when he mapped out new directions in the gospel/rhythm and blues synthesis that was already well underway. It was his musical example, more than anyone else's, that led black music to soul and inspired numerous white musicians along the way. The second resulted from his recordings of popular song and country music. In particular, the country recordings opened up new expressive possibilities to a new generation of country performers.

Summary

In the fifteen years after World War II, rhythm and blues got a name, a host of new styles, and a much bigger audience. Electric blues, jump bands, Latinish R&B from New Orleans, doo-wop, and the blues/gospel fusions of Ray Charles were all new sounds.

All these new styles sounded black, but they covered a lot of territory. There's a big gap between doo-wop ballads and electric blues or New Orleans R&B. Still, there was also a lot of interplay among the styles. From one perspective, the blues got rhythm, rhythm got the blues, and most of it got the spirit via gospel. Country blues became electric blues when it added an electric guitar and a heavier beat, via a full rhythm section. Swing added the riffs, blues forms and shuffle rhythm of pre-war boogie woogie: out of this mix came the jump bands. Slow doo-wop applied black gospel style to pop ballads; up-tempo doo-wop did the same to jump band R&B. Among solo singers, gospel also mixed with pop and blues.

During the fifties, the audience for rhythm and blues grew rapidly. By the end of the decade, black acts were regular visitors to the pop charts. The most popular R&B style was doo-wop; the most popular artist was Fats Domino. The crossover audience for electric blues was smaller, but still considerably larger than that for country blues a generation previously. All of this success was a prelude to the musical and commercial triumphs of the sixties, a golden age for black popular music.

KEY TERMS

Rhythm and blues (R&B)	Blues-Latin fusion	Blues-gospel fusion
Crossover	Power chord	Verse-refrain (verse-chorus) form
Jump band	Electric blues	
Triplet	Doo-wop	

CHAPTER QUESTIONS

1. Make a list of all the rhythm and blues styles discussed in the chapter. Then create a three-column table with these headings: style, rhythm, blues. Place each of the styles from your list under the style column. Then describe, in your own words, the nature and extent of "rhythm" and "blues" influence on the style in the appropriate column.

2. Compare gospel influence on Sam Cooke, Ray Charles, the Penguins, the Platters, the Coasters, and the Flamingos.

3. Compare the beats in "Rocket 88," "Ain't That a Shame," "Hoochie Coochie Man," and "Bo Diddley." Which are four-beat based? Which are closer to an eight-beat feel?

4. Listen to the doo-wop songs discussed in this chapter. Describe similarities and differences between early and late doo-wop, and between fast, medium, and slow doo-wop.

5. Listen to the blues recordings by Hooker, Waters, and Elmore James and the Robert Johnson recording in the previous chapter. Compare them, in order to determine why all four exemplify "deep blues." Then trace the transformation of Johnson's "country blues" into electric blues, by noting the differences from recording to recording.

c h a p t e r   4

Rock and Roll

What is rock and roll? In the late fifties, the answer might have been: "the new music that teenagers are listening to." The roster of rock and roll musicians would have included Frankie Avalon and Paul Anka, Pat Boone and Chuck Berry, Eddie Cochran and the Coasters, Bo Diddley, Bobby Darin and Fats Domino, and, above all, Elvis. However, this list encompasses a broad range of musical styles—despite the fact that all of the artists were popularly labeled as "rock and roll." We need to make a finer distinction.

The music of Chuck Berry, Elvis Presley, Little Richard, Jerry Lee Lewis, the Everly Brothers, and Buddy Holly is the heart and soul of rock and roll. Their music represents only a small fraction of the new music of the late fifties, but it is its core. From their music came the attitudes and musical qualities that would shape rock.

What sets this core music apart? Above all, it was its *beat,* the beat that, when fully matured, would give rock its rhythm. But there were other elements: Elvis's singing, Berry's guitar playing, Little Richard's manic performing style, Holly's new instrumental sounds and song forms. All would coalesce into a vibrant new music.

Using their music as a point of reference, we can see that rock and roll music had a lifespan of about fourteen years. It began in 1951, when Alan Freed started calling the rhythm and blues he was playing on Cleveland's WJW "rock and roll"; it ended in 1964, irreversibly transformed into the new musical language called rock. Its history has three chapters:

- 1951–early 1956. The idea of rock and roll began filtering through American society, but the musical style had not coalesced.

- 1956–1959: The three golden years when the style came together: from Little Richard's "Tutti Frutti" in early 1956 to Buddy Holly's plane crash on February 3, 1959—"the day the music died," in singer/songwriter Don McLean's memorable words.

- 1959–1964: The Beatles, the Beach Boys, et al. complete rock and roll's assimilation into the mainstream and transformation into rock.

We begin with a search for the beginning of rock and roll.

The Beginnings of Rock and Roll

When did rock and roll begin? There are several answers to this question, none of them definitive. However, all of them tell us something about the widely debated origins of this music.

The answer depends a great deal on the context in which the question is asked. Does it have to do with the term itself: Did rock and roll begin when people labeled rhythm and blues "rock and roll"? Or did it begin when young white singers began covering rhythm and blues songs? Or when the media acknowledged a new kind of music and its new stars? Or when what was called rock and roll brought new sounds to the pop charts?

The term came into popular music via blues lyrics. In these songs, "rockin'" and "rockin' and rollin'" were euphemisms for sexual intercourse. One of the first "race record" hits was Trixie Smith's "My Man Rocks Me (With One Steady Roll)." The lyrics to Wynonie Harris's 1948 hit "Good Rockin' Tonight" make the sexual reference as explicit as it could be and still get in the stores and on the jukeboxes in the late forties: "I'm gonna hold my baby as tight as I can, tonight she'll know I'm a mighty man."

ALAN FREED It was disc jockey Alan Freed who attached "rock and roll" to a musical style. Freed was an early and influential advocate of rhythm and blues. Unlike most of the disc jockeys of the era, he refused to play white cover versions of rhythm and blues hits, a practice which gained him respect among black musicians but made him enemies in the business. While broadcasting over WJW in Cleveland in 1951, he began using the term as a euphemism of a different kind: through him, "rock and roll" became a code word among whites for rhythm and blues.

Freed's "Moondog's Rock and Roll Party" developed a large audience among both whites and blacks, so he took his advocacy of rhythm and blues one step further, into promotion. He put together touring stage shows of rhythm and blues artists, which played to integrated audiences. His first big event, the Moondog Coronation Ball, took place in 1952. Twenty-five thousand people, the majority of them white, showed up at a facility that could accommodate only a small fraction of that number. The ensuing pandemonium was the first of many "incidents" in Freed's career as a promoter.

Freed linked the term "rock and roll" to rhythm and blues, so it's no wonder that Fats Domino and Dave Bartholomew, the mastermind of so many New Orleans rhythm and blues hits, commented that rock and roll was rhythm and blues. Bartholomew said, undoubtedly with some bitterness, "We had rhythm and blues for many, many a year, and here come in a couple of white people and they call it rock and roll, and it was rhythm and blues all the time!"

As rhythm and blues began to find a white audience, white musicians began to tap into this new sound. In the early fifties, groups such as Bill Haley and the Comets and the Crew Cuts started performing rhythm and blues songs. Haley was a country and western musician who began covering rhythm and blues hits such as Jackie Brenston's "Rocket 88." This proved successful enough that he made a career out of it. His biggest hit before "Rock Around the Clock" was a 1954 cover of Joe Turner's "Shake, Rattle and Roll." The Crew Cuts were a vocal group formed in 1952 by four members of the Toronto Cathedral School Choir. They began to hit the charts in 1954 with a series of hits, including their cover of "Sh-Boom," a song recorded earlier that year by the black vocal group, the Chords (see Chapter 3).

"Rock Around the Clock" and "Sh-Boom" show the two main sources of early rock and roll songs. The Crew Cuts' "Sh-Boom" was a cover, "Rock Around the Clock," was a new song written in the style of an R&B song. "Rock Around the Clock," was the work of the white songwriters Jimmy DeKnight and Max Freedman, who had previously scored with Jimmy Preston's 1949 R&B hit "Rock the Joint."

The Birth of Rock and Roll

Five solo acts and one duo brought rock and roll into existence and defined both its essence and its range:

- Chuck Berry put together its key musical elements: he gave rock and roll its style.
- Elvis Presley personified rock and roll: he gave the music its most memorable voice, its most indelible image, and its strongest commercial presence.
- Little Richard brought in the beat and performed with an outrageousness that inspired generations of rockers.
- Jerry Lee Lewis reinforced the beat and brought unrestrained abandon into rock and roll.
- The Everly Brothers refined that harmony and brought country storytelling to rock and roll.
- Buddy Holly was the bridge between rock and roll and rock: he gave rock its basic instrumentation, new forms and harmonies, and its main way of creating the future out of the past.

Five of them seemed to share a common karma, finding success very quickly, and then suffering death or a career-damaging experience almost as quickly. In 1955, Berry had his first hit, "Maybellene." His rock and roll-defining records, such as "Roll Over Beethoven," would begin to appear in the following year. Little Richard gave 1956 a wake-up call with "Tutti Frutti." Elvis became a national celebrity with "Heartbreak Hotel" a few months later. Lewis and Holly would score with No. 1 hits the following year.

Their decline was just as sudden. Little Richard traded the stage for the pulpit in the middle of a 1957 Australian tour. It was the first of several vacillations between secular and sacred careers. The next year, Lewis married his 13-year-old cousin and saw his career go into a tailspin. Elvis's induction into the army that same year put a huge two-year hole in his career. In 1959, Holly died in an infamous plane crash, while Berry had a scrape with the law that eventually put him in jail for two years. Only the Everly Brothers escaped the 1950s more or less unscathed; their career remained strong until the British Invasion. In that brief window of time, however, the six acts defined rock and roll, put it on the map, and set it on its course.

Chuck Berry

Chuck Berry was the architect of rock and roll. He assembled it out of blues, boogie woogie, rhythm and blues, and country, blending them into rock and roll's most distinctive voice—in both words and music. He gave rock and roll its two most distinctive features: its beat and its most prominent instrumental sound, an assertive guitar. No one contributed more.

Berry's lyrics were genuinely new. Like those of so many other songs of the period, they deal with teen themes: cars, school, rebellion, rock and roll. But that's where the similarity ends. Unlike "Earth Angel" and its countless clones, Berry's lyrics were not sentimental pop pap, watered down for teens. Nor were they the barely articulate sentiments of Gene Vincent: "Be-Bop-A-Lula, she's my baby . . . don't mean maybe."

His lyrics are accessible, yet sophisticated: "Roll over, Beethoven, and tell Tchaikowsky the news." They have catchy new words, like "motorvatin'." They talk about relationships but not love: "Maybellene" and "Brown-Eyed Handsome Man" are good examples. They're instructive: the lyric to "Rock and Roll Music" not only lays out a key ingredient of the style "got a backbeat, you can't lose it," but also distinguishes rock and roll from all the other music in the air. More than anyone else's, Berry lyrics appealed directly to teens because of their clever wordplay.

Berry was controversial because of his scrapes with the law, but his music wasn't—at least, not in the way Elvis's was. How did a black man speak so

Chuck Berry on stage, August 30, 1959. Photo courtesy *CORBIS/Bettmann.*

easily to white teens without either compromising his dignity or threatening the establishment during a period of real racial tension? (1957, the year that Berry recorded "Rock and Roll Music," was also the year that Eisenhower forcibly integrated the Little Rock schools.)

BERRY'S LYRICS Perhaps it's because the lyrics speak with such detachment and humor about their subjects. Berry is usually an impersonal commentator. Even when he is (presumably) the subject of the song, he deflects attention away from himself toward events (the car chase in "Maybellene") or activities (going dancing in "Carol"). Even in "Brown-Eyed Handsome Man," possibly his most autobiographical song, he writes in the third person.

There are no real precedents for Berry's lyrics. They are as clever in their own way as the most sophisticated Cole Porter lyrics, but they speak to a different audience with a different language. Their most direct antecedents are, of course, the lyrics of blues and rhythm and blues. But there is none of the self-deprecation so common in jump band lyrics: no one's out of work, getting arrested, or getting drunk. And they contain none of the posturing ("tonight you'll know I'm a mighty man") or the personal passion ("the sky is cryin'") heard in so much blues and rhythm and blues.

Berry's lyrics talked about new ideas in a new way to a new audience. As such, they were both a model for sixties rock musicians and a standard to be measured against. Yet, as innovative and influential as his lyrics were, Berry's music was even more innovative.

BERRY'S MUSIC Innovation in popular music generally takes one of two forms. It can be something completely different from what already exists, or it can be a new way of combining existing musical elements that are present but separate. The vocal styles of Elvis or Little Richard, James Brown's rhythmic "new bag," and Jimi Hendrix's guitar pyrotechnics are examples of the first kind of innovation. Ray Charles's blues-gospel synthesis, the Beatles' accretion of outside influences, and Berry's rock and roll exemplify the second kind.

Berry created the beat of rock and roll from two blues sources. He took the backbeat from jump band rhythm and blues songs such "Shake, Rattle, and Roll" and its eight-beat rhythm from fast boogie woogie. The idea of merging fast boogie figures with a heavy backbeat was not Berry's. Little Richard had combined the two in late 1955, several months before Berry started doing the same thing.

Berry's innovation was to transfer the boogie pattern, which he had undoubtedly learned from his longtime collaborator, pianist Johnny Johnson, to the electric guitar and bring it to the fore. The electric guitar had become the main instrumental voice of electric blues in the early 1950s. With Berry, however, it also became both the lead instrument of rock and roll and its most aggressive accompanying voice.

Berry's recordings between "Maybellene" and "Johnny B. Goode" document the synthesis that produced rock and roll's beat and texture. "Maybellene" (1955), a radical makeover of the country song, "Ida Red," features a heavy backbeat and Berry's nasty guitar. It is honky-tonk with an attitude.

Berry soon transferred the eight-beat rhythm to the guitar. "Roll Over Beethoven" (1956) begins with one of Berry's patented guitar introductions. However, the guitar stands out only in the guitar solos. The accompaniment pattern that Berry adapted from piano boogie is very much in the background during vocal sections. The boogie figure is more prominent in "Rock and Roll Music" (1957). However, Berry's guitar is almost exclusively an accompaniment instrument in these songs.

In "Johnny B. Goode" (1958), Berry, (undoubtedly) with some skillful overdubbing, puts the whole package together: great solo breaks, plus the boogie pattern prominent under both lead guitar and vocal lines. This recording brings together some of the essential features of rock style: backbeat, eight-beat rhythm, strong rhythm guitar, and assertive lead guitar. It was this sound, above all, that inspired the next generation of rockers.

Berry's guitar-playing innovations went well beyond simply putting the instrument in the spotlight. In his most creative years, he developed a repertoire of now-classic, often-copied guitar lines. Because they were often made up of two notes at a time, they were not as flashy as those of the sixties guitarists. However, the extra note seems integral to his conception: it gives the group sound a density that it would otherwise not have. The single-note lines in his guitar solos are often interesting, but the double-note lines are his trademark. They define his sound as much as the beat and the texture.

Berry's groundbreaking work was done by 1958. Most of his subsequent recordings—"Carol," "Sweet Little Rock and Roller," and "Back in the USA"—mine this same rhythmic and textural vein. They are great songs, but add nothing significantly new. "Memphis," which features a more delicate texture and subtle presentation of rock rhythm, is an intriguing exception.

The lyrics, beat, and guitar sound of Berry's hits stand out as his major innovations. Innovations in other areas, especially form, were more subtle and less radical, but still influential. In his songs, Berry relied heavily on blues form, but ran it through a kaleidoscope that produced a string of variations on its basic pattern. None of his well-known songs use the conventional blues formal plan—rhyme scheme, melody, harmony, phrase length—from start to finish, although almost all of them contain some evidence of blues form. Furthermore, no two songs have exactly the same form; there are subtle differences from song to song.

For example, in "Maybellene," Berry creates what we will call a *refrain-frame* form. The refrain is one chorus of a conventional blues, the kind we learned in the Introduction. However, the verses simply tell the story; they are narratives set over a single chord, not blues form. The verses are interpolated between statements of the refrain, in the following sequence: guitar intro//refrain (blues)//verse//blues refrain//verse//refrain//guitar solo//refrain//verse//refrain//guitar outro. It is an obvious early example of what would become a popular formal option in rock-era music.

It's clear in these and most of his other songs that Berry simply tweaked blues form rather than creating a radically new formal concept. His use of refrain-type blues form has deep roots that reach back to the twenties, and a strong country connection as well. Still, his seemingly limitless variations keep both his sound and the form fresh.

Elvis Presley

Here's a heretical thought. Elvis Presley, the king of rock and roll, sang very little rock and roll. One can listen in vain to his Sun recordings and most of his early hits on RCA for a bona-fide rock and roll sound. Only a few, such as "Hound Dog" and "Jailhouse Rock," have anything approaching a rock rhythm.

Elvis Presley on stage, c. 1957. Drummer D. J. Fontana and bassist Bill Black are seen to his left. Photo courtesy CORBIS/Bettmann.

Sure, several of the songs have a good strong beat, which was clearly important to Elvis. On his recording "Milkcow Blues Boogie," a country song despite the references to blues and boogie, Elvis begins the song as a slow blues, then stops the band: "Hold it, fellas. That don't move. Let's get real, real gone for a change." Immediately, the band shifts into high gear—not a rock beat, but up-tempo.

However, most of his early medium and up-tempo songs use either the shuffle beat of rhythm and blues—e. g., "Good Rockin' Tonight," "Heartbreak Hotel," "All Shook Up"—or a souped-up two-beat rhythm, e. g., "That's All Right" and "Mystery Train." The ballads range from pure pop to doo-wop-style triplets. Is Elvis still the king of rock and roll, even though none of his early recordings have Chuck Berry's rock-defining features?

How can we justify dethroning him? In the history of rock, his royal status is seemingly indisputable, although Ray Charles challenged it early on. Nevertheless, the musical evidence is incontestable. By our limited definition, there's very little rock and roll in Elvis's rock and roll.

Perhaps there's something wrong with our definition, if it doesn't have room for Elvis. However, its purpose was to identify those elements of rock and roll that:

1. distinguished it from other music of the time, and

2. led most directly to sixties–seventies rock.

These elements are seldom present in Elvis's music. It's quite clear in retrospect that if Elvis had been the dominant musical influence on sixties music—if there had been no Chuck Berry, Little Richard, Jerry Lee Lewis, or Buddy Holly—the sound of the sixties would have been far different. There would have been no rock as we know it: no Stones, no Hendrix, no Beatles. Nevertheless, Elvis unquestionably deserves his throne, because he made three unparalleled contributions to rock and roll. Elvis gave rock and roll a presence, an image, and a voice.

For many people growing up in the 1950s, Elvis *was* rock and roll. The two were all but synonymous. Some kids knew about Chuck Berry, Fats Domino, and Little Richard. Fewer had heard of Ray Charles or the Platters or any of the one-hit wonder doo-wop groups. But everyone knew about Elvis—kids, their parents, and just about anyone else who wasn't off in the woods somewhere.

In his discussion of Elvis in *The Story of Rock*, Carl Belz writes:

Elvis Presley is the most important individual rock artist to emerge during the music's early development between 1954 and 1956. His extraordinary popularity surpassed that of any artist who appeared in those years, and it remained as a standard for almost a decade . . . .
For the music industry, Presley was "king" for almost ten years. He was the first rock artist to establish a continuing and independent motion picture career, the first to have a whole series of million-selling single records—before 1960 he had eighteen—and the first to dominate consistently the tastes of the foreign record market, especially in England, where popularity polls listed him among the top favorites for each year until the arrival of the Beatles.

What's interesting about Belz's remarks is that he equates importance only with popularity. His list of Elvis's firsts contain no musical innovations. It is strictly numbers and visibility. While Elvis's popularity was crucial to rock and roll, he brought much more to the music than that.

Elvis gave rock and roll its most memorable visual images. His looks sent girls into hysteria and guys to the mirror, where they greased their hair and combed it into Elvis-like pompadours. His uninhibited, sexually-charged stage persona scandalized adults even as it sent teen pulses racing. These images endure, as the legion of Elvis imitators reminds us.

However, his most lasting musical contribution was his voice. Elvis knew what he had; when he first showed up at Sun Studios and was asked by the secretary there, "Who do you sound like?" he responded, "I don't sound like nobody." Elvis described himself perfectly: he sounds like Elvis and no one else. Before he became a performer, he was one of the great listeners of all time: blues, rhythm and blues, black and white gospel, country, pop, musicals, classical music. He listened to anything he could find, and he distilled all this listening into an absolutely unique vocal sound—not white, not black, but blacker than white.

ELVIS ON SUN RECORDS   Elvis first recorded for the tiny Sun label located in his hometown of Memphis, Tennessee. Listening to Elvis's early recordings, two qualities stand out: the uniqueness of his basic sound, and its remarkable adaptability. Elvis could tailor his sound to the song, yet always sound like himself. He was not one singer, but several, each of them a different version of himself.

This adaptability is evident from the start. "That's All Right" (1954), his first recording for Sun Records, presents "pure" Elvis. It is a heavily blues-tinged "high lonesome" sound: his unique mix of blues and country. He uses this sound again in perhaps the best of his Sun recordings, "Mystery Train" (1955), a thorough makeover of Junior Parker's rhythm and blues hit.

In other songs with a strong, fast beat, such as "Good Rockin' Tonight" (1954) and "Blue Moon of Kentucky" (1954), Elvis sings with a darker sound and begins to add the mannerisms—the little gulps and hiccups—that would make his style too easy to caricature.

Elvis shows a much more tender side in ballads such as "Harbor Lights" (1954), originally a pop hit in 1937. On it we hear sweet, beautifully controlled singing that would be the envy of most crooners, but with a touch of vulnerability that connects his singing to a new generation.

ROCKABILLY Elvis all but created rockabilly style, which fellow Sun Records star Carl Perkins described as "blues with a country beat." For all intents and purposes, it was born when Elvis recorded Arthur Crudup's "That's All Right." Elvis's version of the song fits Perkins's description of rockabilly to the letter: Elvis, guitarist Scotty Moore, and bassist Bill Black take Crudup's medium-tempo swing beat and transform it into the classic rockabilly two-beat: fast, frenetic, but not very funky.

The rockabilly beat is most clearly evident in "Mystery Train." Junior Parker's original version features a down-tempo imitation of a locomotive—a proto-rock sound. Elvis and his bandmates perform the song twice as fast, and Moore adds a souped-up backbeat.

Elvis's rockabilly recordings are the most distinctive of his Sun recordings, because they found a unique niche between country and blues. Elvis's sound, the frenetic two-beat, and the light instrumentation—electric guitar, slapped acoustic bass, little or no percussion—create a highly individual sound world.

Rockabilly, of course, was more than Elvis's few Sun recordings. Musically, it broadened out to include countrified interpretations of rhythm and blues styles and, later, rock and roll. For example, both Bill Haley's "Rock Around the Clock" (which predates "That's All Right") and Perkins's "Blue Suede Shoes" (for many, the rockabilly anthem) have country versions of the heavy four-beat rhythm of rhythm and blues. Jerry Lee Lewis's early hits are straight-ahead rock and roll, as we'll soon discuss in more detail.

Finally, rockabilly was a state of mind—and body. It was the music of liberation for southern white males: what they danced to on Saturday nights when they wanted to "get real, real gone." As Glenn Gass has observed: "Rockabilly was distinctly and proudly southern." Its capital was Memphis, and its capitol building a small storefront located at 706 Union Avenue, where Sam Phillips operated Sun Records. A legion of Johnny B. Goodes, many of whom sang and played with the abandon of black rhythm and blues musicians, beat a path to Phillips's door. He recorded most of the important rockabilly artists: Elvis, Perkins, Lewis. Phillips's reputation in the region was unsurpassed: Roy Orbison came from Texas to re-record his first hit, although he soon bought back his contract.

ELVIS AND RCA Rockabilly ended for Elvis when Sam Phillips sold his contract to RCA. His RCA recordings lost the strong country flavor of his Sun dates. They no longer showcase the "pure" Elvis sound of "Mystery Train" or

"That's All Right," and the lean country-beat blues backup that Moore and Black had provided gave way to much richer accompaniments.

However, Elvis's RCA recordings brought him enormous commercial success: fourteen gold records and a movie contract in less than two years. His two-sided hit, "Hound Dog"/"Don't Be Cruel," was a clear index of the breadth of his appeal. It topped all three charts—pop, R&B, and country—in 1956.

His RCA material had a strong pop orientation. His hits included a series of "love" ballads—"Love Me Tender" (a remake of the Civil War-era song "Aura Lee"), "Loving You," "Love Me"—as well as rocking numbers such as "Heartbreak Hotel." Although Elvis performed with greater abandon than any established pop performer, white or black, the overall sound of his RCA records have little of the bite or drive of Chuck Berry or Jerry Lee Lewis.

Elvis's musical position somewhere between pop and Berry's rock and roll helps account for his popularity. No doubt his looks and his uninhibited performing style—what he called his "wiggling"—had something to do with it. So did his good fortune to be in the right place at the right time: popular music definitely needed a jolt. But it helped that so many aspects of his music sounded familiar to his audiences. In most cases, the only real novelty was the sound of his voice.

Elvis also brought into rock and roll a new attitude: a democratic eclecticism. As we've noted, he listened to everyone. And, unlike his pop predecessors, he didn't seem to pass judgment. If we judge by his recordings, he doesn't value Patti Page more than Arthur Crudup, or Bill Monroe more than Billy Eckstine. This attitude is in stark contrast to the previous generation of pop performers, who generally regarded minority styles with disdain.

Moreover, he reflects this eclecticism in his singing. What the Beatles or Paul Simon would later do externally—by varying the accompaniment—Elvis did internally—with his voice. Elvis was the first to express this democratic attitude in his music, and no one did it more naturally or organically.

Little Richard and Jerry Lee Lewis

Little Richard and Jerry Lee Lewis were the true kindred spirits of rock and roll. They were alike in so many significant ways—even in their differences. Both:

- Grew up poor in the South.
- Were manic performers: If Elvis stretched the boundaries of acceptable performance, Jerry Lee Lewis and Little Richard broke through them and kept on running.
- Played the piano, not the guitar.
- Found a narrow groove, and kept on it during their brief moment in the sun.

Their most obvious differences were their race and their sexual orientation. Little Richard was black, Jerry Lee Lewis was white. Little Richard was flamboyantly homosexual; Jerry Lee Lewis decidedly heterosexual. In this matter, both strayed well outside the sexual norms of the time. Little Richard was overtly gay during a time when few men, and even fewer black men, were out of the closet. Lewis went through a string of wives—three before he reached 24! It was his third marriage, to his 13-year-old cousin, that caused the scandal that torpedoed his career. Not only was she underage, but he had neglected to divorce his previous wife.

Little Richard was the first to hit nationally: "Tutti Frutti," released in late 1955, reached No. 17 on the pop charts in early 1956 and caused enough of a sensation to merit a Pat Boone cover. Lewis's first hit, "Whole Lot of Shakin' Going On," appeared on the charts about a year and a half later—not much time in the larger view of things, but half a lifetime in the brief flourishing of rock and roll.

LITTLE RICHARD Little Richard was the first and the loudest of the early rock and rollers. His flamboyant personality, outrageous appearance (wearing mascara decades before Michael Jackson), dynamic stage presence, and jet-propelled energy established a standard for rock and roll performance that only Elvis and Jerry Lee Lewis approached. He took the stage, literally throwing himself into his work; at one moment casting a leg up onto the top of the piano, then leaping to the ground in a leg split. Little Richard embodied the new style: wild, uninhibited, and sexually charged. From the moment he sang "Womp-bomp-a-loo-bomp, a-lomp-bomp-bomp!" to start "Tutti-Frutti," popular music would never be the same.

Little Richard brought substance as well as style to rock and roll. He introduced several of its most characteristic musical features: its volume, a vocal style that valued power over prettiness, and its beat. His music started loud and stayed that way. It was a conscious decision, as he acknowledged: "I came from a family where my people didn't like R&B. Bing Crosby and Ella Fitzgerald was all I heard. And I knew that there was something that could be louder [sic] than that, but I didn't know where to find it. And I found it was me."

Little Richard in England, c. 1962. Photo courtesy CORBIS/Hulton-Deutsch Collection.

He sang with a voice as abrasive as sandpaper. He hurled his lyrics at the microphone, periodically interrupting them with his trademark falsetto howls and whoops. His singing, like his piano playing, is more percussive than anything else: we are more aware of rhythm than melody, which in most cases is minimal.

Still, it's rhythm where Little Richard made his greatest contribution. He brought the new rock beat—the one that Chuck Berry would consolidate—into rock and roll. Listen to a group of mid-fifties rhythm and blues songs and interpolate a Little Richard hit: it immediately stands out because of its beat. Rock and roll had a name before Little Richard hit; after "Tutti Frutti," however, it also had its beat.

Little Richard has acknowledged the source of the beat: boogie woogie. His gospel roots are evident in every one of the melismatic flourishes. But his combination of boogie, gospel, and blues—and his own personality—gave the mix an unprecedented aggressiveness. His music was loud, fast, and in the face of everyone who listened to it.

Little Richard made his mark in a series of songs released between late 1955 and early 1958. Many of them were about girls: "Long Tall Sally," "The Girl Can't Help It" (the girl in this case was blonde bombshell Jayne Mansfield, the star of the film for which the song was written; Little Richard also appeared onscreen), "Lucille," "Good Golly, Miss Molly," and "Jenny, Jenny" stand out.

He found his sound right away in "Tutti Frutti" and kept it pretty much the same throughout his three years in the limelight. His songs seem to offer little variation, mainly because his vocal style is so consistent, but also because they are fast and loud and rely so heavily on standard blues form. "Long Tall Sally" could be grafted onto "Tutti Frutti" without dropping a beat—they are that much alike.

His later hits such as "Lucille" (1957) have a more New Orleans flavor, because their repetitive bass riff, played by bass, guitar, and saxes, replaces the walking bass of the earlier songs. The heavy bass line and slower tempo forecast the rhythmic feel of sixties rock.

There is no questioning Little Richard's importance to rock and roll. He embodied its spirit more outrageously and flamboyantly than any other performer of the era. He gave it one of its most identifiable and influential vocal sounds. And he blazed its rhythmic trail. If he had been a good-looking white heterosexual guitar player, he would have been the undisputed king of rock and roll. His music found a slim groove and stayed there, but what a groove it was!—and is! He's still at it as of 1999.

JERRY LEE LEWIS   There were ten rock-era acts inducted into the Rock and Roll Hall of Fame in 1986, the first year of induction. The roster included Chuck Berry, James Brown, Ray Charles, Sam Cooke, Fats Domino, the Everly Brothers, Buddy Holly, Jerry Lee Lewis, Elvis Presley, and Little Richard. No one had a shorter career, fewer hits, or less influence than Jerry Lee Lewis. So why was he a member of the inaugural class?

For all intents and purposes, Lewis's rock and roll career lasted just over a year. He began recording late in 1956 with a country song, "Crazy Arms." He recorded his first rock and roll song, "Whole Lot of Shakin' Going On," in March 1957, and scored big. It went to the top of the R&B and C&W charts, and reached #3 on the pop chart. He had three more big hits, "Great Balls of

*Jerry Lee Lewis, August
1957. PHOTO COURTESY
CORBIS/BETTMANN.*

Fire," "Breathless," and "High School Confidential," within a year. Then he watched his career go down in flames after he married his underage cousin.

Still, if any performer ever deserved rock immortality for a single song, it would be Lewis for "Great Balls of Fire." It was rock and roll's first recorded orgasm—or as close to it as anyone could get in the 1950s: "kiss me, baby . . . HOOOOOO . . . feels good!!!!" The recording was overtly sexual to a degree that surpassed even Elvis and Little Richard.

The song is 1 minute 48 seconds of ecstasy, from the opening words of the lyric to the last four chords. Unlike most of the impersonal, teen-themed songs of the period, this song shouts its message loud and clear. And the music, with its pulsing beat, sends the same message, just as loudly and just as clearly.

"Great Balls of Fire" was the aural counterpart to Elvis's gyrations. It made the link between the original and musical meanings of rock and roll explicit. Songs with strong sexual overtones were common in blues and rhythm and blues, but most were different from Lewis's song. Elvis's cover of "Good Rockin' Tonight" points this out. The lyric talks about what will happen: "Tonight you'll know . . . ." By contrast, Lewis's lyric is of the moment; he's right in the middle of the experience he's describing. Moreover, his singing and playing imply that he's experienced—that he knows what he's talking about. Elvis, who was 19 when he recorded "Good Rockin' Tonight," sounds callow by comparison. Lewis was a white man singing blatantly about lust and using rock and roll as a subtext. It was a moment of liberation for rock and roll, a prelude to the sixties.

Among the first great rock and rollers, only Lewis matched Little Richard's musical frenzy. His voice was not as assertive as Little Richard's, whose sound cut through a band like a buzzsaw, but he made up for it by attacking the piano, pounding out rock and roll chords and swooping up and down the keyboard with his trademark glissandos. For that alone, he's worth remembering.

However, he also cemented the connection between country music and rock and roll. He framed his rock and roll days with country music. "Crazy Arms," his first recording, was a cover of Ray Price's No. 1 country hit from early 1956. And after a decade of one-nighters, he made a comeback in 1968 as a country singer with hits such as "What's Made Milwaukee Famous (Has Made a Loser out of Me)." If Elvis's rockabilly recordings opened the door between country and rock and roll, then Jerry Lee Lewis's hits walked right through it.

The Everly Brothers and Buddy Holly

It's hard to imagine two rock and roll acts more different in temperament from Jerry Lee Lewis and Little Richard than the Everly Brothers and Buddy Holly. They were shy where Jerry Lee and Little Richard were flamboyant. Their music was different, too—Holly's was more varied and innovative, the Everly Brothers' more melodic. Together, they showed that rock and roll also had a gentler side.

THE EVERLY BROTHERS   The Everly Brothers stand out in the history of rock and roll for two related reasons: they completed rock and roll's country connection and they popularized rock song. The brothers had begun their career as country entertainers not long after they started school. Their parents, Ike and Margaret Everly, had featured the boys on their radio show, broadcast from Iowa, during the mid-forties. After their parents retired, the brothers went to Nashville, where they wrote songs and tried to secure a recording contract. They finally did, with Cadence Records, a small label that recorded mostly pop and jazz. Their first hits were teen-themed country songs that crossed over to the pop charts. "Bye, Bye, Love" and "Wake Up, Little Susie" were among the biggest hits of 1957. These songs relate to rock and roll mainly in their subject matter. Musically, they relate much more to country music—especially their sweet-voiced close harmony.

Quickly, their music moved closer to rock and roll. As it did, they created—with the help of Felice and Boudleaux Bryant, who wrote most of their early hits—a new sound, the rock ballad. As we have heard in the music of Chuck Berry, Little Richard, and Jerry Lee Lewis, early rock and roll songs—real rock and roll—were set over a driving, uptempo eight-beat rhythm. Slower songs were usually "Earth Angel"-type songs, with muted triplets in the background. With their 1958 hit, "All I Have to Do Is Dream," the Everly Brothers changed that. The song has a flowing melody, the melody is the dominant strand in the texture, and the tempo is slow—all like "Earth Angel." What's different is the beat—a gentle rock beat. The Everlys' singing is the perfect complement—sweet but not saccharine.

The Everly Brothers' music represented the quietest side of the rock revolution, but songs such as "All I Have to Do Is Dream" and "Devoted to You" marked the real beginning of the end for pre-rock pop. Prior to these songs, traditionalists could dismiss rock and roll as crude, noisy, vulgar, dance music for tasteless teens. But these songs signal the emergence of a new, rock beat-based pop: rock and roll was meeting pop on its own terms—and holding its own.

Out of this new melodic rock ballad style would come songs such as the Shirelles' "Will You Still Love Me Tomorrow?" and the Beatles' "Yesterday," and countless others. The hard rockers may have represented rock and roll's cutting edge, but it was groups such as the Everly Brothers that would ensure rock's complete domination of popular music within a decade. Their music made sure that there was something for almost everyone.

BUDDY HOLLY Buddy Holly occupies a unique position in the history of rock: he is the musical bridge between fifties rock and roll and sixties rock. In the music of Chuck Berry, Elvis, Little Richard, and Jerry Lee Lewis, rock and roll coalesced out of several diverse styles, as we have seen. Their achievement was to form a new style out of existing sources. Buddy Holly's achievement was just the opposite. Using this newly formed style as his point of departure, he opened up rock and roll to new sounds, forms, harmonies, and rhythms. All would resurface in the 1960s, especially in the music of the Beatles and Bob Dylan, and become the main inspiration for the eclecticism that characterized so much sixties rock.

What makes Holly's achievement even more remarkable is that it happened in such a short time. He began rock and roll's second generation less than two years after the style had begun to come together. By the time he began recording, he had assimilated the music of his heroes and was using it as a springboard for rock-based innovations. Moreover, his career lasted only a year and a half, from August 1957, when "That'll Be the Day" topped the charts, to February 1959, when he died at age 22. No one got more done in less time.

Holly was an unlikely rock star. With his horn-rimmed glasses, he looked more like a nerd than a sex symbol. His singing voice is high, somewhat thin and reedy, the most ordinary sound of the rock and roll greats. Saturated with hiccups, stutters, and other Elvis-isms, it sound more than anything else like Elvis-lite: a gifted teen who wants to sound like Elvis but lacks Elvis's vocal presence or expressive range. (Of course, that was true of many other early rock stars.) Curiously, all this seemed to work in his favor. His looks, voice, and reserved stage manner gave him an everyman quality. Seeing him perform, the implicit message was that one didn't need super looks, a great voice, and a total lack of inhibition to be a rock star.

This image resonated beautifully with the images portrayed in the lyrics. From "That'll Be the Day" to "Think It Over," so many of the songs deal with the insecurities of teen relationships. Male teens may have wanted to be another Elvis, but they could put themselves in Buddy Holly's shoes much more easily. Many did, in garages around the United States and in England.

Holly hid a curious, open, and imaginative mind beneath his shy, rather gawky exterior. It was fueled by the diverse musical influences that he encountered growing up. The first was country music. Lubbock, Holly's hometown, is in west Texas, just below the panhandle and close to the New Mexico border. Texas had been home to Jimmie Rodgers toward the end of his life and the home base of Western swing king Bob Wills, so progressive country music was definitely in the air.

Holly also listened to rhythm and blues intently. A friend recalls sitting with him in his car late on Saturday nights so that they could listen to an R&B show on a station out of Shreveport, Louisiana. Not surprisingly, then, numerous R&B elements pop up in his songs: the "Bo Diddley beat" of "Not Fade Away" is an obvious example.

Elvis was a more powerful and immediate influence. He performed in Lubbock twice during 1955, in the spring and fall, and both times Holly and his friend Bob Montgomery opened the show. This direct contact not only influenced his singing but also strengthened his resolve to pursue a career in music. By the time Elvis returned in the fall, Holly was pumping Elvis about how to get a recording contract.

In 1956, Holly went to Nashville to record for Decca records, with indifferent results. After returning home, he headed west, to Clovis, New Mexico, where Norman Petty operated a well-equipped studio—the best in the region. In Petty, Holly found a soulmate, someone interested in record production and in expanding the sound world of rock and roll. Although their relationship ended badly, their work together helped lay the groundwork for the recording innovations of the Beatles and other major sixties artists.

Country, Elvis-isms, rock and roll, and rhythm and blues all figure in Holly's music, but it was much more than just a synthesis of these styles. His hit recordings are a catalog of innovations and adaptations. For "That'll Be the Day," Holly borrows the chorus/verse/chorus form of Chuck Berry's "Maybellene" and sets it to new chords. Like so many rock and roll songs, "That'll Be the Day" relies heavily on the three basic chords found in the blues, but the song presents them in an unusual sequences, starting on the IV chord.

"Not Fade Away" was a much bolder statement. Its rhythmic point of departure was the "Bo Diddley beat," itself firmly rooted in the clave rhythm of Afro-Cuban music. In this song, the rhythm is a slight alteration of the typical clave pattern. The persistent call-and-response exchanges between Holly and the backup singers also recall Bo Diddley's self-titled hit.

Despite this connection, however, this song is philosophically different from the rock and roll of Berry, Little Richard, and Lewis. Their rock and roll is dance music—loud, assertive dance music. This song is not. A typical rock and roll song reinforces three regular rhythms: the eight-beat rock rhythm (e.g., Berry's guitar), the beat (usually kept by the bass), and the backbeat. Here, none of these rhythms is consistently present.

Allison's drumming is especially unconventional here. He marks the clave rhythm on the hi-hat and keeps time intermittently on a deadened drum, a sound which suggests the conga drum much more than the standard drum set.

Throughout the song, almost all of the accents play against the beat and measure instead of confirming it. The backup vocalists don't sing on the first note of the clave pattern, so they never mark the beginning of the measure. And Holly gives a strong accent on the last beat of the second measure of the pattern. Moreover, there is no bass or rhythm guitar. No one marks time, so we don't get our rhythmic bearings until Holly sings the lead vocal line. This kind of rhythmic ambiguity was unprecedented in rock and roll.

"Not Fade Away" introduces into rock and roll the idea that a song can be more than dance music. It can tell a story—here at something less than full volume. It's an about-face from the music's original message and a door opening to a new sound world.

"Well . . . All Right" looks even further into the future. In its use of acoustic instead of electric guitars, alternation of modal and conventional harmonies (compare the chords of the first two phrases), melodies that build phrase by phrase toward a high point at the end of a section, and delicate rhythm accompaniment, "Well . . . All Right" leapfrogs the entire folk revival to anticipate the folk rock of the later sixties. It would have sounded completely at home on an album from that era.

Buddy Holly stands apart among the early rock and rollers. If the others showed the world what rock and roll was, he showed them what it could—and would—become. His songs were an obvious inspiration for the innovative music of the Beatles, Dylan, Simon and Garfunkel, and many others. Add to his impressive musical achievement the sense of loss that his death created, and it's easy to understand the veneration that he has enjoyed.

Summary

At the beginning of the chapter, we posed the question, "What is rock and roll?" If we embrace all the music that was called rock and roll during the 1950s, we have a muddy answer to the question. However, if we look back from the future and ask "What music of the fifties led most directly to rock?" our answer quickly comes into sharper focus: it is mainly the music of the six acts discussed in this chapter.

In three short years, rock and roll came together as a distinct style. Elvis was its front man: On record, in person, on television, and in the movies, he was its most recognizable voice and most powerful image. Little Richard gave the music its beat, its volume, its assertiveness, and its most outrageous persona; Jerry Lee Lewis followed right behind. Chuck Berry transferred the beat to the electric guitar, rock's most outspoken instrumental voice, and created rock and roll's most emulated sound. The Everly Brothers opened up a gentler side, while Buddy Holly opened the door to the eclectic sound world of sixties rock.

In words and music, rock and roll became the voice of a new generation. Especially in the lyrics of Berry and Holly, it spoke simply but subtly of teen issues—mostly issues of the heart. And the music, with its energy and presence, was the teenagers' sound badge. The songs coming out of transistors and car radios were as much a part of their identity as their hair styles, clothes, and cars.

In 1959, with its first great musicians and the industry itself mired in scandal, rock and roll seemed destined to fade away. However, the music had come too far too fast for that to happen. In fact, the opposite took place. Rock and roll's posture, its rhythms and textures, its singing and sound world would begin to infiltrate almost every other popular style: rhythm and blues, country and folk, pop, jazz. It reached beyond America's borders, as England and then the rest of the world discovered this new music.

K E Y   T E R M S

Rock and roll	**Double-note guitar lines**	**Bo Diddley beat**
Teen themes	**Rockabilly**	
Backbeat	**Close harmony**	

CHAPTER QUESTIONS

1. Search for the first rock and roll record, using the following plan. Listen to one of the Rolling Stones' songs from Chapter 8, and keep the recording handy. Then listen to "Rocket 88," "Sh-Boom," "Rock Around the Clock," "That's All Right," "Tutti-Frutti," and "Johnny B. Goode." Compare each of the recordings to the Rolling Stones' recording. Then decide which of these is the most likely candidate for the first rock and roll record. Justify your decision by linking your chosen recording to the Stones' recording.

2. Locate a video of early rock and roll performers, and compare clips of Elvis, Chuck Berry, Little Richard, and Jerry Lee Lewis. Then compare these four with pop performers, either from television video or movie musicals. Then imagine that you were 14 in 1957, and consider how you might have reacted to Elvis and the others, and why your parents might have been horrified (or not).

3. Trace the consolidation of rock style in the four Chuck Berry recordings, listening for the heavy backbeat, rhythm guitar pattern, and Berry's solos. Then locate his recording of "Nadine" and note similarities and differences.

4. Compare Buddy Holly and his music to Berry, Elvis, and the others. How did they influence him and his music? How was his persona different from theirs? How was his music different? What was innovative about it?

c h a p t e r   5

Coming Together
Rock and Rhythm and Blues in the Early Sixties

In 1959, real rock and roll was reeling, not rocking, and black pop was mostly doo-wop. At the same time, the music establishment realized that there was money to be made in rock and roll—or what passed for rock and roll in their recording studios—even as they attacked rock and roll and R&B through Congress and the courts. Record company executives promoted "teen idols" like Frankie Avalon and Fabian. Although they used Elvis—his look, if not his sound—as a model, they were at best pale imitations. Their product was pop, packaged in pegged pants and pompadours.

Corruption of the music and corruption within the music industry seemed to signal the demise of rock and roll, just as its detractors had predicted. However, the music had come too far to simply fade away. So had rhythm and blues, which was on the verge of musical and commercial breakthroughs.

Perhaps because there was no surpassingly important act (e.g., Elvis, the Beatles), it has been customary to portray the early sixties as an uneventful period in rock history. In fact, the opposite is true. The early 1960s were a time of transition: to a new generation, a new set of attitudes, and new kinds of music. How this transition occurred is a fascinating story in itself. Add to that a substantial and varied legacy: some memorable one-hit wonders, and much of the work of major acts such as the Shirelles, Phil Spector, the Drifters, and Roy Orbison. Both the process and the results merit our attention.

The Integration of Popular Music

On November 30, 1963, *Billboard* suspended its R&B singles chart. Their decision was a sensible reaction to the enormous crossover between the R&B and pop charts: for the last few years, they had become so similar that the R&B chart had become redundant. It was a unique moment in the history of popular music. At no time before or since has America's taste in popular music been so integrated.

Chart integration was one dimension of the multi-dimensional integration of rock's segment of the music industry. Racial integration not only showed up on playlists, but also in record production—and occasionally on the bandstand. White producers such as Phil Spector showcased black acts; black producers such as Berry Gordy hired white symphony musicians to back his singers.

Rock also began to integrate sexually, although much more slowly, and never as fully as it did racially. Rock and roll was music for "guys": all its early stars were male. So was rhythm and blues, for the most part. Doo-wop groups were, with few exceptions, male, and so were most of the top solo acts. However, the early sixties saw the emergence of girl groups such as the Shirelles and Ronettes, as well as Motown stars such as Mary Wells and Martha and the Vandellas. Behind the scenes, Carole King, Cynthia Weil, and other female songwriters turned out hit after hit, while Deborah Chessler trailblazed the path for women producers.

Musical Integration

The best evidence of musical integration came from the songs of the girl groups and the Drifters. Its most obvious features, the singers and their singing styles, were black. However, there was also considerable white input: directly from producers such as Phil Spector and songwriters such as Carole King, and indirectly from the infusion of traditional pop elements. Although clearly black in sight and sound, the overall result was a true musical fusion of white and black, not simply a black take on white music (like most doo-wop hits) or a white take on black music (e.g., Pat Boone covering Little Richard).

This music was also evidence of a curious role reversal. In the early days of rhythm and blues and rock and roll, whites covered black songs. Thus whites were in the foreground, blacks in the background. Less than a decade later, it was black artists who were out in front and whites who were in the background. That trend would continue throughout the sixties: consider the integrated house band at Stax.

The success of this new black pop style was a significant moment in the history of rock. It was the first time that a black style, not just a black artist, was competing on equal terms with white music: a significant moment in rock history.

Still, black pop was the musical exception, not the rule. In the early sixties rock and roll and rhythm and blues evolved along separate, if parallel, paths, even though they kept company on the charts. Rock and roll would become rock, in all its variety. Rhythm and blues would become mainly Motown and soul. Like racial integration, musical integration went only so far: the Shirelles and the Drifters sound quite different from the Beach Boys and Roy Orbison.

The New Sounds of the Early Sixties

Despite these differences, all of it was music of a new generation. Regardless of its source, the new music of the early 1960s shared musical features that distinguished it from virtually all the music of the 1950s and before. In addition, the major figures of this period continued a fundamental reconception of popular song. Every aspect of songwriting and production, from first moment of inspiration to final product, underwent major change. We discuss these innovations below.

Musical Innovations

Among the most important musical innovations of the early sixties were:

- electric bass
- a new beat
- diffusion of melody
- more democratic texture
- new song forms

Some changes were radical, others slight, but all contributed to a new sound. We can examine each briefly.

ELECTRIC BASS The crucial new instrument in the transition to rock was the electric bass. Most of the first rock and roll bands had simply adapted electric blues band instrumentation to the new music. As the music developed, bands needed a stronger, more flexible bass voice. As a result, the electric bass gradually replaced the acoustic bass used in the first rock and roll bands. By 1960, it was the instrument of choice for most rock bassists.

A NEW BEAT The most obvious and pervasive evidence of the influence of rock and roll was its beat. This new eight-beat rhythm came in many forms, some quite different from Chuck Berry's original formulation. However, its presence was a clear signal that a song was up-to-date.

DIFFUSION OF MELODY Another important development in the new music of the early sixties was the distribution of melodic interest throughout the group. The idea of distributing melodic interest had become increasingly popular during the fifties, as we noted in the previous chapters. By 1960, it had become standard operating procedure. The melodic signature of a song could appear almost anywhere: not only in the lead line but also in a backup vocal ("Duke of Earl") or instrumental part ("Oh, Pretty Woman").

A MORE DEMOCRATIC TEXTURE Pre-rock pop had a clear hierarchy of importance: the lead singer at the apex, the rhythm section at the base, with subordinate, well-defined timekeeping responsibilities. Rock and roll and much of the postwar rhythm and blues had begun to break down this hierarchy by making the rhythm section and background riffs more prominent. The process accelerated in the important rock of the early sixties. In much of this music, most of the participants had something important to say, at least some of the time. As we'll hear in several examples, textures were more balanced and interdependent. Increasingly, it became impossible to subtract instruments or voices and still retain the essence of the song.

NEW SONG FORMS The venerable verse/chorus form had resurfaced in rock and roll, through the music of Chuck Berry, Buddy Holly, and others. There were two widely used variants of this form:

- *Refrain-frame*. In songs with "refrain-frame" forms, such as "Maybellene" and "That'll Be the Day," the refrain frames narrative sections. It appears at the beginning and end of the song, and pops up periodically to remind us what the song is about.

- *End-weighted*. Songs with end-weighted forms, such as "Johnny B. Goode," begin with a narrative, then build to the main point of the song. Typically, it is the title phrase of the lyric, set to the *hook*, i. e., the most accessible and memorable melodic idea.

Refrain-frame and end-weighted forms, used only occasionally in the mid-fifties, became normative in the early sixties. They replaced, or at least modified, the more traditional blues and AABA pop song forms.

Moreover, as their use became more widespread, the *idea* of form changed. Instead of a template into which songwriters poured a melody, form became a set of basic principles. As a result, there was much greater formal variety from song to song. All of the songs studied in this chapter use some variant of these forms, but each is quite different in its realization of the basic outline.

Reconceiving Popular Song

Hand in hand with the musical innovations of the early sixties came a fundamental reconception of popular song. Every crucial element, what it is, how it is created, and how it reaches its audience, underwent major revision. To appreciate the magnitude of this reconception, we need to examine how popular music reached its audience before the rock era.

The popular songs of the twenties, thirties, and forties generally went from inspiration to hit in several stages:

1. A songwriter or songwriting team (composer and lyricist) wrote the song.

2. An arranger scored the song for the group that would perform it: the orchestra for a Broadway or Hollywood musical, a dance band, or a studio orchestra supporting a singer such as Frank Sinatra.

3. Once a song caught on, it was "out there," for anyone to perform. Typically, several bands would record different versions of the song, all about the same time. Live performances—in a nightclub, at a dance, over the radio—would be even more varied.

4. At the same time, the song's publisher would print a piano/vocal setting of the song. This would offer a simplified version of the melody and harmony of the song, appropriate for home use.

As a result, the song would exist simultaneously in several forms. For instance, listeners in 1935 could hear Irving Berlin's hit song "Cheek to Cheek," featured in the film *Top Hat*, on records by Fred Astaire, Ginger Rogers, and several others, performed live on radio broadcasts, and in night clubs and restaurants, or they could buy the sheet music and play it themselves.

Two aspects of this process stand out. First, there was no one person who controlled the sound of the song. Second, there was no authoritative version. The songwriter and his lyricist wrote the words, melody, harmony, and basic rhythms of the song. However, their published version of the song did not specify the instruments to be used in an ideal performance, the vocal style of the singer, the overall form of the performance, and many other features. Moreover, the songwriter effectively lost artistic control of the song when he finished it. Arrangers and performers could change almost any aspect of the song—and usually did.

By the early 1960s, every aspect of this process had changed. Increasingly, the progress of a song from idea to finished product typically went like this:

1. Songwriters within a band would write a song, then flesh it out with the rest of the band in rehearsal.

2. They would bring it into the recording studio, where a producer would oversee the entire recording process: the basic recording, overdubbing, mixing, etc.

3. A "single" was released performed by that band and (possibly) would become a hit.

4. The hit record would be played on the radio throughout the country. Other groups would rarely cover it.

A simplified sheet music version might appear. However, most people learned the sound and style of a song from the recording. If they used the sheet music at all, it was only as a bare-bones guide.

This new process produced two far-reaching changes: First, the creators of the song generally retained some control of the end result throughout the entire creative cycle. Second, there was, as a result, a definitive version of a song: the original recording by the group or team that conceived it. The song became the sound captured on record: not just the melody and chords, but the complete sound experience. Unlike earlier popular songs, the recording was the document.

Everything about the recording—its beat, the choice of instruments, the sound of the singer(s), signature riffs, accompaniments—helped define the song. (By way of example, eight of the ten songs discussed in this chapter can be immediately identified by a distinctive combination of sounds, rhythms, and riffs—before the first word of the melody is sung!) Any other version of it, whether a cover recording or a sheet music reduction, lacked the authority of the original.

Moreover, songs often represented a more unified conception. It could be the musical vision of one individual or a collaboration between songwriter, performer, and producer, with one person often filling two of the roles. In either circumstance, the song represented a collectively conceived viewpoint, worked out mainly in one place (a recording studio) within a narrow time frame (over the course of a recording session).

Steady improvement in recording technology made this new creative process possible. The most far-reaching innovation was multitrack recording, which enabled producers to assemble a song layer by layer. Experimentation through trial and error was possible on a much broader scale at every stage of the process, from initial idea to final mix. This more-or-less continuous evolution of a song was a far cry from the severely segmented assembly of a recorded performance in pre-rock pop.

THE PRODUCER The shift to the recording as authoritative document elevated the status of the producer. Producers had been part of rock and roll since the beginning, but in the early sixties they assumed an increasingly important creative role.

Jerry Leiber and Mike Stoller were among the first to elevate record production to an art. By the time their first major act—the Coasters—recorded "Young Blood," Leiber and Stoller were independent producers for Atlantic records, often writing the songs and supervising all aspects of the recording. They were meticulous in both planning and production, often recording up to sixty takes to obtain the result they sought. A remark of theirs summarizes the wholesale change in the creative process: "We don't write songs, we write records." They carried this idea into their work with the Drifters.

At about the same time, Roy Orbison found a soulmate in producer Fred Foster, who gave a symphonic, lush backup to Orbison's often soaring vocals. Brian Wilson, lead singer, primary songwriter, and bass player with the Beach Boys, began producing the Beach Boys' recordings almost as soon as their career got off the ground. He directed the group's major recording sessions, and melded their distinctive vocal and backup sound. Berry Gordy went a step further, developing the Motown sound, which is immediately recognizable regardless of the singer(s).

Despite their importance, all of these men remained pretty much in the background. It was Phil Spector, a former Leiber and Stoller assistant, who would become the first celebrity producer. Spector, rock's first producing prodigy, developed his trademark "wall of sound" through massive overdubbing. Much more than in the Motown recordings, the singers were secondary and all but interchangeable; a distinctive, technology-driven orchestration was his sound signature.

Rhythm and Blues in the Early Sixties

Almost all rhythm and blues styles got a face-lift in the early sixties. Most of the new styles of the fifties continued to evolve. Doo-wop disappeared; a new black pop replaced it. The "rhythm" segment of rhythm and blues got a new, more active beat. Only electric blues held on to its shuffle groove.

A New Rock-Based Pop

Black pop was the most significant new music to emerge at the beginning of the 1960s, both commercially and musically. Groups such as the Shirelles, the Drifters, the Miracles, and Martha and the Vandellas brought a new sound to the top of the charts. The style had much in common with doo-wop: the

gospel-inspired vocal sound and the pop orientation stand out. The most obvious differences were a more animated beat, usually based on an eight-beat
rhythm; and the use of the new storytelling forms. However, all of the changes
discussed are part of the new black pop sound.

THE SHIRELLES If there's one song that epitomizes the new black pop style,
it could very well be the Shirelles' "Will You Love Me Tomorrow," a No. 1 hit
in 1960. The Shirelles, a black female vocal group from New Jersey, enjoyed a
string of hits in the early sixties. Their first hit was written by Carole King and
her first husband, Gerry Goffin, two of many talented songwriters working in
the Brill Building. It was released on Scepter records, at the time a mom-and-
pop record company (literally!) started by the mother of a high-school class-
mate of the Shirelles.

The principal players and their roles show an industry in transition. The
creative division of labor—Goffin and King wrote a song for others to sing—
was the old way of doing things, but the song explored a contemporary theme,
and the group who sang it was the first of the R&B "girl groups" to crack the
pop charts.

"Will You Love Me Tomorrow" talked about love and its absence with open
eyes, rather than the starry eyes of "Earth Angel." More importantly, it introduced
a woman's point of view. Its message—the emotional uncertainty of a new relationship: is this love at first sight or a one-night stand?—is presented in plain,
direct language. This kind of directness presages the realism of sixties rock.

The form of the song helps communicate its message. On the surface, it
seems like a typical AABA pop song. But there are two key differences: its

---

The Brill Building

The Brill Building, Goffin and King's professional address at the time, was
Tin Pan Alley's (i.e., traditional pop music's) last stand. Located at 1619
Broadway in New York, it was home to several publishers whose songwriting staffs supplied teen idols and others with a string of hits in the late
fifties and early sixties. Hal David and Burt Bacharach, Neil Sedaka, and
Bobby Darin were among other notable songwriters who worked for Brill
Building publishers. The "Brill Building sound" became associated with
the lighthearted, teen-pop hits that were crafted there and then issued by
the many small labels located in and around New York City.

The hiring of songwriters just to write songs was business as usual for
music publishers. However, these songwriters were young, and the songs
that they wrote were directed at a young audience. Further, they wrote
songs mainly for recording; sheet music sales continued to diminish in
importance. Indeed, for many of these songwriters, their Brill Building
employment was simply an apprenticeship. Darin, Sedaka, and King all
went on to important careers as performers and recording artists.
Bacharach and David found a unique alternative to performing their own
material: they wrote most of their hits for Dionne Warwick—with her
sound in mind.

length and the end-weighting of the A sections. Each A section contains sixteen measures, twice the normal length. This additional length gives room for a different balance within the A section. The opening material is verse-like; the theme of the song comes at the end of the phrase. In this respect, it's much more like the Motown recordings presented in Chapter 1 than "Earth Angel" or "Sh-Boom."

The Shirelles' singing lacks the polish of the Supremes, the virtuosity and passion of Aretha, or the vocal richness of the Raelettes. Instead, it has an endearing amateurishness—a mix of innocence and worldliness—that gives the performance an everyday realism that complements the text beautifully.

The accompaniment is an early version of the musical mix that characterized the new pop of the era. The delicate but straightforward rock rhythm has little of the rhythmic interplay that we will hear in subsequent examples. Its relative simplicity reminds us that rock rhythm was still new in 1961. At the same time, the intricate and prominent string counterpoint modernizes the sumptuous string writing of pre-rock pop.

THE DRIFTERS   During the early 1960s, the Drifters kept the Shirelles company at the top of the charts. They shared common musical ground as well: both were black vocal groups who sang new-style pop songs written by young white songwriters, mostly from the Brill Building. But there are significant differences. Gender is the most obvious, experience the most meaningful.

In rock and roll time, the Drifters were greybeards by the time they recorded "Save the Last Dance for Me" and "On Broadway," their two major hits from the early sixties. Indeed, the Drifters who recorded "Save the Last Dance for Me" were the group's second incarnation. The original Drifters, formed in 1953 to back Clyde McPhatter, enjoyed immediate success as an R&B act. After McPhatter went solo in 1955, the group went through several personnel changes and eventually disbanded in 1958. Their manager, who owned the name, reformed the group in 1959 with four new singers—Ben E. King sang lead—and engaged Leiber and Stoller to produce their records. As before, they were immediately successful, this time on the pop charts: they had five top ten hits between 1959 and 1964.

Their experience, and Leiber and Stoller's, shows. Both "Save the Last Dance for Me" and "On Broadway" are beautifully performed and flawlessly produced. Leiber and Stoller's skill is evident in both the large-scale design and the details that flesh it out. In both songs, the basic "feel" of the music resonates with the scene painted in the lyric.

In "Save the Last Dance for Me," the background seems to capture both the tenuousness of the singer's hold on his partner and lightfootedness (and lightheadedness) he feels when dancing with her. Every element contributes to this effect: Latinish beat; discreet strings; high-pitched percussion; acoustic guitar and bass; Latin-inspired bass line, whose rhythm comes from the rhumba via New Orleans; and the double-time guitar chords. All provide a cushion for the gently flowing melody to ride on.

King left the group to go solo shortly after "Save the Last Dance for Me" climbed to No. 1. He was replaced by the grittier Rudy Lewis, who was the lead singer in "On Broadway."

"On Broadway" is a much darker song, a tale of a lonely young musician with talent—and not much else—getting his first taste of life in New York. The sparse instrumentation (notice how the beat is delicately passed among several percussion instruments) echoes his own loneliness, while the static quality of the harmony supports the "to-be-continued" aspect of the story. The repetition of the melody at successively higher pitches seems to parallel the guitar player's growing resolve, while the jarring juxtaposition of guitar solo and string melody dramatize the contrast between his rough edges and the city's slickness.

The purposeful manipulation of the entire sound world of a song to underscore its basic idea had seldom occurred prior to rock. (When it did, it happened mainly in the best Broadway musicals and film scores.) Nor was it evident in most of the first rock and roll records. Its appearance here and subsequently—most spectacularly in the music of the Beatles—is evidence of both the imagination of the songwriters, performers, and producers and the new understanding that a song is the sound world created on the recording, not just the lyrics, melody, and harmony.

A New Rhythm for Rhythm and Blues

Curiously, fifties rhythm and blues resisted rock and roll's beat. Past, present, and future stars did little to move rhythm and blues into the rock era. Fats Domino had found a groove with his trademark triplets early in the 1950s and stayed in it for the rest of the decade. Ray Charles, the artist who could have shown the way to the new beat, chose not to. Instead, he crossed over to country and pop. James Brown was still in the early stages of his career and had not yet found his "brand new bag." With so little internal impetus, rhythm and blues came to rock rhythm reluctantly. Not surprisingly, its main source was New Orleans.

ROCKING FROM NEW ORLEANS Fats Domino to the contrary, New Orleans was the most likely place for rhythm and blues to acquire a rock beat. As we have heard, Professor Longhair anticipated rock rhythm as early as the late forties, while Little Richard was the first to hammer it out, during his New Orleans-based Specialty sessions. So it was definitely in the New Orleans air during the 1950s. Other New Orleans musicians followed somewhat tentatively in Little Richard's footsteps. Huey (Piano) Smith's aptly titled 1957 recording "Rocking Pneumonia and the Boogie Woogie Flu" teetered on the boundary between shuffle and rock rhythms.

By the early 1960s, however, New Orleans rhythm and blues had absorbed rock rhythm and turned it into its own special groove. It appeared in songs such as Ernie K-Doe's "Mother-in-Law" and Chris Kenner's "I Like It Like That" (which hit No. 1 and No. 2 on both R&B and pop charts at different times in 1961). Both K-Doe (born Kador, he legally changed his name to K-Doe) and Kenner were one-hit wonders, but Allen Toussaint, the man who produced their records, remains one of the giants of early rock. Like so many New Orleans pianists, Toussaint was a disciple of Professor Longhair. In the mid-fifties, he became a session player for Dave Bartholomew and began a long apprenticeship with him. By 1960, he had added songwriting, arranging, and producing to his professional skills. In 1961, he hit the jackpot with K-Doe and Kenner.

When rhythm and blues musicians finally got around to using rock rhythm, they made the beat less explicit, so that it sounded quite different from conventional rock beats. Recall that in the first rock and roll recordings, the eight-beat rhythm was very much in the forefront. It was most prominent in Chuck Berry's guitar or Little Richard and Jerry Lee Lewis's piano, and also reinforced in the drum part. Indeed, its prominence was a big part of the message of the song.

That's not the case in rhythm and blues with a rock feel. In "I Like It Like That," for example, the eight-beat timekeeping—when it's present—is much more subtle than in a conventional rock and roll song: it's heard faintly on a closed hi-hat. The other drum figures, an active bass line with a free rhythm, the backup vocal riffs, and the piano patterns overlay the eight-beat rhythm. The result is a much more open rhythmic texture, with lighter reinforcement of the rock beat and considerably more syncopation.

This rock-rhythm groove, where everyone feels the beat so that no one needs to hammer it out, brings popular music much closer to the kind of cooperative rhythmic interaction heard in West African music. It would lead to the rhythms of soul.

MELODY VS. RHYTHM IN R&B A comparison of "I Like It Like That" with "Will You Still Love Me Tomorrow" shows not only the musical, but also the philosophical differences between melodically-oriented black pop and rock-based rhythm and blues. In "Will You Love Me Tomorrow," for example, the melody builds continuously through the phrase until it arrives at the hook. This melodic tension and release reinforces the story told in the lyric. In the songs by the Shirelles and the Drifters, the tension that is inherent in the lyric reverberates through the music. The conflict—how will the story end?—sustains our interest.

There is no conflict in the lyric of "I Like It Like That," because there's not much of a story. So, for the music to keep our attention, it must sustain interest in other ways. Here, it's the complexity and variety of the rhythmic texture—the qualities that give the song a good beat—and the varied texture. Both encourage—almost demand—physical participation from listeners, so that they also ride the groove.

This kind of music is philosophically different from melodically oriented songs, where there is a story to be told. Storytelling songs ask listeners for empathy with the protagonist. We can relate to the vulnerability of the young woman depicted in "Will You Love Me Tomorrow." By contrast, songs like "I Like It Like That" demand surrender of their listeners: surrender of their personalities to the group. "Is" blend into the "we" that makes and experiences the music. For the moment, at least, band and audience are one; there are no individuals. Instead of empathy, we have ecstasy, where all give themselves up to the groove.

Twisting the Night Away

In the 1950s, rock and roll was a dance music for teens. Adults were still fox-trotting their way across the dance floor. The song that would change all that was "The Twist," a two-time hit for a one-hit wonder, Chubby Checker.

Checker, who started life as Ernest Evans, was part of pop promoter Dick Clark's stable of artists. Clark was always on the lookout for new dance sensations, because he hosted the popular *American Bandstand*, a dance-oriented television program for teens. When he discovered Hank Ballard's obscure 1958 recording of a novelty number called "The Twist," he had Checker record it for a local Philadelphia label. Clark, who had a financial interest in the label, then promoted the song vigorously on his show. The song was an immediate

Chubby Checker on stage in England, c. 1962. PHOTO COUR-TESY CORBIS/HULTON-DEUTSCH COLLECTION.

sensation, and it had staying power as well: it was the only rock era song to reach the top of the charts twice, first in 1960/1961, then again in 1962.

"The Twist" got everybody dancing to rock and roll. It was easy to learn, even for adults—and they did, from the Kennedys on down. Suddenly, dancing the twist (and the frug, watusi, and subsequent dance sensations) was the "in" thing to do.

Dance Instruction Songs

"The Twist" continues the tradition of "dance-instruction" songs by African-American popular musicians. The earliest date back to the teens: "Ballin' the Jack" is a still-familiar example. "Pine Top's Boogie Woogie" is a slightly more recent example (see Chapter 2). The song's lyric shows the crucial role television played in popularizing this new dance (and most others of the era). Earlier dance-instruction songs had given verbal directions, e.g., Pine Top's "mess around." However, Checker simply sings "Do like this." He presumes that his listeners will have seen him, or be able to see him, do the dance.

The song itself is stripped down and souped-up Chuck Berry. It's a straight-forward blues, with heavy marking of the beat and rock rhythm. There's a lot of energy, but not much subtlety, as is appropriate for a dance song.

"The Twist" belongs to those "right time/right place" moments that are so much a part of rock history. Neither the song nor Checker's performance are exceptional, but its timing was impeccable.

From Rock and Roll to Rock

Rock and roll underwent a changing of the guard in the early sixties. After leaving the army, Elvis left rock and roll behind to concentrate on his acting career. He still recorded, but his music had lost the cutting edge of his earliest work. Jerry Lee Lewis lived hard and toured hard, staying busy, if not in the limelight. Chuck Berry started the 1960s in court and found himself in jail soon after. Only the Everly Brothers continued steadily along the career path they'd marked out earlier. Joining them were acts such as Roy Orbison and the Beach Boys.

"Louie, Louie"

Rock critic Dave Marsh claimed that "Louie, Louie" was the "world's most famous rock and roll song" and argued his case in a book that examined both the history and (as he put it) the mythology of the song. Most famous or not, "Louie, Louie" was one of the first real rock songs, in attitude as well as style. It brought back the nastiness of early rock and roll, a welcome antidote to the saccharine pop-rock schlock that passed for rock and roll. The lyrics of the song, which remain impossible to decipher, have only added to the legend.

The Kingsmen were important because they proved that almost anyone had a shot at rock stardom. Their song's simple but memorable three-chord vamp was easy to learn, and the words didn't matter, except to the FCC, who couldn't figure out what they said, but figured it had to be obscene. As a result, "Louie, Louie" launched literally thousands of garage bands.

Still, the Kingsmen were basically a one-shot wonder. They had two other songs chart, but had dissolved by 1967. It was a lesson learned by many other bands: sometimes staying on top is harder than getting there. They also taught rock another lesson: don't stray too far from your roots.

Roy Orbison

Roy Orbison, a shy Texan, was the last rockabilly, the first country rocker, and one of the architects of the symphonic pop-rock sound of the early sixties. After recording his first sides at Norman Petty's Clovis, New Mexico, studio, Orbison migrated to Tennessee in 1956. During stops in Memphis and Nashville, he had rubbed shoulders with all of the important figures in white rock and roll by the end of the decade: Elvis, Buddy Holly, Jerry Lee Lewis, Sam Phillips, Norman Petty, and the Everly Brothers.

His music—especially that produced at the peak of his career— would blend all these influences, but first it went through another important phase. After a brief flirtation with RCA, Orbison signed with Monument records, where he found a soulmate in producer Fred Foster. Together, they cultivated a more melodramatic version of the rock ballad introduced by the Everly Brothers in songs such as "Only the Lonely" (1960).

"Meanwoman Blues" (1963) and his classic, "Oh, Pretty Woman" (1964), update rockabilly and showcase one of the great voices of the rock era. "Mean Woman Blues" is country rock—hard country rock—recorded over a decade before there was such a thing. It blends Orbison's unmistakably southern singing—his own blend of blues and country—with a good, basic rock beat, the kind heard in so much country of the eighties and nineties. The instrumental interlude shows that Orbison had been listening to the radio recently: it layers a bluesy guitar solo over the riff from the Surfari's "Wipeout," played on a saxophone. Orbison's recording brings honky-tonk into the rock era, where the driving rhythm and dense texture amplify the swagger of the lyric.

Orbison's masterpiece was "Oh, Pretty Woman" (more commonly known as "Pretty Woman"). The song shows many of the changes that transformed rock and roll into rock, e.g., a new take on rock rhythm and the opening guitar riff, which immediately identifies the song.

The most noteworthy feature of the song is its form. Earlier in the chapter, we had discussed the increased formal flexibility that surfaced in the new music of the early sixties. "Pretty Woman" illustrates this flexibility better than any other song discussed to this point. More than that, the memorable events seem to respond almost cinematically to the images described in the lyric. Like a good soundtrack, they capture the basic mood of the story and highlight the constantly shifting emotions.

The story is a cliché of romantic comedies, music videos, and television commercials: boy sees beautiful girl, boy makes some kind of contact with girl, boy is apparently rebuffed, but gets the girl in the end.

Here are some of the highlights:

0'02"   The opening guitar riff is assertive, yet the chord that it outlines, and the silence that follows, asks a question that is not answered conclusively until the final notes of the song. The periodic return of the guitar riff not only outlines the form of the song but keeps us focused on the main issue in the song: will the pretty woman like the hero?

0'14"–0'40"   The first two sections of the vocal line begin by setting the scene. But both end by dangling on the V chord. The second time, the suspensful ending highlights the crucial question: "Are you lonely, just like me?"

1'06"   At this point, the "hero" of the song hits on the pretty woman. A new melody, with short, pleading phrases in a higher register, underscores the intensity of his interest.

1'34"   Orbison extends the pleading section by dropping down into a lower register as he attempts to persuade her more intimately, in both words and music. This extension is the first clear signal that Orbison is molding the form to fit the pacing of his story: a more conventional song would have returned to the opening section before the extension.

Roy Orbison in 1964, resting backstage during a British tour. PHOTO COURTESY
CORBIS/HULTON-DEUTSCH COLLECTION.

1'55"   He continues to press his case as the opening vocal section
returns. However, the suspenseful ending is expanded enormously as
the hero seems to lose the pretty woman, then discovers that she's
returning. The sudden ending after the big buildup is, in effect, a
quick fade to black as the hero and the pretty woman come together.

In "Pretty Woman," Orbison molded the form to the story, not the other
way around. He underscored the feelings of his protagonist musically, in both
the guitar riff and the melody. His hero's success with the pretty woman owes
much to the persuasiveness of the music.

Orbison's flexible approach to form and musical reinforcement of the story
line would become increasingly common in rock. Few would connect the
music with the story as closely and powerfully as Orbison did here.

The Beach Boys

Rock and roll came from the center of the United States: New Orleans,
Memphis, Texas, Chicago. However, it quickly spread to both coasts and
beyond. While Dick Clark was filling the airwaves with teen idols and
Philadelphia teens twisting the night away, rock and roll was taking root elsewhere, most notably Southern California and England.

During the early 1960s, rock and roll became part of a new subculture,
southern California surfers. While surfers rode the waves and basked in the
sun, the Surfaris, the Ventures, Jan and Dean, and numerous other bands

created the sound track for their lifestyle. The most important and innovative of these groups was the Beach Boys. Their band was a family affair. The original group consisted of three brothers, Carl, Dennis, and Brian Wilson; their cousin, Mike Love; and a friend, Al Jardine.

Surf music was a milestone in the history of rock. It was the first important rock style to develop without the direct involvement of one of rock and roll's founding fathers. The torch was passed by record, rather than by personal contact.

The Beach Boys' first recordings point out their debt to Chuck Berry. They appropriated Berry riffs—even entire songs ("Surfin', U.S.A.")-borrowed almost note-for-note. But Berry's music is simply a foundation. Their vocal sound owes more to the Four Freshmen, a jazz-influenced singing group that was popular during the fifties. This unlikely mix was one reason for their distinctive sound. Another was the imagination of Brian Wilson.

The Beach Boys' image and the message of their songs kept Wilson's creativity in the background. In their recordings released between 1963 and 1965, the Beach Boys glorified the surfer lifestyle. The "fun in the sun" lyrics of the songs—surfing, cars, girls—suggest a mindless hedonism, which was enormously appealing not only to southern Californians but to teens everywhere.

The lyrics belie the considerable sophistication of the music: harmonies and key changes that range well beyond the three-chord rock progressions of so many bands, the beautifully interwoven vocal parts, sharp contrasts in texture that outline the form of the song, varied timekeeping, and other more subtle features.

This sophistication was mainly the work of Brian Wilson, who wrote most of the songs, sang and played in the band, and produced their recordings. In their peak years, the sound of the Beach Boys was Brian Wilson's conception. Wilson's imagination and craft went on behind the scenes, just as he himself retreated from public performance after a nervous breakdown in 1965.

Two recordings from 1964, "I Get Around" and "Dance, Dance, Dance," show the key elements of their style and the variety possible within it. "I Get Around" was one of their biggest hits, reaching the top of the charts in June, 1964. The song begins with just voices, presenting the essence of the Beach Boys' vocal sound. In order, there is unison singing, tight harmonies, and a soaring single-line melody juxtaposed with harmonized riffs: all sung with no vibrato. The refrain follows, with both the main melody and the high, wordless obbligato supported by a driving rock rhythm played by the entire band.

The "blocks-of-sound" approach continues in the verse sections. These are set off from the refrain by the substitution of an open-sounding, loping rhythm for the straightforward rock rhythm of the refrain. Even the instrumental solos have a characteristic, clearly defined sound. The short interlude in the verse combines a doubled organ and bass line with double-time drums, while the guitar solo is supported with sustained vocal harmonies.

"Dance, Dance, Dance," released later in 1964, shows the same level of sophistication in a different package. The song begins with a bass riff, which, in addition to starting the song off in a nice groove, showcases the liberation of the bass. Unlike "I'll Get Around," this song uses the end-weighted verse/refrain form. Two features are worthy of note: the addition of instruments to mark the beginning of the refrain, and the use of an exotic harmony and the sustained low/high vocal sounds that push the final "Dance, Dance, Dance" to the end of the phrase. Again, there is the trademark vocal sound:

soaring melody over harmonized riffs, and a parallel instrumental effect in the guitar solo: a twangy lead line contrasts with the more straightforward Chuck Berry-ish rhythm riff.

What stands out musically in both recordings is the way in which Wilson sustains interest throughout the songs by constantly varying the musical setting. The basic Beach Boys sound—a vibrato-less vocal style underpinned by an updated rock and roll beat—was so distinctive that it would have quickly become stale if Wilson had simply put songs in gear and stayed there. But he is constantly shifting some element: adding or subtracting instruments, changing keys, making an instrument more or less active. This variety keeps the sound fresh, even as its basic features remain consistent throughout. Without it, the Beach Boys would likely have gone the way of the Ventures, another southern California group with a distinctive sound: two or three hits and out.

Orbison and the Beach Boys dramatize two of the ongoing dialectics in rock: outside/inside and new/old. While Orbison helped diversify the sound of early rock, much as Buddy Holly did with rock and roll, the Beach Boys helped define rock by creating a highly personal style and staying within it, much as their hero, Chuck Berry, did. And while Orbison was the last important link to rock and roll's first generation, the Beach Boys were the beginning of a new era: re-regionalizing rock and roll to southern California and speeding its transformation into rock.

Summary

The early 1960s were a time of transition. Rock and roll matured into rock, and black music updated two of the important currents in 1950s rhythm and blues. The pop/gospel crossover music of Sam Cooke and the doo-wop groups evolved into the truly integrated black pop styles of the Shirelles, the Drifters, and several of the early Motown groups. The new rock-based rhythm and blues would become uptempo soul, as heard in the music of James Brown, Sam and Dave, Otis Redding, and others. At the same time, acts such as the Beach Boys and Roy Orbison purged rock and roll of its anachronisms. The result was rock, a new kind of popular music.

By the beginning of 1965, rock had begun to take over popular music. Rock acts—most notably, the Beatles, the myriad Motown groups, and the Beach Boys—dominated the airwaves and singles charts and gained a presence on album charts, pop's last bastion. Everything of substance was new: how the music was created and preserved, the ideas and attitudes it expressed, its beat and rhythms, sounds, harmonies, textures, and forms. Pop, even the warmed-over pop of the teen idols, was out of place in rock's brave new sound world.

K E Y T E R M S		
Electric bass	Democratic texture	Songwriter
Rock (eight-beat) rhythm	Refrain-frame song form	Arranger
Diffusion of melody	End-weighted song form	Producer

Rock-based pop   **New Orleans R&B**   **Formal flexibility**

Brill Building   **The Twist**   **Surf music**

Girl groups   **Multitrack recording**

CHAPTER QUESTIONS

1. Listen to the bass on any of the recordings discussed in this chapter. Then compare the role of the bass in these recordings to its role in the early rhythm and blues and rock and roll recordings in the previous two chapters. Has its role changed? If so, how?

2. Compare "Will You Love Me Tomorrow" to "Earth Angel." Describe similarities and differences in the language and message of the lyric, the singing style, and the musical setting.

3. Trace the influence of Chuck Berry on the Beach Boys by identifying features in either of the Beach Boys' recordings that are also heard on the Berry recordings.

4. Compare either of the Drifters' songs to Sam Cooke's "You Send Me," or any of the Buddy Holly recordings to Elvis's "Hound Dog." Describe the differences in musical setting: instrumentation and use of the instruments, rhythmic background, and overall polish of the recording. What conclusions can you draw about the increasing role of the producer?

5. Compare the first 30 seconds of "Oh, Pretty Woman" and "Louie, Louie" to any song or group of songs in the previous two chapters. Focus particularly on the beat and the role of the guitar. What earlier songs are they most like? What differences do you notice? Based on the contemporary music that you listen to, do the differences suggest the direction of rock evolution?

Society and Popular Music

1964–1974

This overview resumes the account of rock-era music and the context in which it developed. It begins with the British Invasion and stops just before punk, funk, and disco emerge as significant new popular styles. Again, we will examine social trends and changes in the music industry and describe how they affected the growth of rock, in not only the United States but the United Kingdom as well.

Social Trends

Economic and Social Conditions

As 1964 began, both the United States and the United Kingdom had strong economies. Following World War II, the American economy had grown steadily; as a leader of the "free world," the United States had also helped rebuild European nations, including Great Britain. When the sixties began, both countries were enjoying robust growth. Teenagers—who in the past had to hold down a job to help add to the family coffers—had leisure time and cash to spend. However, by 1974, the economies in both countries were reeling. Double digit inflation, increased unemployment, and the gas rationing brought on by the Arab oil embargo showed how interdependent the global economy had become and how fragile prosperity had become.

Hand in hand with economic hard times went distrust of government. Lyndon Johnson's first full term in office began with great expectations: government *could* change society for the better. Much significant legislation did get passed. Richard Nixon's term in office ended in 1974 with his resignation. There were no scandals of comparable magnitude in the United Kingdom, but the failure of the welfare state prompted widespread dissatisfaction. One consequence was that conservatives replaced liberals in both the United States and the United Kingdom, beginning in the late sixties.

Vietnam

If any single event symbolized the roller coaster ride of the sixties and early seventies, it was the Vietnam War. What had begun as a minor commitment of American "observers" during Kennedy's administration had escalated into a full-scale war by mid-decade, with over 500,000 American troops involved. The U.S. military command tried unsuccessfully to bludgeon the Viet Cong into submission, but failed: The war ended in a stalemate in 1973.

At first, the majority of Americans supported the war. However, as the horror of U.S. tactics—most notoriously, the My Lai massacre —and the deception of government and military leaders became public, public sentiment turned against the war. More than any other event of the period, it soured the American public against government.

Generation Gap

The reaction of young people to the Vietnam War underscored a growing division in American society between the younger and older generations: the so-called "generation gap." Most older Americans had served proudly in either World War II or Korea; for them, military service was the duty of all citizens, and Americans should never question their military, particularly in times of conflict. Younger Americans were less ready to die for what they viewed as a pointless and cruel war. They openly questioned the military's motives, and actively protested the government's involvement in Vietnam.

The younger generation's motto was simple: "Don't trust anyone over 30." (This would be a problem a few years later when many of them crossed this life landmark!) Different fashions, hairstyles, language, and music all worked to separate the generations. For older Americans—used to the placid family life of the fifties—these were alarming times; the young seemed to be out of control and bent on destroying all the core American values.

Race Relations and Minority Rights

The mid-sixties were the best of times and the worst of times for race relations in the United States. The 1964 Civil Rights Act and the 1965 Voting Rights Act restored and expanded the equal rights given blacks during emancipation one hundred years earlier.

However, the legislation could not change attitudes overnight. Many whites, especially Southerners, felt that no change was necessary. Others, including many blacks and white students, felt that change came far too slowly. The result was a series of confrontations (such as the march from Selma to Montgomery, Alabama, led by Martin Luther King, where protesters were attacked by state troopers), demonstrations, and race riots: 329 between 1964 and 1969, which left 220 dead and caused millions of dollars in property damage.

Again, younger white Americans tended to be more vocal in their support of racial equality than their older counterparts. This lack of agreement over the severity of the problem, and the necessity to address it, was another element that added to the growing generation gap.

The civil rights movement spearheaded a more widespread push for equal rights in other areas. Most prominent were the women's movement and gay liberation, but there were also equal rights movements among Chicanos and Native Americans. While laudable in their goals, these movements further polarized society, leading to many more explosive confrontations.

Rev. Martin Luther King, Jr. greets the crowd at the famous March on Washington, 1963. PHOTO
COURTESY CORBIS/HULTON-DEUTSCH COLLECTION.

Drugs

Popular musicians have had a long history of drug use and abuse. It seems to
run in cycles: alcohol was popular in the twenties, when it was illegal; heroin
was popular in the forties and fifties, especially among jazz musicians.
Marijuana use also dates back to earlier in the century. Seemingly, it has
always been part of the popular music lifestyle—at least for some.

In the 1960s, LSD became the latest fad among musicians and their listeners. LSD is a consciousness-expanding drug synthesized by Swiss chemist
Albert Hoffman. During a routine synthesis in 1943, he absorbed some of the
drug through his fingers and experienced the first acid trip. By 1962, poet Alan
Ginsberg, novelist Ken Kesey, and Harvard psychologist Timothy Leary were
among those who had tried LSD, more commonly called acid. Leary and Kesey
advocated its use: Leary by exhorting people to "turn on, tune in, drop out,"
and Kesey through his "Electric Kool Aide Acid Tests." By 1965, rock musicians, including Bob Dylan, had experimented with acid. By 1967, the Beatles,
bands in the Bay Area, and many others were tripping regularly.

Two things distinguish the LSD cycle from earlier ones. Unlike alcohol or
heroin, LSD is physically non-addictive; and LSD dramatically reshaped the
sound of the music. There was no "liquor jazz" or "heroin bebop," but there
was acid rock. Acid rock and acid-influenced rock reflected the consciousness-
expanding and time-suspending sensations produced by an acid trip. In its use
of unusual sonorities, it was often more colorful than basic rock and roll.
Moreover, it made use of drones and other repetitive patterns, and it sprawled—
songs often unfolded on a grand scale, especially in live performance (just ask
a Deadhead!). Acid use peaked in the late sixties. It seemed to lose its appeal
when general disillusionment replaced the goodwill of sixties "peace and love."

Jerry Garcia poses at the corner of Haight and Ashbury Streets, the heart of San Francisco's hippie neighborhood, in 1966. Photo courtesy CORBIS/ TED STRESHINSKY.

Music Business and Technology

Recording

Multitrack recording, already used by recording pioneers in the fifties, became standard operating procedure in the sixties. Four-track decks, introduced in the late fifties, were the standard until 1967, when larger studios opted for eight-track machines. The size of the board quickly escalated: 16-track machines were introduced the following year, and by 1972 the 24-track machine was the industry choice.

The richly textured songs of the Beatles, the Beach Boys, and other groups of the mid-sixties were made possible by a process called "bouncing down." Part of the song would be recorded onto four tracks; this would be mixed down into a single track—or perhaps two—which would open up the other tracks for additional parts. In analog recording, however, re-recording results in signal degradation, so excessive bouncing produces a record with inferior sound quality. Precisely because of that, the development of 16- and 24-track boards was inevitable. Multitrack recording produced better sounding records, or at least records closer to the sound desired by the producer.

There were four additional consequences of multitrack recording, all of them of crucial importance to rock music:

- *The creative process changed*. With the advent of multitrack recording, musicians no longer had to bring the whole package to the studio: either a self-contained group, or arrangements to be recorded during the session. Instead, musicians and their producer could assemble a recording in several stages, layering elements in stages. Any pre-mixing decisions could be reversed. So long as a group could afford studio time, almost unlimited trial and error was possible.

- *The producer became a central player*. Increasingly, producers shaped the sound of a recording. Some bands had outside producers: the Beatles/George Martin partnership is certainly the best known. Others found their producer within the band: Brian Wilson assumed that role with the Beach Boys. Stevie Wonder took the process even farther, not only producing his own recording but layering in almost all the tracks himself.

- *The recording became a document separate from live performance*. As recording became more sophisticated, the sounds of recordings became increasingly difficult—and expensive—to replicate in live performance. Particularly after the Beatles' *Sgt. Pepper*, the *recording* had become the document. The song was the sound captured on record, with all its subtleties.

- *The recording industry became less monolithic and centralized*. Anyone with a vision, a sound in their ear, money for a studio, and access to a good recording engineer and some good musicians could establish his own center. This process had begun in the fifties, with independent producers in New Orleans, Memphis, Chicago, and elsewhere. It accelerated in the sixties. Memphis remained an important regional center, but for soul, not rockabilly. A more unlikely center was Muscle Shoals, Alabama, home to Rick Hall's Fame Recording Studio, which produced some of the biggest soul records of the sixties. Detroit was home to Berry Gordy's Motown sound. In the early seventies, they received competition from Gamble and Huff's "The Sound of Philadelphia." San Francisco; Austin, Texas; Atlanta; and Nashville were other cities that became important recording centers.

The Instruments of Rock

Recording helped shape the sound of rock. So did its instruments. There were three kinds of developments:

- new instruments
- new sounds coming from existing instruments
- improved—and louder—amplification.

By 1964, the electric guitar and electric bass were standard equipment in a rock band. The newest sounds were keyboard instruments: portable electric organs and electric pianos, most notably the Fender Rhodes, a staple of jazz rock bands. The venerable Hammond B-3 electronic organ, a fixture in black churches, resurfaced in R&B and rock recordings during the latter part of the sixties.

However, the real breakthrough in keyboard instruments came in 1971, with the introduction of the Minimoog synthesizer. This portable version of the classical Moog synthesizer soon became a favorite of rock keyboardists like Rick Wakeman and Keith Emerson. An analog synthesizer, like the Moog, creates sounds out of wave-forms; the keyboard merely activates the sound. Keyboardists could access "patches," specific configurations of wave forms, and then manipulate them with pitch wheels, ribbons, and other devices. Some patches replicated existing sounds, e.g., strings, while others considerably expanded the sound palette of popular music. Tangerine Dream and Brian Eno were pioneers in this direction. Further improvements after 1975 would secure an even more central place for the synthesizer in popular music.

The electric guitar and electric bass were essentially the same instruments in 1974 that they were in 1964, but they sounded completely different. The biggest single change in their sound was the loudness. The development of powerful amplifiers, most notably the Marshall stacks that were part of the gear of almost every important rock guitarist, made it possible to play instruments at ear-shattering volumes. This in turn made stadium concerts feasible.

The expanded sound palette of rock bands was also due to innovative performing techniques. Three stand out:

- signal looping
- distortion
- percussive sounds

In solid-body instruments, like the Fender Stratocaster, the vibration from the plucked string is immediately converted into an electric signal. As such, it could be manipulated before being run through the amplifier. One manipulation was signal looping, which enabled the guitarist to sustain a note indefinitely. With this technique, the electric guitar becomes a completely different instrument. It can play sustained notes and soaring melodic lines; it is no longer limited by the quick decay of the acoustic instrument.

Another popular sound modification was distortion. Distortion first surfaced—on purpose—in early fifties blues and R&B, as has been noted. However, rock guitarists, most notably Jimi Hendrix, harnessed distortion—with the help of a fuzz box and the amplifier manufacturers. It became, in both guitar and bass, part of the sound of hard rock; extreme distortion became the sound signature of heavy metal.

While white guitarists experimented with distortion and feedback, black guitarists created new sounds by depressing the strings only part of the way. When strummed, the guitar produced a sound more percussive than pitched. This "choked" guitar sound was used by James Brown's guitarist, and became a staple of the "Superfly"-type music of the early seventies—as well as disco toward the end of the decade.

Bass players were even more inventive. Larry Graham (originally of Sly and the Family Stone) and Bootsy Collins (of James Brown's, then George Clinton's bands) started snapping, pulling, and tapping the strings, to produce more percussive sounds. More than any other instrument, the bass has gone from a melodic to a percussive instrument in the hands of black musicians.

Rock Outlets

One signal of rock's emergence as the most popular and significant music of the sixties and seventies was its domination of the media. New technology made it more available, while acceptance by the music power structure—business, after all, is business—created new kinds of access.

Massive amplification made live performance to huge crowds possible. Woodstock, a 1969 concert which attracted (by some counts) 300,000 people, was the most spectacular example, but by 1966, the stadium had replaced the theater and the club as the venue for major rock acts. Powerful amplification made possible the spectacle rock of Alice Cooper, Kiss, David Bowie, and other stars of the early seventies.

As it had been in the fifties and early sixties, television was the springboard to stardom for several rock groups: The Beatles' appearance on the *Ed Sullivan Show* certainly boosted their popularity in the United States. Dance shows, the other fifties holdover, continued. The new wrinkle was a made-for-TV rock band, the Monkees. The stars of a sitcom built around their career, they were extremely popular in the mid-sixties.

Radio went through another cycle in the ongoing tug-of-war between disc jockeys who want to play the music they like versus station managers and owners who want nicely packaged playlists that "guarantee" big audiences. "Underground" radio emerged on FM stations in the late sixties as a major outlet for the new rock of the time. It was especially important in San Francisco, where bands like the Jefferson Airplane, Santana, and the Grateful Dead got significant airplay. By the mid-seventies, radio programming was again controlled by the suits: AOR (album-oriented rock) replaced the free-form programming of the underground DJs.

In the early sixties, the film industry was as conservative musically as any branch of the media. That changed in the sixties. Rock-era music infiltrated the film industry in three ways: as the basis of a feature film, as background music for films, and through documentaries that recorded live performances. The breakthrough rock film, of course, was the Beatles' *A Hard Day's Night*. The film was as novel and fresh in its "day in the life" storyline, visual imagery, and low-key tone as the Beatles' music. A 1968 film, *The Graduate*, used the music of Simon and Garfunkel in the sound track. It helped break the ice in the film industry regarding the use of rock—and gave a real boost to the career of Simon and Garfunkel. Cutting-edge black music gave a contemporary sound to the "blaxploitation" films of the early seventies: *Shaft* and *Superfly* are notable in this regard. Finally, rock performers were captured in live performance: *Monterey Pop*, a documentary about the 1967 festival, was the first; the film of *Woodstock* helped its owners recoup expenses.

Finally, new playback media, most enduringly the cassette, made popular music more portable and transportable. Cassette decks and eight-track players became popular accessories in automobiles. Rock could be heard almost anywhere—and it was.

chapter 6

Motown and Soul

Black Music in the Sixties

Black music arrived in the mid-sixties. Vibrant new sounds filled the air. The Supremes, the Temptations, and other Motown groups routinely kept pace with the British bands at the top of the charts. Aretha Franklin, James Brown, and the Stax soul stars also found a large, integrated audience. It was a glorious period in American music.

Black music reached this artistic and commercial peak just as the civil rights movement crested. The sixties began full of promise as much of the nation—from President John F. Kennedy on down—finally joined civil rights crusaders in the march toward racial equality. Many Americans were inspired by the words and deeds of Martin Luther King, Jr. and other civil rights leaders. When racial equality became the law, racial harmony seemed possible.

However, the afterglow from these legislative successes was short-lived. In 1968, everything went sour. The pivotal event was the assassination of Dr. King, which left many wondering whether "the dream died with the dreamer," as Stax producer Al Bell put it. Race riots in Detroit and Watts and the confrontation between liberals and radicals during the 1968 Democratic convention replaced the idealism of the civil rights movement with disillusionment. The nation quickly discovered that laws do not change attitudes overnight. Nevertheless, the civil rights movement and the legislation it prompted profoundly redefined race relations in the United States.

The new black music of the 1960s reshaped the popular music landscape just as profoundly. Even as it carved its new identity, it penetrated deeply into the fabric of popular music. The sounds of soul would resonate through much of the music of the late sixties and seventies—black and white—and continue to shape popular music into the present.

Moreover, African-American popular music began to lose the racial stigma which it carried for generations. For the first time in its history, it was no longer low-class, wrong-side-of-the-tracks music. In theory, at least, the playing field had become level, just as it had in society as a whole.

In the 1970s, the popular music audience realigned along racial lines to some degree. Nevertheless, popular music did not retreat to a pre-soul past, just as the nation could not return to the federally sanctioned injustices of segregation.

The great black music of the sixties came mainly from two cities, Detroit and Memphis. Detroit was the home of Berry Gordy's Motown empire. Memphis was "soul city" in the sixties, just as it had been the mecca for rockabillies in the fifties. As before, it was a single recording studio that was the magnet: In the 1960s, Jim Stewart and Estelle Axton's Stax Records eclipsed Sam Phillips's Sun Records as the cutting edge sound from Memphis.

Two stars transcended these geographical boundaries. Aretha Franklin, whose career took off with the support of the Stax house band, linked the two, symbolically and musically. James Brown followed his own path, geographically (from Georgia to the world via Cincinnati's King Records) and musically.

All of this music was called "soul" at the time. In fact, however, there were two distinct, if related, styles: the black pop of Motown and the real soul music of Aretha, James Brown, and the Stax artists.

Motown

Berry Gordy began Motown with a vision and transformed it into a sound. He conceived of a new black pop sound that would cross racial boundaries and become as popular with whites as it was with blacks. It went from dream to reality in less than a decade.

Gordy's vision came into focus during the fifties. His first musical love was jazz. It was deep enough that he started a jazz record store. He went out of business after a couple of years, because many of his customers came in to buy R&B records that he *didn't* stock. He learned a crucial lesson from that experience: there was much more money to be made from pop.

Armed with that insight, he began writing songs for Jackie Wilson at the beginning of Wilson's solo career; several were hits. Although encouraged by his songwriting success, Gordy realized that the only way that he could gain complete artistic control of his music was to form his own record company.

Gordy started Motown in 1959 with little more than his dream and his drive. He knew that storytelling songs sold, and he soon learned how to sell them. Motown's first No. 1 R&B hit (the Miracles' "Shop Around") came in 1961; a No. 1 pop hit the following year (the Marvelettes' "Mr. Postman"). By that time, he had largely ceded the day-to-day creative work to others, but remained in control of the overall operation.

By 1964, the roster of Motown performers included Mary Wells, Martha and the Vandellas, the Supremes, Stevie Wonder, Marvin Gaye, the Miracles, the Temptations, and the Four Tops. By mid-decade, three out of every four Motown releases charted—unprecedented success for a record label.

The late 1960s and early 1970s saw the expansion of both its artists' roster and musical horizons. The most notable additions were Gladys Knight and the Pips and the Jackson 5. Around the same time, Gordy reluctantly gave Marvin Gaye and Stevie Wonder artistic control over their recordings. The results include some of the most significant music ever to appear on the label.

Motown was a unique phenomenon in popular music. Gordy was the first African American to create and manage a major record label, and the empire

The Supremes ask you to "Stop in the Name of Love," *1965. Photo courtesy CORBIS/BETTMANN.*

that he created was like no other. The Motown sound was a collective effort. It was hundreds of people—Gordy, his singers, songwriters, producers, musicians, plus all the business and clerical staff—all working together to produce a reliable product.

Motown was structured like a pyramid, with Gordy at the top. Songwriter-producers, most notably Smokey Robinson, the Holland-Dozier-Holland team, and, later, Norman Whitfield, were next in importance. Immediately beneath them were the house musicians who put the sound on tape and the staff arrangers who orchestrated the songs. Of these musicians, bassist James Jamerson, drummer Benny Benjamin, and guitarist Robert White played a crucial role. Only then did the singers figure into the equation.

There is no question that the acts were the most visible part of Motown. Gordy, who ran what amounted to a finishing school for his groups, made sure they were well-dressed, well-rehearsed, and presentable in every way. And there is no question that they were essential to the artistic and commercial success of the label. However, in terms of defining the Motown sound—the quality that often identified the style before a note was sung—they were among the most interchangeable parts. Indeed, one act would often cover another act's hit. The essence of the sound was in the songwriting, the producing, the conception of the studio musicians, and—above all—Gordy's overriding vision.

The Evolution of the Motown Sound

Gordy's "Sound of Young America" was a black pop style carefully calculated to appeal to the widest possible young audience. As we discovered in Chapter 1, Motown songs had something for everyone: good stories, conveyed in clearly outlined forms that underscored their main ideas; catchy lyrics; melodic hooks; an enticing but not overpowering beat; the sophistication of pre-rock pop and jazz, blended with the innocence of young voices. Listeners could sing along with them and dance to them.

In the earlier discussion we focused on its musical qualities, as heard in songs of 1964, the year that Motown took off. Our discussion here expands the idea of black pop to include the lyrics and how they coordinate with the music, and considers the evolution of the Motown Sound in the late sixties and early seventies, mainly in the music of Marvin Gaye.

The lyrics of Motown songs told stories about the joys and insecurities of young love, in language that young people of all races could understand and identify with. Often, they managed to be wide-eyed and somewhat worldly at the same time.

The language of the lyrics was everyday speech, but the lyrics were far from ordinary. Sometimes they were direct, as if the singer was telling us something important in her life; Holland/Dozier/Holland's "Come See About Me" is a terrific example. Other songs, especially those of Smokey Robinson, contained vivid images, often presented in a rapid-fire string of similes. Recall lines from "The Way You Do the Things You Do," such as "the way you smile so bright/you know you could have been a candle."

"My Guy," a No. 1 hit in 1964 for Mary Wells and her signature song, is also a signature Smokey Robinson song. It features striking similes: quick rhymes like "I'm sticking to my guy like a stamp to a letter" and "no muscle-bound man could take my hand from my guy" ripple through the lyric. The song can also flesh out our picture of the Motown sound in the mid-sixties.

The song has deep pop roots. The horn introduction was "borrowed" from Eddie Heywood's 1956 pop hit, "Canadian Sunset," and the form of the song is an elongated version of the venerable AABA form.

Still, Robinson adheres to the spirit of the Motown end-weighted form while putting a new spin on it. Like "My Girl," the song has a two-word title phrase that's attached to a melodic hook. However, instead of clustering all the statements of the hook at the end of a section, he sprinkles them in along the way. The two short phrases at the beginning of the section and the longer one that finishes up the section all end with "my guy."

The larger proportions also help emphasize the hook. The bridge (the B section in an AABA form) is short, offering just a brief contrast. As a result, the weight of the song remains on "my guy." The repeated tagline at the song's end—"there's not a man today/who can take me away/from my guy"—serves as a final hammering home of the lyrical theme. It's a very clever way of modernizing conventional pop forms.

Other features of the song also bear the Motown stamp: a different version of the Motown shuffle (the loping two-beat bass line gives the rhythm a real lilt); the unobtrusive background riffs from organ, then horns; the periodic vocal responses with the title phrase.

"My Guy" reaffirms and enriches our earlier impression of Motown (see Chapter 1). Among the key points are:

1. Like the music, lyrics are simple and appealing, yet catchy enough to retain our interest: the boy/girl subject matter is universal and the story is told in everyday language, but the images are vivid and memorable.

2. The song has clear connections to traditional white pop, yet departs significantly from pop formulas heard in doo-wop. The overall form—the beat, the harmony, and the signature instrumental riff—have clear pop links, but all have been "Motownized."

3. "My Guy" adheres to the general principles of the Motown sound while maintaining its own individuality. Both the form and the beat of the song are different from the earlier three songs. However, the time-keeping strategy remains: the airy two-beat/shuffle mix heard here is certainly the most distinctive Motown beat. And the idea of shaping forms so that the climax comes at the end of a section is still realized with the usual procedures—e.g., richer and faster moving harmonies—even though it is done differently in this song.

In words and music, Motown had found the center of popular music. It was slicker than doo-wop, earthier than pop, and more innovative than either. By 1964, it didn't matter to many whites that Motown artists were black; they simply enjoyed the music. But it did matter to blacks, who understood how significant Motown's breakthrough was.

From Romance to Reality

For all its appeal, however, Motown's 1964 hits lacked the emotional depth of soul—"My Girl" is a long way from Percy Sledge's "When a Man Loves a Woman"—or the social relevance that the times seemed to demand. Talented individual artists—such as the boy-wonder harmonica virtuoso, Stevie Wonder, and vocalist Marvin Gaye—felt restrained by the cookie-cutter production philosophy of Motown, and Gordy's unwillingness to branch into other subjects beyond teen love.

As the 1960s progressed, however, Motown matured: emotionally, socially, and musically. Some of Motown's best songs of the era shifted from romance to reality—the Supremes' "Love Child" and the Temptations' "Cloud Nine" are good examples. And, especially in the work of Gladys Knight and Marvin Gaye, Motown's music acquired the expressive power of soul. No song better illustrates this increased emotional content better than "I Heard It Through the Grapevine."

Two versions of "I Heard It Through the Grapevine," by Gladys Knight and Marvin Gaye, offer a classic illustration of Motown's increased range and emotional depth. Although Gaye was rumored to have recorded his version first, Gladys Knight's recording appeared first, in 1967; Gaye's version came out well over a year later. Both versions were major hits. The song was written by Norman Whitfield and Barrett Strong, another successful songwriting team at Motown. Whitfield, perhaps the most innovative producer on Motown's staff during the late sixties, also produced both recordings.

What's remarkable about the two recordings, apart from their inherent high quality, is the way Whitfield tailors the context to fit the personality of the singer. With its churchy piano part and spare accompaniment, Gladys Knight's version sounds like a hellfire and damnation sermon, a perfect fit for the gospel-rooted intensity of her singing. The setting for Gaye's version is richer, but darker and more atmospheric. Paired with Gaye's pain-drenched singing, the recording projects a completely different emotional response to the partner's infidelity: a cry of anguish instead of Gladys Knight's hands-on-the-hips indignation.

These two versions demonstrate, as well as any pair of recordings can, the inherent flexibility of what Gordy called the Motown "formula." Motown has been accused of being a musical assembly line, because of Gordy's rigid control over the final product. Yet his hit recordings make clear that the songs were not stamped out. Their differences are more than cosmetic. There was sufficient room to "customize" material so that artist, song, and arrangement blend together to produce a recording that followed the Motown template and, at the same time, had a well-defined identity.

If "I Heard It Through the Grapevine" describes the fury and pain of love gone wrong, then "Ain't Nothing Like the Real Thing" conveys the ecstasy of love in full flower. The song, written and produced by Nick Ashford and Valerie Simpson, was a top hit (No. 8 pop, No. 1 R & B) in 1968. The featured performers were Marvin Gaye and Tammi Terrell. During his career at Motown, Gaye recorded with several female partners, including Diana Ross. By most accounts, however, his most successful duet recordings were with Tammi Terrell, who died of a brain tumor in 1970. One reason for their success was their obvious onstage chemistry, which many presumed mirrored their off-stage relationship. (One problem for Gaye: he was married to Berry Gordy's sister Anna at the time!)

Personal complications aside, Gaye and Terrell had no trouble expressing their feelings in song. Their voices are expressive and well-matched, and the message of the song is clear in both lyric and delivery.

The musical backdrop provided by Ashford and Simpson shows the evolution of the Motown sound, principally in the expansion of form and the enrichment of the texture. The form of the song is an updated version of the venerable "refrain-frame" form heard earlier in "Maybellene" and "That'll Be the Day." In the refrain, the singers tell us what they feel, and in the story-telling interludes, they tell us why, with a characteristic Motown twist.

The first interlude is straight verse. However, in the second verse, a new section ("no other sound . . .") extends the second verse, building to the biggest climax in the song—it seems that no Motown song would be complete without a strong push like that. In any event, this extension makes the song seem much more expansive, because it breaks up the refrain/verse alternation.

"Ain't Nothing Like the Real Thing" has a wonderfully lush instrumental texture: cushiony violins, flutes, a rhythm section augmented with conga drums. The rhythmic texture offers an early, if transitional, example of what would become the new beat of the 1970s. Although the title phrase moves at eight-beat speed (as we noted in Chapter 1), the underlying rhythms move twice as fast. This faster layer is present from the very beginning, when the drummer plays a rhythm that moves four times as fast as the beat. This faster rhythm is picked up in the bass line, flute fills, and conga rhythm. Even many of the freer, more syncopated rhythms, such as the piano break after the refrain and the vocal lines in the verse, map onto this faster rhythm, rather than the eight-beat rhythm of the title phrase.

Sixteen-Beat Rhythms and Rhythmic Play

Here's an easy way to experience the difference between a rock beat and the quicker "sixteen- beat" rhythm heard on "Ain't Nothing Like the Real Thing." Begin by tapping the beat, clapping the backbeat, and saying the words, "Rock and roll and rock and roll and . . ." over and over. (Remember that the clap comes on "roll.") The words move at the same speed as the title phrase, so you should be able to shift back and forth between "rock and roll and . . ." and "Ain't Nothing Like the Real Thing."

Stop saying the words, but keep the beat and backbeat going. Then substitute the words, "Par-lia-ment and fun-ka-de-lic." The clap of your backbeat should come on "funk"—appropriately enough, since funk uses this more active rhythm more often than not. If you say the words in time with the song, you'll find that your "sixteen-beat" rhythm lines up with the drum part. (As before, the number "16" refers to the fastest equally emphasized layer. Here, that layer moves four times as fast as the beat, or 16 "beats" per measure—by analogy with "two-beat," "four-beat," and "eight-beat.")

Sixteen-beat rhythms (the term is used by keyboard manufacturers and others in the music industry) offer much greater opportunities for rhythmic play than the conventional eight-beat rhythms of rock. Here's why:

For each beat in an eight-beat rhythm, performers have four rhythmic options. They can play on the first half of the beat, on the second half of the beat, on both halves of the beat, or not at all. These are diagrammed below (X = sound; O = silence).

X O

O X

X X

O

In sixteen-beat rhythms, there are four times as many possibilities, as seen in the following diagram.

XXXX; OOOO

XXXO; XXOX; XOXX; OXXX

XXOO; XOXO; XOOX; OXXO; OXOX; OOXX

XOOO; OXOO; OOXO; OOOX

Here's an illustration, taken from the beginning of the verse of "Ain't Nothing Like the Real Thing," that shows the increased rhythmic possibilities of sixteen-beat based rhythms. If we were to set the lyric to an eight-beat rhythm, it would be absolutely undifferentiated and rather stiff, such as

(continued)

I've got your pic- ture han- gin' on my wall

0 X X X X X X X X X X

However, when set over a sixteen-beat rhythmic base, there is more differentiation at the end of the phrase and a nice syncopation on "wall." This gives us a much more speech-like rhythm such as

I've got your pic ture hang in' on my wall

O O X O X O X O X O X O X O O O X X X O X X

This geometric increase in rhythmic options led to much more complex rhythmic textures, not only in Motown songs, but also in some soul, late sixties rock, jazz fusion, Brazilian-influenced music, and the proto-funk of Sly and the Family Stone.

The subtle use of a sixteen-beat rhythm shows a transitional phase in the development of this new beat. By 1971, the transition is complete: Gaye's "What's Going On" is built only on a sixteen-beat rhythm.

MARVIN GAYE: WHAT'S GOING ON From the start, Marvin Gaye had chafed at the tight control Berry Gordy exercised over his career. Gaye, who had a deep interest in jazz, wanted to branch out in that direction. Gordy, who rightfully viewed Gaye as Motown's sexiest male act, wanted him to mine the same vein that had brought him success with songs like "How Sweet It Is (To Be Loved By You)" and the two hits we've just discussed. After extensive wrangling, Gaye got Gordy's approval to create his own album.

The result was *What's Going On*. Released in 1971, it was a commercial and artistic success. It took a hard look at life in Motown—the city—with songs like "Inner City Blues" and the title track. At the same time, the music behind the words and ideas developed in range and complexity, to support the deepened emotional weight of the songs. Both the album and three singles from it hit the top ten.

Marvin Gaye on stage, c. 1975. Photo courtesy Corbis/Neal Preston.

Gaye's lyric in the title track is part lament, part exhortation. It alludes to Vietnam, race relations, and the generation gap—burning issues throughout the country at the time. In the title phrase, "What's Going On," he simply shakes his head. At the same time, he urges us to find the answer to our problems in love, not hate. The music, with its lush texture, rich, jazz-inspired harmonies, and subtle and active rhythms, sends a similar message. (The same basic sound would be used in much of the black romantic music of the seventies and eighties—Roberta Flack, Bill Withers, Ashford and Simpson—in addition to Gaye himself.)

"What's Going On" enriches the Motown sound of the sixties. The rhythm, now based on a sixteen-beat pattern, is more active, and the conga drum gives it more presence than the hi-hat timekeeping heard on "My Girl" et al. Harmony and texture are also richer: the chord formed under the opening sax solo, or the choral sound under Gaye (instead of back-up singers) show this. The song unfolds more slowly, in long phrases. Everything is on a grander scale. Overall, the musical backdrop is more sophisticated. The best Motown songs have had dense, melodically rich textures, as we have seen, but this song goes a big step further in that direction.

"What's Going On" retains Motown's easy points of entry: the title riff, the straightforward lyrics, the groove. And it removes a veneer of sophistication by introducing the crowd noises and generally loosening up the texture. On the cover of the album, Gaye is wearing everyday clothes for a winter day, not the tuxedo which he and other male Motown singers typically wore in performance; the music sends a similar signal. In every respect, it is an enhanced version of the Motown sound, the product of its evolution throughout the sixties.

Gaye's album, and its success, was one sign of major changes at Motown. Stevie Wonder, a popular member of the Motown stable since his early teens, assumed artistic control of his music shortly after Gaye did. He would enjoy his greatest success in the 1970s. The Supremes split in 1970, and Diana Ross launched her career as a solo artist, with considerable help from Gordy and considerable resentment from the other Supremes. Motown's hottest new group was the child-novelty act, the Jackson 5, who had a string of No. 1 hits in the early seventies. Several of the nine Jackson children went on to major solo careers; Michael's was the most notable.

Despite its continued commercial success, Motown's moment had passed. It had ceded that special place it occupied in the sixties, when the songs of the Supremes, the Temptations, and the other great acts were among the freshest sounds in popular music, and one signal of a major musical revolution. By 1971, it had created the bulk of its legacy.

Soul

While Motown was turning out hit after hit, another new black music found its way onto the airwaves: soul. Like Motown, soul music was a synthesis, a new sound created from several sources. Unlike Motown, however, the sources were almost exclusively black. Soul combined the emotional depth and range of the blues, the fervor of gospel, and the energy of rhythm and blues and rock. The result was one of the most memorable and influential styles of the rock era.

The story of soul music in the sixties is mainly about two cities, Memphis, Tennessee, and Muscle Shoals, Alabama; and two transcendental stars, James Brown and Aretha Franklin.

Southern Soul Music

If Gordy's Motown operation was as sleek and well-oiled as a Cadillac, the southern soul scene was more like a souped-up, beat-up pickup truck that, despite appearances, ran exceedingly well. Owners and musicians learned the music business as they went, usually the hard way. A dispute between Stax and Atlantic, who distributed their records, over ownership of the rights to the songs left a bad taste in everyone's mouth. Rick Hall, convinced that he was the man responsible for the southern soul sound, went through five rhythm sections in as many years. Lawsuits, disagreements, bad blood, fights and other evidence of ill will, shady dealings, and hard feelings touched almost everyone. Yet, despite all the internal bickering, late night partying, session skipping, and other unprofessionalisms, some great music was made and recorded.

Southern soul generally came in two speeds, fast and slow. The uptempo songs build on the groove found in the rock-influenced rhythm and blues of the early sixties. Some are upbeat as well as uptempo, while others sermonize or upbraid. The slow songs, an intensification of rhythm and blues and rock and roll ballads, almost always dealt with the pain of love. We introduce soul with one example of each, Sam and Dave's "Soul Man," recorded for Stax records, and Percy Sledge's "When a Man Loves a Woman," recorded in Muscle Shoals at the Fame Recording Studio for Atlantic Records.

Stax Records

Memphis, Tennessee, rockabilly's home base in the fifties, became soul's spiritual center in the sixties, mainly through Jim Stewart and Estelle Axton's Stax Records (Stax is an acronym for Stewart and Axton). In many respects, Stax records was set up like Motown: it had owners, producers, staff songwriters, a house band, and interchangeable singers. (This organizational arrangement distinguished their operations from most of the rock produced by white bands, such as the Beatles and Rolling Stones. These groups wrote their own material; there was no such thing as a house sound for their record label.)

Nevertheless, there were key differences from Motown. The Stax sound seemed more a collective effort than a decision from above. Instead of playing from written arrangements, the Stax musicians would listen to a song a few times and construct what amounted to a "head" arrangement (i.e., created on the spot—off the top of their head[s]). They would play the song through and briefly discuss among themselves who should do what. Then they would be ready to record, often within minutes.

Moreover, the operation was thoroughly integrated. Stewart and Axton (who were brother and sister) were white. Producer Al Bell, songwriters Isaac Hayes and David Porter, who penned "Soul Man" and many other Stax hits, and the headliners—Otis Redding, Rufus and Carla Thomas, Sam and Dave, et al.—were black. The house rhythm section, which recorded under its own name as Booker T. and the M. G.s, included two blacks, keyboardist Booker T. Jones and drummer Al Jackson, and two whites, guitarist Steve Cropper and bassist Donald "Duck" Dunn. The horn players—who became famous on their own as the Memphis Horns—were all white. In the cocoon that was the Stax recording studio, race didn't seem to matter, even if it mattered a great deal as soon as they stepped out onto the street.

SAM AND DAVE: SOUL MAN   Sam and Dave (Sam Moore and Dave Prater) were the premier vocal duo of the Southern soul scene. Like so many of the other Southern soul singers, they sang with the raw intensity of impassioned black gospel, untouched by pop prettiness. The partnership, with its frequent exchanges and raw harmonies (compare the open intervals in the refrain of "Soul Man" to the sweeter-sounding harmonies of the Everly Brothers' "All I Have to Do Is Dream") underscored their gospel heritage—as if it weren't obvious enough from the first notes that they sang.

A superficial overview of Sam and Dave's "Soul Man," a huge hit for them in 1967, reveals its basic similarity to the Motown template, and—for that matter—to many rock songs of the sixties. It begins with an instrumental riff and continues with several vocal sections, each containing a verse and refrain. A reprise of the opening instrumental riff leads to a short instrumental interlude which shifts the song to a higher key for the last repetition of the vocal section.

However, there are differences that distinguish this as a Stax production. The raw power of "Soul Man" demands vocals and an accompaniment of comparable strength and directness—and that's what it gets. The song begins in an almost suspended state—a brief guitar riff, accompanied only by a backbeat, shifting through four chords. The band immediately finds its groove, however. The groove has four components, none of which is interesting enough to stand alone:

- A bass line moving at eight-beat speed (i.e., marking the rock rhythm)
- A drum part marking the backbeat and reinforcing the rock rhythm of the bass
- Sustained notes and riffs in the horns
- A double-time guitar riff

Sam and Dave, c. 1966. Photo courtesy Joyce Moore.

These rather simple parts interlock to set up an infectious groove, which they sustain all the way through the verse. There is no change of harmony, no change of role or melodic material, just the groove, pure and simple. Over this relentless rhythm, Sam Moore, the lead vocalist, struts his "Soul Man" stuff, timing it so that there is a constant call-and-response between his part and the guitar riff.

This accompaniment is placed front and center, much more so than in a Motown arrangement. The bass, the brass (playing a single note in each verse), and the guitar riff are all in the forefront, literally driving the song. The result is a sound with little nuance but lots of power: all primary colors.

The refrain is even simpler: just the vocal refrain, a fast horn riff in response, drums, bass playing a repeated note that shifts down and back again, and the sparest of guitar riffs. So, even though the basic form of the song recalls the Motown/rock era template, the balance of the elements is completely different. Rhythm and a raw aggressive sound are in the front. Subtleties of melody (the vocal line is as much spoken as sung) harmony, and orchestration are not in evidence.

PERCY SLEDGE: "WHEN A MAN LOVES A WOMAN" If "Soul Man" offers an extended advertisement for the ecstasy of love, then Percy Sledge's "When a Man Loves a Woman" is a lament of love gone wrong. It is as intense an expression of emotional pain as "Soul Man" is of pleasure.

Sledge was born in Leighton, Alabama, a small town not far from Muscle Shoals, where he recorded "When a Man Loves a Woman" in 1966. Quin Ivy, a local disc jockey and all-around entrepreneur, had discovered Sledge singing in a local group called the Esquires Combo. Ivy engineered a solo artist contract with Atlantic and arranged the recording date that produced Sledge's first and biggest hit.

Sledge's rapid ascension to stardom proved once again how the black church was such a fertile training ground for soul. It seemed that many blacks (and not a few whites) sang gospel—not just the suave stylings of the Soul Stirrers but the raw, impassioned singing first secularized by Ray Charles. There were enough good singers to provide a seemingly endless stream of talent.

Like the Motown acts who were lucky enough to live in Detroit, stardom for a soul singer seemed to be as much a matter of being born in the right place at the right time as talent. While there was no question that Otis Redding, Percy Sledge, and Wilson Pickett deserved their fame, there were certainly other talented southern blacks who could have achieved stardom if they had found themselves around music business people who could nurture their talent.

Soul ballads, of which "When a Man Loves a Woman" is perhaps *the* classic example, have an entirely different dynamic from uptempo songs. Here the band is accompanist rather than partner, more like a frame to a painting than an indivisible part of the mix. The opening is about as unobtrusive as it can be in the rock era: walking bass, slow triplets and backbeat on the drums, sustained chords on a Farfisa organ (one of the wave of electronic keyboards that came on the market during the sixties). Other layers accumulate during the course of the song: guitar noodles, backup vocals, then horns on the final chorus. Their accompanying role is defined not so much by their volume—eventually the band all but overpowers Sledge—as by the complete lack of rhythmic or melodic interest in their parts. Only the guitarist is doing anything other

Atlantic Records, Stax, and Fame Recording Studio

Atlantic Records' arrangement with Stax and Rick Hall's Fame Recording Studio showed how much the music business had changed in less than a decade. Recall that after RCA bought Elvis's contract from Sam Phillips, the men in charge turned Elvis over to their house producers in Nashville. They had little understanding of, and even less interest in, the unique chemistry between Elvis and Phillips.

Jerry Wexler, who joined Atlantic in 1953 as a producer and talent scout, had helped Atlantic grow from a small independent label into one of the major players in the record industry by signing and/or producing a string of successful R&B acts: Ray Charles, the Coasters, the Drifters, and others. Wexler was in tune with R&B; his keen ear and love for the music, were a big factor in Atlantic's success.

In 1960, he reached an agreement to distribute Stax Records, thus giving this small regional label access to markets in the U.S. and abroad. Later in the decade, he began to record acts that he had signed to Atlantic (and its subsidiary Atco) at Stax's studios in Memphis and at Fame Recording Studio in Muscle Shoals, a small town in northwestern Alabama.

The idea of farming out production responsibilities was nothing new for Wexler and Atlantic. In the mid-fifties, Atlantic had signed Leiber and Stoller to a contract to produce the Coasters' records and worked a similar deal with them for the Drifters' early sixties hits. With Stax, and with Rick Hall at Fame, he went a step further. In effect, he hired the southern soul sound—not just the producer, but the band and all the other components—and gave them pretty much free rein. The legacy is music of power and passion, undiluted by pop pretensions.

In the eighties and nineties, this practice has become business as usual: the major labels are umbrella organizations that incorporate a large number of small, specialized labels. These labels are run by people close to the music scene that they record: the rap label Def Jam has had such an arrangement with Columbia/Sony. Wexler's arrangement with Stax and Fame was the first important example of a record company going to the source to capture a sound.

than sustaining a chord or marking time, and his part remains pretty much in the background. As a result, the sound spotlight shines straight on Sledge.

Although this was Sledge's first recording, he "let it all hang out," as the catch phrase of the day put it. There is no emotional reserve in his singing. What you hear is what he feels, with no buffer in between. Such naked emotion had only been heard previously in the blues—and Ray Charles's blues/gospel synthesis—but, as in Charles's best work, it is amplified through gospel style. Like the blues, the phrases start high and finish low, but the strain from singing so high in his range projects the pain that is inherent in the song.

The powerful emotion captured in this song touched a lot of nerves, black and white, here and abroad. The song was No. 1 on both the R&B and pop charts in 1966, and remains one of the great soul anthems.

OTIS REDDING The king of southern soul singers was Otis Redding. Redding, who grew up in Georgia, first tried to break into the music business in Macon; he eventually ended up singing behind Little Richard. After he secured an Atlantic recording contract, he turned out a string of R&B hits at Stax. He broke through to the pop market with a scintillating performance at the 1967 Monterey Pop festival, where he won over a new, largely white audience for his music. Tragedy struck soon after: he died in a plane crash later that year. The posthumously released "(Sittin' on the) Dock of the Bay," written with Steve Cropper in Monterey, was his biggest hit. (Ironically, it was one of his least soulful recordings.)

Redding took the blues/gospel fusion a step further than either Charles or Sledge did: if they were lead singers in the choir, then Redding was the preacher. Especially in uptempo numbers, his singing is more than impassioned speech, but less than singing with precise pitch. It is as if the emotion of the moment is too strong to be constrained by "correct" notes. "I Can't Turn You Loose," one of his classic soul recordings, showcases his unique delivery, sandwiched between the Memphis horns and the M.G.s.

The song also gives us another, harder-edged version of the southern soul sound. The song begins with not one, but two, memorable melodic hooks, both of them instrumental. There is a wide-open space between the low range guitar/bass riff and the horn riff: that's where Redding sings. This is an extreme example of the soul sound: heavy on the bottom and top, and basically empty in the middle (except, of course, for Redding's singing). The only chord sounds come from the piano, heard faintly in a high register.

The rhythm is also typical of soul style: strong beatkeeping from the drums, frequent syncopations in both riffs that fight against the beat (the famous offbeat horn riff at the end of each big section is the quintessential example of this), and Redding darting in and out of a steady rhythm with the kind of rhythmic freedom that all the great soul singers had.

This performance has a harder edge than most soul recordings, because of Redding's gritty singing, and because the guitar is so prominent and has a little distortion. Perhaps the edge comes from rock: one of Redding's big hits was a cover of the Rolling Stones' "Satisfaction."

The heyday of southern soul was brief—about four years, from 1965 to 1968. The bullet that killed Dr. Martin Luther King, Jr.—ironically in Memphis—also seemed to pass through the heart of soul. The major southern soul studios were integrated operations: The Stax rhythm section was half black/half white, and the house musicians at Rick Hall's Fame studio were almost all white. In the wake of the racial tensions triggered by Dr. King's assassination, business ground to a halt at Fame and slowed down at Stax.

Audience attitudes seemed to change as well. Most of the soul stars saw their careers nosedive. Only vocalist Al Green had a major career after the glory years, although Isaac Hayes had a brief moment in the sun when he began to perform the instrumental music he created. Nevertheless, soul left an indelible imprint on the music of the rock era.

Aretha Franklin

Sam and Dave, Percy Sledge, Otis Redding, and almost all the other soul acts were southern men. The greatest of the soul singers, however, was Aretha Franklin, neither a man nor a Southerner. She was—and *is*—the queen of soul and one of the great artists in the history of popular music.

If any performer grew up with a destiny to fulfill, it was Aretha. Her father, C. L. Franklin, was one of the most charismatic preachers in the country. Although his home base was in Detroit (interestingly, Berry Gordy recorded his sermons on a Motown subsidiary), he toured the nation, attracting throngs to the black churches where he preached. Franklin was also a lavish and gracious host. The cream of the black entertainment world, both sacred and secular, passed through his house. Growing up, Aretha heard everyone from gospel star Mahalia Jackson to the virtuosic and elegant jazz pianist Art Tatum.

Although shy as a child (throughout her career, only her singing has been extroverted) and the daughter of a wealthy man, Aretha was anything but sheltered. As a teenager, she went on the road with her father, but not her mother, who had left when she was six. In those few years, she crammed a lifetime of experience. Before she set off for New York at eighteen to begin her secular career, she had repeatedly experienced the discrimination that went with being black in the 1950s, endured endless bus rides from town to town, and given birth to two children. So when she sang about love and respect, her feelings came directly from her own experience.

Aretha Franklin's secular career began in 1960, when she signed a contract with Columbia Records. Her producer was John Hammond, perhaps the most knowledgeable and sensitive advocate of black music in the music business (a pioneering jazz critic, he had signed many top acts for Columbia). Although he recruited her for the label, the company didn't know how to tap her talent. Some of her recordings show her as a bluesy pop singer, a la Dinah Washington, who was very hot around 1960; others capture her singing pop treacle accompanied by syrupy strings. Jerry Leiber suggested that Aretha was "suffering from upward mobility." Although she produced some good work, her career went nowhere.

In 1966, Atlantic Records' producer Jerry Wexler bought her contract. He took her to Muscle Shoals in January of 1967 for what in retrospect proved to be one of the most famous recording sessions of all time. Within seconds after she sat down at the piano to play through "I Never Loved a Man (The Way I Love You)," everyone in the studio knew they were in the presence of someone special. Although put together on the fly (the horns were in the studio's office working out the riffs while Aretha was rehearsing with the rhythm section), the song was recorded in only a couple of takes. Its obvious success sparked a camaraderie among those present at the session—which was fueled by liberal amounts of alcohol. Unfortunately, that proved too rich a mixture: A fight between studio owner Rich Hall and Ted White, Aretha's husband and manager at the time, broke out sometime in the wee hours. With that, the session was called off, Aretha headed back to Detroit, where she all but disappeared for weeks, and Wexler went back to New York with one-and-a-half songs. He finally got Aretha to return to finish the second song, and the rest is history.

In "I Never Loved a Man," Aretha took soul to a new level by opening her soul. She sings with directness and immediacy, with a power and personal involvement that had never before been heard in popular music. Nothing stands between her and her audience.

Her vocal virtuosity makes this possible. Its components—the subtle nuances, the effortlessly soaring leaps, the sharp edge to her basic vocal timbre, the speech-like timing of her delivery—are expressive tools, not ends in themselves. As with all great virtuosos—in any kind of music—her extraordinary skill is organic. Emotion spills out in her singing, unimpeded by technical limitations. The sound caught the ear of the world. The song rocketed to the top of the rhythm and blues charts and crossed over to pop as well, making her an overnight sensation.

Many of Aretha's first hits explored the heartbreak of love, like most soul ballads of the time. However, her first uptempo hits, most notably Otis Redding's "Respect" and her own "Think," emotionally redefined fast soul. What had frequently been a forum for sexual braggadocio became the backdrop to a demand for dignity in "Respect" and a tongue-lashing in "Think." In both songs, the groove is as good as it gets, but it assists a call to arms rather than an invitation to sensual pleasure. "Respect," in fact, took on a meaning beyond the intent of its lyric: it became an anthem for the women's movement, which was just gathering momentum.

The musical formula for "Respect" is much the same as for "Soul Man" and "I Can't Turn You Loose": interlocked rhythm section, with horns playing riffs or sustained chords. The two major differences are Aretha's singing and the backup vocals, which give the song a churchier sound. The most memorable and individual section of the song is the stop-time passage when Aretha spells out what she wants—"R-E-S-P-E-C-T . . . "—so that there's absolutely no misunderstanding. What had been a straightforward verse/refrain song suddenly shifts up a gear. The remainder of the song features dense texture previously heard in the refrain: a series of riffs from the backup vocalists—"sock it to me," "just a little bit," and finally the repeated "re-re-re-re" (not only the first syllable of "respect" but also Aretha's nickname)— piled on top of the beat and horn riffs, with Aretha commenting on it all from above.

Having quickly established her credentials as the "queen of soul," Aretha began to explore other musical territory. She has been one of the artists of the rock era who can convincingly cover songs by other artists. Her versions of Burt Bacharach's "I Say a Little Prayer," Sam Cooke's "You Send Me," Nina Simone's "Young, Gifted, and Black," and Paul Simon's gospel-influenced "Bridge Over Troubled Water" are all standouts. Several of her own songs gave further evidence of her expressive range: in "Rock Steady," she tips her hat to James Brown, while "Daydreaming" is as tender and romantic a song as any of the early seventies.

Aretha's music is deeply personal and, at the same time, universal. The responsive listener feels her communicate one-on-one, yet her message transcends such a relationship. The best of Aretha's music seems to demand both empathy and ecstasy. We can give ourselves up to the groove even as we listen to her tough time tales. No one in the rock era has fused both qualities more powerfully and seamlessly than she did.

James Brown

James Brown was the godfather of soul, the man who nurtured it longer than anyone else and whose music has had more influence than any other soul artist. Brown's career has spanned almost the entire history of the rock era. His first hit recording, "Please Please Please," appeared on the R&B charts in 1956. We continue to hear his music today in multiple forms: more rappers have "sampled" his music than any other artist's.

It took Brown almost a decade to arrive at the original sound of "Papa's Got a Brand New Bag," his 1965 hit that was his most significant musical

James Brown, c. early 1960s. Photo courtesy CORBIS/BETTMANN.

breakthrough. The majority of his hits in the fifties were typical slow rhythm and blues ballads. Other than James's singing, there is little in these recordings that suggests the originality of his work in the sixties.

Brown came to his new sound by subtraction. He gradually eliminated anything not essential to maintaining the rhythmic flow of a song: repeated guitar riffs, repetitive bass lines, keyboard chords, busy drum parts, and the like. With "Papa's Got a Brand New Bag," the process is complete. Underneath Brown's short vocal riffs, the horns play short riffs, the baritone sax a single note, the guitar a chord on the backbeat (except for the double-time repeated chord at the end of each statement of the refrain—a brief moment in the spotlight), the bass short groups of notes separated by silence, while the drummer plays a rock rhythm on the hi-hat and bass drum kicks on the offbeat. The little timekeeping that's audible comes from the drummer.

In both cases, the drummer's light timekeeping is like aural graph paper, onto which Brown and his band draw their rhythmic design. The open sound that results from this bare minimum texture was not Brown's new "bag" (i.e., style or sound), but one of the most original conceptions of the rock era.

In his other breakthrough hit, "I Got You (I Feel Good)" (1965), the regular rhythm is just as spare: the drummer marks the rock beat layer on a closed hi-hat. The instrumental texture that surrounds it (the horn riffs, the bass line, drum fills) alternates between simple reinforcement of the eight-beat rhythm (e.g., the riff in response to "I feel good") and total conflict with the beat (the completely syncopated riff that ends the opening section). Brown's vocal line is freer: sometimes he's right with the beat, and other times he simply soars over it.

Both "Papa's Got a Brand New Bag" and "I Got You (I Feel Good)" alternate blues-form refrains with sections that don't use blues form. The transitions between sections are sharply drawn; so are the shifts within sections.

Compare, for example, the opening of "I Feel Good" with the stop-time passage at the end of the first section, or the change in rhythmic texture underneath the sax solo. Further, each section has its own well-defined character, which usually remains the same throughout. By sharply defining the character of each section and the boundaries between sections, Brown creates forms that seem assembled from blocks. This differentiates them from the Motown songs, which proceed in waves of sound.

In "Papa's Got a Brand New Bag" and "I Got You (I Feel Good)," Brown emphasized rhythm, texture, and the soul of his singing over melody and harmony. In "Cold Sweat" (1967), he goes a step further. The basic approach is the same: riffs layered over light timekeeping. However, there is virtually no harmonic movement: one chord lasts the entire opening section, and the bridge alternates between two chords. At the same time, the texture is more active. The guitar part adds fast-moving rhythmic counterpoint. Of special interest is the new "choked" guitar sound: the guitarist strums across the strings while holding his hand across the neck, "choking" out the sound to create a percussive scraping sound. The guitar becomes, in effect, a percussion instrument, with more rhythm than pitch. Moreover, its pattern is active and highly syncopated, enriching the rhythmic texture more than any other line. Other strands—drums, bass, baritone sax, other horns—are also more consistently syncopated than in the previous songs. Because the texture is more active, Brown sings less, especially in the contrasting section. Here Brown seems to sing only when he feels like it. He is content to ride the band's rhythmic wave.

The combination of an active, syncopated rhythm texture and harmonic stasis creates a sense of open-ended time. Much more than in "I Like It Like That," we are immersed in an "eternal present." Because they create and maintain a groove, sections are infinitely extensible: they don't go anywhere, they just are.

Brown's minimalist approach to rock rhythm and static harmony create a strong sense of open-ended time. There is no shuffle rhythm to mark the beat and no harmonic movement to mark the measure. Because the rock-layer timekeeping is light, we are barely aware of it. As a result, we are not as aware of the regular passage of time as we are of the groove. This was a huge conceptual breakthrough, anticipated only infrequently by such songs as John Lee Hooker's "Boogie Chillen'" and Bo Diddley's "Bo Diddley." Brown goes further than either of them.

Brown's music, especially "Cold Sweat" and much of the work that followed it, bring us closer to its African roots than it had ever been before. Indeed, John Chernoff reported in his 1971 book, *African Rhythm and African Sensibility*, that African musicians felt more at home with James Brown's music than with any other popular musician of the time. His music was profoundly influential. With its emphasis on intricate rhythms and de-emphasis of melody and harmony, it would create the blueprint for funk, jazz fusion, and—later—rap.

With its deep roots in gospel, blues, rhythm and blues, and jazz, and its blending and modernizing of these styles, the music of James Brown epitomizes soul. In its originality and individuality, it stands apart from all the other music of the 1960s. No one had a more distinctive sound, and few have had a more lasting influence.

Summary

In the film *Good Morning, Vietnam*, Robin Williams portrays Adrian Cronauer, an Air Force disk jockey brought in to improve morale among the troops. Cronauer junks the staff-approved tame white pre-rock pop, replacing it with an integrated playlist that includes James Brown, Motown, and the Beach Boys. While he's on the air, the film cuts away to scenes of the soldiers on and off duty listening to the music that he's playing. They are smiling, dancing, moving to the groove. Music is the film's most powerful symbol of the huge generation gap between the old guard and the young troops.

Berry Gordy's "Sound of Young America" was also a *symbol* of young America. More than any other aspect of American culture, music, and especially Motown and soul, brought home the arrival of a new generation and the profound changes taking place in American society. The new black music was fresh and it was good. And it was popular, among young people of all races. At least while they listened to it, race no longer mattered, except in a good way. This was no longer "wrong side of the tracks" music. Its broad acceptance was one important sign of the wholesale shift in attitude that would characterize the sixties.

For a brief time in the mid-1960s, it seemed that divisions of race, class, and culture were about to be eliminated. That didn't happen, but the changes that took place during that time were irreversible. The one-color world of mid-century film and television was gone forever; the music that was its soundtrack is largely forgotten. The black music of the 1960s helped bridge the gap between that world and the multicultural society we now see in both the media and real life. It lives on: the best of it sounds as good today as when it was released.

K E Y   T E R M S

Motown	**Groove**	**Soul ballad**
Tagline	**Soul**	**Choked-guitar sound**
Two-beat/shuffle mix	**Instrumental riff**	**Open-ended time**
Sixteen-beat rhythm	**Double-time guitar riff**	

C H A P T E R   Q U E S T I O N S

1. Update the profile of the Motown sound from Chapter 1 by observing its elements in the two versions of "I Heard It Through the Grapevine," "Ain't Nothing Like the Real Thing," and "What's Going On." Find changes in at least three elements.

2. Review the insert on sixteen-beat rhythms. Map out ten beats of sixteen-beat-based lyrics. A couple should come from songs discussed in this chapter. The remainder can come from music discussed in subsequent chapters or your listening outside of class.

3. During the sixties, all black music was referred to as "soul music." We have suggested a more limited definition. To test this, compare "Soul Man" to any of the Motown songs. Using the list of the elements as a checklist, discover five differences between the two.

4. Compare Aretha's singing to the other singers discussed in this chapter—male as well as female. Try to put into words the differences in sound, inflection, and melodic elaboration.

5. James Brown has been called (by himself and others) the "Godfather of Soul." Yet his music, as evidenced in the three songs discussed here, sounds different from the up-tempo soul songs. Identify three common features between Brown's music and that of the soul singers, and three differences.

c h a p t e r   7

Rock Grows Up

Bob Dylan and the Beatles

Rock grew up almost overnight. It came to maturity in a two-year span, from the beginning of 1964 to the end of 1965. Appropriately enough, the U.S. release of two Beatles' albums: *Meet the Beatles* (January 1964) and *Rubber Soul* (December 1965) frame this time span. *Meet the Beatles* was the group's first U.S. album to chart; *Rubber Soul* was the first to plot the significant new direction that would lead to their creative peak. Among other important developments during this period were Dylan's reconversion to electric music, the breakthrough of the Rolling Stones, a series of proto-metal hits by the Kinks, and the Beach Boys and Roy Orbison hits discussed in the previous chapter.

The two albums also tell us about two crucial changes during this rapid maturation. The runaway success of *Meet the Beatles* signaled the start of the British invasion and rock's takeover of the pop market. *Rubber Soul*, inspired in large part by Dylan, made clear in both words and music that rock had progressed far beyond teen dance music. This was now a music with something important to say, and it had a new way of saying it.

Two observations about geography and popular music.

1. Rock started in the heart of America, from New Orleans, Memphis, and Chicago. There is a rock-like irony that the four most influential acts of sixties rock would come from along the English-speaking periphery: England (Beatles and Rolling Stones), the northernmost part of the Midwest (Dylan), and Pacific Northwest (Hendrix). It was also an early sign that rock would become the closest thing we have to a universal musical language.

2. The last time British music had significantly touched American popular music was almost a century earlier, with the Gilbert and Sullivan operettas. However, these were strictly imports. Unlike the British bands in the 1960s, Gilbert and Sullivan had not assimilated any American popular music.

There are obvious differences between Dylan and the Beatles: solo performer vs. group; private vs. public persona; seat-of-the-pants vs. state-of-the art record production; talking, barely melodic songs vs. tuneful melodies.

However, they were alike in at least two crucial ways: they came to rock from the outside, and they stretched rock to its outer limits. Outside for Dylan meant starting his professional career as a folksinger. Outside for the Beatles meant, more than anything else, Liverpool, England. The idea of foreigners redefining American popular music—and thereby internationalizing it—was without significant precedent.

Both Dylan and the Beatles stretched the stylistic boundaries of rock even as the Rolling Stones and other groups were defining its essence. Songs such as Dylan's "I Want You" and the Beatles' "Norwegian Wood" are part of the world of rock simply because they are by these artists and they express a rock-era sensibility. Neither song creates the sound world of classic rock: a rock beat, loud guitars, heavy riffs, and so on.

In this chapter, we will explore these boundaries, mainly in the work of Dylan and the Beatles. Chapter 8 will be its complement: a look at the core of rock style. We begin with Dylan and the folk revival.

Bob Dylan

Bringing It All Back Home was the first of Dylan's albums to include electric music. One side of the LP was acoustic; the other electric. As Bob Spitz points out, the title signals Dylan's return to rock and roll. To Alan Lomax, Pete Seeger, and the folkies who thought he'd committed musical blasphemy, this was the beginning of the end. But looked at in relation to the rest of his career, it was the end of the beginning. It was the next-to-last act in the first public phase of a career that would go through several twists and turns.

To understand Dylan strictly as a product of the folk revival is like starting to watch a film in the second reel. You might be able to piece together the beginning of the story from the rest of the film, but there's a good chance that you wouldn't completely understand the plot. In Dylan's case, you would have missed two crucial influences: rock and roll and the Beats. For Dylan, born Robert Zimmerman in Hibbing, Minnesota, rock and roll was his first love. He had played in rock and roll bands while in high school and when he first arrived at the University of Minnesota. Soon, however, he was spending less time in class than in coffee houses. There, he discovered the Beat poets and folk music. It's impossible to understand his music in the mid-sixties without taking all of these influences into account. Nevertheless, Dylan started his professional career as a folksinger. By late 1960, when he moved to New York, the folk revival was well underway.

The Folk Revival

The folk revival had a short lifespan, even by pop standards. For all intents and purposes, it began in 1958, when the Kingston Trio's recording of "Tom Dooley" topped the pop charts. It ended seven years later, when Dylan went electric at the Newport Folk Festival, and Lomax and Seeger went ballistic.

The folk revival was apolitical at first. Its audience liked the tuneful melodies, pleasantly sung. That soon changed, as this new folk revival quickly rediscovered its past. Historic preservation and social commentary, the two main directions of the folk movement of the thirties and forties, resurfaced within a year.

The restoration of traditional music had two branches. One was the rediscovery of folk musicians, white and black. The other was the re-creation of folk music by contemporary performers. The blues revival of the early sixties was one dimension of the folk revival. Delta bluesmen who hadn't sung professionally in 25 years were suddenly touring college campuses and appearing at folk festivals.

Equally important was the reissue of early recordings. This helped folk traditionalists try to replicate the country and blues styles that they heard on folk recordings. Their search for authenticity went far beyond learning a song out of a songbook. The most notable and popular of these traditionalists was Joan Baez.

We can hear a typical result of this effort in her cover of the Carter family's "Wildwood Flower." Baez's guitar playing closely resembles that of Maybelle Carter. However, her pure-toned singing has none of the Carters' nasal quality or country twang. It is as far from their style as New York is from the southern Appalachians.

The folk revival also gave voice to the protest movement. The drive for racial equality had been gathering momentum since the end of World War II. The gradual dismantling of the "separate but equal" policy and the confrontations that ensued brought the issue into the national spotlight.

In the process, it revived the activist side of the folk movement. Ex-Weaver Pete Seeger joined the fray and gave the civil rights movement its anthem, "We Shall Overcome." He became godfather to a new generation of activists. Like Dylan, they were mainly college students and dropouts who were looking for a cause.

Social commentary presented in folk-style songs gushed forth from the coffee houses of New York's Greenwich Village and college towns around the United States. The audience was young and idealistic. They turned to this music, despite its simplicity, because many of the alternatives were so unappealing and none had the relevance of this music.

A recording of Bob Dylan's "Blowin' in the Wind" by Peter, Paul, and Mary shows the appeal and the musical limitations of these newly composed folk songs. Peter, Paul, and Mary (Peter Yarrow, Noel Paul Stookey, and Mary Travers) were the Kingston Trio of the early sixties: commercial, but with a conscience. They rode the crest of the protest movement: "Blowin' in the Wind" was a No. 2 hit in 1963. Their straightforward presentation of the melody made the words easily comprehensible; their pleasant voices and subdued guitar accompaniment made it palatable to a broad audience.

However, their sound related to the message of the song in only the most generic way. Their other No. 2 hit, "Puff (the Magic Dragon)," sounds virtually identical, although the lyric is a children's story rather than a call to action. It is precisely this situation—folk music's tenuous connection between verbal meaning and musical expression—that Dylan would address by going electric.

Beyond Social Protest

By 1965, Dylan had been sharpening his tongue for several years. The main focus of the protest movement, for Dylan and others, was civil rights: "The Lonesome Death of Hattie Carroll" was one of several songs about the mistreatment of African Americans.

However, Dylan shot verbal darts at a wide range of targets. To cite just one example: in "Talking John Birch Paranoid Blues," Dylan assumes the identity of a superpatriot who finds the "red menace" everywhere, even in the red stripes of the American flag. It is a scathing indictment of the far-right mentality: the caustic talking blues of his idol Woody Guthrie brought up-to-date in subject and image. "Blowin' in the Wind" seems tame by comparison, which may help account for its popularity—and for the negative reaction it received from several of Dylan's fellow folkies.

However, on the album *Bringing It All Back Home*, Dylan's verbal virtuosity served different ends. The biting satire of his essentially impersonal social commentary was gone. In its place came more personal, obscure, and allusive lyrics. We hear this change in two songs from the album, "Mr. Tambourine Man" and "Subterranean Homesick Blues."

"Mr. Tambourine Man" comes from the acoustic side of the album. It features just Dylan's singing and harmonica and guitar accompaniment, plus another guitar playing an obbligato line. The song combines a catchy melody and memorable refrain ("hey Mr. Tambourine Man, play a song for me . . .") with impressionistic lyrics ("evening's empire," "magic swirlin' ship," "skippin' reels of rhyme," "twisted reach of crazy sorrow," "circled by the circus sands") and the perfect sixties symbol: a pied piper leading a group of hip individuals to a new level of consciousness.

The oft-repeated refrain and its "jingly-jangly" accompaniment make "Mr. Tambourine Man" immediately accessible. The opening phrase lodges in our ear and stays there, in part because it's used for both refrain and verse. The hook provided by the melody and repeated refrain keep us anchored as Dylan parades a stream-of-consciousness series of vivid, but elusive, images before us. Individually, they are easy to grasp, but they don't seem to refer to any central storyline. They come so fast that the next one arrives almost before we can ask, "What did he mean by that?" This elusiveness even applies to the refrain: who *is* Mr. Tambourine Man? And what does he have to do with life in the sixties?

The melody reinforces the rambling, dream-like free association of the lyric. The refrain consists of two eight-measure phrases: the most common phrase length in popular music. But in the verse versions of the melody, Dylan expands the phrase in a completely arbitrary way. There is no set pattern for the expansion; phrase length responds directly to the lyric.

"Mr. Tambourine Man" opened popular music up to a radically new kind of lyric. Country, folk, and blues lyrics were direct, as we have seen. Pop song lyrics could be sophisticated, rock and roll lyrics could talk nonsense ("Tutti Frutti") or capture the essence of teenage angst ("That'll Be the Day"). But none had been surreal.

The most direct precedent was the writings of the Beat poets. After hearing Dylan, Beat poet Allen Ginsberg said, "The world is in good hands."

It's fairly safe to assume that the surreal world portrayed in "Mr. Tambourine Man" was shaped by Dylan's experience with LSD. Dylan first dropped acid in the spring of 1964; Dylan recorded *Bringing It All Back Home* in January, 1965. We can certainly infer from the opening lines of "Subterranean Homesick Blues"—"Johnny's in the basement/mixin' up the medicine"—that Dylan was tripping while preparing this album.

"Subterranean Homesick Blues" creates a world of hyperreality: street life seen through a distorted lens. Dylan unleashes a flood of images. They are

The Byrds

The Byrds came together in the summer of 1964 to form what would become the first folk- rock band. The original lineup included guitarists Jim (later Roger) McGuinn, Gene Clark, and David Crosby, bassist Chris Hillman, and drummer Mike Clarke. McGuinn, Clark, and Crosby had formed a folk trio in Los Angeles in late 1963, which went nowhere. Adding Hillman and Clarke changed their sound and put them on the cutting edge of the mix between folk and rock.

A comparison of the two versions of "Mr. Tambourine Man" is instructive. Dylan's version is acoustic. The Byrds' cover uses a full band, including Jim (later Roger) McGuinn's electric 12- string guitar. Dylan's version lasts five-and-a-half minutes; The Byrds' version lasts only two-and-a-half minutes. And even that difference is deceptive, because the Byrds' recording has a slower tempo and includes McGuinn's famous opening riff.

The Byrds' version is also much more like a rock song in form. Two statements of the refrain frame just one of the four verses. This truncated version cut out over half of the lyric—precisely the element that had made the song so special for Dylan fans. But the expanded instrumentation, simpler form, and slower tempo made the song much more accessible. Judging by his next record, the connection between accessibility and commercial success was not lost on Dylan. In fact, it has been reported that the Byrds' success with his song inspired Dylan to switch back to electric guitar.

vivid, but often complex in their meaning. Even when they're obvious, they come so rapidly, and in such jarring juxtaposition, that it's virtually impossible to absorb them in a single pass. The song invades our space, demanding that we get its message even as it goes by too fast. It is as confrontational as "Mr. Tambourine Man" is ethereal.

"Subterranean Homesick Blues" implies a musical basis for Dylan's decision to go electric. Unlike "Mr. Tambourine Man," which is tuneful and has a frequently repeated refrain, in this song neither the lyric nor Dylan's vocal line have an easy point of entry. The melody, such as it is, seems more like rap— or operatic recitative—than any pop style of the sixties. Its antecedents are Guthrie's talking blues and the beat poets. So it's left to the accompaniment, a raunchy honky-tonk beat by way of Chuck Berry's "Maybellene," to set the overall mood of the song and bring the listener in.

For all its easy appeal, however, "Mr. Tambourine Man" did not chart—in Dylan's version. As with "Blowin' in the Wind," it was another group that brought his song to the top of the charts. This time it was the Byrds, whose version hit No. 1 in June, 1965.

Dylan Goes Electric

Dylan officially entered the rock era with his next album, *Highway 61 Revisited*. Recorded in the summer of 1965, the album brought into full flower the power latent in the electric side of *Bringing It All Back Home*. The songs mix blues, country, rock—and even pop, in "Ballad of a Thin Man"—into a new Dylan sound. The title of the album suggests this roots remix. Highway 61 runs through the heart of the Mississippi delta, and the title track is a hard shuffle with strong echoes of "deep blues."

"Like a Rolling Stone," the first track to be recorded, shows how he harnessed his verbal virtuosity to write an accessible rock song. The words still have sting: the song paints an "I-told-you-so" portrait of a young girl who's gone from top to bottom. But they tell a story that we can follow, even on the first hearing.

The song sounds like a rock song from the start: a free-for-all of riffs overlays Dylan's vigorous electrified strumming and a straightforward rock beat on the drums. This sound is maintained throughout the song, with Dylan's harmonica competing with Mike Bloomfield's guitar in the instrumental interludes.

The body of the song consists of four long sections. With each section, verse and refrain alternate, as they do in many rock songs. Dylan immediately puts his own spin on this rock convention: each section has, in effect, two verses and two hooks. The first verse of each section consists of two rapid-fire word streams, saturated with internal rhymes—typical Dylan. But each word stream paints only one picture, and each phrase ends with a short, riff-like idea (e.g., "didn't you, babe?"), followed by a long pause. The slower pacing of the images and the break between phrases allows the listener to stay abreast of Dylan's lyric.

The second verse serves as a long introduction for the first of two melodic hooks: Dylan's voice drips scorn as he sings "how does it feel?" followed by a memorable organ riff; this is repeated, the question left hanging in the air. Dylan then gives a series of equally scornful responses that fill out our picture of the girl's plight. These culminate in the title phrase. By expanding each section internally, Dylan also expands the dimensions of the song: it lasts over six minutes, twice the length of a typical song.

"Like a Rolling Stone" established Dylan's rock credentials and his originality as well as any one song could. No one else could have written a song like this: a cinematic portrayal of a privileged princess who's strung out and trying to survive on the streets. Despite its length, the song would become one of Dylan's most successful singles, briefly reaching No. 2 in the summer of 1965.

However, it was the album, taken as a whole, that would reveal what Dylan would bring to rock. At first hearing, it seems like an unlikely candidate for one of the most influential rock albums of all time. The next five songs on the album are extraordinarily diverse:

- "Tombstone Blues," an uptempo song with a hard honky-tonk beat
- "It Takes a Lot to Laugh, It Takes a Train to Cry," a Dylanesque transformation of the blues, set to a medium groove shuffle rhythm
- "From a Buick 6," a blues-form song with piles of riffs and a honky-tonk beat
- "Ballad of a Thin Man," a ballad with slithery pop-ish harmony and a light shuffle beat
- "Queen Jane Approximately," an early sixties-style rock ballad

There are no recurrent stylistic conventions, such as a basic beat, harmonic approach, or formal plan.

Instead, Dylan used these and the other songs on the album to give rock a freewheelin', anything-goes attitude. In the album, Dylan thumbed his nose at the conventions of pop music and the pop-music business. Songs ranged in length from just over three minutes to well over eleven minutes; most were five minutes or more. The song titles could be descriptive and evocative—or not: "From a Buick 6," for example, has no apparent connection to the song. These are simple outward signs that the songs themselves are unconventional: shockingly original, despite their deep roots in rock and roll, blues, folk, country, and Beat poetry.

The songs seem to have come about almost by spontaneous combustion: they would take shape in the recording studio, with seemingly arbitrary decisions—like Al Kooper playing organ for the first time on "Like a Rolling Stone"—crucially shaping the final result. The songs juxtapose the sublime and the ridiculous, profane the sacred, and package elusive ideas in images that brand themselves on your brain. Above all, they democratize popular music while elevating its message in a way that no music had ever done before: with Dylan, high art did not have to be high-class.

The music was comparably original, in a much more subtle way. His most far-reaching innovation was the evocative use of musical style. He used beats, instruments, harmonies, forms, and the like to create an atmosphere: in

Bob Dylan in the recording studio making his first album, c. 1963.
PHOTO COURTESY CORBIS/BETTMANN.

"Highway 61 Revisited," for example, the rough-and-tumble ensemble sound recalls Delta blues, which contextualizes the title. Earlier generations of pop artists had used style evocatively, but no one before Dylan had let it penetrate so deeply into the fabric of the music.

Blonde on Blonde, his next album, offers more of the same, only more so. Dylan recorded it in Nashville during early 1966, at the suggestion of his producer, Bob Johnston. Most of his collaborators were veteran Nashville session men, most of whom knew nothing about Dylan's music. After an awkward adjustment period, they worked splendidly together, in large part because Dylan brought them into the creative process. He gave very little guidance before they started taping, preferring to let the song take shape as they recorded.

It worked. *Blonde on Blonde* expands Dylan's range in every way: verbally, musically, and—most important—emotionally. The contrasts are even more pronounced: in "Visions of Johanna," he follows doggerelish quick rhymes—gall/all/small/wall/hall—with the thought-provoking "infinity goes up on trial" and the searing "Mona Lisa had the highway blues, you can tell by the way she smiles."

Each song has a distinct musical identity. Dylan's eclecticism embraces an even broader range of mood and style: a funky Salvation Army-type band ("Rainy Day Women #12 & 35), the delicate rock ballad ("Visions of Johanna"), and a gritty electric blues/rhythm and blues mix in "Obviously 5 Believers."

The constant element throughout all of this music was Dylan's voice, his most personal innovation. When he sings, it is not pretty, by conventional pop standards, and much of the time he talks/shouts/rants instead of singing. But it reminded rock that expressive power and personality could count for far more than prettiness. His blues and blues-influenced songs on *Highway 61 Revisited* and *Blonde on Blonde* show this better than any comparable group of songs. In them, Dylan sings with the spirit and feel of the blues. His sound is completely original, yet perfectly appropriate: he sounds like himself, not a white guy trying to sound black.

After a serious motorcycle accident in the summer of 1966 that prompted him to retire briefly, he resumed recording in 1967 with *John Wesley Harding*. He returns periodically to the stage and the studio: 1997 saw the release of the widely acclaimed *Time Out of Mind*. Since 1967, his work has taken many twists and turns, and shaped important trends in rock-era music. For example, his late sixties albums strongly influenced country rock. But none of his later work has had the pervasive impact of the first three electric albums. They remain his most significant contribution to popular music.

The Beatles

The Beatles are rock's classic act, in the fullest sense of the term. Their music has spoken not only to its own time but also every generation since. Their songs are still in the air: They remain more widely known than any other music of the rock era. Their music is a cultural artifact of surpassing importance. No single source—of any kind—tells us more about the sixties than the music of the Beatles.

Not surprisingly, no rock-era act has received more attention—from fans, fellow musicians, and scholars. The brief span of their career encourages this.

Double exposure of Dylan on tour, 1974. Photo courtesy CORBIS/Bettmann.

Their recordings represent a largely finite legacy, like Beethoven's symphonies and sonatas. And like Beethoven's compositions, their recordings document a musical evolution that continued until death—in the Beatles' case, the death of the group.

We can trace the beginning of the Beatles back to the summer of 1957, when John Lennon met Paul McCartney and soon asked him to join his band, the Quarrymen. George Harrison joined them at the end of year; the group was now known as Johnny and the Moondogs. They went through one more name change, the Silver Beetles, and one more drummer, Pete Best, before settling on the Beatles and Ringo Starr, who joined the group after they had signed a recording contract. The major phase of the Beatles' career lasted just under eight years. For all intents and purposes, it began on June 6, 1962, when they auditioned for George Martin, the man who would produce most of their records. It ended on April 10, 1970, when Paul McCartney announced that the Beatles had disbanded. After their breakup, all continued their careers as solo performers. But we remember the Beatles mainly through their recordings, and those were made between 1962 and 1970.

The Influence of the Beatles

Writing in 1973, rock critic Robert Christgau claimed that the main difference between fifties rock and roll and sixties rock was "the energy and influence of the Beatles." His observation is noteworthy, not because of its accuracy (we believe he overstates the case by quite a bit), but because it sheds light on the enormous impact of the Beatles.

In Chapter 4, we observed that Elvis was the front man for rock and roll. The Beatles fulfilled much the same role for rock, at the exact moment the music came of age. Unlike Elvis, however, the Beatles continued to grow musically. Each album offered something new. Uniquely in the history of rock, they were both surpassingly popular and surpassingly good.

Precisely because of their unique position, the Beatles had enormous influence on rock music and the culture in which it flourished. Before studying their music, we will briefly consider their popularity, their immersion in sixties drug culture, and their impact on the recording process.

POPULARITY   During the sixties, the Beatles recordings topped both the singles and album charts. The commercial breakthrough, for the Beatles and for rock, was their *total* domination of the album charts. Although Dylan introduced the idea that the album was the appropriate medium for significant rock, it was the Beatles who made it a commercial reality.

With the Beatles, albums became rock milestones. Before the Beatles, rock records were promoted mainly as singles. Albums were mainly adult territory: musicals, pop singers, jazz, and classical music. Most of the best-selling albums were soundtracks for musicals, e. g., *The Sound of Music, West Side Story*. Rock and roll albums were collections of hits. Similarly, *Meet the Beatles* was a album of singles compiled especially for the U.S. market and was never issued in the United Kingdom. By contrast, *Rubber Soul* is definitely an album, not a compilation. With that album, the process had been reversed: the singles now came from the album. Part of the message in this reversal of form was that this music was important (i.e., adult) enough to be released in album format.

Record sales were only one dimension of their popularity. When their career took off, "Beatlemania" gripped the Western world. At concerts, their fans would drown the group out with their screaming. Beatle sightings would inevitably produce a crush of fans. Their first film, *A Hard Day's Night*, shows the intensity of fan adulation. The film, acclaimed as innovative in its "day in the life" portrayal of the group and refreshing in its lack of pretense, only fanned the flames of their popularity. All this audience attention eventually backfired; the incessant pressure was a major factor in their decision to stop touring.

The mere fact of the Beatles' popularity gave weight to everything they did. Their work was both inspiration and model to a generation of rock musicians. It is likely that even without the Beatles, rock would have eventually become the dominant language of popular music. Because of the Beatles, however, it happened almost overnight. By the end of the decade, rock ruled—in the record stores, on the radio, and onstage.

DRUGS   Drugs were an inescapable fact of musical life in the sixties. Again, the Beatles were not the first. Dylan turned the Beatles on to marijuana, and a friend sent Lennon on his first acid trip by spiking a drink, well after Dylan and others had been tripping regularly. However, the Beatles were among the most prominent drug users.

While we can never know all the details of the Beatles' drug use, it's clear that drugs actively shaped their music. Indeed, it's not too much to say that the Beatles' shifts in style are a direct consequence of the drug they were taking:

> Describing a meeting between Dylan and the Beatles, during which Dylan turned the Beatles on to marijuana for the first time, Ian McDonald reports:
>
> > 28th August 1964 was a watershed for the Beatles. "Till then," McCartney recalls, "we'd been hard Scotch and Coke men. It sort of changed that evening." From now on, the superficial states of mind induced by drink and "speed" gave way to the introspective and sensual moods associated with cannabis and later LSD. As for Dylan, the Beatles' musical vitality prompted his return to the rock-and-roll that had motivated him as a teenager . . . .

alcohol and speed until 1964; marijuana until 1966; acid during the *Sgt. Pepper* and *Magical Mystery Tour* years; and a cutting down or, in Lennon's case, a switch from acid to heroin in the last few years. Our discussion will point out the musical results of their drug use.

More to our point here, the Beatles essentially advertised drug use, at least indirectly. One of the most persistent rumors of the sixties was that "Lucy in the Sky with Diamonds" was a coded reference to LSD. Lennon's adamant denial only helped strengthen everyone's conviction that it was so. In any case, the group's use of drugs made them "cool"—if far from legal or beneficial.

THE TRANSFORMATION OF THE RECORDING PROCESS The Beatles were *the* major players in the transformation of the recording industry. They influenced several developments that made popular music recording in 1970 substantially different from what it had been in 1960. Among the most significant were:

1. *The record becomes the document.* This process was well under way by 1965. The Beatles confirmed this trend by divorcing recorded performance from live performance.

2. *The first studio band.* Beginning with *Rubber Soul*, the Beatles' records explored a sound world built on cutting-edge recording technology. It included more than an orchestra's worth of instruments, everyday sounds such as crowd noises, and special effects such as tapes run in reverse. The result was a stream of recordings that would be difficult, if not impossible, to replicate in live performance.

3. *Multitrack recording.* The Beatles were not the first band to make use of this technology; overdubbing had been around for over a decade. However, they achieved the most spectacular results with it, especially in albums such as *Sgt. Pepper's Lonely Hearts Club Band*, and they inspired legions of imitators.

Rock records—by the Beatles and others—sounded a lot different in 1970 than they did in 1962. They were better produced and offered a broader palette of sounds. They meant more, as well. For many artists, the album became rock's analogue to the classical composition. *Sgt. Pepper*, cited by many as rock's answer to the song cycle, and the Who's rock opera *Tommy* stand out, but there were many others.

The Music of the Beatles

Our discussion of the Beatles begins and ends with two musical questions: what made their music unique; and how did their music change over the course of their career? Other questions about their music—e.g., their influences, and whom they influenced—come out of these questions. These questions must be considered in a broader context, one that includes their overwhelming popularity, the breath of fresh air they brought to popular music, their use of drugs, and the impact of all of these—and more—on their global audience. Still, the focus is on the music.

No group of the rock era is harder to introduce than the Beatles. We can get the gist of Jerry Lee Lewis or Little Richard in a song or two, and we can zero in on the defining features of the Motown sound, no matter who's singing. Closer to our own time, we can admire Prince's stylistic range and realize that several songs are necessary to show it. But, more than any artists of the last forty years, the Beatles elude one-dimensional description, even though their career lasted less than eight years.

There are two reasons for this difficulty: the rapid evolution of their music, and its unparalleled emotional and musical range. If we didn't know their history so well, it would be hard to believe that the band that recorded "Love Me Do" in 1962 and "I Want to Hold Your Hand" a year later had become the retro-band of "Back in the USSR" or the groove merchants of "Get Back," or the soul-, gospel-, and folk-influenced creators of "Don't Let Me Down," "Let It Be," and "Here Comes the Sun," all recorded in 1969. No group changed so much in so short a time.

The five late recordings also hint at the Beatles' range. What other group could shift moods and styles so drastically—from the parody of "Back in the USSR" and the pathos of "Don't Let Me Down" to the (yes) sunniness of "Here Comes the Sun," the spaciness of "Get Back," and the soulfulness and universality of "Let It Be"—and still sound like themselves? And this is just a sample.

To understand the Beatles' music we will address questions of identity, evolution, and range through a survey of several songs. The richness of their music emerges not from one song but many.

As a point of departure, we can make the following observations:

1. The Beatles had their own sound, right from the start.

2. Their uniqueness grew out of their collaborative approach to music-making; they were a group, in the fullest sense of the word.

3. Their music is both simple and sophisticated. Their songs always provide easy points of entry that hook us, yet also contain subtle details that set them apart from the mundane. This blend of simplicity and sophistication is a key to their commercial and artistic success

4. They had the uncanny ability to absorb outside influences—sometimes almost overnight—and integrate them seamlessly into their music.

The Beatles' music went through four phases, each lasting about two years:

- "Beatlemania": from 1962 to the end of 1964
- Dylan-inspired seriousness: 1965–1966

> The Beatles' singing gives us one clue to their popularity. In rock and roll's first decade (1955–1965), there were three overwhelmingly popular singles sources: Elvis, the Beatles, and the various Motown groups. All sang tuneful songs with voices that were rougher than those of pop singers, but not so rough that mainstream youth would find them unpleasant.

- Psychedelia: late 1966–1967
- Return to roots: 1968–1970

Not surprisingly, transitions from one phase to the next are gradual. Still, the differences between representative examples are easily heard.

BEATLEMANIA The first phase of the Beatles' recording career spanned a little more than two years. It began in September 1962, when they recorded their first song, "Love Me Do," and ended early in 1965, when songs like "Ticket to Ride" clearly indicated that their music was exploring new territory.

During this first phase, the Beatles could be characterized as a rock band with a difference. Their instrumentation was conventional. Like so many bands of the early sixties, they were a Hollyesque quartet: two guitars, bass, and drums, with most of the band singing as well as playing. However, their singing was rougher than that of most other bands, especially the pop pap that was standard fare on British radio.

The difference shows up mainly in the songs. It seemed that even their first hits had a feature or two that was special to that song, and to the Beatles. It might be an element that carries through the entire song, or a little detail— or both. In "Love Me Do," for example, the opening phrase of the vocal melody is harmonized mainly with raw-sounding open fifths. "Please, Please Me," their first song with a rock beat, features McCartney's proto-punk bass line, a novelty for the time.

The song that best illustrates the Beatles' first creative period is "I Want to Hold Your Hand," recorded in October 1963. The opening of the song is a compendium of fifties rock and roll. We hear echoes of Chuck Berry's rock-defining boogie pattern in Lennon's rhythm guitar, the distinctive rebound/prebound backbeat of Elvis's version of "Mystery Train" in the handclaps, Little Richard's falsetto whoops on the second "Hand," and the Everly Brothers' close harmony during the elaborate melismatic version of "Hand," just before the final phrase of the melody.

It's not surprising that the Beatles should begin to shape their identity by transforming existing material. They were tremendous fans of Buddy Holly,

> A *fifth* is the distance between the bass notes of the I and V chords, or between the top and bottom notes of either chord. During the early years of rock, more conventional two-part harmony used adjacent tones in the chord. That would soon change: the open fifth would become the basic interval of the power chord.

> There's been speculation that the Beatles' name is in fact a homage to Holly: the Crickets. Over a period of years, the name changed from the Silver Beetles, to the Beetles, and finally to the Beatles.

the first rock star to assimilate and transform rock and roll in his songs. We heard his borrowing of the "Bo Diddley" beat in "Not Fade Away," which the Beatles recorded while fooling around during one of their last recording sessions. So it made sense that the Beatles would follow his lead.

As with Holly's music, "I Want to Hold Your Hand" is more than pastiche of 1950s rock and roll, because the Beatles' use of outside influences responds directly to the musical needs of the song, and because the group's musical personality dominates the individual components.

The two vocal borrowings clearly show this. Both are used to energize the melody. The first phrase of the melody gradually descends, with little undulations—like a water slide. The second phrase simply repeats the first until the final note. Like an electric shock, the sudden leap up galvanizes the melody. The almost-operatic flourishes that follow sustain the energy through the rest of the section. Here, harmonized singing creates more energy, if only because its intricacy keeps the rhythm active and its difficulty implies effort. The florid singing also counterbalances the repetitiveness of the lyrics, so that the third and final statement of the title phrase, which is the simplest of all, sounds like the hook of the song—even though we've already heard the words twice before.

Like most up-and-coming bands around 1960, the Beatles had to play all kinds of music: not only rock and roll, but rhythm and blues, jazzy numbers, Latin dance tunes, and old and new pop songs. Rock was far from an established style, either for musicians or their audience, so bands had to be able to shift gears, often from song to song. McCartney's pop roots went much deeper, because his father was a amateur big-band leader. What separated the Beatles from other sounds of the time was their ability to personalize these influences. Among McCartney's songs, there is no better example than "Yesterday." It is one of the great pop ballads of our century, only belonging in the rock canon because the Beatles wrote and recorded it.

Yesterday McCartney wrote "Yesterday" in January 1964 but recorded the song almost a year and a half later, in June 1965. He had withheld it from two earlier albums because it had come to him one morning virtually complete, and he was afraid that he was simply remembering a song from his past.

That he should feel this way is no surprise, because the song, as written, is a pre-rock pop song. Like many songs of that era, the melody *develops*

> The Beatles' dues-paying experience is one reason that the second coming of the Beatles is very unlikely. Contemporary rock acts are not required to be as flexible stylistically as early rock bands. In our times, a versatile group can cover several rock sub-styles, but may be totally unaware of non-rock music.

The Beatles on the Ed Sullivan Show, June 1, 1966. PHOTO COURTESY CORBIS/BETTMANN.

from a short, simple, riff-like idea: "Yes-ter-day." Each phrase in the opening section ends with a different version of the three-note pattern. The overall form also recalls the past. The song contains six sections, in an AABABA pattern. This is the 32-measure AABA form, so typical of pre-rock pop songs, as it would typically be performed at a dance! When dance musicians performed slow pop ballads, they would usually omit the first two A sections when repeating the melody, so that it wouldn't last too long. It would seem that McCartney simply adapted that practice into the form of the song. Its obvious pop roots help explain why "Yesterday" is the most-covered song of all time.

McCartney brought pop style into the rock era in several ways: There is his singing, which has an innocence miles away from the whisky-soaked worldliness of Frank Sinatra or the effortless, emotionless efficiency of Perry Como. The simple acoustic guitar accompaniment outlines a delicate eight-beat rhythm, not a fox-trot or swing beat.

The string accompaniment is similarly updated. McCartney specifically asked George Martin for a leaner sound—"no Mantovani" (the lush string sound so favored by pop artists and the adults who listened to them)—and he got it; Martin composed a tasteful accompaniment for string quartet, an unusual touch for a popular recording. The result was a fresh new sound, for all of popular music.

"Yesterday" shows the Beatles' music in transition. We can hear McCartney expanding their sound world by both addition and subtraction. Gone is the nuclear rock band: two electric guitars, bass, and drums. In its place are a single guitar and a string quartet.

There also seems to be a stronger connection between words and music. Perhaps it's just coincidence, but McCartney uses an old style to write a romantic (i.e., pop style) ballad whose title word is "Yesterday." An elegant detail also supports this strengthened connection. The first A section is only seven measures long, instead of the typical eight; the second A section begins a measure early. This premature entrance underscores the lyric: "suddenly."

DYLAN-INSPIRED SERIOUSNESS By the time McCartney recorded "Yesterday," the Beatles were well into a new musical phase. Under the influence of Bob Dylan and drugs, their songs had changed significantly. Lyrics were more meaningful, less teen-oriented, and wider-ranging in subject matter and tone. They were expanding their sound world: the sitar and finger cymbals heard in "Norwegian Wood" are a good illustration. As their music matured, it became bolder, and more individual.

The songs from *Rubber Soul* and *Revolver*, the two major albums from this second phase of their career, were, at the same time, more clearly the work of the (new) Beatles—no one else could have made them—and less like each other. The contrast from song to song had clearly deepened. A group of four songs, "Drive My Car," "We Can Work It Out," "Norwegian Wood," and "Eleanor Rigby," show the wholesale transformation of their music.

Drive My Car We tend to remember the Beatles most vividly for their rock-expanding songs—so much so that we tend to forget how good a rock band they were, and how much they improved in that respect over the course of their career. "Drive My Car" gives evidence of that improvement, as well as other key features of their music during its second phase.

One change that's immediately apparent is the lyric: It has an attitude and a much sharper focus. Although lyrics to the early songs talked about "I" and "you," they were essentially impersonal—"I" and "you" could be anyone. By contrast, this lyric is almost cinematic in the portrayal of its two characters. They may have stars in their eyes, but they also have feet of clay. Sexual tension is implicit in the title phrase of the song—much of its humor comes from the possibility for both literal and metaphorical interpretations of "drive my car."

The accompaniment shows how the Beatles collaborated in creating songs. McCartney brought the song in to record without all the details in place. Harrison, who had been listening to Otis Redding's "Respect," suggested that they try to find a similar groove. The result was a soul-inspired riff, played by lead guitar and bass. There is no rhythm guitar part; only the chorus has solid chords, played on the piano. The bass-heavy riffs and extra percussion—cowbell and tambourine—give the song a sound much closer to soul music than white rock.

As before, the Beatles dissolve this outside influence into the mix. The dominant element is Beatles'-style humor. It's present in the lyric and the "car horn" close harmony in the vocal part just before the chorus. The soul elements simply support this humor.

We Can Work It Out   "We Can Work It Out," recorded in October 1965, offers one of the best examples of Lennon and McCartney's collaborative method. Most songwriting teams are made of a lyricist and songwriter. By contrast, both Lennon and McCartney contribute words and music. In this song, McCartney wrote the opening section, Lennon the middle. The abrupt shift in mood and sound comes from two personalities responding to the same theme differently.

McCartney's section is an almost public plea to Jane Asher, his partner at the time. Its urgency is brought home by the compact opening phrases—three measures instead of the more typical four. Lennon's response is far more detached, even supercilious, like advice from an unsympathetic acquaintance. Yet this contrast holds the song together: the song worked out, even if McCartney's relationship didn't.

A TRIP TO SOUTHERN CALIFORNIA; A TRIP IN SOUTHERN CALIFORNIA
An encounter with two members of the Byrds during their 1965 American tour would spark a profound change in the music of the Beatles. Lennon and Harrison spent a day with Roger McGuinn and David Crosby, tripping on LSD, playing twelve-string guitars, and discussing the music of the Indian sitar player Ravi Shankar. Harrison had been intrigued by the sound of the sitar for a while. For Lennon, however, it was a new sound. Lennon quickly translated this experience into "Norwegian Wood": both the sitar and the use of modal scales show the influence of East Indian music.

The Byrds' "Eight Miles High"   The Byrds are credited with creating the first "acid rock" song, "Eight Miles High." There's a certain irony to that association, because the title began as a reference to the cruising altitude of an airliner (it went from "six miles" to "eight miles" in response to the Beatles' hit "Eight Days a Week"), and the Byrds apparently created it while ingesting massive amounts of speed, not LSD. So there are no overt LSD links in the title or its creation. Nevertheless, key elements of its sound found their way into the acid rock of the San Francisco bands.

Regarding the "acid rock" sound: its most prominent elements are the drone-like support of McGuinn's solo and the new, modal-based harmony. Other features include McGuinn's solo, (a flight of fancy presumably inspired by Shankar's sitar playing), the tabla-like drums (the tabla is an Indian percussion instrument) under McGuinn's solo, the dense texture, and the overall air of spontaneity and improvisation. This recording is "loose," especially during the drone-like solos. The acid rock of the San Francisco bands, Hendrix, and others typically featured drones, long solos, and a free and easy sound. However, this music was not the only response to acid. It also begins to figure in the Beatles' music from 1965 on.

Norwegian Wood   In "Norwegian Wood," also recorded in October 1965 for *Rubber Soul*, Lennon and McCartney cast a much more jaded eye on the relationship between the sexes. Apparently, this song was also a collaboration, with Lennon taking the lead, although Lennon later claimed it as solely his own.

Ian McDonald makes the point that "Norwegian Wood" is the first Beatles song where the words are more important than the music. The lyric is simultaneously cryptic—what does the song's title mean, after all?—and clear; in just a few words, Lennon and McCartney create images as sharp and as striking as a photograph. Like an unrelated series of slides, they give us a view of love's underside at the dawn of the free love era.

The music of "Norwegian Wood" departs completely from rock's conventions: the band, the beat, etc. In its place are acoustic guitars and a sitar and a waltz rhythm. It's clear that "Norwegian Wood" was a rock song in attitude, but not basic sound.

Eleanor Rigby A song about the unlamented death of a relationship is unusual enough in popular music. A song about an unlamented death was unprecedented. "Eleanor Rigby," recorded in June 1966, for the album *Revolver*, broke sharply with pop song conventions in both words and music. McCartney relates the story of Eleanor Rigby with a detachment rare in popular music. There is no "you" or "I," even of the generic kind. The story is told strictly in the third person. Her tale is as gloomy as a cold, damp, grey day. Even the chorus is as impersonal as a Greek chorus. It simply asks: "Ah, look at all the lonely people." There's no particular empathy for either Eleanor Rigby or Father McKenzie.

The musical setting is as bleak as the words. A string octet (four violins, two violas, and two cellos), scored by George Martin from McCartney's instructions, replaces the rock band; there are no other instruments. Even more than in "Yesterday," the string sound is spare, not lush—the chords used throughout emulate a rock accompaniment, not Mantovani. Like Eleanor Rigby herself, the melody of both chorus and verse don't go anywhere. Set over alternating modal chords, the chorus is just a sigh. The melody of the verse contains longer phrases, but they too mostly progress from higher to lower notes. Again, because of the modal harmony, we have no sense of movement toward a goal. Lyric, melody, harmony, and the repetitive rhythm of the accompaniment convey the same message: time passes, without apparent purpose.

With "Eleanor Rigby," the Beatles announced that their music—and, by extension, rock—was, or could aspire to be, art. The most obvious clue was the classical-style string accompaniment. However, the subject of the song and the detachment with which it is presented have more in common with classical art songs than pop or rock songs. Having recorded rock's answer to the art song, the Beatles soon created rock's answer to the art song cycle: the concept album.

ANOTHER SIDE TRIP TO CALIFORNIA: THE BEACH BOYS Although the Beatles did not have the mind-altering personal contact with the Beach Boys that they did with the Byrds, they were intensely aware of their music. To cite just one example, "Back in the USSR" salutes Chuck Berry via southern California.

However, their strongest connection—perhaps competition is a better word—was the link between the Beach Boys' 1966 album, *Pet Sounds*, and the Beatles' *Sgt. Pepper*. Up to this point in their careers, the Beach Boys had been a step ahead of the Beatles in terms of production. Brian Wilson had become increasingly involved in production during 1965 and 1966, to the point of withdrawing from live performance to spend time in the studio. His crowning achievement was the song "Good Vibrations," the biggest hit from the album.

"Good Vibrations" immediately raised the "production" bar and expanded the musical possibilities for a single. The song itself is beautifully conceived. The verse floats, with high organ, wisps of bass line, and somewhat later, delicate percussive sounds. All are a far cry from the souped-up Berry-ish sound of their early surf hits. Yet they are a logical, if imaginative, extension of the varied textures of "I Get Around" and "Dance, Dance, Dance." Quite clearly, "Good Vibrations" is no longer rock as dance music. The chorus swaps high register sounds for low register and decisive rhythm for the implied time of the verse. Triplets, played by cellos (!) in their low register, offer one kind of vibration. A theremin—an early electronic instrument—provides a different kind of vibration with a high melodic obbligato behind the vocal. The textural contrast between verse and chorus is dramatic.

The most original feature of the song is a long collage-like extension that begins about halfway through. "Good Vibrations," which is almost twice as long as their early singles, could have ended with a fadeout after the second chorus. Instead, Wilson strings together a series of barely related sections. The first, which features a harpsichordish sound, fragments the chorus. The second, in an abruptly slower tempo and much less active rhythm—as if the song suddenly went to church—introduces new material. The chorus abruptly returns; after some pseudo-classical vocal counterpoint, the song fades out as the theremin line drifts off into the ether.

Wilson recorded the song in four studios over a period of six months. The song, his wonderfully imaginative setting of it, the novel instrumentation, and—above all—the superb production (well before 24-track boards) made "Good Vibrations" unique, and a challenge to the Beatles and all who aspired to a higher standard of production. For the Beatles, *Sgt. Pepper's Lonely Hearts Club Band* would be their response.

PSYCHEDELIA The cover to *Sgt. Pepper's Lonely Hearts Club Band* tells the story. In a "group portrait," the Beatles appear twice, "live" and dressed in band uniforms, and in wax-museum style likenesses. They are surrounded by icons of high and popular culture, mainly from earlier generations: Karl Marx, Laurel and Hardy, and Marilyn Monroe are but a few; Dylan is their only contemporary. That they represent themselves as wax figures or in costume suggest that the Beatles no longer see themselves publicly as they had been in *A Hard Day's Night*. Instead, they are playing roles.

Further, by placing themselves among several generations of cultural icons, they seem to imply that their music is culturally significant; that it connects to the past even as it promises a new postmodern future; and that the division between "high" and "low" art is not divinely ordained.

Indeed, the message seems to be that gaps—both generational and cultural—implode, leaving artistic significance in the eye and ear of the beholder.

LSD helped fuel this relativistic vision of reality. Indeed, this vision is part of the underlying concept of the album. Throughout the album, there are contrasts between the everyday world and the heightened sensibility experienced while tripping on acid.

This contrast is most sharply drawn in "Lucy in the Sky with Diamonds." In this song, Lennon and McCartney give the venerable verse/chorus form an original twist. The verse creates a dreamy state. The lyric contains numerous psychedelic images (e.g., "marmalade skies") and the music floats along in waltz time. It gives the impression of a person in the middle of an acid trip.

By contrast, the chorus is straight-ahead rock and roll, which conveys a sense of normalcy. The repetition of the title phrase suggests a second persona in the song: someone observing the person who's tripping in the verse.

However, the song that best sums up the *Sgt. Pepper* worldview is "A Day in the Life." Here, the contrast between the mundane, everyday world and the elevated consciousness of acid tripping is made even more dramatic. It is projected by the most fundamental opposition in music itself, other than sound and silence: music with words vs. music without words. The texted parts of the song are everyday life, while the strictly instrumental sections depict tripping—they follow "I'd love to turn you on" or a reference to a dream.

This contrast is made even more striking by the nature of the words and music. The text of the song, and the music that supports it, paint four scenes. The first is Lennon's response to a newpaper account of a man who dies in a horrible automobile accident while, Lennon suspects, he was tripping. The second pictures Lennon attending a film—perhaps an allusion to the film, *How I Won the War*, in which he'd acted a few months prior to recording the song. The third depicts Lennon in the workaday world rat race. The last one is a commentary on another, more mundane news article; in Lennon's view, it is news reporting—and, by extension, daily life—at its most trivial: who would bother counting potholes?

The music that underscores this text is, in its most obvious features, as everyday as the text. It begins with just a man and his guitar. The other instruments layer in, but none of them makes a spectacular contribution. This everyday background is opposed with the massive orchestral blob of sound that depicts, in its gradual ascent, the elevation of consciousness. The dense sound, masterfully scored by George Martin, belongs to the world of avant-garde classical music—it recalls the Polish composer Krzystof Penderecki's *Threnody for the Victims of Hiroshima* (1960) and other works of that type, works familiar to classical music insiders but not well-known generally. This creates another strong opposition: well-known vs. obscure, and by implication, the unenlightened (i. e., not turned on) masses vs. those few who are enlightened.

The apparent simplicity of the vocal sections obscures numerous subtle touches. Starr's tasteful drumming and McCartney's inventive bass lines are noteworthy. So is the doubling of the tempo in the "Woke up . . ." section. What had been the rock beat layer is now the beat. This expresses in music the narrator's frantic preparation for work without disturbing the underlying rhythmic fabric of the song. Perhaps the nicest touches, however, are found in the vocal line: the trill heard first on "laugh" and "photograph," then expanded on "nobody was really sure . . ." before floating up to its peak on "lords." It is precisely this melodic gesture—the trill, now set to "turn you on"—that presages the move from the vocal section to the orchestral section, and by extension the beginning of an acid trip. When the trill/leap material returns in the film-viewing vignette, this connection becomes explicit: the melodic leap is followed by the trill, which blends seamlessly into the orchestral texture. As a melodic gesture, the trill/leap sequence is also a beautiful surprise, strictly on its own terms—a sequel of sorts to the leap to "hand" in "I Want to Hold Your Hand."

The final words are for the final chord: an "OM," the clarity of enlightenment after the transition, via the orchestral section, from the mundane life in the "normal" world. It is a striking ending to a beautifully conceived and exquisitely crafted song, a song that is one of the most powerful metaphors for the acid experience ever created.

Return to Roots

The Beatles reached a pinnacle with *Sgt. Pepper's Lonely Hearts Club Band.* Their subsequent efforts, most significantly *Magical Mystery Tour*, were not as successful, either artistically or commercially. By 1968, they had begun to retreat from the grandiose. Instead of attempting to make yet another major artistic statement, they created music that responded to the music around them. From one perspective, the songs from this period are their unique reinterpretations of the styles that were "out there." Gone, for the most part, are the big orchestras, electronic collages, crowd noise. In their place, more often than not, is some straight-ahead, high-class rock and roll.

But there are two crucial differences. First, they brought to their task what seems like a lifetime of experience and exposure. Second, the music around them had also grown up. Rock—in all its manifestations, black and white—was now an established family of styles, in a way it hadn't been five years previously, so they had much more to draw on. Their maturity, and the maturation of rock, give their music a depth and breadth that it could not have had at the beginning of the decade.

The Beatles at Abbey Road studio, May 20, 1967, preparing to record "All You Need Is Love."
PHOTO COURTESY CORBIS/BETTMANN.

Yet, despite the more modest scale of their efforts (notwithstanding *The Beatles*, a double album commonly referred to as the "White Album"), their music has increased musical and emotional range. Influences come from everywhere. Here's a sampling:

- "Back in the USSR" is twice-fried rock and roll: a homage to both Chuck Berry and the Beach Boys (the pseudo-Beach Boys harmonies and allusions to "Moscow girls . . ." ironically recall the sunny surf music that the Boys created).
- "Ob-La-Di, Ob-La-Da" is the Beatles' take on West Indian music. The song is touched by calypso and ska, the Jamaican precursor of reggae, which was known in England all through the sixties.
- "Get Back" was apparently inspired by the American blues/rock band Canned Heat. In any event, it's gentrified boogie band music.
- "Don't Let Me Down" drips with the sounds of Memphis or Muscle Shoals—both the song and Lennon's impassioned singing have a clear connection with soul.
- "The Ballad of John and Yoko" owes part of its sound to country rock—appropriately enough, since ballads, i.e., long storytelling songs, have deep country roots.
- "Something" is a pop ballad: "the greatest love song of the past fifty years," according to Frank Sinatra—who should know.
- "Let It Be" comes straight out of black gospel.

The fact of the Beatles' familiarity with—and comfort in—so many different kinds of music is remarkable enough. However, it is their ability to personalize a style, to integrate it into their conception of the song, to make it work for the song, that sets their music apart from everyone else's.

"Let It Be" is a fine example. The gospel influence is evident from the first piano chord. But neither McCartney nor the choir try to sound black. His singing is wonderfully simple and unaffected. McCartney seems to evoke black gospel in this song out of musical—and emotional—necessity. Of all the vernacular styles in the air during the sixties, none is more universal and spiritual in its message or more uplifting in its spirit. The intimation of black gospel, in the piano and organ accompaniment and in the choir behind McCartney's singing, is strong enough to convey the message of the song, but not so strong that it deflects attention away from his song and his singing of it, which is the central focus of "Let It Be."

"Get Back" is, if anything, an even better illustration of the Beatles' ability to synthesize and personalize the musical world around them. It is perhaps the quintessential "groove" song in their entire recorded output—what song of theirs has a more propulsive beat? The infectiousness of its beat would seem to put it squarely in the rock mainstream, but its sound is unique. Perhaps it is the "dum-diddy" rhythm that Starr plays on the snare, instead of the more conventional rock beat on the sock cymbal (as in "Back in the USSR"). Or perhaps it's Harrison's pulsing afterbeat guitar, overlaid onto Lennon's Chuck Berry-style riff. Regardless of its sources, it's a unique sound, at once squarely in a rock groove and unique unto itself.

The rhythm and excellent solos by Lennon and keyboardist Billy Preston support a wacky lyric, in which the verse seems to have nothing to do with the refrain. There's a good reason: the song began as a satire on British reaction to an impending influx of Kenyan Asian refugees. "Get Back" refers to prevailing public opinion in the United Kingdom—"don't come here." McCartney realized that the song would simply pour oil on the fire and substituted a stream of consciousness set of verses for the original—none of which connect to the refrain.

The two songs suggest the emotional range of the Beatles' later music. Ironically, one reason for the greater range of these songs was the growing divisions within the Beatles. Their increasingly fractious relationship meant that they did as little as possible together. Typically, they would come together to record the basic tracks, and the person who wrote the song would supervise its production. That they created so much high-quality music during this turmoil is remarkable.

Summary

Bob Dylan's first three electric albums represent his most significant contribution to rock music. He gave rock new sounds and new ways of combining old sounds. But his most important contributions were conceptual. Dylan brought a new attitude into popular music: an eclectic egalitarianism, in the service of messages with meaning. Above all, he raised the level of discourse, not only for rock, but for all of popular music. After Dylan, everyone was accountable. Rock acts who took themselves seriously had to respond to him: explaining their musical breakthrough in the mid-sixties, the Beatles said, "We were only trying to please Dylan."

The Beatles began as another rock and roll band. Early in their career, their biggest claim to fame was that they were from England—the first wave of the British invasion. If they had dissolved at the end of 1963, their music would be a sidebar in the history of rock. However, the qualities which had already become evident in their early songs—their gift for melody, their imagination, their ability to capture such a wide range of moods and feelings in music—came into full flower in the remaining six or so years of their association.

It is not too much to say that as their music matured, they redefined popular song: not only what it was, but what it could say. Others were traveling along the same path—we have mentioned the attitude that Dylan brought to popular music and the emotional power of the best soul music—but no rock act did more to shape the new music of the rock era than the Beatles.

Just as significantly, the Beatles legitimized rock music. Through their mass popularity, their aspirations, and, above all, the quality and originality of their music, they did more than any other act to establish rock as the music of a new generation. It is an incomparable legacy.

K E Y   T E R M S

Folk-rock	**Beatlemania**	**Acid rock**
Folk revival	**Studio band**	**Psychedelia**
Social commentary	**Multitrack recording**	**Roots rock**

CHAPTER QUESTIONS

1. Compare the two versions of "Mr. Tambourine Man." Which one do you like better? Why?

2. Profile two or three songs from *Blonde on Blonde*. First compare the basic character of the song, as evidenced in the lyric and the overall musical impression. Then compare specific details—instrumentation, beat, melodic style, and so on—to sharpen your initial impression of the musical differences. Do your findings confirm or refute the discussion in the text?

3. Compare "I Want to Hold Your Hand" to "Get Back." Then explore two questions: How do you know (from listening) that both songs are by the Beatles? How can you describe the differences between early and late Beatles' songs?

4. Pick one Beatles' song—preferably one that you like a lot and one that is not discussed in the book—and write a paragraph or two explaining some of the ways in which the music supports the lyric: how do details of form, rhythm, melody, and so on, underscore the basic mood projected in the words?

5. Listen to either of the early Beach Boys' songs discussed in the Chapter 5 and either "Please Please Me" or "I Want to Hold Your Hand." Then listen to "Good Vibrations" and "A Day in the Life." Then describe as specifically as you can how these songs show rock growing from good "good time" music into art.

chapter 8

From Blues to Rock

In the early 1960s, while the Quarrymen were moulting into the Beatles, other young British musicians were hanging out at Alexis Korner's London-based Blues and Barrelhouse Club. Korner, a "trad" (British-style dixieland jazz) and skiffle musician during the fifties, spearheaded the blues revival in Great Britain as the sixties began.

Korner nurtured a generation of British musicians who had grown up listening to the blues. Their primary contact came from the recordings of Muddy Waters, John Lee Hooker, Howlin' Wolf, and other country and electric bluesmen—highly prized because they were so hard to obtain in Britain. Korner's club, a regular stop for American bluesmen touring England, was a mecca for British blues fans. It gave blues fans a chance to hear—and for a lucky few, to play—"real blues." It was also an outlet for the British blues musicians, a place where they could gain valuable performing experience.

The roster of musicians who played at Korner's club reads like a Who's Who of British rock in the sixties and early seventies. Both the Rolling Stones and Cream were made up of Korner alumni, while key members of Led Zeppelin, the Yardbirds, John Mayall's Bluesbreakers, and other notable bands also paid their dues there.

At first, the British musicians were content to play a pale imitation of the "real thing." However, when Sonny Boy Williamson visited England, he was accompanied by a very young, very green Eric Clapton. This encounter with a real bluesman transformed Clapton as a musician, as he related some years later to blues scholar Robert Palmer:

> It was a frightening experience, because this man was real and we weren't. We didn't know how to back him up, and he put us through some bloody hard paces. I was very young, and it was a real shock. I realized we weren't being true to the music; I had to almost relearn how to play. But it taught me a lot. It taught me the value of that music, which I still feel.

By the time Clapton and his peers "got real," they had transformed their blues experience into a completely new music: rock. This was music with a hard edge, music that confronted and challenged. Although often popular, it was not pop. Nor was it simply heavily amplified blues, although blues attitude and style pervades the music. It was something new.

Another musician who grew up on the other side of the Atlantic had a similar agenda. Jimi Hendrix, following his own path, transformed the blues into the most daring and influential instrumental style of the sixties. Hendrix was born and raised in Seattle, paid his dues touring with blues and rhythm and blues artists, got his solo career going in England, made his first big splash in the United States at the 1967 Monterey Pop Festival, and died in London. His powerful and imaginative playing linked like-minded musicians on both sides of the Atlantic.

Deep Blues and Rock

Rock and roll grew out of the blues, but not what Robert Palmer evocatively called "deep blues": the music of Blind Lemon Jefferson, Robert Johnson, John Lee Hooker, Muddy Waters, and other blues greats. Except for its instrumentation, electric blues barely touched rock and roll. Throughout most of the fifties, electric bluesmen lived in their own world, and the old Delta bluesmen who were still alive were all but forgotten until the blues revival.

The blues revival that paralleled the folk revival of the late fifties and early sixties exposed young rock musicians to the power and emotional depth of deep blues. The British musicians who immersed themselves in the blues took from it several of its most distinctive features: the attitude and posturing of the bluesmen, often obvious in its sexual challenge; lyrics that told their stories in plain, direct language, often with a nasty edge (Muddy Waters's "I Can't Be Satisfied"/the Rolling Stones' "[I Can't Get No] Satisfaction"); a rough, declamatory vocal style; heavy guitar riffs and string-bending blues-scale guitar solos; a strong beat; and a thick, riff-laden texture.

The rock that emerged from the British blues scene took two forms. One was a group-oriented music with lots of riffs and little soloing. The other spotlighted guitar solos, at times to excess. We consider both in turn.

Group-Oriented Rock

Among the horde of British bands that invaded the United States in the mid-sixties were blues-influenced groups such as the Animals, the Kinks, and the Rolling Stones. They had a tougher sound than the Beatles: more prominent and more distorted guitar, a stronger beat, rougher vocals, and, behind it all, a more aggressive attitude.

The Animals' interest in the blues resonated with their working-class upbringing in Newcastle. They were the backup band of choice for the American bluesmen who visited there, and they were among the first British bands to score a U.S. hit with "The House of the Rising Sun" (1964).

The Kinks' long, intermittently successful, and chameleon-like career began with two hits, "All Day and All Night" (1964) and "You Really Got Me" (1965). These songs were among the first to bring the raunchy, blues-drenched branch of British rock to the United States.

The idea of building a song over a short, repetitive guitar riff came directly from electric blues: recall the riff that opens Muddy Waters's "Hoochie-Coochie Man." The new elements in the Kinks' song are the increased distortion, the harmonization of the riff with power chords, the repetition of the riff at successively higher pitches, the driving rock beat, and the move away from blues form.

A "power chord" is a three-note chord comprised of the main note, or "root," plus notes a fifth and an octave above the root. It is not a conventional chord in common practice harmony because it lacks the third.

The Rolling Stones

The most notorious, important, and influential of these British blues-based bands was the Rolling Stones. The original Rolling Stones included lead singer Mick Jagger, guitarists Keith Richards and Brian Jones, bassist Bill Wyman, and drummer Charlie Watts. Jagger and Jones also played other instruments—e.g., extra percussion, harmonica—from time to time.*

The Stones began to take shape in 1960, when Mick Jagger saw Keith Richards standing in a train station with an armful of blues records. It was not their first meeting; both had grown up in Dartford, England, and had attended the same school for one year, when they were six. Their chance meeting eleven years later would be the beginning of their band.

Both spent a lot of time at Korner's club, where they met Brian Jones and Charlie Watts. At the time, Watts was the drummer for Korner's Blues Incorporated, which would also include Jagger after 1961. The band came together in 1962 when they added bassist Bill Wyman via an audition. Keyboardist Ian Stewart was also a member of the band at the time. He stopped performing with the group soon after their career began, but retained a close connection with the Stones and performed on many of their recordings.

Like the other British bands, the Rolling Stones began by covering blues and rock and roll songs. Within a year, Jagger and Richards began writing original songs for the band, inspired by the success of Lennon and McCartney. They had their first U.K. hit in 1963 and reached the top of the American charts for the first time in 1965 with "(I Can't Get No) Satisfaction." By the time they recorded the song, they had pretty well defined their sound, style, and image.

Almost from the outset, the Rolling Stones, astutely guided by their manager, Andrew Oldham, cultivated a "bad-boy" image. Its purpose was to set the group off from the Beatles, and it succeeded because the image so closely mirrored reality. They were provocative, pushy, outrageous, impudent, earthy, and menacing—at a time when others weren't.

Jagger was the first star with an onstage attitude. His singing and strutting reeked sex and aggression. It brought into rock performance the kind of sexual braggadocio that had been part of the blues—especially deep blues—since the twenties.

The sound of the band behind him reinforced this image. Richards's guitar playing has a bite that feeds off Jagger's singing, and the band as a whole has a nasty sound—there's nothing pretty or at all sentimental in their style. In addition, the band favored dense textures and low registers. Watts's drums

---

* Their personnel has remained remarkably stable, with only three changes in over thirty years. Mick Taylor replaced Jones shortly before Jones's death in 1969. He was replaced by Ron Wood in 1990. Bill Wyman left the group in 1992. Daryl Jones has played bass on most of the Stones' tours since then, although he has never been made officially a member of the group.

The Rolling Stones, January 17, 1964. L to r: Brian Jones, Mick Jagger, Keith Richards, Charlie Watts, Bill Wyman. PHOTO COURTESY CORBIS/HULTON-DEUTSCH COLLECTION.

seem to be tuned loosely, to sound darker, and he makes ample use of the kick drum, the lowest-pitched drum in the set. Richards and Jones also favor lower registers for their riffs and accompanying chords.

Typically, the voices are the highest-pitched sound—which is often not the case in the music of Hendrix and the other virtuoso guitarists who exploit the full range of the instrument. The sheer density of the sound and the use of lower registers gives their music a weight more comparable to a heavily amplified blues band or a good New Orleans rhythm and blues sound than the rock of Chuck Berry, the Beatles, or the Beach Boys. The weight of the sound, along with the drive of their rhythmic conception and the insolence of Jagger's singing, gives their music a swagger that no other rock band of the sixties had.

A survey of three of the Rolling Stones' rock-defining hits, "(I Can't Get No) Satisfaction," "Jumping Jack Flash," and "Honky Tonk Women," gives us some insight into the details of their sound, and how their music evolved during the sixties, their most creative period.

"(I CAN'T GET NO) SATISFACTION" For the Stones, "(I Can't Get No) Satisfaction" was a musical as well as a commercial milestone. No other major band so thoroughly distilled their essence into their first major hit. Every aspect of the song—the title, its lyric, its melody and form, Jagger's singing and Richards's guitar playing, the sound of the band, and the relentlessness of its beat—embodied the rebellious image the band wanted to project.

"Satisfaction" begins with one of the most memorable guitar riffs of all time. It sounds menacing, because Richards uses fuzztone (an effect he seldom used subsequently), situates the riff in the lowest register of the guitar, and places a strong, syncopated accent on the highest and longest note of the riff, which pushes against the beat established in the first two notes. If sound can sneer, then it does so in this riff.

The bass line that enters almost immediately reinforces this initial impression. Two features stand out: its melodic and rhythmic independence, and the interval it forms with the guitar on the most accented note of the riff. While the bass line follows its own rhythmic path, it coordinates beautifully with both the guitar line and the beat. Moreover, the peak of the bass riff forms an interval that belongs more to the power chords of the future than the comfortable chords of the past.

When the drum part enters by marking the beat heavily, the interaction of its clear pulse with the out-of-phase guitar and bass riffs suggests a group of leather jacketed toughs moving in a pack, but not in lockstep.

The lyric operates on multiple levels of meaning. Given the Stones' image, their blues background, and Jagger's stage deportment, it's safe to assume that the title phrase refers to more than Jagger's litany of complaints. The coded meaning of the lyric is, of course, sex: Jagger's frustration is certainly more sexual than anything else. The surface meaning of the lyric is no more than dissembling, as if Jagger's waiting for us to ask, "Now, Mick, what's really bothering you?"

Both the opening riff (the melodic hook) and its overall design express the theme of the song musically. With its syncopated accent on the high note, the guitar riff suggests a strong thrust. But the riff avoids the key note of the song. Instead, it starts and returns to a note some distance from the keynote and excludes it completely. The syncopation and the avoidance of the keynote makes musical "satisfaction"—that is, the sense of release that accompanies the arrival on the keynote on a beat—impossible. Musically, then, we "can't get no satisfaction" from the riff.

The form of the song also leaves us unsatisfied, because it defies our formal expectations for a rock-era song. Jagger and Richards perversely jumble the typical sequence of events, never giving us the satisfaction typically provided by the formal landmarks that guide us through a song. Their inspired musical depiction of frustration can be understood by contrasting the form of the song with the more typical forms of the time.

The majority of rock-era songs follow either the refrain-frame or the end-weighted verse/refrain formal outline, as we have seen. Both forms offer frequent reminders of the main point of the song, heard most obviously in the repetition of the title phrase of the song. However, this point is often underscored musically not only by the use of memorable riffs but also increases in density, more active harmonies, and other features. As a result, the refrain stands like a sound pillar (in the refrain-frame forms) or looms as the goal of a long buildup. In either case, it offers a comforting point of arrival.

"(I Can't Get No) Satisfaction" turns these formal plans upside down. It begins like a refrain-frame form—an introductory riff followed by the title phrase in the vocal line. The opening of the song uncannily echoes Roy Orbison's "Oh, Pretty Woman," especially in the guitar riff.

From this point, the song builds gradually to a climax. However, the climax is truncated; Jagger does not complete even one statement of the title phrase. Instead, he spews out his frustration, describing with great indignation things that tick him off. This is verse-type material, sung basically on one note. But Jagger sings it at full volume at the top of his vocal range, and it comes after a long buildup, and right at the point where we would expect the hook of the song. The only group singing follows Jagger's soliloquy and a drum break, and it's throwaway material, as if they're mocking Jagger. In addition, the signature riff of the song is repeated relentlessly under Jagger's high-pitched singing. Its ostinato-like character suggests the throb of a hangover headache—especially because of the use of fuzztone.

This sequence of events frustrates our expectations regarding the form of a rock-era song. At the points where we might expect the title phrase we get: a) an incomplete statement; b) a screamed-out verse-like melodic line; c) another incomplete statement of the title phrase; d) a drum break; and e) throwaway, group-sung riffs. What we don't get is anything resembling a well-prepared hook. Instead, the song is an "endless loop," without the landmarks typically found in other songs of the period. This formal frustration underscores the message of the song on the largest musical scale, just as the riff underscores it on a much smaller scale.

It's likely that Richards and Jagger did not consciously set out to write a song with the message suggested in the interpretation presented here. By Richards's own account, the first component of the song came in the middle of a restless night: he woke up from a troubled sleep long enough to play the opening riff into a tape recorder, then went back to sleep. The words and the working out of the rest of the song came later.

But it really doesn't matter whether they consciously set out to write a song with that message, or even whether our interpretation accurately reflects their intent. The important point is that the musical events easily lend themselves to such an interpretation. Words and music are all of a piece: they support the same basic attitude, each in its own way. It was this attitude and its musical realization that were so innovative, and, ultimately, so influential.

"Jumping Jack Flash" and "Honky Tonk Women," released in 1968 and 1969 respectively, are less boldly innovative in form—and attitude. However, both songs have a quintessential rock beat, in a way that "Satisfaction" doesn't. The crucial difference is that the beat is not marked, as it is in "Satisfaction," and in "Get Off of My Cloud," their other No. 1 hit from 1965. In the later songs, the rhythms are still highly syncopated, but they are reacting mainly to Charlie Watts's regular marking of the eight-beat rock rhythm, not the beat.

Rock's most characteristic groove builds off of regular timekeeping at eight-beat speed, with a strong backbeat but little or no marking of the beat. Other rhythms play off against the eight-beat rhythm, not the beat. It is the interplay between eight-beat timekeeping, the backbeat, and syncopations and other forms of rhythmic conflict that produces the compelling rhythms of rock. Heavy marking of the beat was a retention from fifties rock and roll and R&B. By the late sixties, it was the exception, not the rule, as numerous subsequent examples will show. The Rolling Stones were among the first to lock into this new groove, and no one has done it better.

Like "Jumping Jack Flash," "Honky Tonk Women" uses the end-weighted form common to so many rock-era songs. In this respect, both are more conventional than "Satisfaction." But a comparision of the two songs shows that they realize the basic form in quite different ways. To cite one difference: the chorus in "Jumping Jack Flash" is delineated not only by the melodic change and the addition of voices, but also suddenly active harmony, while in "Honky Tonk Women" the boundary is drawn by the addition of bass and pedal steel guitar. Here the Stones' imagination and innovation is revealed in their manipulation of an established formal plan, rather than the creation of a new kind of form.

The two songs also illustrate common harmonic options in sixties rock. "Jumping Jack Flash" uses modal harmony, while "Honky Tonk Women" puts a new spin on the I/IV/V chords used so frequently in country music.

These three Rolling Stone songs do not show the full range of their music. Almost from the beginning of their career, the Stones also explored a softer side of rock in songs like "As Tears Go By" and "Ruby Tuesday" and, in emulation of the Beatles, its "symphonic" side in "Sympathy for the Devil" and "You Can't Always Get What You Want." Nor do they account for important work later in their career. However, the three examples do shed light on the Rolling Stones' most significant contribution to rock.

No group did more to define rock's core, its essential value, and its new attitude. More important, they brought the musical tools needed to express this attitude. The Stones' sound was the result of teamwork. What they did best, they did as a group. Foremost is their rock-defining groove, which grew out of the interaction among all the band members. The loose, somewhat unkempt texture is a close second. Although Jagger is the visual focus of the band, there is no one whose virtuosity dominates the sound. Finally, there are the sounds—most notably Jagger's singing and Richards's guitar playing—that project the Stones' particular kind of insolence.

THE ROLLING STONES AND THE BEATLES   The Rolling Stones are inextricably paired with the Beatles. Linked by time, place, overwhelming popularity, and surpassing musical importance, they seem opposite in every other respect. The Beatles were children of provincial working class families whose successful career represented several steps up in class. The Rolling Stones came together in London, the center of British culture. They defined their image by stepping *down* in class. Jagger led the way in this respect, dropping out of the prestigious London School of Economics and being portrayed as the devil incarnate by the end of the sixties.

Their career paths followed opposite trajectories. Within a year of their invasion of America, the Beatles were the most visible band in rock. *A Hard Day's Night* and their appearance on the *Ed Sullivan Show* made their images as accessible as their recordings. But they played their last concert in 1966, retreating to the recording studio and growing apart personally and musically, as the "White Album" documented. They disbanded four years later. By contrast, the Stones have stayed together for an eternity—at least in rock years. Moreover, they have continued to remain accessible, mounting elaborate tours that continue to be financially and artistically successful.

In what they communicated and how they communicated it, they were polar opposites—by design. The Beatles exemplified high spirits and good, mostly clean fun; they were pranksters at worst. In contrast, the Stones—by design—crossed the line. They turned impudence into insolence, peace and love into aggression and overt sexuality.

Musically, they seemed bound in a yin/yang relationship. The Beatles stretched rock's boundaries in numerous directions, while the Stones' best work led to the defining of rock's center. At the time, the Beatles' work was trendier. Their constant explorations into new musical territory inspired similar experiments from others, including the Stones, and secured them almost universal critical approval.

In retrospect, however, the Stones' music from the 1960s has been far more influential on post-Beatles rock. So many of the major trends of the seventies and eighties—heavy metal, punk, hard rock—owe much more to the attitudes and sounds that the Rolling Stones introduced than they do to the music of the Beatles. Even more important, the Stones perfected the sound of rock and roll. Their music became the primary reference for any band in search of (in Huey Lewis's words) "the heart of rock and roll."

The point here is not to denigrate the Beatles' considerable achievement. Rather, it is to adjust critical perception to accommodate the also-considerable achievement of the Rolling Stones. When they anointed themselves the "World's Greatest Rock and Roll Band" in the early seventies, the Stones were merely stating what was common knowledge.

Solo-Oriented Rock

While the Stones polished their group-oriented musical style, other musicians on both sides of the Atlantic were developing another strain of blues-influenced rock. Theirs was a more solo-oriented approach. Like the Stones, Eric Clapton, Jeff Beck, Jimmy Page, and, above all, Jimi Hendrix drew heavily on the blues. But these great guitarists took one additional element from blues: the use of the guitar as the bluesman's second voice.

Throughout the recorded history of deep blues, the guitar had been a melody instrument as well as a harmony and rhythm instrument in support of the voice. From Blind Lemon Jefferson on, bluesmen would answer sung phrases with vocal-like guitar lines or showcase the guitar's melodic capabilities in an instrumental solo. It was this last function—the guitar as expressive solo voice—that resonated so deeply with Hendrix, Clapton, and the others, who brought it into rock.

The guitar had been a solo instrument in rock and roll, featured routinely in Chuck Berry and Buddy Holly recordings, as well as in instrumentals such as the Ventures' "Walk, Don't Run" and Dick Dale's early surf music. Chuck Berry's solos remain models of their kind, but they are riff-based. Dale's guitar lines contain novel effects, like the low-register scale that slithers and snakes down the fingerboard. However, none are vocally inspired. In retrospect, they seem somewhat limited in their exploration of the expressive potential of the electric guitar.

During the same period, electric bluesmen such as Guitar Slim, Buddy Guy, and Freddie King (one of Clapton's idols) played the guitar in a style that paralleled their raw, earthy singing, exploiting such novel effects as severe distortion to do so. Drawing inspiration from these blues masters,

Hendrix and Clapton took these newfound capabilities several steps further. In so doing, they transformed the electric guitar into the transcendental solo instrument of rock.

Jimi Hendrix

Jimi Hendrix grew up in Seattle, Washington, which is about as far away from the Mississippi delta as one can get and still be inside the continental United States. However, the blues were as close as his father's record collection, which also included a fair amount of jazz. Both would be profound influences on his playing.

After a hitch in the Army, cut short by a back injury suffered in a parachute jump, Hendrix began his musical apprenticeship by working in the backup bands of a wide variety of black performers: bluesman B. B. King, Little Richard, saxophone great King Curtis, the Isley Brothers, and Jackie Wilson.

In 1966, Hendrix formed his own band, Jimmy James and the Flames. They were heard in New York by ex-Animals bassist-turned-talent scout Chas Chandler, who encouraged Hendrix to come to England. When he arrived, Chandler introduced him to bassist Noel Redding and drummer Mitch Mitchell, who began jamming with Hendrix. Soon they were performing on the London club scene as the Jimi Hendrix Experience. Their first hit, "Hey Joe," released in the fall of 1966, made Hendrix a star almost overnight. Their

Jimi Hendrix, c. 1968. PHOTO COURTESY *CORBIS/HULTON-DEUTSCH COLLECTION.*

first album, *Are You Experienced?*, released early in 1967, secured Hendrix's reputation in England. A spectacular performance at the 1967 Monterey Pop Festival spread his reputation throughout the United States. For the remainder of his too-short career, he cemented his reputation as rock's most influential and innovative soloist.

Hendrix was one of rock's most flamboyant performers. Like the bluesmen who inspired him, he developed many showy ways of playing the guitar, including through his legs, behind his neck, during a somersault, and almost any other place that he could hold the instrument. Onstage, his guitar was an erotic instrument as well as a musical one, No rock musician before him had so graphically connected the guitar with male sexual potency.

However, his most memorable visual moment came at the Monterey Pop Festival, when he drenched his guitar in lighter fluid and set it on fire. His red guitar, flickering with flames, remains one of rock's most enduring visual images.

Arresting as these visual images are, the most important part of Hendrix's legacy is, of course, his music. There he made clear both his deep indebtedness to the blues and his breakthroughs in sound and style that transformed it into a powerful new rock style. We hear first how Hendrix played the blues.

"Red House," a track on Hendrix's first album, is a straightforward electric blues. It uses conventional blues form and the slow shuffle rhythm so common in blues songs. Both the melody and Hendrix's singing are very much in the electric blues mainstream. The words are forgettable and relatively unimportant—in fact, when he performed the song in concert, Hendrix often changed the lyrics to suit the occasion. Especially at this tempo, they could be improvised in performance, and often were. The melody is like so many others: half-sung, half-spoken, starting high, finishing low. Underneath Hendrix's singing, the other two musicians remain locked into their roles—triplets and a heavy backbeat from drummer Mitch Mitchell, boogie-woogie-based bass lines from Noel Redding—throughout most of the song. Its basic sound could be heard spilling out of countless Chicago bars.

These conventional features merely serve as a backdrop to Hendrix's guitar playing; that's where the spotlight shines. From the first note, it's clear that Hendrix's playing comes straight out of the blues, the kind of blues he would have heard when working with B. B. King. But his conception goes beyond that sound in several respects. The very opening phrase has the sharp edge that a little distortion gives. Later in the solo, he sustains several notes (a feat only possible with electrical modification of the signal), adding intensity to them with a fast, wide vibrato, straight out of Robert Johnson, but with the volume turned way up. Interspersed between them are rapid running figures, based mainly on the "blues" pentatonic scale. The ease with which he tosses them off makes clear his virtuosic command of the instrument.

His response figures played on the guitar during the sung sections might be called "hypervocal": vocally-inspired, but well beyond his singing in their expressive range. They are more intensely expressive than his vocal lines, nastier in sound, more inspired melodically, and certainly more agile. In this context, Hendrix's virtuosity is functional, an expressive tool that he uses when a single note doesn't convey the power and energy that he needs.

Hendrix's solo puts all aspects of his breakthrough guitar style on full display: facility, evidenced most clearly in the rapid repeated figures; numerous special effects, such as bent notes, reverb and echo, and extra distortion; and his exploration of the upper range of the instrument. They show the ways in which his style transcended the blues.

If "Red House" connnected Hendrix's music to its blues past, then "Purple Haze" put it squarely in the psychedelic present of 1967 and forecast important future directions. "Purple Haze" is Hendrix's best-known song, for several good reasons: it contains evocative verbal images and memorable melodic material, and it is among his most clearly outlined forms.

"Purple Haze" begins ominously with a power chord gone south. The slight compression of the basic power chord interval removes all of its inherent resonance; the sound is stultified. The interval used in the opening idea (often called a tritone, because it divides the octave in half) has a long and notorious history in music. In medieval times, it was known as "diabolus in musica" (devil in music). Whether Hendrix consciously made this connection, or simply felt intuitively the appropriateness of the interval, there is a diabolical undercurrent in the song. It surfaces in the phrase, "cast a spell on me" (she must be a witch) and is also suggested musically in Hendrix's solos, especially the final one.

One of the hallmarks of the new solo-oriented rock style pioneered by Hendrix and Clapton was a shift in the balance of power: the guitar became more important than the voice. The shift is most obvious in the emphasis on improvised solos, but it is also reflected in the overall design of the song.

Hendrix makes this shift clear right from the start. Typically, rock songs from the sixties begin with a vocal, like "Eleanor Rigby," or a short introduction built from an instrumental riff, like the Rolling Stones' "Satisfaction." So do blues songs like Muddy Waters' "Hoochie Coochie Man."

By contrast, "Purple Haze" begins with not one but three different introductory elements. There is the opening tritone; a series of eight phrases, based mostly on melodic permutations of a four-note rhythm; and finally a nicely grooved guitar figure.

The voice seems secondary when it enters; the instrumental riffs overpower it. Only in the stop-time sections is the voice in the spotlight—in the first of these, Hendrix delivers one of rock's most enduring lines, "'Scuse me, while I kiss the sky." And even here, the voice is immediately answered by another strong, easily remembered riff. The balance shifts even further to the guitar side in the contrasting section. Here, Hendrix half-sings, half-screams "help me, help me," which underscores Hendrix the relatively rational singer being overrun by Hendrix the demonic guitarist. The voice trails off as Hendrix launches into his first solo.

"Purple Haze" is a study in opposites. The most obvious opposition is Hendrix the vocalist vs. Hendrix the guitarist. But there is also an interesting formal opposition: a clearly structured and well-articulated design, especially at the beginning of the song, vs. the almost uncontrollable frenzy that grips Hendrix during his solos. Indeed, the first solo ends abruptly with a return to the original four-note riff: we can almost see/hear Hendrix snap out of his spell, at least for a moment.

The formal design—several sections that juxtapose tight control in ensemble passages with virtuosic abandon in solos—would become a model for heavy metal. So would Hendrix's virtuosity, which metal bands like Led Zeppelin, Aerosmith, and Van Halen also brought into ensemble passages.

"Purple Haze" is also a primer for the new harmonic approach that surfaced in the hard rock of the late sixties. Much rock and roll in the fifties relied on harmonic progressions derived from the major (i.e., "Joy to the World"/"Do-Re-Mi") scale used in pre-rock pop, although blues chords occasionally include notes outside the main scale.

By contrast, Hendrix builds chords in the "groove" (third introductory) section on the notes of a minor pentatonic scale, the same scale he uses for his riffs in the previous section. Along with the modally derived chords in "Jumping Jack Flash" and the power chords of the early Kinks' hits, Hendrix's use of chords based on a pentatonic scale signals the beginning of a new harmonic conception in rock. In combination, both approaches were influential. They helped liberate rock from the tyranny of pop harmony.

In their wake, the major scale-based harmonies of pop became a seldom-used option among many, instead of the common practice. The advances of Hendrix, the Stones, and other like-minded bands also encouraged further harmonic experimentation, as we'll hear in subsequent examples. (Interestingly, white rock has been more adventurous harmonically than black music during the rock era. Even James Brown, the most progressive black artist of the time, does not explore alternative harmonic options to the extent that hard rock bands did.)

If "Purple Haze" best represents Hendrix the composer, then "Voodoo Child," from the Experience's third and final album, *Electric Ladyland*, shows Hendrix the performer at his most inspired and imaginative.

"Voodoo Child" is an ideal showcase for Hendrix's abilities, because it draws on the blues, jazz, and rock-era song that informed his music. These multiple sources of inspiration are evident in both the form and style of the song. It is inspired by the blues, yet also suggests connections with rock-era song in its form, and with jazz in the virtuosity of his improvisation.

The vocal section contains four phrases. The first three could be the lyric for a twelve-bar blues: statement, repetition, rhyming line. The fourth is a refrain, the title phrase that sums up each section of the lyric. In essence, Hendrix appends a refrain onto a twelve-bar blues to bring the form of the song into the rock era.

His harmonization of the form is also a highly individual mix of old and new, mixing a new take on blues harmony with modal progressions.

However, it is Hendrix's brilliant improvisations that are the spiritual focus of the performance. They are virtuosic to a degree matched only by jazz in the popular music tradition before rock. (Indeed, toward the end of his life, Hendrix immersed himself in the music of John Coltrane, one of jazz's great virtuosos as well as its most progressive voice in the sixties, and collaborated with fusion guitarist John McLaughlin, who also recorded with Miles Davis at this time.)

The quality that stands out above all is Hendrix's astounding variety. It is most apparent in his improvisatory strategies and range of sounds. Hendrix does not limit himself to any particular improvisatory style—e.g., a fast-moving single line melody, or variations on a riff. Instead, he roams over the entire range of the instrument, interweaving sustained bent notes, rapid running passages, riffs, and chords in a dizzying sequence.

Just as masterful is the dazzling array of sounds he draws from his guitar—an inventory of the sound possibilities of the instrument. They range from the pitchless strummings of the opening of "Voodoo Child" and the biting sound on the rapid repeated intervals on the bottom strings (at about 2 minutes 30 seconds) to the sustained high-note wails, distorted chords, and hyper-vibrated notes in his solos. And he mixes them together in dizzying sequences that seem completely spontaneous in their unpredictability.

Hendrix plays in technicolor—there are times when almost every note has a sound that's different from the ones around it. Both the degree and frequency of sound variety far exceed that heard in earlier improvisation-based styles—indeed, such variety was not possible before Hendrix began to exploit the potential of the electric guitar.

Hendrix's solos represent a new kind of virtuosity, one that emerges from the particular demands of rock improvisation. In them, he elevated sound variety to a level of interest comparable to pitch and rhythm, and he enormously expanded the vocabulary of available sounds. In a Hendrix solo, how a note sounded became just as important as its pitch and rhythmic placement. In so doing, he built on the expressive sounds of the blues and the virtuosity and melodic inventiveness of jazz, merging and transforming them into the definitive improvising style in rock.

Hendrix's legacy was his playing. It not only helped define rock-based improvisation, but also helped redefine the possibilities of improvisation within popular music. It echoes through much of the music of the seventies and eighties, not only heavy metal and hard rock, but also punk (listen to the quick repeated interval at about 2 minutes, 30 seconds in "Voodoo Child"), funk, and disco. (The pitchless musings at the beginning of the song were quickly mutated into the choked guitar sound heard in black-oriented film and television soundtracks, most notably in Isaac Hayes's music for *Shaft*, plus countless disco and funk songs.) Others have built on it, but none have surpassed it in imagination and originality. It remains the standard of rock guitar playing.

Eric Clapton

The other guitar god of the late sixties was Eric Clapton. Because they were the dominant soloists of their time, Clapton and Hendrix are inextricably linked. Despite their strong connection in time, place, and purpose, they were two quite distinct musical personalities.

Some of the differences between Hendrix and Clapton may have grown out of their early exposure to the blues. Hendrix grew up with the blues, hearing it as part of a broad spectrum of black music that also included jazz and rhythm and blues. Clapton approached the blues with the fervor of a convert, especially after his encounters with American bluesmen.

During the sixties, Clapton refined and purified his blues conception, especially during his short stint with John Mayall's Bluesbreakers in 1965–1966. The purity of this conception was important to him: He had left the Yardbirds just prior to joining Mayall when the band moved away from blues towards psychedelic rock.

By the time he formed Cream in 1966, with bassist Jack Bruce and drummer Ginger Baker, Clapton had developed into rock's premier virtuoso soloist. He was the first major rock performer to play extended, improvised solos, especially in live performances. To accommodate his solo excursions, Cream dispensed with the rhythm guitar. It was the first of the "power trios": lead guitar, bass, and drums, but no chord instrument. Their success proved the viability of this new format.

Cream's version of Robert Johnson's "Crossroads," recorded live at San Francisco's Fillmore Auditorium in 1967, showcases both Clapton's

George Harrison and Eric Clapton perform together at the Concert for Bangladesh, August 1, 1971. Photo courtesy Corbis/Bettmann.

inventiveness and the virtuosic interplay among the band members that made their chordless sound work, at least in live performance. Cream made no attempt to re-create, or even evoke, Johnson's recording. Only the lyrics remain from Johnson's version—and even some of those are changed. Tempo, beat, volume, accompaniment, and virtually every other significant variable are radically changed from the original. However, faithfulness is not the issue here; inspiration is. The song is an excuse to jam.

"Crossroads" is really about Clapton's solo conception. Here, it is as powerful as a piledriver. Clapton's solo has an intensity that is relentless from beginning to end. The two vocal choruses that appear in the middle and toward the end interrupt its drive, but do not deflect it. Clapton begins the solo in a middle register, with riffs and melodic figures that move at a moderate speed, for the most part. Chorus by chorus, he moves up in register and increases the activity of his lines, although he typically signals the beginning of a new chorus with more sustained notes. After the vocal "interlude" (about 2 minutes, 10 seconds), Clapton resumes his solo with renewed intensity: moving higher, using double notes, speeding up the rhythm, adding syncopation. He mixes these in varying proportions until he brings the solo to a climax.

A comparison of Hendrix's solo in "Voodoo Child" with Clapton's solo in "Crossroads" contrasts two quite different approaches to improvisation within rock. Hendrix's solo playing is like a fireworks display. There are new sounds firing off in almost random profusion. Clapton's playing is more focused than flamboyant. As we have heard, it is remarkable for its sustained, inexorable drive to the climax reached just before the final vocal section.

Both players teach important lessons about improvisation in rock. Hendrix's style may have been more influential, but that's partly because many of its features, especially the effects, are easier to imitate. Constructing a solo in Clapton's style takes a special kind of imagination and concentration, plus complete command of the instrument. Constructing a solo as Hendrix did requires a different but no less demanding kind of inspiration.

Cream became a different band in the studio. The demands of AM radio airplay, with its three-minute target, constrained Clapton's solo excursions. Their material gravitated toward the then-fashionable psychedelic rock, although it still retained a strong blues connection. And, through the miracle of overdubbing, the band acquired additional instrumental voices without additional personnel, most notably, Clapton on rhythm guitar.

"Strange Brew," not a singles hit but one of their best-remembered studio recordings, shows the studio side of their musical personality. The lyric has psychedelic overtones—what is the "strange brew"? But the real story is in the music. Here the blues influence runs deep, yet it's transformed into one of the most influential rock sounds of all time.

This transformation process is evident in the song itself, as well as its performance. Words and melody superimpose the refrain/frame form onto a blues progression. Like several of the Chuck Berry songs, it combines the verse/refrain idea with the harmony of the twelve-bar blues. In this instance, the last four measures support the refrain, while the first eight underpin the narrative sections of the lyric. In a nice touch, the first eight bars of the song are instrumental, so that the refrain, which comes at the end of the blues progression, is the first vocal section we hear—as well as the last.

The vocal sections in turn frame Clapton's solo. It is brief: only a single chorus. And, perhaps because it is so brief, Clapton does not get up a head of steam, as he does on "Crossroads." Still, it is a masterpiece in its understated way—almost Clint Eastwood-like in the terseness and impact of its statements.

Playing such as that heard on "Crossroads" and "Strange Brew" put Clapton in the vanguard among rock guitar soloists. Even more innovative, however, are Clapton's riff-derived accompaniment, Bruce's syncopated bass lines, and the loose-jointed rhythm that they create. Clapton's repeated riff is a textural breakthrough for rock. From Chuck Berry on, rhythm guitarists had typically played chords. Usually they surfaced as some kind of boogie-woogie derived pattern (Berry, Holly), strummed (Beatles, Rolling Stones), or arpeggiated (Dylan, Beatles). Clapton's alternative, while certainly based on chords, breaks away from the rhythmic and melodic regularity that is customary in rhythm guitar parts. In this respect, it is more like a repeated riff in an electric blues than anything commonly found in rock and roll.

Similarly, the texture created by the riff, Clapton's lead guitar line, and Bruce's bass line resembles the intertwined melodic strands of the electric blues style heard in the Muddy Waters examples. (The connection shouldn't be surprising because Clapton claimed Waters to be his major influence.) At the same time, the concept is considerably updated, not only by the shift to rock rhythm, but also the emancipation of the bass line.

Bruce's bass line is even freer than Clapton's riff: it is highly syncopated and never settles into a completely predictable pattern. Prior to Bruce, only sixties black music—Motown (especially James Jamerson's bass lines), soul, and James Brown—had routinely featured such freely constructed and synco-pated bass lines.

This freedom also extends to the rhythm. The basic beat is the eight-beat rhythm of rock, but all three instruments occasionally include patterns that move twice as fast as the basic rock beat. The most persistent and obvious is Clapton's riff, but there are also occasional double time patterns in the drum part (a variant of the "fatback" beat so popular in soul music) and the double time break toward the end. The double-time rhythms open up new paths toward greater rhythmic complexity. They also underscore one of rock's most admirable qualities. The best rock has never been content with the status quo; its leading musicians were exploring and stretching its boundaries even as the music was just coming together.

Taking Stock of Rock

The music of the Kinks, Stones, Hendrix, and Cream is rock, without qualifi-cation. All of it, and especially the music of the Stones and Hendrix, has given us some of rock's most indelible sounds and images.

At this point, it may be useful to ask, what is rock? An easy answer is "What you hear on just about any of the songs in this chapter." Certainly, the sound of power chords and heavy riffs, played with distortion on a heavily amplified guitar, could be nothing but rock. But what about the music in the previous three chapters? What do we make of Motown, or Beatles' songs such as "Norwegian Wood" and "Yesterday," or Dylan's own version of "Mr. Tam-bourine Man"? All are also commonly considered rock.

In fact, "rock" has three widely used connotations. The broadest is "all the new music of the rock era." This meaning distinguishes rock from pop, jazz, Broadway musicals, country music, and other pre-rock styles. A second, more restrictive meaning of rock distinguishes the mostly white music of the sixties from black music: rock vs. Motown and soul. The most narrow meaning comes from the music of this chapter: "pure" rock.

We can identify each meaning of rock by what it says and how it says it. At each level, the music expresses certain points of view and makes musical choices. We will examine both aspects, identifying common features, and con-trasting it with the style(s) to which it is being compared.

Rock, the Music of the Rock Era

The music that came to maturity during the 1960s expressed new attitudes in a rich new musical language. Pop's impersonal, often sentimental expressions of love largely disappeared. In their place came Dylan's cryptic songs, love thwarted and love-never-found songs ("When a Man Loves a Woman," "I Heard It Through the Grapevine," "Norwegian Wood," "Satisfaction"), slice-of-life songs ("A Day in the Life," "Honky Tonk Women"), state-of-the-groove songs ("Papa's Got a Brand New Bag"), et al.

These songs were more personal, in part because songwriters so often sang their own songs, and because the songs were the recordings they made. But the rock stars of the sixties often tried to say something in their songs, sometimes spelling it out in direct language ("R-E-S-P-E-C-T"), other times couching it in images and metaphors that challenged their audience. Both their attitudes and the ways they expressed them were a clear departure from the conventions of pop. Mainly for this reason, we consider much of Dylan and the Beatles' music to be rock, even though it may not evidence many of rock's musical elements.

This new music also had common musical ground, features that grouped Dylan with Sam and Dave but not Sammy Davis, the Byrds with James Brown but not Joni James. Two stand out above all: the beat and the singing styles. Most of the songs in these last four chapters have a rock beat. This feature cuts across all the boundaries: white/black, pop-oriented/soulful/statement-making, etc. The basic beat does take wildly different forms. The rock beats in "I Want to Hold Your Hand," "Purple Haze," and "I Feel Good" are realized in quite different ways, but the rhythmic foundation is the same. In the sixties, a rock beat was the surest sign that a song was up-to-date—or trying to be.

There is even more variation among the vocal styles, from Diana Ross's almost breathless singing to Dylan's and Hendrix's barely singing. They are united by what they aren't: pretty, pop-style singing. All, even the Supremes, have at least a little grit, a little soul.

Almost all of these singers would have been "unacceptable" vocal styles for pop. (An important exception: Aretha began her career as a pop singer, and was good at it.) It is difficult to imagine Dylan singing "If I Had You," for example. However, the reverse is also true. Pop vocalists sounded out of place singing rock.

The range of vocal styles is perhaps the most obvious clue to rock's more pragmatic and democratic approach to musical communication. It was pragmatic because the overriding criterion was: does the sound work for this song? It was democratic because anyone could sing a rock song, so long as the sound fit the style and the song. It is difficult, for example, to imagine anyone other than a soul singer singing "When a Man Loves a Woman," and Dylan, for all his vocal limitations, sang Dylan better than anyone else.

Paul McCartney's recording of "Yesterday" clearly exemplifies this new attitude and approach. The song has been covered countless times, more than any other song in history. Many of the singers are more highly trained. But is there a more affecting performance of the song than his original version?

This democratic, pragmatic attitude extends to other musical elements: instrument choice, texture, and form. Virtually all songs use the nuclear rhythm section—guitar, bass, drums—as the point of departure. However, the juxtaposition of finger snaps and symphonic violins in the Motown songs, the cowbell in "Honky Tonk Women," the massed string sound at the end of "A Day in the Life," the crowd noises in several songs: all express in different ways the idea that instrumentation responds directly to the needs of the song or the style. The use of distortion, which turned a liability into a desirability, shows how this idea also extended to the way one played an instrument.

Both the balance within the texture and the widespread distribution of melodic interest offer additional evidence of this approach. Almost every song has at least one instrumental hook; in some cases (e.g., "I Can't Turn You Loose," "Purple Haze") it is the most memorable hook. Further, in most cases, at least one of the instruments is as prominent as the lead vocal line, and on some occasions, the band all but drowns out the singer.

Rock is, at its core, a collective music. A song exists not only in melody and harmony, but in the interplay of all the elements. As a result, a performance requires everyone's participation to be effective. Although a pop song can be effectively performed by a singer and pianist or a full orchestra, a rock performance begins to lose something with the subtraction of even a single part.

Most of the songs discussed in the last several chapters use some variation of a verse/refrain form, either a refrain-frame form or an end-weighted form. Rock's pragmatic approach shows up mainly in its formal flexibility. This is especially evident in songs such as "Satisfaction" and "Pretty Woman," where the basic patterns are altered significantly to underscore the message of the song in music.

To review briefly, we expect rock songs from the sixties to express an emotion or describe a situation in lyrics that are typically direct and unsentimental. We also expect them to:

- be sung in a singing style with at least a touch of grit, and typically quite a bit;

- have a rock beat;

- have a varied mix of instruments, with at least one prominent rhythm instrument;

- have an interdependent texture, with melodic interest shared among voice and instruments; and

- use some version of a verse/refrain form.

All of these qualities reflect the new, more pragmatic attitude toward what rock could say and how it said it.

Rock vs. Rhythm and Blues

"Rock" also commonly identifies much of the rock era music made by white musicians, as opposed to the black music of the same period. As with rock vs. earlier styles, two of the big differences are lyric content and vocal style. Black songs of this period tend to discuss romance, or at least the possibility of romance. In white rock, such songs are the exception, not the rule. Those who sing the black music of the sixties betray some gospel influence. Very little of the white singing has echoes of gospel style: blues, perhaps, but not gospel.

There are other more subtle distinctions. In black music, the bass is the most likely rhythm instrument to stand out; guitar and drums tend to be more in the background. In white rock, the guitar is, of course, king. Black music of the sixties typically includes horn sections; white rock doesn't. In part because the bass is so often the strongest instrumental part, the texture in black music tends to be open, with light timekeeping and a relatively thin middle register sound. White rock, by contrast, tends to have a much thicker sound, because of the prominence of the guitar(s) and heavier timekeeping.

Interestingly, no umbrella term for black music has emerged during the rock era. Rhythm and blues is a holdover from pre-rock times. Much black music of the 1960s and beyond is more than just rhythm and very little of it is blues. Labels for individual genres have arisen: e.g., Motown and soul in the sixties. But there was no new label that encompassed all of black music, as rock (in its second meaning) did for white music.

Rock = Hard Rock

At the heart of white rock is a body of music that is unquestionably rock. One could argue that such songs as Dylan's "Rainy Day Women #12 & 35" and the Beatles' "Eleanor Rigby" are rock only because they are by Dylan and the Beatles. This is, on one level, a rather flimsy assertion, because so many of the style cues are absent: e.g., the beat or the typical instruments. However, no such argument would exist with "Jumping Jack Flash" or "Strange Brew." All of the features we most associate with rock are present: a rock beat; a densely interwoven texture; prominent, distorted guitar; a rough vocal style; and above all the rebellious attitude communicated by the musicians.

This sound was *completely* new. There were, of course, precedents for every feature, but no one had put the whole package together until the mid-sixties, when the Kinks, the Rolling Stones, the Jimi Hendrix Experience, Cream, and other like-minded bands did so. With their music, rock, in its most focused connotation, was defined for all time.

Summary

These three meanings of "rock" are the central reference points in this book. From each meaning, we can look to the past, present, and future. We can observe how the disparate influences described in Chapter 2 coalesced into the family of new styles we call rock. In Chapter 12, we will see how established styles updated their sound with infusions of rock style elements. And throughout the rest of the book, we can relate the music we hear back to this moment, when everything came together to create a vibrant new musical language.

KEY TERMS

Blues Revival	Distortion	Power trio
Trad-jazz	Modal-derived harmony	Collective music
Endless-loop form	Guitar god	Interdependent texture

CHAPTER QUESTIONS

1. Listen to "You Really Got Me," "Jumping Jack Flash," and "Purple Haze." Find the common features among the three songs. Using this information, formulate a set of expectations for a rock song.

2. Compare "Honky Tonk Woman" with "Strange Brew." What differences can you notice between group-oriented and solo-oriented rock besides the guitar solo?

3. Write out the lyrics of "Jumping Jack Flash" and "Honky Tonk Woman" as you listen to the songs. Draw a line separating the verse from the refrain. In each song describe as specifically as you can the sound in the verse and the refrain in each song (the way the beat is marked, the overall rhythmic feel, the instruments used, etc.). Then compare your sets of observations. Do your findings confirm or refute the point made in the text about outlining form?

4. Find 15-20 seconds in the guitar solos of "Voodoo Child" and "Crossroads" that you like. Use these excerpts to formulate your own description of the similarities and differences between Hendrix and Clapton's approach to solo playing in rock. How does your description compare to the one in the text?

5. Create a playlist of about 10 songs from your personal record collection. Try to make the selections as varied as possible. Then, assign them to one of four categories: one of the three meanings of rock, or non-rock. Justify your choices by considering both words and music.

Rock Dresses Up

The music of the two previous chapters highlighted two important trends in sixties rock: artistic aspirations and deepened roots. Although the inspiration for these trends came from opposite ends of the social and cultural spectrum, their relationship was more complementary than oppositional. It was more a matter of how much of each, rather than either/or.

We hear both of these directions realized in numerous ways in the next three chapters. In this chapter we touch on several expressions of rock as significant statement: rock opera, "dark side" rock, rock parody, glam rock, art rock, and progressive rock. In Chapter 10, we see rock expand its roots search, not only in the blues, but also in country music. Heavy metal, discussed in Chapter 11, drew on both blues and art music precedents, sometimes in the same song. We begin with the Who.

The Who

No group of the sixties merged rock's essence with rock as art more effectively than the Who. The Who came together as a group in 1964. A year later, their music began to appear on the British charts. Their early hits, most notably "My Generation" and "Substitute" (both 1966), speak in an ironic tone; indeed, "My Generation" became the anthem for the "live hard/die young/don't trust anyone over 30" crowd. Musically, they were a powerhouse band with a heavy bass sound that betrayed the strong influence of sixties rhythm and blues. Pete Townshend's power chords, John Entwhistle's virtuosic bass playing, and Keith Moon's flamboyant drumming gave Roger Daltrey's searing voice a rock-solid foundation. Still, it seemed that they were no more than a singles band, incapable of anything more than a series of good three-minute songs. That perception began to change with the release of the album *Happy Jack* (1967), which included an extended piece, "A Quick One While He's Away," and was dramatically altered with the release of the "rock opera" *Tommy* in 1969.

Townshend, the most intellectually adventurous member of the band, had been interested in expanding the Who's horizon's beyond pop stardom. When Kit Lambert, the group's producer and manager, suggested almost offhandedly that Townshend compose a rock opera, he took the idea and ran with it.

Opera is the most spectacular and prestigious of classical music genres. Labeling *Tommy* a rock opera immediately implied its highbrow status, even if

The Who on stage, c. 1975. PHOTO COURTESY CORBIS/NEAL PRESTON.

the label was misleading. As Richard Barnes points out, "Strictly speaking, [*Tommy*] isn't a rock opera at all. It has no staging, scenery, acting, or recitative."

It doesn't have much of a plot, either, and what plot there is is difficult to follow. Still, the story—of a deaf, dumb, and blind child who becomes a messiah via pinball wizardry—unfolds in the songs, by fits and starts.

The songs don't pull any punches. The list of subjects addressed in *Tommy* includes (again, according to Barnes) "murder, trauma, bullying, child molestation, sex, drugs, illusion, delusion, altered consciousness, spiritual awakening, religion, charlatanism, success, superstardom, death, betrayal, rejection, and pinball." Not typical fare, even for the late sixties, but certainly a logical extension of the Who's efforts in *Happy Jack*.

Musically, what's remarkable about *Tommy* is not so much the fact that the Who make an artistic statement, but how they make it. Unlike the Beatles and so many who followed in their footsteps, the Who didn't abandon their rock roots, nor merely overlay them with classical music trappings. There are no strings, no synthesizers, or other classical music features associated with so much of the art rock of the period.

Instead, the band remains pretty much self-contained: the most obvious non-rock sounds are Moon's timpani, Entwhistle's French horn, and Townshend's various keyboard sounds. Instead of adding an orchestra's worth of instruments, they vary the sounds within the group. As he shifts from character to character, Daltrey displays extraordinary vocal flexibility, from the soul-drenched grittiness of "Smash the Mirror" to the tenderness of "See Me, Feel Me." Townshend and the rest of the band play classic hard rock in songs like "Sparks," yet the instrumental "Overture" and "Underture" contain steely acoustic guitar playing—alternately gritty and sensitive, and always imaginative.

The other feature that immediately sets *Tommy* apart from standard rock fare is the pacing of the work. The tracks are as long as they need to be. There is no allegiance to the three-minute song. The shortest "song" is "Miracle Cure"; it is 12 seconds long. And it is one of seven tracks well under two minutes. The longest track is the magnificent "Underture" (10 minutes, 9 seconds), which divides the work in half—like the first and second acts of an opera. The irregular rhythm of the tracks is clear evidence that Townshend is responsive to the dramatic demands of his subject, rather than the conventions of popular song.

In *Tommy*, the Who have the best of both worlds, in two ways. They make an artistic statement on a grand scale (75 minutes long) without forsaking, or even downplaying, their rock roots. Moreover, they were able to perform *Tommy* live without hiring a symphony orchestra, because they stayed within the group's basic instrumentation. It was a unique achievement, for the Who and for rock. Their subsequent "operatic" efforts, most notably *Quadrophenia*, did not enjoy similar success, and no other band produced anything comparable.

The lessons they learned creating *Tommy* carried over into all their work. For example, "Won't Get Fooled Again," a hit from their 1971 album, *Who's Next*, shows both their arty and hard-rocking sides. The organ-like keyboard layer, which begins as a series of kaleidoscopically changing chords, makes the opening sound like progressive rock. The opening soon gives way to some nasty rock and roll; and the keyboard part, with its relentless rhythm, works like a rhythm guitar when it's layered in with the rest of the band. In an absolutely unique way, the Who merged rock's heart with its head, reaching down to its roots and up to the sky.

Rock as Art

In this century, one of the first objectives of an emerging popular style is to legitimize itself. Early in the century, this was done by "classicizing" popular music, or reinterpreting classical music in the new popular style. Examples of the former were Scott Joplin's ragtime opera, "Treemonisha," and George Gershwin's *Rhapsody in Blue*. The Chopin-derived popular song "I'm Always Chasing Rainbows" (1918) is an early example of the latter; so was Jack Fina's swing-era hit, "Bumble Boogie," based on Rimsky-Korsakov's "Flight of the Bumble Bee." Rock used a different approach, as we'll see below.

There are two main reasons that this has occurred, one social and cultural, the other musical. An association with classical music made musical social climbing possible. Its use, or at least its obvious influence, narrows or eliminates numerous gaps—racial (white/black), generational (old/young), cultural (traditional/novel), economic (rich/poor), class (highbrow/lowbrow)—that separate the new style from established ones. The musical reason is more mundane but no less compelling. Good musicians are creative. They are often eager to explore new possibilities, or reinterpret the past in terms of a vibrant new present.

Rock emerged at a time when the traditional view of "classical" music was under assault from several directions. Both jazz and the Broadway musical had attained a kind of "art music" status by the late fifties; the orchestral albums of Miles Davis; third stream music, which attempted to fuse jazz and classical music; and Leonard Bernstein's musical *West Side Story* are illustrative. Moreover, "high" art's expressive boundaries had been severely stretched since World War II in such developments as the chance music of John Cage, *musiqué concrete*, the minimalist music of La Monte Young, and, in the visual arts, the abstract expressionism of the "New York School" and the pop art of Andy Warhol.

For many in the avant garde, the function of art was simply to make a significant statement about something. It didn't necessarily require the conventions or materials of high art, e.g., a symphony orchestra. Instead, artists took a pragmatic approach to the means: In the case of Cage, for example, it could be no more than sitting quietly for four-and-a-half minutes.

This attitude seeped into rock, particularly after Dylan. It was *what* you said that counted, rather than what means you used to say it. There were no inherently privileged methods. In fact, one of rock's self-imposed challenges was to create new ways to make a statement. That began with Dylan, as we have seen: words that said something important, set to simple yet powerful music. That also became a kind of art.

A second art-like option emerged in the early seventies: art as spectacle—what was called glam rock. This had classical precedents—especially the lavish operas of the Baroque era—if not direct classical models or sources.

Classical/rock fusions were a third important direction. These were realized in diverse ways by Frank Zappa, progressive rock groups such as Pink Floyd and Yes, and heavy metal bands such as Deep Purple. We consider these options below and in Chapter 11.

Rock's Dark Side

While the Beatles were singing "All You Need Is Love," other rock groups were exploring the darker side of the rock revolution. Three stand out: the Doors, the Velvet Underground, and Frank Zappa's Mothers of Invention. Each explored different territory. The Doors explored (in their words) "the other side": nightmarish conflations of sex and death. The Velvet Underground rode Lou Reed's lyrics to portray the underbelly of life in New York. Zappa visited the dark side with his tongue firmly in his cheek. He was rock's supreme satirist, ready to pop everyone's bubble.

Despite these artists' obvious differences in subject and approach, their songs shared two important features. The words, and the way they were sung, were of primary importance, and the music that supported the lyric explored new territory. The level of musical craft varied widely, but each of the bands tried to match the message of the lyrics in sound.

The Doors

The Doors came together in 1965 through a meeting of two UCLA film students. After Jim Morrison read one of his poems to keyboardist Ray Manzarek, they decided to form a group. They soon added drummer John Densmore and guitarist Robby Krieger. Morrison named the group the Doors after Aldous Huxley's book, *The Doors of Perception*, a reference that was probably lost on much of their audience.

The Doors had a meteoric rise and a slow, painful fall. Their first album, *The Doors*, hit the charts in 1967, reaching No. 2 and establishing the group's reputation almost overnight. Five years later, it was over. Morrison, who had taken a leave of absence from the group and moved to Paris, was found dead in a bathtub. Without Morrison, the group floundered, eventually disbanding two years later.

The Doors performing in Frankfurt, Germany, September 13, 1967. PHOTO COURTESY
CORBIS/BETTMANN.

"Light My Fire" and "The End," two of the best-known songs from their
first album, show the hot/cool tension in early Doors performances. In "Light
My Fire," this tension is apparent from the outset. The opening of the song,
which features Manzarek's busy, classical-sounding organ introduction, creates an emotionally neutral backdrop for Morrison. His lyric, sung in a throaty
style, starts as a come-on. But in the second section of the song, Morrison
links what is patently sexual "fire" to filth ("mire") and death ("pyre").

THE END This contrast is even stronger in "The End," an 11-minute excursion
into Oedipal conflict and its most violent resolution. With its East Indian overtones, the musical setting is more low-key than that heard on "Light My Fire."
The beginning sounds like background music for an acid "trip." The opening of
Morrison's long, rambling discourse is histrionic in the words, if not the music.
The middle section offers an extended metaphor ("ride the snake"), abstruse
images ("the blue bus is calling us") and clichés ("the west is the best"). The juxtaposition of images and the musical drone underneath have an almost hypnot-
ic effect. Morrison's switch to clear narrative is like waking up from a nightmare,
except that the awakened state *is* the nightmare. The musical chaos of the fatal
climax (about 2 minutes after Morrison the narrator announces that "I'm going
to kill you") gives emotional credibility to the song's moment of truth.

Morrison's shock-provoking lyrics and his intense, often histrionic vocal
style convinced his audience that he spoke about the confluence of death,
decadence, and sex from personal experience. The emotional detachment of

the rest of the band, especially Manzarek, only served to bring Morrison's words and singing into sharper relief. For popular music, songs such as "Light My Fire" and "The End" opened the door to life's underbelly.

From their first album, the Doors, and especially Morrison, were on the edge. In fact, Morrison lived out the dramas he wrote about in his songs: extreme alcohol and drug abuse, increasingly flagrant public obscenity, and finally death at 27, allegedly by a heart attack. Morrison's willingness to go to the edge, to immerse himself in a self-destructive lifestyle and publicize it in his music and behavior, to risk—even invite—spectacular failure and public humiliation (rock critic Lester Bangs once described Morrison as a "Bozo Dionysius"), put him in a category by himself. It made almost everyone else's music seem tepid by comparison.

The Velvet Underground

The Velvet Underground invite comparison with the Doors. Both took a long walk on the wild side. But the Doors were based in southern California, while the Velvet Underground were part of the New York scene. The Doors were popular; the Velvet Underground were known only to a few. The Doors, and especially Morrison, who fancied himself a major literary figure, aspired to high art. The Velvet Underground started with the support of the high priest of pop art, Andy Warhol, who created the famous peelable banana cover of their first album.

Lou Reed brought his literary sensibility to the group, as well as his low-key vocal delivery and guitar playing. John Cale, a classically trained violist and composer who had worked with avant-garde minimalist LaMonte Young in the early sixties, was the main source of its original sound. Guitarist Sterling Morrison and drummer Maureen Tucker rounded out the rhythm section.

Warhol produced their early records. To promote the group, he set up the "Exploding Plastic Inevitable," a potent mixture of film, dance, and musical performance. Nico, a blonde European-born actress who was part of Warhol's circle at the time, was with the band for their tour and first album, *The Velvet Underground and Nico* (1967). Given her limited vocal ability, her function within the band might seem to have been only visual ornament. In fact, however, the combination of her icy beauty and lispy, labored singing may have been a Warholesque artistic statement: a poor man's Marilyn Monroe for the rock era.

The Velvet Underground owed an obvious debt to Dylan. Both the primacy of words and Reed's flat, largely uninflected delivery recall Dylan. So does the mood-setting accompaniment, which harks back to Dylan's early electric days (just two years previously).

However, it's clear that Reed and Velvet Underground found their own voice. Reed's lyrics are usually incisive where Dylan's are often elliptical. In "I'm Waiting for My Man," for example, Reed needs only a few short phrases to portray a white guy so strung out that he ventures into Harlem to get his next fix. Each phrase comes to life, as if it were a scene from a film. Where Jim Morrison used a club, Reed used a needle to get his point across.

The musical context has a strong connection with rock, especially Dylan. However, it also grows out of Cale's work with the avant-garde minimalist composer La Monte Young. Indeed, one of the miracles of the Velvet Underground's conception is that the musical backdrop for Reed's vocals can be so powerful, yet allow his words to come out so clearly. The propulsive beat of "I'm Waiting for My Man," a jangly conjunction of sound and rhythm driven by Cale's two-fisted piano playing, is an ideal example.

Even more spectacular is "Heroin," where Cale's viola mutates from a drone into an avant-garde–inspired frenzy to depict the drug coursing through the bloodstream of its user. In its own way, "Heroin" is just as powerful in its evocation of the drug experience as "The End" is in its evocation of the violent resolution of an Oedipal conflict. Both songs use similar techniques—changing tempos, piling on textural layers—to depict a moment of terror or, in the case of "Heroin," a moment of terrible ecstasy.

The Velvet Underground's tenure was even shorter that the Doors'. Cale left after the second album, and the group dissolved soon after. Reed has enjoyed intermittent success as a solo artist and has built a cult following. So did the Velvet Underground, although most of the cult joined after the group's demise. Despite their modest commercial success, the group was a major influence on punk.

Frank Zappa and the Mothers of Invention

The Doors and the Velvet Underground made their reputation by exploring rock's dark side; Frank Zappa and the Mothers of Invention made theirs with dark humor. They took their humor seriously, however: both the words and music of their "songs" can be sophisticated as well as slapstick.

The fun begins with their name, a double pun: Necessity may have been the mother of invention, but "mother" was also street slang for a highly skilled performer—and something else.

Zappa was rock's great iconoclast. He was an equal opportunity satirist, taking potshots at almost everyone in and out of rock, including himself. At the same time, he was one of rock's cleverest and most knowledgeable minds and one of its great innovators. In addition to using rock as a vehicle for satire, he also pioneered multimedia extravaganzas, which he called "freak outs," concept-type albums (McCartney claimed that *Freak Out* [1965] influenced The Beatles' *Sgt. Pepper*), and wholesale eclecticism.

Zappa collected musical influences from everywhere. Among the most important was the French/American avant-garde composer Edgard Varèse. In a Zappa record, one might hear Varèse-influenced music juxtaposed with a fifties rock and roll parody. Such jarring contrasts were one of his innovations. Zappa was also one of the pioneers of jazz-rock fusion, working with violinist Jean-Luc Ponty.

As with the Doors and Velvet Underground, words are the main focus when they are present. You have to listen to Zappa's lyrics; often the music seems to be strictly at the service of the words. Nevertheless, his compositions are in many ways the most sophisticated music of the rock era. They demand great technical proficiency and stylistic flexibility from the musicians who play

A note on the cover of *We're Only in It for the Money* shows how seriously Zappa expected his listeners to take his fun. On it, he demands that they read Kafka's *The Penal Colony* before listening to the album.

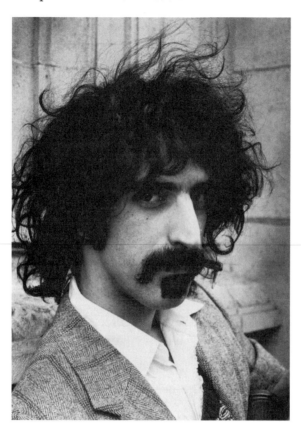

Frank Zappa, February 10, 1971. PHOTO COURTESY CORBIS/HULTON-DEUTSCH COLLECTION.

them. Not surprisingly, his bands included some of the most accomplished and versatile musicians of the era.

Although his first album, *Freak Out*, immediately established him as a unique voice, it was his third album, *We're Only in It for the Money* (1967), that best represented his early work, in the judgment of many commentators. Zappa's tool was a needle, which he used to pop lots of balloons. Deflation begins with the album cover, a sendup of the cover of the Beatles' *Sgt. Pepper*. On it, the group is wearing dresses and the wax figures have become mannequins: one is "giving birth" to a baby doll. Their gallery includes Jimi Hendrix and Lyndon Johnson and assorted cultural icons, many of whose eyes are covered with black rectangles, perhaps to suggest a kind of self-imposed censorship.

We are aware from the outset that *We're Only in It for the Money* is not a conventional album, i.e., a collection of songs. There are, of course, songs. But there are also numerous spoken sections, accompanied by electronic noises (track 1), conventional instruments ("Who Needs the Peace Corps"), or no instruments at all ("Telephone Conversation"). In addition, there are extended instrumental sections.

There is a dazzling virtuosity in the variety. To cite just two examples: The instrumental opening of "The Chrome Plated Megaphone of Destiny" sounds more appropriate for an avant-garde classical music album than a rock disc, while the opening of "Who Needs the Peace Corps" sounds like a children's song.

Zappa's lyrics can be devastating as well as devastatingly funny. The spoken section of "Who Needs the Peace Corps" parodies a definitely uncool guy mapping out his hippie lifestyle in San Francisco.

The biggest zinger, though, is probably "What's the Ugliest Part of Your Body?" The song begins with "Earth Angel"-style background vocals. Their pseudo-innocence only enhances the impact of the punch line. The next few minutes show Zappa's strategy: musical and verbal collage with jarring verbal and musical juxtapositions. He follows the revelation that your mind is the ugliest part of your body with some pompous sermonizing, accompanied by music in an irregular pattern (2 + 2 + 3 quick beats vs. the standard 2 + 2 + 2 + 2 pattern of rock). A question about "Annie" (who is she, and what is she doing in this song, anyway?), accompanied by a slithering melody in waltz rhythm, interrupts the sermon. A piano solo that reaches back to Aaron Copland and ahead to New Age music links the sermon with the next song, which begins with a snotty-toned definition of "discorporate," but not before a woman mutters a snide aside about the limitations of her sexual activity.

It is a dizzying pace, because of the abrupt shifts between segments—the Mothers never miss a beat—and because of the extreme contrast between styles. If it were possible to get whiplash just listening to music, Zappa would be the one to give it to us.

Zappa's lyrics were also often intentionally juvenile and scatalogical, as if to deflate his own high-art intentions. His often silly titles—such as "Peaches en Regalia"—for very sophisticated music was another self-deflating strategy. Many critics missed the seriousness of the music and only focused on the often puerile lyrics—which for Zappa must have been part of the joke. It was as if you had to pass through a series of "tests" to prove yourself a true Zappa fan and listener.

All of this renders Zappa's music, considered as a whole, less accessible than *Sgt. Pepper*. There are certainly accessible moments: The parody songs and monologues stand out (perhaps this is why Zappa scored his only major hit with the silly parody song, "Valley Girl"—hardly his most innovative work). But this is not warm and fuzzy music, or music that you can groove to. As his album cover makes clear, Zappa demands a commitment from his listeners.

That gives the title of the album a certain irony. It's quite clear that money is not a major motivation for Zappa. He and the Mothers were certainly skilled enough to have created music that would have kept them firmly entrenched in the Top 40 charts. But that would have required some selling out and the sacrifice of his unique vision. Zappa did neither during his lifetime. He took it upon himself to become rock's fiercest social critic as well as one of its most imaginative musicians and its greatest humorist; no one else was even close.

"Glitter"/"Glam" Rock:
Rock as Spectacle

Rock has had a strong visual element since Elvis first combed his hair into a pompadour, curled his lips into a sneer, and twitched his hips. It had certainly acquired a theatrical element by the late sixties. Pete Townshend routinely

> There is an interesting precedent for the androgyny of David Bowie and Marc Bolan in eighteenth-century opera. Women's roles were played by *castrati*, male singers who were castrated as boys to preserve their soprano range.

smashed his guitar in performance. Iggy Pop (born James Osterberg), who was fronting the Stooges, took outrageous behavior several steps further. The Stooges exposed themselves, mutilated themselves, vomited on their audience, and worse.

This theatricality was in part a consequence of larger venues. With arena concerts now increasingly common, performers had to appear larger than life to have visual impact. Bands began touring with elaborate sets, special effects (lighting, smoke bombs, fireworks), and larger-than-life costuming.

The most spectacular form of theatrical rock was "glitter" or "glam" rock, which emerged in the early seventies, mainly in the work of David Bowie and T Rex, a group fronted by Marc Bolan.

As rock became more theatrical, the personae of many of its performers became more outrageous. Elvis's hip-wiggling was suggestive enough—for the fifties—that he was shown only from the waist up during some of his early television appearances. But that was tame stuff compared to Jagger's strutting, Hendrix's guitar antics, and Iggy Pop's vulgarity. Although it was outrageous enough to leave audiences wondering about the person's identity—is he really like that in person—it never challenged the ultimate identity question: gender.

Both Bowie and Bolan stripped identity down to this most basic issue. It has been suggested that their androgyny was a response to the excesses of the sexual revolution. However, it can also be understood as an extension of sixties outrageousness. When Morrison exposed himself, he made his gender explicit. When Bowie pranced around onstage in heavy makeup and a big feather boa, he put his gender—or at least his sexual preference—seriously in doubt.

David Bowie

Bowie (born David Jones) began his career in the sixties as a British folksinger. Influenced by Iggy Pop, Marc Bolan, and the Velvet Underground, he began to reinvent his public persona. In 1972, he announced that he was gay. (However, he commented in an interview over a decade later that he "was always a closet heterosexual.") Later that year, he put together an album and a stage show, *The Rise and Fall of Ziggy Stardust and the Spiders from Mars*. It featured Bowie, complete with orange hair, makeup, and futuristic costumes, as Ziggy, a rock star trying to save the world but doomed to fail.

Ziggy was Bowie's first and most outrageous persona. For the rest of his career, he has continually reinvented himself in a variety of guises, all markedly different from each other: "plastic soul" man, techno-pop avant-gardist, etc. Bowie has been rock's ultimate poseur. And that has been his art: assuming so many different personae—not only in appearance and manner, but also in music—that he has made a mystery of his real self. Given Bowie's constantly changing roles during the course of his career, it is small wonder that he has been the most successful film actor among post-Elvis rock stars.

Bowie is intensely involved in all aspects of his roles, including the music. After recording at Philadelphia's Sigma Sound Studios (in the seventies, it was the home of "The Sound of Philadelphia"), he changed his stage show completely—from flair to bare—and incorporated sixties soul classics into his set. But at the same time, there is also detachment. Listening to his music and the words to his songs, we hear both first and third person.

ZIGGY STARDUST The songs from *Ziggy Stardust* provide the musical dimension of Bowie's role playing. Their effect is not as obvious as his appearance, but without them, his persona would be incomplete. The songs have three components: the words, Bowie's singing, and the musical backdrop. All assume multiple roles, as we hear in "Hang on to Yourself."

The lyric is laced with vivid images: "funky-thigh collector," "tigers on vaseline," "bitter comes out better on a stolen guitar." These arrest our ear, without question. But Bowie continually shifts from person to person as he delivers them. He "reports" in the verse—"She's a tongue-twisting storm"—and entreats in the chorus—"Come on, come on, we've really got a good thing going . . . ." His voice changes dramatically from section to section. It's relatively impersonal in the verse, and warm, almost whispered in the chorus.

The music is more subtle in its role-playing. Bowie embeds vocal and instrumental hooks into all his songs. The instrumental hook is the guitar riff; the vocal hook is the whispered chorus, a shock after the pile-driving verse. Both features make the song immediately accessible and memorable.

But there are also subtle clues woven into the song that seem to tell us that, for Bowie, the hooks are the "dumbed down" parts of the music. With such features as the extra beats after the first line of the verse ". . . light machine" and elsewhere, Bowie seems to be hinting that he's capable of a lot more sophistication than he's showing on the surface. Indeed, the spare style of the song was one of the freshest and most influential sounds of the seventies. Like Ziggy, he is descending down to the level of mass taste (even as he's reshaping it) because he wants the effect it creates, not because that's all he can do.

In *Ziggy Stardust*, Bowie creates a persona that demands attention but is shrouded in mystery. What makes his persona so compelling, both in person and on record, is not only its boldness but its comprehensiveness. Precisely because accessibility and ambiguity are present in every aspect of the production—the subject of the show, Bowie's appearance, the lyrics, his singing, the music—Bowie raises role-playing from simple novelty to art. This quality made him one of the unique talents of the rock era.

Bowie was also one of the most influential musicians of the decade. The "lean, clean" sound of "Hang on to Yourself" was a model for punk and new wave musicians.

Rock as Art and Art Rock

Rock began as a dance music. As its musicians aspired to a higher status, rock also became a listening music. People typically danced to "The Twist" but simply sat and listened to "Subterranean Homesick Blues" or "Eleanor Rigby." This change from functional music—music to accompany another activity,

Interestingly, almost all of the progressive rock bands were British. Critic John Rockwell attributes this in part to the relatively greater prestige enjoyed by classical music in British society. In his view, rock musicians who wished to elevate their artistic status could do so by adapting classical values and procedures to rock. He feels that the pressure to do so was far stronger in the United Kingdom.

In the United States, it was jazz fusion that followed a similar path, as we will discover in the next chapter. Guitarist John McLaughlin, a Scotsman who recorded with Miles Davis, straddled the two styles.

such as dancing—to non-functional music—music strictly for listening—raised the esthetic bar. Rock had to have more than a good beat. It had to be inherently interesting on several levels, and challenging to its audience.

Following the lead of the Beatles, a fair amount of late sixties and early seventies rock embraced this new esthetic. Others copied both ideas and materials: the concept album, songs that merged into one another, non-danceable tempos, "real life" voices and noises, electronic sounds and effects, as well as orchestral accompaniments and other classical-sounding expropriations. The results ranged from Procul Harum's "A Whiter Shade of Pale," which mixed rock and Bach, and Keith Emerson's reworking of Mussorgsky's *Pictures at an Exhibition*, to King Crimson's modernist uses of irregular meters and atonality.

Pink Floyd

Certainly the most successful and enduring effort of this kind was Pink Floyd's 1973 album *Dark Side of the Moon*. At the time of this recording, Pink Floyd consisted of guitarist David Gilmour, percussionist Nick Mason, keyboardist Richard Wright, and bassist Roger Waters; Waters wrote most of the songs. In the album, they created an attractive mix of novel electronic effects (the heartbeat that opens the album, the washes of sound in "On the Run"); "life" sounds and voice overdubs ("Speak to Me," "Money"); art rock-features (e.g., seven-beat measures in "Money", a wide range of tempos, connections between songs); and accessible, often soulful rock (most notably the vocal on "The Great Gig in the Sky"). Their formula worked: the album remained on the U.S. Top 200 charts for 741 weeks—over 14 years. No album has charted for a longer period of time.

Progressive rock

Because of the electronic effects and other features associated with art rock, some commentators have labeled Pink Floyd an art, or progressive, rock band. Other commentators have taken a more limited view of progressive rock. They have insisted that true progressive rock requires more extensive adaptations of classical music practices: extended length; traditional compositional techniques, such as counterpoint (two or more independent melodic lines); irregular rhythms; and virtuosity.

With these additional expectations, the roster of progressive rock groups shrinks considerably. Among the noteworthy groups of the early seventies were Emerson, Lake, and Palmer; Genesis; Gentle Giant; Jethro Tull; King

Crimson; and Yes. Of these, Yes was the best known. The band, formed in 1968 by singer Jon Anderson and bassist Chris Squire, underwent two key personnel changes in 1971: keyboardist Rick Wakeman replaced Tony Kaye, and guitarist Steve Howe replaced Tony Banks. Drummer Bill Bruford was an earlier recruit. *Fragile* and *Closer to the Edge* (both 1972), their first two albums with the new lineup, were their most successful; "Roundabout," from *Fragile*, was their most popular single of the decade.

While not mapped out on the broad scale of their later music, "Roundabout" nevertheless provides a helpful introduction to the qualities that defined progressive rock during this period. First, it's clear that the music is the most important dimension of the piece. There are extended instrumental sections throughout, and the lyric of the vocal sections is so vague and non-referential as to be virtually meaningless. However, the words do provide milestones for listeners navigating their way through this lengthy song: "Roundabout" is over eight minutes long, only a third of the length of Yes's longer works (which often covered an entire album side), but about three times the length of the average single.

Its sprawling form, the numerous contrasts, and the flashes of virtuosity also set the song apart from more mainstream rock. "Roundabout" is a big, multi-sectional piece. An extended slow introduction sets it in motion; its return (ca. 4 minutes, 37 seconds) with an organ obbligato marks the midpoint of the piece. There are several changes of texture and key, and occasionally shifts away from the regular four-beat measures. The most striking occurs in the "choral" section (ca. 8 minutes), which has measures with seven beats. Virtuosic ensemble passages, solos, and fills occur throughout: the doubled guitar/bass duet (ca. 6 minutes, 15 seconds), Wakeman's fast fills (ca. 2 minutes, 25 seconds), and Squire's well-grooved bass riff under the first vocal section are good examples.

Despite these departures from common practice, "Roundabout" never loses sight of the fact that it is rock. The gentler sections help the "groove" sections stand out because the contrast is so strong. Indeed, the second melodic idea, which sets "in and around the lake," uncannily anticipates Kool and the Gang's 1981 hit "Celebration"; they even share the same key.

Progressive rock took a good deal of criticism from some quarters as being pretentious, overproduced, and symptomatic of the decline of rock in the seventies. What this song shows, however, is some very capable and inventive musicians at play, stretching rock's boundaries.

Summary

We have surveyed an extraordinarily diverse group of rock acts: the Who, the Doors, Velvet Underground, Frank Zappa and the Mothers of Invention, David Bowie, Pink Floyd, and Yes.

What stands out about their music is the enormous contrast from act to act. There were acts who bared themselves, body and soul (Morrison and the Doors), and acts who hid both behind an artful facade (David Bowie). There were bleak portraits of urban life (Velvet Underground), and parodies of flower power (Frank Zappa). There was music where words mattered intensely (Zappa, the Doors, etc.) and music where words were almost an afterthought (Yes). There was music with cutting edge technology (Pink Floyd), virtuoso music (Yes, Zappa), and music that was artfully basic (Velvet Underground, the Who, David Bowie).

Compared to Top 40 rock, most of it unfolded on a grand scale. *Tommy* was the grandest of all, but we have also heard several 8- to 12-minute songs, songs streamed together, concept albums, and the like. It is one signal that these acts took themselves and their music seriously, even when they were having fun.

These are linked by their desire to make a significant statement about something, and by the distance most—even the Who—had moved from rock and roll. In their attempts to fulfill their artistic aspirations, they took chances—emotionally, intellectually, and musically. They succeeded often enough that their music stands apart from much of the music of the sixties and seventies. The best of it was memorable and influential.

KEY TERMS

Rock parody	Art rock	Avant-garde
Glam rock	Progressive rock	Concept albums

CHAPTER QUESTIONS

1. Quickly write down an answer to this question: "What is art?" Keep it to a paragraph or two. Then review each of the acts discussed in this chapter. To what extent does their music conform to your definition of art?

2. "Art music" is generally music for listening, rather than dancing, marching, working, riding elevators, and so on. Explore this idea by comparing the rhythmic texture, and in particular the marking of the beat, in "The Twist" with songs by three acts that are discussed in this chapter. Summarize what you learned from the comparison. Can it be stated as a hypothesis?

3. Bob Dylan and the Beatles are generally considered the two main sources of artistic aspiration in rock. Review each of the acts discussed in this chapter, and come to an opinion on the extent to which each has been influenced by Dylan, the Beatles, or another source. Justify your decisions, based on what you've learned about the music of Dylan and the Beatles.

4. Read a definition of "art rock" in a reference. Then play devil's advocate and eliminate at least two of the acts discussed from consideration in this chapter because their music doesn't seem to agree with the definition. Identify those features that prompted your decision.

c h a p t e r 1 0

Rock Deepens Its Roots

The flip side of rock's artistic aspirations was the deepening of its roots. Some of those who helped ground rock securely grew up with roots music. Hendrix and the Allman Brothers stand out in this regard. Others absorbed rock's sources into their music through apprenticeships of various kinds. We have already noted the influence of "deep blues" on the Rolling Stones and Eric Clapton and other important British guitarists. In the United States, study of the past and present was more varied: Guitarist Mike Bloomfield hung out in Chicago blues bars; Gram Parsons of the Byrds immersed himself in country music; Jerry Garcia played in a jug band. Their work and the work of like-minded musicians strengthened and updated the connections between rock and its root music: blues and country.

Because they had more direct contact with country music and soul, many American rock bands in the late sixties and early seventies had a sound quite different from British rock. We will survey four key trends:

- The U.S. blues revival and its influence
- The development of an "American" sound in the music of Creedence Clearwater Revival, the Grateful Dead, and the Band
- Southern rock
- Country rock

The Blues Revival

A U.S. blues renaissance also gathered momentum in the late sixties. One important consequence was the increased popularity of urban blues. In particular, B. B. King found his stock soaring. He became the emissary of the blues to white Americans, crossing over several times to the pop charts, most notably with "The Thrill Is Gone." He remains a household name.

There were several centers of blues-related activity. Chicago, naturally, was one; there, Paul Butterfield's blues band, featuring guitarist Mike Bloomfield, held sway. But blues-influenced rock flourished elsewhere in the late sixties, especially in California and the South. We have already mentioned the Doors' interest in the blues; Los Angeles was also home to Canned Heat. In

San Francisco, there was already an active blues scene when Janis Joplin arrived there. However, her impassioned singing brought it national attention. Other San Francisco-based bands, most notably the Grateful Dead and Creedence Clearwater Revival, also borrowed from the blues, but their music included numerous other influences.

Janis Joplin

Janis Joplin migrated to San Francisco during the mid-sixties, like many other young musicians of the time. Born in Port Arthur, Texas, she began performing in coffeehouses in her native state before traveling to California in 1965. There, she began performing with a local blues band, Big Brother and the Holding Company. A rather motley crew, the group made an enormous impact at the 1967 Monterey Pop Festival, thanks to Joplin's dynamic stage performance. Signed to Columbia Records, they cut one album which was widely praised for the quality of Joplin's vocals, while the band was criticized for its ragged playing. Joplin soon separated from the band, and became an important solo act for the rest of her brief life. She died of a heroin overdose in 1970.

Joplin was rock's original blues diva. She was the first white woman to sing with the supercharged passion of Bessie Smith and the other classic blues singers of the twenties. That kind of power had been absent from women's singing in popular music since Smith's demise. However, what distinguished her singing from everyone else's, even the classic blues singers, was the rawness of her sound and the sheer exuberance of her performing style. She had a voice that often sounded like it had been raked over broken glass, although she could also sing as tenderly as any crooner. She combined that with a unique kind of vocal virtuosity. With its stutters, reiterations, rapid fire streams of words, melismas, interpolations, and the like, it is almost operatic in its exhibitionism.

Her cover of Bessie Smith's "Ball and Chain" shows these qualities in abundance. She begins in a subdued manner—a kind of homage to Smith, who

Janis Joplin on stage at the famous Woodstock festival, August 16, 1969. Photo courtesy CORBIS/Henry Diltz.

simply delivered the words with great feeling. But even here, the extroversion that was so much a part of her onstage personality cannot be held completely in check: she hisses out the word "sitting," and adds little melismas within the phrases of the song. To some extent, these flourishes are necessary. Joplin's voice is not as rich as Smith's, and the tempo of the song is slower, so there is musical space that must be filled with sound. But the flourishes are mainly there because they are part of her musical personality, as the rest of the performance shows. As the song unfolds, she becomes less and less restrained, eventually unleashing her full bag of tricks.

Although Joplin thought of herself as a blues singer, most of the songs that she recorded were not blues, at least in the formal sense. Unlike the classic female blues singers of the twenties, who recorded mainly conventional blues songs, Joplin recorded a wide range of material. However, she brought blues feeling and style into everything she recorded, blues or not. "Piece of My Heart" (1967), one of the most popular of her early recordings, shows this. Her delivery of the first phrase of the song ("didn't I make you feel . . .") is straight out of the blues; the wonderfully expressive blue note on "you" is classic.

American Rock and Roll

In the late sixties, San Francisco was the spiritual home of the counterculture, and home to many of its members. Hippies congregated at the intersection of Haight and Ashbury, wishing passersby peace and love, practicing free love, smoking dope, and tripping on LSD.

Providing the soundtrack for all of this activity was an incredibly diverse group of bands. The roster included not only Joplin and Big Brother and the Holding Company, but also Jefferson Airplane, the Steve Miller Band, Santana, Sly and the Family Stone, Moby Grape, Creedence Clearwater Revival, and the Grateful Dead.

The most popular venue was the Fillmore, an old ballroom that Bill Graham used to stage dances, then concerts. The concerts were not a series of three-minute hits, but long, rambling sets, fueled by various kinds of drugs.

We have already discussed Joplin's singing, and we will discuss Santana and Sly and the Family Stone in subsequent chapters. Here we focus on two quite different bands, Creedence Clearwater Revival and the Grateful Dead. Both project an "American spirit" in their music, but in quite different ways.

Like so many British rock bands, the two groups dipped heavily into the blues, rhythm and blues, and fifties rock and roll. However, the ingredient that gives each its American sound—that distinguishes it most clearly from British rock—is country music. Musically, the country influence shows up particularly in the scales on which many of the songs are based, the spun-out melodies, and the guitar riffs. All these influences form a kind of musical stew: we can identify the seasonings, but can appreciate the result fully only by experiencing how they all blend together.

Creedence Clearwater Revival

Unlike many other San Francisco bands, Creedence Clearwater Revival was a Bay Area band because its members grew up there. The four band members—John Fogerty, lead guitar; Tom Fogerty (John's older brother), rhythm guitar;

Stu Cook, bass; and Doug Clifford, drums—grew up in the East Bay, northeast of San Francisco. Beginning in junior high school as the Blue Velvets, they finally incarnated themselves as Creedence Clearwater Revival in 1967, and released their first album a year later. They were immediately successful: for three years they were the hottest singles band in the country.

Regarding the best songs of Creedence Clearwater Revival, Griel Marcus writes "[they] literally define rock and roll—as a musical form, as a recurring event, as a version of the American spirit." Three songs, "Proud Mary," "Fortunate Son," and "Up Around the Bend," show the band at the peak of its powers and reveal their essential Americanness in words and music. The opening riff of "Proud Mary," among rock's most memorable ten-second sound slices, perfectly illustrates the fusion of blues and country influences.

Recall that much country music is harmonized with just three chords—I, IV, and V. These three chords differ only on the notes on which they are built: the first, fourth, and fifth notes of the scale. Many blues songs use these same three chords, as we have learned. However, in most blues songs the basic chords are colored with additional notes, which make the chords sound more African American. In the opening riff of "Proud Mary," however, Fogerty retains the basic, "countryish" form of the chord, and uses it to harmonize the African-American pentatonic scale. This apparent country retention makes Fogerty's riff stand apart from many other pentatonic riffs of the period, especially those of British bands. These were typically harmonized with power chords (e.g., the opening of "Jumping Jack Flash") or not harmonized at all (e.g., Cream's "Sunshine of Your Love").

Both words and music also suggest a seamless mix of black/white roots. "Proud Mary" is, of course, a steamboat traveling up and down the Mississippi. Fogerty's song paints a romantic picture of river life. Moreover, the race of its protagonist is unclear: Fogerty is, of course, white, but "the man" is black slang for a boss.

Most of the time, Fogerty's melody noodles around the first three notes of the Anglo-American pentatonic scale, much like the minstrel songs of Stephen Foster: "Oh, Susanna" and "Old Folks at Home" ("way down upon the Swanee River") are good examples. This choice of notes helps give the song an "American" sound. So do the country-ish guitar riffs.

At the same time, there are clear African-American elements. The texture of the song is dense and highly syncopated: the rhythm guitar pattern plays a key role here. There's a nice bent note on the word "proud"; it is most expressive note in the song, in part because it goes outside the Anglo-American scale. And then there's Fogerty's singing, which resonates with Little Richard's influence.

From the beginning of "Proud Mary" to the end, Fogerty blends the two folk traditions seamlessly. It is their presence, especially the country elements, that help Creedence Clearwater Revival achieve their distinctive, hard-driving rock and roll sound.

"Up Around the Bend," another of their American-themed hits, is, if anything, more country-influenced than "Proud Mary." The striking guitar riff that opens the song simply outlines chords, and the melody of the song uses only the notes of the Anglo-American pentatonic scale. "Fortunate Son," by contrast, has a more modern sound, with power chords and modal harmonies. Perhaps their use has to do with the contemporary subject of the song. It is a scathing indictment of well-to-do young men who used their parents' influence to avoid military service in Vietnam.

CCR was not a typical San Francisco band. They offered tight singles instead of rambling drug-juiced jams. Their Bay Area base was an accident of birth, not a choice, and—unlike the Beach Boys, for instance—they didn't regionalize their sound. Their unique style was all-American.

The Grateful Dead

Keeping Creedence company in the Bay Area were the Grateful Dead. For most of their career, the band consisted of guitarists Jerry Garcia and Bob Weir, harmonica player "Pig Pen" McKernan, bassist Phil Lesh, and drummer Mickey Hart. Lyricist Robert Hunter, who didn't perform with the band, collaborated with Garcia, Lesh, and Weir on most of their memorable songs.

On the surface, it might seem that the Grateful Dead and Creedence Clearwater Revival were as opposite as two "American" bands could be, despite their conjunction in time and place. Where CCR was best known for its short singles, the Grateful Dead made their reputation through long concerts—up to five hours—that featured extended solos, especially by Jerry Garcia. CCR was on the outside of the San Francisco music scene. By contrast, the Dead were the quintessential San Francisco hippie band: they lived communally for years, ingested copious quantities of trendy drugs, and played all the time, often for free, especially in their early years. CCR had a huge, largely anonymous fan base. The Grateful Dead, who didn't chart a single

Grateful Dead, c. 1966.
PHOTO COURTESY
CORBIS/BETTMANN.

until 1987 (!), slowly built an extremely loyal cult following, the Deadheads, who would travel from concert to concert to hear the band, in part because each concert was likely to be different.

Nevertheless, there is an "American-ness" about the Grateful Dead and their music. If CCR explored America's romantic myths and images, then the Dead represented the iconoclastic individualism that is also part of the American character. The Dead followed their own muse, instead of striving for mass popularity. Their route to success was unique in the history of rock.

Their songs often project an American character, in both words and music. Two songs from *Workingman's Dead* (1970), widely regarded as their finest album, are good examples. Both "Uncle John's Band" and "Casey Jones" tap into enduring American images: the country fiddler as pied piper, and trains, respectively. However, they drop autobiographical hints into what would otherwise be rather impersonal accounts, so that both songs mix general and particular, and then and now.

"Uncle John's Band" tells a long, slowly unfolding story, a la Woody Guthrie and Pete Seeger. The music that supports it evokes both the folk revival and Harry Belafonte-ish calypso, until the line "come follow Uncle John's Band." At that point (ca. 3 minutes, 30 seconds), the music abruptly switches to a pseudo-East Indian sound that briefly creates a Haight-Ashbury atmosphere. The implication seems to be that Uncle John's band is a thinly-disguised cover for the Grateful Dead. In "Casey Jones," the song begins with a sniff—presumably of a line of coke. And the references to cocaine and speed suggest that the train and its engineer are a thinly disguised allegory about the dangers of excessive drug consumption—their own included.

Musically, the songs mix white and black influences. This is not surprising, given Garcia's start in a jug band and his ongoing involvement with country music, as well as the Dead's earlier incarnation as a blues band. However, the mix is more eclectic here. From the Anglo-American side there are country, folk, and bluegrass elements in their music. Both songs rely almost exclusively on the major scales and chords of country and folk music, rather than the modal sounds of hard rock. And the mandolinish guitar obbligato on "Uncle John's Band" evokes bluegrass.

The black influences include not only African-American music but Latin and Caribbean sounds, particularly in the rhythms and additional percussion instruments heard on both songs. Then there are special touches that are pure Dead: harmonic surprises, like the sudden shift up to a higher chord in the second phrase of "Casey Jones," the foreshortened rhythms in "Uncle John's Band" at the end of the first two phrases in the melody, and above all, the loose-jointed rhythmic feel of the two songs.

It should be noted that neither of these recordings is "trademark Dead": the sprawling, largely improvisational performances that kept the Deadheads on the road with them. However, the songs, and the album from which they were taken, are representative of the Dead's "American" synthesis. For samples of the Dead in live performance, listen to "Turn on Your Love Light" and "One More Saturday Night."

The Grateful Dead didn't have the "mainstream" American sound of Creedence Clearwater Revival, but they had their own version of an American sound. In their collective persona, the management of their career, and, most of all, in their songs, they followed the less-traveled road. That it included their own blend of Anglo-American and African influences only makes it that much more American.

The Band: "Honorary Americans"

It is a nice irony that the most comprehensively American-sounding band consisted of a drummer from Arkansas and four Canadians. Levon Helm, the drummer, had moved to Canada in 1958 with a group of Arkansas musicians to back Ronnie Hawkins, who started off as a country singer but moved over to rock and roll about the time Helm arrived. Gradually, Canadians replaced the other band members: first guitarist Robbie Robertson in 1961, then keyboard players Richard Manuel and Garth Hudson and bassist Rick Danko. Before long, Helm was the only American left in the band.

The group left Hawkins in 1963 to go out on their own as Levon and the Hawks. Without Helm, the group backed Dylan during 1965, the year that he converted from folk to rock. The group, this time with Helm, would later join Dylan in Woodstock after his motorcycle accident. The group recorded their first album, *Music from Big Pink*, in 1968, and remained together until 1978, when they recorded and filmed *The Last Waltz*.

Their name, the Band, is as downhome, unpretentious, and universal as a pair of blue jeans. On the surface, their music was as unassuming as their name. None of the members was a great singer, and their shows had none of the histrionics that were part of a concert by David Bowie or the Who. But their bland exterior obscured the fact that they were one of the great rock bands of the era. Robertson and the two keyboard players were excellent soloists, and the group had an empathy in performance that few other bands matched. As a result, their live performances were often superior in many ways to their studio recordings.

Like CCR and the Grateful Dead, the Band steeped their music in the past, in both words and music. Lyrics included historical ("The Night They Drove Old Dixie Down") and biblical ("Nazareth" in "The Weight" and "Unfaithful Servant") references, although the songs themselves described contemporary situations. Often the lyrics were obscure, but evocative of the American experience.

Musically, there are references to both distant and recent past: rich country vocal inflections blend with soul-inspired accompaniments, and all of it mixes with rock and roll and rhythm and blues and the rest of the musical stew that is rock-era music.

The music of their songs has many admirable qualities, but perhaps its most distinctive—and American-sounding—feature is its rhythm. Two recordings of "The Weight," the first from the debut album, *Music from Big Pink* (1968), and the second from their 1972 live album, *Rock of Ages*, show both the Band's essence and its evolution.

Like many of the enduring songs by the Band, "The Weight" has a slow tempo. Here it's about 66 beats per minute (the live recording is a little faster), a considerable drop from the 100+ beats per minute of danceable rock songs. The rhythmic foundation is a simple rock beat, kept by drums, rhythm guitar, and piano. However, both the vocal line and all of the instrumental lines contain short phrases that move in double time (i.e., at "sixteen-beat" speed). The word "Nazareth" is a clear example, but it is also heard in many of the bass riffs and the ascending piano arpeggio just before "Take a load off . . . . " In the live recording, double-time riffs are more pervasive: almost all the guitar answers and moving bass parts move at this faster speed. In the studio version, we sense that The Band is straining against the leash of rock rhythm. In the live version they pretty well break free: the texture is far richer.

Sixteen-beat rhythms had already begun to infiltrate popular music, first through Brazilian music (as we'll discover in Chapter 12), then through black music, as we learned previously. Along with Cream and the Allman Brothers, The Band was among the first rock groups to make use of sixteen-beat based rhythms. Few did so with greater variety and imagination.

Southern Rock

Early in their association, Helm took Robertson down South. Overnight, Robertson matched the music that he had grown up loving with places and the people who inhabited them. He came away from the visit with a much stronger sense of the culture behind the music. By his own account, it changed him, although he is at pains to describe exactly how. If a visit changed Robertson that profoundly, imagine what it would be like to grow up there.

To understand Southern rock and the strong regional pride it expressed, we have to remember that rock and roll began as a Southern music: whites who had absorbed the blues; blacks who had some country in their music. Rockabillies, the predecessors of the Southern rockers, had only a brief moment in the sun. As rock and roll became nationalized and internationalized in the process, white Southerners largely disappeared from the limelight. It wasn't until the late sixties that a Southern group offered the country and the world a new, identifiably Southern sound. That group was the Allman Brothers.

There were numerous Southern bands who had successful careers in the seventies: Marshall Tucker, Elvin Bishop, and the Atlanta Rhythm Section were among the most popular. Nevertheless, the story of Southern rock is largely the story of two bands, the Allman Brothers and Lynyrd Skynyrd. There are numerous parallels. Both groups were formed largely from musicians who grew up in northern Florida. As a result, they had deep roots in Southern culture, and the music that was part of that culture. Both faced tragedy: the Allmans had to deal with the deaths of co-leader Duane Allman (in 1971) and bassist Berry Oakley (in 1972) in motorcycle crashes; Lynyrd Skynyrd lost the heart of the band in the deaths of Ronnie Van Zant and Steve and Cassie Gaines in a 1977 plane crash. Both bands were oversized: The Allman Brothers had two lead guitarists, Duane Allman and Dickey Betts, with Gregg Allman on keyboards, Oakley on bass, and two percussionists, Butch Trucks and Jai Johanny Johnson. Lynyrd Skynyrd went one better, with three guitarists plus a keyboard player. Both developed reputations as terrific live bands.

There was also a complementary aspect to their relationship. Lynyrd Skynyrd took off shortly after the deaths of Allman and Oakley. It was as if the torch had been passed: Lynyrd Skynyrd was one of the hottest touring bands throughout the mid-seventies. Musically, the Allman Brothers emphasized the blues/soul side of Southern rock, while Lynyrd Skynyrd marbled country into their sound and attitude. A comparison of two early Allman Brothers' songs, "Black Hearted Woman" and "Every Hungry Woman," with Lynyrd Skynyrd's "Gimme Three Steps" and "Saturday Night Special," brings to light their common ground and musical differences.

THE ALLMAN BROTHERS The Allman Brothers' predilection for black Southern music was a natural extension of their early career. After false starts in Florida and Los Angeles, Gregg and Duane Allman moved back to the South in 1968, to work at Fame Studios in Muscle Shoals, Alabama. Duane Allman became the main session guitarist at Fame Studio, recording with Aretha Franklin, King Curtis, Wilson Pickett, and others.

The brothers formed the Allman Brothers band while Duane was still working at Fame, releasing their self-titled first album in 1969. Although it didn't sell very well, their reputation quickly grew, especially as a live band. Their performance at the Fillmore East, recorded in 1971, remains one of the great live rock recordings.

During Duane's too-brief time with the band, the Allman Brothers drew heavily on black Southern music to create their steamroller sound. In sound, texture, and rhythm, it is a composite of rock, electric blues, and soul. Gregg Allman's songs are cut from the same cloth as blues and soul. Typically, they focus on unfaithful women and awkward love triangles, with "backdoor men" running out of the picture as the wronged man enters. His vocals are blue-eyed blues singing of the first order.

The sound behind Gregg featured his organ playing (a soul link); two lead guitarists, Duane Allman and Dickey Betts, both of whom play the blues well; plus bass, drums, and conga drum (another black music link). With three chord/lead instruments and two percussion layers, the sound is unusually dense, especially because all the instruments are active. The duels and duets between lead guitarists are highlights. To create space for all this activity, the band makes extensive use of sixteen-beat rhythms. The conga consistently moves at the faster layer, and many of the lead guitar lines and accompanying riffs move at double-time speed.

Gregg Allman on stage, August 14, 1975. PHOTO COURTESY CORBIS/BETTMANN.

The soul influence is evident in the greater rhythmic complexity—both songs are highly syncopated. (In the opening of "Black Hearted Woman," the Allman Brothers add another nice rhythmic twist: three-and-a-half-beat measures.) It is also apparent in the use of signature instrumental riffs that serve as the refrain. Both songs are rocked-up blues forms. The blues choruses serve as verses, while the instrumental riffs are the refrains.

Especially because both lead guitarists play in a blues-drenched rock guitar style, there are similarities in style between the Allman Brothers and British blues bands and power trios. However, here the sound is much thicker, because of the additional instruments, and looser, because of the more extensive interplay. In this respect, they are closer to the music of Santana (discussed in Chapter 12). The Allman Brothers' early sound was a special synthesis of rock, blues, soul, and their own inspiration. Among major rock bands of the era, few matched their combination of blues edge, thick sound, and rhythmic drive.

Ironically, the Allman Brothers' greatest commercial success was a hard country single "Ramblin' Man" (1973), written by Dickey Betts, the group's other guitarist. Still, the most important of their legacy came early on, while Duane Allman was still alive.

LYNYRD SKYNYRD It remained for Lynyrd Skynyrd (the name of the band is a parody of Leonard Skinner, the name of a gym teacher whom band members despised) to fully integrate country and blues elements into the distinctive sound of Southern rock. That sound emerged in a series of recordings made between 1973 and 1977. The band featured an unusual (and fluid) lineup of three guitars (Gary Rossington and Allen Collins were the mainstays), keyboard, bass, and drums, all backing singer Ronnie Van Zant.

Their songs are both Southern and rock, in both words and music. "Sweet Home Alabama," the band's signature statement about Southern pride, shows their country roots not only in its defiant defense of place but also in the way it argues the case in song. In the lyric, Van Zant scolds Neil Young for his less-than-flattering portrait of Southern men.

Many other songs grow out of the band members' own experience: hanging out in honky tonks, life on the road, etc. In this respect, the songs come right out of the blues and country music. However, the songs usually suggest more than a bunch of good ol' boys sitting around drinking beer and generally raising hell. There is rock-like complexity behind the down-home exterior. For example, "Saturday Night Special," which tells the story of a killing of passion by a cheated-on man, could be an anthem for gun control. "Gimme Three Steps" is not a flattering self-portrait. It tells the story of an awkward "triangular" encounter from the perspective of a "backdoor man," the interloper in

Country singers occasionally aired out issues in a series of songs. A famous example: Hank Thompson's "The Wild Side of Life" (1951) told the story of a woman who left her family to carouse in bars. Kitty Wells shot back a year later with "It Wasn't God Who Made Honky Tonk Angels," a song about the guys who lead women astray. Both the title of her song and the lyric refer to Thompson's song.

a husband/wife relationship, who would rather make love than war. And running through most of the songs is Van Zant's self-deprecating sense of humor.

With their three guitar plus keyboard lineup, Lynyrd Skynyrd created a sound as thick as the Allman Brothers. And, with all the competing riffs and active bass playing from Leon Wilkeson, there is just about as much rhythmic interplay.

The two bands approached rock differently. With their emphasis on extroverted solos, the Allman Brothers are like Cream or Hendrix. Lynyrd Skynyrd favors more group interaction; in this respect they are more like the Rolling Stones than an augmented power trio.

The sharpest difference, however, is the country influence on Lynyrd Skynyrd. It is not universal. Perhaps because it is such a dark song, "Saturday Night Special," with its pentatonic riffs, sounds more like heavy rock. However, "Gimme Three Steps" and many of their other hits show the influence of country not only in subject, but also in form, the use of basic chords, and the guitar and keyboard riffs.

As exemplified in the music of the Allman Brothers and Lynyrd Skynyrd, Southern rock conveyed a strong sense of regional identity. It's evident in the influence of blues, soul, and country, the singing of Gregg Allman and Ronnie Van Zant, the themes of the songs and the tone of the lyric, and the loose, party-like atmosphere both created in live performance. At the same time, the dense, active, well-grooved texture characteristic of both bands brought a new sound to rock. It was the musical trademark of Southern rock.

Country Rock

In 1968, Gram Parsons, a singer and songwriter from the Southeast, moved to southern California, joined the Byrds and led them into a deep immersion into country music. The result was *Sweethearts of the Rodeo*. The music was miles away from "Eight Miles High"; more than anything else, it sounded like conscientious non-Southerners playing country. Still, it was influential, simply because it was by the Byrds.

Parsons was the main player in the development of country rock, first with the Byrds, then with the Flying Burrito Brothers, and finally as a solo act. Although Parsons's bands enjoyed some success, the group that popularized the sound of country rock was the Eagles.

Formed in 1971 mainly from Linda Ronstadt's backup band, the Eagles became one of the most successful rock groups of the seventies. The original Eagles were Don Henley, drums; Glenn Frey, guitar; Bernie Leadon, country instruments—banjo, steel guitar, etc.; and Randy Meisner, bass. Don Felder, who also played an assortment of country instruments, joined the group in 1974.

The song that helped put both the Eagles and country rock on the map was their first single, the 1972 hit, "Take It Easy." It demonstrates their wonderfully effective fusion of rock and country elements. The lyric is all country: women trouble, trucks, small towns (Winslow, Arizona, is east of Flagstaff), but the music smoothly blends rock and country elements. The song begins with a low-wattage power chord, after which it settles into a nice rock groove.

This particular interpretation of a rock beat is a more relaxed version of the honky-tonk/rock beat synthesis heard earlier in Roy Orbison's "Mean

Glen Frey of the Eagles on stage. PHOTO COURTESY CORBIS/SHELLEY GAZIN.

Woman Blues." It would soon become the most common form of rock rhythm in country rock and rock-influenced country.

Almost everything else also has a country flavor: the guitar licks, the double-time banjo accompaniment, and the singing. The two exceptions are Meisner's occasionally roaming basslines and the beautiful high-register close harmony, which seems to owe more to the Beach Boys than to the Everly Brothers or any country group.

As their career gained momentum, the Eagles moved toward the mainstream, often shedding country elements along the way. Still, songs such as "Lyin' Eyes" (1975) retain a strong country flavor. The band shifted direction rather abruptly in 1975, when guitarist Joe Walsh replaced Bernie Leadon. "Hotel California" (1977), their big hit from this later period, borrows from a "southern" sound of a quite different kind: reggae. It's a skillful adaptation of the reggae feel—as skillful as their earlier assimilation of country—but the Eagles sound like a different band altogether. It was a complete makeover.

Summary

The last and largest of the Woodstock-style concerts took place in the summer of 1973 at Watkins Glen, a raceway in upstate New York. The event, which drew an estimated 600,000 people, featured three groups—the Grateful Dead, the Band, and the Allman Brothers. There is an "all-American" symbolism to the time, place, and bands. Watkins Glen is about halfway between Toronto, where the Band got started, and Woodstock, where they worked with Dylan. The Allman Brothers represented a strong regional accent of American rock; the Grateful Dead captured its free, loose, iconoclastic spirit—a spirit that flourished in northern California.

The groups surveyed in this section—Creedence Clearwater Revival, the Grateful Dead, the Band, the Allman Brothers, Lynyrd Skynyrd, and the Eagles—all have an American sound precisely because they mix rock, black, and country influences. The mixes vary—soul permeates the early Allman Brothers' sound, while direct black influences are all but absent from the Eagles' early music. But the country influence is there, in the storytelling lyrics, down-home, unmannered singing, the harmonies, guitar licks, the occasional pedal guitar and banjo sounds, and occasionally in the straightforward rhythms.

More than any other single element, country music links these disparate styles together. When mixed with black music and rock, it produced, in the work of these groups, rock music of a distinctively American character.

KEY TERMS

Blues revival	**Deadhead**	**Country rock**
American sound	**Southern rock**	

CHAPTER QUESTIONS

1. After you listen to CCR, the Dead, and the Band, refresh your memory regarding the Beach Boys, Roy Orbison, the Byrds, Zappa, Hendrix, and the Velvet Underground. Then consider whether our assertion about an "American" sound is valid. If so, what distinguishes the first three bands from the others (consider both words and music). If not, why?

2. Consider the boundary between soul and rock by listening to the two Allman Brothers' songs, then comparing them to the Clapton and Hendrix recordings, and the recordings by Otis Redding and Sam and Dave. In your opinion, are the songs closer to soul or rock? What elements most influenced your opinion?

3. Consider the state of blues within rock by comparing recordings by Joplin, Hendrix, Clapton, and the Allman Brothers.

4. Try to trace the country connection in "Take It Easy" by comparing it to Roy Orbison's "Mean Woman Blues," as well as "Your Cheatin' Heart" and any of Elvis's rockabilly recordings.

chapter 11

Heavy Metal in the Seventies

No music of the rock era has been more misunderstood than heavy metal. It has been vilified as cretinous music not only by those outside of rock, but also by numerous rock critics and musicians. Until the nineties, surveys of any Top 40/50/100 list of major acts of the rock era generally gave metal groups short shrift. The only names likely to appear were Led Zeppelin, which quickly transcended the boundaries of the genre, and Van Halen, whose music crossed over to the pop charts fairly early in their career. Seminal metal bands, most notably Black Sabbath, are conspicuous by their absence.

For much of its history, heavy metal has existed with its audience in a largely self-contained world. The music's main outlets have been concert performances and recordings. Metal has received relatively little airplay, especially on mainstream recordings.

For many years, its audience was almost exclusively young males, typically disaffected and from middle- or lower-class environments. Immersion in heavy metal has been a rite of passage for many teens around the world. (More recently, the audience for heavy metal has broadened to include both older males—those who grew up with it—and females.) Audience members formed powerful bonds with the acts whom they admired, bonds as strong as any in rock.

Critics of metal have targeted what they perceive as its crudeness and cheapness—e.g., the ponderous riffs of some metal bands or the makeup worn by Kiss and Alice Cooper. Yet metal has been home to many of rock's great virtuosi, from Ritchie Blackmore and Jimmy Page to Eddie Van Halen, Randy Rhoads, and Yngwie Malmsteen. Perhaps more than any other rock style, metal values and demands technical excellence.

There is some confusion regarding the source of the term "heavy metal," as it applies to rock. Everyone agrees that the term appeared in rock as part of the lyric ("heavy metal thunder") in Steppenwolf's 1968 song, "Born to Be Wild." Its history prior to that is less clear. Rock mythology has the term coming most directly from William Burroughs's *Naked Lunch*. That source is myth: Burroughs does not use the phrase anywhere in the book. In any event, it was in common use by the early seventies.

Heavy Metal: Sounds and Influences

Metal's sound signature is distortion—*extreme* distortion. It has other widely-used musical conventions: blues-derived pentatonic and modal scales, often unharmonized; power chords; extended, flamboyant solos; ear-splitting volume; screamed-out, often incomprehensible lyrics; and pounding rhythms, often performed at breakneck speed. Still, the feature that most immediately identifies heavy metal is distortion.

Heavy metal has clear roots in the blues, especially electric blues. Its diabolical overtones, half-sung, half-spoken high register vocal style, lack of harmonic movement, and reliance on riffs easily reach back to Robert Johnson. Power chords and endlessly repeated riffs trace back to John Lee Hooker ("Boogie Chillen'"), heavy distortion to mid-fifties bluesmen. Blues influence is also indirect: it comes into heavy metal through the early music of the Kinks (e.g., "You Really Got Me"), as well as Hendrix, Clapton, and the other blues-based rock guitarists of the late sixties. In transmuting blues rhetoric into heavy metal, bands intensified and stylized these features.

Classical music has been another source of inspiration for many metal artists. From it, they have not only borrowed the idea of virtuosity, but expropriated virtuosic patterns from classical works, as we'll see below. This emphasis on transcendent instrumental skills shows up not only in the guitar solos, but also in the tight ensemble (typically, not a feature of blues style) and pedal-to-the-metal tempos.

Modality has been another seminal influence. Modes are virtually universal in heavy metal; it is hard to imagine a metal song using conventional harmony. There are several good reasons why metal bands used modes. First, they formed the scales of much English folksong: most of the early metal bands were British, so modality was part of their musical heritage. Second, modes were the basis of a fresh new harmonic language within rock, as we heard in the music of the Rolling Stones, the Beatles, and others. Third, the African-American pentatonic scale maps onto most modes, as we have seen. In fact, modes can be understood as an expansion of the melodic resources of the pentatonic scale. Fourth, precisely because it is the basis of so much folksong, as well as Medieval and Renaissance classical music, it connotes archaic, even mythical, times. This meshes smoothly with the gothic element in much heavy metal: consider the beginning to "Stairway to Heaven."

Heavy metal is all of these influences, yet something apart from them and in many cases more than the sum of them. From these influences, metal musicians forged one of the most distinctive styles of the rock era. We will study this style, as realized in the music of the three bands that, more than any others, defined early heavy metal.

Heavy Metal Begins

Joe Elliot, lead vocalist for Def Leppard, was quoted as saying: "In 1971, there were only three bands that mattered—Led Zeppelin, Black Sabbath, and Deep Purple." His statement summarizes the prevailing consensus. Of the three,

Black Sabbath stayed the closest to the musical features that defined early metal. Although Deep Purple could lay down a riff as well as anyone ("Smoke on the Water"), they strayed far enough from metal basics that some critics considered them an art rock band. From the start, Led Zeppelin was much more than "just" a heavy metal band. Their music covered a broad range of styles, even at times within a single song. Accordingly, we will discuss representative examples by each band, to show the signature features of the style in its early years, as well as its range. It should make clear that heavy metal is anything but a monolithic style.

Black Sabbath

Take a poll among serious metal fans: name the first heavy metal band. Chances are that Black Sabbath will receive the most votes. They were not the first band to play in a heavy metal style. Some writers credit Blue Cheer, a very loud San Francisco band. Others cite Led Zeppelin or Iron Butterfly. But Black Sabbath was the first band whose music consistently laid out the most widely-used conventions of the heavy metal world. When you hear Black Sabbath, you're generally hearing heavy metal.

The name Black Sabbath evokes the occult, as it was supposed to do. So did almost everything else about them. Black Sabbath's shows would feature crosses burned onstage and other images of devil worship. The lyrics of their songs often sound like they come straight from a gothic horror film. And the music formed the ideal backdrop for the words and images.

Black Sabbath was the third incarnation of a blues band from Birmingham, England. Vocalist Ozzy Osbourne, guitarist Tony Iommi, bassist "Geezer" Butler, and drummer Bill Ward first came together as Polka Tuck, then changed their name to Earth. By 1969, they had become Black Sabbath; their first album appeared a year later.

Through relentless touring, they developed an international audience. As a result, their second album, *Paranoid* (1971), sold over 4 million copies. They remained the top metal act for the first half of the decade. With the ascendancy of punk and disco in the late seventies, their popularity waned, and Osbourne left Black Sabbath in 1979 to front his own highly successful and notorious group.

In "Black Sabbath," the title song from their first self-titled album, the band throws down the gauntlet. From the rainstorm and bell-tolling that open the song, the song depicts nothing less than a Black Mass. With this song they turned their longstanding interest in the occult into their trademark.

The music supports this vision of the dark side. Like the opening of "Purple Haze," the guitar riff outlines the *diabolus in musica* interval.

Cultivation of the occult may have been new to popular music, but not classical music. The early Romantics also flirted with the diabolic. With his breathtaking virtuosity and cadaver-like appearance, the violinist Niccolo Paganini was thought by many to have made a pact with the devil (long before Robert Johnson). According to his program for the work, Hector Berlioz's *Symphonie Fantastique* depicts a wild opium dream, with goblins, an execution, and a citation from the Mass for the Dead.

Whether its use was intentional or simply inspired intuition, the interval nevertheless implies the whole occult package for the band: devil worship, medieval associations, and the like. They could not have expressed their image in music more succinctly or universally: it would have been understood just as clearly in 1270 as 1970.

The ponderous tempo at the beginning suggests some kind of procession. This impression is strengthened when Osbourne portrays himself as a sacrificial victim. The shift to a faster tempo in the song also has programmatic implications: it suggests people fleeing.

"Black Sabbath" features many of the conventions of heavy metal. In addition to distortion, they include:

1. a high percentage of strictly instrumental performance, including an extended guitar solo;
2. the use of repeated riffs, often played by guitar and bass;
3. the use of modal scales (which we expect);
4. several discrete sections, typically defined by shifts in tempo, riff, and key (here it's just tempo and riff);
5. a dramatic vocal style, in which the boundary between speech and song is often blurred;
6. the lack of harmony; and
7. a very loud dynamic level.

One important reason for the success of heavy metal is the way in which the musical conventions so often support the message of the song. That is certainly the case here. The music carries most of the message of the song: Osbourne's words simply confirm what we already expect. The use of the "devil's interval" is one sign, the slow and fast tempos are another. The absence of conventional harmony helps give the music an archaic sound: both Gregorian chant, the ancient music of the Catholic liturgy, and British folksong began as strictly melodic music. Indeed, early *organum*, the first multivoice European music, was essentially a chant melody harmonized with power chords. The rhythms and the sheer volume of sound reinforce the ritualistic aspect of the metal experience.

One dimension of the connection between intent and musical conventions deserves particular mention. There is, we believe, a causal relationship between distortion, the absence of harmony, and the heavy metal esthetic. Consider that rock, like most music, defines a sound space. The main melodic line and the bassline roughly define the boundaries of the space. The space in-between is typically filled by the rhythm guitar. Other instruments occupy the area around the main line. Power chords played with extreme distortion fill the sound space with overtones and undertones (from the power chords) and white noise (randomly vibrating sounds over a wide range of frequency). Precisely because of this mass of sound, there is, in effect, no sonic room for a rhythm guitar playing chords. The sound would be too thick for comprehensibility.

There is another compelling reason that metal bands have tended to avoid harmony. Progressions of chords generally imply movement toward a goal, even if it's the endlessly recycling one of "Earth Angel" and all its clones. Movement toward a goal, in turn, implies tension (during the movement) and release (at the point of arrival). Pre-rock popular song was *romantic*, above all else, and harmony played a central if seldom acknowledged role in inspiring romantic feelings. Its retentions often continued to do the same job, as we'll hear in the music of both white and black performers in the late sixties and seventies. By contrast, heavy metal is about *power*. Like romance, harmony implies negotiation—will I get to the goal? Metal songs seldom negotiate; more often they slam from one key to the next, as we'll hear especially in Black Sabbath's "Sweet Leaf." The ebb and flow of harmonic tension would in fact *undermine* the metal esthetic. So, both for the image of power and because of the fact of power—the sonically overloaded power chord—metal songs often have little or no harmony. With the best bands, at least, it is not a question of musical insufficiency but esthetic choice.

Two other songs, "Paranoid" and "Sweet Leaf," confirm Black Sabbath's position as the metal-defining band and also show something of their range. "Paranoid," the title track from their album, reveals them in proto-punk mode, an unusual choice for this time. Here, all three instruments emphasize the eight-beat rhythmic layer, with almost no syncopation. The insistence of the rhythm seems designed to reinforce the message of the song: the sonic walls closing in on Osbourne. In other respects, this is a typical heavy metal song in many ways: lots of distortion, bass and guitar working hand in glove, Osbourne singing in a high register, a prominent instrumental accompaniment, power chords fleshing out a modal scale, a guitar solo based strictly on the African-American pentatonic scale.

"Sweet Leaf," a track from their third album, *Master of Reality* (1971), also retains its metal core. The vocal sections at the beginning and end feature two riffs, one underneath Osbourne's vocal line, the other an interlude between his statements. Among the most interesting features of the song is the uptempo instrumental section, beginning at about 2 minutes, 27 seconds. Here the band shifts tempos and keys at the same time, much like a race car driver slamming through the gears. Iommi's guitar solo is also an opportunity for Butler and Ward to strut their stuff; Ward in particular breaks out before settling back into the groove heard in the beginning of the song. This method of creating longer songs by stringing together blocks of sound that are unrelated in tempo and key is heard in much heavy metal music.

Listening to an early Black Sabbath album is like taking Heavy Metal 101. From it, we can learn the basics of the style. For more advanced possibilities, we can study the music of Deep Purple and Led Zeppelin. We will consider Deep Purple first.

Deep Purple

Like Black Sabbath and other British groups, Deep Purple went through several incarnations before finding their groove. Theirs involved not only changes in personnel, but also radical style changes. Their lineup during their most successful period, from 1970 to 1973, included vocalist Ian Gillan, guitarist Ritchie Blackmore, keyboardist Jon Lord, bassist Roger Glover, and drummer Ian Paice. The inclusion of a keyboard in a metal group was unusual. However, Lord was an important creative voice within the group. Among the first recordings of the newly constituted group was Lord's *Concerto for Group and Orchestra*, which Deep Purple recorded with the Royal Philharmonic. At this point, they were marching in step with the classical-influenced art rockers discussed in Chapter 9.

Jon Lord of Deep Purple on stage, April 17, 1973. PHOTO COURTESY CORBIS/NEAL PRESTON.

However, the band soon shifted direction, focusing more on volume (they were listed in the *Guinness Book of World Records* as the loudest rock band) and heavy guitar riffs. Nevertheless, the classical influence was still apparent in both Lord and Blackmore's playing. Both were virtuoso players who borrowed as heavily from the classics as they did from the blues.

Two songs from the album *Machine Head* (1972), "Smoke on the Water" and "Highway Star," show how they combined the two influences. The first shows them in full metal regalia, pounding out one of heavy metal's most memorable anthems. "Highway Star" shows a more direct influence of classical music on their sound.

"Smoke on the Water" is classic metal, at least in the music. (Unusually for a heavy metal song, "Smoke on the Water" recounts a real-life incident, rather than a gothic horror or myth, or an unbalanced state of mind. The event was a fire that occurred during a concert in Montreux, Switzerland, with Frank Zappa.) The song begins with perhaps the most widely recognized metal riff of all time. Underneath it is Glover's bass line, which parallels the guitar riff, but at eight-beat speed, and Paice's sixteen-beat timekeeping. Along with the syncopations in the riff itself, this gives the opening a richer rhythmic texture than "Paranoid." Other metal elements are present: Gillan's hoarse high register vocal, Blackmore's inventive solo, the overall prominence of the instrumental accompaniment. Taken together, these features firmly establish Deep Purple's metal credentials.

If "Smoke on the Water" was solid gold metal, then "Highway Star" was Exhibit A for demonstrating the influence of classical music, and especially the music of J. S. Bach and Vivaldi, on Deep Purple. Blackmore acknowledged his classical sources: "For example, the chord progression in the 'Highway Star' solo . . . is a Bach progression." And the solo is "just arpeggios based on Bach." Lord also adapts the melodic patterns and fast, even rhythms of Bach and Vivaldi to rock. (Both solos are overdubbed with harmony parts, further evidence of the virtuosity of both players. It's difficult enough to play such fast, intricate passages, but even harder to synchronize a second line perfectly with the first.)

Blackmore's solo shows how classical and blues influences come together in heavy metal: side by side, rather than blended. Blackmore's solo begins with blues-based riffs. After gaining considerable momentum, it reaches a climactic point where more energy is required (ca. 4 minutes, 30 seconds). It is at this point that Blackmore shifts into classical high gear. The type of figuration that Blackmore uses here, like its Bach and Vivaldi models, is high energy music. Quite simply, Blackmore wanted speed, and went to Bach and Vivaldi to get it, because they were excellent models for how to play fast and intelligibly at the same time. After about 30 seconds, the solo returns to less active but more emotionally charged blues-based riffs.

In "Highway Star," blues-based and Baroque-inspired musical ideas coexist happily. That's especially true in Blackmore's solo, because its pacing makes the transition seem perfectly natural. Lord's interpolation of classical figuration has more of a "ready-set-go" quality. In both cases, however, the consistency of sound, both in the guitar and keyboard timbres and in the rhythmic undercurrent, helps link them together smoothly.

Deep Purple's infusion of classical elements into heavy metal brought new dimensions to the music. The most emulated was virtuosity, especially among individual performers. A list of rock's most technically proficient guitarists includes a disproportionately high number of heavy metal players. Indeed, for a handful of top guitarists (and those who wished to play at that level) Baroque music became a primary source for musical ideas. In the eighties, Eddie Van Halen, Randy Rhoads, and Yngwie Malmsteen followed in Blackmore's footsteps, as we'll see in Chapter 17.

It also became a goal of bands: precise ensemble playing, often at breakneck speeds, occurs more frequently in heavy metal than any other rock substyle. In fact, the eighties saw the emergence of speed metal: a heavy metal substyle which typically featured dazzling ensemble playing.

Led Zeppelin

Led Zeppelin, although often cited as a seminal heavy metal band, ultimately defies category. From *Led Zeppelin* (1969), their first album, it was clear that heavy metal was just one aspect of their musical personality. *Led Zeppelin* includes two prototypical metal songs ("Good Times Bad Times" and "Communication Breakdown"), two blues covers, a song that's halfway between blues and heavy metal ("How Many More Times"), plus an East Indian-inspired instrumental and ballad/rocker ("Babe I'm Gonna Leave You") with overtones of Flamenco music.

Their center is clearly the blues, and their version of heavy metal that evolved from it. At the same time, there seems to be nothing in their musical world that is not fair game for appropriation. What's particularly interesting in their music, all through their career, is the way one style bleeds into the other. Their music may cover a lot of stylistic territory, but it is not compartmentalized.

Led Zeppelin's front man was vocalist Robert Plant, who was guitarist Jimmy Page's second choice as lead singer, but who turned out to be the ideal voice for the group. Bassist John Paul Jones was, with Page, part of the British music scene in the late sixties; drummer John Bonham was a friend of Plant's from their Birmingham days.

Page and Plant shared a deep interest in the mystic, the mythical, and the occult. This interest would increasingly inform their work, from untitled albums to cryptic covers, sparse liner notes, non-referential lyrics, and numerous archaic musical influences.

The range of their music came mainly from Page, whose personal playlist went well beyond rock, blues, and classical music. Page also produced their albums. His production skills were as important a component of their success as his guitar playing: He brought a wonderful ear for sonority and texture to their music.

Another quality that sets their music apart from every other group of the era is the exploration of extremes. It is inherent in virtually every aspect of their musicmaking. Plant sang higher than Osbourne, Gillan, and most other male vocalists (and many females, too). Their ensemble playing was more daring, their riffs more elaborate and beat-defying: "Black Dog," from their untitled fourth album, is an excellent example. Their production is more elaborate. One writer described Led Zeppelin as a heavy metal band with finesse. That assessment may seem like an oxymoron to metalphobes, but it makes perfect sense to fans, and seems to capture Led Zeppelin's unique ability to mold disparate influences and values into a unified vision.

"Dazed and Confused" and "Stairway to Heaven" are ideal examples of this reconciliation of extremes, because the extremes that characterize their music occur *within* a single song. These songs, and others like them, cover an

Robert Plant of Led Zeppelin, c. 1973.
PHOTO COURTESY CORBIS/ NEAL PRESTON.

enormous emotional and musical range. They can be tender one moment and overpowering the next.

The music of Led Zeppelin evolved considerably from their first album to *Physical Graffiti* (1975). That and the wide range of their music make it difficult to represent their achievement adequately with a discussion of a single album. However, if any one recording allows us to understand their unique place in rock history, it would be the untitled fourth album (1971) (referred to as *Zoso*, for those who can't stand the thought of an untitled album).

By the time this album was recorded, they had moved away from their blues roots and begun to incorporate more outside influences. Each song bears their personal stamp even more clearly than in the first album. There are no electric blues covers; the only track with clear blues overtones is "When the Levee Breaks," which features a harmonica and blues-like ostinato riff. At the other end of the spectrum is the beautiful, haunting "The Battle of Evermore." The song offers clear evidence of the group's mystical/mythical bent. What's most striking perhaps, and certainly out of the ordinary for an "ordinary" heavy metal band, is the acoustic instrument accompaniment: a pillow of plucked and picked sounds.

"Black Dog" is closer to "pure" heavy metal than any other song on the album. It incorporates many of the features we expect from a metal song: Plant's high vocals, a riff by heavily distorted guitar and bass, loud volume, and a strong beat (some of the time.)

There are several differences from prototypical metal. Plant begins singing without accompaniment. The guitar/bass riff that answers Plant is long, convoluted, and full of rhythmic surprises, instead of short and simple. With it, Page immediately raised the skill bar several notches. These and other dramatic contrasts within the song confirm Led Zeppelin's emphasis on extremes.

"Stairway to Heaven" offers the whole Led Zeppelin package in a single song. Here is the sequence of events:

0:00   Opening melody: A modal, folksong-like melody supported by recorders (an archaism that suggests Renaissance or Medieval music) and tender acoustic guitar arpeggiation.

c. 2:15   The addition of electric instruments brings the song into the 1970s without destroying the atmosphere. The instrumental interludes, with their shifting, unresolving harmonies, create a sense of anticipation (so does the vocal phrase "it makes me wonder.")

c. 4:20   It becomes a full-fledged rock song when the drums enter; still, the melody remains the dominant element.

c. 5:55   Page's guitar solo, which grows out of a more expansive instrumental interlude, is pure metal: the sound is distorted, and he is soloing on the African-American pentatonic scale over a simple modal bass line which is repeated again and again.

c. 6:40   Plant enters with a new melodic idea. It resembles a compressed version of the original melody, but it is more active rhythmically, and Plant's singing has traded sensitive balladry for prototypical metal screeching. Somewhat out of place is the Bo-Diddley/Latinish beat that accompanies his singing. The abrupt and abruptly truncated reprise of the final phrase of the first melody brings the song to a surprising close.

Perhaps the best word to describe the change from section to section is "morphing": we know at the beginning, and at the end, that this is a lovely, folk-like ballad, with a haunting refrain that is seemingly centuries old. But gradually, before our very ears, it is transformed into quintessential heavy metal, much like Arnold Schwartzenegger morphed into the terminator. That Led Zeppelin could touch so many stylistic bases in a single song, and move from one to another so smoothly until arriving at a mountainous climax, is a tribute to their artistry. Small wonder that it is one of the enduring rock anthems.

Despite, or perhaps partly because of, the mystery with which they enveloped themselves, Led Zeppelin gained a large, loyal audience. Their tours sold out and broke attendance records, and all of their recordings went platinum. They are still popular, almost two decades after their disbanding. Their recordings continue to sell well and they remain on the playlists of rock stations.

There is no mystery why they have remained popular: Their music is a rare combination of almost unbridled power and subtle artistry, of raw emotion and superbly calculated craft. For some, the mix was too heady: The band never attracted the broad-based audience of the Beatles or Elton John. But for a large core, it was just the right strength. Millions of loyal fans remain unsatiated.

Summary

Heavy metal took the blues and transmuted them into a music of unprecedented power. It was powerful in an absolute sonic sense: no music was louder. There was power from the mastery of craft. Like the alchemists of old, heavy metal performers diligently studied ancient formulas: in this case, the musical patterns of Bach and Vivaldi. These they adapted to rock, then juxtaposed with elemental musical material. Heavy metal evoked supernatural—or at least paranormal—power, especially the group personae of Black Sabbath and Led Zeppelin. At a time when the women's rights movement was in the ascendancy—bras being burned, the National Organization for Women being formed—metal bands projected masculine power, to the point where performers could sport skillfully styled long hair, wear make-up, and sing higher than many women without fear of abandoning their sexual identity, a la David Bowie. And heavy metal wielded power over its audience, creating an extremely loyal fan base. Metalheads were not casual listeners or consumers: Black Sabbath's *Paranoid* went platinum on the strength of the group's tours, not airplay.

What heavy metal gained in power, it often sacrificed in subtlety. It was not typically a vehicle for expressing the pain of love lost or the joy of love found. It was not a music of nuance, except perhaps in the blues-inspired inflections in guitar solos. Even songs that talked about man/woman relationships did so in an almost impersonal, posterized manner.

The music was similarly posterized. Most of the conventions of heavy metal—distortion; massive amplification; use of modes, pentatonic scales, and power chords; its basic rhythms; "power trio" instrumental nucleus—were also part of the vocabulary of all hard rock music, around 1970. What metal bands did was take these features and streamline or amplify them to give them more impact. Metal bands used more distortion and played more loudly. They took rock's shift away from traditional harmony several steps further by using conventional chords sparingly, or in some cases, abandoning harmony altogether. Its guitarists played power chords with more "power"—i.e., greater resonance—and used them almost exclusively, and they developed more flamboyantly virtuosic styles. Its riffs and rhythms were stronger and more pervasive: at times, vocal lines seemed to ride on the riffs, like a whitewater raft.

Above all, the music is *there* more. One of the qualities that distinguishes metal from most other styles is the sheer amount of non-vocal music. Even more important, music is the primary source of heavy metal's overwhelming impact and expressive power. Words seem to serve a largely explanatory role. Most of the audience at a metal concert will know the lyrics to songs, but they *feel* the music.

Many writers have observed that rock is ritual. If so, then heavy metal quickly became rock's most ritualistic music.

K E Y   T E R M S

Heavy metal	**Occult/Devil worship**	**Power chord**
Modes	**Pentatonic scale**	

C H A P T E R   Q U E S T I O N S

1. Practice singing the first two melodic ideas in "Smoke on the Water" (three notes, then four notes) until it's pretty secure. Then locate a tuned guitar. Try playing a power chord by fretting the bottom string with your index finger and fretting the next two strings two frets higher. Then, if that goes easily, try playing the first three-note riff in power chords: Start on the third fret and move up three frets for the second chord, then two more for the third. For the second riff, return to the first chord, go up three, then three more, then back one.

2. Deep Purple has been considered both a metal band and progressive rock band. Explore this idea by comparing "Highway Star" with Yes's "Roundabout" and Black Sabbath's "Sweet Leaf." What aspects of "Highway Star" suggest the progressive rock connection? In your opinion, are they more or less dominant than the heavy metal elements?

3. For metalheads: Select one or two of your favorite metal recordings from the nineties. Then, using Black Sabbath as your primary reference, describe similarities and differences between early metal and the style of your current recording.

4. There has been considerable debate as to whether Led Zeppelin is a metal band. Take a position one way or the other, and support it by citing two or three recordings that prove your point.

Rock and the World

When rock became the dominant popular music, it forced the rest of the musical world to come to terms with it. At the very least, new music had to resemble rock or sound out-of-date. At the same time, rock-oriented musicians took musical inspiration from anywhere they found it. Their approach was strictly pragmatic: if a sound fit their musical needs, they would use it.

What resulted was a tremendous interchange among styles. There were fusions between rock and virtually all of the established styles: pop rock, country rock, jazz rock, Latin rock, art rock, rock musicals. Moreover, musicians working at some distance from the Liverpool–Los Angeles axis mixed rock and rhythm and blues with the music of their own cultures. From these encounters another family of rock hybrids emerged: reggae, Afro-pop, soca, tropicalista, et al. Their music would in turn feed back into rock, continuing the exchange between rock and the rest of the musical world.

In this chapter, we will study five of these interactions. It is just a sampling—a representative selection, not an inclusive one. Nevertheless, even these few examples can suggest the breadth of rock's influence and the willingness of its musicians to absorb outside influences.

Brazilian Music

Brazilian popular music had been a part of American musical life since the teens, when the *maxixe*, a Brazilian social dance, became a minor dance fad. The maxixe was not as sensational as the tango, nor as popular as the fox-trot, but it introduced Brazilian dance music to Americans.

In the thirties and forties, Brazilian music was a novelty. It surfaced in films and on Broadway as part of escapist entertainment, such as the 1933 film, *Flying Down to Rio*. The performer who personified Brazilian music was Carmen Miranda. Miranda combined a flamboyant personality and appearance—a petite woman, she created a signature look with six-inch platform heels and fruit-basket headdresses—with real ability as a singer and dancer. Her music was as exotic as her appearance. The "society sambas" she performed introduced the complex sixteen-beat rhythms of the samba to U.S. audiences.

Bossa Nova

Brazilian music trickled into the popular music mainstream in the early sixties via the *bossa nova* (Portuguese for "new beat"). In the late fifties, a group of Brazilian songwriters, most notably João Gilberto and Antonio Carlos Jobim, created a new Brazilian popular style by thinning out the rhythms of the samba and overlaying them with sinuous melodies and rich, jazz-inspired harmonies.

The American jazz/classical guitarist Charlie Byrd discovered these new sounds coming from Brazil, as did jazz saxophonist Stan Getz. Getz soon recorded with Gilberto and his wife, Astrud. Getz's albums with Byrd and Gilberto enjoyed surprising success, introducing him and the bossa nova to a far broader American audience than either had known previously.

João Gilberto's 1958 Brazilian recording of Jobim's "Desafinado," one of the earliest bossa nova hits, shows essential components of this Brazilian popular style. It has a long, spun-out melody supported by rich, constantly shifting harmonies. Gilberto, who accompanies his singing on the guitar, plays the chords in an irregular, highly syncopated rhythm. The rhythm of his accompaniment is one strand in a texture that also includes a bass note on every (slow) beat, a shaker-like percussion instrument moving four times as fast as the beat, and sharp percussive sounds in a busy offbeat rhythm. Slower-moving string lines and trombone obbligatos complement the faster rhythms of the voice, guitar, and percussion instruments.

Samba

The bossa nova was a stripped-down—and often slowed-down—variant of the samba. It had the same basic rhythm, but was generally more melodious and less dense rhythmically than the Afro-Brazilian sambas from which it was derived.

This music has flourished in lower-class black neighborhoods in Rio de Janeiro, especially during Carnaval, Brazil's counterpart to Mardi Gras. In preparation for the big parades, and the prizes that go to the best groups, samba schools assemble a huge battery of percussionists—up to 300—and for the better part of a year rehearse the intricate samba rhythms, which typically include six or more percussion parts.

"A Felicidade" is a well-known song from the Brazilian/French film *Black Orpheus* (1959), a retelling of the Orpheus legend set in Rio during Carnaval. In this version by João Gilberto, we can hear the affinity between Carnaval-like samba in the opening and the bossa nova style during Gilberto's vocal. The samba sections have many more percussion instruments and a denser sound, but the basic rhythmic feel remains the same from section to section. The sixteen-beat rhythmic foundation of the samba and bossa nova is particularly clear in the samba sections: we hear a bass thump on every beat and a mass of rhythms moving four times that speed.

The film captured a relatively large U.S. audience in the early 1960s; it gave many Americans a helpful point of entry into Brazilian music.

Brazilian Music and the New Beat of the Seventies

Brazilian music crossed over in the sixties partly because both American and Brazilian music had moved much closer to a common ground. The bossa nova represented a simpler and more singable form of the Brazilian samba, while the rhythms of rock-based American popular music had moved closer to Brazilian rhythm.

Like Afro-Cuban rhythms, Brazilian rhythms fit with rock-era rhythms because both divide the beat equally, as we have seen. However, because the samba and bossa nova rhythms divide the beat into four equal parts, they anticipated the use of sixteen-beat rhythms, which began to appear in rock and black music at the end of the sixties. Only at slow tempos were they an alternative to rock rhythm.

The role of Brazilian music in introducing sixteen-beat rhythms is analogous in many respects to the role of Afro-Cuban music in shaping rock rhythm. It, too, was a largely silent partner. The bossa nova and the samba influenced black pop, jazz, and pop most directly. For these styles, the Brazilian rhythms were a "lite" rhythmic alternative: more subtle, less aggressive, and more complex. Other connections are harder to trace.

However, there is one noteworthy difference. Brazilian music was the first and only popular style to use sixteen-beat rhythms before they began to appear in rock. There was no African-American antecedent to these rhythms, like boogie-woogie was for rock.

It is likely that sixteen-beat rhythms would have evolved in time, even if Brazilian music had remained unknown, much as jazz branched off rhythmically from syncopated dance music in the early twenties. However, the fact remains that the bossa nova gave rock era audiences their first real exposure to sixteen-beat rhythms.

Pop and Rock

A marriage between pop and rock seemed unlikely in the early years of rock and roll. The pop establishment scorned rock and roll, dismissing it as primitive jungle music unfit for those with more cultivated sensibilities. In the wake of the British Invasion and Motown's success, however, pop had to jump on the bandwagon or get left in the dust. Even Frank Sinatra, one of the most outspoken critics of rock and roll, hopped on—however reluctantly. His two big hits from the mid-sixties, "Strangers in the Night" and (the strangely-titled) "Something Stupid," use a slow, very discreet rock beat.

The Sinatra songs were simply conventional pop that had been given a rock beat. They were songs for adults, talking about romance in the language of pre-rock pop. Their melodies, harmonies, and forms continued traditional pop practice, and they were sung in a pop style. Only the beat was different.

However, the seeds for a new rock-based pop style had been planted in the early sixties, primarily through collaborations between Brill Building songwriters and groups such as the Shirelles. As in pre-rock pop, this new pop had lyrics that dealt with matters of the heart and melodies that were the center of musical attention. But virtually everything else was different, as we heard in "Will You Love Me Tomorrow."

Burt Bacharach

The most original songwriter to come out of the Brill Building during the early sixties was Burt Bacharach. Bacharach brought to his pop songwriting a rich musical background. It included extensive training in classical music compo-

Dionne Warwick and Frank Sinatra sing together, April 2, 1986. PHOTO COURTESY *CORBIS/*BETTMANN.

sition, training that included study with the noted French composer Darius Milhaud; work as a jazz pianist, including dates with Charlie Parker and Dizzy Gillespie; and pop arranging and conducting for Marlene Dietrich, Vic Damone, and several other pre-rock pop stars. From these experiences, he forged the most original pop/rock fusion of the sixties—indeed of the entire rock era. In a series of hits, he developed a new approach to pop, one that blended rock innovations with his own highly personal musical vision.

Bacharach's songs updated virtually every dimension of traditional pop. They retained the songwriter/performer division of labor, but with a rock-style twist. Although he and his longtime collaborator, lyricist Hal David, wrote songs for others to sing, Bacharach recruited Dionne Warwick to sing most of their hits. Her sound and vocal agility became an integral part of their conception: they wrote songs with her ability in mind. Their creative bond was so strong that David recalled imagining her singing a song as it was being created. Their partnership was a distinctive way of bridging the gap between pre-rock songwriters, who wrote for others to perform, and those rock-era artists who performed their own material.

Like pop songs, Bacharach and David's songs often talk about love. Typically, however, the emotions and language were closer to the emotional insecurity and ambivalence of "Will You Love Me Tomorrow" and the reality of daily life than the rose-colored world of fifties pop.

Bacharach's use of rock-related rhythms required innovations in David's lyrics. The pop songs of the twenties and thirties were themselves innovative in the use of a conversational melodic rhythm. The rhythm of the lyric was about the same, whether spoken or sung. In good lyrics of the time, unequal division of the beat and the occasional syncopation gently amplified the natural inflection and accent of the words as spoken.

With rock's equal division of the beat as their rhythmic point of departure, David had to write lyrics with less pronounced accentuation. The opening line of "I Say a Little Prayer" shows how he addressed the issue. "The moment I wake up" works beautifully over a rock rhythm, but would fail miserably with a swing feel. In this and many other songs, Bacharach and David adapted the conversational style of pop lyrics to rock rhythm—better than anyone else writing at that time.

"I Say a Little Prayer" also shows Bacharach's important musical innovations. These innovations touched every aspect of a song. Here are some highlights.

- *Harmony* Bacharach developed his own harmonic vocabulary, which remains absolutely unique: not pop, jazz, rock, or anything else. In "I Say a Little Prayer," Bacharach ends the simple opening vamp with a surprising chord, which returns at the end of each phrase. So each phrase of the melody begins away from the home key and ends with a question mark. This underscores the sudden emotional insecurity in the lyric at the end of each section, e.g., "To live without you would only mean heartbreak for me."

- *Melody* Many of Bacharach's hits have surprising melodic leaps. The second phrase of the song—"before I put on my make-up"—has two, between "put" and "on," and between "my" and "make." The leaps are expressive, a way to intensify the inflection of the lyric—it is difficult to imagine any other melodic shape that would be as effective. They are also an immediately recognizable part of his style. (Phrases like this show how integral Dionne Warwick was to their success. Such leaps are not easy to sing, especially back-to-back. Warwick, trained at the Hartt School of Music in addition to singing in a gospel choir, negotiates them effortlessly. Few other pop singers could.)

- *Rhythm* In this same phrase (and several other places in the song), Bacharach adds two extra beats to the measure. His flexibility regarding the number of beats in a measure extends his ability to capture speech rhythm in song. In effect, there are no conventions limiting the rhythm of the words; they can be sung almost as naturally as they are spoken.

- *Form* Bacharach also absorbed rock influences to update pop song forms. Like pre-rock pop songs, "I Say a Little Prayer" develops from a riff. However, sections are longer and end-weighted, like so many rock-era songs. Indeed, "I Say a Little Prayer" is end-weighted on three levels: at the end of each sub-section, the first two of which end with the title phrase; at the end of each section, which ends with a huge question mark in both words and music; and at the end of the song, where Bacharach finally comes home harmonically.

Among rock-era pop songwriters, Bacharach's songs stand apart. Their inventiveness and originality were unmatched, although elements of his style—e.g., the wide melodic leaps—were widely imitated by Barry Manilow, Marvin Hamlisch, and others. Bacharach's music has been dismissed by rock critics as kitsch and superficial—not really rock because it wasn't real or gritty enough. Nevertheless, he has many admirers in the rock world, among them Elvis Costello and the countless black artists who have recorded his songs.

Pop Rock in the Seventies

The biggest change in rock-era pop was not "what" but "who." A new generation of songwriters and performers, working largely within the conventions of earlier pop—lyrics about romantic love, mellifluous singing style, discreet accompaniment, and traditional pop harmony and forms—updated pre-rock popular style. The new elements were their younger voices and the use of a subtle rock rhythm. Neither their singing nor the songs had the worldliness or maturity of Sinatra singing "My Way."

Here's a question with a surprising answer: What rock-era artist or group has the most gold records? The answer is not the Beatles or Elton John or . . . It's Barbra Streisand, who has well over 30. Three significant points emerge from this observation. First, she and other pop-oriented stars of the late sixties and seventies (and beyond) were popular (in the commercial sense) as well as pop. The Carpenters were the fifth most popular singles act of the seventies; Neil Diamond ranks well ahead of many of the groups discussed in the previous chapter in both singles and album sales. Barry Manilow's early music was probably more widely known than that of any of the other artists: he earned a fortune writing jingles for McDonald's, Dr. Pepper, and other companies. Later on, he scored several hits under his own name.

Second, the fact of their popularity makes them part of the popular music landscape during the rock era. To discuss the Sex Pistols, who never charted a song in the United States during their career, and ignore Streisand, et al., skews our view of the popular music landscape.

Third, the music they recorded is not an anachronism: old pop songs sung by a new generation. It is true that songs such as Marvin Hamlisch's "The Way We Were," a No. 1 hit for Barbra Streisand in 1973, and Paul Williams's "Rainy Days and Mondays," a No. 2 hit in 1971 for the Carpenters, rely heavily on pop conventions; so does the singing of Streisand and Karen Carpenter.

However, the forms are more expansive, the phrases more end-weighted, and the harmonies more modern. Above all, the use of rock rhythm—even the really light rock rhythm used in both songs—changes the feel of the song. It affects the delivery of the words, the tempo (songs can move more slowly without sounding funereal), and the buoyancy of the melody.

Granted, songs such as the Streisand hit are not rock in the sense that we have understood rock in the last several chapters. However, the style that they represent would not exist without rock. Their existence and their success show us not only the extent of rock's influence, but also the way in which its conventions, if not its attitudes, filtered down into other styles.

Like Bacharach's music, pop rock has not been held in high regard by many rock cognoscenti. Without question, it is miles removed from Dylan's elevated discourse and the emotional strength of the soul singers. But many of the songs by Bacharach and others are beautiful on their own terms. They have worn well and found new life in the nineties.

Jazz-Rock Fusions

Jazz was slow to react to rock. The first jazz-rock fusions didn't appear until the early sixties, when rock and roll was almost a decade old. Given the affinity of jazz and R&B, jazz's slow reaction time was surprising. Indeed, one of the main currents in late fifties jazz was a "back to the roots" movement, inspired by several Ray Charles jazz recordings. Some of the dates paired him with jazz stars like vibraphonist Milt Jackson of the Modern Jazz Quartet.

However, there were several reasons why jazz did not immediately embrace rock and roll. Jazz had finally become an "art" music—music strictly for listening. Mixing with rock and roll would have meant an immediate loss of status. Moreover, like the pop establishment, many jazzmen looked at rock and roll as a crude music. They felt that rock and roll was obvious in its rhythms where jazz was subtle; simple in its three-chord songs where jazz was harmonically intricate; repetitive in its use of riffs vis-à-vis a style where imagination and inventiveness were valued.

Moreover, rock and roll had usurped jazz's place as the music of rebellion. Bebop musicians and their admirers had formed the first counterculture, and jazz was also the music of the Beats, the hipsters of the fifties. Rock and roll threatened both the status and livelihood of jazz musicians. Many reacted by snubbing the new music.

In addition to the threat from rock and roll, jazz was also going through an internal crisis. The music had become so complex that it was in danger of losing its most essential qualities: swing and expressive blues-based inflection. Faced with crises from within and without, jazz sought new directions. One of them was a fusion with rock.

The First Fusions

Jazz musicians began experimenting with rock in the early sixties. Their first attempts were largely exercises in futility: they had the repetition and directness of rock, with little of its power or density. By the mid-sixties, however, musicians such as keyboardist Herbie Hancock had begun to play rock rhythms with jazz-like subtlety and blend them with modal or pentatonic harmonies.

MILES DAVIS In the fifties and sixties, Miles Davis was the god of jazz—or, if not god, at least a major prophet. Davis's music stood out not only because of the originality of his playing, but also because he had charted many of the important new directions in jazz for the better part of two decades. His boldest innovation came in 1968.

In that year, Davis abruptly shifted gears, abandoning straight-ahead (i.e., swing-based) jazz and embracing rock. He completely overhauled the conventions of traditional jazz. Among his innovations were:

1. adding extra keyboardists and percussion to the basic jazz instrumental nucleus;
2. creating dense musical fabrics—as dense as any music of the sixties;
3. using complex rock-based rhythms;
4. slowing down chord rhythms, or even eliminating chord change altogether for long stretches;
5. abandoning the customary theme and variation form in favor of free forms held together only by periodically recurring melodic fragments;
6. taking the spotlight off the soloist—often there was no soloist, just a group groove.

All of these changes are evident in an excerpt from "Pharaoh's Dance," a 20-minute track from Davis's 1970 recording, *Bitches Brew*. By the time of

*Miles Davis in Los
Angeles, March 30, 1958.*
Photo courtesy
CORBIS/Bettmann.

this recording, he had assembled what he called "the damn best rock band in the world." It included three percussionists, acoustic and electric bassists, guitarist John McLaughlin, keyboards Chick Corea and Joe Zawinul (both of whom would soon lead their own jazz-rock fusion bands), plus Davis, bass clarinetist Benny Maupin, and soprano saxophonist Wayne Shorter.

Davis's cast of musicians was enough for three rock bands, but their sound would have been drowned out by a power trio. There is an almost impressionistic aspect to the rich texture they create: instead of the bold strokes of a rock band, where every instrument goes full bore, there are daubs of color—an electric piano riff here, a low drum fill there, a sustained bass clarinet note underneath.

Davis's role in this performance is more impresario than star. He waits over two minutes to play his first note, and when he does play, he simply floats long notes and silences over the groove set up by his musicians. Not until well into his second entrance does he move at the same speed as the rest of the band. While his part stands out during his solo, it is simply one more strand in the texture.

"Pharaoh's Dance" is, more than anything else, an extended jam. According to several musicians on the date, Davis didn't rehearse any of the composition/improvisations and gave only a few vague instructions. The musicians had to infer Davis's concept for the piece with very little information to work with and no chance for trial and error. It worked as well as it did because of

Davis's ability to select compatible musicians, musicians who were tuned in enough to pick up his musical vibrations and skilled enough to realize them in a way that was to Davis's liking.

Indeed, the greatest honor a musician could receive was an invitation to join Davis. Playing with Davis became a rite of passage for the best jazz/rock musicians of the late sixties and seventies. Almost every important leader—Joe Zawinul and Wayne Shorter of Weather Report, John McLaughlin, Chick Corea, Tony Williams, Herbie Hancock, et al.—spent some time with him.

Bitches Brew is a true jazz/rock fusion. It has the rhythm and texture of rock, plus the spontaneity and rhythmic flexibility of jazz. It uses piles of riffs, but in a less repetitive way than in rock. It is a music that draws on both styles but is different from either.

The recording was both successful and influential. It was Davis's only album to chart and go gold, and it had a profound influence on fusion musicians, who built on the innovations heard in this music. However, none of them, even those who had worked with him, approached jazz fusion with Davis's daring.

Jazz/Rock Fusions in the Seventies

Davis's alumni took fusion in numerous new directions: Hancock explored jazz/funk syntheses in the early seventies, with considerable success. Corea focused on varied fusions of jazz, Latin music, and rock in his several incarnations of Return to Forever. Joe Zawinul and Wayne Shorter formed Weather Report, which came close to Davis's collective approach to music making in much of their music. John McLaughlin created a powerful jazz/rock fusion with his Mahavishnu Orchestra.

Other jazz musicians drew inspiration from the more restrained music of singer/songwriters to create a mellower jazz fusion. Gary Burton, Pat Metheny, and Keith Jarrett stand out in this regard. And artists such as George Benson and Grover Washington, Jr. occasionally rode a pop/jazz/R&B fusion to the top of the charts.

Latin Rock

Afro-Cuban music had helped to shape rock and roll from the outset, as we heard in the music of Bo Diddley and Professor Longhair. Less directly, Latin elements—especially its rhythms and instruments—filtered into rock-era popular music, as we heard in the music of Ray Charles and Motown. During the sixties, as rock took hold throughout the world, New York Latin musicians fused rock, R&B, and a variety of Afro-Caribbean musics. Out of their work came such short-lived experiments as *bugalu*. By the early seventies, all of this music would become identified as *salsa*, although salsa remained at its core an updated version of the uptown mambo style of Tito Puente and others (heard in Chapter 2).

However, the most important, and by far the most commercially successful, fusion of Afro-Latin music and rock happened on the other side of the country, in San Francisco. Latin rock was, for all intents and purposes, a one-man movement. Its sole important representative was Mexican American Carlos Santana, an outstanding guitarist if somewhat diffident vocalist and leader. Santana was a major player in the San Francisco rock scene of the late sixties. Although not connected to Afro-Latin music by birth or geography

(New York was still the center of Latin music in the United States), he developed a strong interest in it. He parlayed this into a style that mixed rock and R&B with Latin rhythms and instruments; this style became one of the most original sounds of the rock era.

Santana's cover of Tito Puente's "Oye Como Va," which he recalled hearing Puente perform on a late-night radio broadcast from New York, shows how he blended rock and Afro-Cuban music. From the blues-driven rock bands of the late sixties, he brings his own first-rate electric guitar playing, electric bass, and Hammond organ. Augmenting the drum kit, however, is a full Latin percussion section: most clearly timbales, cowbell, congas, bongos, and guiro (the scraping sound). For the most part, the drum part remains in the background, a small part of the overall percussion mix. It is most prominent at the climaxes.

"Oye Como Va" lends itself nicely to a Latin/rock synthesis. It displays its Latin connection proudly, but is not locked into the rigid conventions of Afro-Cuban music. For instance, the rhythm of the organ riff that opens the song is clave-like, but does not fit well with either the clave or reverse clave rhythms. (Compare this rhythm to the rhythms in "Complicación," in Chapter 2.) Similarly, the bassline in Santana's performance has the openness of an Afro-Cuban bassline: little activity, and much of that off the beat.

At the same time, the rhythmic texture in Santana's recording is far more than rock rhythm played on Latin percussion instruments. The texture is dense, yet spacious-sounding. The rhythmic interplay among percussion instruments—some marking a steady pattern, others (most notably the timbales) dancing over the beat—sounds Latin, even though the underlying rhythm fits better with a basic rock beat than clave rhythms. Still, this hybrid rhythm accommodates the overlay of rock playing nicely. Both the guitar and organ solos work beautifully.

If only because of its link to Puente—and, by extension, Afro-Cuban music—"Oye Como Va" is the most notable of Santana's Latin/rock efforts. Afro-Latin elements filter into much of his other music. They may not be as prominent in other songs as they are in "Oye Como Va," but they are an integral part of the mix much of the time. The extent of their presence, unique among the major acts in the rock era, made Santana the Lone Ranger of Latin rock.

Reggae

Reggae enjoys a unique place in the history of rock. It was the first regional/ rock fusion to gain international recognition, and it was the first rock-era music to become a "roots" music—i.e., an important "outside" influence—for a new generation.

Reggae and its two antecedents, ska and rock steady, came to life during the rock era. In this respect, they are different from blues, Afro-Cuban music, and the other three fusions described in this chapter. All of these were established popular styles well before rock. Jamaican popular music took on a distinct identity only when it absorbed rock and rhythm and blues.

Many of rock's main themes are realized in reggae: the close involvement of music with its culture; the hand-in-glove relationship between music and recording technology; a local music scene that finds an international audience;

patterns of musical influence between mainstream and "outsider" styles. All have been realized in a particularly Jamaican way.

Precisely because its history begins in the rock era, the evolution of reggae parallels the evolution of rock, but in fast-forward, and with some significant editing. What had taken about 25 years to unfold in the United States and in the United Kingdom occurred in Jamaica in about half that time. In this and other ways, it *is* the early history of rock in microcosm.

Jamaican Music in Jamaican Life

A distinctly Jamaican popular music emerged at the most significant time in the country's history: its push toward independence. Jamaica began to break away from Great Britain in the late fifties and became a sovereign country in 1962. Throughout that decade and well into the next, Jamaica experienced the growing pains typical of former colonies.

During that same time period, Jamaican music responded to the country's newly-won independence by also becoming independent. Both the music and the industry that supported it flourished, while the popularity of imported music waned.

No rock-era music has enjoyed a closer relationship with the culture that produced it than reggae. According to reliable sources, there are more recordings made per capita in Jamaica than in any other country in the world.

However, it is the content of the music, not just the sheer quantity of it, that creates such a bond with its Jamaican audience. Reggae has been the voice of its people. Indeed, in the seventies, reggae stars became major players in Jamaican politics. Bob Marley was the target of an assassination attempt in 1975. It occurred just before a national election, on the night before he was to give a concert in support of Prime Minister Michael Manley. Three years later, he gave a reconciliation concert that brought together Manley and Edward Seaga, the opposition leader (and the founder of one of Jamaica's first record companies).

SOUND SYSTEMS   The Jamaican music industry got off the ground in the late fifties. Its early history revolves around sound systems, an integral part of the music scene from the beginning. Sound systems were, in effect, discotheques on wheels: huge hi-fis mounted in (or on) trucks or vans. They would be driven through Kingston and other urban areas. Instant parties would break out wherever they stopped.

Radio was another important source of American music. Kingston was within range of clear channel radio stations in Memphis, New Orleans, Miami, and other southeastern U.S. cities. Rhythm and blues, especially that heard in the South, was popular in Jamaica.

By the end of the decade, however, Jamaicans had begun to make their own records, and during the sixties, the Jamaican music industry grew exponentially.

> Chris Blackwell, a pioneer producer of Jamaican music and the founder of Island Records, wrote about the music scene around 1960: "When I went to New York in those days I used to buy the latest, most obscure 78s . . . . The sound system that had the greatest records drew the biggest crowds."

Many of the early producers started out as sound system DJs. Duke Reid, one of the most prominent, nicknamed himself "The Trojan" after the truck he used to transport his sound system. For Reid and other enterprising DJs, record production was a logical extension of their business.

Record production was a smart business decision for the most skilled and savvy producers, especially Reid, Coxsone Dodd, and, later, Lee Perry. Instead of spending exorbitant sums of money for the hottest U.S. records, they *made* money through record sales. Sound systems, an obvious way to promote their recordings, remained popular through much of the sixties. Indeed, the new government imposed curfews on sound system parties later in the decade, because so many of the songs spoke out against the government or painted such a bleak picture of daily life.

RECORDING TECHNOLOGY   The first Jamaican recordings were primitive by the international standards of the day. However, as their recording industry grew, many Jamaican recording studios upgraded their equipment. By the end of the decade, many Kingston studios were equipped with multitrack recorders.

This advance in technology was crucial to the success of reggae, because reggae is a dense yet delicate music. By way of example: the instrumentation of Bob Marley's Wailers included three guitars, bass guitar, multiple percussion, two keyboard players, plus lead and backup vocals (the "I-Threes"), and occasionally horns. Songs, e.g., Bob Marley's "Is This Love" (discussed below), had as many as eight or nine different parts going on simultaneously. Skillful mixing was required to bring them into balance.

TOASTING   DJs who ran the sound systems would often toast, or talk over the music, in order to attract business. Their commentary touched on every aspect of daily life in Jamaica: from politics to the most personal matters. To make it easier for DJs to toast over a recording, producers often extracted tracks from a recording: the vocal line was always removed, if the song had one, and often the more prominent instrumental parts were also excised. At times, all that was left was the bass and drum parts. Once stripped down, the song could be reassembled to suit the needs of the DJ. This practice, known as "dub," was the forerunner of the sampling that is so much a part of rap and hip-hop—and toasting, of course, anticipated rapping.

MESSAGE THROUGH THE MUSIC   Like the toasting DJs, Jamaican music put its finger on the pulse of the people. That wasn't the case initially. The first ska records copied song subjects as well as musical style from American R&B. However, the subject matter became more local as the music became more homegrown. There were good-time songs, bad-time songs, and, as the decade wore on, more and more songs with social messages. In its subjects, the directness of its lyrics, and strong identification with the concerns of its audience, reggae and rock steady were, in effect, Jamaica's answer to the blues.

In the seventies, reggae, and especially the music of Bob Marley, became the most public symbol of Rastafarianism. Rastafarians are a Jamaican religious cult who see Africa as the promised land and deify Ethiopian emperor Haile Selassie. (Their name means "prince Tafari," Haile Selassie's birth name.) Rastafarians have been on the fringes of Jamaican society, definitely out of the mainstream, but they have had a powerful impact musically and socially, well out of proportion to their number. Non-rastas didn't use ganja (marijuana) as part of their religion, and dreadlocks were not for everyone, although many non-Rastas wore them. Nevertheless, through the music of Marley and others, almost everyone knew about them.

After independence, many Jamaicans emigrated to the United Kingdom. They brought their music with them—first ska, then rock steady and reggae. By the seventies, London had become a home away from home for many Jamaican musicians. As a result, British musicians could easily hear the music live, and they had relatively easy access to recordings.

After it became known internationally, reggae attracted huge followings, especially in Europe and Africa. At the peak of his fame, Bob Marley was as popular as any rock star. A Marley concert in Italy drew 100,000 fans.

The Evolution of Reggae's Rhythm

When reggae emerged as an international music in the early seventies, it brought an absolutely new sound to rock. There was nothing like it at the time. The Jamaican accent of its singers and the high-pitched Rastafarian drums were obvious new elements, but perhaps the most distinctive feature, and certainly the most influential, was its rhythm.

Reggae's beat had no obvious precedents or analogues in early seventies rock. It seemed a fresh inspiration, straight from Kingston. However, there is compelling musical evidence to suggest that reggae's characteristic rhythm is in fact a multi-stage transformation of the shuffle rhythm heard in much fifties rhythm and blues.

If you compare either of the Bob Marley songs discussed below to "Rocket 88" or "Have Mercy, Baby," you may conclude that the connection between reggae and rhythm and blues seems far-fetched, because reggae's rhythmic texture is the complete opposite of a shuffle in many important respects. Shuffle rhythms mark the beat heavily; reggae avoids regular marking of the beat. Shuffle rhythms divide the beat into long/short patterns; reggae rhythms more often divide the beat evenly. Shuffle rhythms are generally thick and bass heavy; reggae rhythms float through time. Yet, numerous Jamaican recordings give evidence that reggae grew out of shuffle rhythm.

The rhythmic road from rhythm and blues to reggae took about ten years to travel; it went through ska and rock steady before arriving at reggae. The trip begins in the late fifties, with the first ska recordings. It is a fascinating journey in style regionalization and transformation.

SKA AND RHYTHM AND BLUES The first stage in the transformation began about 1960 with the first ska recordings. Ska emerged in the late fifties when Jamaicans began infusing *mento,* their local calypso-ish music, with the rhythms and sounds of rhythm and blues. Judging by the music they produced, they absorbed a wide range of black music, although New Orleans-style R&B clearly seems to be the dominant influence.

Throughout the fifties, the most popular rhythm in R&B was the four-beat based shuffle rhythm. This beat found a second home in Jamaica, as we hear in Derrick Morgan's 1959 (Jamaican) No. 1 hit, "Lover Boy." Morgan, who won the talent contest that launched his career singing Little Richard's "Long Tall Sally," was the most popular individual artist during ska's early heyday. "Lover Boy" was one of the very first ska hits.

"Lover Boy" begins with a guitar riff that clearly outlines the characteristic long/short rhythm of the shuffle. The "Jamaicanization" of this rhythm becomes apparent after Morgan begins to sing. In much early ska, the long/short rhythm remains but the emphasis is reversed. That is, the *after-beat*, not the bass note *on* the beat, is the stronger sound. On this recording, strong piano and guitar chords reinforce the afterbeat. The strongest on-the-beat sound is the low piano—and it's not very strong. This heavy afterbeat is the key to the Jamaican approach to rhythm.

The difference between African-American and Jamaican approaches to a shuffle rhythm is shown in Figure 12.1.

On Prince Buster's "Madness," recorded two years later, the difference between beat and afterbeat is so pronounced that the on-the-beat bass note might as well not be present. In this recording, the afterbeat is most heavily reinforced by the trumpet (Prince Buster's instrument). Even more than before, there is no strong bass instrument; the pianist plays what bassline there is now and again.

The second stage of the rhythmic transformation of the shuffle got underway at about the same time, when Jamaican musicians mapped the heavy afterbeat onto the straightforward eight-beat rhythm of early sixties rock and R&B. The mapping took two forms. One was an evening-out of the shuffle rhythm; the other was the isolation and highlighting of the "rebound" backbeat, heard in songs such as the Shirelles' "Will You Love Me Tomorrow." The Figure 12.2 shows both options, and the two excerpts illustrate the "afterbeat" and "rebound" rhythms, respectively.

The Jamaicanized rock rhythm is evident in Laurel Aitken's "Judgment Day." Aitken was another of ska's early stars; "Judgment Day," released in 1959, made his reputation in Jamaica. Aitken soon emigrated to England, where he became one of the stars on the British ska scene.

In this song, the heavy afterbeats occur in the guitar and saxophones. Note that in the guitar part, there is also a sound on the fourth beat. It links up with the afterbeats on either side to form a three-note pattern. This anticipates the composite afterbeat rhythm of reggae (see Figure 12.3).

The "rebound" backbeat of early sixties rock also found a home in Jamaican music. We hear an early and particularly "pure" example in Bunny and Skitter's "Chubby" (1961). Bunny and Skitter were among Jamaican music's first stars. They charted numerous hits from the late fifties on.

"Chubby" has a spare texture: mainly voices in harmony, handclaps, and the high-pitched drum sound associated with the Rastafarians. There are other

FIGURE 12.1
Comparison of African-American and Jamaican shuffle beats

African-American shuffle	X		x	X		x	X		x	X		x
Beat	1			2			3			4		
Beat division	/	/	/	/	/	/	/	/	/	/	/	/
Jamaican shuffle	x		X	x		X	x		X	x		X

Large "x" = louder sound

FIGURE 12.2
Rock and ska rhythms

Rock rhythm, with "rebound" backbeat	x	x	X	X	x	x	X	x
Beat	1		2		3		4	
Beat division	/	/	/	/	/	/	/	/
Ska's "afterbeat" rock rhythm	x	X	x	X	x	X	x	X
Ska's "rebound" backbeat rhythm			X	X			X	X

Large "x" = louder sound

FIGURE 12.3
Guitar rhythm in "Judgment Day"

Guitar part	o	x	o	x	o	x	o	x
Beat	1		2		3		4	

faint percussion sounds, but no chord instruments or horns. The hand clap pattern alternates single and "rebound" backbeats, much like those heard in the Shirelles' "Will You Love Me Tomorrow," but there is little else around the hand claps to orient the rhythm to the beat and measure.

Notably absent from all three afterbeat-based rhythms is a strong bass sound on the beginning of the beat, as is heard in American rhythm and blues. Indeed, there is often no bass instrument in the band. From the early sixties on, the afterbeat became the most prominent regular rhythm in Jamaican music.

The adaptation of the heavy afterbeat to rock was the second step in transforming the rhythm and blues beat into reggae rhythm. The next step occurred in the first rock steady recordings.

ROCK STEADY Rock steady provided the final step in the metamorphosis of the shuffle beat into reggae: layering in afterbeats at two different tempos. We hear both layers in Derrick Morgan's "Tougher than Tough" (1966), by some accounts the first rock steady recording. One layer moves quite slowly—it was a hot summer in 1966—the other moves twice as fast. They are shown below.

Slow tempo beat	1				2			
Rim shot (drum)			X				X	
Fast tempo beat	1		2		3		4	
Piano and ride cymbal		X		X		X		X

The two afterbeat layers combine to create the composite afterbeat rhythm shown below.

Rim shot (drum)		X		X

+

Piano and ride cymbal	X		X	X

=

Composite afterbeat rhythm	X	X	X	X	X	X

This composite afterbeat rhythm is the most consistent regular rhythm in rock steady and reggae. In this respect, it is equivalent to the backbeat and eight-beat rhythmic layer of rock.

To understand its uniqueness, we contrast this composite afterbeat rhythm with the beat of sixties music. In a straightforward rock or soul song, songs have a central tempo. We can find the beat, and thus the tempo, by listening to the interaction of the backbeat and the eight-beat rhythm. The beat falls between them: twice as fast as the backbeat, and half as fast as the eight-beat rock rhythm. So even if no single strand of the rhythmic texture marks the beat, we can still locate it easily.

By contrast, each afterbeat layer in "Tougher than Tough" implies its own tempo. Although the slow tempo is the main rhythmic reference, it is not nearly so obvious (at least to non-Jamaicans) as it is in rock.

Rock steady also added a strong bass voice to Jamaican music. The presence of the bass certainly conformed to standard rock practice, but its function was boldly innovative. Unlike the piano chords and drum layers, the bassline follows no regular pattern, but instead roams freely.

With the creation of the composite afterbeat rhythm and the addition of the bass, the rhythmic foundation of reggae was in place. In reggae, the basic rhythmic texture of rock steady is treated more flexibly, and with greater complexity. Reggae rhythms may layer any of the three ska rhythms—rock-based afterbeat, shuffle-based afterbeat, or the rebound backbeat—over the slow tempo afterbeat rhythm. These produce reggae's "ka-CHUNK-a" rhythmic signature in some form. Moreover, reggae's rhythmic texture is typically denser and more subtle, with several additional rhythmic layers, including Rasta percussion.

RHYTHMIC EVOLUTION: ROCK VS. REGGAE In retrospect, the rhythmic evolution of reggae seems to parallel the rhythmic evolution of rock in its basic pattern, if not in the details. The heavy afterbeats of ska have their counterpart in the triplets heard in Fats Domino's rhythm and blues: both add a distinctive new element, but do not present a new beat. Rock steady pairs up with rock and roll, in that both offer a distinctive new beat in rather simple form. Along the same line, reggae and rock both offer more varied and complex versions of the simple new beat. Both reggae and rock are identified most immediately by their beat, regardless of how it is realized.

GETTING THE MESSAGE "Tougher than Tough" and, by extension, rock steady, anticipates reggae in another important way. Its lyric depicts a mock trial of "rude boys," Jamaica's equivalent of ghetto gangs. The song illustrates how Jamaican music had begun to engage the issues of daily life, rather than offer escape from them, as was the case in the ska recordings.

Many reggae songs were topical: "Get Up, Stand Up" is virtually a Rastafarian call to arms. More often, however, their themes were universal. More than any other music, reggae became rock's conscience in the seventies, as most American and British rock deserted the moral high ground occupied by the rock of the sixties.

Bob Marley and Seventies Reggae

Bob Marley was born in Jamaica in 1945. His recording career began in the early sixties and took off in 1964, after he formed the first edition of his back-up group, the Wailers. By the early seventies, he was extremely popular in Jamaica. However, it wasn't until he signed with Island Records that his reputation spread throughout the world.

His success on record and in concert gave him and his country's music unprecedented exposure. For many people, Bob Marley *was* reggae. Worldwide,

Bob Marley on stage, c. 1980. PHOTO COURTESY *CORBIS/S.I.N.*

he was its most popular artist. He was also the decade's most visible spokesperson for peace and brotherhood, carrying the torch of sixties social activism and idealism into the seventies. He also made his Rastafarian affiliation clear, as we'll hear in "Get Up, Stand Up." While Marley's stance didn't completely legitimize Rastafarianism, it certainly raised its status in Jamaica and elsewhere. However, Marley's music left the deepest impression. It made possible his popularity, which in turn gave him the leverage to work for meaningful change in Jamaican society.

With our previous understanding of reggae rhythm as a point of reference, we can study two songs by Bob Marley, "Get Up, Stand Up," recorded in 1973, and "Is This Love," recorded five years later, in 1978.

Like so much rock-era popular music, the music of Bob Marley and the Wailers was a collective effort. As the lead singer and the composer of most of the group's hits, Marley was its guiding force and most visible member. However, the Barrett brothers (Aston "Familyman" Barrett on bass and Carlton Barrett on drums), percussionist Bunny Livingston, and keyboardist Peter Tosh (shortened from Peter MacIntosh) also played significant roles.

"Get Up, Stand Up" shows Marley's political side. The chorus of the song exhorts Rastafarian true believers to take a stand, while the verses lays out central tenets in the Rastafarian belief system, including the personification of God in Ethiopian emperor Haile Selassie. Like its message, the music is direct—for a reggae song. Its form is the refrain-frame form heard so often in rock-era popular music.

"Is This Love" is much more intimate: Marley is speaking one-on-one with a special woman. In keeping with the content and tone of the lyric, the form of this song sprawls lazily through time, moving at a more relaxed tempo than "Get Up, Stand Up."

Taken together, the two songs show essential qualities of reggae style and the flexibility with which these style elements can be handled. We consider each in turn.

"Get Up, Stand Up" uses the standard reggae beat. Over this basic beat are layered several fragmentary lines. Three stand out:

- The high pitched drum fills that signal the Rastafarian connection
- The keyboard and guitar fills that comment on the vocal lines in the chorus
- The roaming bass lines

Both songs show the continuing evolution of bass playing in Jamaican music: the bass is the least role-bound of the major instruments in a reggae band. Bassists can fill any of three roles. They can double the melody or a higher pitched countermelody; play their own melodic-like figure in opposition to the melody; or support the harmony with bass notes of chords.

In the refrain of "Get Up, Stand Up," the bass line opposes the vocal line with its own melodic figure in a free rhythm. A new, wider-ranging bass riff in a higher register complements the new melody introduced in the verse. The contrast in high and low register between verse and refrain underscores the greater weight of the message contained in the refrain.

The bass, vocal lines, and the instruments that create the reggae beat are several strands in a complex texture. Other lines—e.g., a faint rhythm guitar here, a barely audible shaker there—are woven into a rich but almost transparent tapestry of sound. The same textural approach occurs on an even more elaborate scale in "Is This Love."

A comparison of the rhythm in the two songs suggests the flexibility of reggae rhythm. "Get Up, Stand Up" uses a rock-based afterbeat in the faster layer. By contrast, "Is This Love" layers an elaborate form of the shuffle-based beat. Combined with a slower tempo, it projects a quite different rhythmic feel. Note that in both songs, the slower rhythm is the same. It is only the faster-moving layer that is varied.

The slower layer (whose afterbeat is marked by a sharp guitar "chunk") is the reference tempo, as it is in most rock steady and reggae songs. The vocal line implies the primacy of slower tempo, especially when Marley sings the title phrase over and over: "Is this love, is this love, is this love, is this love that I'm feelin'?"

The gentle pulsations of the drum and tambourine, prompted by the fast shuffle afterbeat rhythm in the organ, keep the rhythm afloat, while the vocal parts—Marley's slow-moving melody and the sustained harmonies of the "I-Threes"—and in-and-out bass slow the beat down to a speed below typical body rhythms—even the heartbeat at rest or the pace of a relaxed stroll. As a result, the rhythm of the song is buoyant and lazy at the same. All of this evokes a feeling of languid lovemaking in the tropics, a perfect musical counterpoint to the lyric of the song.

THE IMPACT OF REGGAE   Reggae enjoyed its greatest popularity during the seventies, when Marley's career reached its peak. His death from cancer in 1981 seemed to precipitate reggae's decline in popularity during the eighties. However, by that time, it had become a major influence on post-1975 rock. It echoes through new wave (the Clash, Elvis Costello), white and black pop (Eagles, Marvin Gaye, Tina Turner), and rap (everyone). (We will discuss several reggae-influenced styles in subsequent chapters.) No other rock-era regional style has touched so many diverse styles.

Its influence went beyond the music: Reggae became rock's conscience in the seventies, as so much American and British rock deserted the moral high ground occupied by the significant rock of the sixties.

Summary

The music surveyed in this chapter can only hint at the extent of the interaction between rock and non-rock styles, once rock became the dominant popular style. Brazilian music gave the most and took the least, as its rhythms and instruments filtered into seventies black music, pop rock, and various jazz fusions. Latin rock flowered briefly, but significantly. Afro-Cuban music continued to influence rock-era music, especially disco. The pop/rock fusions pioneered by the Brill Building songwriters would become commercially important in the late sixties and seventies. The best songs of Bacharach and others would also be creatively significant. Once they got the hang of it, jazz musicians produced some of the boldest musical experiments of the era. Jazz/rock fusions covered a lot of stylistic territory, intersecting not only with rock, but also funk, soul, black pop, and Brazilian music. Reggae had the most profound encounter with rock. It came into existence through Jamaicans' contact with rhythm and blues, and developed its own distinctive voice. In the seventies, reggae returned the favor, influencing a wide range of music.

All five were "outside" styles, either geographically or musically. Precisely because of this, they show—even more than the music of previous chapters—the extent of rock's influence. This trend would continue: by the eighties, rock would be the first global musical language.

KEY TERMS

Maxixe	Bugalu	Ska
Bossa nova	Reggae	Mento
Samba	Toasting	Rebound rhythm
Jazz-rock	Rastafarianism	Afterbeat
Fusion	Shuffle rhythms	Rock steady

CHAPTER QUESTIONS

1. Review sixteen-beat rhythms, then compare either of the Brazilian songs with the sixteen-beat based songs in Chapter 6, or Roberta Flack's "Feel Like Makin' Love" in Chapter 14. Do you hear a connection—rhythmic and otherwise—between the Brazilian songs and black pop? What links them? How are they different?

2. Consider this paradox: Dionne Warwick is considered "black pop"—and there-fore part of rock. Burt Bacharach is considered "pop"—and therefore non-rock, even though Warwick made her reputation singing his songs. Do you feel that this is a fair assessment? Explore this idea further by comparing "I Say a Little Prayer" with a late fifties' or early sixties' recording by Frank Sinatra, Tony Bennett, or another major pop star. What pop elements do the songs have in common? What elements of Bacharach's song evidence that it could not have been written before the rock era?

3. Compare Miles Davis's "best damn rock band in the world" to any of the record-ings by the "World's Greatest Rock and Roll Band." What common ground do you find between "Pharaoh's Dance" and any of the Stones' recordings? Do you think that Davis's recording is rock? If so, why? If not, why?

4. Review clave rhythm and the sound of Latin music by listening to "El Manisero" and "Complicaciòn." Then listen to "Oye Como Va," and detail similarities and differences between it and Latin recordings, then it and other sixties' rock recordings. How strong is the Latin influence, in your opinion?

5. Using the figures in the discussion of reggae and the ska and rock steady excerpts, work through the transformation of the rhythm and blues shuffle into the reggae beat. Try doing it with a partner: one at each tempo. Then clap along with the two Bob Marley recordings, to feel the difference in beat division at the faster speed.

chapter 13

Melody and Meaning

In the late sixties, rock acquired a gentler, if not always kinder, side. While the Rolling Stones, Hendrix, and others were finding the groove, Simon and Garfunkel were "feelin' groovy." They and others developed a kind of contemporary, urban, country music (if that's not an oxymoron). The lyrics and their musical settings were often more sophisticated than the music coming out of Nashville, and the performers seldom sang with a nasal twang. However, the underlying impulses were much the same: words that told a story, often autobiographical, in plain if thoughtful language; melodies that helped tell the story; and generally subdued accompaniments, often with acoustic instruments—even a single guitar.

Much of this music has been called folk rock. The term suggests a merger of contemporary "folk" music with rock elements, as in the Byrds' version of Dylan's "Mr. Tambourine Man." But, even apart from the misleading use of the term "folk," this is too limited a label. Indeed, a good deal of the music has virtually no connection with either rock or folk music: Van Morrison's songs stand out in this regard. And some of it, e.g., Crosby, Stills, Nash, and Young's "Teach Your Children" or the Byrds' entire *Sweethearts of the Rodeo* album, are country in every respect except the pedigree of the performers. The common bond linking most of this music is the focus on the story: a personal tale or commentary, told in song.

The major influence on this body of music was, of course, Bob Dylan. His songs set the tone. In them, he showed a new generation what they could say and how they could say it. However, there were others within the rock tradition who helped shape its sound and sensibility. Buddy Holly, the Everly Brothers, Roy Orbison, and the Brill Building songwriters were important early sources. The Beatles and the Byrds were the most influential of Dylan's contemporaries. Other influences came from everywhere: folk and country especially, but also jazz, blues, pop, Latin music, etc.

In this chapter, we will study three late sixties acts who told stories in song, then sample the singer/songwriters of the early seventies.

Beyond Dylan: The First Generation of Singer/Songwriters

Three popular acts—Simon and Garfunkel, Van Morrison, and Crosby, Stills, Nash, and Young—give some sense of the variety of the music created by the first wave of singer/songwriters. There is one solo singer, Van Morrison; one duo, Simon and Garfunkel; and a group (Crosby, Stills, and Nash) that started off as a trio and briefly grew into a quartet with the addition of Neil Young. Simon and Garfunkel were the closest to folk style: their accompaniments built off of Simon's guitar playing. CSN&Y straddled the boundary between the singer/songwriters and harder rock: their accompaniments often went electric. In his early recordings, Morrison had a predilection for jazz, which he blended into his unique musical personality.

Van Morrison

Van Morrison's *Astral Weeks* (1968) continues to rank as one of the major recordings of the rock era. If they gave Grammys for most unlikely major rock album, *Astral Weeks* would probably win hands down. Morrison came from a different place, and so did his music.

Van Morrison was born in Belfast, Northern Ireland, in 1945. He heard very little rock and roll growing up; instead, he listened to the blues, country, and jazz in his father's record collection. After forming the group Them in Belfast in 1964 and moving to England, Morrison disbanded the group in 1966 and accepted producer Bert Berns's invitation to come to the United States. After Berns's sudden death in 1967, Morrison signed with Warner Brothers and recorded *Astral Weeks*, his most influential recording, soon after.

Astral Weeks was that rare artistic phenomenon, a bona fide original. Everything about the album seems to go against the grain. At a time when record production was becoming more sophisticated by the day (keep in mind the "Good Vibrations"/"A Day in the Life" exchange a year earlier), Morrison recorded the album in two days with a group of studio musicians. Many of them were top jazz artists; none of them played much rock. There is a curious blend of sloppiness and sophistication. Morrison might have tuned his guitar more carefully, and there is an obvious difference of harmonic opinion between bassist Richard Davis and Morrison in "Ballerina" (ca. 1 minute, 43 seconds) and between Morrison and the background strings in "Cyprus Avenue" (ca. 6 minutes) that probably should have been redone or edited. But Morrison's songs are challenging; the playing of Davis, drummer Connie Kay (of the Modern Jazz Quartet), and the other musicians is especially sensitive; and Larry Fallon's delicate string-rich arrangements are an effective backdrop for Morrison's singing.

At the heart of the album are Morrison's songs and his singing of them. They are not songs in any conventional sense. Unlike a Beatles' or Motown song, the melodic line does not have a clear identity apart from the words. There are no nicely sculpted phrases, no ear-catching hooks, as in "My Girl," and there is an irregular flow to the rhythms. It's difficult to imagine people whistling "Cyprus Avenue," as they might whistle "I Heard It Through the

Grapevine." Instead, Morrison seems to have returned to the most basic conception of melody: intensified speech. Much of the time, Morrison's singing seems like an amplification of the kind of inflection that an actress would give her lines, or a poet would use in reading his work. Sometimes the words spill out, carried on a wave of melody.

We have encountered melody as intensified speech previously: in the blues. So had Morrison: Leadbelly was among his favorites. But Morrison is miles from simple emulation of blues singing. Instead the blues tinge his singing slightly; it's a style beyond category.

Precisely because it is closer to rock style than any other song on the album, "Cyprus Avenue" shows how far removed Morrison's songs and his singing are from the rock mainstream. The song is a conventional blues: a series of rhymed couplets, accompanied by a standard blues chord progression. The basic rhythmic feel of the song could be related to rock: Unlike most of the songs on the album, there are four beats in the measure, and each beat is divided into two equal parts.

However, that's where the parallel to rock rhythm ends. There's no backbeat, no strong marking of the eight-beat layer, and very little syncopation, because there's not much beat to push against. Instead, there is Morrison's voice and strummed guitar, Davis's bass in counterpoint, the occasional tinkle of a harpsichord, a cushion of strings, and jazz flute and violins. If a rock band is primary colors, then this setting is delicate pastels. The delicacy is an esthetic necessity, because Morrison's singing is so unrestrained. At least in this song, louder, more powerful rhythms in the accompaniment would have almost surely shackled him.

When the song is well underway, the instrumental parts—violin, flute, harpsichord, bass—swirl around Morrison's voice. This richer setting helps build intensity as Morrison brings his story to a climax. Here Morrison's powerful narrative and the large-scale planning of the instrumental setting give the song tremendous sweep. Details may be spontaneous, improvised, even accidental; Morrison's singing certainly gives the impression of spur-of-the-moment impulse. But the overall momentum from beginning to end suggests a larger vision.

These qualities—the contrast between the power of Morrison's words and singing and the delicacy of the accompaniment; the spontaneity of detail vs. the impact of the song as a whole; the distance from rock conventions—are also evident in the haunting "Beside You."

To understand how different these qualities make Morrison's music, we can compare it to songs with which we're familiar. In almost all songs, words are harnessed to the music. They respect such musical conventions as regular phrases, intelligible melodic ideas, recurrent riffs, steady rhythms, and clearly outlined forms. How many times would you say "my girl" or "I want to hold your hand" or "I can't get no satisfaction" in normal conversation?

In "Beside You," the tables are turned. Morrison's tale spills out, unfettered by any convention, even something as simple as blues couplets. The music, most notably Davis's bass and Jay Berliner's flamenco-inflected guitar, floats along underneath. This song is miles from rock; yet, paradoxically, it is very much of its time.

Here especially Morrison's songwriting and singing emerge as a completely organic and unified conception. Normally we can separate out the elements of a song performance: here are the words, here is the melody, this is the way the singer sings the melody. But with Morrison, they are indivisible; they seem to spring from a single impulse. Of all the qualities of his music evidenced on *Astral Weeks*, this is perhaps the most individual.

Morrison's music makes us confront a fundamental question about style: how can music that is so far removed from rock conventions be rock music? There is no way that any song on the album will be confused with a Cream, Who, or Rolling Stones song. The answer lies, we think, in the idea of rock sensibility. Among the most powerful impulses behind rock-era music was the idea that you could make a meaningful statement without the trappings of art. We heard this in Dylan's music, we heard it in soul. The Beatles' decision to use symphonic strings (e.g, "A Day in the Life") was a choice, not a requirement. If you chose to use the conventions of the period—rock beats, riffs, loud guitars, etc.—fine. Morrison could, and did in an idiosyncratic way: his 1971 rocker "Wild Night" mixes steel guitar with Memphis-style horns. If you chose to use other means, as Morrison often did, that's fine, too. What matters is the emotional commitment and the power of the statement, and Morrison's music has both in abundance.

Morrison has remained a restless seeker throughout his career. He has formed and reformed bands. He has moved from New York to California, back to Ireland, then back to the United States. He has retired and come out of retirement. What he has not done is compromise his musical vision to achieve popular success. He has been popular, particularly in the early seventies: *Moondance*, the album that followed *Astral Weeks*, went platinum, and he has even charted a few singles. But that has not been his goal.

Although others sold better, *Astral Weeks* was nevertheless Morrison's most influential album. Through it, he brought to rock-era music an extraordinarily personal musical vision, one that had to broaden the musical perspective of its audience.

Simon and Garfunkel

Listeners catching a snatch of Simon and Garfunkel's first big hit, "The Sounds of Silence" (1965), might be forgiven for assuming that the duo had "folkified" the Everly Brothers's sound. There was good reason. Close-harmony duet singing was uncommon in both rock and roll and the music of the folk revival, so the Everly Brothers were the obvious precedents (as well as strong influences). Moreover, the singing of Simon and Garfunkel, especially Garfunkel's fragile tenor, bears some resemblance to the sweet harmonies of the Everlys. But the Everly Brothers' music was simply a point of departure for them. They would develop one of the most distinctive styles of the sixties.

Paul Simon and Art Garfunkel grew up together in Queens, New York. As teenagers, billing themselves as Tom and Jerry, they had a minor hit in 1957 with the pop song "Hey Schoolgirl," written by Simon. They split up to attend college. During the late fifties Simon was involved with both the pop songwriting business (he co-wrote a song with Carole King) and the Greenwich Village folk scene. Both experiences would figure prominently in his later work.

Simon and Garfunkel reunited in 1962 and released *Wednesday Morning, 3 AM*, in 1964. "The Sounds of Silence" was on that album. It didn't become a hit, however, until producer Tom Wilson added an electric guitar, bass, and drums backup—without Simon and Garfunkel's permission. The electric version of the song, released in 1965, made their reputation, and led to enormous

Simon & Garfunkel in a characteristic pose, April 28, 1967. PHOTO COURTESY CORBIS/BETTMANN.

success for the rest of the sixties. Among their most noteworthy achievements was Simon's music for *The Graduate*, a 1968 film about a college graduate's (Dustin Hoffman) affair with an older woman. It was one of the first major films to use rock-based music in the soundtrack. Its success opened up the film industry to using rock music in soundtracks.

A closer listening to "The Sounds of Silence" shows how original both Simon's song and Simon and Garfunkel's sound were. The lyric paints a dark portrait of contemporary society—almost like an Edward Hopper painting. It is set to a long melody that builds slowly toward a peak just past the halfway point, then gently descends. In this case, the "sounds of silence" come in waves.

The song shows how Simon drew on his folk and pop experiences in his songwriting. The melody develops from a brief opening idea, much like a pop song does. However, like many folk and folk-style songs, "The Sounds of Silence" has a *strophic* form. That is, the story told in the song unfolds over several verses, all set to the same melody.

The song is also an early example of modal melody and harmony: it predates the Beatles' "Eleanor Rigby" by a year. The vocal harmony highlights the modal flavor, because Simon mixes in the open sound of fifths (the interval used in power chords) with more conventional close harmony.

In all of these ways—the subject and tone of its lyric, the mix of folk and pop elements in the melody, its modal sound—"The Sounds of Silence" helped point out a new direction in songwriting. It also presaged Simon's imaginative style syntheses in the songs he would subsequently write for the duo and, later, for himself.

Simon and Garfunkel's late sixties hits cover a lot of musical turf. The two No. 1 hits stand out: "Mrs. Robinson," written for *The Graduate*, has echoes of Buddy Holly ("Well . . . All Right") and the Beatles; "Bridge Over Troubled Water" (1970) is a great gospel song. However, the most imaginative song of their career may well have been "The Boxer" (1970). In it, Simon narrates the story of a young man adrift in the city. He fills the lyric with vivid images that contrast the timelessness of the basic story—it could as easily be a century old as a year old—with the gritty reality of contemporary urban life.

In "The Boxer," Simon's juxtaposition of current and archaic also includes the music. As in "The Sounds of Silence," Simon tells his story over a long, beautifully paced melody, which is repeated again and again as the story unfolds. However, he adds a wordless refrain, which evokes the "fa-la-la" refrains of the sixteenth- and seventeenth-century English madrigals. The instrumental accompaniment also supports this old/new contrast. The accompaniment of the guitars is both old and new: folk and folk revival. The subtle bass drum rhythm suggests the bodhran, the percussion instrument of Irish traditional bands, and the buzzing and trumpet-like obbligato instruments also evoke the sound of a Renaissance wind band. But the thuds that echo through the texture periodically are up-to-date sounds; so is the wall of sound at the end of the song. The use of musical references, singly, or more often in combination, would become a trademark of Simon's solo music.

Simon and Garfunkel parted ways professionally in 1970. Simon has broadened his palette as songwriter and performer in his solo career, which we will discuss in greater detail below.

Crosby, Stills, Nash, and Young

If Van Morrison's music showed how far rock's boundaries could be stretched, then the music of Crosby, Stills, Nash, and Young showed how difficult it is to draw them in the first place. Their music is beyond category, not because they define a new sound world, as both Morrison and Simon and Garfunkel did, but because they move around so effortlessly in the world which they inhabit. One song might have strong country-rock overtones ("Teach Your Children"), another evoke the Beatles' "Penny Lane" ("Our House"). The unifying elements are the vivid pictures they painted in the words of their songs—social commentary, cautionary tales, personal stories—and their high, close vocal harmony that was almost always present, regardless of the musical setting.

Crosby, Stills, Nash, and Young were among the numerous "supergroups" that surfaced around 1970. They stayed together less than two years, from early 1969 to late 1970. Their rise and fall exemplified the fluidity within the rock world during this time. The group had its roots in Buffalo Springfield, which was formed in 1966. Its charter members included Stephen Stills and Neil Young. They followed the midway path between folk and rock pioneered by the Byrds. After the group split up, Neil Young embarked on a solo career. Meanwhile, Stills met David Crosby of the Byrds and Graham Nash, a member of the Hollies, one of the British Invasion bands, at Cass Elliot's house. After jamming together, they decided to form a group, which they did in 1968. A year later, they invited Young to join the group. Unfortunately, the chemistry suggested by their beautiful harmony singing masked the friction caused by the almost inevitable clash of several strong egos. It led to their dissolution about a year and a half later.

The basic character of the CSNY sound is evident in Buffalo Springfield's biggest hit, "For What It's Worth" (1967). A spacious-sounding musical background—high, keening electric guitar, bass drum, an occasional strum of acoustic guitar—provides an ominous setting for Stills's lyric, a biting commentary on the establishment's reaction to social protest. The tone of the lyrics, their primacy in the texture, and the mix of electric and acoustic instruments would all carry over into their subsequent incarnations.

What's missing is the high harmony. That would appear when Crosby, Stills, and Nash came together. When Young joined the group, he added an edge to the sound, particularly in his guitar playing. These qualities are evident in his song "Ohio." Young wrote the song in a white heat as a response to the shooting of four people by National Guardsmen at Kent State University in 1970.

The lyric is as serious as a heart attack; it is miles in subject and style from conventional pop lyrics. Indeed, it fulfills the prophecy of "For What It's Worth." And where the mood of the earlier song was ominous, this song, with its jangly guitar riff and lumbering beat, seems to evoke the confrontation described in the lyric. The trademark close harmony sets the words of the chorus. Taken together, these qualities render "Ohio" perhaps the quintessential Crosby, Stills, Nash, and Young recording—if such a thing is possible.

Déjà Vu (1970), the group's first and most successful album, covers a lot of stylistic ground. The songs are of markedly different character, from the folk-like simplicity of Stills's "4 + 20" to the raucous, hard-rocking drive of "Everybody I Love You"; from the straightforward country feel of Nash's "Teach Your Children" to the tongue-twisting rhythms and subtle harmonies of Crosby's "Déjà Vu." In fact, there are character shifts within several songs: "Déjà Vu" and Stills's "Carry On" are prime examples. One reason for the contrasts is the organization of the group. The album is not so much a team effort as a group of mini-albums by each of the stars, with the others serving as "guest artists" on the date. All have distinctive voices, especially Crosby and Young, and each man sings his own song.

Ironically, the most successful song from the album was Joni Mitchell's "Woodstock," which Crosby, Stills, and Nash transformed from her ballad into a hard-rocking song. Its driving beat and surly guitar show Young's influence. The high, closely voiced, modal harmonies in the chorus stamp the song as CSNY.

In their brief time together, Crosby, Stills, Nash, and Young carved a small but significant niche for themselves in the world of rock. In addition to developing a "sound" signature, they explored that delicate equilibrium between verbal message and musical impact. They showed that songs could tell a story or send a message and still rock. Of course, they were not unique in this ability, but they did it in an individual way.

After the group split apart, each of its members pursued a solo career. Young's has been by far the most successful. They also recombined intermittently in various groupings: Stills and Young; Crosby, Stills, and Nash; etc. They have reunited as a foursome only once, in the late 1980s; Young left the group (again) shortly after they recorded *American Dream* (1988). However, their legacy rests almost completely in the albums recorded during their brief time together in the late sixties.

The Singer/Songwriters

There is no more eclectic subcategory within rock music than "singer/song-writer." Interpreted literally, "singer/songwriter" identifies those who perform the music they create. That includes almost every rock-era act! However, the term came into use during the early seventies to identify a body of performers who told stories in song, usually by themselves. Their songs were supported by a subdued, often acoustic accompaniment that put the vocal line in the forefront.

Within these general parameters, there has been an astonishing variety. Some songs are intimate, first-person accounts, confessional in tone. Others are *cinema verité* portraits, still others cryptic accounts that leave the identity of the narrator in question. Most are songs in a restricted sense of the term: they have coherent melodies that help tell the story and make musical sense through an inner logic. They are seldom formulaic: formal and melodic imagination finds its greatest outlet in these songs.

The music grouped under the singer/songwriter label represented the continued exploration of the path marked off first by Dylan, the Beatles, and the Byrds, then by the artists discussed above and some in Chapter 9: Lou Reed, Jim Morrison, and Frank Zappa.

There were old and new faces among the singer/songwriters. Carole King was a Brill Building veteran: she had been a professional songwriter for over a decade before releasing her first album. Neil Young and Paul Simon continued their careers as solo performers. They were joined by a new generation of folk-inspired performers, most notably Joni Mitchell and James Taylor. Randy Newman, by contrast, came from a family heavily involved in traditional pop and film music. A survey of their music will give some sense of the extraordinary variety of music grouped under the singer/songwriter umbrella. We begin where we left off, with the music of Neil Young.

Neil Young

If a single incident can sum up the restless spirit and unpredictability that informs Neil Young's music, it's this: his then-record label, Geffen Records, sued him for making recordings that didn't sound like Neil Young! Young's songs have overtones of country, rockabilly, rhythm and blues, techno-based pop, not to mention hard rock and punk. He is seemingly open to everything, and because of this, his music defies category—or, better, it is constantly roaming from category to category.

Young grew up in Winnipeg, Manitoba. He made his way to the United States via Toronto, where he met Stephen Stills and Joni Mitchell, among others. From there, he moved to Los Angeles, where he formed Buffalo Springfield with Stills. After that group broke up, Young embarked on a solo career. He has often worked with a ragged, hard-rock band called Crazy Horse as his accompaniment; he has also, from time to time, performed with various combinations of Crosby, Stills, and Nash. But his solo work has been his most lasting contribution to rock.

Young tells good stories. He paints vivid images in words and music, and develops his plots slowly and elliptically. His portraits are typically dark: greys and browns. They are bleak, yet intensely human.

In "The Loner," perhaps the best-known song from his self-titled first album (1969), Young describes the loner, apparently a certified creep who spends his time lurking and stalking. The heavy-footed, guitar-rich accompaniment reinforces the sense of danger and foreboding. An abrupt shift in the texture—richer harmony, high strings, a smoother rhythmic flow—and cryptic lyrics hint that there may more to the story. As the song unfolds, we learn that the loner is not a pervert, but a man devastated by the breakup of a relationship. A tender instrumental section that serves as both interlude and epilogue suggests even more strongly that we can respond to the loner with empathy rather than fear.

If "The Loner" is fictional, "Tonight's the Night" (1975), is not. Bruce Berry was one of Young's roadies. Like Crazy Horse guitarist Danny Whitten, Berry died of a drug overdose. The song is part eulogy, part cry of despair. Typically, he tells the story in pieces, and allusively, not directly. As we listen to the song, we can visualize with photographic clarity Bruce sitting with Young's guitar, after the gig had finished, doing his best Neil Young imitation. The refrain is even more elusive: does it refer to the night of his death (of course), to getting high (probably), or to something else as well? As in the earlier song, the contrasts in the musical setting underscore the message of the lyrics. In the refrain, the rhythm floats like Young's voice, perhaps suggesting the suspension of time that is part of the drug experience. By contrast, the verse sections have a nice groove, and Young's singing is much more forthright.

These two songs simply scratch the surface of Young's varied output. Over his long career—he has retained his loyal fan base and added new ones with each generation—he has explored a lot of musical territory, and these songs are a small slice of that.

Still, they bring to light essential aspects of his complex, contradictory musical personality. Alone among the major singer/songwriters, Young knew how to rock hard, and did so regularly. Yet, his music may also contain moments of considerable tenderness. Often both dimensions appear within the same song. His quavering voice is not pretty or powerful, yet it is capable of expressing a wide range of emotions. His songs are not obvious, in either words or music, yet their messages have impact and staying power.

James Taylor

If Neil Young's songs grab you by the front of the shirt, James Taylor's tug gently on the sleeve. Taylor was rock's first great conversationalist. Even in songs that express deep feelings, such as "Fire and Rain," Taylor sings as if he's talking with you one-on-one. He sings with emotional reserve, not excess, even when he talks about highly personal and obviously painful subjects.

Taylor grew up in Chapel Hill, North Carolina. His childhood was privileged (his father was dean of the University of North Carolina Medical School and the family was wealthy enough to summer on Martha's Vineyard) and problematic (Taylor committed himself to a mental institution while in his teens). Through his older brother Alex (all four Taylor siblings—James, Alex, Livingston, and Kate—would have professional careers), he discovered folk and country music. After working in and around New York in the mid-sixties, he moved to England, where he recorded his self-titled debut album in 1968 for Apple Records under the auspices of the Beatles. The album didn't do well, so Taylor returned to the United States, while Peter Asher—better known as one-half of the pop duo Peter and Gordon, who had produced his Apple recording—negotiated a contract with Warner Brothers. Taylor's first two albums for Warner Brothers were enormously successful and established his career.

Taylor recorded both originals and covers. This division in recorded output highlights a fascinating paradox in his career. His own songs are quintessential

James Taylor on stage, May 1978. PHOTO COURTESY *CORBIS/*NEAL PRESTON.

singer/songwriter material: autobiographical accounts that are nothing less than public confessions of his troubles and desires. These he delivers in a restrained, almost laconic manner. His covers generally find him with a smile on his face. His originals were more emulated; his covers more successful.

Taylor's early songs, such as "Something in the Way She Moves" and "Fire and Rain," beautifully illustrate the fresh new sound that he brought to rock. Front and center, of course, is his low-key delivery. Surrounding the melody is a musical setting that artfully blends country, folk, and rock. The core rock instrumentation is intact, except that the instruments are acoustic, not electric. Rock rhythm, when it is used (which is most of the time), is muted; the emphasis is on the melody and the chords that support it.

In 1968, the chords, and the arpeggiated elaborations of them that he played on the guitar, were a new blend of old sounds. From country music came the general idea of a few simple chords and pentatonic elaborations. But many of the chords were derived from modal scales: the openings phrases of both songs illustrate this. The result was a fresh family of chords. It was quickly copied. Later songs, such as "Mexico" (1975), mine the same lode, but are richer harmonically and texturally.

In his covers, Taylor adopts a different, more upbeat persona. He substitutes reassurance and authority for the yearning and regret that seem so much a part of his original work. Much of this difference is found in the choice of songs: "You've Got a Friend" and "How Sweet It Is (To Be Loved by You)," the latter a 1964 hit for Marvin Gaye, have upbeat messages. But it's also in how he presents them. The calmness of his delivery and easy flow of the accompaniment in "You've Got a Friend" are the musical version of an arm around the shoulder, while the soul-inspired urgency of his singing in "How Sweet It Is" helps convey the happy message of that song.

Taylor's career peaked in the early seventies, as he scored a series of successes on both album and singles charts. He achieved further celebrity with his marriage to Carly Simon in 1972; they divorced in 1983. He continues to enjoy intermittent commercial success, while keeping a good-sized fan base. And he seems to have left his personal problems, including heroin addiction, in the past.

Taylor's best songs, and his singing of them, brought to rock an unprecedented intimacy and sense of personal connection with the artist. His music epitomized rock's gentler side. With its acoustic instrumentation, novel, modal-based harmonies, and restrained but gritty vocal sound, it added an important new dimension to the sound of rock.

Joni Mitchell

Joni Mitchell was born Roberta Anderson in Alberta, Canada, and grew up in the Canadian plains. She has had equally strong interests in art and music: after high school, she enrolled in the Alberta Institute of Art, and played folk music in the local coffeehouse. Like many Canadians in search of a career, she gravitated to Toronto, where she met and married Chuck Mitchell, also a folksinger, in 1966. The couple moved to Detroit. After her divorce a year later, she moved to New York, where she connected into the folk scene, mainly as a songwriter: Tom Rush and Judy Collins recorded two of her early songs: "The Circle Game" and "Both Sides Now," respectively. Within a year, she had moved to southern California.

Mitchell began recording under her own name in 1968. She found her audience in a series of albums released between 1969 and 1974. Our first hearing might suggest that she was just a folkie who had never found rock: in most songs, the setting is simply voice and acoustic guitar, with perhaps another instrument or two. However, closer listening reveals how far she had distanced herself from folk music. We can hear the originality of her poetic and musical inspiration in a sampling of songs from *Blue*, the most critically acclaimed of these albums.

Joni Mitchell, c. 1980.
PHOTO COURTESY CORBIS/
NEAL PRESTON.

Like Taylor, Mitchell wrote autobiographical songs, but they were cut from quite different cloth. To begin with, almost all of Mitchell's songs have some kind of romantic thread (or at least relationship thread) woven through them. The more striking and meaningful differences are in the nature of the lyrics and melodies. If Taylor converses with his audience, telling tales in everyday language, then Mitchell gives her audience a slice of psychic life. Her lyrics usually juxtapose striking real-life images (e.g., "wreck my stockings in some jukebox dive" from "All I Want" or "I'll even kiss a Sunset pig" from "California") and evocative metaphors (e.g., "but you are in my blood/you're my holy wine" from "A Case of You" or "here is a shell for you/inside you'll hear a sigh/a foggy lullaby" from "Blue"). We hear what's going on around her and what's going on inside her head in a stream-of-consciousness flow.

The melodies of the songs work hand-in-hand with the lyrics. *Blue* contains two groups of songs: those on which Mitchell accompanies herself on the piano, and those which have guitar-based accompaniment, usually with other instruments. Songs with piano accompaniment tend to be rhapsodic, as if words and music simply pour out of her. "Blue" is a good example: the tempo is fluid, not steady; the melody spills out in long phrases; the harmony is unpredictable; the form grows out of the text, not a stereotype. The songs with guitar accompaniment have a firmer pulse: "All I Want," "California," and "A Case of You" all have a subtle, largely implicit version of rock's eight-beat rhythm. ("California" uniquely features drums delicately laying down first a rock rhythm, then a sixteen-beat rhythm on the steel-guitar-accompanied chorus.)

"All I Want" offers an ideal example of the way Mitchell spins out a melody. The song is strophic: the same melody sets three stanzas of text. The first phrase of the melody spirals out of the repeated pitch with which it begins; an answering phrase brings it back to the starting point. The second phrase is a slightly varied version of the first that begins "too soon": the answering phrase lasts two-and-a-half measures instead of four. The "early" entrance of the repetition of the first phrase helps give the impression that the song simply tumbles out of her imagination. A new melodic idea sets the text that begins "I want to be strong . . . ." Shorter phrases and a more active, wide-ranging melodic contour echo the more active and frequent images in the text. They in turn lead to the heart of the song: "do you want . . . ." Here the phrases are even shorter in the beginning; then the melody spins up to its peak on the words "sweet romance," the real issue of the song. Both text and music end the section with a question. The second and third stanzas of text end just as indecisively. A vaguely Middle-Eastern–sounding instrumental prelude/postlude underscores the central message of the song: that she may not get what she wants.

As "All I Want," "Blue," and "California" reveal, Mitchell's songs disdain the conventions of rock and pop. In her songs, ideas shape the forms, not vice versa. Melodies respond to the words, yet follow their own internal logic. Other aspects of the setting—most notably harmony, instrumentation, and rhythm—are individual to a particular song. They remain in a supporting role: the focus is squarely on the words and melody. One measure of Mitchell's genius is the fact that words and melody are separable yet indivisible. Her lyrics are studied simply as poetic texts; her songs are performed as instrumentals. Yet the sum is greater than the parts. Those searching for rock's counterpart to the art songs of classical music need look no further than the music of Joni Mitchell.

After 1974, Mitchell turned in other directions. Through the rest of the seventies, she connected with jazz and the avant garde. This culminated in the collaboration with jazz great Charles Mingus, which was cut short by Mingus's death in 1979. Her seventies experiments anticipated the "world music" movement of the eighties. In the eighties, she continued to explore what some called "jazz-folk" fusions, as well as develop her career in the visual arts, as a photographer and painter.

Carole King

The other major female singer/songwriter of the early seventies was Carole King. Gender aside, King's and Mitchell's careers are a study in opposites. Where Mitchell grew up in the Canadian plains, about as far geographically and culturally as one could be from New York, King was born Carol Klein in Brooklyn. While Mitchell was singing in Canadian coffeehouses, King was at work in the Brill Building, cranking out a string of pop hits with Gerry Goffin, her husband at the time. After her divorce from Goffin in 1968, she began a solo career. She broke through in 1971 with *Tapestry*, which remained on the charts for almost six years. If Mitchell was the quintessential outsider, then King was the ultimate insider, a veteran with over a decade in the music business by the time *Tapestry* was released.

Tapestry is, more than anything else, black pop written and sung by a white woman with real empathy for the sound and style of Motown and soul, and who speaks candidly about life and love from a woman's point of view. Two of the songs on the album were major hits for black female artists in the sixties. We discussed the seminal role of the Shirelles' "Will You Love Me Tomorrow" in the creation of a black pop sound in Chapter 5. "(You Make Me Feel Like) A Natural Woman," which came straight out of church, put Aretha Franklin in the top ten for the fourth time in 1967.

Most of the new songs on *Tapestry* are cut from similar cloth. "You've Got a Friend" projects the optimistic tone heard in so much black pop. There are also musical parallels: with a form that builds to the title-phrase hook, riff-based melody, and rich but mostly traditional harmony, it echoes hundreds of black pop hits. Not surprisingly, then, the song was almost as big a hit on the R&B charts for Roberta Flack and Donny Hathaway as it was for James Taylor on the pop charts. "I Feel the Earth Move," "It's Too Late," and "Where You Lead" with their solid grooves, instrumental and vocal hooks, rich harmony, Motown-style backup vocals, and end-weighted forms, could have been hits for the Temptations or the Supremes. Aretha or Percy Sledge could have covered "Way Over Yonder," and King's excellent gospel-style piano playing would have provided a first-rate accompaniment.

Unlike Mitchell's songs, which document her personal experience, King's songs have an "everywoman" universality as they describe the vagaries of love and life. There is ecstasy ("I Feel the Earth Move," "A Natural Woman"), disillusionment ("It's Too Late"), loneliness ("So Far Away"), and the comfort of companionship ("You've Got a Friend"). They are "real," no-frills songs, sending their messages in plain language. There is no sugarcoating, just frank, heart-to-heart talk. King's timing was perfect. Her songs found receptive ears, especially among women, just as the women's rights movement was gathering momentum. Aretha Franklin's "Respect" had already been adopted as an anthem; Helen Reddy's "I Am Woman" would top the charts in 1972.

The straightforward lyrics were only part of the appeal. King's songs are beautifully crafted: they may follow Motown's formulas, but they are anything but formulaic. "It's Too Late" is an excellent illustration. The song begins with an instrumental introduction that contains a memorable riff, here played by piano and guitar. The verse unfolds over the riff and simple harmonies of the introduction. As the phrase builds toward the title-phrase hook, the harmony becomes richer; moreover, it shifts the song into a new key. The chorus, then, is in a different key than the verse, certainly an unusual strategy. As the chorus winds down, the song shifts back to the original key, signaled by the return of the opening riff. The second statement of the melody begins like the first. However, as the chorus winds down the second time, the harmony takes a sharp turn into a third key, which is the temporary home base for an extended instrumental interlude. (It wasn't easy to keep track of the constant shifting of keys, even for the musicians on the recording. At the end of the song [ca. 3 minutes, 32 seconds], another harmonic fork in the road becomes a point of confusion: guitarist Danny Kortchmar plays the riff that takes the song back to the opening key, while King and the rest of the group stay in the third key.)

Dylan has been regarded as the godfather of the singer/songwriter movement, and rightly so. But songs with melody and meaning had been part of rock since Buddy Holly's brief heyday and King's own "Will You Love Me Tomorrow" in 1961. King's success made clear that the singer/songwriters had roots in pop as well as folk. And it was certainly gratifying to her to step out of the shadows and into the spotlight. She remained there a relatively short time. Her next two albums did well, but neither approached the colossal success of *Tapestry*, which eventually sold over 22 million copies.

Paul Simon

Paul Simon had paired with Carole King in 1958, while both were still teens. Their partnership didn't last long, and during the sixties, while she wrote songs for others, Simon went on to fame and fortune with Art Garfunkel. When Simon and Garfunkel dissolved their partnership in 1970, Simon immediately embarked on a solo career.

What's remarkable about Simon's solo music is that it's so different from the music he wrote and recorded with Garfunkel. Almost all the collaborative songs were necessarily somewhat impersonal: "The Sounds of Silence" is a good illustration, and even "The Boxer" is a story told in the third person. By contrast, Simon usually speaks in the first person in his solo music, and the persona he projected was one of the most distinctive of the time: urban, contemporary, neurotic, yet sophisticated and street-wise—a quintessential New Yorker.

The musical transformation is, if anything, even more striking. In the Simon and Garfunkel songs, the focus is squarely on the voices: their exquisite close harmony. The musical backgrounds are relatively featureless: they begin with Simon's acoustic guitar, and may layer a generic rock band accompaniment, as in "The Sounds of Silence."

By contrast, Simon's solo songs tend to be more complex melodically and harmonically. Moreover, all the elements of the accompaniment—the choice of instruments (and, on occasion, voices), the rhythms, the textures—contribute to the meaning of the song. The sound world that envelops the vocal line is a full partner with lyric and melody in conveying the character of a song.

A survey of Simon's songs recorded in the seventies shows the extraordinary range of styles he has at his command, and the expressive purposes to which he puts them. "Mother and Child Reunion" is a reggae song, "Something So Right" is a gorgeous romantic ballad, "Love Me Like a Rock" and "Slip Slidin' Away" have gospel overtones, "Have a Good Time" has a funky chorus, and "Late in the Evening" has a Latin flavor.

A closer look at a few of these songs shows how Simon uses these styles to connote a particular mood or feeling. "Slip Slidin' Away"—which has the Oak Ridge Boys, a country group with a white gospel background, singing backup vocals—contains a series of parables. The singers' presence amplifies the didactic, almost preachy, quality of Simon's lyric.

"Secular" songs also benefit from Simon's connotative use of musical style. "Something So Right" is a love song celebrating a love that is almost too good to be real. Simon helps depict it by writing a "modern" romantic ballad, a song as rich harmonically as any pre-rock pop song, and more inventive in its twists and turns than most. Sumptuous strings specifically enhance this feeling. There's a beautiful touch in the middle of the song, when rhythm shifts to a fast two-beat as Simon sings "Some people never say the words, 'I love you' . . . ." The more active rhythm suggests the emotional reserve, even bashfulness, of "some people." The return to the original rhythmic feel coincides with the return of the lyric to the main message of the song.

"Have a Good Time" is by turns more subtle and more obvious in the use of style to help tell its story. The lyric paints a picture of the protagonist enjoying himself even though his "life's a mess." As he explains his worldview in the verse, the song lopes along in alternating four- and three-beat measures. This rhythmic imbalance, very rare in popular music, seems to underscore the subject's mixed-up personal life. The sudden shift to a funky, Sly Stone-ish groove in the chorus, where the lyric simply repeats the title phrase, is a switch to "good-time" music. The sharp contrast between the verse, with its relatively sophisticated language and unbalanced rhythm, and the chorus, is striking.

Simon's urbane lyrics and subtle evocations of style are two of four key elements in his style. The others are his beautifully crafted melodies and subtle textures, particularly his handling of rhythm. He is expert at controlling the flow of a song by manipulating timekeeping and density: to cite just one example, the light shuffle rhythm, overlaid with sustained keyboard chords and vocal harmonies, helps project the wistful mood of "Slip Slidin' Away." Almost uniquely among the singer/songwriters, Simon's songs derive mainly from the Beatles' revolutionary reconception of song: a sound environment in which the words and melody are central, but where the rest of texture also embodies the meaning of the song.

How to explain the marked difference between Simon's solo music and his earlier music with Garfunkel? As the discussion of "The Boxer" made clear, Simon had already begun to explore a more varied sound world and wrote more complex songs, in both words and music, toward the end of their partnership. However, the break with Garfunkel may have accelerated the process. Garfunkel had the more distinctive and emotionally resonant voice of the two, as he showed on "Bridge Over Troubled Water." Further, their voices together were one of the most identifiable vocal sounds of the sixties.

Simon lost that vocal identity when the pair broke up. His voice is true, musically and emotionally, but rather neutral, even when compared to the other singer/songwriters. With Young and Mitchell, for example, you have to react to their voice. Many respond to them like others respond to guitar distortion: with immediate identification or complete turnoff. Taylor's voice has more grit than Simon's; it would be difficult to imagine Simon singing a blues or a Motown song as convincingly as Taylor does. So Simon communicates his message as much by what he does around his voice as he does in his singing.

The spirit of exploration—new ideas, new sounds, new forms—that characterized Simon's music in the early seventies grew bolder in subsequent years. His most highly regarded efforts have been the albums *Graceland* (1986) and *The Rhythm of the Saints* (1990). In them, he gave his interest in musical styles a global dimension, recording with South African musicians in *Graceland* and Brazilian and West African musicians in *The Rhythm of the Saints*.

His explorations into other media have been less successful: the film *One Trick Pony* (1978) and *The Capeman* (1998), a Broadway musical that closed after a short run. Their lack of success did not indicate any loss in popularity: in 1991, a free concert in New York's Central Park drew an estimated 750,000 people. Especially in his "world beat" syntheses, Simon remains a vital voice on the contemporary music scene.

Randy Newman

Randy Newman has taken an unusual path in his career as a singer/songwriter: he is the genre's true iconoclast. While others were baring their souls, Newman was inhabiting a string of reprehensible characters: slave traders, rednecks, and assorted other bigots. Unlike the songs of almost all the others—Simon is the occasional exception—Newman's songs are usually ironic. They are devastating satires of people he finds worthy of his barbs. What makes them special, and often confusing to simpler minds, is that they are not heavy-handed caricatures, but complicated portraits in which Newman assumes the character in the song. Both his satirical humor and his assumption of personas quite different from his own distinguish his music from the other singer/songwriters.

Newman grew up in New Orleans, where he absorbed the sound of Fats Domino and the New Orleans piano professors. He had moved to Los Angeles by the time he was a teenager; he began writing songs for Metric Music while still in high school. He was well-connected: three of his uncles, Alfred, Lionel, and Emil Newman, wrote and conducted film music for Hollywood films, and his long-time friend Larry Waronker, who co-produced his first album, would become president of Warner Brothers records.

Newman began recording his own music in 1968. New albums appeared intermittently throughout the 1970s: typically they received rave reviews but sold poorly, although *Little Criminals* (1977) went gold, in part because of the controversy surrounding the novelty hit single, "Short People."

"Sail Away," the title track from his 1972 album, shows the subtlety of Newman's satire. The "voice" in the song is a slave trader giving a sales pitch about life in America to West Africans. In fact, there are multiple voices. We hear not only the slave trader's perception of the "dark continent" ("lions, tigers, and mamba snakes . . ."), but also Newman's own perspective on the various myths and stereotypes regarding life among the slaves ("watermelons and buckwheat cakes"). Behind his voice is an accompaniment of symphonic proportions (Newman performed the song with members of the New York Philharmonic). The serene winds and sumptuous strings could just as easily be providing background music for a patriotic film.

Newman also assumes multiple roles in "Short People." To a jaunty accompaniment, the song's protagonist sings "Short people got . . . no reason to . . . short people got . . . no reason to . . . " delaying the tag line "no reason to live . . . ." The song is of course a satire of bigotry, but also a satire of the mindless, "have-a-nice-day" mentality that infused much commercial music of the seventies. When Newman sings, "Short people are just like you and me . . . ," he is satirizing the other side of bigotry; unthinking liberals who offer false sympathy to those who are different. Newman manages to make fun of bigotry and those who supposedly oppose bigotry in the same song.

"Short People" was the most notorious example of the confusion his music can cause. Some people took him literally, and the song was banned from a few radio stations. During the controversy, Newman took great pains to explain that the song was not an expression of his personal beliefs but rather his way of putting bigotry in the glare of the spotlight, in the rather forlorn hope that the song might enlighten a few listeners. As he said a few years later, "I don't know why, but bigotry has always bothered me more than war or pollution or anything else. . . ."

Newman has been more than just a songwriter: From the beginning of his career, he was also a skilled arranger and orchestrator. In the seventies and eighties, he began to write film scores. Among his credits are the music for *Ragtime*, *The Natural*, and Disney's *Toy Story*. His musical, *Faust*, can be understood as a culmination and synthesis of his work in both areas: as a songwriter and as a film composer.

Summary

The music of the six singer/songwriters discussed in this chapter shows remarkable variety: Young's hard-rocking but thoughtful songs, Taylor's first-person accounts, Mitchell's delicate musings, King's Motown-tinged melodies, Simon's soundscapes, and Newman's satires. Their songs are representative of the stylistic and methodological variety of the singer/songwriters in the late sixties and early seventies, but by no means exhaustive.

These singer/songwriters created a new kind of popular song. Generally, these were songs in the most specific sense: music that set meaningful words to a melody that was the most coherent and prominent element in the texture. In this respect, they were like not only country songs, but also pre-rock pop and the art songs of classical music. And the best of them were as beautifully crafted as music from any era. They may have been miles from the power chords of the metal bands or the steam-driven propulsion of Creedence Clearwater Revival. However, in their attitudes and adventurousness, they captured much of the spirit of the rock era.

An interesting footnote to their earlier music is the varied career directions so many of the singer/songwriters took after 1975. Young careened from style to style; Mitchell embraced jazz and non-Western musics; Simon also explored world musics while venturing into film, then onto Broadway. Newman followed in the footsteps of his uncles, scoring (at last count) seventeen films and mounting the production of *Faust*. They were already a heterogeneous group in 1970; they became even more so in subsequent decades.

If rock needs a beat that moves you, as Lou Reed suggested, then much of the music in this chapter is not rock. It fails this most basic test. However, if rock includes music that expresses the feelings and attitudes of its audience in ways that are not dependent on the conventions of earlier eras, then this is rock.

Granted, Joni Mitchell's "All I Want" is miles away from Led Zeppelin's "Black Dog" in almost every respect. However, rock has always been eclectic; there has always been room for diversity. The message of the music of the singer/songwriters may not be electrically charged, but in its own way, it is powerful. There has always been room in rock for melody and meaningful words.

KEY TERMS

Intensified speech   **Singer/songwriter**   **Brill Building pop**

Rock sensibility   **Jazz-folk fusion**   **World music**

Supergroups

CHAPTER QUESTIONS

1. In this chapter, we encounter songs written and performed by women for the first time. As you listen to the songs by Mitchell and King and compare them with the rest of the songs discussed in this chapter, can you identify gender-based differences? If so, what are they?

2. Bob Dylan is considered the most important forerunner of the singer-songwriter movement. Listen to the lyrics of one or two of his electric songs, and then the lyrics of songs by three other singer-songwriters. How do they compare in subject and style?

3. Compare Simon with and after Garfunkel. What is your perception of the differences in his music? How do you account for them?

4. Consider the question of style boundaries in relation to the music of Van Morrison. Is his music really part of the rock era? Why or why not? If you can, locate one of his more conventional songs, e.g., "Domino" (1970). Do you find him more or less distinctive in this setting than in the songs from *Astral Weeks*?

5. Explore the musical and emotional range of the singer-songwriters by comparing songs by Newman, Young, Mitchell, and one other. Consider the subject of the lyric and the way it is expressed, the singing style of the songwriter, and the musical setting.

c h a p t e r   1 4

Black Music in the Early Seventies

Black music went through a changing of the guard in the early seventies. Berry Gordy, whose Motown empire had defined the sound of black pop in the sixties, faced challenges to his domination of the market. Some came from within: Motown artists like Marvin Gaye and Stevie Wonder demanded and received artistic control of their recordings, so that the "Motown sound" could no longer be defined as one single style performed by every artist on the label. Meanwhile, new producers were beginning to score pop hits, particularly the team of Kenny Gamble and Leon Huff at Philadelphia International records, creating the so-called "Philadelphia sound."

Southern soul fell on hard times with the assassination of Dr. Martin Luther King, Jr., as the fertile but fragile collegiality between black and white artists dissolved into distrust. The raw emotions of soul music continued into the seventies mainly in the music of Aretha Franklin and Al Green. Many other sixties soul acts saw their audiences shrink. However, two new sounds emerged from soul around 1970. One was film music by Isaac Hayes and Curtis Mayfield for so-called "blaxploitation" films, the other a new style of black gospel music.

The most progressive sounds of the seventies came from James Brown and Sly and the Family Stone. Even as Brown's music continued to evolve rhythmically, Stone introduced a new sound that was rhythmically looser, but instrumentally denser than Brown's. Their innovations would soon lead to funk. We will survey each of these developments in turn.

Black Pop

Black pop flourished musically in the early seventies. No one act or company dominated the charts the way Motown did in the mid-sixties, but black pop maintained a strong crossover presence. Moreover, there was much more variety. The Motown sound had given way to the Motown "sounds"; its records were no longer the expression of a single, highly focused musical vision. The

Jackson 5 and Marvin Gaye were a generation apart, and it showed in their music. From a harmonica-playing child prodigy, Stevie Wonder had matured into a powerful songwriter and studio genius.

At about the same time, two other black pop styles carved out a sizable share of the market. One was the distinctive "Philadelphia sound," the work of producers Gamble and Huff and Thom Bell. They developed a more extravagant black pop style, richer sounding than late sixties Motown. Their slickly produced records made stars of the O'Jays, the Spinners, Teddy Pendergrass—even MFSB, their "house band"—and reestablished Philadelphia as an important music center. The other was a more adult black romantic music, popularized mainly by Roberta Flack and Bill Withers.

Motown in the Early Seventies

Perhaps the best way to understand Motown's evolution in the early seventies is generationally. The "Young America" that Gordy had targeted in the early sixties had grown up. At the same time, many of Motown's acts had also matured, and they were anxious to explore new directions. As a result, Motown's freshest sounds came from two sources: new faces (most notably the Jackson 5) or Motown veterans going in new directions (Marvin Gaye, Stevie Wonder, and Diana Ross). The Jackson 5 attracted another generation of young fans, while many of the Motown veterans expanded their audience.

THE JACKSON 5   The Jackson 5 was both Motown product and a product of Motown. Motown's success inspired scores of imitators. Among them was the family of Joseph and Katherine Jackson, living in the industrial city of Gary, Indiana. Joseph Jackson was a crane operator and frustrated musician; Katherine gave birth to nine children, all of whom would eventually have professional musical careers.

The family's first successful incarnation was as the Jackson 5. It consisted of the five oldest boys in the Jackson family: Joseph, Tito, Jermaine, Marlon, and Michael. Their father had started them on their career as the Jackson 5 around 1964, when Michael was only six. Within a few years they were opening for major soul acts. In 1969, they came to the attention of Berry Gordy, most likely through Gladys Knight (although Diana Ross was given credit for "discovering" them). He signed them, they released their first single for Motown, the No. 1 hit "I Want You Back" (1970), and they were on their way.

The Jackson 5 were an immediate sensation: they had three more No. 1 singles in 1970. Among them was "ABC." The themes of the song are as old as rock and roll: school and teen love. However, even more than the teen idols of the late fifties or the Beatles, the Jackson 5, and especially Michael, were speaking for their age group rather than to it. Michael's prepuberty sound gave their performance an innocence that it might not have had with a more mature voice. Certainly, when Michael asks the "girl" to "shake it, shake it, baby," there is none of the sexual innuendo heard in, let's say, Ray Charles's line from "What'd I Say," when he remarks that she sure knows how to "shake that thing."

If their lyrics and vocal style projected an air of childlike innocence (they voiced over their own Saturday morning cartoon beginning in 1971 and received a commendation from Congress in 1972 for their "contributions to

The Jackson 5 appear on "Shindig." PHOTO COURTESY CORBIS/BETTMANN.

American youth"), their music was sophisticated and current. Their father had drilled them relentlessly (Katherine's autobiography, released in the late eighties, detailed his abuses), and Motown, since relocated to Los Angeles, supplied topflight instrumental backing and production.

Like sixties Motown hits, "ABC" balanced accessibility and sophistication. The hook, "A, B, C . . . ," was simple enough to sink deeply, and the bass line underneath the chorus was a simple scale. What brought the song up-to-date was the rhythm and the texture. An augmented rhythm section—drums, congas, tambourine—laid down an active, highly syncopated sixteen-beat rhythm that floated effortlessly under Michael during the verse.

"Never Can Say Goodbye" (1971) is more grown-up. It is a love song for all ages, not just prepubescent teens (Isaac Hayes, among others, would cover the song). Appropriately, the musical setting is even lusher, and the tempo is slower. There are more instruments, most of them delicate (flutes and bells stand out), the texture is richer, and the harmony more elaborate. The melody takes longer to unfold, and builds steadily toward the title phrase. Michael sounds older, but not yet an adult. If listeners were bothered by the incongruity of an apparently inexperienced young man singing about the "heartbreak" of love, they didn't show it at the record counter: the song was a No. 2 hit for the group.

The Jackson 5 was Gordy's last big act, and Motown's only successful new act in the seventies. By the mid-seventies, Berry Gordy was no longer a major creative force in popular music. His reluctance to cede artistic control led to fractious relationships with many of his acts. From the beginning, he had butted heads with the Jacksons' father. By 1976, they had left Motown and re-formed themselves as the Jacksons, although Jermaine, who had married Gordy's daughter Hazel, remained at Motown. All of the remaining Jackson children had solo careers in addition to their on-again/off-again collaborations; Michael's and Janet's have been by far the most successful. Their collective and individual success have made the Jackson family popular music's most enduring family dynasty for the better part of three decades.

On the other side of Motown's generational divide was Marvin Gaye. Gaye had gained control of his career around 1970, as evidenced by his landmark album, *What's Going On* (see Chapter 6). The most successful of his hits for the remainder of his troubled career were blatantly erotic (as well as great songs). Gaye had been Motown's most soulful singer, and soul had been much more direct in its approach to sex: compare Percy Sledge's "When a Man Loves a Woman" to "My Girl" or "My Guy." Gaye's artistic liberation freed his lyrics as well as his music, from "Let's Get It On" (1973) to his last big hit, "Sexual Healing" (1982). His was the most adult music coming out of Motown, older and more worldly by far than the teen-themed songs of the Jackson 5.

Gordy's troubles were not confined to the Jacksons and Gaye. Gladys Knight and the Pips left the label, and enjoyed even greater success on Buddah Records. Diana Ross chafed at Gordy's control of her career and life, and eventually severed their business relationship. Other top Motown acts, most notably the Temptations and the Four Tops, stayed on, but saw their popularity wane. Their run at the top was over by 1973. The single exception was Stevie Wonder.

STEVIE WONDER   There's a certain irony that Motown's most powerful and original talent, and its longest-running success story, is in many ways the antithesis of the Motown image and sound. Stevie Wonder is a solo act; most Motown acts were groups. The visual element was crucial to Motown's success: its groups dressed in gowns or tuxedos and moved through stylized, carefully choreographed routines as they sang their songs. By contrast, our enduring image of Stevie Wonder: a blind man with sunglasses and long braided and beaded hair, dressed in a dashiki, sitting behind a keyboard and rocking from side to side in a random rhythm. Motown recordings were collective enterprises: behind the groups were largely anonymous songwriters and studio musicians. Wonder has created his own recordings from soup to nuts: not only singing and playing all the instruments at times, but also performing the technical tasks—recording, mixing, mastering, etc.

There are also differences in subject and attitude. In the mid-sixties, Motown song lyrics talked mainly about young love, usually in racially neutral, often idealized language. Only reluctantly did they begin to address "real life" in songs like the Supremes' "Love Child." By contrast, Stevie Wonder took on social issues almost from his first album: the vignette of an innocent man's arrest in "Living for the City" (1973) is chilling. Where Gordy waffled politically and socially, even at the height of the civil rights movement, Stevie Wonder has advocated a long list of causes, from his firm push for a national holiday for Martin Luther King, Jr., to rights for the blind and disabled.

Stevie Wonder was born Steveland Morris (by most accounts; Steveland Judkins by others) in 1950. A hospital error at birth left him blind. By age 10, he was a professional performer, singing and playing the harmonica (he also played piano and drums). Within two years, he had signed a Motown contract and was being billed as "Little Stevie Wonder, The 12 Year Old Genius." (The

Stevie Wonder in his days as a child-star, c. 1964. Photo courtesy CORBIS/BETTMANN.

"little" disappeared two years later, but the "Wonder" stuck.) He had a number of hits in the sixties, including "Uptight" (1966) and the beautiful love song, "My Cherie Amour" (1969), but emerged as a major force in popular music only in the early seventies. The reason: when he turned 21 he negotiated a contract with Motown that guaranteed him complete control over his work.

Wonder was the most popular black artist of the seventies. A series of albums, beginning with *Music of My Mind* (1972), established his unique sound and cemented his reputation as a major player in popular music. Each album release was a major event within the black community, and his recordings also enjoyed enormous crossover success.

The widespread popularity of Wonder's music grows out of a style that is broad in its range, highly personal in its sound, and universal in its appeal. Wonder's music is a compendium of current black musical styles: in his songs are the tuneful melodies and rich harmonies of black romantic music; the dense textures and highly syncopated riffs of funk; the improvisatory flights of jazz; and the subtle rhythms of reggae and Latin music. Yet, even though he absorbs influences from all quarters, his style is unique.

"You Are the Sunshine of My Life" and "Superstition," two No. 1 singles from the 1972 album *Talking Book*, show the two main directions in his music. "Superstition" is a funky up-tempo song with a finger-wagging lyric: in it he chastises those who would let their lives be ruled by superstitious beliefs. The melody that carries the lyric grows slowly out of a simple riff. Like so many Motown (and rock-era) songs, it builds inexorably to the title phrase. The harmony shows the two sources of his style: the verse sits on a bed of riffs, all built from the African-American pentatonic scale; there is no harmonic change. By contrast, the transition to the hook is supported by rich, jazz-like harmonies.

The most distinctive element of Stevie Wonder's sound, however, is the rich texture that flows underneath the vocal line. The song begins simply enough, with a rhythmically secure drum part. Onto this, Wonder layers multiple lines: the signature riff, a repeated-note bass line, plus several more riffs in the background, all highly syncopated. Wonder played all the lines on synthesizers, overdubbing until he produced the dense, funky texture that became one of his trademarks. (Wonder was one of the first musicians to develop a sound based almost completely on synthesizers.)

"You Are the Sunshine of My Life" is a love song. Not surprisingly, the focus is more on the melody, which spins out in four eight-measure phrases. Both melody and harmony grow out of pre-rock popular song; the chords supporting the melody are, in effect, souped-up "Heart and Soul" harmonies. But Wonder modernizes the melody by looping it. It has a beginning, but not an ending, because the final phrase leads back to the beginning instead of bringing the song to closure. Because Wonder showcases the melody, the texture is not as dense as in "Superstition," but it is still rich, with the addition of congas to the rhythm section of electric piano, bass, and drums.

Taken together, the two songs show many of the defining features of Stevie Wonder's music:

- lyrics that talk about love and life
- tuneful melodies and riffs
- a harmonic vocabulary appropriated from jazz and popular song via Motown, but applied in a highly imaginative and individual way
- dense textures and complex, syncopated rhythms
- the fresh, new sounds of synthesizers
- soaring above it all, his resonant, upbeat voice

Stevie Wonder is an optimist, a "the-glass-is-half-full" person. Even in his darkest songs, hope is implicit, if not in the lyric, then in the bounce of the beat: how can you be down if your hips are shaking and your foot is tapping the beat? "You Haven't Done Nothin'" (1974), another finger-wagging song (rumor has it that the subject of the song was then-president Richard Nixon), is a good example.

At the other end of the emotional spectrum are "Isn't She Lovely" (1976), a truly happy song celebrating the birth of one of his children, and the tender ballad, "Send One Your Love" (1979), which is saved from sentimentality only by the sincerity of Wonder's voice and the craft of his songwriting and production. That Wonder has such an optimistic outlook on life is remarkable in light of numerous personal problems. Not only has he been blind from birth, but he suffered a devastating automobile accident in 1973 that left him in a coma for several days. He followed this adversity with some of his best music.

The Philadelphia Sound

In the early seventies, it seemed as if Motown had opened a branch office in Philadelphia. The most "Motown-like" records of the period appeared on Gamble and Huff's Philadelphia International label, not Gordy's. The basic formula was the same: lush orchestrations, solid rhythms coming from a rhythm section that had played together for years, jazz-tinged instrumental lines, all supporting vocal groups singing about the ups and downs of love. Only the details were different.

Three men engineered the "Philadelphia sound": Kenny Gamble, Leon Huff, and Thom Bell. All were veterans of the Philadelphia music scene; they had worked together off and on during the early sixties in a group called Kenny

Gamble and the Romeos. By mid-decade, Gamble and Huff had begun producing records together. They enjoyed their first extended success with Jerry
Butler, who revived his career under their guidance. Their big break came in
1971, when Clive Davis, the head of Columbia Records, helped them form
Philadelphia International Records. The connection with Columbia assured
them of widespread distribution, especially in white markets.

The artist roster at Philadelphia International included the O'Jays, Harold
Melvin and the Blue Notes, Teddy Pendergrass (who left the Blue Notes to go
solo), Billy Paul, and MFSB, which was the house band. Their competition
came mainly from Thom Bell, who produced the Stylistics and the Spinners,
a Detroit group that had gone nowhere at Motown, but took off when paired
with Bell in 1972.

Two songs, the O'Jays' "Back Stabbers" (1972) and the Spinners' "Could It
Be I'm Falling in Love" (1973), show how Gamble, Huff, and Bell extended and
updated the black pop style developed at Motown. The instrumental introduction of "Back Stabbers" runs for 40 seconds, far longer than any of the
Motown intros. It begins with a quasi-classical piano tremolo, an ominous
rumble that helps establish the dark mood of the song. The unaccompanied
piano riff that follows simply hangs in sonic space; there is still no regular
beat-keeping. Finally, the rest of the rhythm section enters, with the guitarist
playing a jazz-style riff.

The rhythm sound is fuller than late sixties Motown records, not just
because of the addition of Latin percussion instruments (Motown had been
using them for years), but because there are more of them, and the reinforcement of the beat and eight-beat layer is more prominent. After the conclusion
of the opening phrase, the strings—and, later, brass—enter; all combine to create a lush backdrop for the O'Jays.

The song, cowritten by Huff, advises a hypothetical person to guard
against "friends" who are out to steal his woman. Like so much black pop, the
song is about love, or at least a relationship. What's different about the lyric is
that the narrator is an outside observer, rather than the person in the relationship. In effect, it's "I Heard It Through the Grapevine," told from the other
side of the grapevine, but up close and personal. It was the first of a series of
such songs by the O'Jays.

"Could It Be I'm Falling in Love" is the work of the Spinners and producer
Thom Bell, but the formula is basically the same. The song is richly orchestrated; the harpsichord interlude is the kind of exotic sound that occasionally
appears on Philadelphia recordings. Again, the instrumental introduction
gradually mushrooms, this time from a vibraphone lead to full orchestra. The
active rhythms give what is essentially a ballad a bouncy beat. The melody and
harmony are full of twists and turns. As in most Motown songs, the vocabulary comes from older pop music, but it is much richer here than in any of the
Motown songs we have heard.

The main differences between this and "Back Stabbers" are the lyric, which
is starry-eyed, and the singing of the Spinners. Lead singer Phillip Wynne, who
had joined the group in 1972, floats along effortlessly, and the Spinners mastered falsetto singing so thoroughly their sound seems almost genderless.

What's evident in both recordings is a comprehensive expansion and mod-
ernization of the Motown sound. The instrumental introductions are grander;
the texture is richer; the songs themselves are more complicated; the spotlighted instruments are more contemporary sounding (in the case of the guitar)

or more exotic (in the case of the vibraphone); and there is greater rhythmic freedom, not only in the opening, but also in the syncopated riffs that are the instrumental hooks of the songs.

The formula behind the Philadelphia sound worked well for the better part of the decade. By the late seventies, however, it would be largely superceded by a more obvious version of itself: disco.

Black Romantic Music

Black music also had a generation gap. One important strand in post-war rhythm and blues (not for rock and roll, but for its audience) was popular song sung by people who sounded as if they had lived a little. It attracted a substantial audience among both blacks and whites. Nat Cole was the most successful of these artists, but Billie Holiday, Sarah Vaughan, Dinah Washington, and Billy Eckstine also had faithful followings. Ray Charles's recordings of standards like "Georgia on My Mind" added the grit of soul to the performance of pop material; Otis Redding's "Try a Little Tenderness" went a step further. (By contrast, Aretha's career was almost over before it started because her producers at Columbia had her singing pop.) However, this branch of rhythm and blues went into decline in the mid-sixties, because of the deaths of Holiday, Washington, Sam Cooke, and Nat Cole, and because of the emergence of Motown, which had no mature counterpart.

A new black romantic style emerged around 1970. Some of the music came from Motown, mainly in the music of Marvin Gaye, who was the oldest of the Motown headliners. Philadelphia countered with songs like Billy Paul's "Me and Mrs. Jones." Aretha Franklin showed a more tender side in "Day Dreaming" (1972) and her version of Stevie Wonder's "Until You Come Back to Me" (1974). However, a new group of artists with no direct connection to Motown, Philadelphia, or Southern soul also appeared; Roberta Flack, Bill Withers, and Barry White found the largest audience.

These artists filled the generation gap. They were all over thirty; in fact, Bill Withers didn't even begin his musical career until he was over thirty. Both the songs and their performance presented a more mature view of love—found, enjoyed, abused, or lost—and they presented it with sophistication and subtlety. Melody, supported by rich, pop-influenced harmony, was at the center. Singers caressed the songs; they sang intimately, but with expressive inflection. This was mood music, not big-beat music; any dancing would be slow. The accompaniments were also more subtle and sophisticated, thanks to the use of session musicians, many of whom came out of the jazz tradition.

The new black romantic style differed from the traditional pop and jazz-based romantic music of the fifties in several distinct ways:

- *The relative explicitness of the lyrics* As the song titles suggest, lyrics spoke more directly about love: Marvin Gaye is not talking about a coat when he says "let's get it on." This quality sets them apart from both pre-rock pop, which typically talked about love from afar or obliquely.

- *The use of contemporary rhythms* Latin-tinged rock or (more often) sixteen-beat rhythms typically replaced the fox-trot or swing-based rhythms of the earlier styles. Light timekeeping allowed these more active rhythms to float. There's enough of a beat to move with, but not enough to overwhelm the melody.

- *Open-ended song form* Forms typically avoided big buildups and punctuations. Instead, they seem to spin out without end.

- *An enriched harmonic palette* There is the ebb and flow of harmonic tension characteristic of pre-rock pop, but more contemporary twists and turns that lead the progression away from comfortable resolution.

All of these qualities seem to suggest the essential timelessness of both the pleasure and pain of love. "Feel Like Makin' Love," a No. 1 hit for Roberta Flack in 1974, illustrates all of these qualities.

- *Explicit lyrics* You can hardly get more explicit than the title of this song, and Flack's breathy vocal underlines the sensuality of the message.

- *Contemporary rhythm* The song is propelled by a light 16-beat feel, played by strummed guitar and Latin percussion instruments.

- *Open-ended form and enriched harmony* A delicate keyboard arpeggio starts the song "in the middle." The harmony under the first two phrases of the melody is the venerable "Heart and Soul" progression, but it starts on the third chord of the sequence, so it never resolves. The melody glides into the hook of the song; the harmonies at the beginning ("That's the time") and end ("oh, baby") of the phrase keep the music moving.

Flack recorded the most delicate music within this new romantic style. Bill Withers, by contrast, brought a blue-jeans sensibility to the style. "Use Me," with its spare accompaniment, love-addicted lyric, and—most of all—Withers's moaning, gritty singing, has a "get real" quality that shows the painful side of love.

Barry White, on the other hand, outdid both Motown and the Philadelphia producers in the elaborateness of his production and the explicitness of his message, which recreated the sexual experience in music over and over. White might be best described as the "minister of love." Most of his hit songs begin with a spoken erotic fantasy set over a pulsating rhythm track. Like a black preacher whipping his congregation into a frenzy, he lets the music build, until he finally breaks into song. (The more immediate precedent for his spoken prologues is the music of Isaac Hayes, but the idea of a smooth transition from speech to song goes back to the black church.) All this unfolds on an epic scale: the prologue to "I'm Gonna Love You Just a Little More Baby," his first big hit, lasts about one minute, 20 seconds, and the song proper doesn't get under way until almost two minutes have passed.

The songs themselves are effective, but the prologues display what are usually very private thoughts in public. As such, they lend themselves to parody. In an early *Saturday Night Live* sketch, Chevy Chase lampooned White: billing himself as "Very White," he let the spoken prologues build—as if toward climax—but never sang the song: it was all tension and no release.

This new romantic style had plenty of crossover appeal: Flack, Withers, and White—all very different—charted several Top Ten hits. Even instrumental versions of this style did well. George Benson, a first-rate jazz guitarist as well as a fine singer, became the first artist to have an album top the pop, R&B, and jazz charts simultaneously when *Breezin'* hit No. 1 in 1976.

Soul in the Seventies

By the early seventies, soul had fallen on hard times. After 1970, the hits stopped coming for most of the Southern soul stars. Nevertheless, positive reverberations of the soul style helped diversify the sound of black music in the early seventies. The music of Aretha Franklin and James Brown, soul music's most powerful voices, changed in the seventies. In Aretha's case it came about through an expansion of her stylistic range; in James's case through the continuing rhythmic evolution of his music.

Isaac Hayes and Curtis Mayfield, who worked behind the scenes throughout the sixties in Memphis and Chicago, respectively, became solo performers around 1970, but had even greater success with film scores. Al Green was soul's new voice—and its last great one. As with black pop, a jazz-inflected instrumental music also emerged. This style, exemplified most notably in the music of the Crusaders, also had a large dose of soul. Perhaps the most surprising and inspiring development, though, was the reinvigoration of gospel music and its emergence as a distinct, if secular, popular style.

Al Green

The new voice of soul in the seventies was Al Green. Like virtually all other soul stars, Green grew up singing in church. When he was nine, he and some of his brothers formed a gospel quartet that performed first in and around his Arkansas hometown, about 40 miles west of Memphis, then in Michigan, where his family moved when he was twelve. And like many other soul singers, he began his career in his teens. The crucial event early in his career was his encounter with Willie Mitchell, who owned Hi Records in Memphis. Mitchell became not only his boss, but also his partner, coproducing his records and cowriting many of Green's hits.

Although he had an isolated hit in 1967, Green's career effectively began in 1970. Within a year, he had crossed over to the pop charts: "Let's Stay Together," his biggest hit, topped both the R&B and pop charts in late 1971. He remained a presence on the charts for most of the decade.

Green brought subtlety and sophistication to both his songwriting and singing without sacrificing its soulfulness. All qualities are evident in his first big crossover hit, "Tired of Being Alone" (1971). Its basic design is the refrain-frame form that dates back to "Maybellene," but the verse is in a different key than the chorus, and quite long. In addition, there is an open-ended section where Green simply "goes off." In general design, then, the song is in step with rock-era songwriting, but the details make Green's song distinctive almost to the point of idiosyncrasy.

However, it is his singing—and the man behind the voice—that is the main focus here. Green's voice is a remarkably flexible instrument. He is a tenor: his basic sound is higher-pitched and lighter than most other soul singers. Even more distinctive, however, are the variations in the basic sound. Less than a minute into the recording, we have already heard several different vocal qualities:

- a plaintive sound in the chorus
- a huskier sound for the first phrase of the verse (ca. 23 seconds)
- a more matter-of-fact sound on the second phrase (ca. 35 seconds)

He even changes sound on a single note: each pulsation on the syllable "me" (ca. 30 seconds) features a different shade of vocal color.

This variety is evident even before Green goes into high, head-voice singing, or falsetto (his effortless, floating lines anticipate the buoyant sound of the Bee Gees), or begins to use the moans, stutters, melismas, and other devices that are part of his vocal arsenal. All these dimensions make his singing more varied and subtle than the other soul singers, who tended to rely more on brute power. Al Green is Muhammad Ali to the sixties soul singers' Joe Frazier, Sonny Liston, and George Foreman: his voice can float like a butterfly and sting like a bee, as well as punch with authority.

As a result, Green's singing was intimate: women took its erotic messages personally. His appearance and stage manner certainly encouraged this perception. During his heyday, he had the svelte physique of a welterweight in fighting shape; photographs show him bare chested, even in performance. And he teased his audience with his moves as well as his voice. Women, certain that he was singing only to them, showered him with gifts: bras and panties were thrown on stage as tokens of his female fans' affection and excitement.

Green's sensuality soon led to tragedy. In 1974, one of his girlfriends poured hot grits on him, burning him over several parts of his body, and then shot herself. Green took it as a sign that he had become too worldly—his father had expelled him from the family gospel group while he was in his early teens for listening to "profane music"—so he turned back to religion. In 1976, he started his own church in Memphis, but continued to tour. Another incident, in 1979, when he fell off the stage but escaped serious injury, convinced him to retire from secular music, which he has largely done. Since then, Green has devoted himself mainly to gospel music, although he has appeared and recorded occasionally with other rock artists.

Green was the last and one of the greatest of the soul singers. Certain features of his style, especially the stutters, moans, and yelps, recall the singing of Ray Charles, the artist most responsible for the sound of soul. So, in effect, Green's singing completes the circle. And his decision to enter the ministry closes a larger circle. With "I Got a Woman," Ray Charles took the ingredients of soul out of the church and into popular music. Green helped soul reinvigorate black gospel music.

The Lord Giveth; the Lord Getteth Back

For over a generation, black gospel music had given its emotions, its sounds, and its performers to popular music. Especially after World War II, black churches had become, in effect, schools for rhythm and blues singers. The roster of "gospel-trained" singers reads like a Who's Who of black music. Beginning around 1970, however, gospel music began to get a return on its investment: the music that it had nurtured for so long now began to give back to gospel.

Green's gradual defection from popular music to the ministry was one sign. Another was *Amazing Grace* (1972), a best-selling live album of straight gospel by Aretha Franklin. A third was the emergence of what has been called "inspirational pop." This music in effect reverses the Ray Charles formula: instead of using spiritual music to deliver an earthy message, it uses earthy music to deliver an uplifting, if non-denominational, message. The first of these inspirational songs to have a widespread impact was "Oh Happy Day," a top ten hit in 1969 for the Edwin Hawkins' Singers.

However, the group that best represented this particular strand of black music was the Staple Singers. The Staple Singers were a family affair: father Roebuck Staples, a former blues guitarist, and four children. Mavis Staples, who also enjoyed moderate success as a solo act, sang lead. Their No. 1 hit, "I'll Take You There" (1972), is an ideal illustration of this new soul-gospel style. The song has all the ingredients of soul: a great groove in the rhythm section, working over a simple alternating two-chord accompaniment, horn riffs, backup vocals, and, above all, Mavis's soulful singing. But the message of the song is not about man/woman issues or a good time on Saturday night. Instead, it is about a place where there is racial harmony: "No more smiling faces/lyin' to the races." Without the words, it could be just another soul song. With the words, it's a new genre. "Inspirational pop" found a niche in the pop marketplace in the first half of the seventies, but faded away in the latter part of the decade.

A much more far-reaching development was the infusion of black gospel with pop rhythms and instruments. The message remained holy, and the core of the pre-sixties gospel sound remained: full-sounding choirs, melismatic lead vocal lines, with support from piano and organ. But drums, electric bass, and (often) guitar were added to fill out the accompaniment, and songs were set to the rock-based rhythms of contemporary black music. In the forefront of this movement to "modernize" gospel was Andraé Crouch.

Like so many other gospel (and soul) performers, Crouch grew up in the church: his father had a ministry in Los Angeles. By 1967, he had formed the gospel group, the Disciples. Early members included his sister, Sandra, and Billy Preston, who soon left for a career as a solo performer and session player. By 1971, the group had begun recording for Light Records, a leading Contemporary Christian label. From the start, they had a large crossover following. Crouch tells a story of a performance in Dallas, Texas, to a large, white audience who didn't realize that Crouch and the Disciples were black. After some initial hostility, they "converted" the audience to them as well as their music.

By his own account, Crouch deliberately positioned his music to attract the widest possible audience, not for personal gain, but for his ministry. To achieve this goal, he used the rich harmonic palette of popular song, the rhythms of contemporary black music, and the full rhythm section of virtually all rock-era music. "Soon and Very Soon," a song recorded in 1976, shows how Crouch merged traditional gospel style with contemporary elements. In this song, at least, traditional features are central: the rich-sounding choir, accompanied mainly by the piano and, later, Crouch's melismatic singing. Underneath, however, are bass and drums laying down sixteen-beat based rhythms. The contrasting section has the rich harmonies of pop.

The synthesis of traditional gospel, contemporary black rhythms, and white harmonies heard in this and other songs was successful for Crouch. He was among the most successful of a new generation of gospel performers.

His music also found a non-religious audience. He provided music for Steven Spielberg's *The Color Purple*, Paul Simon and Elvis covered his songs, and he has collaborated with Diana Ross, Madonna, and Michael Jackson.

Crouch was also an integral part of the Contemporary Christian movement. His music not only helped spark a new generation of black gospel music, but also inspired the use of contemporary elements in white religious music. Contemporary Christian music, both black and white, had become by the late seventies a powerful enough force commercially to rate its own

Billboard chart. It remains so, despite little attention from the media and the crossover success of artists such as Amy Grant.

Instrumental Soul

Behind almost every great soul singer was a soulful saxophonist and a rhythm section that could groove. Occasionally, one or the other would step into the spotlight. Booker T and the MGs, Stax's house band, had a string of hits in the sixties, beginning with "Green Onions" (1962). Saxophonist King Curtis, a studio veteran since the fifties (among his work was the famous solo on the Coasters' "Yakety Yak"), also scored with several hits in addition to accompanying a roster of top stars, most notably Aretha Franklin.

The saxophone had been the main instrumental voice of rhythm and blues since the days of Louis Jordan. However, Ray Charles's recordings debuted not only a new vocal style, but also a new instrumental sound: the biting, expressive tone of saxophonists David "Fathead" Newman and Hank Crawford, who provided instrumental counterparts to Charles's gritty vocals. In the sixties, this sound was carried forward not only by Curtis, but also by James Brown's Maceo Parker and Motown's resident gritmeister, Junior Walker. Walker's string of hits—"Shotgun," "(I'm a) Roadrunner," and more—featured his expressive, hard-toned saxophone playing as well as his singing.

Nevertheless, despite Curtis's occasional forays on the charts, the saxophone remained mainly in the background—behind a vocalist or in alternation with him; so did rhythm sections. For the most part, soul remained a vocal music throughout the decade. That changed around 1970, mainly because of the emergence of the Crusaders.

THE CRUSADERS Three of the Crusaders' charter members, saxophonist Wilton Felder, keyboardist Joe Sample, and drummer "Stix" Hooper, began playing together while in high school. While at Southern University, they added trombonist Wayne Henderson to the mixture. After moving to Los Angeles in 1958, they billed themselves as the Jazz Crusaders and tried to forge a career as a jazz act for most of the sixties. However, they had always played rhythm and blues as well, and, after a year off in 1969, dropped "Jazz" from their name and repertoire.

While the jazz influence was still evident in the new Crusaders' work—mainly in their harmonic progressions (and their skill improvising over them)—the music was a lot funkier. The grooves were stronger, and Felder's saxophone playing took on a decided R&B character. These qualities are evident in their first hit, "Put It Where You Want It" (1972), which also featured guitarist Larry Carlton.

Two aspects of the song are especially noteworthy. The groove—which Carlton said was called "the pocket" by the Crusaders—grows out of rich interactions within a dense rhythmic texture. Hooper lays down a standard rock beat with a heavy backbeat. However, the rest of the band sets their own rhythmic agendas: the bass line is usually silent on the first and third beats; the guitar chords often fall on the afterbeat; the opening keyboard riff ends on a strong syncopation; and the droopy guitar melody is completely off the beat. As we have noted previously, a good—even great—groove emerges from the interplay between beatkeeping and rhythmic conflict: this is an especially dense and complex example.

Felder's solo shows him to be a master of rhythm and blues saxophone. He begins with the hard, biting sound that was part of the David Newman/King Curtis style. But he inflects his lines with slurs, slides, hesitations, strained high notes. Although there are no words, his expressive vocabulary certainly recalls the inflections of the great soul singers. Felder's playing influenced a generation of saxophonists—for example, Tom Scott and Grover Washington, Jr. In a more watered-down form, it has become the staple of the contemporary "smooth jazz" sound of the last two decades.

The Crusaders stayed together until 1983, scoring their biggest hit in 1981 with "Street Life," featuring vocalist Randy Crawford. They also have been highly sought-after studio musicians, performing on over 200 gold albums by others. The roster of artists they have supported is a diverse group, including Steely Dan, Van Morrison, B. B. King, Joan Baez, Joni Mitchell, and Barry White.

The Roots of Funk

The black pop and soul-derived styles of the early seventies represented, more than anything else, the final flourishing of the main black styles of the sixties. By contrast, the sound that foretold the future of black music came mainly from James Brown and Sly and the Family Stone. Its driving force was rhythm.

James Brown

In our discussion of James Brown's "Cold Sweat" (see Chapter 6), we noted the qualities that made Brown's music virtually unique in 1967: an overriding emphasis on rhythm, expressed in complex riff-based interactions over static harmony. This formula was Brown's rhythmic mother lode, and he mined it for the next several years.

By 1970, the rhythms of his music had become more active and complex, particularly after bassist "Bootsy" Collins and his guitarist brother "Catfish" joined the band for a brief tenure. In songs such as "Mother Popcorn," "Get Up (I Feel Like Being a) Sex Machine," "Super Bad, Pts. 1 & 2," and "Soul Power, Pts. 1 & 2," there is a cauldron of rhythmic activity.

Two features of the rhythm stand out. First, a sixteen-beat rhythmic foundation is now standard. Even when the only steadily marked rhythm is an eight-beat rhythm, as is the case in "Sex Machine," all the rhythmic interplay is taking place at sixteen-beat speed. The use of the more active sixteen-beat foundation geometrically increases the possibilities for rhythmic conflict (see the discussion of "Ain't Nothing Like the Real Thing" in Chapter 6), and James and his band exploit them fully. Especially noteworthy are Collins's bass lines, which typically play against the beat. His figures further liberate the bass line from the restrictive rhythmic role of fifties rhythm and blues.

In addition, both the bassist and guitarist use an array of percussive sonorities—that is, sounds with sharp attacks and quick decays. The most obvious example is the "choked" guitar sound, a rapid strum made with the strings only partially depressed, that produces more percussion than pitch. Even Brown's vocal delivery, with its sharply articulated consonants and clipped vowels, is percussive.

The funky grooves laid down by Brown's band served as a backdrop for his vocals. Some songs, like "Mother Popcorn," simply talked about good times.

Others, like "Sex Machine" and "Super Bad," were good-natured braggadocio. Also on the playlist were Brown's secular sermons, like "Get Up, Get into It and Get Involved," and "Say It Loud—I'm Black and I'm Proud." These were exhortations to the black community to take charge of their lives. No one delivered stronger or more positive messages than Brown.

Brown's recordings from the seventies enable us to perceive even more clearly his enormous impact on popular music, especially in the last quarter of the century. It can be argued that the dominant theme in the evolution of popular music is, ironically, the ascendancy of rhythm at the expense of melody. Rhythms have become more active and syncopated, while flowing melodies have become the exception, not the rule. We have moved from "no beat" music ("Woodman, Spare That Tree"), through two-beat, four-beat, eight-beat, and finally sixteen-beat rhythms.

Brown's "brand new bag" was a new rhythmic feel for black music, and his seventies music is even more active, percussive, and complex. By example, he led rock and soul toward the new rhythms of the late seventies, thus anticipating funk, rap, and the alternative music funk/punk fusions of the eighties and nineties.

Sly and the Family Stone

Among the acts that Brown influenced was Sly and the Family Stone, an integrated band led by Sly Stone, aka Sylvester Stewart. Stewart grew up in the San Francisco Bay area. His childhood included familiar rites of passage for a black musician: gospel singing as a youngster (he started when he was four), and a local hit as a teenager. However, perhaps because he was in the Bay Area instead of Motown or Memphis, his career followed a different path. His first

Sly Stone in England, September 11, 1968.
PHOTO COURTESY CORBIS/ HULTON-DEUTSCH COLLECTION.

real notoriety came when he was working as a DJ for the two local black music stations. Working with Tom Donahue, a major player in the San Francisco music scene, he began producing records for several San Francisco-based bands, most of them white. He formed an early version of Sly and the Family Stone in 1966. After Stone recruited his cousin, bassist Larry Graham, a year later, the group was complete.

Sly and the Family Stone was an unusual group in almost every respect. It was truly a family affair: Sly's brother Freddie and sister Rosie were integral members. It was fully integrated: its roster included women as well as men, whites as well as blacks (trumpeter Cynthia Robinson was a double reverse minority: female and white). Their music found a large, racially mixed audience, especially after their appearance at Woodstock, where they were, in the minds of many, the hit of the festival. At the peak of their success, between 1969 and 1971, they charted as well on the pop charts as they did on the rhythm and blues charts, even though Stone used none of the tried-and-true crossover strategies.

The group's early songs were all upbeat. Although they come out of gospel (the inspirational messages of "You Can Make It If You Try" or "Everyday People," for example) or the good times of uptempo rhythm and blues and soul (e.g., "Fun" and "Dance to the Music"), they had an appeal that transcended racial boundaries. Then there were the psychedelic overtones in songs like "I Want to Take You Higher" and the good humor that shows through in the phonemically twisted title, "Thank You (Falettinme Be Mice Elf Agin)." By contrast, the songs on their 1971 album, *There's A Riot Goin' On*, are darker in both words and music. They represent not only the backlash from the racial problems of the late sixties but also the crash from what was surely a drug-induced high.

Their music was also a family affair, that is to say, a group conception with no real stars or frontliners. Although Sly Stone was the leader and main vocalist, any given song might feature two lead singers, and usually one of them was a woman. The distribution of musical interest is also well-balanced. Larry Graham's innovative and virtuosic bass playing is the most distinctive element, but many songs also feature heavily amplified, blues-influenced guitar, organ, and/or electric keyboards. In addition, there are sections for voices without instruments. At times, these are extremely intricate, although they sound almost spontaneous: the beginning of "Dance to the Music" is an excellent example. Voices and instruments combine in a loosely interwoven texture: singers talk as well as sing, and horns and rhythm instruments create piles of riffs. It was a unique kind of good-time music, and—later—a singular trip to a darker side.

Sly and the Family Stone's songs were also among the most progressive music of their time, in the sense that they anticipated the new rhythms, sounds, and textures of funk and rap. Two of their early hits, "I Want to Take You Higher" and "Thank You," show the distinctive elements of their style. Two later hits show how it changed.

The first minute or so of "I Want to Take You Higher" shows their full arsenal. The song begins with a bluesy pentatonic guitar/bass riff straight out of Hendrix or Clapton. But the groove that follows is denser and more intricate than virtually all hard rock. The bass is more active and prominent, and the texture is a stack of riffs. None of the riffs is especially complex, but their interaction is: it's James Brown with the empty spaces filled in. Instead of a single spotlighted performer, there are three vocalists heard in the first 30 seconds; we can almost see them toss phrases back and forth on stage. The rhythmic underpinning of all this is a sixteen-beat rhythm. Sly's band was among the first to use the rhythmically richer sixteen-beat foundation almost exclusively, and no one of his time did it with more imagination.

"Thank You" is a "missing link" between James Brown's seminal "Cold Sweat" and George Clinton's funk. The hard rock elements are absent; the guitar sounds include a low wah-wah riff and the occasional high-chord interjection, a la James. They and the rest of the band create an infectious groove over a single chord (again shades of Brown).

The highlighted strand in the texture is Larry Graham's bassline. Graham's playing continued the liberation of the bass from a strict timekeeping role and expanded the sound possibilities of the instrument. Graham was mainly responsible for adding an array of percussive sounds to bassists' repertoire. The two main techniques were plucking the string to create a slapping sound against the fingerboard and slapping the string with the side of the thumb so that the percussion of the slap was almost as prominent as the pitch of the note being played.

Throughout their recorded (that is, recording) history, African Americans have sought percussive ways to play all instruments. The plucked sound of the string bass and the tight strum of the rhythm guitar date back to the twenties. The choked guitar sound heard in Brown's recordings (and in recordings by Stone and other black artists of the early seventies) and especially Graham's enormously influential bass playing were a quantum leap forward in this direction.

"Family Affair" (1971), the group's last No. 1 hit, adapts the style of "Thank You" to a more pop-oriented style. The texture is leaner, there are harmonic progressions, the refrain has an easily remembered hook, and the overall sound is more muted. The bright sounding tambourine and horns are absent, and the tone of the song, especially when Sly is moaning the verse, is much darker. Similarly, "Africa Talks to You 'The Asphalt Jungle'" is a wound-down version of "Thank You" Although this is a one-chord song with a tangle of interwoven riffs, the tempo is slower and the lyric much more depressing and cautionary. It's a curious combination of optimism (in the interplay that produces the groove), pessimism (in the lyric and vocal line), and indifference (in the draggy tempo).

Sly's star shone brightly for about three years. However, a cavalier attitude toward professional responsibilities—such as not showing up for gigs—and legal problems jettisoned his career. A serious drug problem undoubtedly contributed to his professional problems. It has bedeviled his career since: a 1987 arrest for cocaine possession nipped a minor comeback in the bud. Nevertheless, his problems cannot obscure his crucial contribution to the music of the seventies. He and his band (especially bassist Larry Graham) were enormously influential.

Art Funk

Among those profoundly influenced by Sly Stone's music was jazz keyboardist Herbie Hancock. He was among the first jazz musicians to be attracted to rock music. During the sixties he began to explore jazz/rock fusions. One of his first efforts, "Watermelon Man," was a hit for Cuban percussionist Mongo

Santamaria in 1963. Hancock himself recorded a version of it the previous year. His album *Maiden Voyage* (1965) was an experiment in melding jazz with R&B and rock rhythms. In the early seventies, he invented his own particular jazz/rock fusion in a series of albums, beginning with *Headhunters* (1973).

A comparison of Hancock's two versions of "Watermelon Man"—the original 1962 recording and the 1973 remake from *Headhunters*—shows how thoroughly Hancock absorbed Stone's music into his conception. In the first version, he simply grafts a rock beat onto a jazz performance, mainly through repetitive riffs in the rhythm section. After a short introduction, the horns play the melody. Improvised solos follow; after they are finished, there is a reprise of the melody. It is the rock beat that differentiates the song from conventional jazz of the time. The later version ultimately creates a dense, riff-based texture derived directly from Stone. It begins with a single African flute. Other instruments gradually layer in, mostly one by one, until there are about ten strands in the texture. Only the saxophone hints at the original melody; the other instruments play short riffs or percussion lines over what turns out to be a sixteen-beat rhythm.

Hancock continued to explore this jazz/proto-funk fusion in subsequent albums. In the process, he singlehandedly defined what might be called "art funk." It was popular: *Headhunters* went platinum, and his next two albums charted. His earlier albums had sold well by jazz standards, but his particular spin on funk generated a huge jump in sales.

Blaxploitation Music

Finally, there was a short-lived but influential genre that drew on black pop, soul, and funk: the music for "blaxploitation" films such as *Shaft* and *Superfly*. These were action films with black leads, set in the ghetto. They portray the seamier side of life in the inner city, focusing on drug use, prostitution, and crime. The producers of the films wanted appropriate-sounding music and turned to two veteran producers to provide it: Isaac Hayes and Curtis Mayfield. Hayes, who helped mastermind the Stax soul sound, had just begun a solo career with drawn-out arrangements of popular songs like his cover of "By the Time I Get to Phoenix," one of only four tracks on his hot *Hot Buttered Soul* album (1969). Mayfield, based in Chicago, had been the guiding force behind the Impressions, and Jerry Butler, after he left the group. He also became a solo performer in the late sixties.

Hayes scored first with the soundtrack to *Shaft* (1971). The soundtrack album briefly topped the charts and won him a Grammy, and "Theme from Shaft," a single from the album, was a No. 1 hit. (Many more people heard the music than saw the film.) He would follow his score for *Shaft* with several others; he also acted in *Tough Guys*, (1973) and *Truck Turner* (1974). Mayfield followed Hayes with the score to *Superfly* (1972), which also reached the top of the charts that year. He also scored several other films.

The title track single from *Superfly*, which reached the top ten, shows how Mayfield merged the several strains of black music together. The song has the rich orchestration and active, percussion-enriched rhythms of a Philadephia song, added to the brighter beat, the wah-wah guitar, and something of the complex interplay of early funk. Above it all floats Mayfield's soulful voice, in which he tries to give a balanced portrait of the film's antihero. This synthesis also helped pave the way for disco.

Summary

Like rock, black music branched off in many different directions during the early seventies. Black pop matured. The music coming from Motown, especially that of Stevie Wonder, Marvin Gaye, and Diana Ross, was more mature, although the Jackson 5 helped them retain their teen and pre-teen fans. Philadelphia producers Gamble and Huff and Thom Bell challenged Motown's supremacy with music that extended and enriched Motown's pop formula: tuneful melodies, infectious rhythms, and rich orchestrations. Their music was also directed at a more grown-up audience, as was the music of Barry White. Less lavishly produced, but even more jazz-influenced, were hits songs of Roberta Flack (at times in duet with Donny Hathaway) and Bill Withers. The stylistic diversity of this music was the most compelling evidence that all of black music had finally arrived in the rock era.

Meanwhile, soul hung on, but it was going, not coming. Al Green was the last in the line of great soul singers, and he left popular music altogether to return to God. His return could serve as a metaphor for the fate of soul: its sound and style lived on mainly within the black church after 1975.

The cutting edge black music of the early seventies came from the "Godfather of Soul" James Brown, and Sly and the Family Stone. The dense, rhythmically intricate textures of their music would help shape disco, funk, rap, and other music of the late seventies and eighties.

Instrumental, jazz-influenced versions of all these styles also did well: George Benson, Grover Washington, Jr. and others combined romantic rhythm and blues with jazz. The Crusaders were more soulful, while Herbie Hancock created a funk-based instrumental music. All of this music was, by jazz standards, overwhelmingly successful.

Rock had been a hard sell in Hollywood; black music even more so. But Isaac Hayes and Curtis Mayfield broke the ice on the use of contemporary black music in film; in so doing, they created a new, if short-lived, genre.

By 1974, the second wave of successful black music had crested. In the wake of disco, funk, and a new wave of black artists, most of the musicians who had dominated the charts in the early seventies saw their careers decline. Some would reinvent themselves: the most spectacular, of course, was Michael Jackson. Others simply marched on. The music of the early seventies, both white and black, has generally suffered when compared critically with the music of the sixties. Granted, it was not cutting-edge music in most cases, but the best of it made up in craftsmanship and sophistication for what it lacked in innovation. It remains some of the most durable and best-loved music of the rock era.

K E Y   T E R M S

Philadelphia sound	Latin-tinged rock rhythm	Choked guitar sound
Blaxploitation film	Sixteen-beat rhythm	Slap bass style
Synthesizer	Groove	Jazz-funk fusion or art funk
Black romantic music	Funk	

CHAPTER QUESTIONS

1. Listen to "The Backstabbers," then compare it with "My Girl." Find three or four features that demonstrate how the Philadelphia International recordings were an expansion of the Motown sound.

2. Review some of the gospel recordings from Chapter 2, especially the Soul Stirrers' "Jesus, I'll Never Forget," then compare them to "I'll Take You There" and "Soon and Very Soon." Can you isolate the "inspirational" features of the music, evident in both of the more recent songs?

3. Stevie Wonder was the first major artist to perform virtually all the parts on his recordings. Do his recordings seem more unified in their conception as a result of his comprehensive control? Take a position one way or the other, using "Superstition" as a primary reference.

4. The "Sound of Young America" began to show a generation gap in the early seventies. Listen to three or four of the black pop examples, including one of the Jackson 5 recordings and "I'm Gonna Love You Just a Little More, Baby." Compare the message and language of the lyrics, then consider how—and to what extent—the music amplifies, contradicts, or ignores the substance and style of the lyric.

5. Compare one or two of the Sly and the Family Stone recordings with "Sex Machine" and "Cold Sweat." Find three elements that show their common ground and at least two differences between them.

Society and Popular Music

1974–1989

By the mid-seventies, rock was becoming the world's common musical language. Its reach was global, cutting across national boundaries and language barriers: the Swedish group ABBA, the most commercially successful group of the seventies, sang their songs in English. At the same time, Africans began to redeem their legacy: Afro-pop styles flourished in most West African countries.

Rock was also capable of speaking to small, even minuscule, constituencies. It could give voice to groups defined by geography, economic status, class, race, gender, beliefs, and/or any other criterion: reggae began as the voice of Rastafarian Jamaicans, for example. And it had become intertwined with other aspects of culture more deeply than ever before—consider that the idea of punk was born in a London boutique.

Social Trends

The 12 years between 1974 and 1985 saw the beginnings of the global village. Huge increases in international trade created global economic interdependence. A telecommunications breakthrough transported news throughout the world in seconds, rather than hours or days. Popular music was part of this globalization process. Music had always been advertised as a universal language; by 1985, it truly had become that.

Peace and War
Two developments that frame this time period, the end of the Vietnam war and the ascension to power of Mikhail Gorbachev, were crucial steps in the drive toward global peace and stability. The Vietnam war officially ended in 1973.

However, fighting continued, and the last refugees didn't leave until 1975. Vietnam made clear that superpowers could no longer impose their will on smaller nations without using weapons of mass destruction. The Soviets learned much the same lesson in the eighties as a result of their failed invasion of Afghanistan. Even as the Afghan war was going on, Soviet premier Mikhail Gorbachev began the process of opening the Soviet empire to the west and moving away from the rigid and repressive communism of his predecessors.

The end of Vietnam marked the beginning of the most sustained global peace in this century. There have been local wars with international consequences: the most notable was the Arab–Israeli war of the early seventies. But the threat of mutual nuclear annihilation that hovered over the world through the fifties and sixties greatly diminished during this 12-year period.

That did not mean that the impulse toward war dried up. It simply shifted to another arena: trade. The trade war with the most far-reaching consequences was the Arab oil embargo of the seventies. More than any other factor, it fueled the double-digit inflation that devastated economies in the industrialized part of the world during this decade. It even had a direct impact on the popular music industry: many independent record labels closed because the smaller record pressing plants could not get the raw petroleum-based materials they needed to make records.

Money

Money was on the minds of most during the seventies and eighties. The rich were getting richer, but the poor stayed poor. Between 1974 and 1985, the median income of America's poorest 20 percent remained virtually unchanged in real terms, while the median income of the wealthiest 5 percent increased by about 25 percent. The income gap between rich and poor in the United Kingdom was reduced somewhat by the emigration of many rich Britons to avoid heavy taxation. This, of course, placed more of the burden on those who remained behind.

Inflation, which decreased only with a recession in the early eighties, was the economic cue that the bloom was off the rose of sixties optimism. It was not just that the dollar you earned at the beginning of the year might be worth 90 cents or less by the end of it, but also that the inflationary spiral seemed to have no end. This created an atmosphere of economic insecurity; long-range financial planning seemed almost impossible at the time. Inflation's psychological impact was almost as devastating as its economic impact. It was within this atmosphere of disaffection and instability that both punk and disco emerged.

The acquisition of money became almost a religion in the eighties. After his election in 1980, Ronald Reagan removed many governmental restrictions on business. No longer restrained by government regulations, a generation of moneymakers amassed enormous fortunes. Michael Douglas, portraying a ruthless Wall Street speculator in the movie *Wall Street*, encapsulated the new ethic of the new rich in the phrase "Greed is good."

"Insider trading" and "hostile takeover" entered the vocabulary of ordinary Americans. Forced mergers designed to line the pockets of the new capitalists threw thousands of people out of work. The music industry was not exempt from merger mania. By 1980, six companies dominated the recording industry, and one of them, Columbia-CBS, was itself the target of a takeover by Sony, the Japanese electronics giant.

Minorities and Their Rights

In the seventies, the women's movement replaced African-American civil rights as the main minority cause. The drive for women's rights had a long history in the United States. Ironically, the second-class treatment of women active in the civil rights movement—male civil rights leaders often relegated them to menial jobs while they did the "real" work of the movement—helped fuel their drive for equal status; so did Betty Friedan's landmark book, *The Feminine Mystique*, published in 1963. "Women's lib," as its detractors often called it, was more than bra burning. Women sought equal pay for performing the same jobs, equal access to jobs for which they were qualified, responsiveness to their needs (e.g., no penalties for maternity leave) and, above all, respect.

Popular music both reflected the growing voice of women and advanced their cause. Helen Reddy's "I Am Woman" (1972) was an enormous pop hit and became the anthem of the women's movement. Far more powerful women emerged shortly thereafter: Patti Smith, whose music added rage to reason, was a leading voice in the punk movement; Madonna brokered her unique mix of sexual daring, talent, and power into a major career that began in the early eighties. Others assumed roles that had been almost exclusively male: The popular hard-rock group, Heart, for example, was led by two women who sang and played guitar in a manner previously only done by men.

At about the same time, homosexuality came out of the closet. "Gay" became the designation of choice, not only within the homosexual community, but also in the media and in government. The fact that homosexuality was openly discussed represented a major breakthrough for gay rights, as did several legal victories and legislative triumphs. Sgt. Leonard Matlovich, a much-

Gay Rights March, November 2, 1974. Photo courtesy CORBIS/Hulton-Deutsch Collection.

decorated Vietnam veteran, was given a general discharge from the Air Force after publicly announcing his homosexuality. His intent was to challenge the military's ban on homosexuality. In the wake of the furor that followed his dismissal, his discharge was upgraded to "honorable," a clear victory for gays.

Popular music certainly brought homosexuality into the public eye, if only because it openly challenged norms of sexual identity. David Bowie and Marc Bolan made cross-dressing fashionable. Heavy metal bands wore make-up; Kiss took stage make-up to the extreme. Allegations of homosexuality or bisexuality seemed to have little negative effect on performers' popularity: Elton John was the most popular artist of the seventies; Michael Jackson of the eighties.

For racial minorities in both the United States and United Kingdom, the late seventies and early eighties offered good and bad news. In the United States, the disparity between their rich and poor also increased enormously. The most obviously well-to-do minorities were professional athletes and entertainers, and black professionals found increased opportunity and greater mobility. One consequence was the flight of blacks, especially middle- and upper-class blacks, from the ghetto to the suburbs. Those who stayed behind found the ghetto an even more deprived and perilous environment. Rap, which emerged in the late seventies, gave inner-city ghettos a strong new voice.

As the British empire disintegrated after World War II, there was a large influx of immigrants from the West Indies and Africa. Immigration became so heavy in the late fifties and early sixties that the British government revoked its policy of extending naturalization rights to a citizens of any former colony, and began establishing quotas. This was an inevitable backlash, especially toward those with darker skins: not only West Indians and Africans, but Indians and Pakistanis. Nevertheless, some prospered. Athletes such as Olympic sprinter Linford Christie stood out.

Business and Technology in Popular Music

In the spirit of the era, rock became even more of a business than it had been. With the introduction of cable television, the media underwent its most profound change in almost three decades. Applications of digital technology transformed the recording process; its effects were evident from conception to playback.

Corporate Rock

In 1974, Stevie Wonder, who had received $1 million in royalties upon turning 21, signed a seven-year contract with Motown for $14 million. Later that same year, *Billboard* noted that over 80 percent of the best-selling albums and singles came from only six companies. These two announcements showed the extent to which rock had become big business.

Record sales boomed in the seventies: platinum (1 million units sold) succeeded gold (a "mere" 500,000) as the measure of success. Multi-platinum albums became more common: Fleetwood Mac's *Rumours* (1977) sold 13 million units, making it the best-selling album of the decade. Michael Jackson's *Thriller* (1984) has sold three times that amount.

Successful artists demanded, and got, more of the revenues from record sales. Their agents negotiated higher royalties, larger advances, and a host of other benefits. Contracts became complex documents, with numerous riders regarding promotion, international sales, and the like. Wonder, Elton John, Neil Diamond, and other best-selling artists bargained from a position of strength.

Recording had become a more elaborate process, and studio time was expensive. Promotional and production expenses had also risen. It is difficult to imagine a riskier business than the pop industry during this time. Indeed, in a 1971 interview, one record company executive reported that only 10 to 15 percent of all rock albums recouped their original investment.

Still, it was a business, and a profitable one for the strongest companies. Rock and roll's early entrepreneurs—Sam Phillips, Cosimo Massima, the Chess Brothers, Norman Petty—ran largely regional operations with shoestring budgets. Twenty years later, virtually all of popular music was controlled by ten corporations. Six—CBS (now Sony), RCA (now BMG), EMI, Polygram, ABC, and WEA—controlled over four-fifths of the big business. Motown, A&M, United Artists, and 20th Century Fox divided most of the remainder among themselves. Independent labels had to fight for even a small voice.

The six majors, which have remained in place since the seventies, are as international as the music they sell. By 1990, four of the six companies had headquarters outside of the United States. Their operations have been similarly diverse. They have served, in effect, as large holding companies, providing administrative structure for numerous smaller labels targeted to specific markets. The music business, like business in general, had gone through a wave of consolidation, but it did not get homogenized in the process—except on radio. The increasing diversity of the popular music industry was reflected by a substantial jump in the number of *Billboard* charts.

Rock and the Media

New technology played a crucial role in most of the main developments in radio, record playback, television, and film. Improvement in tape playback equipment reshaped radio and improved record sales. Cable television allowed market fragmentation. Film was least affected, except in reaction to television.

AOR/MOR RADIO If the late sixties were the heyday of freeform rock radio, then the seventies and early eighties were the era of the playlist. Most radio stations bought syndicated prepackaged radio shows that played a short list of songs selected from a chart. Turnover on the playlist was minimal: only five new songs were added a week.

Improvements in tape playback, most notably the Dolby noise reduction system, made it possible to record entire radio shows on cartridges—not only the songs, but the DJ patter and commercials as well. For much of the day, technicians who could read the news replaced radio personalities.

This mainstream-style radio programming came in two forms, MOR and AOR. MOR, or "middle of the road," was easy-listening music: favored artists early on were Neil Diamond, Carole King, the Jackson 5, and Elton John, among others. AOR, or "album-oriented rock," was somewhat more aggressive, but a long way from heavy metal. Acts such as the Eagles, Steely Dan, and Fleetwood Mac made these playlists. MOR/AOR programming dominated both AM and FM through the seventies. That would change in the eighties, in part because of the rise of MTV.

CABLE TELEVISION AND MTV   Cable television got its start in the mid-seventies. Cable not only improved the picture quality of network broadcasts, but also made specialty channels economically feasible, because they received income from the cable operators as well as advertisers. One of these specialty stations was MTV.

The idea of using moving images to help promote songs went back to the beginning of talking pictures. In the fifties, rock acts appeared on television variety shows, often "lip-syncing" (or pretending to perform) their songs to a prerecorded soundtrack. Many popular acts also appeared in movies oriented to teen audiences; again, their appearances tended to be some sort of performance sequence (the kids have a party; Chuck Berry shows up and does a song). In 1964, the Beatles' *A Hard Day's Night* showed the commercial and artistic potential of mixing rock with narrative. The Beatles made short films to promote many of their later songs, such as the surrealistic, dream-like film created to promote "Strawberry Fields Forever." Promotional films or videos continued to be made through the seventies. By 1981, cable television had expanded sufficiently to make a network built around music videos practical. MTV went on the air that year.

Although some music videos were simply concert footage, the music video quickly evolved as a distinct medium. They had to appeal visually as well as musically, so acts quickly learned the value of well-produced videos. Duran Duran, who mastered the art of suggestiveness, were the kings of MTV and a major recording act of the eighties mainly on the strength of their videos. However, it was Michael Jackson who established the music video as a new art form, and integrated MTV in the process. Until public demand for Jackson's *Thriller* videos became too much to ignore, MTV had had a lily-white playlist. Their unconvincing rationale for this policy was that they were simply giving their public what they wanted. After 1984, MTV belatedly acknowledged that the public wanted black as well as white acts.

Jimmy Page's band taping a typical MTV video, complete with smoke bombs. PHOTO COURTESY CORBIS/NEAL PRESTON.

The music video was an interesting mixture of innovation and tradition. Music videos have their roots in the musical and other forms of stage entertainment where song is used to advance a story. But videos completely invert the relationship between song and story. Instead of using music to enhance the action on stage, the video uses visual elements to enhance the song.

Music videos brought a visual dimension to rock-era music that had been largely absent during the seventies. The rock musical came and went very quickly. Stage shows, e.g., David Bowie's Ziggy Stardust, were certainly theatrical, but glam rock also passed quickly. The music video has become rock's most enduring combination of music, narrative, and visual images and effects: short-attention-span music theater for the home.

The music video also brought back the idea of the all-around entertainer. Well before the rock era began, performance had become specialized: there were singers, there were actors, and there were dancers. Fred Astaire, remembered mainly for his dancing but also admired for his singing, was an exception. From the beginning of the rock era, movement had been a big part of performance. All the greats moved to their music: Elvis's gyrations were simply the most notorious. Motown's elaborately choreographed routines were slicker, but along the same line. However, both were simply an adjunct to the music.

It was the music videos of Michael Jackson and Madonna that signaled the return of the complete entertainer. Their dancing was virtuosic, theatrical, and expressive. It was as much a part of the video as the song itself. By integrating song, dance, and staging, they revived and updated a venerable tradition, and tailored it to the new medium.

ROCK IN THE MOVIES Hollywood was the last bastion of popular music's old guard. Radio, television, and Broadway embraced rock earlier and more enthusiastically than the film industry did. However, that would change in the late seventies, mainly because of Robert Stigwood.

Stigwood was an aggressive Australian entrepreneur who made his first splash as manager of the Who and Cream. By the early seventies, he was managing numerous British rock acts, among them the Bee Gees. By mid-decade, he was venturing into film. First came the controversial film version of *Tommy* (1975). His biggest success, however, was *Saturday Night Fever* (1977), which made John Travolta a big screen star. *Saturday Night Fever* is arguably the most important rock-era film, not only because it is the biggest-selling soundtrack of all time (over 11,000,000), but because it fed disco into the mainstream. *Blackboard Jungle* made a song, Bill Haley's "Rock Around the Clock," a hit, but it was essentially a cult film. By contrast, *Saturday Night Fever* made a style—and a lifestyle—a huge hit. Stigwood's other two big films from the period were released a year later. *Grease* celebrated fifties rock and roll, while *Sgt. Pepper's Lonely Hearts Club Band* made a film out of the Beatles' album. The three films covered all three decades of the rock era: the fifties, sixties, and seventies.

In the wake of Stigwood's success, films with rock soundtracks flooded the market. In its dance orientation, *Flashdance* (1983) was a notable heir to *Saturday Night Fever*. *Purple Rain* (1984), a more-or-less autobiographical account of a rock star's career, was an overwhelming success for Prince. In its popularity and its portrayal of the life of a rock musician, it was the first important successor to the Beatles' *A Hard Day's Night*.

It was also, with *Saturday Night Fever*, a quintessential example of a classic music-business strategy: cross-marketing. Cross-marketing was the use of recordings to promote films, and vice versa. Recordings would be released prior to the release of the film to build up interest in it, and what amounted to a music video was shown as a preview, well before the release of the film. The film would in turn help popularize the recordings. After 1977, it was a common strategy.

Technology Leaps Forward: Synths, Sequences, Samples, and Sound Systems

In the 16 years between 1974 and 1989, popular music went almost completely electric and completely digital. A new wave of synthesizers appeared throughout the seventies, as did the first applications of digital technology. The early eighties saw the complete arrival of digital technology, and with it, a new way of making music.

SOUND RECORDING IN THE SEVENTIES Although it was an exciting, breakthrough technology, multitrack recording was a cumbersome process in the sixties. Tracks had to be bumped down—mixed and remixed—because there were often only four tracks available. For example, an instrumental accompaniment would be recorded on all four tracks, and then mixed down to one track so vocals could be added. Two developments, the expansion of multitrack recording to 24 tracks and the use of Dolby noise reduction, radically improved the sound of recordings in the seventies. Twenty-four-track recording, the industry standard by 1972, meant that bumping down was almost never necessary. Noise reduction greatly reduced signal degradation at every step of the recording process.

The art and craft of recording took a big jump when 24-track boards became standard equipment in recording studios. This development had two important consequences. First, 24 tracks meant that instruments could be miked with several microphones—this was standard procedure with drum sets—or fed directly into the mixing board. Further, each track could then be altered through post-recording sound modification. Finally, the tracks could be mixed to create a sound difficult, if not impossible, to replicate in live performance. The heavy but crisp backbeat popular from the late seventies on is a familiar example of this process. (It's easily heard on Bruce Springsteen's "Born in the U.S.A.")

The profusion of tracks and noise reduction technology also made *sequencing* practical. Sequencing is the repetition of a recorded musical fragment. It is produced by looping the taped excerpt as many times as desired. Repetitive strands in a texture, e.g., bass lines and drum parts, could easily be sequenced; sequences could also be programmed on synthesizers. "Striping," which allowed performers to synchronize a new sequence with an existing sequenced track, made multitrack sequencing much easier. Sequencing quickly found a home in disco, with its relentless beats and negligible tempo variation. Sequencing made disco records less expensive to produce, which appealed to record company executives. Their support was an important factor in its commercial success.

SYNTHESIZERS Synthesizers became viable performing and recording instruments in the seventies. Early synthesizers, most notably those of Robert Moog, looked like old-fashioned telephone switchboards. Each sound had to be calibrated and connected with patchcords, so they were impractical for live performance and clumsy to use in the studio. Moog's "Minimoog" synthesizer, introduced in 1971, was the first unit to be widely used in performance. Others, by Oberheim and ARP, soon followed. The Minimoog was *monophonic*: it could play only one note at a time. With the application of computer chip technology, however, *polyphonic* synthesizers came on the market, beginning in 1976. These instruments could play several lines at once, and, before long, they were also programmable: That is, settings could be saved, stored in memory, and then recalled when needed.

Synthesizers, far more than any other instrument, enormously expanded the sound resources available to musicians. In addition to replicating the sound of existing instruments, synthesizers added a seemingly infinite number of new sounds—sounds impossible to produce on acoustic instruments. Although keyboardists Keith Emerson and Rick Wakeman had used early synthesizers in performance, the first musicians to fully exploit this new sound were the group Tangerine Dream—Brian Eno, who collaborated off and on with David Bowie and later with U2—and the German duo Kraftwerk.

Early synthesizers were used in rock mainly as replacements for conventional pitched instruments: bass, strings, piano, and organ. However, it was just a matter of time before the beatbox, an electronic counterpart to the drum kit, would come into use. Roland was among the beatbox pioneers. They offered a far wider palette of sounds than a traditional drum set, and were widely used in recordings from the mid-seventies on.

The Digital Revolution

The first digital recordings date from 1970, on Denon, a Japanese label that specializes in classical music. However, it wasn't until microprocessors grew smaller and more powerful that digital technology was incorporated into every step of the recording and playback cycle. The digital revolution began on several fronts in the late seventies, with the introduction of the first commercial digital multitrack recorders, digital synthesizers, digital effects in sound systems, and CDs. By 1985, digital technology had become the industry standard.

Digital technology supplanted analog recording and sound synthesis. In analog recording, magnetic tape or the groove of a record captures the amplitude waveform of the original sound. In analog electronic instruments, like organs and synthesizers, oscillators generate waveforms. Both processes are imperfect in their ability to capture or recreate existing sounds. (Keep in mind that analog synths added an enormous number of new sounds to rock: Stevie Wonder's "Superstition" is a fine illustration.) It was difficult at best to determine, then render, the precise waveforms of existing instruments. Corruption—from physical imperfections in the tape, outside interference, and the like—was an ever-present danger. Tape editing was an art as well as a science, because splicing had to be done mainly by feel.

In digital synthesis, the sound is generated as a stream of 1s and 0s. In digital recording, it is converted to such a stream, or sampled. The sampling rate is very fast, thousands of times per second. Digital information, whether generated or recorded, is essentially incorruptible. One benefit of digital technology is improved sonic clarity. Moreover, sampling made editing much more precise and opened up the possibility of digital manipulation of the sound, e.g., the addition of a parallel voice with a different timbre and pitch.

SAMPLING   Sampling was the most far-reaching change introduced by digital technology. Any sound, or group of sounds, could be sampled. This new process produced two major innovations. One was an array of digital instruments—drum machines, electronic keyboards, and the like. These sounded like recordings of the original acoustic instruments, because that's in fact what they were. The other was the use of fragments from earlier recordings in new ones. Rap artists could pull a favorite instrumental lick or vocal sound from an older recording and incorporate it into the background of their new work.

MIDI AND DIGITAL INSTRUMENTS   In the early years of digital technology, competition was keen, and each company used its own technology. The need for an industry standard soon became apparent. It appeared in 1983, and was dubbed MIDI, an acronym for Musical Instrument Digital Interface. MIDI allows one instrument to play another, or for a master controller to operate several other modules that are "slaved" to it. It gave unprecedented flexibility to keyboardists and other performers in both recording and performance.

Even as industry agreed on a common standard, the instruments themselves were getting smaller and lighter, because microprocessors became even smaller, yet more powerful. Keyboardists were liberated from their cage-like rack; they could strap a keyboard over their shoulder, use it as a controller, and prance around like guitarists or bassists.

TECHNOLOGY FOR THE MASSES   Digital is digital. There can be differences in quality based on the sampling rate, but there is not the huge gap in quality between high- and low-end machines. As a result, high-quality equipment became affordable, for both creators and consumers. By investing judiciously, a musician could make a professional-quality recording at a relatively small cost. This has been the area of greatest development since 1985. With the advent of DAT, hard disk recording, sound generating and editing software, and other technologies, an inexpensive home studio is a reality. In fact, many commercial recordings begin in the home studios of the artists.

c h a p t e r   1 5

Rock, 1974–1980

Rock became a house divided in the mid-seventies. From its humble begin-ning—rehearsed in garages, performed in dives, recorded in tiny studios, with records peddled out of the back of a car—it had become a huge business. Rock acts sold out arenas, recorded in state-of-the-art studios, sold expertly crafted records in the millions, and earned seven-figure advances. For many, compe-tence and complacency replaced the risk-taking, revolutionary fervor that had driven rock in its first 15 years. Even outrageousness was scripted, in the pro-ductions of David Bowie, Kiss, and Elton John. As a result, rock now faced an internal revolt, the punk movement. Punk was, among other things, an attempt to recapture the energy and vitality of rock and roll, to once again pro-voke and outrage the establishment. This time, however, the establishment was rock itself.

The rock of the mid- and late seventies divides most easily into two groups: the music that built on the rock of the early seventies, and the music that reacted against it. We will survey each in turn.

Established Rock Styles in the Mid- and Late Seventies

By the mid-seventies, "established" rock had traded its cutting edge for craft. Progressive rock, heavy metal, country rock, glam rock—styles that had expanded rock's horizons in the early seventies—went into decline. In their place came bands whose music didn't rattle cages. The best of it was of high quality, beautifully crafted, and subtly innovative. The music of the Eagles is perhaps the typical example of this trend. Two of their major hits, "Take It Easy" and "Hotel California," explore new territory. The first was an early country-rock fusion, as we have noted, and the latter was one of the first to integrate the characteristic rhythms of reggae into mainstream popular music. But neither song challenged or confronted prevailing tastes or attitudes. The band had set their sights on commercial success, and they achieved it: in 1976, their first "greatest hits" album was also the first album to be certified platinum.

We will look mainly at three developments in the rock of this period. One is the emergence of a new array of pop styles. Another is the "purification of the groove," the distillation of hard rock style. The most varied development is the continued interaction of white musicians with black music: jazz, soul,

New Orleans, blues, etc. We will also touch on one other development, ambient music, and the role it played in introducing electronic instruments into pop and influencing the growth of "new age" music in the eighties.

Pop Rock in the Seventies

Pop has almost always meant melody, and the songs of the seventies were no exception. Although the Beatles, rock's quintessential pop group, had dissolved in 1970, all its members remained active after the group disbanded. McCartney's group, Wings, was the most popular; Lennon's work, especially with his wife, Yoko Ono, and the Plastic Ono Band, was the most provocative.

Their place was taken not by other sixties acts, but by a new generation of pop stars. Some were shooting stars, acts who enjoyed a brief period of overwhelming success but could not sustain it over several years. Peter Frampton "came alive" for a short while around 1976, but his run lasted only a couple of years. Fleetwood Mac hit even bigger the following year with their album *Rumours*, but none of their subsequent albums even approached its sales—13 million and counting. Others endured roller-coaster–like careers. For example, the Bee Gees' international career began around 1970, went dry for a while, crested in the late seventies with their songs for the *Saturday Night Fever* soundtrack, then continued up and down during the eighties.

The most enduring pop stars of the seventies were Elton John and Rod Stewart. Both are from the British Isles, and both began their careers as solo artists around 1970 and remained major attractions through the eighties. Both made a strong first impression with touching ballads, and both were accused of selling out to the marketplace, of not living up to the potential of their early work.

Their differences are more obvious. Stewart could ask "Do Ya Think I'm Sexy?" with a straight face. Apparently a string of beautiful, high-profile blonde women did: Stewart was in and out of court in a series of palimony suits. John could not claim such obvious sex appeal. In fact, John admitted his bisexuality in 1976, at the peak of his career. Instead, he became rock's Liberace, not only playing the piano skillfully—he remains one of rock's most accomplished pianists—but also dressing in outlandish costumes.

Their singing styles are different, and immediately recognizable. Stewart sounds as if he has sandpaper in his throat. Although he claims Sam Cooke as a main influence, his style seems to owe more to Sam and Dave. At its best, it is soulful and expressive. John's voice does not have such a distinctive trademark, but it is a rich, warm voice, ideally suited to much of his material.

In terms of their enormously successful careers, their most important similarity was that they both understood the mechanics of good pop: tell a good story, or at least set a good mood; provide plenty of hooks—vocal and instrumental; back the melody with a rich, varied texture; and package it all in a form that listeners can easily grasp. We can hear these elements realized in a series of songs by John and Stewart. We begin with John.

Elton John

After scuffling around London for most of the sixties, Elton John, born Reginald Dwight in 1947, hit big in 1970 with his album, *Elton John*. "Your Song," the biggest hit from the album, shows John clearly in command of pop style. The song unfolds slowly, both in Bernie Taupin's lyric and in the melody,

*Elton John in one of his
wilder costumes, 1974.*
PHOTO COURTESY *CORBIS/
NEAL PRESTON.*

which noodles around in Elton's lower register. About halfway through the
first phrase, it begins a climb towards the high point and the hook of the song:
"I hope you don't mind."

With a prominent, even dominant, melody and a form that shifts smoothly
from verse to refrain, "Your Song" recalls the forms—and formulas—of sixties
pop, especially Motown. In its scope, it expands them. The backdrop for
Elton's song is subdued but rich. Elton's piano, an acoustic guitar, and—later—
harp provide harmonic support. A string ensemble overlays voice and harmony
with sustained lines. The rhythm is subtle, a loping, sixteen-beat rhythm that
Elton favored in many of his early ballads. The drums don't enter until
halfway through the song; their delayed entrance is part of a gradual thickening of the texture during the course of the song. This, another favorite John
strategy, helps unify the several statements of the melody into a larger whole.

"Daniel" (1973), one of John's last hits in his early ballad style, has many
of the same features as "Your Song": prominent melody, subtle sixteen-beat
rhythm, cushiony texture. But the backdrop is leaner: a solo flute and mandolin replace the strings and harp, while shakers flesh out the percussion section. Together they give the song a mild Caribbean flavor. In addition, the form
is more expansive: a climactic third section follows two statements of the
opening section, which has its own internal highpoint at the end of the phrase.
This expansion of the form was one dimension of the overall expansion of
mainstream rock style in the seventies: songs got longer through this kind of
stretching.

From the start, Elton had been more than a balladeer. Unlike Mick Jagger,
he cannot sound like he's sneering when he sings. His voice is too wholesome,
even when he tries to get down and dirty. (In fact, that's part of his appeal.)
But he could get in a great groove, especially when he contrasts his highly syncopated, stop-time piano riffs ("stop time" means no one else is playing) with
sections involving the entire band. "Take Me to the Pilot" is an excellent early
example. "Bennie and the Jets," a track on *Goodbye Yellow Brick Road* (1973),
Elton's first double album, is another good example. Here Elton's piano is

joined by bass and drums, but his interludes are often syncopated against the relentless beat, and the opening piano hook is instantly recognizable, much like a great guitar riff.

By the time he recorded the album, Elton had entered the blatantly pop period of his career: the cover depicts him setting out on the yellow brick road in red platform shoes. By his own admission, he inundated himself in pop, in a concerted effort to achieve superstardom. He succeeded.

The musical results were uneven. Elton never lost his gift for melody, but he seemingly forsook some of his musical personality. In his hits of the mid-seventies, he changed, almost chameleon-like, from style to style. In "Your Sister Can't Twist (But She Can Rock 'N Roll)" (1973), he not only flashes back to the fifties, but borrows David Bowie's lean, straight-ahead rock sound. The result anticipates punk's fast tempo and straightforward rock beat, although Elton was punk's favorite whipping boy. "Philadelphia Freedom" (1975) is his take on the Philadelphia International sound; "Island Girl" (also 1975), his interpretation of Caribbean music. The styles are the aural counterpart to the costumes he wore: they obscure the musical personality revealed in his earlier songs.

Elton John has left a mixed legacy. Throughout his career, he has been a superb songwriter and craftsman and a first-rate keyboard player. He knows how to create and perform pop, and it made him the biggest solo act of the seventies. For many people, however, his best work came in the early seventies, before he started dressing both himself and his songs up.

Rod Stewart

Rod Stewart has parlayed his soulfully scratchy singing and a clear understanding of pop craft into one of the most successful careers of the rock era. He scored his first big hit in 1971 with "Maggie May" and was still charting steadily in the nineties. He has understood pop—and pop success—in terms of basic principles rather than specific musical details, so he has been able to adapt his songs to the times without forsaking the qualities that have kept his music on the charts.

His basic principles could easily be the topics in Pop Song Success 101.

First, tell a good story well. In Stewart's best songs, the story presents complex emotions; often they have a bittersweet flavor, which is ideally suited to his voice. It unfolds in a series of vivid images. In "Maggie May," for instance, "Maggie," an older woman, is "everything," but he also notes how the sunlight brings out her wrinkles: he's not wearing rose-colored glasses. "Some Guys Have All the Luck" (1984), which Stewart didn't write, sets up an opposition of lucky and unlucky guys in the refrain, which the verse then explains.

Second, marble the song with good hooks. Like other memorable pop songs, Stewart's songs have melodic hooks that are easy to remember. The vocal line always has one, and typically there are instrumental hooks as well. The most notorious is probably the "snake charmer" synthesizer line in "Do Ya Think I'm Sexy?"

What's noteworthy about the hooks in Stewart's songs is not only that they are repeated again and again—that's standard practice—but that the repetition so often highlights or adds to the individual character of the song. In "Maggie May," for instance, almost every segment of the melody starts with

Rod Stewart on stage, c. 1980. PHOTO COURTESY *CORBIS/*DAVID REED.

the same basic idea. The phrase that sets "you led me away from home" not only repeats a slightly different version of the basic idea, but also extends the form; a more conventional song would have moved to the concluding phrase. In "You're in My Heart" (1978), the repeated refrain highlights the contrast in key and mood between the refrain and the preceding verse. What makes the hooks in Stewart's hits so memorable, then, is that the pattern of repetition is specific to the song, not just a generic gesture.

Third, give each song a personality. The good Stewart songs are familiar enough in general outline to be accessible. Yet each song contains features that give it a distinct identity: not only the melodic hooks, but the expanded form of "Maggie May"; the "easy listening" verse and key shift of "You're in My Heart"; or the nice takeoff on "Earth Angel" harmony and the plucked string synthesizer sound in "Some Guys Have All the Luck." Each song is a period piece: "Maggie May" sounds like early seventies rock, "Some Guys" like early eighties. But the individual character of the songs keeps them from sounding dated, much as the emotional conflicts in the lyrics make the stories timeless.

Fourth, develop your own sound. No matter what the style, you can immediately recognize a Rod Stewart song by his signature voice. That raspy, throaty sound could come from no one else. So, even if the accompaniment is a mechanical disco beat as in "Do Ya Think I'm Sexy?" we still know that the song belongs to him.

In 1989, Stewart released *Storyteller*, a 25-year retrospective of his work. The title explained the reason for his success: in what his songs say, and how he sings them, he is one of pop's best storytellers. An ironic footnote: The song for which he is best remembered is "Do Ya Think I'm Sexy?" He has admitted his bad taste and lack of judgment in recording it, and has put his money where his mouth is by donating royalties (over $1,000,000) from the song to UNICEF.

OTHER POP STARS OF THE SEVENTIES   Among the brightest new stars of the seventies were women singing about love—or, more often, the lack of it—from a woman's point of view. Linda Ronstadt's first big hit, "You're No Good" (1975), was a worthy sequel to Carly Simon's big 1973 hit, "You're So Vain." Ronstadt has one of the most expressive and compelling voices of the rock era. After her initial success, she began to record covers of early rock hits: e.g., her loving and lovely version of Roy Orbison's "Blue Bayou." Since then she has balanced new material with older, and older style material: among others, a country album with Dolly Parton and Emmylou Harris, and several albums of pre-rock pop standards.

Fleetwood Mac was an unusual group for the time—or any time: a rock band with two female lead singers, both of whom had romantic liaisons with members of the band. Christie McVie had married bassist John McVie (the "Mac" of Fleetwood Mac), and Stevie Nicks was involved with guitarist Lindsay Buckingham. Odd man out—or perhaps above it all—was drummer Mick Fleetwood. Both relationships were strained during the time the group recorded *Rumours*, and the songs on the album speak directly to the problems the couples were having. This autobiographical dimension probably accounts for the overwhelming success of the album. Many of the top hits of the decade presented a bleak view of relationships, as we have seen; this album was full of such songs. Of course, it is more than tales of love lost: the bleak background of "Dreams," for example, is an ideal undercurrent for the despair of the lyric. But the album as a whole seemed to resonate with a large audience.

Not all pop songs were about love lost. Even more popular than *Rumours* was the soundtrack to *Saturday Night Fever*, which, among other things, helped catapult the Bee Gees to superstardom. Although the disco music and John Travolta's dancing may be the most vivid memories of the film, the tension that keeps the plot moving ahead is the love triangle between Travolta and his once and future dance partners. The film ends with Travolta and his upscale partner facing each other and the future with a complex mix of hope, doubt, and fear—a far cry from the "live happily ever after" endings of Hollywood musicals. "How Deep Is Your Love," the Bee Gee's love song for the film, plays underneath the scene as it dissolves into the credits. The song succeeds on two levels, as one of the finest love songs of the decade, and a perfect counterpart to the unresolved mood at the end of the film.

The mood captured in "How Deep Is Your Love" begins with the title, a question rather than an answer. In its pop-derived harmony, lush texture, easy rhythm, and flowing melody, the song recalls the black romantic music of the early seventies, and the Bee Gee's pillow-soft falsetto harmonies mesh perfectly with the background. However, it is the form of the song that expresses the question in the title in musical terms and underscores the couple's fragile relationship at the end of the film.

The song begins conventionally enough. After a short instrumental introduction, the verse unfolds slowly, building to the first statement of the title phrase of the song. Most songs of this kind would simply repeat the title phrase a couple of times and end the section. However, in this song, the melody, after spinning around twice more on the title phrase, builds slowly to another big climax. Even richer harmony supports this drive to the "end"— except that the end never comes. Instead, the song returns abruptly to the opening verse, and goes through the same cycle again. This "violation" of conventional song form—verse, bridge, refrain with hook—seems purposeful. The ambiguity of the form (where does it end? it never does, actually) parallels the uncertainty in the couple's relationship. "How Deep Is Your Love" is not only a good song, but a good song for the end of the film.

It's Only Rock and Roll

By mid-decade, rock and roll—as in the kind of music played by "the world's greatest rock and roll band" (aka the Rolling Stones)—had become a timeless music. Bands from the late sixties and early seventies, such as the Rolling Stones, the Who, the Allman Brothers, Lynyrd Skynyrd, the Steve Miller Band, ZZ Top, Boz Scaggs, and Bachman-Turner Overdrive, kept mining the groove that they had found. A new generation of bands began to make their mark by mid-decade: Aerosmith, Bad Company, Foreigner, Ted Nugent, J. Geils Band, and Bob Seger and the Silver Bullet Band stand out.

Although these bands didn't limit themselves to "old time rock and roll" (styles age quickly in the rock era), all enjoyed success revisiting the formula mapped out in songs such as the Stones' "Honky Tonk Women" and Lynyrd Skynyrd's "What's Your Name." They begin with lyrics that tell a "slice of life" story, usually about dealing with women, in "down-home" language. Behind the words is a basic rock band: no less than a two guitar/bass/drums nucleus, and sometimes no more. The lead guitarist will start the song with a catchy riff; he will probably use some distortion. The rest of the band layers in riffs or marks rock rhythm, creating the kind of rhythmic interplay that makes listeners want to move to the groove. There is no pretense or artifice in this

Steve Tyler and Joe Perry of Aerosmith, 1990. PHOTO
COURTESY *CORBIS/S.I.N.*

music, no questions of gender or sexual orientation, and it makes no statements. It is simply good time music.

Ted Nugent's "Cat Scratch Fever" (1977), with its relentless riff, is a textbook example. "Rock'n Me" (1976), by the Steve Miller Band, has a more extended and complex opening riff, but pays homage to Chuck Berry in the eight-beat timekeeping played by the low guitar under the vocal. In most cases, the groove reacted to a rock beat. Occasionally, however, the reference beat was the hard shuffle rhythm of postwar rhythm and blues. Grand Funk's cover of Carole King's "Some Kind of Wonderful" (1975) is a nice, if lean, example of this style.

Most of this music looked back to the recent past. However, in their 1976 hit, "Walk This Way," Aerosmith anticipated a future direction in rock by about ten years. In most respects—lyric, instrumentation, guitar riffs, distortion.—"Walk This Way" is typical of hard-rock songs of the era. The crucial difference is that the riffs and the vocal line move at sixteen-beat speed. They are more active and complex than riffs based on eight-beat rhythms—closer to funk than rock, at least in this respect. This affinity was not lost on the rap group Run-D.M.C., who covered the song a decade later. Their cover helped point the way toward the rock/funk fusion of the late eighties and early nineties in the music of alternative bands like the Red Hot Chili Peppers, Fishbone, and others.

ROCK AND COUNTRY MUSIC   In the last three decades, rock and roll has been like a favorite pair of jeans: not always worn, but always comfortable when they are worn, and always pretty much the same. Rock's basic feel really hasn't changed since the early seventies, although the nature of the rhythmic interplay between beat and riffs allows for limitless variety.

Although older and younger rock musicians occasionally return to it, basic rock and roll has flourished more in country music than any other style. The wholesale assimilation of rock rhythm and rock feel into country music got underway in the late seventies and early eighties. A new generation of country musicians, among them Alabama, Hank Williams, Jr., the Judds, and John Anderson, helped make rock the rhythmic foundation for a new country sound. John Anderson's "Swingin'," which won the Country Music Assocation award for Best Single in 1983, has a classic rock beat. It is mainly the story told in the lyric, and Anderson's voice, that identify it as a country song.

At about the same time, country acts began to cross over to the pop charts. The most popular were crossover acts such as Dolly Parton, whose theme song for the film *9 to 5* was a No. 1 pop hit, and Kenny Rogers, whose "countrypolitan" style added a dash of country to soft rock. But hard country acts, such as Anderson and especially Alabama, also began to appear on pop charts, which almost certainly underestimated the real popularity of country acts. Indeed, a new, more accurate, method of tabulating sales and airplay—Soundscan—introduced in the early nineties coincided with a "sudden" rise in the popularity of country music.

Hard Rock Goes Pop

Several bands, most notably Foreigner and Queen, created a niche for themselves by blending pop, hard rock, and heavy metal. Foreigner's "Cold as Ice" and "Feels Like the First Time" (both 1977) are love songs—or at least

Freddie Mercury of Queen, 1977. PHOTO COURTESY CORBIS/DENIS O'REGAN.

"relationship" songs. Both songs have well-developed melodies, and the harmonic vocabulary extends well beyond three or four chords. The songs also have rich accompaniments featuring choirs and synthesizers, in addition to a basic rock band. The rhythm section alternates between relatively light beat-keeping in the verse, and a heavily marked beat in the chorus. The metal element is cosmetic: guitar riffs and solos played with some distortion.

Queen's "We Are the Champions" (1978) follows much the same plan, except that the guitar is more prominent and Freddie Mercury's singing is more histrionic. All three songs offer convincing evidence that a song needs more than distortion to be heavy metal. In most other respects, the music of Foreigner and Queen is miles from the "pure" metal of Black Sabbath.

"Blue-eyed Soul" and Other White Takes on Black Music

The integrated playlists of sixties rock were ancient history by the mid-seventies. The middle of the road went mainly through white neighborhoods, with occasional detours to Philadelphia and Detroit, where Stevie Wonder consistently crossed over. In the main, however, white musicians sounded white, especially after the punk revolution. Countering this trend were acts such as Steely Dan, Ry Cooder, and Chicago. These and other acts created truly unique styles, immediately recognizable as their own. Despite their obvious differences, they had a common bond: they were white musicians who had absorbed at least some elements of black music directly into their style. Rock was always part of the mix, but so were soul, jazz, Motown, and New Orleans rhythm and blues. We survey some of these distinctive sounds below.

BLOOD, SWEAT, AND TEARS White musicians began to create rock/rhythm and blues/jazz fusions in the mid-sixties, most prominently in the music of Blood, Sweat, and Tears and Chicago. Both groups were formed in 1967. Blood, Sweat, and Tears made the bigger splash initially, with three No. 2 hits in 1969, but Chicago proved to be the more popular band in the seventies.

In many respects, the music of Blood, Sweat, and Tears sounds like a white take on soul music. Certainly the instrumentation of the group took its cue from Ray Charles, James Brown, and the Stax house band: lead vocalist backed by a full rhythm section (including organ), and horns. Singer David Clayton Thomas obviously listened a lot to Ray Charles, although his singing would never be confused with Ray's.

However, there are other influences besides soul. Horn lines and solos borrow from not only the syncopated riffs and sustained chords of soul but also the more complex figuration of jazz, where ensemble lines and individual solos are often streams of fast-moving notes. The rich harmonic palette of their songs draws from jazz, rock, pop, and soul. The opening of "Spinning Wheel" begins with a chord used almost exclusively in jazz; "You've Made Me So Very Happy" could be a soul song harmonically, while "Go Down Gamblin'" begins with a guitar riff that could have been borrowed from Cream. In fact, "Go Down Gamblin'" not only showcases Thomas's gritty singing, but also juxtaposes jazz-influenced horn riffs with rock guitar.

CHICAGO Chicago, guided by James William Guercio (who had previously produced Blood, Sweat, and Tears), followed a similar path: rhythm plus horns, along with a nice mix of rock, pop, rhythm and blues, and jazz. But during their long run of hits in the seventies, the group drew more on pop and rock than soul and jazz. In fact, one of their early hits, "Does Anybody Really Know What Time It Is?," could summarize their career. The song begins with complex jazz-style chords from the horns, played largely in stop time. A short keyboard interlude built from patterns lasting five beats (three plus two), connects the opening to the main part of the song, which begins with a jazz trumpet solo over a foot-tapping shuffle beat. The melody of the song has a simple verse/chorus form, with a catchy title-phrase hook. The harmony and the accompaniment in the verse have strong jazz overtones; the refrain retains the same basic feel, but is simpler. The parallel with the career of the group is clear: both begin boldly and a little "outside," but quickly gravitate toward a more pop-oriented sound.

Chicago's blend of rock, pop, jazz, and soul earned them critical neglect and commercial success during their peak years. Perhaps because they had the jazz/rock/soul/pop fusion to themselves after Thomas left Blood, Sweat, and Tears in 1972 and the group faded from the charts, the rock press has all but ignored them—they don't "fit" anywhere. Their fans didn't ignore them: they were the second most-charted album act and the fourth most-charted singles act of the decade.

STEELY DAN Another unique group developed an even more idiosyncratic mix of rock and jazz—which is often combined with quirky lyrics. Steely Dan, which existed almost exclusively in the studio, was the brainchild of keyboardist Donald Fagen and bassist Walter Becker. Their "band" was the cream of Los Angeles studio musicians.

It's difficult to describe their "style" because each of their songs seemed so different from the next: among their hits was an electronically enhanced "cover" of Duke Ellington's 1927 recording of "East St. Louis Toodle-oo." The two constants in their music seem to be impeccable production—two of their albums won Grammys for "Best Engineered Album"—and stream-of-consciousness lyrics that offered slices of life in LA. There was often a jarring incongruity between the lyrics and the sophisticated music to which they were set. For example, "Rikki Don't Lose That Number" juxtaposes a plea to maintain a barely-begun relationship—a simple account, told in plain language—with a subtle, jazz-inspired music: jazz pianist Horace Silver's "Song for My Father" is the source of the accompaniment pattern. There seems to be both an emotional and social gap between words and music, but the song works. So does "Peg," which accompanies a rather sketchy account of a film star on the rise. In this song, the contrast is between the "outside-looking-in" lyric and its upbeat musical setting with jazz-like flourishes and harmonies (the harmony is a juiced-up blues progression).

Steely Dan's offbeat lyrics, imaginative musical ideas, and meticulous production earned a loyal following. All of their albums sold well, several singles charted, and critics liked them. However, they were one of a kind, and no band has really followed in their stylistic footsteps.

BLUE-EYED SOUL Among the important acts of the seventies were a few white performers who had immersed themselves in the sound of sixties black music: soul, New Orleans rhythm and blues, and James Brown. Joe Cocker, although clearly influenced by Ray Charles, forged his own soulful style. "You Are So Beautiful," a song recorded in 1975, when Cocker's career was on the ropes because of severe alcohol and drug abuse, shows him at his best: his gritty vocal style and direct delivery give his singing great emotional power.

Another Ray Charles-influenced vocalist was Michael McDonald. McDonald, who did session work for Steely Dan in the early seventies, joined the Doobie Brothers in 1975. Within a year, he had helped reshape the sound of the band. To their original rock nucleus, the Doobies added extra percussion and McDonald's keyboard. At the same time, they loosened up the rhythm. As in much black music, beat keeping was lighter, the bass line was free to roam, the texture richer but not thick, the rhythm more syncopated. Over this active texture soared McDonald's hoarse, high range vocal. Their first big hit, "Takin' It to the Streets" (1976), evidences all of these features, as does their Grammy-winning 1979 hit, "What a Fool Believes," although it is more of a mainstream pop song.

RENEWING ROOTS Two of the more interesting figures in seventies rock built their styles on the rock's early roots. Mac Rebbenack, better known as Dr. John, continued the New Orleans piano style of Professor Longhair and Huey "Piano" Smith. His "Right Place Wrong Time" (1973) is a whimsical song that overlays Dr. John's gravelly voice and electronified New Orleans piano with Superfly-like bass, percussion, and horns. It is an updated version of the loose-jointed New Orleans sound that seemed to disappear around 1960.

The music of Ry Cooder was far more eclectic and even more deeply rooted in the past. Cooder has mastered not only the guitar, but numerous other fretted/plucked instruments. In addition, he has explored both black and white folk music, the almost-forgotten hits of the early years of the rock era, and pre-rock popular styles as old as ragtime. Many of the tracks on his albums were versions of folk songs or old classics. Despite the disparate sources of his music, it had a distinctive sound, not so much because of his rather diffident singing, but because of its open yet multi-stranded textures and its rolling rhythms, guided mainly by his highly syncopated guitar patterns. These qualities are evident in his 1979 cover of Doc Pomus's "Little Sister," a hit for Elvis in 1961.

Blood, Sweat, and Tears, Chicago, Dr. John, et al. represent a stylistic mixed bag, without a doubt. There is enormous contrast between Joe Cocker's simple and direct "You Are So Beautiful"—we know exactly what he's feeling—and the elliptical portrait of Steely Dan's "Peg." Still, what dances through the music of all these acts is the direct influence of black music. Above all, it's the rhythmic play common to so much black music, especially jazz, rhythm and blues, and soul. But it's also occasionally the sounds of massed horns and heartfelt vocals. Collectively, they created some of the most distinctive music of the seventies.

All of this music had a high comfort level. Most of the songs discussed above have a distinct personality because they rework and recombine the past in new ways, but they are not especially innovative. Even the shifting rhythms of "Does Anybody Really Know What Time It Is?" or the intricate lines and chords of "Peg" seem to be clever musicians at play, rather than a challenge to accepted norms.

Ambient Music

In a class by itself, at least during the seventies, was the ambient, technologically driven music of Brian Eno. In its use of then-new electronic sounds and sound modification, his own music heralded, better than anyone else's, the technological revolution of the early eighties. In its essential minimalism, it inspired New Age music, the polar opposite of the ear-splitting sounds of heavy metal, punk, and arena rock.

Eno was particularly important for introducing synthesizers into rock music. Although synthesizers had been used as part of popular music production before, they had mainly been used to "imitate" the sound of conventional instruments (such as to replace or augment string sections). Eno was among the first to use the pure sound creation capabilities of the synthesizer to add flavor to a production.

Eno gained critical respect but little popularity for his late seventies albums, such as *Another Green World* (1975) and *Music for Airports* (1978). However, his sonic genius has become widely known through his work with David Bowie, Robert Fripp, the Talking Heads, and U2. In each case, he transformed the sound of the group—U2's soundscapes owe much to his work. Through both his own work and his many collaborations, Eno's influence on the sound of rock in the last quarter century has been profound.

Punk and Its Aftermath

Punk injected an increasingly complacent, corporate-minded rock world with a shot of adrenaline. Surfacing in New York in 1975 and in London a year later, punk replayed rock's early history, shaking up the music establishment with hyperkinetic two-minute songs and outrageous behavior, much as Little Richard and Jerry Lee Lewis had done 20 years before.

There were, of course, crucial differences. What was considered outrageous in 1956 was tame in 1976. What's more, punk was a calculated attempt to outrage, orchestrated by Malcolm McLaren, the svengali manager of the Sex Pistols who was one of punk's loudest promoters. Further, it was a social revolution that used music as a tool, rather than a musical revolution that changed society. Punk was an attitude and a fashion statement before it was a musical style, not the other way around.

Punk was rife with contradictions. It articulated the frustrations of working-class British, yet it was conceived as a business venture. The music itself was both a throwback to rock basics and a complete negation of rock roots. It unleashed forces beyond its control and self-destructed almost overnight, yet it has been the most influential new rock style of the last 25 years.

Punk was a trans-Atlantic revolution, with headquarters in London and New York. Its attitude and style came mainly from London, its sound mainly from New York. However, their connection was much more symbiotic than that simple paradigm might suggest. Among punk's most important influences was the Velvet Underground. They anticipated punk on several levels: the abrasive, minimalistic sound of their music; their embrace of the New York City subculture sensibility and their role in nurturing it; the darkness of songs like "Heroin," which foreshadows punk's "no future" mentality; their image and sound, rejecting the artistic aspirations of the Beatles and other like-minded bands; and the fact that their impresario was an artist—Andy Warhol, who packaged them as part of a multimedia experience (the famous Exploding Plastic Inevitable).

Punk's mastermind was Malcolm McLaren, a former art student who was enamored of anarchist ideas. His business was fashion, but he invested his work with his ideals. In 1971, he opened a clothing store on Kings Road, a part of London where England's disaffected youth hung out. After a visit to New York and exposure to the nascent punk scene there, McLaren renamed his shop Sex and stocked it with torn T-shirts, fetish-inspired leather, and other provocative designs. During his trip to New York, McLaren renewed his acquaintance with the New York Dolls, whom he had first met in England, during one of their tours.

The New York Dolls, led by David Johansen, were America's answer to David Bowie, Marc Bolan, and the rest of the British glam bands. They lacked Bowie's musical craft and vision; their musical heroes were not only the Velvet Underground but also the MC5 and Iggy Pop and the Stooges. In effect, they dressed up the latter groups' proto-punk and made it even more outrageous, wearing makeup and crossdressing outlandishly—they out-Bowied Bowie in this respect—and taking bold risks in performance. Brinksmanship came easily to them, as they were, in the words of one critic, "semi-professional" at best. McLaren, clearly drawn to their outrageous attitude and androgynous appearance, and aware of their "do-it-yourself" garage-band esthetic, managed them briefly.

Rock's first "alternative" scene had sprung up in New York in the wake of the Velvet Underground and the New York Dolls. Much like the folksingers of the sixties, bands performed in small clubs located in Greenwich Village and Soho. The most famous of these clubs was CBGB OMFUG (Country, Blue Grass and Blues, and Other Music for Urban Gourmandizers; usually shortened to simply CBGB), which, despite the name, launched the careers of a host of punk and new wave bands. Among the CBGB graduates were Patti Smith, the Ramones, Talking Heads, Pere Ubu, and Blondie.

Patti Smith, a rock critic turned poet/performer, was the first major figure in the punk movement to emerge from the New York club subculture. Smith was its poet laureate, a performer for whom words were primary. She delivered them directly and with passion. Her recording of Van Morrison's "Gloria" (1975) is a sprawling rendition of the song, in spirit much like Morrison's early work, but rawer. As with many of her own songs, it begins simply: just her chanting the words while a pianist plays a two-chord accompaniment. Gradually the rest of the rhythm section enters, playing first a lazy shuffle, which metamorphizes into a driving rock beat. Smith spills out a mix of Morrison's and her lyrics—she added and reworked the original. The effect is like a train coming down the tracks—even with the stop at the station toward the end.

There is nothing groundbreaking in the sound of her music. Indeed, she wanted to recapture rock's brief glory period in the mid-sixties, to have her music make a statement, not a spectacle. Her work had much of the purity and power of punk: purity in the sense that it returned rock to its "garage-band" spirit, and power in the outrage, such as that heard in "Gloria." But it was not outrageous, at least by the Sex Pistols' standards.

Smith was also important because she was a woman in charge: she played a seminal role in the creation of this new/old style. Partly because of her presence, punk and new wave music was much more receptive to strong women than conventional rock.

The Ramones, another CBGB-based group, created the sound of punk. Their music was high-voltage stuff. The songs were two-minute jolts of electricity: short, fast, and loud. The Ramones were brothers only on the

Joey Ramone on stage, c. 1976. Photo courtesy CORBIS/Denis O'Regan.

bandstand. All had been students at Forest Hills High School in Queens, New York, but were not related. They assumed their almost cartoonish (think Mutant Ninja Turtles) personae—Joey, Johnny, Dee Dee, and Tommy Ramone—when they formed the band in 1974. Their sets at CBGB were famous: in less than half an hour, they would play ten or more songs, all sounding pretty much the same.

The group looked like the Fonz in quadruplicate, and they sounded like the early Beach Boys stoked on speed. Their rock and roll was basic: three (or four) chords, very fast tempos, pile driving rhythms—the whole band pounding out a rock beat with little syncopation and less subtlety—and Dada-esque lyrics set to melodic snippets, sung with a fake Cockney accent.

"Blitzkrieg Bop" (1976) is typical: what is "Blitzkrieg Bop" and what does it have to do with the rest of the song? Are these teenagers making out ("climbing in the back seat/ . . . steam heat") or breaking out ("shoot 'em in the back now")? These questions remained unanswered in the lyric.

The music is basic three-chord rock and roll (I, IV, and V), played loud and fast. It is powerful enough on record, but it is even more powerful in person. Imagine being in a small club packed with like-minded people (punk had a small following by any objective standard, but it seemed big because the bands performed in such small venues), being drowned in a sea of sound.

The title of the song is worth a comment: Although neo-Nazi references were relatively rare in the Ramones' music, Nazi images were a big part of the punk scene in the United Kingdom. Among the provocative fashions sold at McLaren's shop was a short leather skirt with a swastika in studs on the back panel, and Siouxsie (of Siouxsie and the Banshees) regularly sported an armband with a swastika.

Punk in the United Kingdom

In the United Kingdom, punk was a music waiting to happen. All the components were in place, except the sound. Disaffected working-class youth wanted an outlet for their frustration: pierced body parts, technicolor hair, and torn clothes made a statement, but they weren't loud enough and they didn't articulate the message. Many of them hung out in McLaren's shop; a few of them would eventually become the Sex Pistols. McLaren and Vivienne Westwood, his sometime significant other and main designer, had a vision that needed a soundtrack. McLaren's involvement with the New York Dolls had already given him a taste of the music business.

THE SEX PISTOLS Two events helped transform the Sex Pistols from idea to reality. The first was a massive festival of CBGB-based bands in the summer of 1975: 40 bands performed over four weeks. The festival shone a spotlight on what had been—literally—an underground music scene. Suddenly, outsiders learned about this movement. Among the attendees was McLaren. The other event was the Ramones' U.K. tour in 1976. The Sex Pistols, who had just formed, and other U.K. bands could experience the power that stripped-down and souped-up rock and roll could have.

McLaren found the Sex Pistols in his shop. Glen Matlock, the original bassist with the group, worked for McLaren. When he let McLaren know that he and two of his friends, guitarist Steve Jones and drummer Paul Cook, were putting together a band, McLaren found them rehearsal space, took over their management, and recruited a lead singer for them. John Lydon, who became Johnny Rotten (allegedly because of his less-than-meticulous personal hygiene), had been hanging around Sex for a while. McLaren had gotten to know him and felt he had the capacity for outrage that he'd been looking for. (Another Sex shop hanger-on, Sid Vicious [John Ritchie], would eventually replace Matlock.)

In fact, none of the four had much musical skill at the time they formed the band. Jones was more adept at thievery than guitar playing: he stole the group's first sound system. McLaren booked the group into small clubs, where they acquired more of a reputation for outrageous conduct than for musicianship. Word spread about the group through word of mouth, newspaper reviews, and subculture fanzines. (Punk, a fanzine started by two high school friends from suburban Connecticut, gave the new movement its name.)

The Sex Pistols found their musical direction after hearing the Ramones and learning the basics of their instruments. What they had from the beginning, however, was the ability to shock, provoke, confront, and incite to riot. When they added the musical energy of the Ramones to this stew they were ready to overthrow the ruling class. Two of their best-known songs take on the entire establishment. In "Anarchy in the UK," Johnny Rotten opens with "I am an Anti-Christ; I am an anarchist" and ends with a drawn out "destroy." The opening line—almost an anagram—lances both church and state; the final word makes clear their agenda. And Rotten, a skinny kid in wire-rim sunglasses who knew no bounds, sings/screams/snarls the lyric. In "God Save the Queen," we can imagine the sneer on Rotten's face as he delivers the opening line, "God save the queen, the fascist regime."

All of this was music to McLaren's ears. He hated the liberal attitudes of the sixties. Still, he was canny enough to exploit their openness, so that he

The Sex Pistols live in Atlanta, Georgia, c. 1979. Photo courtesy CORBIS/BETTMANN.

could take aim at both the ruling class and the "peace and love" generation. In his mind, punk was nihilistic: "no future" was the motto. Everything seemed to convey destruction or terror. The bondage gear that McLaren sold promoted sex as pain, not pleasure. Although Rotten railed against the "fascist regime," punk's use of the swastika image evoked the ultimate fascist regime. And the Sex Pistols' sets often ended in some kind of fracas: their attitude was more than words and symbols.

The music behind the words was just as provocative. It was not just that it was loud—particularly when heard in the small venues where the punk bands played—or simple—power chords up and down the fretboard. It was the beat. Punk fulfilled the confrontational promise of the very first rock and roll records. Rock and roll's signature was a repetitive eight-beat rhythm, whether pumped out by Chuck Berry or hammered out by Little Richard and Jerry Lee Lewis. It was the subversive element that got the revolutionary message across loud and clear, even when the lyrics didn't (after all, what *is* "Tutti Frutti" about?).

In both Sex Pistols songs, the entire band, not only the guitar, but also the bass and the drummer, on both hi-hat and kick drum, pound out a relentless eight-beat rhythm almost all the way through. Only the periodic guitar riffs interrupt it. By taking this approach, the band in effect distilled rock and roll's revolutionary rhythmic essence and amplified it into its most extreme form. There is no way that the rock beat could be more pervasive or powerful.

The message of the Sex Pistols resonated throughout the United Kingdom. Many working and middle class youths were tired of the rigid class system that they inherited, and foresaw a bleak future. The Sex Pistols' songs encapsulated the frustration and rage they felt. The group achieved their main ambition—to be rock and roll stars.

So did McLaren: through the band, he made a statement, although the fact that he made a statement seemed to be far more important than its message. McLaren had his cake and ate it, too: he made a lot of money off the Sex Pistols, some of which he had to turn over to the band after they sued him. His dishonest management certainly suggests that punk, for him, was more a business proposition than a matter of political principle.

Despite their meteoric rise and fall (Lydon announced the breakup of the group in January 1978), the Sex Pistols were enormously influential: no group in the history of rock had more impact with such a modest career. The reason: they embodied the essence of punk in every respect. No one projected its sense of outrage and its outrageousness more baldly. The Ramones were comparably influential, not only because their fast and loud sound inspired the Sex Pistols and countless other groups, but also because their facelessness—assumed names and punk "uniform" (torn jeans, T shirts)—and cryptic lyrics projected a different form of nihilism: loss of identity and meaning.

New Wave

A so-called "new wave" of bands, mainly in London, New York, and Ohio(!), drew on the energy and attitude of punk to take rock in numerous new directions. Few acts followed the extreme path, in attitude, words, and music, of the Sex Pistols and the Ramones. Instead, most refracted punk's boundary-stretching lyrics, top-to-bottom eight-beat conception, and upbeat tempos through their own musical vision. New wave music went well beyond punk's nihilistic worldview and its monolithic musical approach. Alternatives to rage included quirky humor, parody, psychodrama, nonsense—even relationships. Paralleling this was a variety of musical settings, from ear-shattering rock to folk and classical styles.

Some of the acts, especially those from the United States, were already active before the Sex Pistols made their big splash. Most were based in New York: not only the Ramones and Patti Smith, but also Richard Hell and the Voidoids, Television, and Talking Heads. Ohio was another spawning ground: Pere Ubu, from Cleveland, and Devo, from Dayton, both had careers under way by 1975. In the wake of the Sex Pistols' notoriety and the attention generated by the 1975 CBGB festival, many more emerged. Elvis Costello quickly became the bard of the new wave. The Clash, the Pretenders (fronted by Akron, Ohio native Chrissie Hynde), and the Buzzcocks were among other leading U.K. bands in the late seventies. In the United States, Blondie offered punk pop, while the B-52s, who came from Georgia but were miles musically from Southern rock, both satirized and celebrated the glory days of sixties pop.

THE CLASH The Clash expressed the rage and frustration of punk in songs of political and social protest. They embraced numerous causes, including the plight of Jamaican immigrants. In the summer of 1975, they found themselves in the middle of a riot between Jamaicans and police, which they immortalized in the song "White Riot." The musical influence of Ramones/Sex Pistols–style punk is much less evident, at least at the time of their commercial breakthrough. "Stand by Me (Train in Vain)" (1979), their first big single, is a "relationship" song that uses a simple riff, instead of a driving rock beat, as support for the lyric. There is considerable musical variety on their first major album, *London Calling* (1979); the influence of reggae is much more evident than the influence of punk, especially on songs such as "The Guns of Brixton" and "Revolution Rock." Their music suggests that punk was more a source of inspiration than a model to be followed closely.

PERE UBU Pere Ubu's "The Modern Dance" (1978) has the bright tempo and "clean" rhythm (i.e., not much syncopation or interplay) of punk, and both guitar and bass have lines moving at eight-beat speed. But the background, which also includes drums, keyboard, and the occasional sound effect, is subtle, not overpowering. Melodic snippets, setting barely comprehensible lyrics and sung with psychotically quavery voices, float over the bass-heavy backdrop. Both the emotional tone of the song (are these guys serious, and if so, what are they talking about?) and the careful production and electronic effects are miles away from the unbridled outrage and garage-band esthetic of the Sex Pistols. Still, the punk influence is evident.

TALKING HEADS Another group close to Pere Ubu musically and emotionally was the Talking Heads. Like so many British rock musicians (and McLaren), Talking Heads started out in art school: lead singer David Byrne and drummer Chris Frantz attended the Rhode Island School of Design together before moving to New York. They formed the group in 1975, with Tina Weymouth, Frantz's then-girlfriend (and later wife), playing bass, and added guitarist/keyboardist Jerry Harrison two years later.

"Psycho Killer" (1977), one of their best-known early songs, shows several of the same qualities as Pere Ubu's "The Modern Dance." Rhythm and texture

David Byrne of Talking Heads, c. 1979. Photo courtesy CORBIS/Denis O'Regan.

are simple and clean: the bass line moves mainly at beat speed, while guitar and keyboard move at eight-beat speed. This spare backdrop—perhaps a musical counterpart to the white cell of the psycho ward—is an ideal foil for Byrne's vocal. The lyric is inflammatory: Byrne announces quite clearly that he's crazy ("a real live wire"), and his neutral delivery makes his portrayal especially effective: when will he explode?

The personae projected by Byrne and Pere Ubu almost certainly owe more to David Bowie than they do to punk; so does their singing and the clean instrumental accompaniment (recall Bowie's "Hang on to Yourself"). However, in their lean sound and decidedly anti-pop lyrics, these songs are very much in the spirit of punk.

The music of Talking Heads evolved considerably in the eighties. Much of the change was due to their collaborations with Brian Eno and Byrne's interest in world music. Eno's touch is evident in the luminous synthesizer effects in "Once in a Lifetime" (1980). They form part of a wonderful soundscape: synths in the high register, guitar and keyboards slightly below that, percussion in the middle register, low midrange drum kit, and the occasional bass. What makes it work so well is not just the placement of the voices, but the move away from steady timekeeping, especially in the bass.

"Life During Wartime" (1984), by contrast, shows the impact of Byrne's world-music study in the denser rhythms and additional percussion. The song purposely sets up a strong, disco-flavored beat to an ironic end: Byrne uses the accompaniment as a foil, singing at one point, "This ain't no disco." It is this ironic element, ideally expressed in Byrne's ranting vocal style, that remains the constant in their music.

Two other U.S. bands, Devo and the B-52s, showed that new wave also had a sense of humor. Devo's first hit, "Jocko Homo" (1977), owes much more to Frank Zappa than to the Ramones, in attitude, words, and music. Lines like "What's round at the ends and high in the middle? O-hi-o" not only tip their hats—or whatever they had on their heads—to their home state, but also recall Zappa's bizarre humor. So does the refrain, "Are we not men? We are DEVO." There is a Zappa-like hipness to the music, as well: the fastest rhythms in the outer sections of the song move at rock-beat speed, but there are only seven "beats" per measure instead of eight. It takes considerable virtuosity to pull off this stunt (just as Zappa's humorous songs demanded great musicianship to achieve), and it's functional: its offbeat quality underscores the offbeat nature of the lyric.

"Whip It" (1980), their biggest hit (both as recording and video), is fun of a different kind. The title phrase is a double entendre: "Whip It" seems to mean more than overcoming an obstacle. The musical setting, with its clean, fast rhythm and cheesy organ sound, puts still another spin on the sound of new wave.

The B-52s' "Rock Lobster" is somewhat similar in character: certainly it's also funny, in a nerdy way. Here, "rock" cycles through three meanings: a music, a stone, a crustacean. And the musical setting, with more cheesy organ and a pseudo-scary guitar riff, matches up perfectly with the lyric. Like Devo, the B-52s projected a specific visual image. But where Devo appeared to be some kind of science-fiction space people, the B-52s lovingly recreated the beehive hairdos (from which they took their name) and nylon slacks-and-shirts look of the late fifties.

Groups such as Blondie led new wave's march toward the pop mainstream. Deborah Harry, the lead singer of the group, was new wave's princess, certainly one of its most glamorous stars. Blondie's songs typically tinged pop themes and style with the bounce and boldness of punk. "X Offender" (1978), one of their first hits, shows how the group invigorated pop with punk's energy and sensibility. The pop elements are clear. Like her look, Harry's breathy singing owes more to Marilyn Monroe than Patti Smith. The song has a "relationship" storyline: girl meets boy, circa 1980. Melodic hooks, both instrumental and vocal, are plentiful and easily grasped, and the harmony that supports the melody is far richer (i.e., closer to pop) than the three- and four-chord songs of the Sex Pistols and the Ramones.

However, the song has the bright tempo and the top-to-bottom eight-beat timekeeping of punk. This rhythmic texture, with fast, clipped, repeated notes in all registers, became the generic new sound of pop rock around 1980. The lyric of the song also betrays a punk-influenced sensibility: Mr. Right turns out to be a creep, who "wants the love of a [se]X offender." In this song, there are no stars in Harry's eyes.

ELVIS COSTELLO In the United Kingdom, the most distinctive punk-influenced new voice belonged to Elvis Costello (born Declan McManus). Costello combined a great singer/songwriter's storytelling gift with a punk sensibility, a cheeky way of looking at the world. Musically, Costello was an equal-opportunity borrower: his songs drew on both punk and reggae, the two vital new sounds in the United Kingdom in the late seventies. Yet he was able to fuse these influences into a highly personal style, distinguished by image-rich lyrics and imaginative melodies.

In "Watching the Detectives" (1977), an early hit, he supports a bizarre boy/girl tale with the jaunty rhythm of reggae. Costello's tale unfolds in a string of cryptic images, jarringly juxtaposed like a series of abrupt cuts in a film. Their relation to the title phrase is not immediately obvious; neither is its meaning. Marbled into the texture are a Ventures-style low-register guitar riff and their trademark cheesy organ sound. For Costello, as well as almost all other new wave bands, punk influence also included a retro element. Anything pre-1965 seemed to be fair game: hence, the Ventures-style solo and the organ sound. Here, he uses them to create an eerie backdrop to his story.

By contrast, the story line in "Radio, Radio" (1979) is easy to follow, and the music, from the opening organ hook on, is as accessible as a Blondie song. Costello's genius becomes apparent as the song unfolds. What seems like a simple paean to radio in the verse develops Orwellian overtones (1984 was only five years in the future!) by the chorus. And the complexity of his ideas is matched by the complexity of the form of the song. Although it is a verse/chorus song, with sections clearly marked off by restatements of the opening organ hook, the chorus goes through a tunnel full of twists and turns before returning to the verse.

The setting is likewise a complex realization of the basic punk-pop sound. Costello's texture is almost orchestral. The opening organ hook is thickly textured, the punk band equivalent of a full orchestra. As Costello enters with the verse, the texture thins drastically—only the three rhythm instruments, playing a bottom-heavy version of the eight-beat rhythm. The organ returns in the chorus, along with some special effects, and there is a nice stop-time section at the end. The basic texture has a clear affinity with punk, but the orchestral-like variation in rhythm and texture (also evident in "Watching the Detectives") is a clear departure from the relentless rhythmic drive and unvarying texture of a typical Ramones' song.

The music of the Clash, Talking Heads, Pere Ubu, Devo, Blondie, and Elvis Costello shows both affinities and differences between punk and new wave. All drew on the energy of punk, evident in the active rhythms and lean textures, and borrowed key musical elements. However, their songs express sensibilities quite different from the rage of the Sex Pistols. The music of Devo seems to be at the other end of the emotional spectrum, and the songs of the Talking Heads and Elvis Costello are articulate, not inchoate. The musical elements are similarly transformed. Collectively, this music shows how the same point of departure can, with a fair amount of tweaking, end up in radically different places.

Summary

By 1980, Sid Vicious was dead, the Sex Pistols were history, and the Ramones were still trying to find their way onto the charts. Indifference and the demands of the marketplace quickly blunted punk's cutting edge. Like the queen and her allegedly fascist regime, rock survived Johnny Rotten's onslaught. However, punk gave rock new looks, new energy, and a leaner and cleaner sound. Above all, punk and new wave revitalized rock, injecting it with the impudence and energy of its early years. Few punk groups were as outrageous—or as capable of outrage—as the Sex Pistols. Still, punk and new wave music was fresh, forward, and often funny.

Punk quickly bled into other rock styles. From the start, Bruce Springsteen and U2 built their sound on the power and purity of punk's beat, as we'll discover in Chapter 17. Later, punk/funk and punk/disco fusions would generate some of the most interesting music of the eighties.

At the same time, the rock that *was* popular was, at its best, expressive, imaginative, and beautifully crafted. It was also enormously varied: Aerosmith, the Bee Gees, Chicago, the Doobie Brothers, the Eagles. With few exceptions, however, this was essentially conservative music. As Elton John demonstrated again and again, it built on the (mostly) recent past, rather than pointing to the future. And punk, for all its energy and attitude, was musically a neo-conservative movement. It offered a new way to present an old beat—rock's eight-beat rhythm—not a new beat. The newest sounds of the eighties and nineties—rap, the new pop, dance music, speed metal, alternative punk/funk fusions—would find their beat elsewhere; in funk and disco. We discover how in the next two chapters.

KEY TERMS

Pop-rock

Hard rock

Countrypolitan

Jazz-rhythm and blues-rock fusion

Ambient sound

Punk rock

Alternative scene

New wave

CHAPTER QUESTIONS

1. Explore the idea of a "saturated eight-beat" rhythmic texture by comparing the Sex Pistols' and Ramones' recordings to recordings by Berry and Lewis. What instruments mark the eight-beat rhythm in the earlier recordings? What instruments mark the eight-beat rhythm in the punk recordings? How much does this "saturated eight-beat" rhythm contribute to punk's confrontational attitude?

2. Explore the idea that Bowie was a major influence on new wave music by listening again to "Hang On to Yourself" and "Blitzkrieg Bop," then relating them to songs by Devo, Talking Heads, and Elvis Costello. In your opinion, who was more influential? Why?

3. "Pure" punk, as evidenced by the music of the Sex Pistols, is provocative and confrontational. The music of the "new wave" bands explores a much more varied landscape. Compare either of the Sex Pistols' songs to at least two other songs by different bands. Consider the differences in the verbal messages and the musical setting. To what extent do you feel that punk's attitude is retained in the new wave songs? How is it modified? How does the music change with the message? What does it keep from punk; what does it discard or change?

4. During the seventies, one of the music industry's recurrent themes was identifying a successor to the Beatles. To what extent did Elton John achieve their combination of overwhelming popularity and musical innovation and excellence? Do you feel that there were other viable candidates? If so, who, and why?

5. To what extent do you see the impact of the women's movement in the music discussed in this chapter? Consider particularly the songs of Patti Smith, Linda Ronstadt, Blondie, and Fleetwood Mac. Do you feel that any of them express a particularly feminine sensibility? If so, in what ways? How do they compare to the women singer/songwriters in Chapter 13? To the "male" music discussed in this chapter?

6. We have suggested that the musical interplay that produced a great rock beat was more or less common knowledge by 1970. This common knowledge, which we can call the "purification of the groove," is expressed in various ways in much of the rock of the seventies. Explore this idea in three or four songs from the middle and late seventies. Do you agree with our suggestion? If yes, consider the different ways it's expressed in the songs you chose. If no, then explain why you don't think so.

c h a p t e r   1 6

Black, Brown, and Beige

Black Music in the Late Seventies, Disco, and the New Middle Ground of the Eighties

For some African Americans, the seventies and eighties were the best of times. For others, they were worse than before. The civil rights legislation of the sixties had given black Americans unprecedented opportunity. Educational opportunities rose dramatically, corporate and professional doors opened, and incomes rose. The most affluent and successful blacks were professional athletes and entertainers, but they were not alone. Other blacks found opportunity in industry, the professions, government service, and the military. Julius Erving, Magic Johnson, Diana Ross, and Stevie Wonder were household names in 1981; by 1991, so were Supreme Court Justice Clarence Thomas and military leader Colin Powell. The ranks of middle- and upper-class blacks grew.

Accompanying this newfound prosperity was another black migration: to the suburbs. Before the civil rights movement, almost all blacks had lived in segregated neighborhoods, both in cities and towns. However, in the wake of legislation that outlawed housing discrimination, many well-to-do blacks moved out of these black neighborhoods. Among those left behind were families that could not afford to move. Welfare rolls swelled, and some black sections of major cities turned into urban wastelands. New York City's South Bronx became in many respects as culturally isolated as the Mississippi Delta, even though Manhattan was only a short subway ride away.

Black music in the seventies and eighties mirrored these social changes. Black artists continued to cross over to the (white) pop charts, especially in the eighties. A few, most notably Michael Jackson and Prince, enjoyed enormous commercial success. Their music helped create a new pop middle ground that virtually ended the distinction between white and black music. Their success signaled that finally, for a few blacks, and on some levels, race was simply a fact, not an issue.

At the other end of the social and musical spectrum were funk and rap, two styles with a strong black identity. Funk never crossed over; its audience remained largely black. Nevertheless, it would play a crucial role in shaping the crossover music of the seventies and eighties and rap and the alternative music of the late eighties.

Between these extremes came other black music, some by new artists and some by established acts, much of it with broad appeal:

- The funky, yet melodic music of Earth, Wind, and Fire;
- A new generation of black balladeers, including Lionel Richie and Luther Vandross;
- The soulful singing of Sister Sledge.

All of these trends—and more—will be discussed in this chapter.

Funk

One man put "one nation under a groove," but he needed two bands to do it. George Clinton was the mastermind behind both Parliament and Funkadelic. The two bands shared personnel; Funkadelic came into existence because of a legal problem over the use of the name Parliament.

Clinton converted to funk well after his career had started. He had formed the Parliaments in 1955; for years, they remained an obscure doo-wop group, with only a few recordings. They changed with the times, however. By 1967, when they first charted, the Parliaments had become a soul group. In the early seventies, Clinton found his signature groove, with help from several ex-members of James Brown's band, most notably bassist Bootsy Collins and his brother, guitarist "Catfish," saxophonist Maceo Parker, and drummer "Kash" Waddy. Clinton's 40-plus member group, which he called "A Parliafunkadelicament Thang," was a school for funk musicians, much like Miles Davis's groups in the sixties were a rite of passage for so many important jazz musicians.

The word "funk" followed a similar long and winding road to its seventies musical meaning. Its use dates back to the turn of the century, but it came into widespread musical use only in the mid-fifties. Around that time, jazz musicians began to use it to describe jazz that had "returned to its roots," that is, borrowed from blues and/or gospel. Ray Charles's jazz excursions exemplified this funky style. In the sixties, it also acquired another connotation: hip, especially in an outrageous way, as in, "funky threads" (fashionable clothes). Clinton's funk was both: earthy and outrageous.

Funk developed mainly from the music of James Brown and Sly and the Family Stone. In his mid-seventies music with Parliament and Funkadelic, Clinton refined and expanded upon Stone and Brown's proto-funk music. He retained key features of Stone's music, including its signature vocal phrase, complex grooves over single chords, and dense texture. The texture became even thicker because Clinton added several keyboard layers and horn riffs that were even more prominent. From Brown's music, Clinton took the idea of stringing together blocks of sound. Once Stone established the groove in a song, he would stay in it. Brown, however, shifted between a series of grooves, each built over a different chord. Clinton also took from Brown—and the glam rockers—the idea of putting on a show. Clinton's stage shows were spectacles: the band wore outlandish costumes, and there were fancy light shows, fog, spaceships dropping down from the ceiling, and other outrageous effects.

"Up for the Down Stroke," Parliament's first big hit, shows how Clinton put his own spin on Brown's and Stone's music. The song begins with five strands: a handclap backbeat; a rock beat on the drums; an occasional bass note; a double-time guitar riff; some band members talking.

The most prominent strand is the guitar riff, which is the most active and syncopated part of the texture. Precisely because the guitar part is the most prominent layer, the rhythmic "feel" of the song is not based on an eight-beat rhythm, but the more active guitar line. In this part of the song, it's a loping sixteen-beat rhythm.

When voices enter with the title phrase, the texture immediately thickens, not just because of the vocal line, but also with the addition of several layers of keyboard riffs and chords, another guitar part, then horns. At this point, the song is classic funk:

- the dense texture assembled from piles of riffs;
- the light beatkeeping (the rock beat on the sock cymbal and the backbeat are the only regular rhythms here);
- a vocal line sung by several people that consists of a single phrase repeated again and again;
- the groove over a single chord;
- above all, the highly syncopated and active rhythms moving at sixteen-beat speed.

The answering vocal phrase—"ev'rybody get up"—is an ideal example of a funk-style riff. It moves at sixteen-beat speed, and ends with a syncopation on "up."

At 51 seconds, there is a shift to a new chord; the section is an instrumental "bridge" (James Brown frequently refers to such sections as the bridge: for example, in "Sex Machine"). During the second bridge (at 1 minute, 32 seconds), the drummer confirms the sixteen-beat rhythm. However, the sixteen-beat "feel" is present throughout the song in the rhythms of the riffs, whether or not the drummer (or anyone else) actually plays a steady sixteen beat pattern. The shift in rhythmic texture, like the change from one chord to another, simply helps define the building blocks of the song.

The groove, the richness of the texture, the voices singing/chanting in unison, and the lyric work together to create a good-time feeling. In this song, at least, "we're havin' a party, y'all . . . ." Clinton felt that his music should lift the spirit, yet reflect the reality of life as a black person in the seventies. Even though it was outrageous and provocative, Clinton's music smiled in the face of adversity. Clinton called the increasingly black urban areas "Chocolate Cities," showing his sense of humor. But, he also pointed out that many chocolate cities were surrounded by "vanilla suburbs," showing his grim awareness of ghetto life. What was implicit in Clinton's funk would become explicit in rap.

Clinton's bands were the most outrageous of the funk bands of the seventies. Other notable groups included War, who discussed a long list of political and social issues in their songs, the Ohio Players, the Brothers Johnson, Graham Central Station (led by ex-Sly and the Family Stone bassist Larry Graham), Cameo, Mandrill, the Bar-Kays, and Con Funk Shun. Kool and the Gang was the most noteworthy of the bands who straddled the boundary between funk and disco, while Herbie Hancock's progressive recordings of the seventies and early eighties filtered funk through a jazz perspective.

And, although funk was mainly black music for black audiences, a few white bands also contributed. Among them were the Average White Band, remembered for their angularly melodic instrumental, "Pick Up the Pieces" (1976), and Wild Cherry, whose big hit, "Play That Funky Music" (1976), was a self-fulfilling prophecy.

Clinton began a solo career in the early eighties. In his No. 1 R&B hit "Atomic Dog" (1983), he went techno, substituting synthesizers for horns and rhythm instruments. But the groove is basically the same, and so are his messages: he embeds a parable-like message under layers of his wacky humor ("why must I feel like that/why must I chase the cat/nothin' but the dog in me").

Despite the success of "Atomic Dog," Clinton's solo career never took off. However, his influence was pervasive: next to James Brown, he and his groups were probably the most sampled artists of the eighties and early '90s.

Funk, like punk, quickly rippled into other styles. Funk-inspired rhythms merged with a more melodic style to create a new black crossover music. The music of Earth, Wind, and Fire best exemplified this new sound, but it was also evident in the music of Rufus, with Chaka Khan. Funk also fed into disco, and it was the main source of rap, which first appeared on record in 1979 with the debut recording of the Sugarhill Gang.

Disco

Disco was the ultimate inside/outside music. Originally the province of numerous minorities—blacks, Latinos, gays—it became everyone's dance music in the wake of the enormous success of the film *Saturday Night Fever*. Discotheques, night clubs that featured recorded dance music instead of live music, had been around since the sixties. As the French name implies, they were especially popular in Europe, perhaps because good live bands were not as plentiful.

Disco emerged as a distinct musical style in 1974, with the release of such songs as the Hues Corporation's "Rock the Boat." Within a year, Van McCoy's "The Hustle" and a string of hits by KC and the Sunshine Band topped the pop charts briefly. At the same time, Barry White was releasing his songs of sexual passion. These were similar in many respects to early disco hits, but were more suitable for the bedroom than the dance floor. Still, their influence is evident on songs like Donna Summer's 1976 hit, "Love to Love You Baby," with its provocative moaning.

Within a couple of years, however, the disco scene had become popular enough to attract notice in the press. The storyline for *Saturday Night Fever* grew out of a magazine article about Brooklyn youths living for Saturday night at the disco. Sparked by the film's overwhelming success, disco came up from the underground. By the late seventies, discos such as New York's Studio 54 were the places where everyone *had* to be seen. All kinds of music—even Beethoven (Walter Murphy's travesty "A Fifth of Beethoven")—throbbed to a

Disco dancers dance "the night away" in New York, March 15, 1979. PHOTO COURTESY *CORBIS/BETTMANN.*

disco beat, radio stations went to all-disco playlists, and even Sesame Street's Grover donned a John Travolta-style white suit.

The music was increasingly popular, but the acts were not. Of the major styles of the seventies, disco was certainly the most faceless. Disco spawned more one- and two-hit wonders—e.g., the Hues Corporation, Van McCoy — than any other music of the seventies. Disco's most memorable visual images are of dancers in glittery costumes and platform shoes, not the performers, who, after all, seldom appeared live. It was a style that existed mainly on record. With few exceptions—the Bee Gees, Donna Summer, Chic—we remember the songs more than the artists: Alicia Bridges's "I Love the Nightlife (Disco Round)" is a good example ("I want some 'akkk-shooon'").

Disco was producers' music. Producers had been key players in record production since the beginning of the rock era: Rock would not have been the same without producers like Sam Phillips or Leiber and Stoller. In large part because it was a style that was even "performed" on record—among disco's most important artists were the club disc jockeys who blended one recording seamlessly into the next—producers became the major players. Singers were often just hired hands, not stars.

Van McCoy's "The Hustle," the first big disco hit, shows how the producer's role had grown; it also showcases essential features of disco style. Disco effectively blended Philadelphia International's richly orchestrated style with a more obvious form of funk rhythm to produce a new kind of dance music. Its rich orchestration, with strings, flutes, vibes, plus full horn section and solo trumpet, recalls Gamble and Huff's lush backdrops behind the Philadelphia International artists, as does the harmony. In many respects, including the almost complete absence of voices, the song seems almost a clone of MFSB's 1974 hit, "TSOP (The Sound of Philadelphia)." Indeed, both seem to be instrumentals in search of a lead vocal.

"The Hustle" also introduces disco's rhythmic backbone: a sixteen-beat rhythm played on a closed sock cymbal, undergirded by four-on-the-floor thumps on the bass drum. Layered over this are additional percussion parts—shakers and conga drum reinforce the sixteen-beat rhythm—and riffs in the bass line, guitar, and flutes. In its dense texture, sixteen beat rhythm, and layers of riffs, this early disco sound is clearly related to funk. But the beat is more obvious, because of the bass drum thumps, and the ratio of syncopated riffs to timekeeping is balanced much more toward the timekeeping side.

It's also important to note that the tempo is brighter than is typical in either Philadelphia International–style or P-Funk songs. Most disco songs had a beat that pulsed somewhere between 120 and 126 beats a minute: the close similarity in tempo was necessary if club DJs were to blend one song into another.

"The Hustle" also shows how disco began to blur rock's racial divide. There had certainly been integrated groups prior to disco, and countless studio orchestras were racially mixed—think of Stax or Motown, or Billy Preston doing session work for the Beatles. However, the dominant sound within a group was usually identifiable as white or black. That was often not the case with disco hits such as "The Hustle." Although its style is derived from black sources, there is nothing about the song that sounds distinctively black—no funky riffs, soulful singing, etc. Both McCoy and the studio orchestra could be white or black—McCoy, in fact, was a black man. Although there had certainly been individual recordings, especially instrumentals, that were racially neutral, disco was the first style to straddle this racial dividing line.

The first band to put a face on disco reinforced this message. Harry Casey's KC and the Sunshine Band was a nine piece band; Casey (aka KC) and his partner Richard Finch were the only two whites. The group was disco's first big act, with four top singles during 1975–1976. "That's the Way (I Like It)" (1975), the second of its number one hits, is a funk-inspired song, with these characteristic features:

- oft-repeated title phrase sung over one chord (noteworthy mainly for the exchange of "uh-hunh's")

- dense, percussion-heavy texture, with guitar, conga, and drummer laying down a sixteen-beat rhythm

- layers of riffs (including the vocal line, which might as well be an instrumental part for all its verbal interest!)

- free-moving bass line

But the tempo is faster than is customary in P-Funk–style funk, and the rhythmic feel not quite as loose. These qualities move it more toward disco.

In its racial neutrality, the rise of Afro-Cuban music in Cuba during the twenties bears a remarkable similarity to disco. Cubans of African descent popularized the *son*, the musical ancestor of the mambo and salsa, through radio broadcasts. White Cubans apparently didn't know and/or didn't care whether the bands were white or black. They just liked the music.

In the wake of their success came a rash of disco hits. Some were by one-hit wonders—how many people remember the Andrea True Connection? A few were by acts who helped shape the sound and style through a string of hits: Donna Summer, Chic, Gloria Gaynor, the Village People. Ironically, the Bee Gees, the group most associated with disco, was the one major act that did not limit themselves to that style.

The Bee Gees supplied six songs for *Saturday Night Fever*. Yet, their music for the film clearly stands apart from the stream of late-seventies disco hits, from "The Hustle" to Chic's "Good Times." The differences are many. Two are especially noteworthy. One, all six tracks are *songs* in the limited sense: they are more than just title phrases repeated again and again, with verses or moans thrown in for variety. Two, only "You Should Be Dancing" is in "correct" disco tempo. "How Deep Is Your Love" is a beautiful love ballad, and "Night Fever" is more an evocation of the sound of disco than a disco song—a kind of disco mood music. The other songs are too slow to be mixed with conventional disco songs by a club DJ, although they are certainly satisfactory on their own terms.

"You Should Be Dancing" is in many ways the most interesting disco song of the era, because it departs in so many ways from the conventions of the

The Bee Gees, c. 1975. PHOTO COURTESY CORBIS/NEAL PRESTON.

style. From the start, it is clear from the thump of the bass, the choked guitar, and the battery of percussion instruments that this is a disco song: they lay down disco's characteristic rhythmic foundation. However, the vocal section of the song is classic Motown: a verse over static harmony; a transition over more active chords; and the title phrase hook over a return to the opening harmony. The magic lies in the seamless integration of disco rhythm and pop melody: the song works as both disco dance music and a popular song.

Another interesting feature of "You Should Be Dancing" is the percussion "jam" that begins at about two minutes, 45 seconds. The clearest precedent for this is the *inspiracion*, the group improvisation of percussionists in Afro-Cuban music. It is commonly heard in "uptown" mambos and salsa. The Latin component of disco was not as obvious as the black or gay elements, but it was present. One of the tracks on the *Saturday Night Fever* soundtrack is "Salsation," a pseudo-salsa disco song. The extensive percussion sections, active rhythms, and occasional percussion interlude also point to the influence of Afro-Cuban music.

The Gibb brothers are obviously white—even their jumpsuits are white! Yet their distinctive high falsetto sound comes right out of Motown groups such as the Temptations and the Four Tops and, before them, doo-wop groups too numerous to mention. No major white act of the seventies more clearly evoked the sound of black pop.

In this racially neutral climate, several black acts positioned themselves musically for maximum success. Donna Summer, Kool and the Gang, Gloria Gaynor, the Trammps, and Chic all enjoyed a few moments in the sun during disco's peak years. Of these, Chic was the quintessential disco act. Like so many disco acts, Chic was producer-driven: bassist Bernard Edwards and guitarist Nile Rodgers orchestrated the group's sound.

What separated Chic from so many other disco acts is the balance between melody, beatkeeping, and background. Because they are music for dancing, disco songs tend to be rhythmically obvious: typically there is strong time-keeping at four-beat and sixteen-beat speeds. Other rhythmic layers wrap around these easy points of reference. The melody, if there is one, usually appears in the forefront, because melodies normally stand out as a matter of course. However, in songs such as "Le Freak" (1978), Edwards and Rodgers created a rich texture, with active, syncopated guitar and bass patterns, voices, sixteen-beat rhythm on the sock-cymbal and four-beat rhythm on the bass drum, sustained keyboard, and prominent string lines that vary between active countermelody and sustained notes and chords. Compared to "You Should Be Dancing," it's a lean texture, but there's still a lot going on. In addition, they mix the tracks so that the guitar, strings, and bass stand out. As a result, both timekeeping and vocal melody are present, but they do not overwhelm the other parts of the texture. The result is disco's most elegant sound, as chic as their name or their dress.

Chic's songs celebrated the disco experience. "Le Freak" was the Twist of the late seventies, a "dance exhortation" song. "Good Times," similar in many ways to "Le Freak," but with a chord progression that never comes to rest, captures the suspension of time in the disco, where the music never stops. Chic's music, and that of the other good disco acts, was most successful when it was simply music for dancing.

Donna Summer's "Bad Girls" (1979) shows disco's limitations when it strayed outside of the discotheque. The song is about prostitutes. The lyric

Donna Summer, January 9, 1979. PHOTO COURTESY *CORBIS/*BETTMANN.

won't make anyone forget Joni Mitchell or Curtis Mayfield, but it does paint a clear picture of life on the street. However, it's set to a disco soundtrack—a good one, to be sure, but emotionally incompatible with the subject of the song. Far more credible is Alicia Bridges's "I Love the Nightlife (Disco Round)" (1978), which tells the story of a woman who opts for a night at the disco instead of spending time with her good-for-nothing ex-boyfriend. But the song is not a disco song musically, in spite of its subject. (It's a fine song, but it doesn't have either the beat or the tempo of "The Hustle" or the other disco songs.)

Disco had a devoted gay following well before it crossed over to mainstream audiences. A few groups, most notably the Village People, pandered to the gay audience. Producer Jacques Morali conjured up the idea for the group in a gay bar. He eventually hired six beefcake types, three whites, two blacks, and a Latino, who parodied macho male stereotypes while singing songs laced with gay in-jokes and coded messages. "Y.M.C.A." (1979), for example, may have seemed harmless enough to most Americans. However, those aware of gay culture would realize that urban YMCAs were meeting places for gays, and that many of the "many ways to have a good time" involved "hang(ing) out with all the 'boys'," i.e., gay sexual encounters. Their music in effect publicized the gay subculture that frequented discos.

Disco generated strong feelings, both pro and con. Many who disliked the music may have had another agenda: theirs was a racist and bigoted reaction to disco's "multiple minority" fan base (Latinos, blacks, and gays) and its racially blended sound. Still, disco haters were themselves a minority, even among whites. For a brief time, the music was immensely popular.

Disco's popularity peaked in the late seventies; it waned quickly as the eighties began. However, its period of peak influence began even as it disappeared from the charts, as it merged with punk, funk, and other styles to inspire much of the important music of the early eighties.

Disco made two significant contributions to eighties popular music. It laid the groundwork for the racially undifferentiated pop middle ground of the eighties, and it solidified the place of sixteen-beat rhythms in popular music.

The New Rhythms of the Eighties

As we have noted, sixteen-beat rhythm patterns had been used since about 1970 by artists as diverse as Sly Stone, Roberta Flack, Elton John, and Aerosmith. But only with disco were they presented so obviously and unmistakably—in music for dancing.

The Brothers Johnson's "Stomp," a No. 1 R&B hit in 1980, dramatically illustrates both the underlying affinity between disco and funk and the key differences between them. "Stomp" begins as a disco song. It has disco's trademark four-on-the-floor/sixteen-beat rhythm, a singable melody with shifting harmonies underneath, and a rich texture that includes horns and strings. For over two minutes, it sounds as though the Brothers Johnson, one of the leading funk bands in the seventies, has simply sold out to disco.

However, at about two minutes, twenty seconds, the band suddenly shifts over to a funk groove. The chords stop changing, the heavy beatkeeping on the bass drum stops, the bassist plays complex slapped riffs, and a fast-moving vocal line enters soon after. The funk interlude is brief; the disco beat returns at about two-and-a-half minutes.

"Stomp" underscores two basic points.

1. The underlying rhythmic affinity of funk and disco is evident from the seamless transition from one style to the other;

2. Funk includes much more rhythmic play, and less obvious timekeeping, plus more static harmonies, than disco.

Funk and disco were two sources of the new rhythms of the eighties. The others were the saturated eight-beat rhythms of punk and new wave and the distinctive afterbeat rhythm of reggae, which could be superimposed on either an eight-beat or a sixteen-beat foundation. In their various combinations, they helped define many of the decade's new sounds.

Brothers and Sisters:
Crossing Over in Style(s)

Throughout the sixties and early seventies, black music had followed two quite different paths:

- Black pop began with Motown and continued in Philadelphia and with Roberta Flack and other black romantics.

- Soul began in Memphis and with James Brown and mutated into funk.

Each was different from the other, and both were different from white music. This began to change in mid-decade, most obviously in disco, but also in the work of other artists. Style fusions occurred not only within black music, but in the use of rock style underneath black vocalists.

Crossing Over in the Seventies

In 1975, just as disco was taking off, Patti LaBelle released "Lady Marmalade." LaBelle had fronted the Blue Belles, a girl group, in the sixties, but had spent almost a decade in artistic limbo. She reconstituted her group as LaBelle and put her career in gear again with this song, which topped both the R&B and pop charts.

"Lady Marmalade," a vignette about a Creole prostitute in New Orleans, has lots of crossover appeal. The most apparent is the hook: it's sung in French, but you don't have to be bilingual to catch its drift. The background, with its horn riffs, busy bass line, organ countermelody, and rhythmic play against the strong marking of the beat, sounds like it was cooked up in a sixties soul kitchen, but the extra keyboards and percussion give it a slightly more contemporary sound. This sound had achieved wide currency not only in the soul records of the sixties and early seventies, but also in the music of Blood, Sweat, and Tears and Chicago.

The Pointer Sisters' "Fire" (1979) blends black vocals with white rock—which is not surprising, because Bruce Springsteen wrote the song. The instrumental background, which features prominent guitars laying down a nice riff over an eight-beat rhythm, could have just as easily accompanied an Elton John song. But the group's vocals and the churchy organ line are clearly black. The mix of rock guitar and black vocal style just as clearly had crossover appeal: the song did better on the pop chart (No. 2) than it did on the R&B chart!

Sister Sledge used a similar formula during their brief run at the top. "We Are Family" (1979) mixes an uplifting message, soulful vocals, and a disco-inspired accompaniment. A particularly nice touch is the downshift to a funky eight-beat rhythm during the verse. The shift back up to the disco-ish rhythm enlivens the anthemic refrain.

EARTH, WIND, AND FIRE One of the freshest sounds of the mid-seventies was the music of Earth, Wind, and Fire. The group was the creation of percussionist/producer Maurice White: the name of the group comes from the three elements present in White's astrological chart. White had paid his dues as a session player for Chess Records and as the drummer for jazz pianist Ramsey Lewis in the sixties. He formed Earth, Wind, and Fire in 1969 after leaving Lewis. They charted for the first time in 1973, and by mid-decade were regularly visiting the top of both singles and album charts and packing arenas with elaborate stage shows, one of which was designed by magician Doug Henning.

Earth, Wind, and Fire was a large group. The roster fluctuated between eight and ten musicians, among them vocalist Philip Bailey and two of White's brothers, Fred and Verdine. Like the Sly Stone and other funk bands, the instrumentation included a full rhythm section, extra percussion, and horns, in addition to the vocal parts. Not surprisingly, then, one dimension of their sound is the complex rhythms and riffs of funk. However, White's jazz background is evident in intricate horn riffs—as virtuosic as any in the rock era—shifting harmonies, and extended forms. The group conveyed the often inspirational messages of their songs through catchy melodies and hooks.

Their music moved through most of the black styles of the seventies, even as it created a distinctive sound. Songs such as "That's the Way of the World" (1975) and "After the Love Is Gone" (1979) hold their own with the black ballads of the era. "Getaway" (1977) sounds like a kissing cousin to disco, although it lacks the bass drum thump on every beat. "Serpentine Fire" (1977) has the riff-laden texture of funk, although it also has a singable melody, while "September" (1978), with its Latinized rock beat, roaming bass, high horn riffs, and upbeat hook, has no parallel in other music of the time.

"Serpentine Fire" shows key elements of Earth, Wind, and Fire's style. The vocal line finds the middle path between the repeated title phrase of funk and the verse/refrain pattern of black (and a lot of other) pop. The story unfolds slowly, carried on a narrow-ranged, almost blues-like melody, which is supported by a single chord. This merges the static harmony of funk with the storytelling of pop. The title phrase is in a higher register and more active, but still sung over only one chord; only with the Amen-like "oh-yeahs" do we hear rich vocal harmony. As with many of their songs, the melody is funkier than pop, and more pop-like than funk.

Like many of their songs, "Serpentine Fire" is upbeat and uplifting. Part of the message is, of course, in the lyric ("When I see your face like the morning sun . . . shine"), but where it really comes through is in the musical setting. Here, the upbeat mood is mainly a product of register and rhythm: both are "up."

The overall sound of Earth, Wind, and Fire is bright in large part because both individual instruments and the overall texture are concentrated in a high register. This is clearest in the falsetto singing of Philip Bailey and the high horn riffs (compare these to the earlier funk and disco recordings). But there is also an absence of consistent low-register sounds. The bassist roams freely, playing only intermittently, and there is only an occasional twanged note or vocal line in a medium low-register. Everything else—keyboard, guitar, and percussion, in addition to voices and horns—is in a middle or high register.

The rhythm is also "up": that is, almost all of the activity moves at rock beat speed or faster. Regular rhythms mark both four-beat and eight-beat levels; there are none slower than the beat. Most of the other parts play off these regular rhythms, although horn riffs typically move twice as fast.

The combination of predominantly middle- and upper-register sounds with a bright tempo and medium-to-fast rhythms gives the song (and others like it) the group's characteristic upbeat sound. It was a sound with broad appeal throughout the seventies. After 1975 their albums consistently went platinum and, among black acts, only Stevie Wonder charted more in the 1970s.

Earth, Wind, and Fire is often compared and contrasted with George Clinton's P-Funk empire. Certainly, there are parallels: both had big bands, put on elaborate stage shows, and created music with compelling rhythmic grooves. But there is also a discernible difference in spirit; it is much like the difference between gospel music and the blues. Although their music is clearly secular, it is inspirational, by design: Maurice White claimed that "We [Earth, Wind and Fire] are actually being used as tools by the Creator." Like the blues, Clinton's message is earthier, and often bleaker.

Black Pop in the Early Eighties

A new generation of black pop singers also emerged in the early eighties. Among them were Natalie Cole (daughter of the great Nat Cole), Lionel

Richie, Luther Vandross, James Ingram, Al Jarreau, and Deniece Williams. In addition, many stars of earlier decades also found success. Stevie Wonder, Diana Ross, Marvin Gaye, Patti LaBelle (her biggest hit was a duet with ex-Doobie Brother Michael McDonald), George Benson, Gladys Knight, Bill Withers, and Aretha Franklin all charted during the early eighties.

Black pop was in many respects the most conservative music of the decade, in that the songs favored the melodic and harmonic approach of earlier romantic styles. "Smooth jazz," the instrumental counterpart to black pop, also flourished. A new generation of saxophonists, both black and white, followed Grover Washington, Jr.'s path to commercial reward. Kenny G. was the most successful.

Romance—an ultimately optimistic view of love and life—remained a frequent topic. As in the seventies, black pop was the only music consistently engaged with romantic love. (White and middle ground pop concentrated more on its absence.)

After a decade with the Commodores, Lionel Richie began a solo career in 1981. He became one of the most commercially successful singers of the decade; both albums and singles sold well—better than any black artists except Michael Jackson, Prince, and Whitney Houston. His 1986 hit "Love Will Conquer All" shows how black romantic pop absorbed new sounds and rhythms while remaining true to the musical language of love.

"Love Will Conquer All" puts a new spin on the romantic ballad. The obvious novelty is the setting. Here, synths substitute for strings, piano, and many other conventional instruments; only drums and bass retain their original sound. The song could easily be a case study in how synthesizers expanded the sound palette of popular music. The new colors are more pastel than primary—there are no spectacular effects—but there is more variety than is typically available with conventional instruments.

In most other respects, the song adheres to traditional Motown values (Richie was, after all, a Motown artist). The song has a good but unobtrusive beat, a singable melody, expressive pre-rock style harmony, a melodically saturated texture—augmented with a variety of synth chords, melodic wisps, and riffs—and subtle enrichment of the rhythmic texture with delicate percussion sounds. The final product: a Motown sound for the eighties.

Richie enjoyed great crossover success, charting almost as well on the pop charts as he did on the R&B charts. However, Michael Jackson and Prince went even further, effectively wiping out the black/white boundary commercially and musically.

The New Middle Ground of the Eighties

A new pop style emerged in the early eighties, one dramatically different in almost every respect from the music of the previous decade. Five qualities distinguish it:

- *It wiped out discrimination by sex, sexual preference, and race.* None of its top stars were heterosexual white males: its leading acts were Michael Jackson, Prince, and Madonna. Other successful performers included Boy George, Cyndi Lauper, and Tina Turner, making a comeback as a rock goddess.

- *It exploited new media resources.* Michael Jackson was not the first to make music videos, but he raised the music video to an art form. Video and film were essential in boosting both Prince and Madonna to superstardom.

- *It was a musical melting pot.* Punk, disco, reggae, funk, pop, and black romantic music—in short, almost every current style—fed into it.

- *Synthesizers played an increasingly important role in the sound of the music.* Some replaced guitars, basses, and conventional keyboards as the main sources of harmony; synthesized percussion sounds enriched, or even replaced, drum kits and other acoustic instruments; and sustained synth sounds put a lot of string players out of work.

- *It was incredibly popular.* Michael Jackson's *Thriller* album easily surpassed the sales of the previous best-selling album. Prince and Madonna also had impressive sales figures. As rock critic Robert Christgau pointed out, the sheer volume of sales was part of its significance.

Precisely because its artists drew from so many sources, there was no single "middle ground sound." It was not defined by a distinctive kind of beat-keeping, like punk; or a rhythmic feel, like funk; or a special sound quality, like the distortion of heavy metal. Indeed, all three are used in middle ground music: the opening of Prince's "When Doves Cry" or Eddie Van Halen's solo in Michael Jackson's "Beat It" are familiar examples of metal-style guitar playing.

Instead, it was a set of principles that defined the music that topped the charts during the eighties. The songs typically have intelligible lyrics that tell a story, usually about love, or its absence, or a slice of life; they are set to a singable melody. The melody in turn is embedded in a rich, riff-laden texture; most layers—if not all—are played on synthesizers. The songs typically have a good beat—easy to find and danceable, neither too monotonous nor too ambiguous.

Within these guidelines, there was a lot of room to operate. One of the most striking features of albums such as Michael Jackson's *Thriller* and Prince's *Sign O' the Times* is how different each song is from the others.

In effect, the middle ground took the Motown idea of good pop even further than Richie. The music remained accessible, but the lyrics were franker, the backgrounds more electronic, the beats more varied. It was fitting that the king of this new middle ground pop style was a Motown graduate, Michael Jackson.

The New Pop Royalty

Each of the three artists who most fully defined the new pop were multidimensional. Michael Jackson was the complete performing machine: songwriter, singer, dancer. Prince was the complete creative machine: songwriter, singer, multi-instrumentalist, producer, film star. Madonna wrote, produced, sang, and danced in her videos. That they were multidimensional is part of their importance. Michael Jackson is, without question, the finest all-around performer of the rock era. Prince gave Stevie Wonder's one-man band a visual dimension. And no woman before Madonna had so thoroughly challenged the place of women in rock or was so obviously in control of her career.

MICHAEL JACKSON Although only 24 when *Thriller* (1982) was released, Michael Jackson was the veteran of the "royal" three: he had been a professional entertainer for three-fourths of his life and a star for half of it. Even though he had released solo singles in the early seventies, Jackson's solo career didn't take off until 1978, when he starred in the film version of *The Wiz*. During the filming, he met composer/arranger/producer Quincy Jones, who collaborated with him on *Off the Wall* (1979), his first major album, and *Thriller*. Jones's skill and creativity proved to be the ideal complement to Jackson's abilities.

Dance—or at least movement—had been part of rock since Elvis the Pelvis (as he was called in the press) and his scandalous hips. The stylized choreography of the Motown groups was an important part of their image, and James Brown's stage shows featured "the hardest working man in show business" moving and grooving all over the stage. But no performer before Jackson had danced with his virtuosity and expressiveness.

As with so many other rock artists, Michael Jackson was fortunate to be in the right place at the right time. MTV had gone on the air in 1981. It was the perfect medium for a performer like Jackson, whose talent as a dancer more than matches his singing ability. Jackson's dancing was crucial to his success, because his medium of expression was the music video. Before *Thriller*, music videos had been essentially promotional tools. By contrast, Jackson's were mini-movies that told the story of the song visually as well as aurally. In fact, it was Jackson who broke MTV's color barrier, because the demand for his videos was so strong. Prior to 1983, when the videos began to be aired, MTV had pursued a "white-only" policy. The few black artists who

Michael Jackson shows off his glove, July 7, 1984.
PHOTO COURTESY CORBIS/
BETTMANN.

appeared in videos were shunted off to the side, as jazz-rock pianist Herbie Hancock ruefully noted.

This visual, almost theatrical, dimension is implicit in the music: each song on *Thriller* creates such a distinctive atmosphere that it seems to demand visual depiction. The most obvious example, of course, is the opening of "Thriller," with the squeaky door and the footsteps. But the song succeeds in sustaining the suspense with its relentless bass riff, busy percussion, and the slowly rising melody that finally spills over on the title phrase. Without the skillful orchestration of the rest of the song by Quincy Jones's production team, the opening—and Vincent Price's mid-song rap—would have been cheap effects.

The other songs on the album also capture the tone of the lyric in the musical setting. The hard-edged riffs that open "Wanna Be Startin' Somethin'" anticipate the schoolyard-style provocation in the lyric. With its punk-derived beat and Eddie Van Halen's guitar, the setting for "Beat It" underscores the message of the lyric.

By contrast, in "The Girl Is Mine," the loping beat (a shuffle beat on top of a rock beat), the use of pre-rock pop harmony, and the soft synth sounds, reinforces the friendly rivalry between Jackson and Paul McCartney. In another direction, "Billie Jean" characterizes the emptiness of the "groupie"-style relationships in a setting that mixes an open middle range—just a simple synthesizer riff—with the irritation of a persistent bass riff and percussion sound. Other songs create similarly distinctive settings.

There is no doubt that *Thriller* would have been a successful album without the videos. But it also seems certain that the videos, and the fact that the songs were so "video-ready," played a crucial role in its overwhelming success. *Thriller* has been the crowning achievement of Jackson's career; nothing before or since matched its success.

PRINCE Jackson's major competition as the king of eighties pop was Prince. Prince Rogers Nelson was born in 1958, the same year as Jackson. Although not a child star, he was more precocious than Jackson as both musician and producer. He played all the instruments on his first five albums and produced them as well. Stevie Wonder had pioneered this electronic version of the one-man band earlier in the decade; Prince grew up with it.

Prince charted from the start: "Soft and Wet," a single from *For You* (1978), released when he was only twenty, appeared on both pop and R&B charts. He achieved superstardom in the early eighties, especially after the phenomenal success of his film *Purple Rain* (1984).

Set in Minneapolis, Prince's hometown, it is a more or less autobiographical account of the contemporary pop musician's life. The album topped the charts for almost half a year and sold well over ten million units; five tracks also charted as singles. Subsequent albums, including the sound track to the film *Batman* (1989), did well enough to make Prince the most consistently successful artist of the eighties. The double album *Sign O' the Times* (1987) was perhaps his "statement" album, the album on which he showcased the full range of his musical ability.

Listening to a Prince album can be like taking a course in rock history. Not only is Prince a master of many instruments and multitrack recording, but he is also the master of virtually all rock-era styles. For Prince, style mastery is not simply the ability to cover a style; he seldom does just that. Instead, he draws on disparate style elements and mixes them together to evoke a particular mood. For him, beat patterns, sounds, and rhythmic textures are like ingredients in a gourmet dish; they are used to flavor the song. More important, he also adds original ideas to create the *nouvelle cuisine* of eighties pop.

"Soft and Wet," his first hit, underpins erotic lyrics, pop brightness, the remarkable range of Prince's singing—from stratospheric falsetto to gravelly bass—and virtuoso keyboard playing with a terrific funk groove. Three hits from the early eighties show him straying well beyond his black roots; they give some sense of his range and originality.

"When U Were Mine" (1980), with its signature synth riff, straightforward eight-beat rhythm, and twangy guitar, sounds much like the new wave music of the time; Elvis Costello would have felt right at home with the musical setting. What makes it stand apart from other new wave music is his soulful falsetto singing, the amount of syncopation (unusually high for new wave songs), and the textural variety.

The mix of white and black elements anticipates the punk/funk fusion of the eighties, while the contrast between the almost naked sound of the verse, with its open-sound, power-chord intervals and minimal accompaniment, and the synth-enriched transitions and breaks, as well as the rhythmic variety from section to section, illustrates Prince's aural imagination.

"Little Red Corvette" (1982) is a wonderful example of the new pop of the eighties. The title riff is a great hook. The rhythm, with the sandpaper-like percussion instrument sound laying down an eight-beat rhythm and the syncopation of the hook, is remarkably varied. As in "When U Were Mine," Prince weaves together elements that seems miles apart stylistically: his clearly black vocal style, the cushiony synth sounds, and mildly distorted rock guitar. Three quite distinct styles merge together seamlessly into one conception. And, as in the previous song, there is considerable textural variety.

"When Doves Cry" (1984), one of the hits from *Purple Rain*, makes an especially good case for the originality of Prince's musical imagination. Here, Prince begins by mixing metal-style guitar with a drum track filled with scattershot percussion sounds. What's missing is a bass line; its absence is the most striking feature of the texture. Vocal and percussive sounds occasionally dip into a lower register, but the song has no bottom: it is the ultimate liberation of the bass. Furthermore, the lack of a bass part is not just a novelty. It seems to have an expressive purpose: to reinforce the emptiness conveyed in the lyric, with its stark contrast between fantasy ("the sweat of your body covers me") and reality ("you just leave me standing").

These three songs just scratch the surface of Prince's musical range. Because he is at home in almost any style, and because he has so much music to draw from, each of his songs tends to have a quite distinct character. Yet, they follow much the same plan as the best rock-era pop. Like not only Jackson's *Thriller*, but also the music of the Beatles and Motown, Prince's songs have both easy points of entry—infectious beats, easily followed stories, catchy riffs, imaginative sounds—and complex, varied textures that reward repeated listening.

For all his musical creativity, Prince has probably received more attention—or at least notoriety—for his sexual provocativeness and bizarre personal life. His lyrics—even his titles—are saturated with strong, often explicit sexual messages. In his stage shows, he would often strip down to underpants, and suggestive gestures ripple through his videos.

Yet Prince has led an extremely reclusive private life, even to the point of obliterating his identity. Since 1990, he has been most often referred to as "the artist formerly known as Prince"; he identifies himself with a sign that combines the symbols for male and female.

Nevertheless, these eccentricities cannot obscure or diminish Prince's remarkable musical achievement: there has been no more multitalented, multidimensional musician in the history of rock.

MADONNA   Madonna matched Prince pretty much step for step in sexual daring. In her public life, she portrayed herself as a provocative woman, totally in control of herself and those around her. Some were disgusted by her overt sexuality; others felt threatened by her aggressive posture. However, many others found her public persona liberating: it helped level the playing field in the battle of the sexes. Here was a woman in complete charge of her career: producing her albums and videos, writing her songs, choreographing her performances. Without question, her success signaled a kind of sexual equality within the pop music business: women no longer had to be front persons for men.

Like Michael Jackson, Madonna is an excellent dancer. Given her dancing ability and sexual daring, it was clear that she needed to be seen as well as heard. And she was: her videos got considerable airplay on MTV, and she also starred in several films during the eighties, among them *Desperately Seeking Susan*.

Madonna on tour, July 13, 1987. Photo courtesy CORBIS/Bettmann.

At the same time, she had a string of top-selling albums throughout the eighties, including the provocatively titled *Like a Virgin* (1984) and *Like a Prayer* (1989). The titles are provocative because they contrast her given name, Madonna Ciccone, and her blatantly sexual image with the religious meaning of "Madonna": for Catholics, the madonna is the Virgin Mary.

For all her sexual boldness and business shrewdness, Madonna's music is essentially conservative. Many of her hit songs simply graft contemporary rhythms and synth sounds onto traditional pop-style melodies, harmonies, and forms. "Borderline" (1983), from her self-titled debut album, is a perfect early example. The song sounds up-to-date because of the layered texture, rich in synth sounds and based on a sixteen-beat rhythm. But the melody and the chords underneath it reach back to rock's past; the verse of the song could as easily have come from the late sixties as the early eighties, while the chorus ("Borderline . . . ") echoes fifties teen pop.

Madonna's music of the late eighties kept the same basic approach; the differences are mainly cosmetic. For instance, the title track of her 1989 album, *Like A Prayer*, begins with a string of jarring juxtapositions: metal-ish guitar figures; pure choral singing; and finally Madonna's vocal, with a quasi-religious accompaniment, voices, and sustained organ synth sounds. The active rhythms that animate the chorus of the song gradually seep into the texture, until they take over completely. At this point, the rhythmic texture has a late eighties pop sound: it recalls Steve Winwood's 1986 hit "Higher Love." But, change the beat to a simple rock or shuffle rhythm, and Frankie Avalon or Fabian could be singing this song.

This familiar-but-different approach to music making parallels Madonna's frequent changes in appearance—blonde one year, brunette the next. The look changes, but the person underneath stays pretty much the same. It was a clever, and very successful, approach to pop success.

The Ballad Sound of the Eighties

Perhaps the most distinctive new sound of this new middle ground was a new reggae-influenced ballad style. The evidence of reggae's influence is not only in the slower tempos but also the liberation of the bass line and the subtle, active synth and percussion rhythms, often with the trademark reggae rebound.

Reggae filtered into British rock during the mid-seventies. Jamaicans in the United Kingdom stayed abreast of musical trends in their homeland. Jimmy Cliff, Bob Marley, and other Jamaican musicians attracted a loyal following in the United Kingdom, first among Jamaican expatriates and then among white British musicians. Eric Clapton's cover of Marley's "I Shot the Sheriff" (1974) spurred the assimilation of reggae into rock. By the late seventies, new British talents, among them Elvis Costello and the Clash, had begun to incorporate reggae rhythms into their music, as we noted in Chapter 15.

Both punk and reggae were outsiders' music with a strong protest streak. Rhythmically, however, the two styles are as different as day and night. Punk is *rhythmically explicit* because it saturates the rhythmic texture with eight-beat timekeeping. Reggae, by contrast, is *rhythmically implicit*, because the most consistent rhythms are all afterbeats. The other rhythm lines, especially the bass, move freely, creating a rhythmic fabric of unparalleled lightness.

The group most responsible for mainstreaming reggae was undoubtedly the Police. From their very first U.S. hit, "Roxanne" (1979), they incorporated reggae rhythms into their music. Indeed, their early hits take their underlying rhythm from either reggae or punk—or, in songs like "Can't Stand Losing You," both in alternation.

In "Every Breath You Take" (1983), a beautiful ballad and the Police's biggest hit, there is a merger of sorts between punk and reggae. The rhythmic feel is the saturated eight-beat timekeeping of punk. The reggae influence is much less direct. It's suggested in the slower tempo, soft dynamic level, the clipped attacks, and the moving guitar line, all of which lighten the sound considerably.

Other ballads from the early and mid-eighties use reggae rhythm more obviously. Cyndi Lauper's "Time After Time" (1983), Tina Turner's "What's Love Got to Do with It" (1984), and the Cars' "Drive" (1985) all show how reggae rhythm was at the root of a new kind of pop ballad.

A comparison of Cyndi Lauper's "Time after Time" and Tina Turner's "What's Love Got to Do with It" shows both the range of this new ballad style and its reggae-inspired backdrop. The two songs offer sharply different takes on love. "Time after Time" is guardedly hopeful, and Lauper's singing sounds as young and wide-eyed as her look. Turner's song, and her singing, project an embittered, even cynical, emotional stance, forged during years—decades—of disappointment in love. Despite the emotional difference between the songs, the setting is much the same: slow tempo, sustained synth chords, synth obbligatos, reggae-inspired offbeat rhythms (the rebound rhythm in "What's Love Got to Do with It" is in the background, but quite distinct), and a free-roaming bass.

These two songs show how the boundary between black and white music was erased in the eighties. Recall the discussion at the end of Chapter 8, where it was noted that the differences between black and white went well beyond such obvious features as vocal style: it was also evident in such features as the rhythmic texture and the most prominent rhythm instruments (guitar vs. bass). Here, there is a clear difference between Turner's singing, which is obviously black, and Lauper's, which is obviously white. But the setting is "race neutral": the same basic sound works for both equally well.

As in "Every Breath You Take," the influence of reggae in the Cars' "Drive" has more to do with the overall rhythmic feel of the song than reggae's specific offbeat rhythm. However, the basic elements of the ballad sound are still there: light, high-pitched fast-moving rhythms, a bass line that does not mark the beat, synth melodic figures, and sustained synth chords.

The use of synths in place of strings is characteristic of this new ballad sound. There is an obvious reason for the substitution: a single musician can take the place of several, thus reducing costs. But there also seems to be an expressive dimension as well. The last three songs talk about love with reservation or regret. Perhaps the emotionally gray synth sound is more appropriate for the mood of the song than a warmer string sound would be.

Even though none of the artists were affiliated with Motown Records, the new ballad style that they exemplify extends the Motown legacy in still another direction. One of the great Motown achievements was floating the melodies of love songs on buoyant rhythms. This was achieved by freeing up the bass, marking faster-than-beat rhythms lightly, and presenting the harmony with some delicacy. The reggae-inspired rhythms and textures of these eighties songs follow the same plan, only more so, and get the same result. Such a sound was possible only in the eighties, after the textural possibilities of the new sixteen-beat rhythms had been thoroughly assimilated.

Summary

There is an uncanny resemblance between funk, disco, and the new middle ground, and the early years of rock. Funk had its counterpart in the jump bands and, even more, the loose-jointed sound of New Orleans R&B. All were rhythm-oriented styles. The songs were usually about good times, and they often had salacious lyrics. Further, none of the styles crossed over to any great extent.

Disco, like rock and roll, was a black-derived dance music that introduced—or at least popularized—a new beat. And both were racially integrated styles. Alternative forms of the new beat came from outside the U.S.-U.K. axis: Afro-Cuban and Brazilian music helped shape a more complex alternative to rock rhythm in the late fifties and early sixties; reggae helped shape a gentler, more complex variant of sixteen-beat rhythms. And just as the Beatles and the Motown acts best exemplified rock-based pop in the mid-sixties, so did Michael Jackson, Prince, Madonna, et al.

Of course, there are numerous differences as well. Here are some of the most crucial. The new styles of the seventies emerged *within* the prevailing style—rock—rather than in opposition to it. Further, there was no counterpart to punk: an intense, rebellious, musically reactionary version of the prevailing style. Racial and sexual attitudes were much less confining: Madonna or Prince would not have gotten any airplay in the sixties without cleaning up their acts. Disco and the middle ground pop of the eighties went far beyond the "equal opportunity" of the sixties, best symbolized by Motown's ascendancy. Both were, for all intents and purposes, racially neutral styles. And, finally, the popular music landscape was far more fragmented in the eighties than it was in the sixties. The next two chapters consider some of the important alternatives to eighties pop.

K E Y   T E R M S

Funk	**Disco**	**New middle ground**
Bridge	**Four-on-the-floor/sixteen-beat rhythm**	**Public persona**
Groove		

C H A P T E R   Q U E S T I O N S

1. Listen to "Stomp," noting the shift between disco and funk-style sections. Then sharpen your understanding of the differences between the two by considering the common features between "Up for the Down Stroke" and the funk section, and the common ground between the disco section and "Le Freak."

2. In terms of marking the beat, "Bad Girls" and "What's Love Got to Do with It" are polar opposites. React to the suggestion in the book that the storytelling in "Bad Girls" is hampered by the strong beatkeeping. Do you agree or disagree? Do you think it's possible to tell a good story in music with such a dance- oriented musical setting? Why or Why not?

3. Explore the idea that the music of Earth, Wind, and Fire is both a synthesis and expansion of black pop and soul/funk in the late sixties and early seventies. What

evidence is there of this in "Serpentine Fire" or in other EWF songs? Are you convinced?

4. Take one of these positions: a. I like Michael Jackson's music more than Prince's; b. I like Prince's music more than MJ's. c. I don't like either one. d. I like them both equally. Support your position by giving your impression of two songs by each artist.

5. Trace black pop from early doo-wop through Motown and PI to the songs by Lionel Richie and Tina Turner. Do you feel that the later songs and their settings are more sophisticated? Justify your opinion by referring to the words and music. In particular, explore two ideas: that the musical setting for romantic song had become racially neutral; and that the reggae-inspired settings continue the liberation from the strong timekeeping first observed in Motown.

chapter 17

Old Wine, New Bottles

Rock in the Eighties

The early eighties saw the dawning of a new age in rock music. It had little to do with Aquarius: as the beginning of the decade, rock was much more about money than love, and nothing was free. Instead, it had much more to do with the arrival of a new generation of musicians, playing a new kind of music.

The top artists of the decade were almost exclusively musicians whose careers had begun—or at least taken off—after 1974: Springsteen, U2, Talking Heads, Prince, Madonna, and Van Halen. Sixties stars such as Bob Dylan, Paul McCartney, and Eric Clapton assumed the role of elder statespersons. Many of the seventies stars essentially reinvented themselves, often as solo artists: Michael Jackson, above all, but also David Bowie, Don Henley of the Eagles, Phil Collins and Peter Gabriel of Genesis, Steve Winwood of Traffic, and Ozzy Osbourne of Black Sabbath. Indeed, heavy metal essentially reinvented itself: only the distortion remained the same.

Like the middle ground music discussed in Chapter 16, the new rock of the early eighties converted the energy of punk and disco into a kaleidoscopic new sound world. Virtually all of it revealed the impact of the new digital technology. The sonic spaciousness of U2's music, the fresh palette of synth sounds, and, most pervasively, rich, subtly-layered textures: all showed the impact of digital-based sound generation and processing.

In the early eighties, the unenhanced two guitar/bass/drums rock band was a truly retro sound, but it was neither gone nor forgotten. Indeed, by mid-decade, it was an increasingly popular alternative. Among the major new trends of the late eighties was a neo-traditional movement. The movement had several dimensions. It spawned an "alternative" style, based on what rock used to be. In addition, it revitalized careers of rock stars from the sixties and early seventies and breathed new life into older styles, most notably the blues and Dylanesque "statement songs."

These styles emerged or returned in counterpoint to the pop middle ground discussed in Chapter 16. Since rock became the dominant popular music in the sixties, it had not been one style, but several, as we have seen. However, the musical landscape had never been as fragmented as it was in the eighties. There may have been a middle ground, but there was no mainstream.

Perhaps the most flagrant example of the pure-profit mentality of the music industry was the CD. From the start, CDs cost about twice as much as cassettes or vinyl, still a widely used recording medium in the early eighties. Initially, this high price reflected not only the novelty of CDs and their superior sound and durability, but also the relatively high costs of production. Pressing plants routinely threw away large numbers of defective CDs. However, the price of CDs has remained higher than cassettes, even though production is much more efficient and materials less expensive: Blank CDs now retail for as little as 79¢, much less than blank cassettes.

Rock of Significance

In 1984, U2 bassist Adam Clayton performed on the Band Aid single, "Do They Know It's Christmas?" The project, undertaken to raise money for famine victims in Ethiopia, triggered a series of fundraising events. Among them were an all-star recording session organized by Quincy Jones after the 1984 Grammy Awards gala that produced the USA for Africa single/album/video "We Are the World," and the 1985 mega-event Live Aid. Live Aid, an all-star concert from two venues—London and Philadelphia—that was broadcast around the world, raised over $40 million, also for victims of the Ethiopian famine. Farm Aid and tours for Amnesty International followed later in the decade. Rock had rediscovered its conscience.

The big stars of Live Aid were U2. Their appearance and the success of their 1987 album *Joshua Tree* cemented their reputation as *the* band of the eighties, a distinction conferred on them by *Rolling Stone* in 1985. The only other act of comparable stature was Bruce Springsteen. Springsteen's social activism predated U2's: he had participated in a benefit concert sponsored by MUSE (Musicians United for Safe Energy) in 1979, had performed a series of six benefit concerts for Vietnam veterans in 1981, and was one of the voices on "We Are the World."

Springsteen and U2 were linked by more than their willingness to participate in fundraising events and their overwhelming critical acclaim and popularity. Both acts were willing to confront difficult social issues in their music, and both created powerful and direct musical languages to get their message across. Together, they epitomized a return to rock of significance: rock with something meaningful to say and with the musical means to make it sound important.

Bruce Springsteen

In 1974, critic Jon Landau wrote of Bruce Springsteen, "I saw rock and roll's future and its name is Bruce Springsteen." Landau knew a good thing when he saw it; soon after, he became Springsteen's manager. In the seventies, especially after "Born to Run," Springsteen attracted a loyal if not large following. With *Born in the U.S.A.* (1984), which sold well over 10 million units, he became a dominant figure in rock.

From the start, Springsteen has not been afraid to speak his mind. His music is not deliberately provocative, like punk, or weird, clever, or pandering to popular taste. In the words of Howard Cosell, Springsteen simply "tells it

Bruce Springsteen on stage, October 13, 1986. PHOTO COURTESY CORBIS/NEAL PRESTON.

like it is." Moreover, he sings his music with an emotional commitment that few artists have matched. His messages resonated with a large audience; for many, he was a real working-class hero.

Springsteen's two "born" songs, "Born to Run" (1975) and "Born in the U.S.A." (1984), show that the power of his songs lies in both words and music. His lyrics are slices of life often set in and around his hometown of Asbury Park, New Jersey. His music is about as subtle as a sledgehammer, yet sophisticated in subtle details that enrich its sound world.

While not part of the CBGB clique, Springsteen was aware of the underground rock scene in New York. (He would write "Because the Night" for Patti Smith.) In "Born to Run," the rhythmic drive that would soon become punk's trademark is already present. Here, however, it is used within a big rock conception, rather than the leaner sound of the CBGB groups.

The first twelve seconds of "Born to Run" are a window into Springsteen's popular style. The song begins with a double-time drum flourish, and immediately settles into the saturated eight-beat rhythm that would typify punk and new wave: most of the band, from the bass to the high keyboard, are laying down a driving rock beat. Over this is a simple, if lengthy, guitar riff. However, Springsteen echoes the guitar riff with a chime-like sound and thickens the texture with a saxophone line.

The most prominent features of the opening are simple and direct—and powerful because of that. The beat comes at the listener like a freight train; we hear lots of timekeeping and little syncopation. And the riff is easily remembered. Coloring this basic rock conception are more subtle details: the high-range timekeeping in the keyboard, the chimes doubling the guitar. This mixture of simple, powerful rhythms and riffs with sophisticated "orchestration" is one key to Springsteen's sound.

The rest of the song confirms this opening impression. In the verse, Springsteen sets his lyric to a simple melodic idea, supported by basic three-chord harmony and a stripped-down rock beat. But the transition to the title phrase floats the beat (the bass gives up on its relentless rock beat until the hook), introduces more complex chords, and surrounds the vocal line with a sonic halo—an array of high, tinkling sounds. The contrasting vocal line and instrumental interlude after the saxophone solo are more of the same: a pile-driving beat and simple two-note riffs, followed by a serpentine crawl through a series of chords far removed from I, IV, and V. The mix of simplicity and sophistication is simply happening on a grander scale.

A drawn-out legal battle involving Landau and Springsteen's first producer, Mike Appel, kept Springsteen out of the studios for about three years. He returned with a string of critically acclaimed and mildly popular albums: *Darkness on the Edge of Town* (1978), *The River* (1980), and the acoustic *Nebraska* (1982). He finally broke through to a mass audience in 1984 with *Born in the U.S.A.*

The title track of *Born in the U.S.A.* again mixes a strong story line, simple riffs and rhythms, and subtle details. The song tells the story of a Vietnam veteran through powerful, almost posterized images: "sent me off to a foreign land/to go and kill the yellow man." Musically, it is at the same time more direct in its power and more sophisticated in its setting than "Born to Run." It begins with a simple instrumental riff and a heavy backbeat. The riff eventually becomes the title phrase—"Born in the U.S.A."—but it runs through the song like a mantra, even while Springsteen narrates his story. A heavy backbeat—the fundamental rhythmic element of all popular music—also persists through the entire song. Subtle details strengthen both the backbeat and the riff: there is electronic enhancement of the backbeat, so that it sounds uncomfortably close to a rifle shot; and the doubling of the riff with a high piano line. The other instruments layer in and out of the song, but the riff and backbeat are constants—even through Max Weinberg's "war zone" drum solo.

The relative economy of materials creates a spacious, clear texture: high riff, mid range vocal, bass and drums at times. Precisely because of this, "Born in the U.S.A." *sounds* big, and important. The prominence and persistence of the riff and the backbeat give the song enormous power, in support of Springsteen's trenchant lyric.

U2

Springsteen's European counterpart was the Irish band U2. Like Springsteen, they tackled social and political issues close to home. And like Springsteen, they cultivated a big sound to serve as a backdrop for the message in the lyrics.

There are clear differences, however. Bono's voice is more Irish bard than workingman's blues singer; it is not nearly as gritty as Springsteen's. U2's songs are more melodic; they have overtones of Irish folk music. The preferred beat is not a rock beat, but a synthesis of punk's hard edge and eight-beat bass and disco's steady sixteen-beat rhythm in guitar and drums. And the band creates a roomful of sound with a different strategy: active drums and guitar lines, instead of riffs. However, the overall effect is much the same: a potent message encased in a powerful musical setting.

U2's remarkably stable lineup comprises lead vocalist/guitarist Bono (Vox) (born Paul Hewson), guitarist/keyboardist The Edge (born David Evans), bassist Adam Clayton, and drummer Larry Mullen. U2 was formed in 1978. In their first two albums, *Boy* (1980) and *October* (1981), the group addressed personal issues, among them relationships and their faith. Beginning with *War* (1983), their music took on a more political and social cast. "Sunday Bloody

Sunday" (1983), for example, recounts an especially bloody incident in the ongoing strife between Catholics and Protestants in Northern Ireland. By 1985, *Rolling Stone*, had dubbed them the band of the eighties, but it wasn't until *Joshua Tree* (1987) that they achieved the overwhelming commercial success to match their critical acclaim.

A quick tour through four of their songs will show the defining features of their sound and the way it evolved through the eighties. In "Gloria" (1981) the band sets up Bono's vocal with a four-strand texture, separated into low, middle, and high:

- repeated notes at eight-beat speed in the bass and beat-keeping on the bass drum (low)
- a rock beat on the sock cymbal (mid range)
- an angular guitar line, also moving at eight-beat speed (high)

The sound is a sharp contrast from typical low- or mid-range rock guitar riffs, such as the opening of "Born to Run," or, for that matter, "Walk This Way."

This instrumental texture covers a wide registral span, with high-speed, high-pitched guitar figures, insistent drum patterns, and a strong bass. There is strong reinforcement of both the beat and an eight-beat rhythm, with very little syncopation—mostly in the irregular accents of The Edge's guitar line.

The resulting texture is both spacious and assertive. In the chorus, the bassist stops his persistent timekeeping, the drummer shifts to a disco-derived sixteen-beat rhythm, and the guitarist plays a less relentless line filled with harmonics, which explore an even higher register. It is a beautiful backdrop for Bono's choir-boy–like singing of the title word, "Gloria"; the rich reverberation evokes the resonance of a cathedral.

U2 in a posed, group shot, March 9, 1982. Photo courtesy CORBIS/Neal Preston.

During an extended instrumental interlude beginning around two minutes, 20 seconds, the eight-beat bass is combined with the sixteen-beat drums and choked guitar: this trademark sound supports a slow-moving guitar solo. The "open" sound that results from the registral spacing of the instruments and the prominent timekeeping at beat, eight-beat, and sixteen-beat levels are two trademarks of U2's sound.

"Sunday Bloody Sunday" is more programmatic. The opening drum figure overlays a disco beat with periodic raps on the snare drum, which simulate the sound of gunfire. Perhaps because of the darker mood of the song, The Edge's guitar figure is in mid range instead of the more typical high register. This allows Bono's vocal line to soar over the top of it, although synthesizer lines and electric violin—the latter again suggesting U2's Celtic roots—fill in the higher registers. The bass line consists mainly of bursts of notes, rather than a steady rhythm. This too suggests gunfire. As with Springsteen, the power of the songs comes from the combined impact of the words ("broken bottles under children's feet") and the rhythmically straightforward yet evocative instrumental accompaniment.

Beginning with *The Unforgettable Fire*, U2 engaged Brian Eno to co-produce their albums. He collaborated with them on four albums in the eighties and early nineties, including their megahit, *Joshua Tree*. With his input, their spacious sound became even more "symphonic." For example, in "Pride (in the Name of Love)" (1984), The Edge's guitar part becomes a minimalist guitar pattern—more than a chord, less than a line. This is supported by another choked guitar pattern; both move at sixteen-beat speed. With the addition of the bass and drums and a considerable amount of reverb, the group sounds as massive as a forty piece orchestra. Their sound is not so much loud, as full. The quick-moving rhythms blend into a blur of sound, much like the spokes on a wagon wheel blur into a seemingly solid form. All of this supports Bono's impassioned vocal line.

Eno's influence is even more apparent in "Where the Streets Have No Name" (1987), from *Joshua Tree*. The melody of "Where the Streets Have No Name" is simpler that those of the earlier examples; stripped of its sonic environment, it could perhaps pass for a Woody Guthrie song. Two fast-moving, subtly changing guitar lines create a kind of surround-sound context for the melody. In this song, however, the group's active texture is in turn enveloped by remnants of the "Hearts of Space" synthesizer sounds that open the song. The result is a slow-moving melody, encased in fast-moving accompaniment from the ground, which is in turn encased in slow synthesizer sounds. All of this gives U2's sound even more depth and richness.

Beyond Punk: New and New/Old Rock

Punk had sprung up in opposition to mainstream rock, but the rift between them quickly closed. There was no better evidence of this reconciliation than the bright new punk-tinged sound of groups such as the (appropriately-named) Go-Gos, which was nevertheless almost anti-punk in spirit. More traditional rock also flourished, both in the recycling of "rock and roll" and in new takes on older styles, as in the music of Dire Straits and Tom Petty.

We Got the Beat

Rock got a "beatlift" around 1980. The new sound was lean, clean, vibrant, and colored with an array of synthesizer timbres and effects. It harnessed the energy of punk, but its most direct antecedent was the music of David Bowie, himself one of punk's seminal influences. From these sources, it distilled a purer form of rock rhythm, typically spread throughout the texture, from bass and kick drum to high-pitched percussion and synth parts. Its leanness and cleanness came in large part from an open-sounding mid range: crisp single-note lines and sustained chords replaced thick guitar chords and riffs.

Bowie himself was a major contributor to this new sound. So were new wave artists such as Elvis Costello, Blondie, the Pretenders, Talking Heads, Devo, and the B-52s. However, there were also groups that had neither punk's rage nor new wave's weirdness.

The Go-Go's "We Got the Beat" (1981) could easily be the signature song of this new rock sound. Like a typical Ramones' song, it has a simple lyric, mostly the repeated title phrase. And it has punk's saturated eight-beat rhythmic texture: not only in the drum part, but also in repeated notes and chords from top (high piano chords) to bottom (bass and low guitar). But the spirit of the song is completely different: it is almost mindlessly happy—much closer to fities rock and roll than it is to punk or new wave. However, the rhythmic approach clearly places it in the eighties.

So does the makeup of the band. The Go-Go's were among the first of the all-girl rock groups. "We Got the Beat" also shows how the point of punk's rhythmic innovation (saturated eight-beat timekeeping) had been turned completely on its head within five years. In the Sex Pistols' music, the rhythm was aggressive and confrontational. Here it's simply bouncy: after all, lead singer Belinda Carlisle had been a cheerleader in high school. It's as if someone put a yellow smiley face on Johnny Rotten.

This new sound also filtered into the music of such diverse groups as Roxy Music and Van Halen. Van Halen's "Jump" (1983) shows how quickly it had become common currency. Van Halen had been considered one of the major new heavy metal bands, largely because of Eddie Van Halen's guitar wizardry. But "Jump" is not a metal song; Van Halen's solo is just a teaser, a hint of what he's capable of. For most of the song, including the opening signature riff, synths rule: they provide most of the accompaniment for David Lee Roth's vocal, including the repeated note, eight-beat bass line that is the calling card of this new rock sound. Like "We Got the Beat," this is a good-humored song; we can almost see Roth smirking as he sings the song.

A diverse group of acts emerging after 1980 also hopped on this new sonic bandwagon. Among them were the Eurythmics, Cyndi Lauper, and the Smiths. There was plenty of room for variation within this basic approach, as the roster of acts cited above implies. Yet the music sounds distinctly different from almost all of the music of the seventies and before, mainly because of the livelier, cleaner rhythmic textures and the expanded sound palette created by the new synth timbres.

Rock and Roll Forever—Continued

Old-time rock (and roll) continued to flourish in numerous forms. The Rolling Stones breathed life into their career in the early eighties, while boogie bands such as ZZ Top kept trucking along. Also, many newer rock acts such as John Cougar Mellencamp, Tom Petty and the Heartbreakers, and Dire Straits strengthened their toehold in the market. Flashing back to an even more distant past was a rockabilly revival led by the Stray Cats.

JOHN MELLENCAMP Among the newer rock acts, John Mellencamp was perhaps the most down-to-earth—literally. "Rain on the Scarecrow" (1986), one of his most powerful songs, tells the plight of the small time farmer through a tale about a family that's losing its farm. So it's not surprising that Mellencamp was one of the main forces behind the Farm Aid benefits.

Mellencamp was known as John Cougar at the beginning of his career ("Cougar" was his first manager's invention; Mellencamp learned about it only after seeing the name on the cover of his debut album.). He began his career in the mid-seventies, but it didn't take off until the early eighties. His breakthrough album was *American Fool* (1982), which included the No. 1 single, "Jack and Diane."

The song places him squarely in the American rock and roll tradition: he tells a great story, and the song rocks—at least in the instrumental sections. There are numerous nice touches. The boldest is the use of an instrumental section, with both guitar and keyboard hooks, to frame the vocal sections of the song. The narrative sections of the song have a reduced accompaniment, mainly acoustic guitar, so that Mellencamp's morality play can be clearly heard.

Perhaps the most original touch is the Greek chorus effect that begins around two-and-a-half minutes. Here, singers in harmony, accompanied only by drums, emphasize the main point of the song: Kids may have to grow up very quickly. (There are certainly autobiographical overtones: Mellencamp eloped with his girlfriend, who was pregnant, when he was seventeen.)

Mellencamp's 1987 hit, "Paper in Fire," shows even more clearly his connection with, and expansion of, the American rock and roll tradition exemplified by Creedence Clearwater Revival, the Grateful Dead, and the Band. As in "Jack and Diane," Mellencamp encases an excellent story, which unfolds slowly and suspensefully, in a well-grooved rock and roll setting. Through the instrumentation of the song, Mellencamp deepens the country/blues fusion that typified the "American" sound, around 1970. Among the backup instruments are a banjo (bluegrass), slide guitar (deep blues), and accordion (Zydeco).

A mid-nineties incarnation of Mellencamp's backup band made this fusion even more obvious: it included a fiddle player, two auxiliary percussionists, one of whom is black, and a black keyboard player; both black musicians also serve as backup singers.

TOM PETTY Another major American rock and roller was Tom Petty. His "Stop Draggin' My Heart Around" (1981) is a splendid example of an eighties' take on straight-ahead rock and roll. The song features Stevie Nicks, on sabbatical from Fleetwood Mac (she also recorded a solo album around this time). Her singing here—nasal, with both black and country overtones—is the right sound for the bitter tone of the lyric and the melancholy mood of the song, which Petty's lonesome guitar solo helps establish. There are echoes of the Who in the opening and Southern rock in the use of the organ, which complements the soulfulness of Nicks's singing. The song is essentially timeless: apart from the high quality of the recording, it could have appeared any time after 1973.

Petty had built his career firmly on the music of the sixties. "Refugee" (1979) clearly shows the influence of Bob Dylan in the lyric and his singing of it. However, the instrumental backup, with its prominent organ, is a much

Tom Petty on stage,
October 13, 1986. PHOTO
COURTESY *CORBIS/NEAL*
PRESTON.

fuller sound than Dylan typically used. Moreover, Petty was more than an accomplished retro-rocker: "Don't Come Around Here No More" (1985) shows him combining sitar-like sounds (shades of the Beatles) with contemporary electronic percussion sounds.

OTHER NEO-TRADITIONALISTS   Among the most imaginative of the traditionally oriented bands was Dire Straits, an English/Scottish band led by lead vocalist and guitarist Mark Knopfler, who also wrote most of their music. Their best songs combined great stories with impeccable musicianship, a good groove, and Knopfler's expressive guitar playing. "Sultans of Swing" (1978), their first U.S. hit, combines a Dylan-like account of a New Orleans jazz band, sung in a Dylanesque style, with a clean Bowie-ish accompaniment. (The use of rock rhythm effectively distances the narrator from the subject). Their 1985 hit, "Walk of Life," is at once more contemporary and more retro. Instead of mixing sixties and seventies influences, it combines eighties synth sounds with the feel of fifties rock and roll.

The neo-traditional music of John Cougar Mellencamp, Tom Petty, and Dire Straits, with its deep roots in the music of the sixties and early seventies, anticipated the return of so many major acts of the sixties. In fact, Petty himself joined Dylan's Traveling Wilburys. The group, which also included Roy Orbison, George Harrison, and Jeff Lynne, epitomized the rock audience's newfound reverence for its past.

Solo Acts

Among the most distinctive voices of the eighties were two U.K. artists, Peter Gabriel and Sting. Both had begun their careers as members of major acts. Gabriel was the driving force behind Genesis in the early seventies. During his tenure, they were an art-rock band. (After Gabriel left and Phil Collins took over his role of lead vocalist and songwriter, their music became more pop-oriented.) Sting (Gordon Sumner) was a founding member of the Police; he dissolved the group in the mid-eighties to pursue a solo career. Both created high-class, pop-related—and often popular—music. Their music was distinguished by a higher level of discourse about love and relationships than was typical of pop. And both infused their music with non-pop influences. Gabriel incorporated African and Far Eastern influences into his music, while Sting, who had begun his career as a jazz bassist, came full circle in the mid-eighties by including top jazz musicians in his band.

PETER GABRIEL Gabriel's solo career, which began in 1975, got underway slowly—at least in terms of pop success. His first four albums, all entitled *Peter Gabriel*, met with only modest success; he began to chart only in the early eighties. In 1982, he sponsored the World of Music, Art, and Dance Festival, which included arts from Africa and the Far East. Gabriel spearheaded the movement to bring regional musics, especially from Africa, to the attention of Western audiences.

"World beat" influences suffuse *So* (1986), his most successful album. Among the guest artists on the album are African and Brazilian percussionists and Senegalese vocalist Youssou N'Dour. "Sledgehammer," the most successful song on the album, is the least representative of Gabriel's work during this period. The lyric harks back to the "manly man" posturing often heard in deep blues and soul music; the horn section and the great groove reinforce the soul connection. Only the warbly Asian flute sound at the beginning suggests Gabriel's world music interest. The song's huge success was undoubtedly helped by the incredibly innovative video made to promote it; it remains one of the greatest music videos ever made.

More typical of Gabriel's blend of sophisticated pop and world music is "In Your Eyes." In its synth-rich texture and dense, active percussion, the song certainly is in step with the eighties pop of Madonna and Prince. However, the lyric talks about an almost spiritual love—a far cry from Prince's "I Want Your Sex." And it unfolds on a much grander scale: A single statement of the form takes over two minutes. Each of the three main sections of the form—verse, bridge, and chorus—is clearly defined by a pronounced change in accompaniment; this also contributes to the impression of grandness. The world beat influence is subtly evident in the percussion sounds (including a talking drum) woven into the texture, and much more obviously in Youssou N'Dour's vocal, which soars above an African-tinged rhythmic groove, beginning around four-and-a-half minutes.

STING Just as Gabriel colored his music with African sounds to create a unique style, so did Sting infuse his music with jazz elements to create his own sound. After dissolving the Police, he fronted a band that included jazz saxophonist Branford Marsalis and percussionist Omar Hakim. And like Gabriel, he wove the outside elements seamlessly into a sophisticated pop-related style; they are evident but not dominant.

In his 1985 hit, "If You Love Somebody, Set Them Free," the influence of jazz is evident in the shifting harmonies, especially from the verse to the bridge and from the chorus to a striking contrasting section, subtle shifts in rhythm, and Marsalis's fills. As in "In Your Eyes," the form is expansive. There is a strong hook—the reiteration of the end of the title phrase by the backup vocalists—but there is more than the simple verse/chorus form, repeated again and again. The lyric, which urges liberation instead of possession, advocates a noble view of love. Although the musical result is quite different because of the jazz influence, the underlying similarity in approach between Sting and Gabriel is striking.

Heavy Metal

Heavy metal, such a powerful force in rock during the early seventies, seemed to be merely a cartoonish parody of itself by mid-decade. The most visible metal band was Kiss, who all but made their reputation on their clownish makeup and over-the-top stage show. However, metal didn't go away, it simply went on the road.

Although dismissed or ignored by rock critics—Lester Bangs pronounced it all but dead in the late seventies—heavy metal developed a loyal and steadily increasing fan base through the late seventies and eighties through frequent touring. Fans packed arenas to hear their favorite bands, bought their recordings, and kept up to date through fanzines. Exposure on radio and MTV was minimal, especially early in the decade.

By the end of the decade, it was clear that heavy metal was the most popular genre in a heavily segmented rock marketplace. To cite just one piece of evidence, Guns N' Roses' debut album, *Appetite for Destruction* (1987), sold over 10 million units. Numerous other metal bands, among them Van Halen, Def Leppard, Metallica, and Living Colour, also racked up platinum/ multi-platinum record sales.

Teen and post-teen males made up most of heavy metal's fan base. In the wake of the economic hard times in both the United Kingdom and United States, many faced a bleak future. They felt out of the loop, especially during the eighties, when the gap between rich and poor widened so dramatically. They responded to the recurrent themes in heavy metal: the occult, sexual dominance (often to the point of misogyny), rage, frustration, protest, and—above all—power. Band names tell the story: Megadeth, AC/DC, Motörhead, Judas Priest, Iron Maiden, Twisted Sister, Scorpions—all worthy sequels to the original: Black Sabbath.

And it was the music above all that conveyed the power. Most characteristically, it was loud to the point where a listener *felt* it as much as heard it. Moreover, the sound was heavily distorted, a sign both of power (distortion originally came from overdriving amplifiers) and defiance (distortion was originally an undesirable by-product of amplification, to be avoided if possible).

Performances were a communion between musicians and their audience. Bands preached to the converted. Fans knew the words to songs, even though they were often unintelligible (they learned the lyrics from record jackets). Stage shows were typically spectacles on a grand scale, comparable to an elaborate pagan ritual. In response, metalheads engaged in headbanging, heavy metal's version of dancing. In the familiarity of the audience/congregation with the songs, in their involvement in the performance, and in the sense of power which they experienced during the event, a heavy metal concert was more like a religious rite than anything else.

All of this occurred outside the purview of the mainstream media. Few "unconverted" listeners were willing to go past the distortion, the lyrics, and the visual images. The music, and what it stood for, was almost universally misunderstood and underappreciated. Those who attended the symphony would probably have been horrified to learn of the wholescale expropriation of classical music by metal guitarists such as Eddie Van Halen, Randy Rhoads, Yngwie Malmsteen, James Hetfield, and Dave Mustaine. They might well be scandalized at the suggestion that Eddie Van Halen expanded the sound possibilities and raised the level of virtuosity on his instrument more than any performer in any genre—classical, jazz, rock, or country—since the "diabolical" nineteenth-century violinist Niccolo Paganini and his pianist counterpart, Franz Liszt. For the most part, heavy metal remains insulated in its own world: the bands and their fans.

Van Halen's self-titled debut album (1978) signaled the beginning of a new era in heavy metal. It paid homage to heavy metal's roots, pointed out several new directions, and raised the standard of performance significantly. Two cover songs flash back to heavy metal's roots. "Ice Cream Man" is a braggart's blues, an ideal vehicle for David Lee Roth's swaggering, sneering vocal style. The other is the Kinks' "You Really Got Me," at once a homage to this seminal proto-metal band and a measure of how quickly metal had evolved. The use of heavy distortion, the rhythmic assurance of the band, and especially Eddie Van Halen's guitar breaks and solo, date the performance in 1978, not before.

"Eruption," a solo flight by Eddie Van Halen, is a minute-and-42-second treatise on contemporary rock guitar playing. It is a virtuoso performance, not only in the obvious technical dexterity, but also in the imaginative sound possibilities, including the tapping (at the very end) for which Van Halen became justly famous. It served notice that the rock guitar bar had been raised several notches. Through this single recording, Van Halen advanced rock guitar playing more than anyone since Hendrix.

The remainder of the album explores common themes in heavy metal music, especially the dark side, in both present and future tense ("Runnin' with the Devil," "Atomic Punk") and male dominance in the battle of the sexes ("Jamie's Cryin'," "Ain't Talkin' 'bout Love"). It also suggests the way in which heavy metal would interact with other styles. Although the distortion in Van Halen's opening riff certainly establishes his metal credentials, "Runnin' with the Devil" is, at heart, a pop song. It follows the typical verse/chorus pattern used in countless rock songs, and there is relatively little solo space for Van Halen. In this respect, it anticipates Van Halen's pop crossover, evidenced, as we have seen, by "Jump" and his appearance on *Thriller*. "Atomic Punk" fuses metal with—what else—punk. It too would be a widely followed path in the eighties. The last song, "On Fire," is the "purest" example of heavy metal style. It puts the spotlight squarely on Eddie Van Halen, both in solo sections and in the fills between vocal phrases.

In its use of heavy metal's recurrent themes (power, sexual domination, the occult, etc.), in its tribute to metal's antecedents, and in its presentation of metal both as a pure style and in various alloys, Van Halen bridged the gap between heavy metal's first generation and the metal bands of the eighties.

Van Halen, December 14, 1982. PHOTO COURTESY CORBIS/NEAL PRESTON.

Heavy metal was never a monolithic style, as we have seen, but in the eighties, it became even more diverse. Sub-styles, often based on a single feature, proliferated. By the end of the decade there was speed metal, thrash metal, death metal, industrial metal, and more. Its diversity was also due to its blending with other styles; during the eighties, heavy metal came in several grades of purity. Distortion remained metal's sound signature, but "pure" heavy metal was far more than a rock song played with distortion.

As evidenced in the music of top eighties bands such as Metallica and Megadeth, a heavy metal song is a far cry from standard rock, rhythm and blues, or pop fare. Here are some of the most striking differences:

1. Distortion is typically more extreme. Because it is the most easily borrowed feature of heavy metal style, serious metal bands compensated by increasing the distortion to the point that the notes being played may be almost impossible to discern because of the halo of white noise around them.

2. Instrumentation is basic: one or two guitars, bass, and drums. Use of additional instruments—synths, saxes, extra percussion—is a stylistic impurity, as we noted in the earlier discussion of Van Halen's "Jump."

3. It is not tuneful music. This is especially evident in the vocal line, which is typically more incantation than melody. The vocalist chants, wails, even spits out the words. He seldom sings a catchy melodic phrase.

4. The ratio of instrumental sections to vocal sections is much higher than in most other rock-based styles. In addition to extended solos, where the

lead guitarist shows off his prowess, there are also other long passages with no vocal lines. These typically consist of a series of intricate riffs.

5. In the tradition of Black Sabbath, it is not music that uses conventional harmony. Bands may play power chords, but complete harmonies and chord progressions are the exception rather than the rule. Instead, the music tends to be linear, with both solos and group riffs built on modes. Variety in pitch choice comes about through shifts from one mode to another, or by shifting the central tone of a mode. (It should be noted that the avoidance of conventional harmony in heavy metal is a choice, not a limitation. Numerous metal songs begin with delicate slow introductions; these often contain sophisticated harmony. Apparently, eighties metal bands, like their predecessors from the early seventies, felt that the use of standard or even alternative chord progressions would undermine the power of their music.)

6. The best metal bands are virtuosic: not only the guitarists who solo, but the entire band, who create and perform intricate riffs, often at breathtakingly fast tempos, with a level of precision comparable to a fine string quartet or jazz combo.

7. Metal "songs" tend to be long, sprawling, multi-sectional works. They avoid the standard verse/bridge/chorus formula of rock-era music. Instead, the work typically consists of blocks of sound, often in different tempos and with different key centers, all arranged in complex, unpredictable sequences.

A comparison of two heavy metal songs, Def Leppard's "Photograph" (1983) and Metallica's "One" (1988), shows the difference between heavy metal with a clear pop interface and heavy metal that is distinct from other rock styles.

Def Leppard, part of the new wave of British heavy metal bands, were stars from the start. Their 1980 debut album, *On Through the Night*, charted in both the United Kingdom and United States, and subsequent albums, most notably *Pyromania* (1983) and *Hysteria* (1987), went multiplatinum. They were photogenic, and MTV aired their music videos. The group was regarded as among the most wholesome heavy metal bands of the eighties (if "wholesome heavy metal" is not a contradiction). They were "The Heavy Metal Band You Can Bring Home to Mother," according to a *Goldmine* article.

"Photograph," one of the hits (and hit videos) from *Pyromania*, shows that the band's popularity is due to their music as well as their good looks. Essentially the song grafts heavy metal features onto a pop conception. The lyric is innocuous enough, at least by eighties standards, and the overall form of the song—verse/bridge/chorus with title phrase hook, with smooth harmonies under the hook—is designed to be as predictable and catchy as any Elton John song.

While Def Leppard, Van Halen, and Bon Jovi were bringing metal to the pop charts, Metallica was toiling in relatively obscurity. Formed in 1981, the group, formed by guitarist James Hetfield and drummer Lars Ulrich, built an ardent cult following during the eighties: Record sales were brisk, although the band got almost no exposure on radio or television. The group eventually broke through on radio in 1988 with "One," a single from . . . *And Justice for All*, which peaked at No. 6 on the charts.

Even a cursory listening to "One" shows that the market came to Metallica, not the other way around. "One" is a grim anti-war statement that unfolds on a large scale: The work is well over seven minutes long. It makes few concessions to pop, in lyrics, music, or length. The form of the work is multisectional.

0'00"	The chatter of machine guns and other war noises
0'19"	One guitar enters with a relatively subdued accompaniment
0'37"	Other guitar enters soloing over the accompaniment
0'53"	Drums enter
1'14"	Slightly louder variation of the accompaniment
1'30"	New flamenco-ish melody
1'45"	Singers enter with verse
2'11"	First metal sounds—just a hint—in chorus of this section
2'18"	Return to flamenco-ish melody
2'34"	Voices return with verse, then "metal" chorus
3'14"	Flamenco-ish melody plus high guitar obbligato
3'35"	Return to metalish-chorus
3'53"	Vocal line gives way to a new riff
4'19"	"Machine gun" rhythm, played by the drums, overlays riff
4'33"	"Machine gun" riff with power chords from the guitars
4'50"	New chanted vocal line, with lyric that recounts the horrors of war
5'20"	"Machine gun" instrumental section; double time feel in drums over "machine gun" riff
5'44"	Guitar solo heavily indebted to Baroque music (rapid arpeggiations, etc.)
6"36"	Guitar duet
7'02"	Return to machine gun riffs; shifts between tonal centers for the rest of the song
7'23"	Abrupt ending

The differences between "One" and "Photograph" are striking. With its teen-love lyric, easy-to-follow form, and frequent repetition of the vocal hook, "Photograph" accommodates the listener. By contrast, "One" challenges the listener. Its gritty message appears in spurts: the opening war sounds, the vocal sections (especially the second one), and the machine gun riff. The work is mainly instrumental, and even during the vocal sections, the guitar is at minimum an equal partner. There is relatively little repetition; in fact it is almost two quite different songs joined together at the hip.

In its sprawling form, relatively little emphasis on vocal lines, musical sophistication (e.g., there are several shifts from four-beat to three-beat measures; the first occurs around 1 minute, 15 seconds), and deep contrast from tender beginning to powerful conclusion, "One" demands a lot from its listeners. The music is as uncompromising and grim as its message.

Although "Photograph" and "One" are just a small sampling, we can still infer from them a great deal about heavy metal and its reception during that decade. Clearest, perhaps, is that music identified as heavy metal spanned a lot of stylistic territory. "Photograph" is mainstream rock with a great guitar

There are intriguing parallels between heavy metal in the eighties and another counterculture music: bebop. (Bebop was the avant-garde jazz of the forties, developed mainly by black musicians.) Both were true outsiders' music, supported initially by relatively small but loyal fan bases. Both challenged prevailing standards of appearance: metal stars' ratted hair, makeup, bare chests, tattoos, and the like were anticipated by the zoot suits of the bop hipsters. Both cultivated aggressive, confrontational sounds: the heavy distortion of metal bands has its parallel in the hard, penetrating sound of Charlie Parker's saxophone playing. Both required considerable technical skill to negotiate intricate solo and ensemble passages. Both borrowed heavily from classical music: the "sampling" of Baroque figuration by metal guitarists was preceded by the harmonic sophistication of bebop, which had its most direct precedents in the music of the French composers Debussy and Ravel. And both were largely misunderstood during their emergence.

riff and a good amount of distortion. "One," by contrast, is stylistically far removed from the other rock styles surveyed in this chapter; it is in many respects the most complex and challenging rock music of the decade.

Precisely because of its complexity, more mainstream critics and audiences may have dismissed heavy metal simply because they didn't understand it: it was not that the music was too simple, but rather that it was too sophisticated, despite its heavy artillery. The "pure" heavy metal music of Metallica and like-minded bands provides few of the musical cues that listeners (including critics) can latch onto.

Moreover, heavy metal confronts rather than comforts. So those who are not fans of metal may react to what they *can* easily understand: the visual spectacles, the words, the heavy distortion and ear-splitting volume, the fervor of the crowd. Too often, this was enough to turn them off, so they threw the baby out with the bathwater, so to speak. They didn't bother to listen beyond the distortion. They didn't recognize that metal musicians work diligently to develop their skills: after all, Eddie Van Halen and Randy Rhoads did not become virtuosi overnight.

No rock music of the eighties was less understood or less appreciated than heavy metal. However, even though critics and audiences may have scorned it early on, musicians didn't. Not only did it develop into one of the important directions of the late eighties and early nineties, it also bled into the exciting new fusions of the alternative bands that began to surface at the end of the decade.

Alternatives and Anachronisms: Neo-Traditional Trends in the Late Eighties

One of the most intriguing trends of the late eighties was a neo-traditional movement. On one level at least, it may simply have been a response to the political and social conservatism of the decade in both the United Kingdom

One sign of the reverence for rock's past was the establishment of the Rock and Roll Hall of Fame. The organization inducted its first class in 1986, and opened a spectacular museum in downtown Cleveland in 1993.

and the United States. More directly, it certainly reflected the aging of the children of the sixties. Those who had not trusted anyone over thirty were now in their late thirties or early forties; many had traded peace signs for pieces of property and ideals for deals.

But the movement was more than an exercise in nostalgia. In addition to the return—even the reunion—of major acts of the sixties and early seventies, there were two other developments that also turned back the clock. One was a revival of two styles that helped shape sixties rock: blues and social protest song. In both cases, the major players were younger musicians, rather than veterans of the fifties and sixties. The other development was a return to the clean two guitar/bass/drums sound of the sixties. It too was led by young talent, most notably R.E.M.

The Revival of Rock's Old Guard

A casual listener during the latter half of the eighties might have felt caught in a time warp. The Who and Led Zeppelin reunited specifically for the Live Aid benefit, and many of the stars who appeared in these benefits were revered celebrities, including Bob Dylan and Paul McCartney. The spirit of the occasion was "us for them," rather than the sixties attitude "us against them."

Other icons from the sixties and early seventies also charted. Some resurfaced as solo artists: Steve Winwood, Peter Gabriel, Don Henley, Robert Plant, Robbie Robertson, and Keith Richards all found success apart from the groups that had brought them to prominence. Others simply resumed their careers. The Grateful Dead charted a single for their first and only time in 1987, and Roy Orbison, Bob Dylan, Lou Reed, Bonnie Raitt, and Neil Young found new life and deepened respect.

Perhaps the most influential of the old guard was Neil Young, whose 1989 album *Freedom* showed that he had lost none of his fire. "Rockin' in the Free World," one of the important tracks from the album, juxtaposes scathing social commentary with his frenzied guitar playing, all backed by a pile-driving band. His indictment of President Bush, "We've got a thousand points of light for the homeless man," is set into relief by a spare accompaniment: only bass and drums. Young's mixture of searing words with powerful rock made him a model for the alternative bands of the nineties.

The resurgence of rock's old guard also brought long overdue recognition to Bonnie Raitt. Raitt's career had begun in the early seventies, after she dropped out of Radcliffe to play in the clubs around Boston. It included a long apprenticeship with blues musicians; their influence is evident in her singing and slide guitar playing. She had won the respect of musicians and a small group of fans for the sincerity and earthiness of her music, but didn't break through until 1989, when her album *Nick of Time* topped the charts and won several Grammys, including Album of the Year.

Part of her success was undoubtedly due to the then-current enthusiasm for old-time rock and roll. However, another crucial ingredient was her new partnership with producer Don Was. Was provided Raitt's straightforward songs of the heart and her bluesy, emotionally charged singing with sympathetic and imaginative backing. "Thing Called Love," one of the hits from *Nick of Time*, is a good example of their work together. The song travels one of rock's well-worn grooves—the vagaries of romance—but with some nice touches in the lyric (rhyming "Queen of Sheba" with "ain't no amoeba," for example). She delivers it in her rough-hewn, worldly voice, and interpolates some nice slide guitar licks.

Was supports her vocal with a hard shuffle beat, onto which he overlays reggae rhythms. It's most noticeable in the bass line and the emphasis on the reggae rebound pattern. The reggae connection becomes perfectly clear around two minutes, 28 seconds, when only bass, rhythm guitar, and percussion play. Was's fresh settings of Raitt's honest songs, with their familiar themes and forms, was a winning combination. Their subsequent collaborations have been almost as successful.

Revivals of Rock's Antecedents

Rock also revisited the early sixties by resurrecting two of rock's most influential antecedents, the blues and the socially conscious song. The blues revival that began in the mid-eighties gave a boost to the careers of established bluesmen and introduced new stars. Later in the decade, a new generation of socially aware female singer/songwriters would evoke the spirit of early Bob Dylan.

THE BLUES REVIVAL   The eighties blues revival brought new breadth to the blues. Blues' elder statesmen flourished: Albert Collins made a memorable appearance in the 1987 film *Adventures in Babysitting*, and Bonnie Raitt would team with John Lee Hooker to win a 1989 Grammy for best traditional blues recording.

However, it was the younger generation who stretched its boundaries. Its leaders were Stevie Ray Vaughan and Robert Cray. Both were true bluesmen: soulful singers and masterful guitarists. Both drew on two generations of the blues: not only the electric blues of the fifties, but also the blues/rock fusions of the late sixties and early seventies. (In fact, one of Vaughan's *tours de force* was a faithful cover of Jimi Hendrix's "Voodoo Child.")

Vaughan, who is white, was the more traditional of the two, although both strayed from traditional blues forms. Vaughan's "White Boots" (1990) is more good-time rock and roll than the blues, but "Ain't Gone 'n' Give up on Love" is basic blues, and a showcase for Vaughan's superb blues guitar.

Cray was truly a bluesman for the eighties. His songs capture the spirit and feel of the blues, yet they seldom use traditional blues forms or rhythms. In addition, he expanded the emotional range of the blues: Cray was a bluesman with a conscience. "Right Next Door (Because of Me)" revisits a timeless subject of blues songs, man/woman troubles. But Cray puts a different twist on it. He blames himself for the breakup of a couple's marriage because he couldn't help coming on to the wife. The musical setting also puts a contemporary spin on the sound of the blues. Cray's singing is authentic blues, and he has a blues band behind him. However, the song uses the verse/chorus form of rock-era song, rather than blues form, and the melody floats along on an active, sixteen-beat based rhythm.

In "Smoking Gun" (1986), Cray puts himself on the other side of the equation; here he's the victim, not the seducer. And again, the song has the sound and form of rock, not the blues. Still, in both songs (and in his other recordings), Cray's singing is direct and full of emotion, as only the blues can be. Like Vaughan, Cray was equally at home with more traditional blues, as he proved in recordings with B. B. King and other older bluesmen. But Cray, Vaughan, and other younger bluesmen once again stretched the boundaries of blues style without losing its core, just as an earlier generation had done in the sixties.

SINGER/SONGWRITERS REDUX Tracy Chapman was one of the surprise stars of the late eighties. Chapman might be considered the anti-Madonna: black, not white; inspired by white music, not black; plain, not glamorous; shy, not exhibitionistic; sincere, not slick; deep-voiced, not shrill. The opening of her 1988 song, "Talkin' Bout a Revolution," seems to turn the clock back a quarter century. Supported only by a simple guitar accompaniment, Chapman sings of revolution: it could be a coffeehouse in Greenwich Village in 1963 instead of a coffeehouse in Boston in 1988. (Chapman had been a student at Tufts University, just outside of Boston.)

The rest of the song brings us into the eighties: as the accompaniment fills out, it's clear that the production is more polished than the free-for-all that characterized Dylan's early electric music. But the background does nothing to obscure the urgency of her message. In the eighties, the income gap between rich and poor had widened considerably. Chapman's lyric shines a spotlight on the pervasive discontent among America's lower classes, which had been so blithely ignored by the Reagan administration.

Chapman's success was one more signal that rock, or at least an important segment of it, had reclaimed and updated the revolutionary spirit of the sixties. She and Suzanne Vega also inspired a new group of female singer/songwriters who created thoughtful, folk-inspired songs. Vega's breakthrough song "Luka" (1987) is a personal statement, not political. However, its subject, child abuse, is far from typical pop fare.

A Neo-Traditional Alternative

By the early eighties, the classic sixties rock band sound was an anachronism. By the end of the decade, it was an increasingly popular alternative. This neo-traditional trend achieved much the same result as the blues and socially aware singer/songwriter revival. It also reached back to the past—in this case, sixties rock—recapturing and updating the sound of the past.

R.E.M. started what would become the alternative movement with songs whose sound owed more to the Byrds than banks of synthesizers. The band, formed in 1980 by guitarist Peter Buck and vocalist Michael Stipe in Athens, Georgia, began as one of the numerous do-it-yourself groups that sprang up in punk's wake. They became the exemplars of the underground rock scene of the period, playing college bars and parties while waiting for their break.

Their early songs show the influence of new wave music. "Radio Free Europe" (1981), one of their first hits, has the bright tempo, clean rhythm, and lean sound associated with David Bowie and new wave bands. The lyric, by contrast, is as elliptical as the music is clear. The words are intelligible but what do they mean? By their own admission, the band has deliberately written non-specific lyrics. As Michael Stipe said in a late-eighties interview, " . . . I've always left myself pretty open to interpretation."

Their approach to lyric writing may not have changed much during the eighties, but their sound did. Around mid-decade, they devolved into a sound

R.E.M., 1984. Photo courtesy *CORBIS/S.I.N.*

that synthesized several sixties styles. In "The One I Love" (1987), their first top ten single, the dominant sound is a jangly Rickenbacker guitar sound that recalls the Byrd's Roger McGuinn. In addition, bass and drums lay down a basic sixties rock beat, and the Ventures-style guitar riff that opens the song returns between vocal sections. The overall effect is remarkable in its purity: except for the superior quality of the recording, it sounds straight out of the sixties. As in the earlier song, this straightforward setting contrasts with a rather epigrammatic lyric. The main point is clear enough, but there's no story to give it context.

R.E.M's music represented the most traditional alternative in what would become the alternative movement of the nineties. Other alternative bands would incorporate metal, funk, rap, and punk into their music. But R.E.M. was among the first. In their determination to follow their own creative path, even if it led back to the past instead of forward into the future, the group set the tone for the alternative movement. And the simplicity of their sound—basic instrumentation, clear textures, little if any electronic wizardry—was a model for the alternative bands that followed, even if they followed different musical paths.

Summary

If there is a common thread running through this chapter, it is that rock regained its sense of purpose in the eighties. After more than a decade in pursuit of market share and multiplatinum sales, many major rock acts returned to the values that had been so important during its formative years. Once again, rock had something to say.

U2, Springsteen, John Mellencamp, Metallica, Sting, Peter Gabriel, R.E.M., Tracy Chapman, Bonnie Raitt, Robert Cray, Neil Young: What unites these artists is a seriousness of purpose. They have found quite different ways of expressing it—there's some distance between Metallica and Bonnie Raitt, or U2 and Tracy Chapman. But none of their music is trivial. Some of it (e.g., Metallica's "One") is overtly political. Some of it explores interpersonal relationships with eyes wide open. But almost all of it challenges listeners instead of catering to them.

The artists presented their messages in music firmly grounded in the past, yet often innovative in subtle or not so subtle ways. R.E.M. flashed back to the sixties and Neil Young proclaimed that there would be "Rockin' in the Free World." With Brian Eno's help, U2 created a spacious new sound world; so did Metallica. But the roots of both build on rock's traditional elements. And all of it, even the most straightforward rock and roll, was beautifully produced.

Interestingly, almost all of these acts have been extremely active in social causes: many participated in Live Aid, Farm Aid, and other fundraising events. Even those who did not create music with an explicit social message still worked behind the scenes on matters important to them. R.E.M. let Greenpeace set up booths at their concerts; Bonnie Raitt set up the Rhythm and Blues Foundation to help early rhythm and blues musicians who had not profited from the success of their records.

Rock was now the culture, not the counterculture. It was no longer the dominant music of the era. The middle ground pop artists discussed in the previous chapter typically sold more records, got more airplay, and appeared more frequently on MTV. But rock regained its self-respect and renewed its sense of purpose. Instead of dropping out and dropping acid, the major acts of the eighties did something—speaking their mind, raising money, working for causes important to them. Both the music and the musicians had matured.

K E Y   T E R M S

Rock with a message	**Blues revival**	**Singer/songwriter revival**
Neo-traditionalist	**Heavy Metal**	**Alternative rock**

C H A P T E R   Q U E S T I O N S

1. Explore the evolution of U2's "symphonic" sound by studying the musical background in the four songs discussed in the text. Can you pinpoint differences from song to song? Can you hear the influence of Brian Eno in the last two songs?

2. Test this assumption: Heavy metal, as evidenced in the music of Metallica and other like-minded bands, was the most serious rock of the eighties. Compare both the lyrics and the musical setting of "One" (and any other metal songs you choose) to other music discussed in this chapter. What is your conclusion? Why?

3. Justify or challenge the suggestion in the text that Robert Cray is a "modern" bluesman. Consider both the content of the lyrics to his songs and the blues retentions—or lack of them in the music.

4. Compare Van Halen's "Eruption" and cover of "You Really Got Me" to "Voodoo Child" and the Kinks' original. Draw conclusions on both the relative virtuosity of Hendrix and Van Halen and the transformation of hard rock into heavy metal.

5. Study the changes in record production during the eighties by comparing recordings from this chapter to recordings from the sixties and seventies. What differences, if any, are obvious to you?

chapter 18

We Are the World

Rap, World Beat, and Alternative

In this chapter, we survey three of the most innovative new directions of the eighties: rap, world beat, and the multigenre fusion musics most often labeled "alternative."

All were "outside" styles. They sprang up in unlikely places, such as Guadaloupe, Seattle, and the South Bronx. And mass acceptance seemed to take second place to the message of their music, although none spurned success. All grew in popularity throughout the eighties and into the nineties: in fact, *Rolling Stone*, referring to one form of alternative music, called the nineties the "hip-hop" decade.

Rap, which had taken shape in the South Bronx in the seventies, quickly spread to other black neighborhoods during the early eighties. It began to reach the suburbs during the late eighties when rap groups such as Run-D.M.C. and Public Enemy attracted a white audience, and white imitators, as well.

At about the same time, a host of new popular styles from Africa and the Caribbean emerged on the world scene: highlife, *juju, mbalax,* and *soukous* from West Africa; township pop from South Africa; and ska, soca, and *zouk* from the Caribbean. Like reggae in the seventies, all borrowed from rock and rhythm and blues to create new pop sounds, and all gained global recognition mainly through expatriate musicians performing in Europe. In addition, Afro-Cuban and Afro-Brazilian music continued to evolve. Along with other rock/ethnic fusions, these regional styles became known as "World Beat" or "World Music" in the eighties.

Back in the United States, a wave of new bands effectively erased stylistic boundaries. They forged new sounds by blending heavy metal, punk, funk, rap, and earlier rock and rhythm and blues styles in varying proportions. By the early nineties, much of this music was called "alternative." Perhaps alternatives would be more accurate, because the music was so eclectic, even within the music of a single band, such as Nirvana.

Yet there were common bonds. Among the features that distinguished these alternatives from other music of the time were a disdain for the conventions of pop lyrics; a back-to-rock-basics approach to music making; little use for drum machines and other forms of digital sound generation; and complex, funky rhythms. Within these general tendencies, there was considerable variety, as we will see.

Rap

Without question, rap is the most radically new music of the rock era. It challenged the most basic assumptions about popular music: what it is, how it's created, who makes it, what it says, how it says it.

Rap is poetry delivered over a musical background. Rapping is more than speaking and less than singing. A rapper's voice has more resonance than everyday speech, and he or she delivers the text with a definite rhythm, but does not sing definite pitches. In effect, the rapper's voice is a completely new kind of musical instrument: a percussion instrument that delivers text! (Or maybe it is not so new: many African peoples used talking drums for communication.)

The novelty of rapping is at the center of an ongoing controversy: Is rap music? Its detractors point out that raps often lack melody, so it cannot be music. Of course, this perspective misses the point entirely. Rap needs only to be rap; there is no cultural law that says that a work of art that includes musical sounds must have a melody. Rap is, for popular culture, virtually a new medium of expression. Those who dismiss it as "non-music" fail to appreciate its novelty.

The musical accompaniment for the rapper was just as innovative. Rap's most direct roots are in the "toasts" of Jamaican disc jockeys, delivered over the song they were about to play. The first rap hit, the Sugarhill Gang's "Rapper's Delight" (1979), used Chic's "Good Times" as the musical background. This took toasting a big step further, in effect extending the "introduction" through the entire recording.

Before long, rap DJs began playing their turntables like an instrument, instead of simply playing the discs. They developed several techniques, among them scratching and "back-spinning," to alter the musical accompaniment. To scratch, they interrupted the spinning of the turntable by placing a finger on the disc and moved it back and forth in a regular rhythm. This produced a

There are numerous precedents in twentieth century "art music" for rap's most striking breaks with the past—rapping, sampling, electronic sound generation. Charles Ives used scraps of vernacular music—hymn tunes, popular songs, ragtime, patriotic music—in much of his music. Arnold Schönberg's *Pierrot Lunaire* (1912) uses *Sprechstimme*—more than speech, less than singing. Stravinsky "sampled" Pergolesi in his ballet "Pulcinella" (1920). Edgard Varese's *Ionisation* (1931) is a percussion piece. And there are countless compositions for electronic tape.

high-pitched percussive rhythm. To "back-spin" a record, DJs isolated a musical fragment—a riff, a bass figure—that they wanted to repeat. They found the place on the recording where the riff began. Then, at the end of the sample, they quickly spun the turntable backwards to that spot—without dropping a beat. (Electronic sampling would later make it possible to create this effect with even greater precision.)

Rap introduced the idea of constructing a musical environment completely out of previously recorded material. Rap's "instrument" was the sound system; the turntable was its "keyboard." Through sampling and sequencing, rap producers took a more active role in shaping the backdrop. Instead of waiting for the perfect song, they sampled sounds that they liked from any available source (James Brown and George Clinton were two favorites) and assembled them into sound collages.

Samples were chosen not only for their intrinsic interest; they were also a form of code. Listeners familiar with the source of the sample could find additional meaning in a rap by associating the rap with the source of the sample.

Rapping and sampling have influenced several other styles—we will hear rapping in some of the alternative music later in the chapter. Rapping is the more obvious influence, sampling the more pervasive.

Hip-Hop Culture

Rap's social stance was as radical as its musical approach. Like the blues and reggae, rap was born in a hostile, impoverished environment: The South Bronx was the postmodern urban counterpart to the Mississippi Delta. That part of the Bronx had been a group of multi-racial neighborhoods until the construction of the Cross Bronx Expressway in the late sixties and early seventies. The demolition of 60,000 homes accelerated white flight. Most of those who remained behind were minorities: African Americans, Latinos, Afro-Caribbeans.

New York City's mid-seventies fiscal crisis accelerated the decay of the region. By the late seventies, an already difficult living environment had become even worse. The established media depicted minority areas such as the South Bronx and the Bedford-Stuyvesant section of Brooklyn as desolate, war-torn wastelands. Horrific images appeared on news broadcasts—the coverage of the looting that took place during the 1977 power blackout was especially gruesome—and in films such as *Fort Apache, the Bronx* (1981). Hip-hop culture certainly didn't soft-pedal the grimness of the ghetto, but its very existence affirmed the vitality and resilience of the African-American spirit in even the most hostile environments.

Rap emerged as one expression of hip-hop culture. "Hip-hop" denoted ways of talking, gesturing, dressing, posturing—it was a way of life for many ghetto teens and young adults. It produced three expressive outlets: not only rap, but also graffiti painting and breakdancing. All three were "street" arts. They could pop up on the spur of the moment. All hip-hop artists needed was a street corner, a boom box, or cans of spray paint. Although performances could happen anywhere, anytime, they were far from unplanned events. Rappers, breakdancers, and graffiti artists put considerable effort into honing their craft. Rappers wrote out their poems and memorized them; breakdancers perfected their moves; graffiti artists carefully sketched out their artworks before sneaking into train yards to paint the subway cars.

Rap came along at the right time, so far as the recording industry was concerned. Instead of trying to produce rap themselves, the big record companies simply entered into agreements with rap labels, trading their distribution and advertising muscle for a share of the profits. Producers retained artistic autonomy, which helps account for rap's cutting edge. This is in sharp contrast to the early days of rock and roll.

Hip-hop culture defiantly confronted the prevailing view of the ghetto as a cultural desert by creating vital new forms of expression, forms that challenged both existing artistic conventions and the law. DJs would get power for their sound systems by tapping into street lamps; graffiti artists had to evade police to spraypaint subway cars. (Subway cars were the "canvas" of choice because they were in motion, making the art dynamic, and because they advertised the artists throughout the five boroughs.) That hip-hop culture would not only flourish, but also produce innovative forms of expression was—and is—a testament to the spirit of its creators.

The work of hip-hop artists, especially rappers, gave their audience an insider's view of ghetto life. Rap lyrics would "tell it like it is." For instance, in "The Message" (1980), Grandmaster Flash paints a grim picture of day-to-day existence for poor urban blacks: "broken glass everywhere/ people pissing on the stairs you know they just don't care . . . it's like a jungle sometimes/makes me wonder how I keep from goin' under."

The brutal directness of rap lyrics and the bleakness of its musical setting were radical departures from almost all earlier black popular music. Unlike Stevie Wonder's socially aware songs, such as "Living in the City," there was no melody or harmony to soften the impact of the words.

Rap was not the first plainspoken black music, as we remember from our study of the blues. But no earlier style had talked about urban life in such harsh terms, and—more important—no style had refused to tone down its message in order to gain access to the mainstream. Rappers dealt with the world outside the ghetto on their own terms. It was the exact opposite of Motown's strategy, and it worked: Public Enemy, one of the most outspoken rap groups, was the first to gain a mass audience.

Although rappers often painted an uncompromising portrait of ghetto life, they still projected a strong sense of identity: It may be the ghetto, but it's *our* ghetto, and don't *come* here if you're not *from* here. Crucial to every rapper was his "crew" or "posse," and rap videos routinely located the rapper and his crew in their "(neighbor)hood." This strong sense of location sent out three messages: to the rapper and his crew, it affirmed their sense of identity; to rappers in other locations, it identified their turf; to the outside world, it challenged the sameness of the media ghetto stereotype. The message: Just as not all blacks look alike, neither do all black neighborhoods look alike.

Although virtually every aspect of rap was radically different from earlier music, it was not without links to earlier styles and practices. Most of the themes of rap songs—hard times, male preening, even misogyny—are also found in earlier styles. They occur in "toasting" in the United States and Jamaica and the boasts of calypsonians, in blues songs, both black and white (see Dylan's "Subterranean Homesick Blues," a good proto-rap song), and more directly in the music of James Brown ("Sex Machine"), Sly and the Family Stone, and George Clinton.

The practice of talking over a steady vamp has a long history in popular music. It was common in country blues (e.g., "Boogie Chillen"), and in the fifties, Beat poets read their work over a jazz background. Along the same line, the practice of adapting a "found" object or piece of equipment to a new musical purpose is embedded deeply in African-American culture. The diddley bow, bottleneck guitar, washtub bass, and washboard (heard in much zydeco music) are "found instrument" precedents of the turntable. These connections show rap's evolutionary history. They should not obscure its revolutionary nature: an aggressive, urban, uncomprising voice for African Americans living in the "jungle," and a radically new musical genre.

Rap in the Eighties

Rap "debuted" as a popular music in the fall of 1979, with the release of the Sugarhill Gang's "Rapper's Delight." The idea to record rap commercially came from Sylvia and Joe Robinson, who owned a small and, up to that point, unsuccessful independent label. They had heard rappers in clubs and at parties, and recruited their son, Joey, to find some. He found Guy O'Brien, Michael Wright, and Henry Jackson. The Robinsons renamed their record company Sugar Hill (Sugar Hill was the elite section of Harlem) and hit big right away. "Rapper's Delight" was the group's first and biggest hit. Soon, youths all over North America (it was No. 1 in Canada) were memorizing the raps and chanting them. (Some bought the 12-inch extended play disc, which lasted 14-and-a-half minutes.)

Both the rap and the production show rap's street origins. The rap is part "Rap 101," part good-natured, stylized boasting among friends (who's got more money, finer women, etc.), and part slice of life. The production is smooth, as if a skillful DJ were seamlessly melding two songs together, but not as complicated as the sonic canvases that would come later.

Rap quickly matured, in both words and music. The most innovative of the early rap groups was Grandmaster Flash and the Furious Five. The group consisted of DJ Grandmaster Flash (Joseph Saddler, born in Barbados but raised in New York) and five rappers/dancers, among them Melle Mel (Melvin Glover). Flash was the first turntable virtuoso. He mastered several difficult techniques: not only back-spinning but also "cutting" (connecting two songs without dropping a beat) and "phasing" (adjusting the speed of the turntable). All would later become standard sampling techniques. The group's 1981 hit "The Adventures of Grandmaster Flash and the Wheels of Steel" put these techniques on display: it included samples from not only "Good Times" but Blondie's "Rapture" and Queen's "Another One Bites the Dust." (Clearly, Flash was an equal-opportunity sampler.)

The group's 1982 hit "The Message" shows how quickly rap evolved in both content and musical style. The rap pulls no punches in its depiction of ghetto life. Indeed, the rapid fire images come at the listener like a boxer's combination. The musical setting is a masterful collage of electronic sounds: percussion, bass, and array of synth licks, many of them reminiscent of the instrumental arrangements of George Clinton. It is far more sophisticated than the mixing of two rhythm tracks. And it is far more purposeful: The emptiness of the background not only spotlights the rap but reinforces its bleak message.

Rap quickly spread from New York City to black neighborhoods throughout the United States. For the first half of the eighties, its audience was mainly black. However, that changed in mid-decade, as rap began to tap into the white suburban youth market.

The catalyst was Run-D.M.C., another New York rap group—but from middle class Queens instead of the South Bronx. "Run" was Joseph Simmons; "D.M.C." was Darryl McDaniels. Simmons's older brother Russell had started Def Jam Records with a white partner, Rich Rubin. It was Rubin's idea to team the group with the white rock band Aerosmith in a cover of their earlier hit "Walk This Way" (1986). The recording and video also included Aerosmith's lead singer Steven Tyler and guitarist Joe Perry.

They approached the song much like an architect planning an addition to a house. The song is basically unchanged. The add-ons include some scratching here and there; the rap of the verse by Run-D.M.C. (Tyler sticks his nose in during the chorus); an expansion of the drum beat frame; and Perry's extended Hendrix-ish solo. Of course, the rap of the verse, with its rapid exchanges, remakes the song.

"Walk This Way" helped rap enter the mainstream in several ways. First, it was popular—more so on the pop charts (No. 4) than the R&B charts (No. 8). Second, it bridged the gap between rock and rap—for both the musicians and their audiences. Indeed, in its direct attitude and avoidance of pop trappings, rap could be thought of as the black alternative to the alternative movement that was just gathering momentum. Third, the video of the song, which received considerable airplay, brought the hip-hop look to the malls. Baseball caps worn backwards and untied athletic shoes became almost as common among white students as black. However, even though it paved the way for the widespread acceptance of rap, "Walk This Way" was still a hybrid. "Pure" rap would cross over the following year, in the music of Public Enemy.

PUBLIC ENEMY   Public Enemy was Chuck D (Carlton Ridenhour) and Flavor Flav (William Drayton), rappers; Terminator X (Norman Rogers), DJ; and Professor Griff (Richard Griffin), "Minister of Information." They were rap's breakthrough group. Their second album, *It Takes a Nation of Millions to Hold Us Back* (1988), sold over a million units and helped secure a permanent presence for rap in the popular music landscape.

Public Enemy found success without compromising their beliefs. The members were supporters of the Nation of Islam: excerpts from speeches by Malcolm X and Louis Farrakhan (whom Chuck D labeled a prophet) often begin their raps. They billed themselves as "prophets of rage." Black Muslim rhetoric filled their stage shows, mainly via their Minister of Information.

In 1989, they found themselves in the middle of an ugly controversy when, in a *Washington Times* interview, Professor Griff blamed Jews for "the majority of wickedness around the globe." (That comment probably didn't sit too well with Rubin, a Jewish man who had encouraged Chuck D to begin his career as a rapper.) The group disbanded for a time in the wake of the fallout from Griff's pronouncement. Nevertheless, even in that brief window, Public Enemy had escalated the level of rap's rhetoric, from social commentary to social confrontation.

Public Enemy, c. 1995. PHOTO COURTESY CORBIS/S.I.N.

Public Enemy was the rap corollary to rock's breakthrough artists of the sixties. Their music combined Dylan's provocative political and social agenda, the Rolling Stones' relentless groove, and tuneful, orchestra-like textural sound collages that recalled the Beatles. (Comparisons PE might reject out of hand.) All these qualities are, of course, translated into the new vocabulary of rap.

Their innovative approach is evident in two rap hits, "Bring the Noise" (1988) and "Fight the Power" (1989). Chuck D's raps are militant; they revive the language of the sixties black power movement. The groove is built on an up-tempo sixteen-beat rhythm, rather than the eight-beat rhythm of rock. But, like the Stones' best rockers, it is aggressive, relentless, and varied.

The most musically innovative feature of their music is the background, which is considerably richer than even Grandmaster Flash's work. The range of sounds is considerably expanded to include not only speeches by black Muslims but extra-musical noises such as the sound of bottles breaking. These are woven with a host of samples (there's a nice James Brown sample on "Fight the Power") into a dense collage of sound.

Some of the samples are tuneful, if fragmentary. They are evident in both the verse and "chorus" of the rap. In fact, during the choruses, which are signaled by a new, more dense texture, the rappers' voices are a relatively small part of the mix. In both "Fight the Power" and "Bring the Noise," the most prominent feature is the musical hook. Unlike a traditional rock song, it is not a single sung riff, but composites of several samples. Both the density and (for rap) tunefulness of the background evoke, however faintly, the Beatles' *Sgt. Pepper*-vintage music.

Both songs have four points of entry: the raps, which feature the pronouncements of Chuck D and the Ed McMahon-ish asides and intros of Flavor Flav; the beat; the melodic snippets; and the texture, which is almost visible in its density and variety. Public Enemy's success must be attributed in part to this multi-level accessibility.

By the end of the eighties, rap and hip-hop were firmly established in youth culture throughout North America. In addition, rap had become not one style but several. The music of Ice-T (e.g., the bone-chilling "Colors," an account of gang life in Los Angeles) brought gangsta rap to the covers of news magazines, who asked how far pop music should go in depicting violent situations. Queen Latifah made a case and a place for women rappers. White rappers such as Vanilla Ice, whose self-proclaimed street credibility was debunked by an investigative reporter, capitalized on rap's crossover success. Groups such as De La Soul situated raps in backgrounds that were richly melodic, if heavily sampled: "Me, Myself, and I," a 1989 hit, owes more of its melodic material to George Clinton than to anyone in the group. Both rapping and sampling had become part of the vocabulary of popular music; they could be, and were, used in many other styles, as we'll discover below.

The creation and commercial acceptance of rap—which has increased in the nineties—is one of the most remarkable chapters in the history of rock-era music. In many ways it parallels the birth of rock itself: a truly outside music at first that eventually gains a secure place for itself in popular music. Unlike rock, however, it remains an almost exclusively black music. In addition, it represents a unique expressive genre: part poetry, part posturing, part dancing, part music. And in its heavy dependence on sampling—to the exclusion of live instrumental performance—it signals a new musical generation.

World Beat

Among the freshest new sounds of the eighties came the music known collectively as "world beat." For the most part, these were Afrocentric regional popular styles from Africa and the Caribbean that gained a global presence. All were influenced by rock-era music, at least to some degree. Many found an international audience during the eighties, and both styles and artists were woven into the fabric of U.S./U.K. songs: recall Youssou N'Dour's appearance on Peter Gabriel's "In Your Eyes."

Most of the styles were not new. Calypso, for example, had been a part of life in Trinidad since at least the beginning of the century, and African popular styles had appeared by mid-century. And many were not new to North American audiences. Calypso had been a short-lived fad in the United States in the late fifties. South Africans Miriam Makeba and Hugh Masakela had brief moments in the sun during the sixties. Reggae was, in effect, the first "world beat" music. However, it wasn't until the eighties, when other Caribbean music and African popular music broke through internationally, that the idea of "world beat" took hold.

The emergence of world beat in the eighties came about through the coincidence of several trends and developments. Some were extramusical: social, geographical, and economic; others were strictly musical. Perhaps the most far-reaching was the independence movement in both Africa and the Caribbean.

Almost all of the countries—Ghana, Trinidad and Tobago, Nigeria, South Africa—had formerly been colonies of England or France (Zaire had been a colony of Belgium, while Guadaloupe and Martinique are now part of France.) Most had gained their independence only in the sixties and seventies.

As the countries shook off colonial rule, traditional music became an expression of national identity, especially in Africa. For example, Kwame Nkrumah, Ghana's first president, made the restoration of traditional music a matter of governmental policy. In addition, both England and France had liberal policies regarding immigration from former colonies, as the United States had with Puerto Rico. As a result, London, Paris, and New York became the centers of world beat, because of the large expatriate colonies in all three cities. Like Spanish Harlem in the forties and fifties, these European capitals were homes away from home for both musicians and audience. And with a current population of over two million Caribbeans, New York is the largest Caribbean city anywhere in the world.

Expatriates supported complete music industries dedicated to regional music, such as *zouk*, *soukous*, and *juju*, including: venues for live performance, radio programming, recording facilities, and retail outlets. These communities also made world music somewhat more accessible to whites. Like the white New Yorkers who went to Harlem to buy race records in the twenties and thirties, adventurous British and French whites went to these neighborhoods in search of the music that they'd heard on the radio or perhaps in concert.

Audiences at home also grew. Especially after independence, urban populations swelled as people migrated from country to town. Like the migration from the Mississippi Delta to southside Chicago, the African and Caribbean migrations brought both musicians and audiences to the cities.

Another factor in the spread of world music was the success of reggae. As a result, record companies were eager to find the "next reggae." For example, in the early eighties, Island Records signed Nigerian singer King Sunny Ade to a multi-record contract, hoping that *juju*, his music, would be the next big wave in world music, and that he would be the next Bob Marley. Neither happened, but the move did give *juju*—and Ade—considerable international exposure

With swelling expatriate populations, improved awareness of other cultures, better distribution of recordings, and growing musical affinities with rock-era music, world beat seemed to reach a critical mass in the early eighties.

The Sound of World Beat

There was also an important musical reason for world beat's increased popularity: it wasn't until the eighties that popular music caught up with African and Caribbean music rhythmically. Virtually all the major Caribbean and African regional styles have a dense rhythmic texture, with many layers of percussion, and fast rhythms that move at sixteen-beat speed. Not until disco brought sixteen-beat rhythms and dense percussion textures into the mainstream could world beat be understood as a novel (if more complex) variant of an existing sound rather than an exotic alternative.

Also by the eighties, world beat styles had developed not only an affinity with more mainstream popular music, but with each other. This development wasn't surprising. All are Afrocentric cultures. During colonial times, Caribbean cultures were allowed to retain much of their African musical heritage, and African nations simply revived theirs. That accounts for the rich rhythms and batteries of percussion instruments. The colonizing countries introduced simple European music, most significantly hymns (from the missionaries), brass band music, and ballroom dance music. That accounts for the pervasive use of simple harmonic progressions, most often I-V or I-IV-V.

Afro-Cuban music, from Don Azpiazù's "Peanut Vendor" to the mambos of the fifties, helped shape the sounds of both African and Caribbean music. In the fifties, it was the dominant popular style in the Caribbean, and it caught on in Africa via recordings. African musicians were especially drawn to Afro-Cuban music because of its rich rhythmic texture, which was more like their traditional music than any other popular style, with the possible exception of Brazilian music. Calypso and many African styles—e.g., *juju*, highlife—borrowed the horn riffs of mambo. The final common bond came during the sixties: all took the rhythm section from rock and rhythm and blues.

The most obvious differences between African and Afro-Caribbean musics and U.S./U.K. rock-era music is, of course, the language of the lyric. Many songs, especially African songs, are in native tongues. Others use creole languages (e.g., French creole in *zouk*) or dialects (e.g., calypso). The sound, vocal style, and pronunciation of the singer also help differentiate "world beat" music from other rock-era styles.

One might expect Afrocentric world beat music to sound more African than other rock genres. To some extent, that's true. Both African and Caribbean styles typically feature several percussion instruments. The use of traditional African instruments, e.g., talking drums, is a clear expression of the old/new fusion that characterizes so much of this music. (However, the use of modern instruments—guitar, electric bass, horns—quickly distinguishes popular, urban styles from traditional musics.) The performing style is also closer to traditional African singing than it is to much rock/rhythm and blues singing and playing. Singers (and instrumentalists) perform with almost no inflection, at least by rock and rhythm and blues standards. The blues- and gospel-based expressive devices—e.g., James Brown's whoops—that typify so much rock-era music are largely absent. Instead, the music bubbles along on its buoyant rhythms.

Paradoxically, however, it is harmony, the most European of elements, that is the most obvious musical difference between world beat and other rock-era styles. At a time when rock, and especially heavy metal, had gone modal, and funk and rap often grooved over a single chord, African and Caribbean musician used the same chord vocabulary as simple hymns, dances, and marches. However, the function of these simple harmonies was radically reinterpreted, especially in Africa.

African Popular Music

All along the upper west coast of Africa, from Senegal to Zaire, native popular musics have flourished for the last thirty years. Each country has its own popular style; indeed, many "national" styles actually emerge from a people within a country, such as the Wolof in Senegal. Nigeria is home to *juju* and Afrobeat; Ghana has highlife. *Makossa* is a popular local dance music in Cameroon; so is *soukous* in Zaire. *Gbegbe* grew up alongside other African popular styles in the Ivory Coast; *mbalax* is native to Senegal.

Some styles are updated versions of older popular styles. Highlife, for example, dates back to mid-century, but was modernized with the addition of electric guitars and other changes. Other styles are transformations of traditional music. Gbegbe was created in the seventies by musicians wishing to give their traditional music a modern sound. This was an expression of national pride in the wake of independence and renewed attention to African culture.

National styles moved freely from country to country. *Juju* has flourished in Ghana and Sierra Leone, as well as Nigeria. Not surprisingly, perhaps, the colonial language has had some effect on the dissemination of a style. Highlife is more popular in English-speaking countries; *soukous* more popular in French-speaking nations. But cross-fertilization transcends tribal, national, and linguistic barriers. In Africa and within the expatriate communities in Europe, musicians listen to and learn from each other. As a result, there are common elements in much West African music. Some of them distinguish it not only from U.S./U.K. rock-era music but also Afrocentric Caribbean styles.

We can hear many of these features in a *soukous* recording from the mid-eighties, entitled "Boya Ye." It features Zairean vocalist M'Bilia Bel, who had a large following in Africa and Western Europe. Among those heard from the outset are the core instrumentation and playing style, the rhythmic texture, and the simple harmony. Typically, instrumental accompaniment includes at least two guitars, bass, several percussion instruments, and a synthesizer programmed to sound much like an electric guitar. This multiple guitar—bass—multiple percussion nucleus is a common lineup throughout west Africa. It may be supplemented with horns and keyboards, depending on the style.

Even more distinctive are the guitar and bass sounds and the patterns they play. Compared to rock guitarists, both accompanying guitarists are very restrained. There's no edge or distortion to the sound, and both lay down riff-like vamps that they repeat over and over. Similarly, the bassist plays a relatively high riff that oscillates between two chords. He is neither marking the beat nor playing a line that roams freely. All move faster than the beat, as do the percussion parts; it is this activity that provides the cushion for M'Bilia Bel's vocal line.

The raw materials of the melody and harmony of the song should sound familiar to Western ears: The melody is built from the pitches in a major scale, the one used in so much classical and popular music. (The long phrases in the vocal line are like a garland around a descending scale.) The harmony draws on the same pitches: It consists only of an alternation between I and V.

However, the way melody and harmony are used is radically different from standard European practice. In more conventional usage, European harmony and melody progress to moments of arrival within a song. For instance, the Temptations' "My Girl" had a restricted harmonic vocabulary (I, ii, IV, V), and it too began with an alternation of two chords. But the progression and the rhythm of the chords directed our ear to the title phrase, "my girl"; so did the rise and fall of the melody and its relation to the harmony. Both helped us focus our attention on the hook of the song. Each time we heard it, we felt that we had arrived at an important milestone.

In "Boya Ye," however, there is not the same sense of arrival, because the harmonic alternation never changes and the melodic lines float serenely above it and the buoyant rhythms of the accompaniment. Almost all of the melodic lines start high and eventually settle on the tonic pitch, like a leaf falling to the ground. Unlike "My Girl," where the drives to the hook create a multi-level hierarchy, "Boya Ye" simply spins out over the two-chord vamp. Although melodic ideas return, a larger architecture is not obvious, as it is in verse/chorus-type songs. Instead, there is a wonderful sense that time has been suspended, as if we came in during the middle and left before the end.

This sense—that time has been suspended—expresses a traditional west African esthetic, much like we heard in the Yoruba chorus (Chapter 2). There, everything was, of course, African. Here, the raw materials are about as European as they can be—a major scale (think "Joy to the World") and I and V chords—but their meaning has been radically changed. Instead of "going" somewhere (back to the I chord), they just "are."

This sense of suspended time is not unique to African popular music. We have experienced it in the music of Miles Davis, U2, and Sly and the Family Stone, among others. But when it has occurred in American or British music, a different harmonic approach has been used: a single chord, a power chord, a pattern that doesn't even imply a chord. It is the reinterpretation of European harmony, rather than the creation of alternative harmonic options, that distinguishes west African popular music from both traditional pop harmony and rock-era alternatives.

Other traditional African values are also evident in "Boya Ye." Perhaps the most pervasive is the sense of group, rather than individual, sound. All the rhythm section members suppress their individuality to create a beautifully interwoven texture: the bass riff, percussion parts, and guitar vamps continue through the entire (long) song. Even the instrumental solos and response figures share the spirit. They are understated lines and riffs, rather than opportunities for virtuosic display.

Distinctive mixes of traditional African values and outside, more modern influences have given west African urban music an immediately identifiable sound. Perhaps because so many songs were not in English (and because some of those that were in English discussed such non-rock concerns as free education in Nigeria [the title and subject of a song by Prince Nico Mbarga]), it did not achieve the wide currency of other world beat styles in the seventies and eighties. Still, it attracted a loyal following, not only in Africa and among African expatriates, but also among non-Africans.

Afrocentric Caribbean Popular Music

The Caribbean (and its North American outposts, especially New York) is a unique musical melting pot. Its total land area is smaller than some states, and its population is less than 40 million people. The islands are separated not only by water, but also by language, colonial history, racial makeup (for instance, Trinidad has almost as many citizens of East Indian descent as African), and political system. They are linked by their geographical proximity, the African roots of so much of their population, and their accessibility to mass media from neighboring countries and the United States.

As a result, no other region in the world—except for cities with large expatriate populations—has such a mix and a mixing of styles. By the eighties, the music of the Caribbean had become even more diverse and, at the same time, more interbred than the music of west Africa. Every political entity seems to have at least one distinctive musical style. In addition to son and rumba from Cuba and reggae and ska from Jamaica, there is biguine from Martinique, merengue from the Dominican Republic, mereng (meréngue) from Haiti, bomba from Puerto Rico, calypso from Trinidad, and numerous others.

Hybrid styles have also flourished. Especially in recent years, there have been a host of Caribbean fusions, which blend regional and international styles. Soca is an updated form of calypso, and *zouk*, from the French Antilles, is a hybrid style which mixes contemporary sounds with cadence, itself reputedly a mix of Haitian music and calypso.

CALYPSO AND SOCA Except for Cuban music and reggae, calypso is the best-known Caribbean music. Its history in Trinidad dates back to the nineteenth century, and it has been familiar to U.S. audiences since mid-century. The first U.S. calypso hit was a 1945 cover of Lord Invader's "Rum and Coca Cola" by the Andrews Sisters. About ten years later, Harry Belafonte sparked a calypso craze with "Day O" (the opening of the song is still one of the more famous moments in popular music). It lasted about five years, by which time calypso was firmly lodged in American ears.

For Americans, calypso is "fun-in-the-sun" music, but for calypsonians (calypso singers) and their fans, it has been much more. Without question, it is "good time" music. As with Carnaval and the samba schools in Brazil (and Mardi Gras in New Orleans), calypso bands point toward Carnival, a month-long event during which there are numerous competitions. Musically, calypso songs are typically upbeat. There don't seem to be counterparts in calypso to reggae songs like "Is This Love" (discussed in Chapter 11) or the romantic bossa novas of Brazil.

A typical calypso song moves at about march (or disco) tempo. A battery of percussion instruments and the rest of the rhythm section lay down the groove, typically anchored by calypso's "DUMMMMMM ba/dum bum" rhythmic signature:

A horn section and, on occasion, pans (steel drums) will play riffs and lines on top of it. Over all of this is the calypsonian telling his story to a song supported by simple European harmony.

Some musical features, such as the core instrumentation, thick rhythmic texture, bright tempo, and simple harmony, are common to many Caribbean (and African) styles. Others, most obviously the rhythmic signature and the pans, are closely linked to calypso.

The sunny musical settings of most calypso songs may obscure the sharp edge of the lyrics. Although there are plenty of party-hearty calypso lyrics, calypsonians have also used their stage as a forum for social commentary and preemptive strikes in the war between the sexes. Almost all calypsonians are male, and many include songs in their repertoire that are frankly misogynistic. Here's an excerpt from a traditional calypso song lyric that could be "Exhibit A" for the prosecution in a battered-woman case:

> Every now and then, cuff them down,
> They'll love you long and they'll love you strong.
> Black up dey eye, bruise up dey knee,
> and they will love you eternally.

Other lyrics have directed their venom against social inequities. These often had such a sharp bite that during the colonial era, English governors kept censors on staff.

Among the most outspoken (and most popular) calypsonians is Black Stalin (Leroy Calliste). Competing in the annual Carnival competitions, Stalin won the "National Champion Monarch" award four times between 1979 and 1991. His music embraces numerous political and social issues: the plight of calypsonians, Caribbean unity, black identity, class struggles.

FIGURE 18.1
Calypso rhythm

Beat	1				2			
Beat division	*	*	*	*	*	*	*	*
Calypso Rhythm	X			X	X		X	

In "Play One" (1979), one of his prize-winning songs, he pays tribute to three influential calypsonians, including the great pan player Winston Spree, while lambasting the committee that organizes the carnival for ripping off the musicians while lining their own pockets. The song also shows typical musical features of calypso:

- the distinctive rhythm
- the sound of pans (steel drums)
- the bright tempo
- the dense, active rhythm texture
- a band consisting of big rhythm section + horns.

Soca is a modern variant of calypso. It emerged in the late 1970s, when calypsonian Lord Shorty decided to modernize the sound of calypso by mixing it with more contemporary rhythms. Soca differs from calypso in both words and music. In calypso, text is important. As we heard in "Play One," there's typically some kind of message or comment. By contrast, soca lyrics seem to say only one thing: "jam and wine," that is, "party and dance," and they usually say it as simply as possible. Counterbalancing its simple, party-time verbal message is a more sophisticated musical setting.

We can hear both trends in a skillful 1987 cover of the 1983 soca hit, "Hot, Hot, Hot," by Buster Poindexter and His Banshees of Blue. The original version of the song was by Arrow, one of the leaders in the soca movement. Buster Poindexter was a reincarnation of David Johansen, who made his first

There are several intriguing correspondences among deep blues, rap, Jamaican dance hall, and calypso. All developed in culturally isolated Afrocentric communities of extreme poverty and hardship. Bluesmen, rappers, dance hall DJs, and calypsonians all assume *personae*: Leadbelly, Howlin' Wolf, Muddy Waters; Grandmaster Flash, LL Cool J; MC Hammer; Sir Lord Comic, King Stitt, Prince Jammy; Lord Kitchener, Arrow, Black Stalin. The sound signatures of all three styles came from "found" objects: the neck of a beer bottle (slide guitar), a turntable (scratching), leftover rhythm tracks (dubs), oil drums (pans). And two kinds of song lyrics are popular in all three genres: topical songs, often with scathing social commentary; and man/woman songs which promote the status of the male, often to the point of misogyny.

splash as a member of the New York Dolls in the early seventies. International influence is evident in the more active and syncopated bass line, heavier back-beat, and the greater variety in setting, including a stop-time section.

Perhaps because of the singlemindedness of its musical message, calypso and soca are only part-time musics, even in Trinidad. There, the streets and airwaves are full of it during the weeks leading up to Carnival. For the rest of the year, however, soca and calypso must compete with American rhythm and blues, reggae, and other international styles.

AFRICAN VS. AFRO-CARIBBEAN POPULAR MUSIC It is, of course, diffi-cult to generalize about the music of two large regions on the basis of two songs. Still, a comparison with "Boya Ye" with "Play One" points up similari-ties and differences between calypso and *soukous*—and, by extension, much Afro-Caribbean and African popular music. Common features include percus-sion-augmented rhythm sections, active rhythms, and simple harmony. Noteworthy differences include:

1. *The role of the bass*—in calypso, it's lower and more prominent.

2. *Marking of the beat*—calypso clearly marks the beat, while in *soukous*, the most prominent rhythms move faster than the beat.

3. *Harmony and melody*—*soukous* sticks to two alternating chords, while calypso harmony is more varied (although there are plenty of I-IV-V calypso/soca songs, e.g., "Hot, Hot, Hot"). Also, in calypso, the melody often comes out of the underlying harmony. In the chorus (and intro) of "Play One," the melody is made up mainly of chord tones sung (or played) one after the other. This was not the case in "Boya Ye," as we noted earlier.

4. *Number and role of guitars*—African bands typically include at least two guitars, each playing a riff-like vamp, while in calypso, guitars are typically neither as prominent nor plentiful.

5. *Form*—"Boya Ye" simply spins out, while "Play One" has a clear verse/chorus form.

Compared to other music of the eighties, calypso and *soukous* sound more alike than different—neither sound as much like heavy metal, funk, rap, alter-native, or Michael Jackson as they do each other. But, as the list above shows, there are more subtle, but telling, differences between the two.

World Beat Fusions

As regional styles gained international recognition, rock became even more of a global music. Musicians from the United States and United Kingdom began to incorporate African and Caribbean elements into their music (recall Youssou N'Dour's voice on Peter Gabriel's "In Your Eyes"), and their regional counterparts did just the opposite.

A pair of songs show how varied these global interactions can be when they come from different directions. One is Paul Simon's "Diamonds on the Soles of Her Shoes," from his 1986 Grammy-winning *Graceland album*. The other is "Without a Smile," from Youssou N'Dour's 1994 album, *The Guide (Wommat)*. Simon enriched his songs with South African choral singing and instrumental backup. N'Dour, a native of Senegal and a descendant of Wolof griots, recruited saxophonist Branford Marsalis to play on this track. The two songs are both world beat fusions, but they are opposite in so many ways. Here are some of the differences.

- *Language* Simon's song is in English. N'Dour's song is in Wolof. The differences in the language affect both vocal sound and delivery: The thick consonants of Wolof interrupt the flow periodically.

- *Subject of the lyric* "Diamonds on the Soles of Her Shoes" is another of Simon's quirky relationship songs. "Without a Smile" is traditional in subject. A translation of the opening lines reads "Who has seen my cows/who has seen my goats/these leafless trees/and this dry land." The lyric goes on to talk about moving to a less arid region.

- *Setting* Backing Simon are, in order, Ladysmith Black Mambazo, the pre-eminent South African a cappella choir, and a band comprised of South African musicians. The most familiar African choral sound comes from South Africa. Like black gospel in the United States, it grows out of Africa's contact with Christianity, and like black gospel, it branched off into secular music. The South African rhythm section creates much the same sound as the *soukous* band: floating rhythms with multiple guitar lines (the guitarists play with a particularly African sonority).

  Despite the subject of the song, N'Dour's setting is straight out of black pop: If we didn't know the lyric, we might well think that N'Dour is singing a love song. Marsalis's saxophone obbligato would be a treat on any "smooth jazz" record.

- *"Home style" retentions* N'Dour integrates a drum corp, the Sing-Sing Rythms [sic] into his song, while the bassist on Simon's track plays in a liberated melodic style more common in U.S./U.K. music than in African music.

As this short list suggests, global fusions can produce wildly varying results. However, both represented a kind of "vinegar and oil" approach to stylistic mixing: that is, the African and international elements were clearly distinct, although they blended together beautifully.

Kassav', a Paris-based *zouk* band, explored another, more integrated, approach to world beat fusion. Their music, *zouk*, was already a fusion: a more high-tech version of *cadence*, the dance music of the French Antilles. With African pop so close at hand, they decided to take fusion a step further: they were leaders in creating fusions of Caribbean, African, and contemporary music, such as *soukouszouk*. During the eighties, Kassav' was the hot band in the Paris dance club scene, and also extremely popular in Africa and the Caribbean. Yet, perhaps because they sang in French creole, they were barely known in the English-speaking world, even though they had a recording contract with a major label (Sony) and an international reputation.

"Wép," a song from their 1989 album *Majestic Zouk* ("wép" means "hey" in French creole), illustrates how they seamlessly blended African and Caribbean styles with disco and techno into a new Afrocentric style with strong pop connections. A couple of examples: The basic beat comes from calypso, but the bass guitar figures are more reminiscent of the floating African lines, and the "four-on-the-floor" bass drum comes straight from disco (the disco influence is even stronger when the bass begins to mark the beat later in the song).

The horn riffs are common to both African and Afro-Caribbean styles, so the fusion there is automatic. Synths figures, mainly in a high register, replace the guitar riffs of African music. As these features suggest, the emphasis is on blending regional styles into a new, international fusion.

These five examples are just the tip of the world beat iceberg. Still, taken as a group, they give some sense of the regional identities of these newly global popular styles, and the ways in which they can be blended into new sounds. For both regional and more mainstream pop artists, outside elements can be used as a seasoning or a main ingredient in a fresh, flavorful musical stew. Its impact has not been as significant as reggae in the United Kingdom and United States, but it is no longer a collection of exotic sounds, as calypso was earlier in the rock era. The emergence of world beat, and its interaction with U.S. and U.K. artists, was still another signal that the music of the rock era was truly a global musical language.

Alternative

Among the most eclectic and electric sounds of the late eighties and early nineties was the music created by bands such as the Red Hot Chili Peppers, Primus, Jane's Addiction, Nirvana, Living Colour, the Spin Doctors, Pearl Jam, the Black Crowes, and many others. Like the pop middle ground surveyed in Chapter 16, it thoroughly integrated black and white music. But all of it was almost militantly anti-pop.

These fusions went under a variety of names: alternative, grunge, punk/funk fusion, black rock, retro, etc. The songs expressed wildly different attitudes, from rage to razor-sharp humor. However, they share stylistic common ground, which comes mainly from two features. One is deep roots in soul and sixties hard rock. This connection is evident in the complex, active, syncopated rhythms and the reaffirmation of the basic rock band: a guitar or two, bass, and drums. The other is some mix of the major non-pop styles of the late seventies and eighties: punk, funk, heavy metal, and rap. From punk, they took power and attitude. From funk, they took complex, active sixteen-beat based rhythms. From heavy metal, they took bold guitar playing, extreme distortion and virtuosity: Les Claypool of Primus is a strong candidate for the Van Halen of the electric bass. They occasionally overlaid these mixes with rap-inspired voice parts, more spoken than sung.

In 1985, none of these sources was new. Neither was the idea of forging new styles by mixing black and white sources: That is rock's most time-honored tradition. What gave the music a late eighties sound was its thorough integration of rock and soul, and the currency of its sources. We hear the interplay of both features in a series of examples.

RED HOT CHILI PEPPERS The Red Hot Chili Peppers set the tone for this new sound. A white rock band formed in 1983, they received their training in funk from the highest authorities. George Clinton produced their 1985 album _Freaky Styley_, which also featured Maceo Parker and Fred Wesley, both veterans of James Brown's band. Neither their self-titled debut album or _Freaky Styley_ went anywhere commercially, but their next album, _The Uplift Mofo Party Plan_ (1987) did.

Among the popular tracks from the album was "Fight like a Brave." The song shows how the group fused their diverse influences into a new conception. It begins with a heavy, syncopated guitar riff (metal). Singer Anthony Kiedes enters with a quasi-rap over a single chord (funk); a quick, metal-like series of power chords signals the end of the phrase. The rap serves as the verse of the song. A shift to a new key (but still basically just one chord) signals the arrival of the chorus. The vocal line, a series of short riffs, is sung, not chanted, by the entire band. (Both the riff-built chorus over a single chord and the group singing are straight out of P-Funk.) The accompaniment underneath the singing becomes more active, especially in the bass. Both the verse and chorus overlay a basic rock with double-time riffs and patterns, much like the Parliament recordings of the seventies. But there is, of course, more edge to the sound: That is the rock/punk/metal contribution. The song continues with a simulated radio message, a popular device in rap (cf. Public Enemy above), underpinned by a funk-style bass solo. This in turn segues smoothly into a metal-inspired guitar solo. The song ends with a return to the rap verse and group chorus, with a guitar obbligato at the end.

"Fight Like a Brave" shows not only the mix of several disparate styles but also how successfully the Red Hot Chili Peppers (and other like-minded groups) managed the mix. The juxtapositions of funk and metal do not jar—not even the interlude in the middle of the song. Instead, they merge into one of the freshest sounds of the eighties. The Chili Peppers continued to mine this groove in their last album of the eighties, *Mother's Milk* (1989). For example, the opening track, "Good Time Boys," features a similar combination of styles and adds a rap-like collage of musical fragments.

Other groups offered slightly different takes on this black/white fusion. Jane's Addiction's "Had a Dad" (1988) has a similar groove, but swings more toward punk in Perry Farrell's singing, and toward metal in David Navarro's guitar playing.

Perhaps the purest example of metal/funk fusion—and certainly among the most virtuosic—came in the music of Primus. For example, "Tommy the Cat," from their debut album, *Suck on This* (1989), features a metal-style solo by guitarist Larry Lalonde over a funk-style bass line by Les Claypool and the busy drumming of Tim Alexander. Claypool's dazzling bass solo—part Bootsy Collins, part Jaco Pastorius, and part Claypool—is in turn interrupted by Lalonde's metal-style riff. The bass had been the virtuoso instrument in funk, the guitar in heavy metal. In Primus's music they collide, and creative sparks fly. Their virtuosity is an interesting complement to the zaniness of the lyric of the song, and Claypool's bizarre vocal style. Although the lyric and its delivery are more cartoon than parody, they—and the high level of instrumental skill—resonate with Zappa-esque quirkiness: a kind of trickle-down rock irony.

LIVING COLOUR The Black Rock Coalition, a New York-based group of bands led by Living Colour, approached the black/white fusion from a different direction: reclaiming rock's black legacy. Vernon Reid, the guitarist in Living Colour, asserted in a *Rolling Stone* interview that "Rock and roll is black music, and we are its heirs." While it is hard to imagine more influential guitarists than Chuck Berry and Jimi Hendrix, or a more flamboyant personality in rock's early years than Little Richard, rock had, over time, certainly become a music played by and for whites. Living Colour sought to open the door once again for black rock musicians. They succeeded, with songs that articulated black concerns, that had clear roots in black music, and that borrowed freely from white rock.

"Cult of Personality" (1988), the group's first big hit, begins with a rap-like sound bite from Malcolm X. The "language that everybody here can easily understand" is a Led Zeppelin–style heavy guitar and bass riff, but with even more distortion. The lyric is a decidedly different take on the braggadocio of the bluesman (and, by this time, the rapper). Comparisons to the best and worst of major twentieth century personalities (e.g., Stalin and Gandhi) are a long way from Wynonie Harris's "mighty, mighty man." That, and the other excerpts from famous political speeches, overlay what is essentially a man/woman song with a layer of social commentary. Vernon Reid's furious solo underscores the message of the lyric.

"Cult of Personality" merges black and white by juxtaposing rap-like sound bites and Corey Glover's bluesy vocals with Zeppelin-style group riffs and Reid's metal-style solo. "Middle Man," another 1988 hit, is even more eclectic. It harks back to the double-time feel of sixties power trios—but with more of an edge—and includes funk-style slap bass, a heavily distorted signature riff, James Brown-style guitar fills on a single chord, an extended guitar solo, and "wall of distortion" chords that could easily be transported to a metal song. All of this supports a blues-type lyric: the bluesman as alienated loner.

Alternative in the Early Nineties

Red Hot Chili Peppers, Jane's Addiction, Primus, and Living Colour all attracted substantial followings. Despite exposure on MTV and on tour, however, none of the bands crossed over to the pop charts with any frequency. Alternative broke through commercially in the early nineties with Seattle's "grunge" bands, Nirvana and Pearl Jam.

GRUNGE From Elvis on, rock history has been filled with surprising success stories. Nirvana's overnight success was more surprising than most, for several reasons:

- The band bought into the alternative notion that both words and music should be uncompromising.

- They made their mark with virtually no industry support: they recorded their debut album, *Bleach* (1989), for $606.17, which would only pay for a couple of hours in a professional studio.

- The Pacific Northwest was an unlikely locale for an important music scene.

Nevertheless, grunge put the music industry on notice that alternative was music to be reckoned with—not only for what it said and sounded like, but because of how many were listening. *Nevermind* (1991), Nirvana's breakthrough album, eventually sold over 10 million units. Pearl Jam enjoyed comparable success, also selling over 10 million units of their first two albums.

Grunge was the punkiest of the rock/metal/punk/funk/rap fusions. "Territorial Pissings," a track from *Nevermind*, is pure punk, turbocharged by

Nirvana, c. 1990. Photo courtesy CORBIS/S.I.N

the extreme distortion of heavy metal. The track that perhaps best exemplifies both the group's punk attitude and eclectic musical approach is the opening track, "Smells Like Teen Spirit."

The song begins with a heavily distorted double-time riff that recalls sixties power trios. However, it abruptly shifts to a bleak, spare texture, over the same chord sequence as the beginning. This texture soon supports Kurt Cobain's vocal line. This sound is fleshed out in the surrealistic bridge, where the band simply intones "hello" over and over. The opening riff returns, with vocals on top. A metal-ish instrumental break is the only departure from the mantra-like chord progression. Cobain's guitar solo in the middle of the song paraphrases the vocal line of the verse, but the setting blends the energy and rhythmic feel of the opening with the melody of the quieter-sung section. The song continues to alternate between quiet verse and raging chorus.

"Smells Like Teen Spirit" is a punk song in spirit: It expresses rage, alienation, and frustration in both words and music. But the eclectic mix of styles—power trio intro, understated verse, metal breaks, etc.—serves an expressive purpose here. It extends the emotional range of punk, if only because the quiet of the verse makes the louder sections—especially the chorus, with its short vocal riffs—more powerful by contrast. Classic punk drove in only one gear; here Nirvana, shifts back and forth between several.

Pearl Jam was similarly eclectic, although with deeper roots in sixties rock and funk. A sampling of songs from its second album, *VS.* (1993), shows the band's considerable range. Songs such as "Animal" and "Blood" are excellent examples of a sixties rock/funk fusion (the choked guitar in "Blood" induces flashbacks to "Shaft" and "Superfly"); "W.M.A." careens between punk, a world beat-ish drum part, metal flourishes, and dense, funky rhythms, all underneath Eddie Vedder's lonesome wail. By contrast, "Elderly Woman Behind the Counter in a Small Town" (an unusual title for *any* kind of popular song) evokes sixties folk-rock. And as with Nirvana, the style shifts and blends seem to have specific expressive intents. The band seldom gets in a groove and stays there. More often, they use different styles to control the emotional pacing of a song.

Nirvana and Pearl Jam were certainly among the most emotionally charged of the alternative bands. Both groups invested their music with the energy and attitude of punk, and both enhanced this punk core with the power of heavy metal, the activity and complexity of funk, and the nastiness of sixties power trio rock. And both heightened its impact by building strong contrasts into songs and albums.

Their music speaks to and for the desperation of an alienated generation. Indeed, Cobain performed the ultimate act of desperation, committing suicide in 1994 after several previous attempts. Eddie Vedder coped precariously with success: Among his more bizarre acts was wearing masks to photo shoots.

RETRO TRENDS If grunge represented a step forward in the alternative fusions, then the music of groups such as the Black Crowes and the Spin Doctors were a step back. Theirs was a retro trend, updating sounds from the sixties rather than seeking new syntheses. The Black Crowes' cover of Otis Redding's "Hard to Handle" (1991) is a good example; so is the Spin Doctors' "Little Miss Can't Be Wrong" (1991). The new element in their basically sixties sound is guitar distortion, which gives their music a sharper edge.

K E Y   T E R M S

Rap	**Cutting**	*Juju*
Sampling	**Phasing**	**Highlife**
Toast	**Gangsta rap**	**Ska**
Back-spin	**World beat**	**Meréngue**
Hip-hop culture	**Calypso**	**World beat fusion**
Graffiti	*Zouk*	**Alternative**
Break dancing	*Soukous*	**Grunge**

C H A P T E R   Q U E S T I O N S

1. Make copies of maps of the Caribbean and the west coast of Africa. Then locate each of the countries associated with a style mentioned in the text.

2. Is rap music? This has been a hotly debated question since the emergence of rap. To answer this question for yourself, read two or three definitions of music in dictionaries or encyclopedias, then consider rap as music, in light of the definitions. What do you discover?

3. Rap has also been considered monotonous and unvarying. Explore this idea by comparing the settings of four or five rap and rap-influenced songs discussed in this chapter, including at least one by Public Enemy. What did you discover?

4. Study the rhythmic evolution of hard rock by comparing the rhythmic textures of the alternative songs to hard rock from the sixties and seventies.

5. The grunge music has been labeled the punk of the nineties. Test this idea by comparing "Smells Like Teen Spirit" to either of the Sex Pistols' songs discussed in Chapter 15. What carries over from seventies punk? What's new?

Final Thoughts

Rock began back in 1951 as Alan Freed's "cover" term for rhythm and blues. Within forty years, it had taken over the world. By the nineties, rock had become the first global musical language in history. It was not just that one could hear rock almost anywhere in the world. Other music has been exported worldwide: for example, there are symphony orchestras in Korea, Argentina, and South Africa. What made it a truly global *language*—a living, evolving language—was that musicians all around the world were mixing rock with their local music to create new sounds. We have sampled several such mergers in this chapter, most spectacularly in the *zouk*/Afro-pop/disco fusions of Kassav'. You can hear thousands more by surfing the Internet: rock/Middle Eastern fusions, Korean pop rock . . . the list is seemingly endless. Visit Malaysia, Mali, Mexico, or Martinique and you will hear international stars and local talent on the radio, often side by side. Technological advances in the media, which have truly turned the world into a global village, make these interchanges possible. Rock's inherent openness to new sounds and influences make them happen.

That's the good news.

But in the nineties, there are signs that rock—indeed, popular music—faces the most serious creative crisis of the century. Neither business nor technology is the culprit. The suits have been there from the beginning and always will be there. And there will always be tensions between the demands of the marketplace and the demands of the muse. Indeed, in one absolutely crucial area, availability, the music business is *far* better off than it was forty years ago—or even ten. We can access music from anywhere, order CDs of music from Germany, Nigeria, Japan, and get them in a couple of days. Those of us who grew up in the fifties are grateful. We know that the days of driving around in a car in the often vain hope of catching an earful of R&B on clear channel radio—as Buddy Holly often did—are ancient history.

Technology is neutral: it can be used for good or not so good. For every drum loop that replaces a live musician, there is someone working in a home studio creating *exactly* the sound she hears. Technological improvement imposes no limitations on imagination, and particularly since the digital revolution it has simplified and enriched the creative process in numerous ways: new electronic sounds, sound clips from around the world, and the high quality and relative ease of home recording are just a few.

Instead, the crisis comes from within the music itself. There are three issues: rock is fragmented, rock is fully evolved, and rock seems to have lost its soul. Go into a well-stocked record score, or open an issue of *Billboard* and look at the charts—all 20+ of them. The diversity is exciting, and overwhelming. However, in today's popular music world, there is no central body of music that almost everyone knows, as there was in the sixties, with The Beatles and Motown, or even the eighties, with Michael Jackson. In this respect, rock in the nineties resembles popular music after World War II, when Broadway musicals, bebop, rhythm and blues, honky tonk, mambo, and a host of other styles competed for a share of the market.

To put the evolution of rock in perspective, flash back 100 years, then come forward. The syncopations of ragtime were in the air, but the most popular songs were flowing melodies like "Take Me out to the Ball Game." Today's music is much more about rhythm and less about melody, as any rap song and a lot of other music evidence. Throughout the century, rhythm has driven the evolution of popular music. Decade by decade, the rhythms of popular music have become more African and more active: from the two-beat rhythm of the fox-trot through the four-beat rhythms of jazz, swing, and rhythm and blues; the eight-beat rhythm of rock; and the sixteen beat rhythms of much music since the seventies.

Where do we go from here? Two options have surfaced in the nineties. One is the beat heard in new jack swing, which layers a fast shuffle rhythm on top of a rock beat. The other appears in "jungle" and other techno styles. This layers sixteen-beat rhythms over a rock beat, so that the fastest rhythms move eight times as fast as the beat—it is, in effect, a "thirty-two-beat" rhythm. such patterns move so rapidly they can only be produced on a drum machine—or perhaps by a human drummer high on speed.

The problem with both options is that the most active layer moves too quickly. One can sing or rap to a sixteen-beat rhythm and still be intelligible. That's not possible with these faster rhythms unless the tempo is undanceably slow.

So it would seem that we are at an evolutionary impasse. The desire for more active, Afrocentric rhythms that has, more than any other single factor, directed the evolution of rock era music has apparently run up against a brick wall.

Moreover, the music of the last twenty years has distanced itself from the blues. More specifically, it has abandoned the blues' expressive vocabulary. For much of the century, every new style borrowed from the blues: syncopated dance music and jazz in the 1910s, the new popular songs of the 1920s, swing in the 1930s, rhythm and blues in the 1940s, rock and roll in the 1950s, and rock (in its broadest meaning) in the 1960s. However, almost all of the new music that appeared after 1975 had, at best, an indirect connection with the blues. Reggae and rap replaced the blues as rock's "roots" music, at least to some extent. While both are capable of powerful messages, neither can convey the deep emotions that are so much a part of the blues.

For much of the century, blues has been the soul of popular music. Periodic blues revivals notwithstanding, its direct influence on recent music is all but nonexistent. There is no princess ready to ascend to the throne of the "Queen of Soul," as Aretha Franklin so convincingly demonstrated in a recent meeting of pop music divas.

Popular music can continue business as usual. There is plenty of great music yet to be created in current and even older styles, as Bob Dylan's recent resurgence testifies. This can go on indefinitely.

However, what seems to be missing in today's music is the sense of being on the creative cutting edge, of being part of something really new. For about fifteen years—1955 to 1970—and especially in the latter part of the sixties, many—almost everyone, it seemed—sensed that the music coming from Abbey Road, Motown, Haight-Ashbury, Stax, and so many other places was radically different from what had come before, that much of it was important somehow, and that it was theirs. Today, the cutting edge seems manufactured by the media.

Where will the new creative impulse come from? An unlikely possibility is greater sophistication and complexity in today's musical styles. Classical music discovered that mass acceptance diminishes as complexity increases early in this century. So did jazz around mid-century. A more likely source would be from the numerous regional fusions. Reggae, which transformed rhythm and blues into something quite new, has already pointed the way.

Or it may come from a completely different source—anywhere in the world. We look forward to its arrival.

Glossary

a cappella singing, usually by a group, without instrumental accompaniment

AAB form a three-part form in which the first two sections are more or less identical and the third is different. AAB form was used extensively by rock-era songwriters.

AABA form a four-part form in which the first, second, and fourth sections are identical and the third is different. AABA form was the most widely used song form between 1920 and 1955.

accent a musical event that stands out from its neighbors because of a change in one or more musical elements. The most common sources of accent are intensity (the event is louder), duration (longer), density (the event contains more parts), or pitch (higher or lower).

acoustic bass See *string bass*. The term came into use after the invention of the electric bass.

acoustic recording an early recording process in which sound vibrations were transferred directly to the recording medium (cylinder or disc) by means of a large horn or cone. In the twenties, it was replaced by *electric recording*.

Afro-Brazilian music created by Brazilians of African descent. Also, the influence of their creations.

Afro-Cuban music created by Cubans of African descent.

amplification the process of increasing the intensity of a performer's sound by external means.

amplifier a piece of equipment that can increase the strength of an electrical signal.

Anglo-American an American of English ancestry.

AOR (album-oriented radio) a type of FM radio format that emphasized a restricted playlist.

arpeggio a *chord* whose pitches are performed one after the other, instead of simultaneously.

art music music created strictly for concert listening. Art music serves no functional purpose; its value lies solely in its inherent musical worth. Classical music is, by and large, art music; so is much *jazz*, and some musical theater and *rock*.

art rock a rock substyle that sought to elevate rock from teen entertainment to artistic statement, often by drawing on or reworking classical compositions (e.g., Emerson, Lake, and Palmer's version of Mussorgsky's *Pictures at an Exhibition*). Art rock was often distinguished by the use of electronic effects and mood-music-like textures far removed from the propulsive rhythms of early rock.

backbeat a percussive accent occurring regularly on the second beat of beat pairs: 1 **2** 1 **2** or 1 **2** or 1 **2** 3 **4**.

banjo a four- (or five-) stringed instrument, with a skin head stretched over a wooden or metal hoop, that is strummed or plucked. The banjo has been used principally in minstrel show music, early *jazz* and *syncopated dance music*, and *old-time music* and bluegrass.

bass the generic term for the lowest pitched instrument in a popular music ensemble.

beat 1. the rhythmic quality of a piece of music that invites a physical response ("that song has a good beat"); 2. the (usually) regular marking of time at walking/dancing/moving speed (usually between seventy-two and 144 beats per second); 3. the rhythmic foundation of a style or sub-style, distinguished by the consistent use of regular rhythms and rhythmic patterns: a *two-beat*, a *rock* beat, a *shuffle* beat.

bebop See *bop*

big band the large *jazz* ensemble of the *swing* era that typically contains a complete rhythm section and three *horn* sections: three to five *trumpets*, three to five *trombones*, and four to five *saxophones*.

Billboard a prominent music business magazine, *Billboard* is the primary source for *chart* information for a variety of musical styles.

blue notes a variable microtonal lowering of the third, seventh, and sometimes fifth degrees of the major scale.

blues 1. a melancholy mood or feeling ("I've got the blues"); 2. a style characterized principally by highly inflected, often speech-like melodic lines; 3. a song in *blues form*. See also *country blues*; *electric blues*.

blues form a standard blues form consists of a rhymed couplet, with the first line repeated. Each line lasts four measures, so each couplet is matched to 12 measures of music. Each 12-measure unit forms one *chorus*; a typical blues song contains several choruses.

boogie woogie a *blues* piano style characterized by repetitive bass figures, usually in a shuffle rhythm.

bop a *jazz* style that developed in the forties, characterized by fast tempos, irregular streams of notes, and considerable rhythmic conflict.

bossa nova a *samba*-based, jazz-influenced Brazilian popular song style that became popular in the United States in the early 1960s.

bottleneck originally the neck of a beer bottle worn over a finger of a guitarist's left hand; when placed in contact with the strings, it produced a sliding or whining sound, ideally suited to accompanying the *blues*. Later, narrow metal cylinders replaced bottlenecks. Also, used generally to describe a *guitar* played using a bottleneck or bottleneck-like device.

bridge 1. a wooden arch that conducts the vibrations of a string instrument to the resonating cavity; 2. the C section of a song.

brushes two groups of thin wires bound together to make narrow fans. Brushes are used by percussionists in lieu of sticks when a more delicate sound is desired.

cadence a conventional harmonic progression whose goal *chord* marks the end of a musical section.

cakewalk a dance fad of the 1890s; music to accompany the dance.

call and response a rapid exchange, usually of *riffs*, between two different *timbres*: solo voice/*guitar*; solo voice/choir; *saxophones/trumpets*; etc.

calypso the popular music of Trinidad. Calypso has been part of Trinidadian musical life throughout the twentieth century. It became popular in the United States during the late fifties, and enjoyed an international resurgence of popularity in the eighties.

cha-cha-chá a Latin dance that became popular in the 1950s. Its name comes from the signature rhythm that ends each phrase.

chart a listing of the most popular songs during a given time period. Charts have been compiled from sheet music, record sales, and radio airplay. There are separate charts for different types of music.

chord a group of *pitches* considered as a single unit. The notes of a chord may be played simultaneously, or they may be played in a series as an *arpeggio*.

chord progression a series of *chords*. Many of the chord progressions in popular music follow well-used patterns: e.g., the chord progressions for "Heart and Soul" or "La Bamba."

chorus 1. a large singing group; 2. in *verse-chorus* and *rock* songs, that part of a song in which both melody and lyrics are repeated; 3. in *blues* and *Tin Pan Alley* songs, one statement of the melody.

clarinet a mid- to high-range woodwind instrument. It was the high front line instrument in *New Orleans jazz* and a solo instrument in thirties *jazz*.

classical music *art music* by European composers like Bach, Mozart, Beethoven, and Stravinsky, or music by any composer in the European tradition of music for concert performance.

clave the characteristic rhythm of *Afro-Cuban* music. It can be represented as: X x x X x x X x x x X x X x x x "xs" show an *eight-beat rhythm*; "Xs" are accented notes. To create a reverse clave rhythm, switch the two measures.

claves two cylindrical sticks about 1 inch in diameter used to tap out the clave rhythm.

collective improvisation an improvisational context in which more than one performer is improvising a melody-like line. Collective improvisation is standard practice in *New Orleans jazz*, *free jazz*, and much rock-era jazz *fusion*.

conga drum a large (two-and-a-half-feet high), cigar-shaped drum, which is open at the bottom and covered by a drum head on top. It is one of the essential instruments of *Afro-Cuban* music, and has been used in addition to or in place of *drum sets* during the rock era.

contour the pattern of rise and fall in a melodic line, or any other part (e.g., a walking bass) considered melodically.

cornet a trumpet-like instrument that was widely used in military bands and early *jazz*. It is stockier, and the sound is not as brilliant as that of the trumpet.

country blues a family of African-American folk *blues* styles that flourished in the rural South. Country blues differs from commercial blues mainly in its accompanying instrument—usually acoustic *guitar*—and its tendency toward less regular forms.

country music a commercial form of the music of white Southerners, which began with the advent of commercial radio in the early twenties. The different styles of country music mix elements of the traditional *folk music* of the South with other popular styles, such as *jazz*, pop-song, and *rock*.

country rock a hybrid style that merged *country music* and *rock*. Country rock developed in the late sixties, chiefly through the efforts of Gram Parsons.

crooner a male singer who sings with a *sweet* sound in a conversational, low-key manner. *Amplification* made crooning possible. Bing Crosby was the most successful of the early crooners.

crossover a term used to identify a song or artist associated with one popularity chart (e.g., *rhythm and blues*) who attains popularity on another chart. Early in his career, Elvis was the ultimate crossover artist, placing songs on *pop*, rhythm and blues, and *country* charts.

cymbal a metal, circular plate, with a slightly raised indentation, often mounted on a pole, that, when struck, makes a ringing or bell-like sound.

delineator a minstrel performer who purported to portray African Americans in an authentic manner.

density the measure of the amount of musical activity occurring simultaneously in a composition.

diatonic scale a scale made up of seven different *pitches*. The opening of "Joy to the World" uses a descending form of one of the diatonic scales. (There are eight notes in the opening; the first and last belong to the same pitch family.) There are three kinds of diatonic scales commonly used in popular music: *major*, *minor*, and *modal*.

disco a dance music that rose to popularity in the mid-seventies. Disco songs typically had a relentless beat, a complex rhythmic *texture*, usually with a *sixteen-beat rhythm*, and rich orchestration, typically an augmented *rhythm section*, horns, and strings.

distortion electronic timbral alteration. In some *rock* styles, distortion is intentional; intense distortion is the most immediately identifiable feature of *heavy metal*.

Dixieland jazz See *New Orleans jazz*.

dobro an instrument associated with *country music*, with the body of an acoustic guitar and a resonating device placed in the sound hole. Like the *steel guitar*, the dobro is played horizontally and the strings are stopped with a metal bar.

doo-wop a rhythm and blues style of the fifties, typically featuring vocal groups singing pop standards.

drum kit See *drum set*

drum set a group of percussion instruments set up so they can be played by a single performer. The standard drum set includes a bass drum, struck by a pedal operated by the drummer's right foot; a *snare drum*; two or more *tom-toms*; a *hi-hat* operated by the drummer's left foot; and two or more suspended *cymbals*.

duration the length in time of a musical event.

dynamics levels or changes in *intensity*. The dynamic level of a Ramones' song is very loud.

eight-beat rhythm a rhythm that divides each beat of a four-beat measure into two equal parts. It is the characteristic rhythmic foundation of *rock*.

electric bass a solid body, *guitar*-shaped *bass* instrument. It is tuned like a *string bass*. The electric bass came into widespread use in popular music around 1960.

electric blues a post-World War II *blues* style characterized by the use of a full *rhythm section*, including *electric guitar*. It is the most popular form of contemporary blues.

electric guitar an electrically amplified *guitar*. The first electric guitars retained the hollow body of an acoustic guitar and added a *pickup* to convert the string vibration into an electrical signal. By 1960, the solid-body guitar, with no resonating cavity, had emerged as the primary design for electric instruments.

electric piano a *keyboard* instrument popular in the sixties and seventies that combines electronic sound generation with a piano-like action. The most popular model was the Fender Rhodes. With the application of microchip technology, electric pianos have largely been replaced by digital keyboards.

electric recording a recording procedure developed in the twenties that converts sound into an electrical signal before recording and converts the electrical signal back into sound for playback. Electric recording, with its far superior sound quality, immediately made *acoustic recording* obsolete.

endless loop form a form in which one section flows into another without a *cadence* to emphatically divide them.

endman a comic in a minstrel troupe. Minstrel performers sat in a semicircle onstage; an endman sat at one end or the other.

endweighted form a verse/chorus form in which the *chorus* is highlighted as the goal of each large section. It has been a popular formal approach in the *rock* era. The Temptations' "My Girl" is a typical example of endweighted form.

fiddle the informal name given to the *violin* by folk musicians. Fiddle tunes are the traditional dance tunes played primarily in the Southern Appalachians.

fifth the interval between the first and fifth notes of a *major scale*.

flute a metal wind instrument in the shape of a cylindrical tube. It is open at one end and has an opening at the other that the performer blows across.

folk music music made by a group of people (e.g., Cajuns, Navahos, or whites from rural Appalachia), mostly without formal musical training, primarily for their own amusement or for the amusement of others in the group. Within the group, folk music is transmitted orally. Within the popular tradition, folk music has also referred to folk songs sung by commercial musicians (e.g., the Kingston Trio) or music with elements of folk style (e.g., the folk rock of the late sixties).

form the organization of a musical work in time.

four-beat rhythm a rhythmic foundation in which each beat receives equal emphasis; the common rhythmic basis for *jazz*.

fox-trot a popular dance created in the teens by Irene and Vernon Castle. Also, a song with a *two-beat* rhythmic foundation suitable for dancing the fox-trot.

free jazz a jazz style that developed in the late fifties that abandoned the rhythmic, harmonic, and formal conventions of fifties *jazz*.

front line the horns (or other *melody*-line instruments, like the *vibraphone*) in a *jazz* combo. The term comes from the position of the horn players on the bandstand: they stand in a line in front of the rhythm instruments.

functional music music created to support some other activity. Dance music, marching music, and exercise music are all functional.

funk a *rhythm and blues*-derived style that developed in the seventies, primarily under the guidance of George Clinton. It is characterized mainly by dense *textures* (bands may include eight or more musicians, and complex, often *sixteen-beat rhythms*).

fusion a term applied to much of the *jazz-rock* interactions since the seventies. Fusion often combined the improvisational fluency and harmonic interest of jazz with an *eight-* or *sixteen-beat* rhythmic foundation and a group-oriented, rather than solo-oriented, approach.

glam rock a *rock* style of the early seventies in which theatrical elements—make-up, outlandish dress, etc.—were prominent. David Bowie, in his various incarnations, is considered by many as the major figure in glam rock.

glissando a change of *pitch* that is as blurred as it can be. On a *trombone* or a *synthesizer*, the change of *pitch* is continuous. On a piano, the discrete pitches are blurred because the change of pitch is so rapid. The glissando was a favorite device of Jerry Lee Lewis.

gospel a family of religious music styles: there is white and black gospel music. Black gospel music has had the more profound influence on popular music, by far. Created around 1930 by Thomas Dorsey and others, gospel has influenced popular singing, especially *rhythm and blues*, since the early fifties.

griot a member of an African tribe who serves as tribe historian, doctor, and leading musician.

guitar a six-stringed instrument that is either strummed or plucked. In popular music, guitars come in many forms, both acoustic and electric.

habanera a dance created in Cuba during the early nineteenth century. It became popular in both Europe and South America. Its characteristic rhythm resurfaced in the Argentine *tango* and the *cakewalk*.

Hammond organ a brand of electric organ invented in the thirties. It became a fixture in African-American *gospel* music, and has been used occasionally as a *jazz* and *rock keyboard* instrument.

hard country an updated version of *honky-tonk* style popular since the late sixties.

hard rock a family of *rock* styles characterized by loud dynamic levels; a strong beat; aggressive, blues-influenced vocal styles; and prominent guitar lines, often with distortion and other modifications of the basic sound.

harmony *chords,* and the study of *chord progressions.*

head in *jazz* performance, the statement of the *melody.*

"Heart and Soul" progression a four-chord progression (I, vi, IV, V) that is repeated through one phrase of a song. The name comes from the popular thirties song, "Heart and Soul," although the progression was widely used in popular song through the fifties.

heavy metal a *hard rock* style that developed around 1970. Heavy metal rock features often ear-splitting volume, heavy use of *distortion*, virtuosic guitar and ensemble playing, and extensive use of *power chords*.

hi-hat a pair of *cymbals* attached to a vertical stand. A pedal operated by the drummer's left foot brings the cymbals together, then apart.

hierarchical form a form in which small units coalesce into larger units, which can form still larger units. The *verse-chorus* songs of the *rock* era are excellent examples of hierarchical form.

hillbilly a derogatory term for white rural southerners. Hillbilly also identified early *country* music.

hokum a novelty *blues* style popular in the twenties and thirties.

honky-tonk 1. a rough bar; 2. *country music* associated with honky-tonks. Honky-tonk, which developed around 1940, was distinguished from other country music of the period in its use of drums, a heavy *backbeat*, and *electric guitar*.

hook a catchy melodic idea in a *rock*-era song. It usually comes in the *chorus*, where it can be repeated frequently.

horn a generic term for wind instruments. The horn section of a *funk* band, for example, may contain *saxophones, trumpets*, and *trombones*.

improvisation the act of creating music spontaneously, rather than performing a previously learned song the same way every time. Improvisation is one of the key elements in *jazz*.

inflection moment-to-moment changes in *dynamic* level. Aretha Franklin sings in a highly inflected style.

instrumentation literally, the instruments chosen to perform a particular score; broadly, the instrumental and vocal accompaniment for a recording.

intensity the degree of loudness of a musical sound.

interlocutor the straight man in a minstrel show. The interlocutor would sit in the middle of the semicircle and ask questions of the *endmen*, who would give comic replies.

interval the distance between two *pitches*.

jam to perform music without rehearsal. Such performances are called jam sessions.

jazz a group of popular-related styles primarily for listening. Jazz is usally distinguished from the other popular music of an era by greater rhythmic freedom (more *syncopation* and/or less insistent beatkeeping), extensive *improvisation*, and more adventurous harmony. There are two families of jazz styles: those based on a *four-beat rhythm*, and those based on a *rock* or *sixteen-beat rhythm*.

jazz rock a sixties style that mixed jazz and *rock* in varying proportions. By the early seventies, jazz rock was more commonly known as *fusion*.

juju the popular music of Nigeria.

jump band in the late forties, a small band—*rhythm section* plus a few horns—that played a *rhythm and blues* style influenced by *big band swing*. Saxophonist/vocalist Louis Jordan was a key performer in this style.

keyboard a generic term for an instrument—piano, organ, *synthesizer*, etc.—played by depressing keys. It also refers specifically to electronic keyboard instruments, especially synthesizers.

libretto the text of an *opera*, musical, or other sung dramatic work.

looping electronically sustaining a note well beyond its normal duration; a technique commonly used by electric guitarists.

mambo a Latin dance fad of the late forties and fifties that combined the rhythms of the *Afro-Cuban son* with the *horn* sounds of *big band jazz*.

major scale the most commonly used scale in eighteenth- and nineteenth-century European classical music and in popular music before 1960. Major scales are the raw material from which both *melody* and conventional *harmony* are derived. The popular Christmas song "Joy to the World" is a descending major scale.

mandolin a small plucked string instrument of European origin. It is used chiefly in bluegrass.

march music for marching, or a composition in the style of march music.

marimba a pitched *percussion* instrument It has wooden bars laid out like a piano *keyboard*, with resonators under each bar. The bars are struck with mallets.

measure a consistent grouping of beats. A *waltz* has measures containing three beats; a *march* has measures with two beats.

melisma several *pitches* sung to a single syllable. In popular music, melisma has been most widely used by African-American musicians, especially blues and *gospel*-influenced artists.

melody the most musically interesting part of a musical *texture*. The melody is typically distinguished from other parts by the interest and individuality of its contour and rhythm.

microphone a device that converts soundwaves into an electrical signal. The microphone has been in use in popular music since the twenties.

minor scale next to the major scale, the most widely used scale in eighteenth- and nineteenth-century European music. It has been used only rarely in the *rock* era.

minstrelsy a form of stage entertainment distinguished by cruel parodies of African Americans. Minstrelsy was popular from the early 1840s to the end of the nineteenth century.

mixing the process of integrating the many tracks from a multitrack recording into a finished recording.

modal related to *modes*.

mode a particular form of a *scale*, distinguished by the pattern of large and small *intervals* within the *scale*. The term usually identifies scales other than major or minor. In *rock*, modal scales have been a popular alternative to major and *pentatonic scales* since the mid-sixties.

montuno in *Afro-Cuban* music: 1. a syncopated accompanying figure, usually played on the piano, that is repeated indefinitely; 2. another term for the chorus section of a song.

Motown slang for Detroit. Also the music produced there in the sixties and early seventies, chiefly by Berry Gordy, for his record label of the same name.

multitrack recording the process of recording each part of a performance separately, then *mixing* them into a complete performance. The Beatles, along with their producer George Martin, were among the first to take full advantage of multitrack recording techniques.

multisectional form compositions (usually instrumental) with three or more sections. Marches and rags typically use multisectional form.

New Orleans jazz Style of *jazz* performance based on the early bands that performed in and around New Orleans; revived in the late forties, it is based on collective *improvisation* and quick *tempos*. The *front-line* instruments usually include cornet or *trumpet*, *clarinet*, and *trombone*, with a *rhythm section* usually including *banjo*, *tuba*, and sometimes piano. Also referred to as *Dixieland jazz*.

new wave a *punk*-influenced *rock* movement of the late seventies that typically featured reduced *instrumentation*, a relatively thin *texture*, and active, *eight-beat rhythms*. An early new wave band was Talking Heads.

Newyorican New Yorkers of Puerto Rican descent; something related to or created by them.

octave the *interval* between two pitches that vibrate in a 2:1 ratio. Pitches that vibrate in such a simple ratio to each other share the same letter name.

old time music the earliest recorded *country music* of the twenties and thirties; refers in general to the style and repertory of older country musicians.

opera a music drama in which the entire *libretto* (text) is sung.

oral tradition aspects of a group's culture—songs, stories, etc.—that are passed from generation to generation by singing, talking, or playing, rather than in written form.

outlaw a term that came into use in the seventies to describe the music of Willie Nelson, Waylon Jennings, and other like-minded *country* artists. Outlaw artists rejected Nashville and its slick production style.

overdubbing the process of recording an additional part onto an existing recording.

part one strand in the musical texture. A *rock* power trio has four parts: vocal line, *guitar, bass,* and *drums*. A single part can be performed by more than one musician, as in the string parts in *Motown* recordings.

pentatonic scale a scale with five notes per octave. Two pentatonic scales are used widely in popular music: the Anglo-American pentatonic scale, heard in minstrel songs (Foster's "Oh, Susanna!" begins with such a scale) and some *country* music; and the African-American pentatonic *scale,* heard in *blues* and blues-influenced styles.

percussion a family of instruments whose sounds are produced primarily by striking some kind of vibrating medium. There are two branches of the percussion instrument family: instruments with indefinite *pitch,* like *drums* and cymbals; and instruments with definite pitch, like *marimbas* and *vibraphones*.

phrase the unit of musical thought, roughly equivalent to a clause or sentence in verbal language.

pickup a device that connects an acoustic string instrument to an *amplifier,* allowing the instrument to be amplified directly instead of through a *microphone*.

pitch the relative highness or lowness of a musical sound. The pitch of a sound is determined by the frequency with which it vibrates.

power chord a three-note *chord* made up of a note, plus the *fifth* and *octave* above it. Power chords mark off a midway point between *melody* and *harmony,* because they do not include the third, an essential component of conventional harmony. Power chords are widely used in *hard rock,* especially *heavy metal*.

punk a *rock* style that emerged in the late seventies characterized musically by relatively simple *instrumentation*, rhythms, and production. The Ramones were one of the best-known punk bands.

race record a term that came into use in the early twenties to describe recordings by African-American artists intended for sale primarily in the African-American community.

ragtime a popular style at the turn of the twentieth century, ragtime mixed European *forms*, *harmony*, and *textures* with African-inspired *syncopation*. Ragtime began as a piano music, but soon the term was applied to any music—song and dance as well as piano music—that had some syncopation.

rap a musical style of the eighties and nineties characterized by a rhymed text spoken in a heightened voice over a repetitive, mostly rhythmic accompaniment.

rebound backbeat a *backbeat* which is emphasized by two percussive accents, rather than one.

refrain an alternate term for the parts of a song in which both lyric and *melody* are repeated.

"refrain-frame" form a form in which statements of the refrain frame the verse. Buddy Holly's "That'll Be the Day" is an example of refrain-frame form.

reggae the most widely known popular music from Jamaica. Reggae developed around 1970 from *ska* and *rock steady,* and quickly became popular in England, America, Europe, and Africa.

rhymed couplet two lines of poetry that rhyme.

rhythm and blues a term used since the mid-forties to describe African-American popular styles, especially those influenced by *blues* and/or dance music.

rhythm section that part of a musical group that supplies the rhythmic and harmonic foundation of a performance. A rhythm section usually includes at least one chord instrument (*guitar*, piano, *keyboard*, etc.), a bass instrument, and a *percussion* instrument (typically the *drum set*).

ride cymbal the cymbal on which a *bop* or post-hop *jazz* drummer plays a ride pattern, most commonly "dummmmm, dump a dummmm . . . ."

riff a short (two to eight pitches), rhythmically interesting melodic idea.

rock 1. an umbrella term to describe the family of styles that share an eight-beat rhythmic foundation; 2. music made by musicians associated with rock. (Many of the Beatles' songs, for example, do not use a rock beat, but they are classified as rock because they are by the Beatles.)

rock and roll a transitional style that emerged in the mid-fifties as the precursor of *rock.*

rock musical a musical that uses *rock* rhythms and generally incorporates some of its ideas and attitudes; *Hair* was a prototypical rock musical.

rockabilly a fifties style, performed mainly by white Southerners, that combined elements of *country music* with *rock and roll*.

rock steady a Jamaican popular music that emerged in the mid-sixties. It was an important stage in the transformation of ska into *reggae*.

rumba an *Afro-Cuban* inspired dance popularized in this country during the early thirties.

salsa the term that came into use in the sixties and seventies to describe an updated form of the *mambo*. It is (now) the most popular traditional form of *Afro-Cuban* music in both the United States and Cuba.

samba the most popular *Afro-Brazilian* dance music of the century, both in Brazil and elsewhere. The samba has been popular in the United States since the early 1930s. The *sixteen-beat rhythms* of samba influenced the new *jazz* and African-American popular styles of the 1970s and 1980s.

sampling a recording technique used since the early eighties, in which a short excerpt from an earlier recorded performance is recorded ("sampled") and interpolated into a new recording. Sampling has become a common technique in African-American dance music and *rap*.

saxophone a family of keyed brass instruments with *clarinet*-like mouthpieces. The tenor or alto saxophone has been one of the lead melody instruments in *jazz* since the thirties.

scale a conventional arrangement of *pitches* in a series separated by small *intervals*. The two most widely used families of scales in popular music are *diatonic* scales, with seven pitches per *octave*, and *pentatonic* scales, with five pitches per octave.

scratching a sound produced by rotating an LP record back and forth on a turntable while the needle is in a groove. The tone arm picks up the vibration as if the record were spinning. The performer can control both the pitch and the rhythm of the sound produced in this way by the speed and duration of the movement. Scratching is part of the sound world of *rap* and other African-American popular styles of the eighties and nineties.

sequencing a recording technique in which an excerpt of music, e.g., a rhythm track, is recorded several times in succession.

sheet music music in notated form. Popular songs were sold exclusively in sheet music until the advent of recording in the 1890s.

shuffle a *four-beat rhythm* in which each beat is reinforced with a long/short pattern. Shuffle rhythms were most common in post-World War II *jump band* styles and *rhythm and blues*.

singer/songwriter a term that came into use around 1970 to describe songwriters who performed their own music. The music of singer/songwriters was generally characterized by an emphasis on *melody*, a folk-like accompaniment, and a relatively low *dynamic* level.

sixteen-beat rhythm a rhythmic foundation in which the most active layer is a division of the four-beat measure into four equal parts; the rhythmic basis for contemporary styles such as *disco* and *funk*.

ska a Jamaican popular music that developed around 1960. It was derived mainly from American *rhythm and blues*.

slap bass a technique used by electric bassists in which the strings are slapped, usually with the right thumb, instead of plucked, producing a more percussive sound. Slapping is a common technique in *funk* and funk-influenced music.

snare drum a shallow, two-headed drum with rattling wires placed underneath the lower head.

soca "soul-calypso" a more modern version of *calypso* which blends more mainstream popular styles (e.g., disco) with calypso.

sock cymbal See *hi-hat*

soft rock a family of *rock* styles characterized mainly by sweeter singing styles, more melodious, even *Tin Pan Alley*-ish vocal lines, richer instrumentation, and a gentle *dynamic* level.

son the most characteristic style of *Afro-Cuban* music. The son was popular in Cuba during the early part of the century. Some of the Cuban musicians who migrated to New York in the thirties and forties blended son with *big band swing* to produce the *mambo*.

song interpreter singers, like Billie Holiday and Frank Sinatra, who transform popular song into personal statements, often thoroughly altering the contour and rhythm of the *melody*.

soukous a popular music of Zaire.

soul a term used widely in the sixties by both African-Americans and whites to describe popular music by African-Americans, particularly music, like that of James Brown, marginally influenced by pop or white rock styles.

spiritual a kind of African-American, religious folksong that flourished in the nineteenth century. Spirituals were introduced to white audiences after the Civil War by groups like the Fisk Jubilee Singers.

standard a *Tin Pan Alley* song of enduring popularity.

steel guitar an electric version of the Hawaiian guitar that has been a popular instrument in *country music* since the mid-thirties. The steel guitar rests on the performer's knees, or on a stand just above the knees. The strings are stopped with a metal bar held in one hand and plucked with the other hand. A more modern and complex version of this instrument is the pedal steel guitar, which may have several necks, as well as foot-activated pedals and knee-operated levers that allow for changing the *pitch* or volume.

string band a small group in early *country music* consisting mainly of string instruments of various types: *fiddle, banjo,* and *guitar* were the most widely used.

String bass the largest and lowest-*pitched* of the stringed instruments.

strophic a song form in which two or more verses of text are sung to the same *melody*. A hymn is strophic.

sweet As opposed to *swing*, so-called sweet bands played songs in a *two-beat rhythm*, with little *syncopation*, slow *tempos*, and flowing *melodies*.

swing 1. the sense of rhythmic play, the result of various kinds of rhythmic conflict, that characterizes good *jazz* performance; 2. music, often jazz or jazz-influenced, based on a clearly marked *four-beat rhythm*; 3. an era in popular music extending from about 1935 to 1945 that featured *big bands* playing swing-based songs.

syncopated dance music a post-*ragtime* orchestral dance music popular in the teens and early twenties. It was characterized by the use of syncopated rhythms over a *two-beat rhythm*.

syncopation an accent that comes between the beats of a regular rhythm, rather than with them.

synthesizer a family of electronic instruments in which sounds are produced electronically, either by generating a wave form within the machine or by recording acoustic sounds (e.g., the tones of a piano) digitally. Most, but not all, synthesizers are operated by a *keyboard*.

tango an Argentine dance seemingly based on the *habanera* that has been popular in Europe and the United States since the teens. In the United States, it was the first of the Latin dance fads.

tempo the speed of the *beat*.

texture the relationship of the *parts* in a musical performance.

timbales a pair of shallow, single-headed drums tuned to different pitches. Timbales are a customary component of the *percussion* section of an *Afro-Cuban* band.

timbre the distinctive tone quality of a voice or instrument.

Tin Pan Alley a nickname for a section of East 28th Street in New York City where many music publishers had their offices. Also, the styles of the songs created in the first half of the century for these publishers: a *Tin Pan Alley* song refers to a song by Irving Berlin, George Gershwin, et al.

tom-tom a two-headed drum of varying depth that has become an integral part of the *drum set*. Most drummers use at least two tom-toms, which they play with drumsticks. The smallest is still larger (and lower in pitch) than a *snare drum*, while the largest is smaller than a bass drum.

trio a group of three musicians.

triplet a rhythm that divides the *beat* into three equal parts. Triplets were commonly used in slow *doo-wop* and *soul* songs.

trombone the tenor and baritone voices in the brass section. Trombones use slides (instead of valves) for changes in *pitch*. The trombone was a staple of the marching band, early *jazz* bands, and pre-*rock* dance orchestras. It appears occasionally in contemporary *horn* sections.

trumpet the high voice in the brass section. The trumpet consists of a mouthpiece, a long, slightly conical tube that bends back on itself and then out in the original version, where it ends in a flared bell. Valves permit a trumpeter to make adjustments in *pitch*.

tuba the bass voice of the brass section. The tuba contains a long, wide-bored tube, which gives it a mellow sound. It has been used infrequently in popular music, most importantly as the bass instrument of the *rhythm section* during the twenties. By 1935 it had been replaced by the *string bass*.

tumbao a syncopated bass pattern characteristic of *Afro-Cuban* music.

turkey trot a popular animal dance of the early twentieth century. Like many of the other animal dances of the period, the turkey trot was considered scandalous because it encouraged "lingering close contact" between the dancers.

twelve-bar blues See *blues form*

two-beat rhythm the division of the measure into two primary *beats* or *accents*; the rhythmic basis of the *fox-trot* and other early syncopated instrumental styles.

vaudeville a form of stage entertainment popular from the 1880s to about 1930. A vaudeville show consisted of a series of acts: singers, dancers, novelty performers, comics, etc. Vaudeville differed from the revue and musical comedy in that there was no attempt to link vaudeville acts into a dramatically coherent whole.

vernacular speech common everyday speech, usually rich in slang.

verse-chorus song the most popular song form of the late nineteenth century. The verse tells a story in several stages (this section is *strophic*, i.e., different words are set to the same melody), while the *chorus*, which comes at the end of each verse, repeats both words and *melody* to reinforce the main message of the song. In early verse-chorus songs, the chorus was often sung by a small group, usually a quartet.

vibraphone a pitched *percussion* instrument. The vibraphone consists of a group of metal bars arranged like a piano *keyboard*, with tubular resonators underneath. Dampers, activated by a foot pedal, allow the player to control how long each note sounds. The vibraphone has been used mainly in jazz as an alternative to *horns* in the *front line*, although it was also popular at *Motown*.

vibrato a slight oscillation in the basic *pitch* of a musical sound. Vibrato is used by most popular singers and instrumentalists (except for pianists and percussionists).

violin a high-pitched stringed instrument that is usually played with a bow. In popular music, the violin has been used in several quite different ways. It has been played *fiddle*-style by early minstrels and *country* performers. It is played in the classical manner in *sweet* dance orchestras, film soundtracks, richly orchestrated pop vocal arrangements, and other situations in which a lush, warm sound is desirable. It has also been used as a solo *jazz* instrument.

walking bass a bass line in which the performer plays one note every *beat*.

waltz A dance originally from Eastern Europe featuring a three-beat rhythmic basis, with emphasis on the first beat.

western swing a Texas *country* style popular in the thirties and early forties. Western swing added drums, *horns,* piano, and *steel guitar* to the *instrumentation* of the standard country band. This horrified traditionalists but delighted others.

zouk a *calypso*-derived dance music from the French Caribbean islands of Guadaloupe and Martinique.

Bibliography

ENCYCLOPEDIAS, DICTIONARIES, AND OTHER REFERENCES

Clarke, Donald, ed. *The Penguin Encyclopedia of Popular Music*. 2nd ed. London: Penguin Books, 1999. [A fine, affordable one-volume reference. Good on contemporary peripheral figures and subjects, e.g., salsa artists.]

Gammond, Peter. *The Oxford Companion to Popular Music*. Oxford: Oxford University Press, 1991. [Another good one-volume reference. Similar in approach to the Penguin Encyclopedia but not as opinionated.]

Hardy, Paul and Dave Laing. *The Da Capo Companion to 20th-Century Popular Music*. New York: Da Capo Press, 1995. [A one-volume reference, strictly biographical.]

Larkin, Colin, ed. *The Encyclopedia of Popular Music*. 3rd ed. London: Macmillan Publishing, 1999. [Not really an encyclopedia; it consists mainly of biographies, weighted toward the contemporary British scene. Various subvolumes have been created from this material and published by Virgin Books, enabling you to get the information at a much cheaper price.]

Oliver, Paul, Max Harrison, and William Bolcom. *The New Grove Gospel, Blues and Jazz*. New York: W. W. Norton, 1986. [Compiled from entries in The New Grove's Dictionaries, available in paperback.]

Sadie, Stanley and H. Wiley Hitchcock, eds. *The New Grove's Dictionary of American Music*. London: Macmillan, 1986. [Although not devoted exclusively to popular music, TNGDAM contains entries on major artists, styles, terms, instruments, recording, and many other related subjects. New Grove's dictionary entries have helpful bibliographies as appropriate.]

SURVEYS THAT INCLUDE POPULAR MUSIC

Clarke, Donald. *The Rise and Fall of Popular Music*. New York: St. Martin's Press, 1995. [Lots of information and strong opinions.]

Hamm, Charles. *Music in the New World*. New York: W. W. Norton, 1983. [Hamm's survey, designed to be used with the New World recordings, covers a great variety of American music.]

Kingman, Daniel. *American Music: A Panorama*. Concise edition. New York: Schirmer Books, 1998. [A wide-ranging book covering folk, popular, classical, and jazz styles.]

Roberts, John Storm. *Black Music of Two Worlds*. 2nd ed. New York: Schirmer Books, 1998. [Classic study of African and African-American music.]

Southern, Eileen. *The Music of Black Americans*. 2nd ed. New York: W. W. Norton, 1983. [The definitive history of African-American music in the United States. Particularly informative about minstrelsy, ragtime, early jazz, and African Americans in entertainment around the turn of the century.]

Stewart, Earl L. *African-American Music: An Introduction*. New York: Schirmer Books, 1998. [Covers classical, jazz, gospel, and popular music in easy-to-understand text.]

MUSIC BUSINESS AND TECHNOLOGY

Brabec, Jeff and Todd. *Music, Money and Success*. New York: Schirmer Books, 1994. [Thorough guide to the music industry.]

Goodman, Fred. *The Mansion on the Hill, Dylan, Young, Geffen, Springsteen, and the Head-On Collision of Rock and Commerce*. New York: Vintage Books, 1998. [A fascinating account of the inner workings of the music business.]

Sanjek, Russell, updated by David Sanjek. *Pennies from Heaven: The American Popular Music Business in the Twentieth Century*. New York: Da Capo Press, 1996. [A detailed account of how the American music business has developed over the last 100 years.]

CHART INFORMATION

Whitburn, Joel. *The Billboard Book of Top 40 Albums*. 2nd ed. Menomonee Falls, WI: Record Research, 1991.

———*The Billboard Book of Top 40 Hits*. 4th ed. Menomonee Falls, WI: Record Research, 1989.

———*Pop Memories, 1890–1954*. Menomonee Falls, WI: Record Research, 1986. [A listing of the top singles from the beginning of commercial sound recording to the dawn of the rock era. Organized by artist, with song cross-references.]

White, Adam. *The Billboard Book of Gold and Platinum Records*. New York: Billboard Publications, 1990. [Covers much the same ground as the Whitburn books, but with different statistics.]

TECHNOLOGY

Marco, Guy A., ed. *Encyclopedia of Recorded Sound in the United States*. New York: Garland, 1993.

Trynka, Paul, ed. *Rock Hardware: 40 Years of Rock Instrumentation*. San Francisco, CA: Miller Freeman Books, 1996. [A thorough account not only of the main instruments of rock, but also amplification and recording.]

Rock Sources and Related Styles

NINETEENTH-CENTURY ROOTS

van der Merwe, Peter. *Origins of the Popular Style: The Antecedents of Twentieth-Century Popular Music*. New York: Oxford, 1989. [A thorough and provocative study of the roots of contemporary popular styles in folk and nineteenth-century popular music.]

AFRICAN POP

Stapleton, Chris and Chris May. *African Rock: The Pop Music of a Continent*. New York: Dutton, 1990. [A thorough survey of African popular music through the eighties.]

AFRICAN TRADITIONAL MUSIC

Chernoff, John. *African Rhythm and African Sensibility*. Chicago: University of Chicago Press, 1979.

BLACK GOSPEL

Heilbut, Anthony. *The Gospel Sound*. New York: Limelight Editions, 1985. [The best survey of early black gospel music.]

BLUES AND RELATED STYLES

Cohn, Lawrence, ed. *Nothing But the Blues*. New York: Abbeville Press, 1993. [A fine collection of articles by leading scholars on the blues.]

Davis, Francis. *The History of the Blues*. New York: Hyperion Books, 1995. [Davis takes a broad view of the blues, from "deep blues" to "titular blues." Contains information not to be found elsewhere.]

Oliver, Paul. *The Story of the Blues*. Radnor, PA: Chilton Books, 1982. [An excellent account of country blues.]

Palmer, Robert. *Deep Blues*. New York: Penguin Books, 1982. [A powerfully written study of country and early electric blues.]

Santelli, Robert. *Big Book of the Blues*. New York: Penguin Books, 1993. [Biographical dictionary of leading blues players from the twenties to today.]

COUNTRY MUSIC

Carlin, Richard. *The Big Book of Country Music*. New York: Penguin Books, 1995. [Complete guide to artists and genres in country from the turn of the century to today.]

Country Music Foundation. *Encyclopedia of Country Music*. New York: Oxford University Press, 1999. [A to Z biographical dictionary of country figures.]

Guralnick, Peter. *Lost Highway: Journeys and Arrivals of American Musicians*. New York: Harper Perennial, 1994.

Malone, Bill C. *Country Music, USA*. Revised and enlarged edition. Austin, TX: University of Texas Press, 1985. [The definitive history of country music. Malone also compiled the Smithsonian country music anthology, for which he wrote extensive commentary.]

JAZZ

Gridley, Mark C. *Jazz Styles*. 3rd ed. Englewood Cliffs, NJ: Prentice Hall, 1988. [Gridley combines a comprehensive history of jazz with careful analysis of jazz styles past and present.]

Nicholson, Stuart. *Jazz-Rock: A History*. New York: Schirmer Books, 1998. [Thorough history of how jazz and rock have intermingled from the early sixties through today.]

Porter, Lewis. *Jazz: A Century of Change*. New York: Schirmer Books, 1997. [Readings on jazz history.]

Schuller, Gunther. *Early Jazz: Its Roots and Musical Development*. New York: Oxford University Press, 1978. [The definitive study of jazz through 1930 and a model for the study of any music whose history is documented primarily in recordings.]

LATIN AND CARIBBEAN MUSIC

Chang, Kevin O'Brien and Wayne Chen. *Reggae Routes: The Story of Jamaican Music*. Philadephia: Temple University Press, 1998. [A survey of Jamaican music, with annotated discography.]

Manuel, Peter. *Caribbean Currents: from Rumba to Reggae*. Philadephia: Temple University Press, 1995. [A comprehensive survey of Caribbean musical styles.]

————. *Popular Musics of the Western World*. New York: Oxford University Press, 1988. [This broad survey of popular musics includes helpful discussions of Latin and Caribbean styles.]

McGowan, Chris, and Ricardo Pessanha. *The Brazilian Sound: Samba, Bossa Nova, and the Popular Music of Brazil*. Philadelphia: Temple University Press, 1998. [A thorough and helpful guide to Brazilian music.]

Potash, Chris, ed. *Reggae, Rasta Revolution: Jamaican Music from Ska to Dub*. New York: Schirmer Books, 1997. [Anthology of writings on many aspects of Jamaican pop music.]

Roberts, John Storm. *The Latin Tinge*. 2nd ed. New York: Oxford University Press, 1999. [A full-length study of Latin music in the United States.]

————. *Latin Jazz: The First of the Fusions, 1880–Today*. New York: Schirmer Books, 1999. [Traces the intermingling of Latin and jazz styles in the United States.]

POPULAR SONG

Hamm, Charles. *Yesterdays: Popular Song in America*. New York: W. W. Norton, 1979. [Hamm traces the history of popular song over the last 200 years. His book is particularly informative about nineteenth-century and early twentieth-century song.]

Jasen, David A. and Gene Jones. *Spreadin' Rhythm Around: Black Popular Songwriters, 1880–1930*. New York: Schirmer Books, 1998. [Fine introduction to many forgotten songwriters of the early twentieth century.]

Wilder, Alec. *American Popular Song*. New York: Oxford University Press, 1972. [The most thorough and authoritative analysis of the work of the great Tin Pan Alley songwriters.]

Rock

ROCK REFERENCES

Frame, Pete. *The Complete Rock Family Trees*. London: Omnibus Press, 1993. [Genealogies of rock bands, with commentary.]

Helander, Brock. *The Rock Who's Who*. 2nd ed. New York: Schirmer Books, 1996. [Less comprehensive than *The New Rolling Stone Encyclopedia*, but the entries are more extensive.]

Romanowski, Patricia and Holly George-Warren, eds. *The New Rolling Stone Encyclopedia of Rock & Roll*. rev. ed. New York: Rolling Stone Press, 1995. [Broad coverage, with discographies.]

ROCK SURVEYS

Belz, Carl. *The Story of Rock*. 2nd ed. New York: Harper and Row, 1973. [Gillett in *The Sound of the City* and Belz both tell the story of the early years of rock. Both have strong opinions and convincing points of view about the music and the industry that supported it.]

DeCurtis, Anthony and James Henke, eds. *The* Rolling Stone *Illustrated History of Rock and Roll*. 3rd ed. New York: Random House, 1992. [A useful companion to *Rock of Ages*, this book contains profiles of important artists and styles. Discussions focus more on the music. Entries include thorough discographies.]

Eddy, Chuck. *The Accidental Evolution of Rock 'n' Roll: A Misguided Tour Through Popular Music*. New York: Da Capo Press, 1997.

Friedlander, Paul. *Rock and Roll, A Social History*. Boulder, CO: Westview Press, 1996. [A thoughtful survey of rock music, heavily weighted toward the fifties and sixties.]

Gillett, Charlie. *The Sound of the City*. Revised and expanded edition. New York: Pantheon Books, 1983, reprint New York: Da Capo Press, 1996.

Palmer, Robert. *Rock and Roll, An Unruly History*. New York: Harmony Books, 1995. [A companion to the video series, filled with memorable quotations and useful insights into both the music and the cultures which produced it.]

Ward, Ed, Geoffrey Stokes, and Ken Tucker. *Rock of Ages*. New York: Summit Books, 1986. [A history of rock through the early eighties. Mostly an account of the major trends and events; little discussion of the music.]

Rock Styles and Substyles

EARLY ROCK AND ROLL AND RHYTHM AND BLUES

Dawson, Jim and Steve Propes. *What Was the First Rock and Roll Record?* Winchester, MA: Faber and Faber, 1992. [Fifty candidates for the first rock and roll record.]

Escott, Colin, ed. *All Roots Lead to Rock*. New York: Schirmer Books, 1999. [Portraits of early figures from rock, R&B, and related styles.]

———. *Tattooed On Their Tongues: A Journey through the Backrooms of American Music*. New York: Schirmer Books, 1995. [Biographies of a mixed group of rock performers.]

Guralnick, Peter. *Feel Like Going Home: Portraits in Blues and Rock and Roll*. New ed. New York: Harper Perennial, 1994.

Tosches, Nick. *Unsung Heroes of Rock and Roll: The Birth of Rock in the Wild Years Before Elvis*. New York: Harmony Books, 1984.

FOLK REVIVAL

Cantwell, Robert. *When We Were Good: The Folk Revival*. Cambridge, MA: Harvard University Press, 1996.

FUNK

Vincent, Rickey. *Funk: the Music, the People, the Rhythm of the One*. New York: St. Martin's Press, 1996.

HEAVY METAL

Walser, Robert. *Running with the Devil: Power, Gender, and Madness in Heavy Metal Music*. Hanover, NH: Wesleyan University Press, 1993.

PROGRESSIVE ROCK

Macan, Edward. *Rocking the Classics: English Progressive Rock and the Counter-culture*. New York: Oxford University Press, 1997.

PUNK

Henry, Tricia. *Break All Rules!: Punk Rock and the Making of a Style*. Ann Arbor, MI: UMI Research Press, 1989.

Heylin, Clinton. *From the Velvets to the Voidoids: A Pre-Punk History for a Post-Punk World*. New York: Penguin Books, 1993.

Savage, Jon. *England's Dreaming: Anarchy, Sex Pistols, Punk Rock, and Beyond*. Paperback edition. New York: St. Martin's Press, 1993.

SOUL

Guralnick, Peter. *Sweet Soul Music*. New edition. New York: Harper Perennial, 1994.

RAP

Rose, Tricia. *Black Noise: Rap Music and Black Culture in Contemporary America*. Hanover, NH: Wesleyan University Press, 1994.

Stancell, Steven. *Rap Whoz Who*. New York: Schirmer Books, 1996. [A to Z of rap artists.]

TECHNO

Reynolds, Simon. *Generation Ecstasy*. Boston: Little, Brown, 1998.

Analysis, Aesthetics, and Cultural Studies

AESTHETICS AND CULTURAL STUDIES

Bayles, Martha. *Hole in our Soul: The Loss of Beauty and Meaning in American Popular Music*. Chicago: University of Chicago Press, 1994.

Frith, Simon. *Sound Effects: Youth, Leisure, and the Politics of Rock'n'Roll*. 1st American ed. New York: Pantheon Books, 1981.

Gracyk, Theodore. *Rhythm and Noise: An Aesthetics of Rock*. Durham, NC: Duke University Press, 1996.

Keil, Charles and Steven Feld. *Music Grooves*. Chicago: University of Chicago Press, 1994.

Longhurst, Brian. *Popular Music and Society*. Cambridge, England: Polity Press, 1995.

Marcus, Greil. *Mystery Train: Images of America in Rock 'n' Roll Music*. New York: E. P. Dutton, 1975.

McClary, Susan. *Feminine Endings*. Minneapolis: University of Minnesota Press, 1991. [Although primarily a study of classical music, this book is useful as a demonstration of method and for an insightful essay on Madonna.]

Wicke, Peter. *Rock Music: Culture, Aesthetics and Sociology*. Cambridge, England: Cambridge University Press, 1990.

ROCK AND POPULAR MUSIC ANALYSIS

Covach, John and Graeme Boone, eds. *Understanding Rock: Essays in Musical Analysis*. New York: Oxford University Press, 1997.

Gill, Chris. *Guitar Legends*. New York: Harper Perennial, 1995. [Detailed discussions of the musical styles of major rock guitarists.]

Middleton, Richard. *Studying Popular Music*. Bristol, PA: Open University Press, 1990. [Offers several useful perspectives on the study of popular music, particularly the music of the rock era.]

Discography

We've included on the supplemental CD set many of the key examples discussed in the text. Unfortunately, some songs were impossible to include because the original artist and/or the record label were not willing to license them to us. The following anthologies help fill the gaps. We've keyed the songs to the chapters in the text where they are described.

THE *ROLLING STONE* COLLECTION: 25 YEARS OF ESSENTIAL ROCK

CHAPTER	ARTIST	SONG TITLE
7	Bob Dylan	Like a Rolling Stone
8	Cream	Crossroads
9	The Who	Won't Get Fooled Again
10	Creedence Clearwater Revival	Fortunate Son
10	Creedence Clearwater Revival	Up Around the Bend
10	Grateful Dead	Casey Jones
10	The Band	The Weight
10	The Eagles	Take It Easy
13	Buffalo Springfield	For What It's Worth
13	Crosby, Stills, Nash & Young	Ohio
13	Joni Mitchell	California
13	James Taylor	Mexico
13	Neil Young	The Loner
13	Neil Young	Tonight's the Night
13	Randy Newman	Sail Away
14	Stevie Wonder	Superstition
14	Sly and the Family Stone	Thank You (Falettinme Be Mice Elf Again)
15	Elton John	Daniel
15	Rod Stewart	Maggie May
15	Ry Cooder	Little Sister
15	Talking Heads	Life During Wartime
15	Ramones	Blitzkrieg Bop
15	Sex Pistols	God Save the Queen
15	The Clash	Stand By Me (Train in Vain)
15	Elvis Costello	Watching the Detectives

THE *ROLLING STONE* COLLECTION (CONTINUED)

CHAPTER	ARTIST	SONG TITLE
16	Prince	When U Were Mine
16	Prince	When Doves Cry
16	Prince	Little Red Corvette
16	Madonna	Borderline
17	Bruce Springsteen	Born to Run
17	Bruce Springsteen	Born in the USA
17	U2	Pride in the Name of Love
17	Dire Straits	Sultans of Swing
17	Tracy Chapman	Talkin' 'Bout a Revolution
17	Stevie Ray Vaughan	White Boots
17	Robert Cray	Smoking Gun
17	Sting	If You Love Somebody, Set Them Free
17	Bonnie Raitt	Thing Called Love
18	Living Colour	Cult of Personality
18	Paul Simon	Diamonds on the Soles of Her Shoes
18	Public Enemy	Fight the Power
18	Grandmaster Flash	The Message
18	Run-D.M.C.	Walk This Way
18	Black Crowes	Hard to Handle

SOUNDS OF THE EIGHTIES: THE *ROLLING STONE* COLLECTION

CHAPTER	ARTIST	SONG TITLE
15	Rod Stewart	Some Guys Have All the Luck
15	Talking Heads	Once in a Lifetime
15	Devo	Whip It
16	George Clinton	Atomic Dog
16	Cyndi Lauper	Time After Time
16	Tina Turner	What's Love Got to Do with It?
16	The Cars	Drive
17	U2	Gloria
17	U2	Sunday Bloody Sunday
17	U2	Where the Streets Have No Name
17	Go-Gos	We Got the Beat

SOUNDS OF THE EIGHTIES (CONTINUED)

CHAPTER	ARTIST	SONG TITLE
17	Van Halen	Jump
17	John Mellencamp	Jack and Diane
17	John Mellencamp	Paper in Fire
17	Tom Petty	Stop Draggin' My Heart Around
17	Tom Petty	Don't Come Around Here No More
17	Peter Gabriel	Sledgehammer
17	Def Leppard	Photograph
17	Metallica	One
17	Neil Young	Rockin' in the Free World
17	Robert Cray	Right Next Door Because of Me
17	Suzanne Vega	Luka
17	R.E.M.	Radio Free Europe
17	R.E.M.	The One I Love
18	Public Enemy	Bring the Noise
18	De La Soul	Me, Myself, and I
18	Buster Poindexter	Hot, Hot, Hot
18	Red Hot Chili Peppers	Fight Like a Brave
18	Jane's Addiction	Had a Dad
18	Living Colour	Middle Man

SOUNDS OF THE SEVENTIES: THE *ROLLING STONE* COLLECTION

CHAPTER	ARTIST	SONG TITLE
9	The Who	Won't Get Fooled Again
10	Creedence Clearwater Revival	Up Around the Bend
10	Grateful Dead	Uncle John's Band
10	Lynyrd Skynyrd	Saturday Night Special
11	Black Sabbath	Paranoid
11	Deep Purple	Smoke on the Water
12	Santana	Oye Como Va
13	Joni Mitchell	California
13	Carole King	It's Too Late
13	Paul Simon	Slip Slidin' Away
13	Randy Newman	Short People
14	Jackson 5	Never Can Say Goodbye

SOUNDS OF THE SEVENTIES (CONTINUED)

CHAPTER	ARTIST	SONG TITLE
14	O'Jays	The Backstabbers
14	Spinners	Could It Be I'm Falling in Love
14	Al Green	Tired Of Being Alone
14	Staple Singers	I'll Take You There
14	Sly and the Family Stone	Thank You (Falettinme Be Mice Elf Again)
14	Sly and the Family Stone	Family Affair
14	Curtis Mayfield	Superfly
15	Elton John	Your Song
15	Elton John	Bennie and the Jets
15	Rod Stewart	You're in My Heart
15	Linda Ronstadt	You're No Good
15	Bee Gees	How Deep Is Your Love
15	Ted Nugent	Cat Scratch Fever
15	Foreigner	Cold As Ice
15	Queen	We Are the Champions
15	Steely Dan	Rikki Don't Lose That Number
15	Steely Dan	Peg
15	Joe Cocker	You Are So Beautiful
15	Doobie Brothers	Takin' It to the Streets
15	Dr. John	Right Place Wrong Time
15	Patti Smith	Gloria
15	Ramones	Blitzkrieg Bop
15	Sex Pistols	Anarchy in the UK
15	The Clash	Stand By Me (Train in Vain)
15	The Clash	The Guns of Brixton
15	Pere Ubu	The Modern Dance
15	Talking Heads	Psycho Killer
15	Devo	Jocko Homo
15	B-52s	Rock Lobster
15	Blondie	X-Offender
15	Elvis Costello	Watching the Detectives
15	Elvis Costello	Radio, Radio
16	Parliament	Up for the Down Stroke
16	George Clinton	Atomic Dog

SOUNDS OF THE SEVENTIES (CONTINUED)

CHAPTER	ARTIST	SONG TITLE
16	Van McCoy	The Hustle
16	KC and the Sunshine Band	That's the Way I Like It
16	Chic	Le Freak
16	Donna Summer	Bad Girls
16	Alicia Bridges	I Love the Nightlife (Disco Round)
16	Village People	YMCA
16	Patti LaBelle	Lady Marmalade
16	Pointer Sisters	Fire
16	Sister Sledge	We Are Family
16	Earth, Wind, and Fire	Serpentine Fire

AND THE BEAT GOES ON: CD SET

CHAPTER	ARTIST	SONG TITLE
2	Yoruba Chorus	Yoruba Chorus
2	Kool and the Gang	Ladies Night
2	Henry Russell	Woodman, Spare That Tree
2	Ben Jarrell	Old Joe Clark
2	Dan Emmett/Robert Winans	Boatmen's Dance
2	Scott Joplin	Maple Leaf Rag
2	Fletcher Henderson	Copenhagen
2	King Oliver	Dippermouth Blues
2	Bing Crosby	If I Had You
2	Joe Turner and Pete Johnson	Roll 'em, Pete
2	Count Basie	Jumpin' At the Woodside
2	The Carter Family	Wildwood Flower
2	Bob Wills	Steel Guitar Rag
2	Hank Williams, Sr.	Your Cheatin' Heart
2	Golden Gate Gospel Quartet	Golden Gate Gospel Train
2	Don Azpiazù	El Manisero
2	Tito Puente	Complicación
3	Louis Jordan	Choo-Choo-Ch-Boogie
3	Joe Turner	Shake, Rattle and Roll
3	The Dominos	Have Mercy, Baby
4	Chuck Berry	Johnny B. Goode

AND THE BEAT GOES ON (CONTINUED)

CHAPTER	ARTIST	SONG TITLE
4	Buddy Holly	That'll Be the Day
6	Marvin Gaye	I Heard It Through the Grapevine
6	James Brown	Papa's Got a Brand New Bag
6	James Brown	Cold Sweat
12	Joao Gilberto	Desafinado
14	Sly and the Family Stone	Africa Talks to You 'The Asphalt Jungle'
14	Herbie Hancock	Watermelon Man
14	Herbie Hancock	Watermelon Man seventies' version

THE R&B BOX RHINO R271806

CHAPTER	ARTIST	SONG TITLE
3	Jackie Brenston	Rocket 88
3	Professor Longhair	Tipitina
3	Bo Diddley	Bo Diddley
3	The Five Keys	The Glory of Love
3	The Chords	Sh-Boom
3	The Penguins	Earth Angel
3	The Coasters	Young Blood
3	The Flamingos	I Only Have Eyes for You
5	Chris Kenner	I Like It Like That
6	Percy Sledge	When a Man Loves a Woman

HITSVILLE USA: THE MOTOWN SINGLES COLLECTION, 1959-1971 MOTOWN 3746363122

This set includes all the Motown songs in Chapters 1, 6, and 14.
The remaining songs are available on the following albums:

CHAP.	SONG TITLE	ALBUM NAME	CATALOG NUMBER
Intro	Green Onions	*Booker T. and the M.G.s: Green Onions*	Atlantic 7567-82255-2
2	Back Water Blues	*Smithsonian Collection of Classic Blues Singers*	RD 101; A4 23981
2	Come on in My Kitchen	*Robert Johnson: The Complete Recordings*	Columbia C2K 64916
2	It's Tight Like That	*Good Morning Blues*	Charly CD DIG 18; LC 8477
2	Pine Top's Boogie Woogie	*Good Morning Blues*	Charly CD DIG 18; LC 8477
2	I Gotta Right to Sing the Blues	*Smithsonian Collection of Classic Jazz*	RD 033-1
2	Waiting for a Train	*Smithsonian Collection of Classic Country Music*	RD 042; DMC4-0914

INDIVIDUAL SONGS

CHAP.	SONG TITLE	ALBUM NAME	CATALOG NUMBER
2	This Land Is Your Land	*Folkways: The Original Vision*	Smithsonian Folkways CD SF 40001
2	Jesus, I'll Never Forget	*Jubilation: Great Gospel Performances, Vol. 2*	Rhino R2 70289
2	Move On Up a Little Higher	*Jubilation: Great Gospel Performances, Vol. 1*	Rhino R2 70288
2	The Old Ship of Zion	*Jubilation: Great Gospel Performances, Vol. 1*	Rhino R2 70288
3	Ain't That a Shame	*Billboard: Top Rock 'n' Roll Hits, 1955*	Rhino R2 70598
3	Hoochie Coochie Man	*They Call Me Muddy Waters*	Blue City CD 2652232
3	Longhair's Blues-Rhumba	*Professor Longhair: New Orleans Piano*	Atlantic 7225-2
3	The Platters' songs	*The Very Best of the Platters*	Mercury 314 510 317-2
3	You Send Me Sam	*Cooke: The Man and His Music*	RCA PCD1-7127
3	Ray Charles' Songs	*Ray Charles Live*	Atlantic
4	Rock Around the Clock	*Billboard: Top Rock 'n' Roll Hits, 1955*	Rhino R2 70598
4	Chuck Berry's songs	*Chuck Berry: The Great Twenty-Eight*	Chess CHD-92500
4	Elvis' Songs	*Elvis Presley: The Sun Sessions* *Elvis Presley: Elvis' Golden Records*	RCA 6414-2-R RCA PCD1-5196
4	Little Richard's songs	*Little Richard: 18 Greatest Hits*	Rhino R2 75899
4	Great Balls of Fire	*Jerry Lee Lewis: All Killer No Filler*	Rhino R2 71216
4	All I Have to Do Is Dream	*Everly Brothers: Cadence Classics*	Rhino R2 5258
4	Buddy Holly Songs	*Buddy Holly: From the Master Tapes*	MCA DIDX-203; MCAD-5540
5	Will You Still Love Me Tomorrow	*Shirelles: 16 Greatest Hits*	FST records FCD-4414
5	Drifters' songs	*The Drifters' Golden Hits*	Atlantic 8153-2
5	The Twist	*Billboard: Top Rock 'n' Roll Hits, 1960*	Rhino R2 70621
5	Louie, Louie	*Billboard: Top Rock 'n' Roll Hits, 1963*	Rhino R2 70624
5	Roy Orbison songs	*Roy Orbison: The All-Time Greatest Hits*	Sony AGK 45116
5	Beach Boys' songs	*The Beach Boys: Made In USA*	Capitol CDP 7 46324 2
6	Soul Man	*The Best of Sam and Dave*	Atlantic 7 81279-2
6	I Can't Turn You Loose	*The Very Best of Otis Redding*	Rhino R2 71147
6	Aretha Franklin songs	*Aretha Franklin: Queen of Soul*	Rhino R2 71063
6	James Brown's songs	*James Brown: Star Time*	Polydor 849 108-2
7	Wildwood Flower	*Joan Baez: Volume 1*	Vanguard VMD-2077
7	Blowin' in the Wind	*The Best of Peter, Paul, and Mary*	Warner 3105-2
7	Byrds' songs	*The Byrds: 20 Essential Tracks from the Boxed Set*	Columbia CK 47884
7	Dylan's songs	*Bob Dylan: Bringing It All Back Home* *Highway 61 revisited* *Blonde on Blonde*	Columbia CK 9128 Columbia CK 32168 Columbia CGK 841
7	Beatles' songs	*The Beatles, 1962-1966* *The Beatles, 1966-1970*	Capitol CDP 0777 7 97036 2 3 Capitol CDP 0777 7 97039 2 0

INDIVIDUAL SONGS

CHAP.	SONG TITLE	ALBUM NAME	CATALOG NUMBER
8	You Really Got Me	*The Kinks: Greatest Hits*	Rhino R2 70086
8	Rolling Stones' Songs	*The Rolling Stones: Hot Rocks, 1964-1971*	Abkco 66672
8	Hendrix's songs	*Jimi Hendrix: The Ultimate Experience*	MCA MCAD-10829
8	Cream's songs	*Strange Brew: The Very Best of Cream*	Polydor 811-639-2
9	*Tommy*	*The Who: Tommy*	MCA MCAD-11417
9	The Doors' songs	*The Doors*	Elektra 74007-2
9	Velvet Underground Songs	*The Velvet Underground and Nico*	Polydor 31453 1250 2
9	Zappa songs	*Frank Zappa and the Mothers of Invention: We're Only In It for the Money*	Rykodisc RCD 10503
9	Hang On to Yourself	*David Bowie: Ziggy Stardust*	Rykodisc RCD 10134
9	Dark Side of the Moon	*Pink Floyd: Dark Side of the Moon*	Capitol CDP 0777 7 46001 2
9	Roundabout	*Yes: Fragile*	Atlantic 82667-2
10	Piece of My Heart	*Janis Joplin's Greatest Hits*	Columbia CK 31350
10	Proud Mary	*Creedence Clearwater Revival: Chronicle*	Fantasy FCD 623-CCR2 X
10	The Weight	*The Band: The Night They Drove Old Dixie Down*	Capitol CDL 57260
10	Allman Brothers' songs	*The Allman Brothers Band*	Polydor 823 653-2
10	Lynyrd Skynyrd songs	*Lynyrd Skynyrd: Gold and Platinum*	MCA MCAD2-6898
11	Black Sabbath songs	*Black Sabbath: We Sold Our Soul for Rock 'n' Roll*	Warner 2923-2
11	Highway Star	*Deep Purple: Machine Head*	Warner 3100-2
11	Led Zeppelin songs	*Led Zeppelin IV*	Atlantic 19129-2
12	A Felicidade	*Brasil: A Century of Song*	Blue Jacket 5003-2
12	I Say a Little Prayer	*Dionne Warwick: Her All-Time Greatest Hits*	Rhino R2 71100
12	Ska songs	*Roots of Reggae, Vol. 1: Ska* *Tougher Than Tough: The Story of Jamaican Music*	Rhino R2 72438 Mango CD 518 400-403 2
12	Bob Marley songs	*Bob Marley and the Wailers: Legend*	Tuff Gong 422-846 210-2
13	Van Morrison songs	*Van Morrison: Astral Weeks*	Warner 1768-2
13	Simon and Garfunkel songs	*Simon and Garfunkel's Greatest Hits*	Columbia CK 31350
13	Déjà Vu	*Crosby, Stills, Nash & Young: Déjà Vu*	Atlantic 82649-2
13	James Taylor songs	*James Taylor: Greatest Hits*	Warner 3113-2
13	Joni Mitchell songs	*Joni Mitchell: Blue*	Reprise 2038-2
13	It's Too Late	*Carole King: Tapestry*	Ode EK 34946
13	Paul Simon songs	*Paul Simon: Negotiations and Love Songs*	Warner 9 25789-2
14	You Are the Sunshine of My Life	*Stevie Wonder: Talking Book*	Motown 3746303192
14	Feel Like Makin' Love	*The Best of Roberta Flack*	Atlantic 19317-2
14	Use Me	*Bill Withers' Greatest Hits*	Columbia CK 37199
14	I'm Gonna Love You Just a Little More, Baby	*Barry White: All-Time Greatest Hits*	Mercury 314-522-459-2

INDIVIDUAL SONGS

CHAP.	SONG TITLE	ALBUM NAME	CATALOG NUMBER
14	Soon and Very Soon	*Andraé Crouch: The Light Years*	Light 51416 1156 2
14	Put It Where You Want It	*The Crusaders: The Golden Years*	GRP GRD-3-5007
14	Sly and The Family Stone songs	*Sly and the Family Stone: Greatest Hits* *There's a Riot Goin' On*	Epic EK 30325 Epic 30986
15	Dreams	*Fleetwood Mac: Rumours*	Warner 3010-2
15	Walk This Way	*Aerosmith's Greatest Hits*	Columbia CK 36865
15	Swingin'	*John Anderson: Greatest Hits*	Warner 9 25169-2
15	Spinning Wheel	*Blood, Sweat & Tears: Greatest Hits*	Columbia CK 31170
15	Does Anybody Really Know What Time It Is	*Chicago's Greatest Hits*	Chicago CRD-3009
15	Another Green World	*Brian Eno: Another Green World*	EG EGCD 21
15	The Guns of Brixton	*The Clash: London Calling*	Epic EGK 36328
16	Up for the Down Stroke	*Funk Classics*	Rebound Records 440 011 1103
16	You Should Be Dancing	*Saturday Night Fever*	Polydor 800 068-2
16	Stomp	*Funk Classics*	Rebound Records 440 011 1103
16	Love Will Conquer All	*Lionel Richie: Truly-The Love Songs*	Motown 304530816-2
16	Michael Jackson's songs	*Michael Jackson: Thriller*	Epic EK 38112
16	Like A Prayer	*Madonna: Like a Prayer*	Sire W2 25844
16	Police songs	*The Police: Every Breath You Take*	A&M 31454 0380 2
17	In Your Eyes	*Peter Gabriel: So*	Geffen 9 2408802
17	Van Halen songs	*Van Halen*	Warner 3075-2
18	Rapper's Delight	*The Best of Sugarhill*	Gang Rhino R2 71986
18	The Adventures of GF & The Wheels Of Steel	*The Adventures of Grandmaster Flash... More of the Best*	Rhino R2 72467
18	Boya Ye	*African Moves*	Rounder CD 11513
18	Play One	*Black Stalin: Roots, Rock, Soca*	Rounder CD 5038
18	Without a Smile	*Youssou N'Dour: The Guide*	Columbia OK 53828
18	Wéep	*Kassav': Majestic Zouk*	Columbia CK 45353
18	Tommy the Cat	*Primus: Suck on This*	Caroline Carol CD 1620
18	Smells Like Teen Spirit	*Nirvana: Nevermind*	DGC DGCD 24425
18	W.M.A.	*Pearl Jam*	Epic Associated ZK 53136

Index

Index

Contents of Compact Disc

(packaged separately)

Michael Campbell and James Brody
Rock and Roll: An Introduction
ISBN: 0-02-864727-0 (Book)
ISBN: 0-02-865331-9 (CD Set)

"The Way You Do the Things You Do"
The Temptations

"My Girl"
The Temptations

"Come See About Me"
The Supremes

"Ain't Nothing Like the Real Thing"
Marvin Gaye

"Back Water Blues"
Bessie Smith

"Come On In My Kitchen"
Robert Johnson

"It's Tight Like That"
Georgia Tom and Tampa Red

"Tutti Frutti"
Little Richard

"Pine Top's Boogie Woogie"
Pine Top Smith

"I Gotta Right to Sing the Blues"
Louis Armstrong

"Waiting for a Train"
Jimmie Rodgers

"Your Cheatin' Heart"
Hank Williams

"This Land Is Your Land"
Woody Guthrie

"Jesus, I'll Never Forget"
Sam Cooke/Soul Stirrers

"Move on up a Little Higher"
Mahalia Jackson

"The Old Ship of Zion"
Roberta Martin

"Great Balls of Fire"
Jerry Lee Lewis

"Rocket 88"
Jackie Brenston

"Ain't That a Shame"
Fats Domino

"Boogie Chillen'"
John Lee Hooker

"Hoochie Coochie Man"
Muddy Waters

"Bo Diddley"
Bo Diddley

"Earth Angel"
The Penguines

"You Send Me"
Sam Cooke

"Roll Over Beethoven"
Chuck Berry

"All I Have to Do Is Dream"
The Everly Brothers

"Will You Still Love Me Tomorrow?"
The Shirelles

"Mean Woman Blues"
Roy Orbison

"Not Fade Away"
Buddy Holly

"Oh, Pretty Woman"
Roy Orbison

"Mr. Tambourine Man"
The Byrds

"I Feel Good"
James Brown

"A Felicidade"
João Gilberto

"Oye Como Va"
Santana

"Lover Boy"
Derrick Morgan

"Madness"
Prince Buster

"Judgment Day"
Laurel Aitken

"Chubby"
Bunny and Skitter

"Tougher Than Tough"
Derrick Morgan

"Back Stabbers"
The O'Jays

"Soon and Very Soon"
Andraé Crouch

"Boya Ye"
M'Bilia Bel

"Without a Smile"
Youssou N'Dour

"Thank You (Falettin me Be Mice Elf Again)"
Sly and the Family Stone

"Spinning Wheel"
Blood, Sweat, and Tears

"Up for the Down Stroke"
Parliament

Schirmer Books
An imprint of Macmillan Library Reference USA
1633 Broadway
New York, NY 10019